Social Problems

Social Problems

SEVENTH EDITION

James M. Henslin
Southern Illinois University, Edwardsville

PEARSON

Prentice
Hall

Upper Saddle River, New Jersey 07458

Library of Congress Cataloging-in-Publication Data
Henslin, James M.
    Social problems / James M. Henslin.—7th ed.
        p. cm.
    Includes bibliographical references and index.
    ISBN 0-13-193082-6
1. Social problems.   2. Deviant behavior.   3. Equality.   4. Social change.
5. Symbolic interactionism. 6. Functionalism (Social sciences)   7. United States—
Social conditions—1980– I. Title.
HM585.H45 2006
361.1—dc22   2005004927

Editorial Director: Leah Jewell
AVP, Publisher: Nancy Roberts
VP, Director of Production and Manufacturing:
    Barbara Kittle
Director of Marketing: Brandy Dawson
Manufacturing Manager: Nick Sklitsis
Prepress and Manufacturing Buyer: Mary Ann Gloriande
Senior Marketing Manager: Marissa Feliberty
Editorial Production/Supervision: Bruce Hobart/
    Pine Tree Composition
Production Liaison: Cheryl Keenan
Editorial Assistant: Lee Peterson
Marketing Assistant: Anthony DeCosta
Copyeditor: Karen Slaght

Creative Design Director: Leslie Osher
Art Director: Nancy Wells
Interior and Cover Design: Jill Lehan
Illustrator (Interior): Pine Tree Composition
Director, Image Resource Center: Melinda Reo
Manager, Rights and Permissions: Zina Arabia
Manager, Visual Research: Beth Brenzel
Image Permission Coordinator: Frances Toepfer
Photo Researcher: Teri Stratford
Cover Image Specialist: Karen Sanatar
Cover Art: Stock Illustration Source/Teofilo Olivieri
Media Editor: Kate Ramunda
Media Production Manager: Lynn Pearlman

This book was set in 10/12 Gaillard Roman by Pine Tree Composition and was printed
and bound by Courier Companies, Inc. The cover was printed by Phoenix Color Corp.

Pearson Education LTD.
Pearson Education Singapore, Pte. Ltd
Pearson Education, Canada, Ltd
Pearson Education—Japan
Pearson Education Australia PTY, Limited

Pearson Education North Asia Ltd
Pearson Educación de Mexico, S.A. de C.V
Pearson Education Malaysia, Pte. Ltd
Pearson Education, Upper Saddle River, New Jersey

10 9 8 7 6 5 4 3 2 1

ISBN 0-13-193082-6

For those yet to enter this scene not of their own making—
may they live in a better world.

CONTENTS

PART IV   Social Change and Megaproblems

11 THE CHANGING FAMILY   352

12 URBAN PROBLEMS   388

BOXES

THINKING CRITICALLY ABOUT SOCIAL PROBLEMS

SPOTLIGHT ON RESEARCH

PREFACE

It is a pleasure to see this text go into its seventh edition. Doing the revisions for this new edition was a demanding task, but it was also enormously gratifying to be able to read the latest research and to evaluate the social trends that give direction to social problems. I trust that your students, like the many before them, will react positively to this text, and that it will help you to have provocative discussions of the major issues that face the country.

As in earlier editions, I have kept the focus on both theory and research. Adopters have commented that they appreciate how consistently I apply sociological theories to social problems, and that the theories are presented so clearly that they are easy for students to understand. In addition, I consistently emphasize the *social* nature of social problems—how objective conditions are inadequate to make a social problem, that subjective concerns are also essential. This theoretical framing is especially significant for students. As the students go through life, the specific facts of social problems are going to change, but from this course they can take with them a sociological framework for interpreting the changing conditions of the society that they will experience.

To prepare this edition required the usual: keeping abreast of the latest research and integrating those findings into the analysis of each social problem. But for this edition there was also the pleasure of the unusual: Major researchers on social problems agreed to share with students a sort of insider's perspective. In this new feature, *Spotlight on Research*, the researchers take the reader into the field with them. They let students look over their shoulder as they explain how they became interested in a social problem and how they did their research.

It was a privilege to oversee and to work with such experienced researchers. It was also a pleasure to know that their contributions will increase the students' awareness of how research on social problems is actually done. The authors of this new boxed feature are:

> Edward Laumann, studying human sexuality—and the stigma that comes from this research, Chapter 3
> Ruth Horowitz, getting an insider's perspective on Chicano gangs, Chapter 5
> William Chambliss, discussing his personal journey into sociology, Chapter 6
> Herbert Gans, doing research on the exploitation of people in poverty, Chapter 7
> Nazli Kibria, studying the identity problems of Asian Americans, Chapter 8
> Rafael Ezekiel, studying neo-Nazis and Klans, Chapter 8
> Kirsten Dellinger, exploring the meanings of sexual harassment, Chapter 9
> William Cockerham, solving a medical mystery, Chapter 10
> Kathleen Ferraro, gaining an insider's view of intimate violence, Chapter 11
> Eli Anderson, doing research in the inner city, Chapter 12
> Carl Haub, doing research on population and food, Chapter 13
> Robert Gottlieb, discovering changing meanings of the environment, Chapter 14

Scope and Coverage of the Seventh Edition

Social Problems is an enjoyable course to teach, and many students find it to be the most exciting course in sociology. Certainly the topics are fascinating, ranging from such controversial matters as prostitution and pornography to such deeply embedded problems as racism, poverty, and gender. Some of the issues are intensely personal, such as abortion, suicide, and being the victim of violent crime; others, such as war and the loss of jobs, center on global stratification and the globalization of capitalism. All are significant, vital for our present and for our future.

The benefits of this course for students are similarly wide-ranging. Not only do students gain a sociological understanding of social problems, but also they are able to explore—and evaluate—their own opinions about specific social problems and the controversies that affect their orientations to life. As the course progresses, students become more aware of the social forces that shape their orientations, gaining insight into how their particular situation in life penetrates their thinking and shapes their views of the world.

The Sociological Task: The Goal of Objectivity

This process of insight and self-discovery—so essential to good sociology—is one of the most rewarding aspects of teaching Social Problems. But teaching this class is also a challenge, for it requires objectivity in the midst of deep controversy, something that is difficult to achieve. I am disturbed at the promotion of ideology that increasingly passes for teaching sociology. Students are a captive audience, and in my opinion using the classroom to promote particular points of view on social problems is unfair. It seems to me that the sociological task is to present competing views on what makes something a social problem and the various approaches to solving it. The instructor's personal position on a social problem depends on his or her ideology and belief system. These are subjective, and the instructor's views, like those of others, are only one of a huge array of ideologies and belief systems available in contemporary society. As committed as the instructor might be to a particular point of view—and as difficult as it is to push one's own opinions aside—this is precisely what objectivity requires. If not, then we might as well be up front and change the name from sociology to ideology.

In this text, I have tried to do precisely this—to present both sides of issues fairly and objectively. I have no hidden agenda, no axes to grind. I know, of course, that total objectivity, no matter how ardently it may be desired or pursued, is impossible; but I think that objectivity should be the hallmark of *Social Problems,* and I have tried to attain it. The most obvious example is found in Chapter 1, where I use abortion as the substantive issue to illustrate basic sociological principles. Beginning with this controversy jump-starts the course, placing us squarely in the midst of one of the most debated and heated issues in U.S. society. It also brings deep-seated attitudes to the surface. Used creatively, this approach allows us to illustrate the social origin of ideas, which is so essential to understanding social problems. To be fair to students, however, instructors need to take a neutral stance—no matter how strong their own attitudes may be. Because this is extremely difficult to do in such emotional and volatile matters as abortion, from time to time we need to remind ourselves that our attitudes, too, are rooted in social structure.

If I have been successful in this endeavor, both students and instructors who are on the extreme opposite ends of this issue—those who favor abortion on demand and those who oppose abortion under any circumstances—should feel that their position is adequately represented. They also will likely feel that I have somehow represented the other side too favorably. To check whether I had succeeded in attaining objectivity in this crucial matter, I asked national officers of both pro-choice and right-to-life organizations to comment on this first chapter. *Both sides* responded that I had been "trapped" into being too fair to the other side. I also asked my classes, after they had read the chapter, where they thought I stood on abortion. I was astonished—and pleased—when half replied that I was pro-choice and half that I was right-to-life.

The goal of this book, then, is to present objectively the major research findings on social problems, to explain their theoretical interpretation, and to describe clearly the underlying assumptions and implications of competing points of view. In endeavoring to reach this goal, I have strived to present the best of the sociology of social problems and to introduce competing views fairly. To again use Chapter 1 as an illustration: I use the terms *proabortion* and *antiabortion,* which, though far from perfect, are more neutrally descriptive than those preferred by proponents of either position—*prochoice* and *freedom of choice,* on one hand, and *prolife* and *right to life* on the other. While not everyone will be happy with my choice of terms—and they certainly cannot do justice to the many nuances and positions inherent in both sides of this crucial issue—I feel that they are the more neutral and objective labels.

If I have been successful, readers should find themselves content when they encounter views with which they are in agreement and uncomfortable as they confront those with which they personally disagree. This should hold true for readers of all persuasions, whether "radical," "liberal," "conservative"—or any other label currently in fashion. It should also make for a more exciting class.

Method of Presentation: Incorporating Theory into the Discussions

Readers will find this book more theoretical than many. As one reviewer said, most texts in social problems simply mention theory in an initial chapter and then dispense with it thereafter, whereas this text follows through with the "theoretical promise" of its introductory chapters. Theory, however, can be vague, abstract, and difficult to understand. This is not necessary, and to overcome this problem I embed the theories in clarifying contexts. For example, when I introduce the three basic theories in Chapter 2—symbolic interaction theory, functional theory, and conflict theory—I make them concrete by applying each to the social problem of discrimination against the elderly in U.S. society. In the following chapters, I consistently apply these theories to *each* social problem. This approach helps give students a cohesive understanding of what otherwise might appear to be a disparate collection of problematic events and issues. The effect is cumulative, for each new chapter allows students to broaden their understanding of these perspectives. The single exception to applying each theory to each social problem is Chapter 3. Here I treat three social problems, and, because at this point students are becoming familiar with these theories, it is more effective to apply a single theory in greater detail to each of these aspects of human sexuality.

Chapter Organization and Features

A major impediment to learning is the seemingly whimsical way in which authors of textbooks present social problems. In the typical case, the analysis is jumbled—the order differs markedly from one chapter to the next, with students finding no regularity of structure. To overcome this, I utilize a consistent structure within the chapters. This provides a "road map" to guide students through each social problem and lets them know what to expect in each chapter. After the first three chapters, I use the following framework to analyze each social problem:

> *Opening Vignette* Intended to arouse student interest in the social problem and to stimulate the desire to read more, this brief opening story presents essential elements of the social problem.

The Problem in Sociological Perspective Here I present a broad sociological background that sets the stage for understanding the social problem.

The Scope of the Problem This section presents basic data on the extent or scope of the problem. It allows students to grasp the problem's wider ramifications.

Looking at the Problem Theoretically Here I present a theoretical analysis of the problem or some major aspect of it. I consistently begin on the more personal level, with symbolic interaction theory, move from there to functional theory, and conclude with the perspective of conflict theory.

Research Findings Discussed here are both current and classic sociological studies—and, where relevant, research from other academic disciplines as well. To allow students to become more familiar with primary research, I present some sociological studies in detail. In addition, the feature written by researchers themselves, *Spotlight on Research,* helps students to understand how the researcher's personal background leads to interest in a social problem and how research is actually done.

Social Policy This section focuses on actions that have been taken or could be taken to try to solve the social problem. I often spell out the assumptions on which these policies are based and the dilemmas that they create.

The Future of the Problem Because students are intensely interested in knowing what lies ahead of them in life, I conclude with an overview of the direction that the problem is likely to take, given what we now know about the problem's dimensions and trends.

Summary To reinforce what the students are learning, I provide a succinct point-by-point summary of the main ideas in the chapter. Students also find this summary helpful for review purposes, especially in preparing for tests. Many students also find it useful as a *preview* of the chapter, reading the summary *before* they read the chapter.

Key Terms When a term first appears in the text, it is set in bold type and is defined in context. Key terms are also listed and defined at the end of each chapter.

Thinking Critically about the Chapter At the end of each chapter are several questions designed to help students evaluate what they have read. These questions are also useful to stimulate class discussions.

Suggestions for Using This Text

Authors of social problem texts, as well as those who teach this course, must decide whether they want to begin with the more "micro" or the more "macro" problems. Each approach is popular, and each has much to commend it. In my own teaching, I prefer to begin at the micro level. I begin by focusing on problems of personal concern to students—issues about which they are already curious and have questions they want answered. In my experience, this approach provides a more compelling context for helping students become familiar with the sociological perspective and sociological theory. From there, I move to an examination of broader social problems, those whose more apparent connections to global events often make them seem more remote. This is nothing more than a preference, of course, and it is equally logical to begin with problems that involve large-scale social change and then to wrap up the course with a focus on more individualistic problems. Instructors who wish to begin with the more macro problems can simply move Part II of this text to the end of their course. Nothing else will be affected.

Because this book is written for students, I have resisted the urge to insert qualifying footnotes, the kind that read: "A fuller amplification of this position would include reference to the works of so-and-so," or "This theoretical position is really much more complex than I can describe here, but because of lack of space. . . ." Such qualifiers are directed to a professional audience, and though they might serve to fend off some potential attack on the work, such "disclaimers" do not benefit students.

Invitation for You to Respond

This text flows from years of teaching the basic course in social problems. Especially formative have been the reactions of my students, who questioned and reconsidered their views of social problems. This text also incorporates feedback that instructors have graciously shared with me. I have designed the book to help make your course more successful—so it would both challenge students' thinking and make the sociological perspective clear and readily understandable. As we all know, results count, however, not intentions. What matters, then, is how this text actually works in your classroom. Consequently, I would greatly appreciate your feedback—whether positive or negative. Because your reactions are based on your own classroom experience, I will find them useful. My e-mail address is listed on the next page.

Acknowledgments

Finally, as is the custom in prefatory rituals, I wish to acknowledge the contributions of others to this book, especially Nancy Roberts for encouraging me to continue to work on this project and for overseeing the last several editions. I am especially appreciative of her enthusiastic endorsement of my suggestion that in this edition we have researchers on social problems share their experiences. To these researchers also go my hearty thanks. I also wish to thank Jenifer Kunz for her invaluable help with the initial research for this revision and Bruce Hobart for managing the production of the book at Pine Tree. Finally, I wish to thank the following reviewers for their many suggestions:

Reviewers of previous editions:
   Gary Burbridge, *Grand Rapids Community College*
   Carole A. Campbell, *California State University—Long Beach*
   Cheryl Childers, *Washburn University*
   Al Cook, *Trinity Valley Community College*
   David D. Friedrichs, *University of Scranton*
   Michele Gigliotti, *Broward Community College*
   Rosalind Gottfried, *San Joaquin Delta College*
   Charles Hall, *Purdue University*
   Rosa Haritos, *University of North Carolina at Chapel Hill*
   Rachel Ivie, *South Plains College*
   Cardell Jacobson, *Brigham Young University*
   Joseph F. Jones, *Portland State University*
   Victor M. Kogan, *Saint Martin's College*
   Paul Magee, *North Lake College*
   Marguerite Marin, *Gonzaga University*
   John Mitrano, *Central Connecticut State University*
   Sharon Erickson Nepstad, *University of Colorado—Boulder*

Kevin R. Ousley, *East Carolina University*
Dennis L. Peck, *The University of Alabama*
Richard P. Rettig, *University of Central Oklahoma*
Barbara L. Richardson, *Eastern Michigan University*
Edwin Rosenberg, *Appalachian State University*
K. S. Thompson, *Northern Michigan University*
Richard T. Vick, *Idaho State University*

Reviewers of this edition:
Susan Claxton, *Floyd College*
Carl M. Hand, *Valdosta State University*
Muketiwa Wilbrod Madzura, *Normandale Community College*
James P. Sikora, *Illinois Wesleyan University*

Finally, my heartfelt best wishes to both instructors and students. I hope that this text provides understanding and insight into the major problems facing our country, many of which have global ramifications—and all of which have an impact on our own lives.

May our children live in a better world!

Jim Henslin
Department of Sociology
Southern Illinois University
Edwardsville, Illinois 62026
henslin@aol.com

TO THE INSTRUCTOR, FROM THE PUBLISHER

A wide variety of ancillaries are available from Prentice Hall to help you and your students in using this text. These ancillaries include:

Instructor's Resource Manual with Tests.   For each chapter in the text, this manual provides a detailed outline, list of objectives, discussion questions, and classroom activities. In addition, test questions in multiple-choice and short answer formats are available for each chapter; the answers to all questions are page-referenced to the text.

TestGEN-EQ.   This computerized software allows instructors to create their own personalized exams, to edit any or all of the test questions and to add new questions. Other special features of this program include random generation of test questions, creation of alternative versions of the same test, scrambling question sequence, and test preview before printing.

ABCNEWS   *ABC News/Prentice Hall Video Library for Sociology.*   Prentice Hall and ABC News are working together to bring to you the best and most comprehensive video material available in the college market. Through its wide variety of award-winning programs—*Nightline, This Week, World News Tonight,* and *20/20*—ABC offers a resource for feature and documentary-style videos related to the chapters in *Social Problems, Seventh Edition.* The programs have high production quality, present substantial content, and are hosted by well-versed, well-known anchors.

Prentice Hall Color Transparencies: Social Problems.   Full color illustrations, charts, and other visual materials from the text as well as outside sources have been selected to make up this useful in-class tool. Please see your Prentice Hall sales representative for more details.

Instructor Resource CD-ROM.   Pulling together all of the print and media assets available to instructors, this interactive CD allows you to have all of the ancillaries in one place. In addition, you can insert media—PowerPoint® slides, graphs, charts, maps—into your interactive classroom presentations

OneKey.   A one-stop shop for both professors and students, this innovative, premium Web site will help professors more effectively prepare lectures and help students more efficiently review the course material. For professors, it will include PowerPoint™ presentations, all of the instructor supplements, testing software, and videos. For students, it will include videos, flashcards, quizzes, and concept tips. Professor access to OneKey can be gained by contacting your Prentice Hall representative or by visiting http://www.prenhall.com/onekey for registration. Students can access OneKey when professors order a special package of *Social Problems, Seventh Edition,* with a free OneKey access code wrapped with the text.

OneSearch with Research Navigator™: Sociology.   This guide focuses on using **Research Navigator™**—Prentice Hall's own gateway to databases—including *The New York Times* Search-by-Subject Archive, *ContentSelect™* Academic Journal Database powered by EBSCO, *The Financial Times,* and the *Best of the Web* Link Library. It also includes extensive appendices on documenting online sources and on avoiding plagiarism. This guide, along with the Research Navigator™ access code, is free to students when packaged with *Social Problems, Seventh Edition.*

SocNotes Plus. A useful and exciting super study guide, *SocNotes Plus* is Prentice Hall's one-stop resource for students studying social problems. Designed around the chapters in *Social Problems, Seventh Edition,* this resource helps students keep their course notes and lecture information in order.

SocNotes Plus is FREE when packaged with new copies of this text. Please see your local Prentice Hall representative for more details.

Companion Website™. This online study guide provides unique support to help students with their studies in social problems. Featuring a variety of interactive learning tools, including online quizzes with immediate feedback, this site is a comprehensive resource organized according to the chapters in *Social Problems, Seventh Edition.* It can be found at www.prenhall.com/henslin

 TIME Special Edition: Sociology. Prentice Hall and **TIME** Magazine are pleased to offer you and your students a chance to examine today's most current and compelling issues in an exciting new way. **TIME** Special Edition Sociology offers a selection of 20 TIME articles on today's most current issues and debates in Sociology. **TIME** Special Edition provides your students the full coverage, accessible writing, and bold photographs that **TIME** is known for. Free when packaged with *Social Problems, Seventh Edition,* it is perfect for discussion groups, in-class debates, or research assignments. Please see your local Prentice Hall representative for more information.

10 Ways to Fight Hate Brochure. Produced by the Southern Poverty Law Center, this free supplement walks students through 10 steps that they can take on their own campus or in their own neighborhood to fight hate everyday.

The New York Times/Prentice Hall eThemes of the Times. The New York Times and Prentice Hall are sponsoring e*Themes of the Times,* a program designed to enhance student access to current information relevant to the classroom. Through this program, the core subject matter provided in the text is supplemented by a collection of timely articles downloaded from one of the world's most distinguished newspapers, *The New York Times.* These articles demonstrate the vital, ongoing connection between what is learned in the classroom and what is happening in the world around us. Access to *The New York Times/Prentice Hall eThemes of the Times* is available on the *Social Problems, Seventh Edition,* Companion Website™.

CHAPTER 1

How Sociologists View Social Problems: The Abortion Dilemma

"**B**UT YOU DON'T UNDERSTAND! IT'S NOT A baby!" Lisa shouted once again. She had reached the point of desperation. The argument with her grandmother seemed to have gone on forever.

With tears in her eyes, her grandmother said, "You don't know what you're doing, Lisa. You're taking the life of an innocent baby!"

"No! There's only one life involved here—mine!" replied Lisa. "It's my body and my life. I've worked too hard for that manager's job to let this pregnancy ruin everything."

"But Lisa, you have a new responsibility—to the baby."

"Don't judge my life by your standards. You never wanted a career. All you ever wanted was to raise a family."

"That's not the point," her grandmother pressed. "You're carrying a baby, and now you want to kill it."

"How can you talk like that? This is just a medical procedure, like when you had your gallstones taken out."

"I can't believe my own granddaughter is saying that butchering a baby is like having gallstones removed!"

Lisa and her grandmother looked at each other, knowing they were worlds apart. They both began to cry inside.

The Sociological Imagination

When people have problems, they usually see them in highly personal—and often, emotional—terms. Their perspective is limited primarily to their immediate situation, and they fail to see the broader context in which those problems arise. Because people seldom connect their personal lives with the larger social context, like Lisa and her grandmother, they tend to blame themselves and one another for their troubles.

What Is the Sociological Imagination?

The term **sociological imagination** refers to looking at people's behavior and attitudes in the context of the social forces that shape them. C. Wright Mills, the sociologist who developed this concept, emphasized that changes in society have profound influences on people's lives. As with Lisa and her grandmother, people get caught on various sides of social issues. Until 1973, legal abortions were unavailable in the United States, and almost everyone thought of abortion as a despicable act. When the law changed, however, and doctors were allowed to perform abortions, many people's attitudes changed.

The *sociological imagination*, then, is an emphasis on how the larger events swirling around us have an impact on how we think, feel, and act. Mills used the term **personal troubles** to refer to how these larger events trouble people's lives. We get so caught up in what is bothering us, however, that seldom are we aware of how these larger social forces underlie our personal troubles.

Applying the Sociological Imagination

To better understand this connection between personal troubles and larger social forces, let's apply the sociological imagination to Lisa and her grandmother. Lisa's values reflect developments in our society that were not part of her grandmother's consciousness when she grew up. Lisa's views have been shaped by the women's movement, which stresses that each woman has the right to make choices and exercise judgment about her own body. From this perspective, which has become part of Lisa's outlook on the world, a woman has the right to terminate her pregnancy. In the extreme, proponents of this view state that a woman's right in this area is absolute, that she can choose to have an abortion at any point in her pregnancy—without informing her husband if she is married or her parents if she is a minor.

The sociological imagination also sensitizes us to the social forces that shaped Lisa's grandmother's point of view. When she was growing up, not only was abortion illegal, but it was also considered so shameful that people did not even talk openly about it. Every woman was expected to become a mother, and almost all girls grew up with marriage and motherhood as their *foremost* goal. Careers and advanced education were secondary to a woman being a wife and mother, her fulfillment in life. Like Lisa's grandmother, almost everyone agreed that abortion was murder, and women who had abortions had to keep their crime a secret. Some who had abortions, which was a crime, rode to their destination blindfolded in a taxi and endured kitchen-table surgery that carried a high risk of postoperative infection and death.

Yet neither Lisa nor her grandmother sees this finely woven net that has swept them up and turned their lives upside down. Instead, the impact of social change hits them on a personal level—affecting what they think and feel and how they relate to one another.

More on How the Social Context Influences Our Attitudes and Behavior

In contrast, the sociological imagination (also called the **sociological perspective**) invites us to look at our lives afresh to understand how the social context shapes our ideas and behaviors. This social context includes such broad events as war, terrorism, and other historical turmoil. It also includes our broad *social locations,* such as our gender, race-ethnicity, religion, social class, and even the era in which we grow up. The smaller *social locations* in which we find ourselves, such as our age and marital status, are also part of this social context. Together, such factors shape the way we look at life.

How Having an Abortion Is Influenced by Social Location

Table 1-1 on the next page illustrates how significant social location is in abortion. You can see that age, race-ethnicity, marital status, and even the region of the country make a difference in whether a woman has an abortion. This table shows that half (497 of 1,000) of girls under the age of 15 who get pregnant have an abortion. Those who are the next most likely to have abortions are other teenagers and women in their early 20s. The rate of abortion keeps dropping with age, but increases in the late 30s, and then, when women reach their 40s, it increases sharply. As you can also see, African-American women are more likely to have abortions than are white women. The most striking difference, however—cutting across age and race-ethnicity—is marital status: Unmarried women are *five* times more likely than married women to obtain an abortion.

Suppose, then, that you are a married women in her late 20s. Can you see how much more likely you would be to have an abortion if you were single than if you were married? Similarly, suppose that you are an unmarried white teenager, and you get pregnant. Can you see how much less likely you would be to have an abortion than if you were an African-American teenager who got pregnant? No one is a robot, of course. We all have our own minds, and we use them. Consequently, you never know in any individual case whether that person will have an abortion. But as Table 1-1 makes apparent, we tend to make up our minds along predictable, well-traveled social avenues.

In Sum

Sociologists stress the need to use the sociological imagination to understand social problems. It helps make us aware of how the social context—from our historical era to our smaller social locations—influences our ideas, behaviors, and personal troubles. Just as with Lisa and her grandmother, this context also shapes our views of what is or is not a social problem and of what action we think ought to be taken. Let's look more closely at how this shaping occurs.

TABLE 1-1 Who Has Abortions?

	NUMBER OF ABORTIONS	PERCENT OF ALL ABORTIONS	ABORTIONS PER 1,000 BIRTHS	PERCENTAGE OF PREGNANCIES THAT END IN ABORTION
AGE				
Under 15	9,000	1%	497	50%
15–19	241,000	18%	337	34%
20–24	423,000	32%	297	30%
25–29	308,000	23%	221	22%
30–34	188,000	14%	171	17%
35–39	111,000	8%	200	20%
40 and over	36,000	3%	283	28%
RACE/ETHNICITY[1]				
White	743,000	56%	190	19%
Black and other	572,000	44%	403	40%
MARITAL STATUS				
Married	253,000	19%	86	9%
Unmarried	1,062,000	81%	444	44%
REGION				
Northeast	327,000	25%	NA[2]	NA
West	350,000	26%	NA	NA
South	420,000	32%	NA	NA
Midwest	220,000	17%	NA	NA
WEEKS OF GESTATION				
Less than 9	750,000	57%	NA	NA
9–10	272,000	21%	NA	NA
11–12	139,000	11%	NA	NA
13 or more	154,000	12%	NA	NA
NUMBER OF PRIOR ABORTIONS				
None	682,000	52%	NA	NA
1	365,000	28%	NA	NA
2 or more	268,000	20%	NA	NA

[1]This is the rather strange classification used in the source.
[2]Not Available or Not Applicable.
Source: By the author. Based on *Statistical Abstract* 2003:Tables 83, 95, 104.

What Is a Social Problem?

THE ESSENTIAL ELEMENTS OF A SOCIAL PROBLEM

Objective Conditions and Subjective Concerns

Basically, a **social problem** is some aspect of society that people are concerned about and would like changed. Social problems begin with an **objective condition,** some aspect of society that can be measured or experienced. With abortion, this objective condition includes whether abortions are legal, who obtains them, and under what circumstances. The second key element of a social problem is **subjective concern,** the concern that a significant number of people (or a number of significant people) have about the condition. Subjective concern about abortion includes some people's distress that abortion is not more freely available and that some women must give birth to unwanted children. It also includes other people's distress that any woman would ter-

A Global Glimpse

SEX-SELECTION ABORTION IN INDIA: ONLY FEMALES ELIGIBLE

As you know, science has provided physicians with prenatal tests that reveal the sex of the fetus. In amniocentesis, which can be done during the second trimester of pregnancy, a sonogram locates the fetus. The physician then inserts a needle through the abdomen and withdraws amniotic fluid from the uterus. In CVS (chorionic villi sampling), which can be done as early as the tenth week of pregnancy, the doctor uses a catheter to remove cells from the developing placenta. Now combine these powerful diagnostic tools with a society that is pro-son and anti-daughter.

"May you be the mother of a hundred sons" is the toast made to brides in India, where the birth of a son causes rejoicing and the birth of a daughter brings sadness.

Why? A son continues the family name, preserves wealth and property within the family, takes care of aged parents (the elderly have no Social Security), and performs the parents' funeral rites. Hinduism even teaches that a sonless father cannot achieve salvation.

A daughter, in contrast, is a liability. Men want to marry only virgins, and the parents of a daughter bear the burden of having to protect her virginity. At marriage, they also must pay a dowry to her husband. A common saying in India reflects the female's low status: "To bring up a daughter is like watering a neighbor's plant."

One consequence of these conditions is that female infanticide, killing newborn girl babies, is common in India.

Because these diagnostic techniques reveal the sex of the fetus, many Indians are practicing gender-selective abortion instead of female infanticide. If the test reveals that the fetus is female, they choose to abort it. Some clinics even put up billboards that proclaim, "Invest Rs.500 now, save Rs.50,000 later." This means that by paying Rs.500 (500 Indian rupees) to abort a female, a family can save a dowry of 50,000 rupees in years to come.

Some mothers-to-be resist, of course. To overcome their reluctance, nurses in one clinic show pregnant women the fetuses of twin girls that they keep under the counter. The thought of double vigilance and two dowries is usually sufficient to convince them to have an abortion.

An accident happened in one clinic that made national headlines: A *male* fetus was unintentionally aborted. Protests spread across India, and the Indian legislature passed a law forbidding doctors to tell would-be parents the sex of their fetuses. Physicians who violate the law can be sent to prison and banned from their profession.

An eminent physician disagrees with the law. He says, "The need for a male child is an economic need in our society, and our feminists who are raising such hue and cry about female feticide should realize that it is better to get rid of an unwanted child than to make it suffer all its life."

What do you think?

Based on Kusum 1993; Holman 1994; Raghunathan 2003.

---

minate the life of her unborn child. To see how subjective concerns about abortion differ in another part of the world, see the Global Glimpse box above.

Social Problems Are Dynamic

As society changes, so do objective conditions and subjective concerns. This means that social problems are dynamic. As I mentioned, abortion was illegal in the United States until 1973. In that year, the U.S. Supreme Court made a landmark decision known as *Roe v. Wade*, by which the Court legalized abortion. Before this decision, the social problem of abortion was quite unlike what it is today. The primary objective condition was that abortion was illegal. The subjective concerns centered on women who wanted abortions but could not get them, that mostly untrained people performed abortions, and that women died from botched, underground surgeries. As growing numbers of people became concerned, they worked to change the law. They were successful, and this transformed the problem: Large numbers of people became upset that abortion had become legal. Convinced that abortion is murder, they began their own campaign to change the law. Those who favor legal abortion oppose each step they take. We'll look more closely at this in a moment, but you can see how a social problem is dynamic, how it takes shape as groups react to one another.

Social Problems Are Relative

Social Problems Involve Competing Definitions

As you can see from the example of abortion, what people consider to be a social problem depends on their values. *A social problem for some may be a solution for others.* The *Roe v. Wade* decision of 1973 was a solution for some but a disaster for others. Similarly, mugging is not a social problem for muggers. The billions of dollars spent on warfare are not a social problem for McDonnell Douglas and other corporations that profit from arming the world. Nuclear power is not a social problem for the corporations that use it to generate electricity. From the Issues in Social Problems box below and from Table 1-2, you can see that how people define abortion leads to contrasting views of this social problem.

In a dynamic world of contrasting definitions, whose definition of a social problem wins? The answer centers around **power,** the ability to get your way despite obstacles. After abortion became legal in 1973, most observers assumed that the social problem was over—the opponents of abortion had lost, and they would quietly fade away. As you know, this assumption was naive. Feelings were so strong that groups that had been hostile to one another for centuries, such as Roman Catholics and Baptists,

---

Issues in Social Problems
THE RELATIVITY OF SOCIAL PROBLEMS

"A problem for some is a solution for others" could have been the title of this box. What a specific condition of society means to us depends on our socialization, on what we have learned. Even though we may agree with others on many aspects of life, we can still disagree sharply about the meaning of some objective condition. And these meanings are not written in stone, As we are exposed to different ideas and information, our position on a social problem can change.

This relativity is illustrated in the case of abortion, whose central issue is how people define the status of the unborn. Is the fetus a human being, as the antiabortionists believe, or only a "potential" human, as the proabortionists believe?

Let's look at these two main opposing views.

THE FETUS IS NOT A HUMAN BEING

This is the position of most people who believe that abortion is a woman's right. "The fetus is a potential person that looks increasingly human as it develops" (NARAL). It follows, then, that abortion is not killing but merely a medical procedure. It is the woman's right to have an abortion for whatever reason she desires—from financial pressures to health problems—as well as to help attain goals, whether those be to limit family size, to finish school, to win a promotion at work, or to fulfill any other plans that she might have. The state, therefore, should permit abortion on demand.

THE FETUS IS A HUMAN BEING

This is the position of most people who oppose abortion. It follows, then, that abortion is murder, a killing of unborn babies. To simply want an abortion cannot justify killing a baby. A woman has no right to abortion, for it is not just her body that is involved but also the life of another human—her own child. The exception is when another human life, the mother's, lies in the balance. The state has no business legalizing murder, and abortion should be illegal.

What do you think?

TABLE 1-2 How Definitions of Abortion Affect People's Views

WHO DOES THE DEFINING?	THE RESULTING VIEWS				
	WHAT ABORTION IS	WHAT IS ABORTED	THE WOMAN	THE ACT OF ABORTION	THE ONE WHO PERFORMS THE ABORTION
People Who Favor Abortion	A woman's right	Fetus	Independent individual	A service to women	Skilled technician
People Who Oppose Abortion	Murder	Baby	Mother	Killing a baby	Murderer
People Who Do Abortions	Part of my work	Fetus	Client	A medical procedure	Professional

Source: Modified from Roe 1989.

began to work together to oppose abortion. Shocked at what they considered the killing of babies, they took to the streets and to the courts, fighting pitched battles over an issue that lies at the heart of social divisions in U.S. society.

In Sum

This little overview of how the objective conditions and subjective concerns about abortion have changed in the United States is important, for it helps us to understand how social problems develop. Sociologists have found that social problems go through four stages, which they call *the natural history of a social problem*. Let's continue with the example of abortion to see how this process occurs.

(A Note on Unsatisfactory Terms)

Before we do, we need to pause to consider the matter of terms. Definitions and terms are always signficant, but especially so when we deal with highly sensitve issues

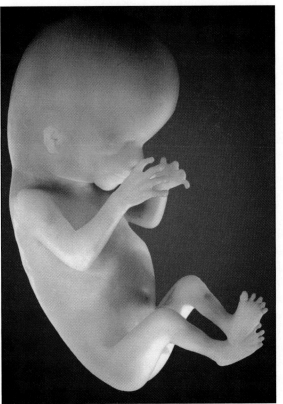

How people define the unborn is the essence of their position on abortion. Pictured here is a fetus of about eleven weeks gestation. Those on one side of the abortion controversy use terms such as "product of conception," while those on the other side call it a baby.

such as abortion. As I'm sure you noticed, in the box on the relativity of social problems I used the terms *antiabortion* and *proabortion*. Terms can represent attitudes and positions and provoke strong emotional response. Although these terms are not entirely satisfactory, and neither side prefers them, I shall use the term *antiabortion* to refer to those who oppose the legal right to abortion and *proabortion* to refer to those who favor it. Intended to be neutral, these terms are less value laden than *prochoice* and *prolife*, which the two sides prefer. If I have succeeded in my intentions in this chapter, even if readers do not like this choice of terms, both those who favor the legal right to abortion and those who oppose it will feel that I have fairly presented their side. For more information on these terms, see the Preface.

The Natural History of Social Problems

How Attitudes toward
Abortion Are Influenced
by Social Location

The first major change occurred in 1970 when Hawaii, in an unprecedented move, legalized abortion. Several states had liberalized their abortion laws at that point, but they still kept abortion illegal except under special circumstances, such as when pregnancy endangered the mother's health. Hawaii's law, in contrast, defined abortion as a private, noncriminal act.

What made Hawaii receptive to such radical change? Before we look at the natural history of abortion, let's take a brief look at the Hawaiian situation (Steinhoff and Diamond 1977). First, more than three-quarters of the population lived on the island of Oahu, where they had a tradition of personally knowing their politicians and participating in political hearings. Second, two-income families had become common, and half the women over age 16 worked. Finally, during an epidemic of German measles in 1964 and 1965, many Hawaiian obstetricians had aborted fetuses to prevent them from being born with deformities. This was a turning point for the physicians, and the rate of abortion never fell back to its pre-1964 level.

Social Problems Go
through Four Stages

With this brief background, let's trace how this issue developed in Hawaii, as well as in the United States as a whole. We shall see that social problems go through four stages.

THE FIRST STAGE: DEFINING THE PROBLEM, THE EMERGENCE OF LEADERS, AND BEGINNING TO ORGANIZE

How Social Problems
Begin

As you have just seen, for a social problem to come into being, people have to become upset about some objective condition. This involves a shift in outlook, a questioning of something that had been taken for granted. This change in perspective can come about in a number of ways. For example, if values change, an old, established pattern will no longer look the same. This is what happened with abortion. The 1960s brought extensive, wrenching social change to the United States. Young people—primarily teenagers and those in their 20s—challenged established values. Amidst political uproar, accompanied by widespread demonstrations, many new values were adopted. The women's movement was part of this challenge to established ideas. As this movement gained followers, more and more women felt that they should not have to become criminals to terminate a pregnancy. They became convinced that they had the right to legal abortions.

Defining the Problem
and the Emergence
of Leaders

As people discussed their concerns about abortion being illegal, leaders emerged who helped to crystallize the issues. State Senator Vincent Yano, a Roman Catholic and the father of ten, argued that if abortion were a sin, it would be better to have no abortion law than to have one that allowed it under certain circumstances (Steinhoff and Diamond 1977). This reasoning allowed Yano to maintain his religious opposition to abortion while favoring the repeal of Hawaii's law against abortion.

Organizing Around
the Issue

Another leader emerged, Joan Hayes, a former Washington lobbyist. She felt that simply to liberalize the laws against abortion would be to duck what she saw as the major issue: the right of a woman to choose whether to have a baby. Hayes understood the use of power—and the value of arousing a concerned public. She invited leaders in medicine, business, labor, politics, religion, and the media to a citizens' seminar on abortion sponsored by the American Association of University Women.

THE SECOND STAGE: CRAFTING THE OFFICIAL RESPONSE

The Stages Overlap

The stages of a social problem don't have neat ending and beginning points. Their edges are blurry, and they overlap. In this case, between 1967 and 1968, legislators had introduced several bills to soften the law against abortion. These bills, which would have broadened the circumstances under which abortion would be legal, were actually attempts to redefine abortion. Thus, the stages of defining the social problem and officially responding to it were intertwined.

The turning point came when Senator Yano announced that he would support the repeal of the abortion law. This stimulated other official responses as organizations, from the Chamber of Commerce to the Roman Catholic church, endorsed or rejected the repeal. Public forums and legislative hearings were held, generating huge amounts of publicity. This publicity served as a vital bridge between the public at large and the advocates of repeal. As Hawaiians became keenly aware of the abortion issue, polls showed that most wanted to repeal the law against abortion. In 1970, Hawaii did just that.

THE THIRD STAGE: REACTING TO THE OFFICIAL RESPONSE

Official Response Engenders Controversy and Opposition

As sometimes happens, the official response to a social problem becomes defined as a social problem. This is what happened with abortion, especially after 1973, when the U.S. Supreme Court concurred with the Hawaiian legislation and struck down all state laws that prohibited abortion. Indignant about what they saw as murder, antiabortion groups picketed and used political pressure to try to sway public opinion and turn legislative defeat into victory.

Besides inspiring new opposition, official response also can change the definition of the social problem that is held by those who promoted the reform in the first place. In this case, proabortion groups noted that despite their Supreme Court victory, most

FIGURE 1-1 *Abortions and Live Births*

Source: By the author. Based on *Statistical Abstract* 2003:Tables 83, 95, 104.

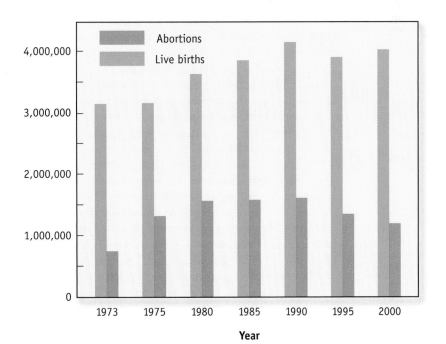

counties did not offer abortions, and many women who wanted abortions could not obtain them. Consequently, they began to promote abortion clinics to make abortion more readily accessible.

Figure 1-1 on page 9 shows the success of these efforts. In 1973, the first year of legal abortion, 745,000 abortions were performed. This number quickly climbed to one million, then to a million and a half, where it reached a plateau. From 1979 to 1994, the total ran between 1,500,000 and 1,600,000 each year, but beginning in 1995 the number began to drop. It now is about 1,300,000 a year. Figure 1-2 presents another overview of abortion. There you can see that the abortion ratio climbed sharply, hit its peak in 1983, and then began to drop. Today, for every 100 live births there are about 32 abortions.

THE FOURTH STAGE: DEVELOPING ALTERNATIVE STRATEGIES

Alternative Strategies Pit Group Against Group

The many abortions after the Supreme Court's ruling led to a pitched battle that still rages. Let's look at some of the alternative strategies developed by the pro- and antiabortion groups.

Antiabortion groups have tried to persuade states to restrict the Supreme Court's ruling. They have succeeded in eliminating federal funding of abortions for military personnel and their dependents, federal prisoners, and workers with the Peace Corps. They also have succeeded in eliminating health insurance coverage of abortions for federal employees. Their major victory on the federal level took place in 1976, when opponents of abortion persuaded Congress to pass the Hyde Amendment, which prohibits Medicaid funding for abortions except to save a woman's life. When the Supreme Court upheld this amendment in 1980 (Lewis 1988), the number of abortions paid for by federal funds plummeted from 300,000 a year to just 17. Despite repeated attempts to change the Hyde Amendment, the antiabortion forces have succeeded in retaining it.

Alternative Strategies of the Antiabortionists

A highly effective strategy of the antiabortion groups is the establishment of a national network of "crisis pregnancy centers." Women who call "pregnancy hotlines" (sometimes called life lines or birth lines) are offered free pregnancy testing. When they accept it, they are directed to counselors who encourage them to give birth. The counselors inform women about fetal development, talk to them about the financial help and social support available to them during pregnancy. They also advise the women about finding adoptive parents or obtaining financial support after the birth. Some activists also operate maternity homes and provide adoption services.

Neither side on this social problem is a single, organized group. Rather, this is a social movement, and it has swept up people from every background, some of whom are moderate, others radical, and most somewhere in between.

The moderates choose moderate alternative strategies. They run newspaper ads and write their representatives. Those in between picket abortion clinics. Some took their cue from the civil rights movement of the 1950s and practiced passive resistance. Lying immobile in front of abortion clinics, they allowed the police to carry them to jail. In the late 1980s, antiabortion groups practiced massive nonviolent civil disobedience, and thousands of demonstrators were arrested. This social movement is so large and active that more abortion protesters have been arrested than the number of people arrested in the entire civil rights movement (Allen 1988; Lacayo 1991; Kirkpatrick 1992).

Radical activists, in contrast, lean toward radical methods. They have thrown blood on abortion clinics, pulled the plug on abortion machines, jammed locks with superglue, set off stink bombs, and telephoned women at night with recordings of babies screaming. Radical activists also have burned and bombed abortion clinics. In the town in which I taught, Edwardsville, Illinois, a group kidnapped a physician and threatened

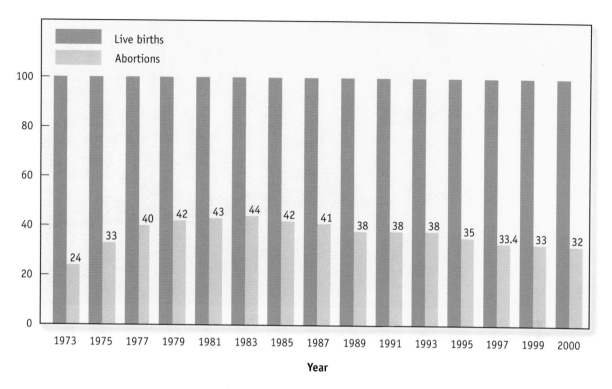

FIGURE 1-2 *Number of Abortions per 100 Live Births*
Source: By the author. Based on *Statistical Abstract* 1988:Tables 81, 103; 1994:Table 111; 1998:Tables 104, 115; 2003:Tables 84, 104.

his life if he did not shut down his abortion clinics. Radical activists have shot and killed four abortion doctors, acts that have been condemned by both proabortionists and antiabortionists alike.

Alternative Strategies of the Proabortionists

Proabortion groups, too, have developed alternative strategies. Their counterattack has taken three primary forms: campaigning for proabortion politicians, lobbying lawmakers to vote against restrictive legislation, and seeking broad-based support by publicizing their position. They have stressed a dual message: Abortion is a woman's private decision in which government should not be involved, and "without the right to choose abortion, any other guarantees of liberty have little meaning for women" (Michelman 1988). They have recruited women who had abortions when it was back-alley business to alert the public to what it would be like if the right to abortion were taken away. Their message: rich women flying to countries where abortion is legal, poor women victimized by unqualified underground abortionists, and thousands of women dying from illegal abortions (Krieger 1985).

Mutual Accusations

Each side paints the other as grotesque, uncaring, and evil. Proabortionists accuse antiabortionists of being concerned about fetuses but not about pregnant women. They also point to the killing of physicians as evidence of hypocrisy—that people who say they stand for life kill others. For their part, antiabortionists accuse proabortionists of suppressing information about the health risks of abortion—and of murdering helpless, innocent, unborn children.

In the midst of this controversy, the U.S. Supreme Court remains the final arbiter of abortion. Short of a constitutional amendment, no matter what laws the states, or even Congress, should pass, the Supreme Court decides whether those laws are constitutional. Consequently, both proabortionists and antiabortionists try to influence how

The nine men and women who serve for life on the U.S. Supreme Court determine the constitutionality of the laws passed by the states and the U.S. Congress. Because their interpretations of the U.S. Constitution are not objective (although they are supposed to be) but are, instead, biased by their political and personal views, their rulings on matters concerning abortion are uncertain.

the Senate votes on Supreme Court nominees. Presidents for the past couple of decades have taken strong positions on abortion and have proposed nominees for the Supreme Court that reflect their position. We can expect this stacking of the Court to continue.

The 1989 Webster Decision

Three Supreme Court decisions since the 1973 *Roe v. Wade* decision are especially significant. The first is *Webster v. Reproductive Services*. In 1989, by a 5-to-4 vote, the Supreme Court ruled that

1. States have no obligation to finance abortion: They can prohibit the use of public funds for abortions and abortion counseling, and they can ban abortions at public hospitals.
2. States have a compelling interest to protect fetal life: Before doctors can abort a fetus that is 20 weeks or over, they must perform tests to determine its viability (capacity to live outside the uterus).

The 1992 Casey *vs.* Planned Parenthood Decision

The second significant decision is *Casey v. Planned Parenthood*. In 1992, by a vote of 6 to 3, the Supreme Court upheld a Pennsylvania law requiring that a woman under age 18 obtain the consent of at least one parent, that a 24-hour waiting period between confirming a pregnancy and having an abortion be enforced, and that the woman be given materials describing the fetus, as well as a list of agencies offering adoption services and alternatives to abortion. By a 5-to-4 vote, however, the Court also ruled that a wife has no obligation to inform her husband of her intention to have an abortion. *Casey* allows states to pass laws that restrict abortion—unless such laws impose an "undue burden" on a woman's ability to have an abortion.

The 1993 Freedom of Access to Clinic Entrances Act

A third significant legal decision occurred in 1993, this time in favor of the proabortion forces. In that year, they won a major victory when Congress passed the Freedom

You

have the freedom to choose.
And now, you have another
safe abortion choice.

The Early Option Pill has
been approved by the FDA.

It safely and effectively terminates a pregnancy, and offers yet another option for women. Mifepristone, the medical breakthrough known as RU-486 in Europe, is now available in the U.S. Taken in the first 49 days of pregnancy, the Early Option Pill works to block the effects of a hormone needed to sustain pregnancy. In U.S. clinical studies, 96% of women said they would recommend it to a friend. To find out if the option used by over half a million women in Europe is right for you—or for a referral to a quality provider—call the National Abortion Federation (NAF) hotline. At NAF, our members have provided quality care to women for over 20 years.

Find out if the Early Option Pill is an option for you: 1-800-772-9100 | www.earlyoptions.org

From the text, you know the two opposing definitions of reality that apply to this ad. For the proabortionists ("pro-choice"), this ad represents expanding freedom of reproductive choices for women. For the antiabortionists ("pro-life"), this ad represents another way that women kill their unborn children. With such starkly different views of reality, these two sides can never come together.

**Five Contributions
of Sociology**

of Access to Clinic Entrances Act. This law impedes demonstrations, for it requires picketers and other demonstrators to remain 300 feet away from the entrances to abortion clinics. If they don't, they face up to three years in prison. The Supreme Court has ruled that this Act does not violate freedom of speech. This was a significant victory for the proabortion side, practically eliminating the picketing of abortion clinics.

Neither the proabortionists nor the antiabortionists can be satisfied, as *there is no middle ground.* Both sides consider their alternative strategies as only nibbling at the problem. Each wants total victory. The antiabortion groups advocate a constitutional amendment that would define human life as beginning at conception and abortion as murder. In almost a mirror image, the proabortion groups want Congress to pass a Freedom of Choice Act that would remove all state restrictions on abortion.

The activists in this ongoing social problem illustrate how interest groups develop alternative strategies as they line up on opposing sides of a social problem. In the case of abortion, the final results are still unclear and probably never will be final. On both sides are highly motivated people. Each side considers the other unreasonable. Each is rationally and emotionally dedicated to its view of morality: One talks about killing babies, the other about forcing women to bear unwanted children, even those conceived from incest and rape. With no middle ground to bridge the chasm, there is no end in sight to this determined struggle.

The Role of Sociology in Social Problems

SOCIOLOGY AS A TOOL FOR BREAKING THROUGH EMOTIONS AND DEFENSES

Sociology, the study of social behavior, helps us see past the passions that surround a social problem. Most people think of their world in individualistic and moral terms. In the chapter's opening vignette, for example, Lisa may think that her grandmother is narrow-minded, and her grandmother may wonder how Lisa acquired such casual morals. Personal defenses and moral viewpoints are real, but they cannot explain social problems.

There are five ways by which sociology can penetrate such emotions and defenses to yield a better understanding of social problems. The first is to determine the extent of a social problem by *measuring its objective conditions.* For abortion, sociologists can gather information on the number of abortions performed in clinics and hospitals. They can also determine why women have or do not have abortions, how women adjust to their decision to abort or to bear a child, and how their husbands or boyfriends react.

Second, sociologists can *measure subjective concerns;* that is, they can determine people's attitudes about social problems (Becker 1966). Such information is useful in evaluating potential policies. To establish sound public policy involves much more than measuring public opinion, of course, but accurate measurements can guide policy makers. An example of measuring subjective concern is Table 1-3, which shows Americans' attitudes about abortion. Note how people's attitudes are related to their age, education, income, and where they live.

Third, sociologists can *apply the sociological imagination;* that is, they can place social problems into their broad social context. For example, abortion is related to people's attitudes about sexuality and sex roles. Abortion is also related to profound differences of opinion about privacy, what human life is, when life begins and ends, the role of the medical profession in terminating life, the role of religious institutions in a pluralistic society, the concept of individual freedom versus responsibility to the group, ideas about desirable standards of living and parenting, and what is and is not moral (Lerner et al. 1990).

Fourth, sociologists can *identify different ways to intervene* in a social problem, *and,* fifth, they can *evaluate likely consequences of social policies* (Becker 1966). For example, sociologists can estimate how different social policies on abortion will affect the birth rate, population growth, and expenditures for welfare and education.

These five tasks are much more easily listed than performed. Although sociologists gather extensive information on social problems, making accurate predictions from those data is difficult. People sometimes change their behaviors unexpectedly, which can throw off the best predictions of social scientists. Sociology, however, is especially useful for clarifying issues in social problems. Clarification, of course, requires facts, which leads to the question of how sociologists get dependable information. Can they simply depend on common sense?

SOCIOLOGY AND COMMON SENSE

People have "gut feelings" about the world. Based on their experiences, they "just know" what is and is not true. People use **common sense,** the ideas common to a society (or to some group within a society) to make sense out of their experience in life. Their commonsense interpretations also give them ideas about social problems. As a result, everybody develops opinions about what causes a social problem, and what ought to be done about it.

Common Sense Is Not Enough

Common sense, though, is not enough, for it is based on impressions that may not be correct. Let's see how common sense holds up when it comes to abortion. Commonsense views about abortion include the ideas that abortion is a last resort, that women who get abortions do not know how to use contraceptives, and certainly, that women who get abortions did not want to get pregnant.

Although these three commonsense ideas appear obvious, they are not necessarily true. For example, abortion is not always a last resort. In Russia, abortion is a major means of birth control, and the average Russian woman has six abortions during her lifetime (Yablonsky 1981; Eberstadt 1988). Abortion is so common in Russia that there are twice as many abortions as births (Kinkade 1997; Library of Congress 1999).

Sociological Research Probes Beneath the Surface

Nor is it that women who have abortions don't know how to use contraceptives. Sociologist Kristin Luker (1975), who studied an abortion clinic in California, found that many women did not use contraceptives, even though they knew how to use them and did not want to get pregnant. They avoided contraceptives, Luker discovered, because they interfered with intimacy, were expensive, were disapproved of by their boyfriends, or caused adverse side effects. Some even avoided contraceptives to protect their self-concept. If they used contraceptives, they would think of themselves as "available" or sexually promiscuous, but without them they looked at sex as some-

TABLE 1-3 Should Abortion Be Legal or Illegal?
This question was asked of a representative sample of Americans:
"Do you think abortions should be legal under any circumstances, legal only under certain circumstances, or illegal in all circumstances?"

	ALWAYS LEGAL	LEGAL UNDER CERTAIN CIRCUMSTANCES	NEVER LEGAL
National	24%	57%	18%
Sex			
Male	22	64	13
Female	25	51	22
Race-Ethnicity			
White	25	57	17
Nonwhite	20	56	20
Black	19	58	21
Age			
18–29 years	20	58	22
30–49 years	27	55	16
50–64 years	30	53	16
50 years and older	22	59	17
65 years and older	13	66	18
Education			
College postgraduate	37	50	12
College graduate	35	51	13
Some college	24	62	13
High school graduate or less	16	58	24
Income			
$75,000 and over	33	57	9
$50,000–74,999	29	58	11
$30,000–49,999	22	58	19
$20,000–29,999	20	61	19
Under $20,000	14	53	30
Community			
Urban area	33	49	17
Suburban area	21	61	16
Rural area	17	59	23
Region			
East	28	54	17
Midwest	24	58	16
South	18	58	23
West	27	57	13
Politics			
Republican	14	57	27
Democrat	31	57	11
Independent	26	58	15

Source: Table 2.101 of *Sourcebook of Criminal Justice Statistics,* 2003.

Life takes many twists and turns, and is sometimes stranger than fiction. Shown here is Norma McCorvey, the "Jane Roe" of the landmark 1972 Roe v. Wade U.S. Supreme Court decision. McCorvey now works with antiabortion groups. This photo was taken at a rally in Dallas, Texas.

thing that "just happened." Luker's study shows that some women take chances—and they get pregnant and have abortions.

Sociologist Leon Dash (1990), who studied pregnancy among teenagers in Washington, D.C., found that the third commonsense idea is also not necessarily true. Some girls get pregnant deliberately. Some want children so that, as they said, "I can have something to hold onto that I can call my own." Some boyfriends also urge their girlfriends to get pregnant. They say that this will make them "feel like a man." And, as Luker discovered, some women get pregnant to test their boyfriend's commitment. Often the relationship sours, and the young women decide not to bear the child. In short, contrary to a middle-class perspective, many poor, young, unmarried women get pregnant because they *want* to.

Principles underlying sociological research.   Luker's and Dash's studies illustrate that our commonsense ideas may not be correct, but how can sociological research provide the understanding that we need to deal with social problems? This is because sociologists

1. *Use scientific methods* to provide objective, systematic research, rather than basing findings on personal experience, assumption, or opinion.
2. *Do not base their conclusions on emotions or personal values.* To do so would obscure our perspective and prevent us from seeing things objectively. Even if sociologists discover things that contradict their own values, they are obligated ethically to report those findings.
3. *Use the sociological imagination.* To discover the underlying causes of social problems, sociologists interpret them from the framework of the larger picture. In contrast, as we saw with Lisa and her grandmother, people's common sense leads them to perceive matters on a personal level, rather than in the context of larger social patterns.

That sociologists can do objective research does not mean that sociology has all the answers. Sociologists can suggest consequences that may result if some particular social policy is developed, but they have no expertise for determining which social policy *should* be followed. To decide social policy depends on people's values, on the outcomes that they want to see. Because sociology cannot determine that one set of values is superior to another, it provides no basis for making value decisions. In short, from sociology we can estimate likely outcomes of specific social policies, but we cannot determine which social policy should be chosen. We'll come back to this in a moment, but first let's look at how sociologists do their research.

METHODS FOR STUDYING SOCIAL PROBLEMS

How Do Sociologists Study Social Problems?

Designing a Study: Research Begins with Questions To Be Answered

To investigate social problems, sociologists choose from several **methods** (ways of doing research). Which method they choose depends on two things: the questions they want to investigate and what is practical. First, they must determine what they want to find out about a social problem, for *the method depends on the goal.* Suppose that a sociologist wants to find out how people form their ideas about abortion. This will call for a different method of research than if a sociologist wants to find out whether college-educated women have fewer abortions than do high-school dropouts. In this short review, we shall first distinguish how sociologists design their studies, then describe how they gather their information.

Most studies fall into one of four common **research designs:** case studies, surveys, experiments, and field studies. Let's look at each.

Four Basic Research Designs:

1. Case Studies

The **case study** is intended to gain in-depth information on some specific situation. As the name implies, the researcher focuses on one *case*—an individual, an event, or even an organization such as an abortion clinic or a crisis pregnancy center. Suppose that you want in-depth information about how women experience abortion. You want to know what conflicts and emotions women experience as they wrestle with the decision, to whom they talk about it, how they feel during the abortion, and how they adjust afterward. A case study could provide this type of detail.

2. Surveys

If you focused on just one woman, however, you wouldn't know whether her experiences are similar to those of other women who had abortions. The **survey** overcomes this limitation. In a survey, you focus on a **sample** of the target group you want to study. (Sociologists call the target group your **population.**) Samples are intended to represent the entire group that is being studied. You probably would want to **generalize**—that is, to apply your findings to people who were not included in your sample. The best way to do this is to use a **random sample,** a sample in which everyone in your population has an equal chance of being included in your study. Random samples are powerful. National surveys on attitudes toward abortion poll only about 2,000 people, yet this sample can represent accurately the opinions of 300,000,000 Americans.

3. Experiments

If you were to use an **experiment,** you would divide people who have certain characteristics (such as Latinas between ages 18 and 21 with two years of college) into two groups. You would expose half of them to some experience. These people are called the **experimental group.** You would do this to see how their reactions differ from those of the other half, who do not have this experience (the **control group**). How the experimental group responds is thought to be generalizable to people who share their characteristics.

Experiments are rare in the study of social problems, partly because ethics do not allow sociologists to create problems for people. For example, sociologists cannot randomly assign some pregnant women to give birth and others to obtain abortions in order to study their reactions. Sociologists, however, can use experiments in more limited ways. For example, if sociologists want to learn how some particular information affects people's attitudes toward abortion, they could measure a group's attitudes, have a random half of that group listen to a woman tell about her abortion, and then measure the attitudes of both groups.

4. Field Studies

In **field studies** (or **participant observation**), researchers go into a setting that they want to learn more about. (This is called "going into the field.") For example, Magda Denes (1976) wanted to know what an abortion hospital was like—for the women and the staff—so she obtained permission to be present and observe. The result was a moving book, *In Necessity and Sorrow.* Denes believes that women should be able to choose abortion, but in the abortion hospital she found sadness everywhere. She describes picking up fetuses from the trash barrel, their little arms broken, cut, and bleeding. A doctor tells her how the fetus stops moving about half an hour after he injects the saline solution, but the women rarely mention this change within them. A single woman talks about her affair with a married man who does not know that she is having an abortion. No other research method could obtain information like this.

Because each research design has its strengths and weaknesses, sociologists often use more than one design. Luker and Denes, for example, each studied women in a single abortion clinic. Their studies could be followed up with surveys of women from many abortion clinics.

After choosing a research design, sociologists decide how to gather their information. Four basic methods are available: interviews, questionnaires, documents, and observations.

Four Techniques of Gathering Information

1. Interviews

Sociologists who use **interviews** ask people questions on the topics they want to explore. There are two basic types of interviews. In a **structured interview,** the researcher asks everyone the same questions (for example, "What is your relationship to the man who made you pregnant?"). In an **unstructured interview,** the researcher lets people talk about their experiences in depth, but makes certain that everyone covers specific areas (contraceptive history, family relations, why abortion is desired, and so on). Look at the Thinking Critically box on the next page. To learn how women interpret their abortion, I used unstructured interviews. The women could talk about their experiences in any way they wanted, and I never knew where that would lead. Structured interviews would not have tapped such in-depth feelings and perspectives.

2. Questionnaires

In the second method, **questionnaires,** people answer written questions. The questions can be either *open ended* (people answer in their own words) or *closed ended* (people must choose from a list of prepared answers). An open-ended question might be, "What is your relationship to the man who made you pregnant?" The woman would state the relationship in her own words. A closed-ended form of this question might ask the person to check one of these choices: husband, boyfriend, casual acquaintance, other. The answers to closed-ended questions are easier to compare, but open-ended questions tap a richer world, eliciting comments and even topics that the researcher did not anticipate.

3. Documents

Documents, written sources or records, often provide a rich source of data about social problems. The documents can be formal. Kristin Luker, for example, analyzed the records of 500 women who came to the abortion clinic that she studied. Informal documents are also useful. Journals, blogs, and letters can reveal people's attitudes and provide insight into how they cope with troubles.

4. Observation

The fourth method, **observation,** is just what the term implies: Sociologists observe what is occurring in a setting. They watch and listen to what is taking place, recording their observations, including conversations and statements that people make. Sociologists sometimes use tape recorders, but when recording would interfere with what people are doing, they take notes, either as something occurs or afterward. When observation is *overt,* sociologists identify themselves as researchers, but when it is *covert,* people in the setting are unaware that sociologists are studying them.

Sociologists often combine these methods. For example, Luker used three of these methods: observation, interviews, and documents. Not only did she observe women and abortion providers in the clinic, but also she interviewed women who were having abortions, and she examined the clinic's records on its patients.

Striving for Accuracy and Objectivity

Sociologists strive for objectivity. They do not want their data to be biased. For example, it is obvious that if a sociologist were to ask, "What is your opinion about killing babies by abortion?" the study would be biased in an antiabortion direction. No one, whether proabortion or antiabortion, favors killing babies. This sort of question would not constitute scientific research. Nor would this question, which would bias answers the other way: "What is your opinion on forcing a woman to have a baby when she wants an abortion?"

To be neutral, a sociologist might choose a closed-ended question, such as, "Do you favor or oppose abortion?" Or a sociologist might ask an open-ended question, such as, "What is your opinion about abortion?" You can see that these questions are neutral, not tilting answers in any direction. In either of these questions, the researcher might specify the trimester being considered. The safeguard against prejudicial re-

Thinking Critically about Social Problems
COPING WITH GUILT AFTER AN ABORTION

Having an abortion solves the immediate problem of an unwanted pregnancy, but it also creates new problems. One is how to define the abortion. For those who view the fetus as nonhuman, this can be relatively simple. For those who view the fetus as a human, however (as well as for those with mixed views, which appears to characterize most women), the situation is more complicated.

How do women cope? While abortions were still illegal (1971), I interviewed 22 college women who had abortions. These women used four major techniques to help them cope:

1. Some women think of abortion as *the lesser of two evils*. They view abortion as preferable to having a child and ruining their own life or the lives of people they love; as preferable to shifting the responsibility for rearing the child onto others; or as preferable to resenting the child for having been born. One woman said:

   We saved ourselves and a child and very numerous other people from a lot of hurt because of this. And besides that, it was the only thing I could do—the only thing that I wanted to do, let's put it that way.

2. Some women look at abortion as a *positive good* in and of itself:

   (My mom) thought it'd be the best thing. . . . After my mom told me, I started to talk to my girlfriend, and she decided it would probably be the best thing for me, too. . . . I told (my boyfriend). . . . He thought that would be the best thing. . . . I always told myself that, you know, I'd probably get one if I didn't get married, 'cause to me that would be the best thing for me.

3. Some women see themselves as having *no responsibility because they had no choice*:

   He (boyfriend) insisted that I do this. I was against it. . . . I knew that I didn't want to . . . but when you have someone saying, "Well, this is what I want you to do"—and he didn't want to get married, and he wouldn't let me just have the child like I wanted to do—so I really didn't have a whole lot of choices. You know what I mean?

4. Some women think in terms of *a future pregnancy that will replace the "pregnancy-abortion"*:

   The mistake is past, if it was a mistake. At any rate, we can do nothing about it now. Now we have to look to the future. In another year John and I will hopefully have the start of our own family. Thoughts of being a mother have entered my mind frequently since the abortion. I really look forward to that day!

search—for sociologists, too, have their own values and opinions about social problems—is the publication of research results. In their articles and books, sociologists include details on the methods they used. Other sociologists examine these publications and are quick to point out flaws.

To highlight the research that sociologists do and to better understand how research is actually conducted, I asked researchers to share their experiences with us. For a summary of this feature, see the Spotlight on Research box on page 21.

SHOULD SOCIOLOGISTS TAKE SIDES?

Sociology Cannot Decide Moral Issues

These research methods allow us to gather objective information, but they do not reveal what attitude or social policy is "correct." This takes us back to the issue I mentioned earlier, that of sociology not having the capacity to specify that some value is superior to another. Abortion, for example, is interwoven with thorny philosophical and religious issues concerning "great questions": morality, freedom, responsibility, life, death, and ultimate existence. Sociologists can study people's ideas about these topics, but sociology has no way to determine the ultimate meaning that may underlie such issues.

What, Then, Should Be the Role of Sociologists?

"*That's the worst set of opinions I've heard in my entire life.*"

Sociologists strive for objectivity and accuracy in their research. To attain this goal, they must put away their personal opinions or biases.

The Debate Over Neutrality versus Taking a Stand

Agreement Can Camouflage Hidden Values

To take a position on a social problem is to take sides—and because sociology is not equipped to make judgments about values and morality, it cannot tell us what side to take. Even so, the question of taking sides on social problems is debated hotly among sociologists, for, like other thoughtful people, sociologists have their own concerns and ideas about social problems.

The issue is clear-cut. Should sociologists, because they are scientists, forget their personal concerns and strive to remain dispassionate, detached, and value-free? If so, they would merely report the facts and not take sides on the social issues that affect our society. Or should they use their professional authority to promote the side of an issue that they see as right? For example, should they try to help the "oppressed," the "down and out," the poor, and others who are on the receiving end of social problems?

Those who champion neutrality take the position that sociologists enjoy no superior vantage point from which to make moral judgments. Sociologists do have knowledge and skills to offer, but not morality. In their study of social problems, sociologists can indicate the potential consequences of different social policies, but they should not promote any particular policy or solution as correct. To do so would be to hide a moral position under the guise of sociology.

On the other side of this issue are sociologists who are convinced that they have the moral obligation to take a stand. "If sociology is not useful for helping to reform society," they ask, "of what value is it?" They stress that sociologists are in a strategic position to relate the surface manifestations of a social problem (such as poverty) to deeper social causes (such as the control of a country's resources by the wealthy and powerful). They say that sociologists should do their studies—and always side with those who are being hurt and exploited. Those on the extreme end of this side of this debate also say that sociologists have the moral obligation to make the oppressed aware of their condition and to organize them to do battle against those who oppress them.

Besides this vital issue of taking sides—which goes unresolved in sociology—there is yet another question about the role of sociologists in the study of social problems. We turn to it now.

SHOULD SOCIOLOGISTS DEFINE SOCIAL PROBLEMS?

What if a sociologist is concerned about a problem, but most people are either unaware or ignoring it? According to our definition (page 4), this would not be a social problem, because a social problem requires not only an objective condition (the "facts") but also subjective concern (people being upset and wanting to change those conditions). Some sociologists, however, argue that sociologists are in a better position than most people to spot the serious problems in society and that they should bring them to the public's attention (Merton and Nisbet 1976; Young 1985). For example, when sociologist Donald Cressey (1967) served on the National Task Force on Organized Crime, he urged the task force to arouse public concern.

Few who know much about organized crime would fault Cressey. After all, organized crime can harm our society. Because most of us probably agree with Cressey on this issue, we may fail to recognize the controversy that this position entails.

SPOTLIGHT ON RESEARCH

Looking Behind the Scenes

Sociologists do a lot of research on social problems. In fact, this is one of their favorite areas of study. As we review the major social problems in this text, you will be introduced to both classic research and to the most recent research findings.

To acquaint you with some of these researchers, ten of the chapters have a boxed feature titled, *Spotlight on Research*. Each box features a researcher who has studied a particular social problem. These boxes are unique, for the researchers themselves have written them.

The research that you will read about in *Spotlight on Research* is incredibly varied. With these researchers, you will visit a violent youth gang in Chicago, a bar in Chicago's inner city where gangsters hang out, and neo-Nazis in Detroit. You'll even be present at a Klan rally. In a study of workers at two magazines, you will learn how views of sexual harassment differ from one work setting to another. You will also learn how ideas about the environment are changing to include city life. One researcher lets you know how his picking beans in the fields of Washington led to a

lifetime of doing research on crime. Another researcher shares how her own abuse at the hands of her husband while she was yet a student motivated her to do research on intimate violence.

As these experts reflect on their research, they open the curtains to let you look behind the scenes. This lets you see how research is actually conducted. To help provide a broader context to appreciate their research, I open each box by sharing a little about the researcher's background and how the researcher became interested in a particular social problem.

I think that you'll enjoy these reports. The "inside" information that these researchers share gives a unique flavor to the text. From these boxes, you will learn things about research that are not available anywhere else. I am grateful to these researchers for taking time out of their research and teaching to share their experiences with us. It was a pleasure corresponding with them and gaining insight into their work.

Uncovering Hidden Values

To make this hidden value evident, we need to turn from things that most of us agree on and consider controversial matters. What if a sociologist were convinced that we should require abortion for all unmarried pregnant teenagers? Arguments can be made for and against this position, but should sociology promote such a point of view? Or consider an even more extreme case. What if a sociologist, after analyzing the soaring costs of Social Security and Medicare, were to become convinced that the solution is to euthanize the physically and mentally handicapped, or everyone over the age of 80? Would professional activity on behalf of these views be appropriate?

THE WORKING CONSENSUS

The Debate Is Divisive

This question of taking sides as *professionals* divided U.S. sociology during the Vietnam War—and it has done so again with Gulf War II. Some sociologists are convinced that the American Sociological Association should make public antiwar pronouncements; others, in contrast, feel just as strongly that such a position is out of order. Although issues change, this broad cleavage among sociologists remains. Some say that sociologists should work toward changing society in order to help the less powerful; others are just as convinced that sociology's proper role is to investigate and report objectively. They say that if sociologists want to take sides on any issue, they should do so as *private citizens*, not as sociologists.

The Value of the Debate

This debate keeps sociologists sensitive to the boundaries between objectivity and partisanship. Although there is little room for middle ground, most sociologists attempt to resolve this dilemma by separating evidence on social problems from their own values and opinions. What they observe and measure, they attempt to report dispassionately and to analyze as accurately as possible. They try to be explicit when they move from neutral description to a value position.

Areas of Agreement

Despite their disagreements about taking sides on social problems, sociologists agree that they are in a unique position to study social problems and that they should produce thorough and objective studies. Sociologists do possess the tools to provide such studies, but they do not possess the expertise or moral superiority to serve as "social problem gurus." When they do, they are reflecting their own values, not values that come from sociology.

A Personal Note

As the author of this book, it is my sincere hope that the coming chapters help you to acquire a sociological imagination that will allow you to work toward creative solutions for the pressing problems we face. Sociologists can provide facts on objective conditions, sensitize you to the broader context that nourishes social problems, and suggest the likely consequences of intervention. Your decisions about what should be done about a social problem, however, will have to be made according to *your* values.

SUMMARY

1. Sociologists use what is called the *sociological imagination* (or perspective) to view the social problems that affect people's lives. This means that they look at how people's behavior and attitudes are shaped by their social locations.

2. A *social problem* is some aspect of society that people are concerned about and would like changed. It consists of *objective conditions*, aspects of society that are measurable, and *subjective concerns*, the feelings and attitudes that people have about those conditions. Social problems are relative— one group's solution may be another group's problem.

3. Social problems go through a *natural history* of four stages that often overlap: defining the problem, crafting an official response, reacting to the official response, and pursuing alternative strategies.

4. Sociologists are able to make five contributions to the study of social problems: to help determine the extent of a social problem; to clarify people's attitudes toward social problems; to apply the sociological imagination to social problems; to identify potential social policies for dealing with social problems; and to evaluate likely consequences of those policies.

5. The sociological understanding of a social problem differs from a commonsense understanding because the sociological perspective is not based on emotions or personal values. Instead, sociologists examine how social problems affect people, view the causes of social problems as located in society rather than in individuals, and use scientific methods to gather information about social problems.

6. To study social problems, sociologists use four major *research designs: surveys, case studies, experiments,* and *field studies*. Sociologists gather information in four basic ways: *interviews, questionnaires, documents,* and *observations*. These methods are often used in combination.

7. Because social problems can be viewed from so many vantage points, sociologists disagree on whether they should choose sides as professionals. Nor do sociologists agree on whether they should attempt to shape people's ideas of what their social problems really are. They do agree, however, that sociological studies must provide objective, accurate, and verifiable data.

KEY TERMS

Case study   A type of research design that focuses on a single case. The case or subject of the study can be an individual, an event, or an organization such as a church, hospital, or abortion clinic.

Common sense   The ideas common to a society or to some group within a society that are used to make sense out of human experience.

Control group   See *Experiment*.

Documents   Written sources or records used as a source of information.

Experiment   A research design that divides a group into an *experimental group* (those who are exposed to some experience) and a *control group* (those who are not exposed to the experience); measurements are taken before and after to determine the effects of the experience.

Experimental group   See *Experiment.*

Field study (or Participant observation)   Making direct observations in a setting that one wishes to study.

Generalize   To apply to other groups the findings that were learned from one group of people.

Interview   A method of gathering information whereby the researcher asks questions. In a *structured* interview, specific questions are asked, whereas in an *unstructured* interview, people are simply encouraged to talk about their experiences, with the researcher making certain that specific areas are covered.

Methods (Research methods or Methodology)   Ways of doing research.

Objective condition   An aspect of society that can be measured or experienced. See also *Subjective concern.*

Observation   A means of gathering information whereby the researcher directly observes what is occurring in a setting. In the *overt* form, people know they are being studied; in the *covert* form, they do not.

Participant observation   See *Field study.*

Personal trouble   An individual's own experience of a social problem.

Population   The target group that one wishes to study.

Power   The ability to get one's way despite obstacles.

Questionnaire   The use of written questions to gather information. *Closed-ended* questions provide specific choices, while *open-ended* questions allow people to answer in their own words.

Random sample   A sample that gives everyone in the group being studied an equal chance of being included in the study.

Research design   Any of four major approaches that sociologists use to study social life. For social problems, these are primarily *case studies, experiments, field studies,* and *surveys.*

Sample   A relatively small number of people intended to represent a larger group.

Social problem   An aspect of society that large numbers of people are concerned about and would like changed.

Sociological imagination (or perspective)   A framework of thought that looks at the broad, social context of what happens to people. This perspective helps people transcend personal values and emotions in order to see the larger picture that affects their situation.

Sociological perspective   See *Sociological imagination.*

Sociology   The overarching social science in which the emphasis is on how groups affect human behavior.

Structured interview   See *Interview.*

Subjective concern   The concern or distress that people feel about some aspect of society. See also *Objective condition.*

Survey   A type of research design that involves a sample of respondents from a target population. The sample is intended to represent the larger group from which it is selected.

Unstructured interview   See *Interview.*

FOR REFERENCE

Contexts. Published by the American Sociological Association, this magazine summarizes sociological research in an informal and informative manner; many topics are covered, not just social problems.

Social Problems: Official Journal of the Society for the Study of Social Problems, the organization for sociologists and other social scientists who are concerned about social problems. Available in most college libraries, the journal presents research and theorizing on social problems.

Mother Jones: A magazine with radical and muckraking reporting that covers controversial aspects of social problems.

The Public Interest: A journal whose less-sensational coverage balances the approach of *Mother Jones.*

THINKING CRITICALLY ABOUT CHAPTER 1

1. Identify a social problem that you have observed and apply the sociological imagination to it.
   - What makes this situation/condition a social problem? (Explain how it matches the definition of a social problem outlined in this chapter.)
   - What are the values of the people involved in this social problem? (Be sure to look at *both* sides of the problem, not just the one that matches your ideas of what is right.)
   - What social forces shaped the parties' points of view?
   - What objective conditions changed to arouse subjective concerns?

2. Who do you think is winning the battle between the proabortion and antiabortion activists? Why? Use the court decisions cited in this chapter to support your answer.

3. Identify a social problem that you have observed. Which methods for studying this social problem do you think would be most appropriate? Why?

4. Do you think that sociologists have a responsibility to take sides on social problems? Why or why not?

Interpreting Social Problems:
Aging

IN 1928, CHARLES HART, WHO WAS WORKING on his Ph.D. in anthropology, did fieldwork with the Tiwi, a preliterate people who live on an island off the northern coast of Australia. Because the Tiwi are uncomfortable around people who do not belong to a clan, they assigned Hart to the bird (Jabijabui) clan and said that a particular woman was his mother. Hart described the woman as "toothless, almost blind, withered," and said she was "physically quite revolting and mentally rather senile." He then described this remarkable event:

How seriously they took my presence in their kinship system is something I never will be sure about. . . . However, toward the end of my time on the islands an incident occurred that surprised me because it suggested that some of them had been taking my presence in the kinship system much more seriously than I had thought. I was approached by a group of about eight or nine senior men. . . . They were the senior members of the jabijabui clan and they had decided among themselves that the time had come to get rid of the decrepit old woman who had first called me son and whom I now called mother. . . . As I knew, they said, it was Tiwi custom, when an old woman became too feeble to look after herself, to "cover her up." This could only be done by her sons and her brothers and all of them had to agree beforehand, since once it was done

they did not want any dissension among the brothers or clansmen, as that might lead to a feud. My "mother" was now completely blind, she was constantly falling over logs or into fires, and they, her senior clansmen, were in agreement that she would be better out of the way. Did I agree?

I already knew about "covering up." The Tiwi, like many other hunting and gathering peoples, sometimes got rid of their ancient and decrepit females. The method was to dig a hole in the ground in some lonely place, put the old woman in the hole and fill it in with earth until only her head was showing. Everybody went away for a day or two and then went back to the hole to discover to their great surprise, that the old woman was dead, having been too feeble to raise her arms from the earth. Nobody had "killed" her; her death in Tiwi eyes was a natural one. She had been alive when her relatives last saw her. I had never seen it done, though I knew it was the custom, so I asked my brothers if it was necessary for me to attend the "covering up."

They said no and they would do it, but only after they had my agreement. Of course I agreed, and a week or two later we heard in our camp that my "mother" was dead, and we all wailed and put on the trimmings of mourning.

C. W. M. Hart in Hart and Pilling 1979:125–126.

The Frail Aged: A Universal Problem

I don't know about you, but I was shocked when I read Hart's account. He does not see any moral issue about agreeing that the old woman should be "covered up." His concern was not having to watch the woman die. In our society, too, there are people who feel that the elderly have outlived any social usefulness they might once have had, and that we should devise our own forms of "covering up." Why spend precious resources (all that money) on people who have only a few years—or just a few months—more to live? goes their reasoning. Wouldn't we be better off having some way to usher them off the stage of life—with dignity, of course?

Such opinions are met with considerably different reactions. Some agree that the frail elderly have outlived their usefulness and that society is better off without them. For others, such thinking sends chills down their spine. If such programs were ever initiated, what people would be placed in the position of deciding who is "socially valuable" and who is not? If the frail elderly are targeted, might others also be considered "useless"—or at least of "less value" and, for the good of the general society, in need of being "covered up?"

Although few groups choose "covering up" as their solution, every society must deal with the problem of people who grow old and frail. You may have noted that the Tiwi "cover up" only old women. It is common throughout the world for females to be discriminated against—in some places, even in death. This topic is so significant that we shall spend an entire chapter (9) on gender discrimination. In this present chapter, in which we consider how theories help us to understand social life, we shall explore the social problem of the elderly.

Sociological Theories and Social Problems

What Is a Theory?

As sociologists do research on social problems, they uncover a lot of "facts." If you have just a jumble of "facts," however, you have little understanding of what those "facts" mean. To make sense of things, those "facts" have to be put in some order. Sociologists use theories to provide this order. Theories help them understand how facts are related to one another. A **theory** explains how two or more concepts (or "facts") are related, such as age and suicide. A theory, then, gives us a framework for organizing facts, and in so doing it provides a way of interpreting reality.

The Theories That Sociologists Use

In this chapter, we shall look at the three main theories that sociologists use—symbolic interactionism, functionalism, and conflict theory. Before we begin, you may want to look at an overview of these theories, which are summarized in Table 2-1. Because each theory focuses on some particular "slice" of a social problem, each provides a different perspective on the problem. As you study these theories, keep in mind

TABLE 2-1 A Summary of the Theories

	SYMBOLIC INTERACTIONISM	FUNCTIONALISM	CONFLICT THEORY
WHAT IS SOCIETY?	People's patterns of behavior; always in flux	Groups within the same social system whose parts work together to benefit the whole	Groups within the same social system competing with one another
WHAT ARE THE KEY TERMS?	Symbols Interaction Communication Meanings Definitions	Structure Function System Equilibrium Goals	Competition Conflict Special Interests Power Exploitation
WHAT IS A SOCIAL PROBLEM?	Whatever a group decides is a social problem is a social problem for that group	The failure of some part to fulfill its function, which interferes with the smooth functioning of the system	The natural and inevitable outcome as interest groups compete for scarce or limited resources
HOW DOES SOMETHING BECOME A SOCIAL PROBLEM?	One set of definitions becomes accepted; competing views are rejected	Some part of the system fails, usually because of rapid social change	Authority and power are used by the powerful to exploit the weaker groups

Source: By the author.

that each theory is like a spotlight shining onto a dark area, illuminating only a particular part of the landscape. Taken together, these theories throw much more light on problems that we want to understand.

Symbolic Interactionism and Social Problems

Images and Meanings of Old Age

Biologically, old age creeps up on us all. As the years pass, we feel our bodies change. Sociologically, however, old age comes suddenly—at retirement, with the first Social Security check, or upon admittance to an old-age home. Our images of old age are largely unpleasant. We use phrases such as old and sick, old and crabby, old and dependent, old and useless. Take your pick. None is pleasant.

Symbols Change: How the Meaning of Old Age Changed in the U.S.

Yet during an earlier period of the United States, "old" suggested wisdom, generosity, even graciousness and beauty. Why did earlier generations have ideas so different from ours? To find out, Andrew Achenbaum (1978) traced the history of old age in the United States. He found that in the early 1800s old people were valued because so few Americans reached an advanced age. With most people dying young, those who made it to old age were admired for their accomplishment. They were thought to have accumulated valuable knowledge about life. At this time, work, too, was viewed differently, and to quit working simply because of age was considered foolish. Because the elderly were more skilled at their jobs, they also gained the respect of younger workers.

How did such a fundamental shift occur in the meaning of old age, so that today "old" has such negative meanings? Social change in the late 1800s turned the situation on its head. As sanitation and medical care improved, many more people reached old age. No longer was being elderly a distinction. Ideas about work changed, too. As machine-driven tools were invented and mass production techniques developed, work was "deskilled." With it no longer being difficult to learn how to do a job, the old workers were no more knowledgeable or productive than the young. As the elderly lost their uniqueness, their social value declined. Old age began to suggest uselessness rather than usefulness, foolishness rather than wisdom. In short, old age went from being an asset to being a liability.

Symbolic Interactionism Defined

Old age, then, means different things to different people—which brings us to the essence of the symbolic interactionist perspective. We all see the world through **symbols,** things to which we attach meaning and that we use to communicate with one another. **Symbolic interactionism** is the sociological theory that examines the symbols that people use.

Symbols Affect Perception

When we first see a person advanced in years, we classify him or her as an "old person." We tend to see the characteristics that our culture assigns to this symbol—wrinkled, unstylish, over the hill. Because people internalize the symbols that dominate their culture, many elderly also see themselves in such terms. In contrast, someone from a culture in which old age symbolizes wisdom or power or privilege tends to perceive an old person in a different light—and so does the old person.

In short, symbolic interactionists stress that symbols, such as the terms we use to classify people, give us our view of the world. As we use the symbols that our culture provides to communicate with one another, we share and reinforce the ways we look at life. We also tend to perceive both ourselves and others according to these symbols. The images on television, the printed and spoken word, our body language, our gestures, our tone of voice, our clothing, even our hairstyles—all are symbols by which we communicate outlooks on life.

Social Problems from a Symbolic Interactionist Perspective

From our brief review of what it meant to be elderly during Colonial times, we can see that symbols change as society changes. Because the term *social problem* is also a symbol, what people consider to be a social problem also changes over time. *From the perspective of symbolic interactionism, then, social problems are what people in a society define as social problems.* What we now take for granted, we may later see as a problem; what we now see as a problem, we may later take for granted.

How Problems Change: From Personal to Social Problem

Old age also provides an excellent example of how social problems change. Earlier in our society, when most people died young, some people survived the odds and reached advanced age. If they had problems because of their age, those problems were matters for them or their family to handle. They were no one else's responsibility. Old age was a *personal* problem, not a *social* problem. Now that so many people reach old age, we perceive of these people as a group. We tend to lump individuals together with others who have similar characteristics, and we consider social action (laws and policies) to be appropriate for solving their problems. In short, *what was once a personal problem has become a social problem.*

In Sum

When symbolic interactionists look at social problems, then, they stress the changing definitions that underlie them. To understand any social problem, we must search for the underlying definitions, or symbols, by which people view their social worlds.

THE DEVELOPMENT OF SYMBOLIC INTERACTIONISM

Symbols Are Essential for Social Life

Symbolic interactionism began with the pioneering psychologist William James (1842–1910), who analyzed how people use symbols to describe their experiences (Turner 1978). Symbols are essential for our lives, because they allow us to think about other people and objects, even when those people and objects are not present. We also symbolize our own self (that is, we think about our self in a certain way, such as young, attractive, and personable). How we symbolize our self affects our behavior. For example, as we saw in chapter 1, some women risk unwanted pregnancies because the use of contraceptives would conflict with their self-image.

The Looking-Glass Self

To such insights, Charles Horton Cooley (1864–1929) added this major principle: By interacting with others, *people come to see themselves as they think others see them.* He summarized this principle in the following couplet:

Each to each a looking-glass
Reflects the other that doth pass.

Cooley argued that our interactions with others create a **looking-glass self.** By this, he meant that our self has three elements: (1) how we think we appear to others; (2) how we think others feel about what they perceive; and (3) how we feel about this reflected image. According to Cooley, our self-esteem depends on this looking-glass self. So it does, too, for the elderly. If a society reflects a negative image to its old people, the elderly tend to think of themselves negatively.

Taking the Role of the Other

George Herbert Mead (1863–1931) concluded that symbols are so important that without them there would be no social life as we know it. He also concluded that symbols are the foundation of our self-concept, which evolves during childhood. During this time of life, we learn to **take the role of the other.** That is, we become capable of putting ourselves in someone else's shoes, able to empathize with how that person feels and thinks and to anticipate how he or she will act. This is followed by another stage in acquiring a self—learning to take the role of people in general—which Mead called the **generalized other.**

The Generalized Other

To illustrate these terms, consider baseball, one of Mead's favorite examples. Suppose that you are playing in the state championship. It is the bottom of the ninth, there are two outs, the bases are loaded, the score is tied, and you are at bat. The pressure is intense. Although you may not do so at this point, you can take the role of the other; that is, you do understand how the pitcher feels as he or she winds up. You are feeling your own pressures, of course, and you probably are aware of the generalized other; that is, how others in general—your teammates, the opposing team, your family, and the fans—will feel if you strike out or get a hit.

Symbols Are Social Creations

Each of us must make sense out of life, and the symbols that our culture provides are the key for how we fit things together. Consider the onset of "old age." Our cultural symbols are so significant that decisions about when old age begins are more rooted in social experiences than in biology. As symbolic interactionists emphasize, there is nothing magical about turning 65, or any other age, that automatically makes someone "old" and disqualifies that person from certain activities. This arbitrary benchmark can be traced to Otto von Bismarck (1815–1898), the architect of the German empire. In order to weaken the appeal of socialism in Germany, Bismarck pioneered the idea of social security. He arbitrarily chose 65 as the mandatory retirement age, partly to force some of his generals out of power. Bismarck's decision, rooted in nineteenth-century politics, continues to affect our twenty-first-century perception of age.

The Social Construction of Reality

Symbolic interactionists stress that we do not unthinkingly label our experiences. Rather, to make sense out of life, we reflect on what happens to us. We have many symbols available to us, and those that we choose give meaning to our experiences. This process of interpreting events, of making sense of life, is called the **social construction of reality.**

Constructing the Meaning of Suicide

To help make this idea clearer, let's look at suicide. After someone commits suicide, the surviving family members and friends wrestle with why it happened. To find the answer, they ask such questions as, "Am I to blame for not picking up on hints of suicide?" "Should I feel guilty?" "What could I have done differently?" As the survivors work out answers to such questions, they are socially constructing their reality; that is, they are trying to bring order to their experience. In doing so, they use symbols that their culture provides. If a Japanese officer falls on his sword after losing a battle, for example, his family uses their culture's symbols of honor and duty to understand why he took his life. Our culture provides a different set of symbols for people to use to interpret suicide. The symbols may differ, but in both cases, Japanese and American, each is involved in the social construction of reality. For more examples, see the Issues in Social Problems box on suicide on the next page.

In Sum

As symbolic interactionists stress, to socially construct reality is an ordinary part of everyday life. We all try to make sense of our experiences—whether that means figuring out why we received an A or an F in this class, why we got promoted—or fired—at work, or even why we like or dislike some television program. In short, reality does not come with built-in meanings, and we all use the symbols provided by our culture to make sense out of life.

APPLYING SYMBOLIC INTERACTIONISM

The idea discussed in Chapter 1, that an objective condition of society may be considered a social problem by some groups but not by others, embodies the symbolic interactionist perspective. Social problems do not exist like stones,

As symbolic interactionists stress, our age does not contain built-in meanings. Consequently, the meanings of being old vary from one society to another—and, within large societies such as the United States, even from one group to another. Shown here is a father in Samburu, Northern Kenya. In this area, old men marry teenage brides. The boy is the man's son.

Issues in Social Problems

MAKING SENSE OF SUICIDE: LABELS AND THE SOCIAL CONSTRUCTION OF REALITY

After someone commits suicide, people who were close to that person try to make sense out of what happened. As their shock wears off, they mentally relive events associated with the dead person. As they think about these events, looking at them in the new light of the suicide, they ask a lot of questions. The main one is "Why?" Just why did the individual take his or her life? As they explore the "why," they confront the horrifying possibility that they themselves could have been part of the reason. "Perhaps if I had done something different, he (she) would not have committed suicide" becomes a burning issue.

This search for meaning and for cause leads survivors to reconstruct the past, which can be a tortured process. Listen to this father of a twenty-five-year-old who killed himself with a handgun. You can hear the questions that plague him as he reconstructs events in his search for satisfactory answers regarding his son's death:

> I've wondered where it began if it was suicide. Was it in grade school? Or college? Or was it all this girl? Could I have done something different? Or wouldn't it have helped? Wondering which is right and which is wrong. . . . I think this thing or that thing could have been done to change the course of events. But you just don't know. I even thought, "If we hadn't moved from St. Louis to Crestview years ago."

We all attain meaning for what happens to us in life by using the labels that our culture provides. Sociologists call this process the *social construction of reality*. When it comes to death by suicide, our culture does not offer satisfactory labels, leaving people perplexed as they search for meaning.

Consider another type of death. When people die from disease, family members don't face such a challenge to the self. Seldom does the label *disease* trigger the question, "Could I have done something different?" This label points to causes beyond us—to germs and chances in life and things of this sort.

Similarly, the cultural label of *normal* points to causes beyond us. When the label *suicide* is attached to a death, however, we are denied this category, too. Because the death is "not normal," we are forced into a search for its meaning, which can end up in a severe challenge to the self. Listen to this survivor as he explains why he can't use this label:

> If he'd been driving and killed in a car wreck—that's an everyday thing. But this was special, and there had to be something wrong—whether with me or the family—if a car wreck, *a normal way people die*—and his personality—figured he'd never do something like that, and couldn't really believe he could have done it. It's an *unusual way,* and *is evidently caused by something or other*—some kind of a problem.

Our culture offers many labels, or categories, to help people adjust to the death of a loved one. Among them is "God's will." This label, if it can be used, removes causation clearly beyond the survivor of the deceased, allowing easier acceptance of the event. If God called the individual home, the survivor certainly bears no responsibility for the death. The family members of a suicide, however, are denied this category, too. Listen to this woman as she struggles with the meaning of her husband's death:

> Well, I would have felt in my own mind that God had called him from the earth and that He had a reason for calling him, and that we could have accepted it as Christians that it was the will of God, and that we could feel in our hearts that God, in his tenderness, had taken him up with him. I can't feel that this was the will of God.

From these examples, you can see that culture provides labels (symbols, categories, concepts, words, terms) that people use to interpret the events of their life. By looking at how the survivors of suicide search for meaning, we can observe the *social construction of reality* as it occurs. We can see that the usual labels offered by our culture are denied these people, leaving them with uncertainty. These examples should also make us more aware of how *we* use our culture's labels to provide meaning for our own experiences—and how, if our culture gave us different labels, we would interpret our experiences differently. The *social construction of reality,* sometimes a difficult concept to understand, is a regular part of our everyday lives.

Based on Henslin 1970.

Social Problems Depend on Definitions

independent of whoever observes them. Rather, from among all the objective conditions in society, people pick some out and define them as problems. As we have seen, the elderly do not automatically constitute a social problem. It depends on how they are viewed. The aged can be admired and respected—or regarded as worthless. In short, *social problems are socially constructed*.

As we discussed, because meanings change over time, the objective conditions that people define as social problems also change. Just as the meaning of being old once made a major shift, so it could again. If the elderly were to grow wealthier and more powerful, for example, then more positive features of social life would be associated with old age, and the elderly would receive admiration and respect. They would no longer be considered a social problem.

Labels Affect Perception and Behavior

As emphasized in the Issues in Social Problems box on suicide, symbolic interactionists stress the significance of **labeling**—stereotyping, or putting a tag on someone, and acting accordingly. For example, the label "old age" is sometimes used to explain health problems. Medical professionals may write off an elderly woman's mental or physical problems as being due to her age (perhaps labeling her "senile"). This label lets them feel comfortable about not treating her, or about giving her placebos (fake medicine). They may think, "What else can you expect with such an old woman?" In many cases, medical treatment could alleviate the problems that are written off as "that's-the-way-people-are-when-they-get-old." For example, using the labels "malnutrition" and "Alzheimer's disease" to account for someone's memory loss and confusion implies the need to search for physiological causes and treatment. In contrast, the labels "old" and "senile" do not imply such a search. Labels, then, affect how we perceive and react to problems.

SYMBOLIC INTERACTIONISM AND SOCIAL PROBLEMS: A SUMMARY

In Sum

Symbolic interactionists stress that social problems are socially constructed; that is, people decide to place the label *social problem* on some objective condition. If they don't place the label on that objective condition, it is not a social problem. If they do, it is. To understand social problems, then, we must focus on how objective conditions become socially constructed into social problems. Symbolic interactionists also stress that to understand any social problem, we must take into account what that problem means to the people who are involved in it.

Functionalism and Social Problems

Functionalism Defined

The second major theory that sociologists use to interpret social problems is **functionalism** (or **functional analysis**). Functionalists compare society to a self-adjusting machine that is composed of many parts. Each part of a machine has a *function*. When a part is working properly, it fulfills its function, and the machine hums along. Functionalists also use the analogy of an animal. An animal has many organs, and when an organ is working properly, it contributes to the well-being of the animal. Society, they say, like a machine or animal, is also composed of many parts. Each part of society has a function, and when a part is working properly, it contributes to the well-being (stability or equilibrium) of society.

The Parts of Society Are Interrelated

Consider just two social services that are designed to help the elderly. Of the vast sums spent on the elderly's health care, some goes into medical research. This, in turn, benefits people in other age groups. Similarly, it is not only the 35 million retired and disabled workers who collect Social Security that benefit from this program but also the 65,000 people who work for this federal agency (*Statistical Abstract* 2003:Tables

500, 543). Their families also gain, and their spending, in turn, benefits businesses across the nation. In other words, functionalists stress how one part of society contributes to other parts of society.

Social Problems from a Functionalist Perspective

Think of society as a single machine with many parts. If each part does its job, the machine runs smoothly. If one part fails, the whole machine can suffer. Functionalists call these failures **dysfunctions.** If a dysfunction creates instability or disequilibrium in society, it is a social problem. *From the functionalist perspective, then, a social problem is the failure of a part, which then interferes with society's smooth functioning.* For example, one component of the social problem of the aged is the red tape they confront when they try to get help. Red tape interferes with the allocation of resources to the elderly. Another problem is "rip-off" nursing homes: Instead of money going to the elderly who are the most dependent, it goes into the pockets of unscrupulous operators.

THE DEVELOPMENT OF FUNCTIONALISM

Comte: Society Is Similar to a Biological Organism

Functionalism is rooted in the origins of sociology (Turner 1978). Auguste Comte (1798–1857), who is called the founder of sociology, developed his ideas during the unrest that followed the French Revolution. Comte concluded that society is like an animal: Just as an animal has tissues and organs that are interrelated and function together, so does society. For a society to function smoothly, its parts must be in balance.

Spencer: Structure and Function

Herbert Spencer (1820–1903) emphasized that the parts of society work together in a **structure.** As with each part of an animal, each part of society helps meet the needs of the structure. Spencer called the part's contribution its **function.** Because the parts fit together in a larger system, a change in one part brings about changes in other parts.

Functionalists analyze functions and dysfunctions of human actions. One of the latent (unintended) functions of some medical research has been to enable more people to live into old age. This, in turn, has both functions (positive consequences) and dysfunctions (negative consequences) for other parts of society.

Durkheim: Normal and Pathological States

Emile Durkheim (1858–1917) further developed the idea that a society has needs that must be met if it is going to function well. When its parts fulfill their functions, he said, society is in a "normal" state; if its parts do not fulfill their functions, society is in an "abnormal" or "pathological" state. To understand society, functionalists say that we need to look at both **structure**—how the parts of a society are related to one another—and **function**—how each part contributes to society.

Merton: Functions and Dysfunctions

The final functionalist I shall mention is Robert Merton (1910-2003). Merton defined *functions* as the beneficial consequences of people's actions. Functions help a social system to maintain equilibrium, such as by helping it adapt to social change. Functions can be either manifest or latent. A **manifest function** is an action that is *intended* to help some part of the system. For example, Social Security is intended to make life better for the elderly. Improvement of life, then, is a *manifest* function of Social Security. Merton emphasized that our actions also have **latent functions;** these consequences help a system adjust, but are *unintended*. For example, the salaries paid to the tens of thousands of employees of the Social Security Administration help to stabilize our economy. Because this beneficial consequence of Social Security is not intended, however, it is a *latent* function.

Social Problems as Dysfunctions

Merton (1968) stressed that human actions also have **dysfunctions,** consequences that disrupt a system's equilibrium. A part that fails to meet its functions is part of a social problem.

Because consequences of people's actions that disrupt a system's equilibrium usually are unintended, Merton called them **latent dysfunctions.** For example, the Social Security Administration has hundreds of rules dealing with incredible details. If the thousands of employees of this agency were to follow each procedure exactly, the resulting red tape would interfere with their ability to serve the elderly. The rules are not intended to have this effect, however, so they are *latent* dysfunctions.

In Sum

Functionalists sensitize us to think in terms of systems, to see whatever we are studying as part of a larger unit. When we examine one part, we look at its functions to see how it is related to other parts of the system. Let's apply these terms of functionalism to the social problem of aging.

APPLYING FUNCTIONALISM TO SOCIAL PROBLEMS

How a Change in One Part of Society Creates a Social Problem in Another Part

From the functionalist perspective, society is viewed as a social system composed of interconnected parts that function together. When those parts work well, each contributes to the equilibrium of society. When they do not, we have a social problem.

We already have seen how economic changes caused a shift in the meaning of old age. When machine production made many of the elderly's skills outdated, the elderly came to be seen as a dependent group that needed to be taken care of. From the functionalist perspective, a change in one part of society (in this case, production) changed an interrelated part of society (elderly workers), and a new social problem arose.

Disengagement Theory

Now let's see how "functions" applies to this social problem. Some functionalists stress that society needs to pass its positions of responsibility (jobs) from one group (the elderly) to another group (younger people). To entice the elderly to leave their positions, dangled before them are Social Security benefits and pensions. In exchange for these benefits, the elderly transfer their jobs to younger people. In this view, called **disengagement theory,** the elderly get paid for not working and, in return, the younger people take over their jobs (Cumming and Henry 1961; Cockerham 1991). Everyone benefits by the exchange—the self-regulating machine makes the proper adjustments.

Nursing Homes as a Functional Adjustment to Social Change

Nursing homes, too, have helped society adjust to social change. Care of the elderly used to fall primarily upon women's shoulders. Because women worked at home and few people made it to old age, this was not a general problem. But then, just when more women were beginning to work outside the home, life expectancy was increasing and there were more frail elderly who needed care. Nursing homes were developed to replace the daughters and daughters-in-law who had become unavailable to care for the increasing numbers of frail elderly. Today, about 4 percent of Americans over the age of 65 live in nursing homes (*Statistical Abstract* 2003:Tables 11, 185). Most of these residents are *not* typical of older people: Most are ill, very old, or have no family. Again, the machine adjusted to change.

Latent Functions of Nursing Homes

As they analyze social problems, functionalists also look for *latent* functions. Researchers interviewed the adult children of the residents of a well-run middle-class nursing home. Forty-five percent of the children reported that their affection had been strained by the burden of caring for a frail parent who had health problems. This burden was lifted when they placed their parent in the nursing home. As time passed, the love that had been obscured by duty gradually recovered. As one 57-year-old daughter reported: "My mother demanded rather than earned respect and love. We had a poor past relationship—a love/hate relationship. Now I can do for her because I want to. I can finally love her because I want to" (Smith and Bengston 1979:441). Because love was not intended, it is a *latent* function.

Dysfunctions of Nursing Homes

Functionalists also study *dysfunctions.* Unlike the nursing home in this study, which was middle class and well run, few nursing homes are pleasant places. They sometimes are called "houses of death" or "human junkyards." Many stink of urine, and it is depressing to see so many sad people clustered together. After being admitted to a nursing home, most elderly people decline physically and mentally. A chief reason is the dehumanized way they are treated: segregated from the outside world, denied privacy, and under rigid controls. Many nursing homes control their residents chemically, by giving them psychotropic drugs such as Thorazine and Prozac (Gurvich and Cunningham 2000). "Chemical restraints" keep elderly patients quiet, but they also can reduce them to an empty shell of their former selves. This particular dysfunction, elderly people being abandoned in abusive nursing homes, is concentrated among the poor elderly who have no close family and friends.

Research on nursing homes shows that abuse is common (McCarthy 2002). Sociologists Karl Pillemer and David Moore (1989) surveyed nursing homes in New Hampshire. Thirty-one percent of the staff reported that during the past year they had seen physical abuse—patients being pushed, grabbed, shoved, pinched, kicked, or slapped. Eighty-one percent said they had seen psychological abuse—patients being cursed, insulted, yelled at, or threatened. When asked if they themselves had ever abused patients, 10 percent admitted that they had physically abused them, and 40 percent admitted to psychological abuse. Pillemer and Moore found that the most abusive staff members were those who were thinking about quitting their jobs and those who thought of patients as being childlike.

The publicity given to problems in nursing homes has made the public painfully aware of such dysfunctions. Consequently, the decision to place an elderly family member in a nursing home can be agonizing. Even though an aged parent may be too sick to be cared for at home, placing your parent in a nursing home is often viewed as a callous denial of love and duty. To see how two major units of society, the government and the family, can work together to provide high-quality care for the elderly, see the Global Glimpse box on the next page.

FUNCTIONALISM AND SOCIAL PROBLEMS: A SUMMARY

In Sum

For an overview of functionalism, see Table 2-2 on page 37. Note that functionalists begin by looking at one aspect of a social system, in this case, the column marked "Action." This action occurs in some part of the social system, such as business or

A Global Glimpse

THE COMING TIDAL WAVE: JAPAN'S ELDERLY

With one of the world's lowest birth rates, Japan's population is aging faster than that of any other nation. In 1950, only 66 Japanese turned 100. Now it is 1,700 a year. To see how rapidly Japan's population of elderly is growing, look at the following table. In just a few years, one of every four Japanese will be age 65 or older.

PERCENT OF JAPAN'S POPULATION AGE 65 AND OLDER

1950	1970	1990	2000	2020
4	7	12	16	24

Japanese policy makers are concerned about the future of their health-care services, especially because about half of the Japanese elderly will be age 75 and over. More than 1 million elderly Japanese are expected to be bedridden, and another million to be senile. By the year 2020, Japan's medical bill is likely to run six times higher than it is now. How will Japan be able to meet the health needs of this coming tidal wave of elderly?

This question must be placed within the context of Japanese culture, specifically, the obligations of one generation to another. The Japanese believe that because parents took care of children, children are obligated to care for their parents. Unlike in the United States, *most* aged Japanese live with their adult children. As the proportion of elderly mushrooms, will the Japanese family be able to carry on its traditional caregiving and protective roles?

Because Europe faces similar problems, Japanese leaders decided that they could learn from Europe's social service system. But when they saw a lower work ethic, higher taxes, and reduced savings—all leading to less ability to compete in global markets—the Japanese worked out their own plan. To reduce inequality among the aged, the government has begun to unify the country's pension systems and has increased spending for social security. To accommodate the elderly who have no families and those who are the sickest, the government is building nursing homes. To improve the quality of life for all elderly, the government is building 10,000 day service centers, available to the poor and rich alike. The government will also provide transportation to physiotherapy centers, and offer free testing for the early detection of cancer and heart disease. The government has also created a new position called "home helper." After passing a government examination, 100,000 specialists will help the elderly at home.

These government-funded services and facilities are not designed to replace the family's care but, rather, to supplement the family's efforts at caring for the elderly, thus strengthening the family.

Gnawing at these ambitious plans, however, is economic reality. Japan is in the midst of a depression that they can't budge. With huge federal deficits and persistent unemployment, some of these plans will have to be shelved. Regardless of economic conditions or if the society is ready, the tidal wave of elderly is on its way and will arrive on schedule.

Based on Freed 1994; Nishio 1994; Otten 1995; Mackellar and Horlacher 2000.

government. The manifest function is the intended beneficial consequence of the action. If a beneficial consequence occurs but was not intended, it is a latent function. If there is an unintended harmful consequence, this is a latent dysfunction.

Functionalists assume that society is like a well-oiled, self-adjusting machine. They examine how the parts of that machine (or social system) are interrelated and how those parts adjust to one another. As society undergoes change, a social problem arises when some part or parts of society do not adjust to the change and are not functioning properly.

Conflict Theory and Social Problems

The Essence of Conflict Theory

We couldn't disagree more, reply conflict theorists. The parts of society are *not* working together harmoniously. What is really happening is that its parts are competing with one another for scarce resources. This competition between society's parts is so

TABLE 2-2 Old Age: A Functionalist Overview

RELATED PARTS OF THE SOCIAL SYSTEM*	ACTION	MANIFEST FUNCTION	LATENT FUNCTION	LATENT DYSFUNCTION
Economic (business)	Pension and retirement benefits	Provide income and leisure time for the aged	Jobs for younger workers	Displacement of the elderly; loss of self-esteem; loss of purpose
Political (government)	Social Security system	Stable income for the aged; dignity in old age	65,000 people employed by the Social Security Administration	Income is inadequate; many recipients live on the edge of poverty
Medical	Technological developments; gerontological specialties	Longer lives for the population	A larger proportion of the elderly in the population	Makes the Social Security system much more expensive
	Medicare and Medicaid	Provide good health care for the elderly	Financing bonanza for the medical profession	"Rip-off" nursing homes
Family	Grown children live apart from their parents	Independence of both younger and older generations	Institutionalized care for the elderly; greater mobility for younger workers	Isolation of elderly parents; loneliness and despair

*As used here, "parts" of the social system are social institutions.
Source: By the author.

severe that conflict is barely kept in check. The elderly, for example, are competing with younger people for scarce resources—income (pensions) and costly medical care. As the competition heats up, the future may bring conflict between the young and the elderly that will throw society into turmoil. In short, the guiding principle of social life is disequilibrium and conflict, not equilibrium and harmony, as the functionalists say.

From the conflict perspective, social problems are the natural and inevitable outcome of social struggle. No matter what a social problem may look like on the surface, at its essence lies a conflict between the powerful and the powerless. As the powerful exploit society's resources and oppress the powerless, they create such social problems as poverty and discrimination. As the exploited react to their oppression, still other social problems emerge: street crime, escapist drug abuse, suicide, homicide, riots, revolution, terrorism. To understand social problems, then, we first need to understand that they are the natural state of society. Then we need to penetrate their surface manifestations and expose the basic conflict that underlies them.

THE DEVELOPMENT OF CONFLICT THEORY

Social Problems from a Conflict Perspective

Marx: Capitalism, Oppression, and the Struggle of Workers

Karl Marx (1818–1883), called the founder of **conflict theory,** witnessed the industrial revolution that transformed Europe. Cities mushroomed as peasants left the land to seek work. The new industrialists put the peasants—and their children—to work at near-starvation wages. As poverty and exploitation grew, political unrest followed, and upheaval swept across Europe.

Shocked by such suffering and inhumanity, Marx concluded that the hallmark of history is a struggle for power. In this struggle, some group holds the top position, and it oppresses those under it. He also concluded that a major turning point in this historical struggle occurred when **capitalism** became dominant in the Western world—that is, when a small group of people gained control over the means of production and made profit their goal. As machinery replaced workers' tools, the **capitalists,** or owners of the factories and equipment, gained an exploitive advantage.

Because they owned the means of production and thousands of peasants had crowded into the cities in a desperate search for work, the capitalists were able to impose miserable working conditions and fire workers at will. These capitalists also controlled the politicians, and when workers rebelled, they could count on the police to use violence to bring them under control. In this struggle, capitalists sometimes made concessions to workers. These concessions were not signs of cooperation, but, rather, they were strategic devices to control workers and weaken their political solidarity. The day of reckoning will finally come, and it will be bloody. The workers will overthrow their oppressors and establish a classless society in which the goal will be not profits for the few, but, rather, the good of the many.

In Marx's time, workers were at the mercy of their employers. They lacked what we take for granted today—a minimum wage, eight-hour workdays, five-day workweeks, paid vacations, medical benefits, sick leave, unemployment compensation, pensions, Social Security, even the right to strike. Conflict theorists remind us that such benefits exist not because of the generous hearts of the rich but because workers fought for them—sometimes to the death.

It is difficult for us to grasp what conditions were like for workers in early capitalism. With the daily wage the equivalent of a loaf or two of bread, workers could not afford what we would call homes. The more lucky ones slept 20 to a room, acquaintances and entire families sprawled out on the floor. The less fortunate ones, as in this photo, made do with even less. It was conditions like this that motivated Karl Marx to do his research.

Simmel: Subordination, Superordination, and Exchange

Other sociologists have extended conflict theory beyond workers and capitalists. Sociologist Georg Simmel (1858–1918), for example, analyzed the relationships of people who are in higher positions (superordinates) and people in lower positions (subordinates). He noted that because subordinates have some power, the more powerful must take them into consideration as they make decisions designed to protect their positions of privilege (Coser 1977). Consequently, superordinate–subordinate relationships are marked not by one-way naked power but by exchange. If employers wish to lower the benefits of a pension plan, for example, they must get unions to agree—and the workers will insist on a trade-off, such as increased job security.

Positive Features of Social Conflict

Conflict, noted Simmel, also has positive features. For example, when they face an external threat, the members of a group tend to pull together. Similarly, if several groups face a common enemy, they tend to become more cohesive (Giddens 1969; Turner 1978). In times of war, for instance, antagonistic groups often shelve their differences in order to work together for the good of the nation. Workers might give up their right to strike, as U.S. workers did during World War II, while employers might agree to binding arbitration on all disputes. To prevent sabotage during World War II, the U.S. Justice Department even asked Lucky Luciano, the head of the Mafia, to spy on dock workers. Lucianco did so.

Coser: Close Relationships Breed Conflict

Sociologist Lewis Coser (1913-2003) emphasized that conflict is especially likely to develop among people who have close relationships. This is because they are connected by a network of power, responsibilities, and rewards. New decisions, which are constantly necessary, often upset the precarious balances they have worked out. Whether we refer to bosses and workers or to a husband and wife, each is part of a balance of power in which the members have determined how they will share responsibilities and rewards. Because their relationship is precariously balanced, actions by either party can upset their arrangement of power.

The U.S. elderly, who today are a potent political force, were not a political group until Dr. Francis Everett Townsend (shown here) organized them in the 1930s. Townsend, a retired physician, gained national prominence when in the midst of the Great Depression he proposed a $200 a month pension plan for all the nation's elderly. Potential revolutionaries ("commies," as they were called) were arousing people all over the country, and Townsend, too, frightened politicians. Townsend also spearheaded campaigns against congressional members who objected to his plan.

APPLYING CONFLICT THEORY TO SOCIAL PROBLEMS

As we apply the conflict perspective to the elderly, let's see how Social Security came about. In this drama, the three major groups are elderly workers, younger workers, and employers. The fourth group is Congress, which, from this perspective, represented the interests of the employers.

How a Social Problem Was Born: Industrialization Pits Two Groups Against One Another

From the point of view of conflict theory, old people became a social problem when those in power found it advantageous to push them aside. When the industrial revolution spread across the United States, owners of big business found old people a nuisance. They earned more than younger workers, and they were not as docile. The owners fired many of the elderly, replacing them with younger workers. This was before Social Security, and most elderly people who lost their jobs or who were no longer able to work were left in poverty. During the 1920s, for example, two-thirds of all Americans over 65 could not support themselves (Holtzman 1963; Hudson 1978). In short, industrialization transformed the aged from a productive and respected group to a deprived and disgraced group.

Fighting Back: The Townsend Movement

Then the Great Depression struck, and many elderly suffered even more. In 1930, in the midst of national despair, Francis Everett Townsend, a physician, started a movement to rally the elderly into a political force. He soon had one-third of all Americans over 65 enrolled in his Townsend clubs, demanding benefits from the government (Holtzman 1963). His plan was for the federal government to impose a national sales tax of 2 percent to provide $200 a month for every person over 60. This is the equivalent of about $2,200 a month today. Townsend argued that the elderly's increased spending would generate new businesses and lift the nation out of the depression.

By 1934, the Townsend clubs had gathered hundreds of thousands of signatures on petitions, and the Townsend Plan went before Congress. In this election year, Congress felt vulnerable to a grassroots revolt by old people, but Congress felt in a bind: The Townsend Plan called for a high monthly pension during a period of unprecedented unemployment when the country was strapped for money. Many also feared that if younger people knew that the government was going to give them a pension when they were old, it would sap their incentive to work and save (Schottland 1963). Congress looked for a way to reject the plan without appearing to oppose old-age pensions. When President Franklin Roosevelt announced his own, more modest Social Security plan in June 1934, Congress embraced it.

Although the Townsend clubs did not get their plan passed, they did force Congress to pass Social Security. The clubs then fought to improve Social Security. Benefits were not scheduled to begin until 1942, and millions of workers would be left uncovered. As the depression lingered, dragging even more old people into poverty, the clubs stepped up their political pressure. As a result, Congress voted to begin paying Social Security benefits in 1940 and to increase old-age assistance grants (the amounts paid to the destitute elderly).

In Sum

When conflict theorists analyze a social problem, they look for conflict among competing interest groups. In this example, they emphasize that today's Social Security benefits are not the result of generous hearts in Congress, but from the political power of the elderly, who had banded together to push their own interests. Congress gave as little as it thought it could get by with, and only when the elderly put more pressure on Congress did it increase benefits—and that reluctantly. For those benefits the elderly paid dearly—their removal from the workforce—for Congress set a mandatory retirement age of 65. This gave employers the goal they wanted, a younger workforce (Williamson et al. 1985).

CONFLICT THEORY AND SOCIAL PROBLEMS: A SUMMARY

Competition, Power, and Exploitation Make Social Problems Natural and Inevitable

At the root of a social problem lies conflict over the distribution of power and privilege. This means that social problems are inevitable, for it is inevitable that groups will come in conflict with one another as they try to maintain or to gain power and privilege. Most conflict is limited—not a battle to the death, but a fairly orderly, focused affair. Retired Americans, for example, have not fought bloody battles in the streets, but they have formed a political lobby to compete with other groups. Understanding that power and privilege lie at the root of social problems helps to penetrate the surface and to pinpoint what any particular social problem is all about.

Two Types of Social Problems

From the conflict perspective, social problems come in two forms. One is the troubles experienced by people who are exploited by the powerful. The other is the troubles experienced by the powerful when the exploited resist, rebel, or appeal to higher values. Although their resources are limited, the exploited do find ways to resist. Some go on hunger strikes or campaign for political office. Others attack those in power. As we saw with the Townsend movement, the elderly—a group weak in and of itself—were able to seize the initiative during a troubled period and force a change to improve their circumstances.

In Sum: Each Theory Highlights Different Aspects of a Social Problem

As you can see, each theoretical perspective provides a unique interpretation of social life. In the coming chapters, we will apply these three theoretical perspectives to the social problems that we analyze. To conclude this chapter, let's look at the probable future of the social problem of the elderly.

As the number of elderly increase, so do the costs of their health care. Cost is only one issue. Another is the quality of care, including the need to treat the elderly with respect. As is evident from the photo of this woman, in some medical settings even basic dignity is stripped from the elderly.

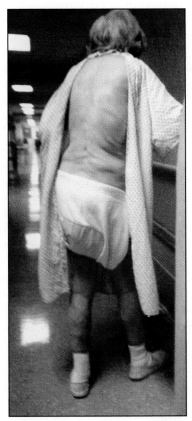

The Future of the Problem: The Pendulum Swings

Images of poor, ill, neglected grandparents have been used to promote programs for elderly Americans. But such images are no longer broadly accurate. Economic growth and the expansion of federal programs have reduced the poverty rate for the aged to the point that it is now *below* the nation's average. To get an idea of how tremendously their poverty has dropped, consider this: In 1970, 25 percent of the elderly were poor, but today it is just 10 percent (*Statistical Abstract* 1990:Table 746; 2003:Table 703).

This turnaround is so remarkable that some people think that the elderly are now receiving more than their fair share—an attitude that reflects a primary shift in the subjective concerns of this social problem. Although people are pleased that poverty among the elderly has declined, some think that the decline may have come at the cost of other groups. Figure 2-1 on the next page shows the objective conditions, the decline in the proportion of the elderly who live in poverty and the increase in the proportion of children who live in poverty. The elderly reply that their moving out of poverty has not

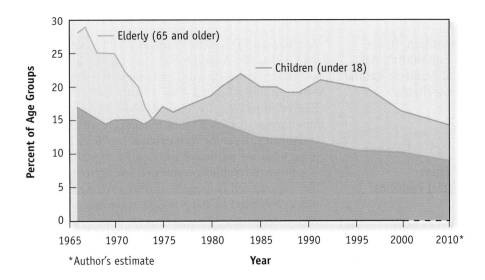

FIGURE 2-1   *The Poverty Rates of Children and the Elderly*
Source: *Congressional Research Services: Statistical Abstract* 1994:Tables 728, 731; 2003:Table 703.

A Disturbing Trend

More Than Their Fair Share?

caused anyone else to move into poverty, that no one should live in poverty, and that they want to reduce the poverty of all age groups.

This change in subjective concern—that the elderly are demanding, and getting, more than their fair share of society's resources—often centers on the costs of health care. Look at Figure 2-2. You can see how the costs of Medicare and Medicaid have skyrocketed. These costs have zoomed past the wildest projections of earlier years. Another subjective concern is the cost of Social Security. In 1950, Social Security payments ran only $784 million, but today they run $453 billion. People are alarmed when they see that the current payout is almost *600 times* the amount paid in 1950 (*Statistical Abstract* 1998 and 2003:Table 544).

Changes in Our Population Mix

Despite the rapid run up in the costs of Social Security, Medicare, and Medicaid, there is no sign that these costs will level off. Today, about one of eight Americans (12.3 percent of the U.S. population) is age 65 or over. As you can see from Figure 2-3 on page 44, in just a few years this proportion will double, and one of four Americans will be elderly. This growth will hit Social Security and health care hard.

Choices Between Children and Old People?

This changing balance of age groups exacerbates the problem. The data shown in Figure 2-1 make some fear that Congress has chosen old people over children, and they want to trim Social Security, Medicare, and other programs for the elderly on the basis that they go beyond the nation's ability to pay. Some reductions have been made. Social Security income, for example, used to be tax free but is now taxable. Despite such measures, as you saw from Figure 2-2, medical costs continue to mushroom.

The Emerging Struggle

To protect their gains, older Americans have organized a powerful political lobby. This group, the American Association of Retired Persons (AARP), boasts 35 million members and a staff of 1,200. It is difficult for politicians, whose foremost goal appears to be to get reelected, to ignore such numbers. Could a battle between younger people and the elderly be on its way? Consider the activities of the Gray Panthers, whose position is summarized in the Issues in Social Problems box on page 45.

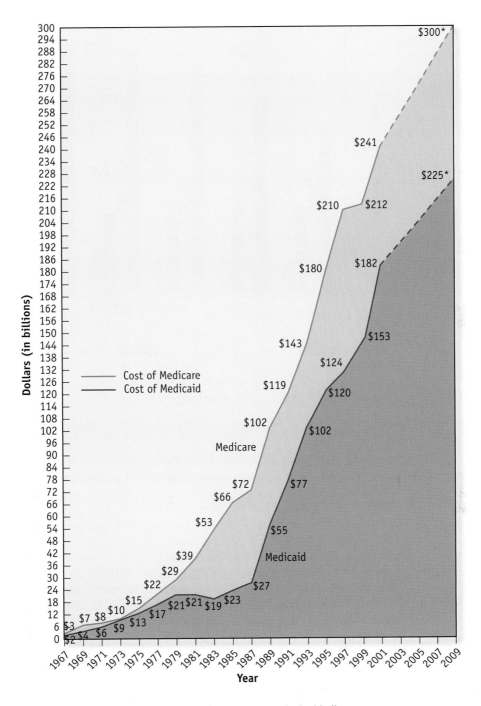

FIGURE 2-2   *Health Care Costs for the Elderly (and Disabled)*
Medicare funds are provided to the elderly and disabled by the federal government.
Medicaid is intended for the needy and is financed by federal, state, and local govern-
ments. Although these two programs began at modest levels, their costs have soared.
By 2001, Medicare and Medicaid ran about 80 times higher than in 1967.
* The author's estimate.

Source: *Statistical Abstract* 1992:Table 147; 1994:Table 159; 1997:Tables 164, 165; 2003:Tables 140,
146.

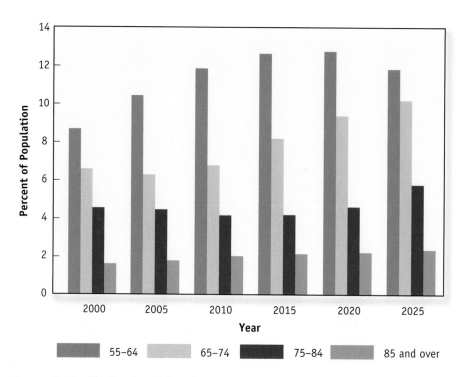

FIGURE 2-3   *The Graying of America*
Source: *Statistical Abstract* 2003:Tables 11, 12.

Social Security as a Gigantic Chain Letter

Some form of conflict does seem inevitable, for the interests of younger and older groups are on a collision course. There are two major problems. The first is that the money a worker "contributes" to Social Security is not put into the worker's own account. Instead, as money comes in from workers across the nation, it is paid out to those who are already retired—a sort of chain-letter arrangement by which the young support the old. The second problem is that the number of people who collect Social Security benefits is growing, but the proportion of working people—those who pay for these benefits out of their wages—is shrinking. We are seeing a major shift in the **dependency ratio,** the number of workers compared with the number of Social Security recipients. Presently, just under five working-age Americans pay Social Security taxes to support each person collecting Social Security. In about a generation, this ratio will drop to about 3 to 1 (Melloan 1994; *Statistical Abstract* 2003:Tables 541, 543).

Coming: An Intergenerational Showdown

Many are counting on the Social Security Trust Fund to prevent an intergenerational showdown. This fund supposedly consists of several trillions of dollars that have been collected in Social Security taxes in excess of payments to retirees. The problem is that the trust fund exists in name only. Those trillions of dollars disappear as fast as they come in, for the federal government "borrows" them, spends them on whatever it desires, and gives Social Security gigantic IOUs called U.S. Treasury notes (Henslin 2005). The day of reckoning between the generations can't be far off.

To close this chapter, let's see what different pictures emerge when we apply the three sociological perspectives to the struggle between the generations (see Thinking Critically box on page 46).

Issues in Social Problems

THE GRAY PANTHERS

WHO WE ARE

We are a group of people—old and young—drawn together by deeply felt common concerns for human liberation and social change. The old and young live outside the mainstream of society. **Ageism**—discrimination against persons on the basis of chronological age—deprives both groups of power and influence.

Besides being a movement of older and younger persons, as Gray Panthers we consider ourselves distinctive in the following ways:

We are against ageism that forces any group to live roles that are defined purely on the basis of age. We view aging as a total life process in which the individual develops from birth to death. Therefore, we are concerned about the needs of all age groups and ageism directed at any age group.

We have a strong sense of militancy. Our concern is not only for education and services, but for effective nonviolent action with an awareness of timing and urgency.

We advocate a radical approach to social change by attacking those forces that corrupt our institutions, attitudes, and values, such as materialism, racism, sexism, paternalism, militarism, and extreme nationalism.

WHAT WE WANT

1. To develop a new and positive self-awareness in our culture that can regard the total life span as a continuing process in maturity and fulfillment.
2. To strive for new options for lifestyles for older and younger people that will challenge the present paternalism in our institutions and culture, and to help eliminate the poverty and powerlessness in which most older and younger people are forced to live, and to change society's destructive attitudes about aging.
3. To make responsible use of our freedom to bring about social change, to develop a list of priorities among social issues, and to struggle nonviolently for social change that will bring greater human freedom, justice, dignity, and peace.
4. To build a new power base in our society uniting presently disenfranchised and oppressed groups, realizing the common qualities and concerns of age and youth working in coalition with other movements with similar goals and principles.
5. To reinforce and support each other in our quest for liberation and to celebrate our shared humanity.

Reprinted by permission of The Gray Panthers.

SUMMARY

1. The frameworks that sociologists use to interpret their findings are called *theories*. To interpret social problems, sociologists use three major theories: *symbolic interactionism, functionalism,* and *conflict theory.* Each theory provides a different interpretation of society and of social problems. No one theory is "right." Rather, taken together, these perspectives give us a more complete grasp of the whole.

2. Symbolic interactionists see social problems not as objective conditions but as definitions or views that are collectively held about some matter; that is, if people view something as a social problem, it is a social problem. As people's definitions or symbols change, so do their ideas about social problems.

3. Functionalists see society as a self-correcting, orderly system, much like a well-oiled machine. Its parts work together to bring the whole into equilibrium. Each part performs a function (hence, the term *functional* analysis) that contributes to the system. When a part is functioning imperfectly, it creates problems for the system. Those dysfunctions are called social problems.

4. Conflict theorists see social problems as a natural outcome of power arrangements. Those in power try to preserve the social order and their own privileged position within it. They take the needs of other groups into consideration only when it is in their own interest to do so. As they exploit others, the powerful create social problems, such as poverty and discrimination. Other social problems, such as revolution, crime, suicide, and drug abuse, represent reactions to oppression by those who have been exploited.

Thinking Critically about Social Problems

APPLYING THE THEORIES: UNDERSTANDING THE INTERGENERATIONAL BATTLE

Theories often appear vague and abstract. To help overcome this obstacle, as I introduced each theory in this chapter I applied it to the social problem of aging in U.S. society. Because these theories will be used throughout this text, it is important to understand them. Let's apply these three perspectives to the potential battle between the generations—because you are likely to experience this cutting edge of the social problem of aging. Because each theory yields a unique interpretation of a social problem, we can compare the different understandings they give us of this coming intergenerational struggle.

Symbolic Interactionism: Symbols are the essence of social life, including social problems. We use symbols to interpret the events we experience. If we were to use different symbols, we would understand our experiences differently. Just as the meaning of old age shifted during industrialization, so this symbol is shifting again. Today's elderly have grown more affluent, and they are choosing new lifestyles: Their condos, motor homes, and vacationing in exotic destinations make their new affluence highly visible. As a consequence, people's ideas of the elderly are changing. The struggle that is shaping up between the generations will provide a new set of symbols, one that will guide how we think about and act toward old people.

Functionalism: We can look at the elderly and the young as two major parts within the same social system. Because each part must work together if society is to func-

tion smoothly, these parts must also fit together well. If one of them takes too much of a society's resources, it creates an imbalance between the parts. Whenever an imbalance occurs, the parts must adjust in order for the larger unit (in this case, society) to attain equilibrium. Just as giving more resources to the elderly during the past two generations was an adjustment, so now, if those resources have become disproportionate, it will require another adjustment. Although the adjustment process will be difficult, both the elderly and the young are essential parts of society. The final result will be a harmonious balance between them.

Conflict Theory: Of course, there is a battle shaping up. The groups within a society are marked by unequal power and privilege, and each will struggle for its own interests. The AARP will push its own agenda, striving for greater advantage and as many resources as it can get. Their concern will be their own interests, regardless of how their gains may affect younger people. For their part, younger people will do the same, pursuing their own interests to the exclusion of other groups. Whenever one group gains a larger share of society's limited resources, others will resent those gains. The coming struggle between the generations is likely to be fierce, and the group with more power will win. Regardless of the outcome of this current competition for resources, conflict will continue in future generations.

KEY TERMS

Ageism   Discrimination against people on the basis of their age; this concept is not limited to older people.

Capitalism   An economic system based on private ownership of property and the investment of capital for the purpose of profit.

Capitalists   Owners of the means of production (land, factories, tools) who buy the labor of workers.

Conflict theory   A sociological theory that views society as a system in competition and conflict. Each group in society attempts to further its own interests, even at the expense of others. As these interests collide, the social order becomes unstable. Those in power exploit people and resources for their own benefit. Social problems stem from exploitation and resistance to exploitation.

Dependency ratio   The number of workers compared with the number of Social Security recipients.

Disengagement theory The view that society prevents disruption by having the elderly vacate (or disengage from) their positions of responsibility so that the younger generation can step into their shoes.

Dysfunction When some part of a social system disrupts the equilibrium of the system or interferes with the functioning of another part in the system, it is a dysfunction. See also *Functionalism*.

Function The contribution of a part to a system; or, people's actions that contribute to the equilibrium of a social system. See also *Functionalism*.

Functional analysis See *Functionalism*.

Functional perspective See *Functionalism*.

Functional theory See *Functionalism*.

Functionalism (also called *functional analysis, functional theory*, and the *functional perspective*). A sociological theory that views society as a system of interconnected parts, each contributing in some way to the equilibrium of the system. The contribution of each part is called its function; hence the term *functionalism*. Functionalists view social problems as the failure of some part of the system to function correctly.

Generalized other Basically, the community or groups in general that someone considers important, and whose views and attitudes the individual takes into account as he or she considers a course of action.

Labeling Stereotyping, or putting a tag on someone, and treating him or her accordingly.

Latent dysfunctions The *unintended* consequences of people's actions that *disrupt* the equilibrium of a system or the adjustment of its parts. See also *Functionalism*.

Latent functions The *unintended* consequences of people's actions that contribute to the equilibrium of a social system or the functioning of its parts. See also *Functionalism*.

Looking-glass self Our self-images are dependent on what we think others think of us. We see ourselves, in other words, as a reflection in the eyes of others; hence the term *looking-glass self*.

Manifest function The consequences of people's actions that are *intended* to contribute to the adaptation, adjustment, or equilibrium of a system or its parts. See also *Functionalism*.

Social construction of reality The attempt to make sense of life by giving meaning to one's experiences.

Structure The interrelations between the parts or subunits of society.

Symbol Items of social life to which we give meaning and that we then use to communicate with one another. They include signs, gestures, words, and even our posture and appearance.

Symbolic interactionism A sociological theory that views society as consisting of the patterns common to a group of people. Because these patterns depend on people's symbols or definitions, and because people's views change, society is always in flux. Within this framework, social problems are not considered objective conditions but, rather, the issues that people have decided to call social problems.

Taking the role of the other To mentally put oneself in another's place, seeing how things look from that perspective and anticipating how that person will act.

Theory An explanation of how two or more concepts, such as age and suicide, are related to one another.

THINKING CRITICALLY ABOUT CHAPTER 2

1. Of the three main theories identified in this chapter, which one do you think does the best job of explaining social problems? Why?

2. Think of a personal problem between two people.
   - How would symbolic interactionists explain this problem?
   - How would functionalists explain the problem?
   - How would conflict theorists explain the problem?

3. What do you think are the biggest problems that we are likely to face regarding the "graying of America" (the aging of the U.S. population)? Propose solutions to these problems.
   - Why do you feel your solutions might work?
   - What might prevent your solutions from working?

CHAPTER 3

Human Sexual Behavior

IN THE SPRING OF 2001, Hillary and Julie Goodridge of Massachusetts were denied a marriage license because they were of the same sex. They and six other couples sued the state. A lower court ruled against the seven couples, but on February 3, 2004, the state Supreme Court ruled that marriage between people of the same sex did not violate the Massachusetts constitution.

The governor of the state, Mitt Romney, announced that he would support a constitutional amendment that the state legislature had already passed. It would limit marriage to one man and one woman.

A state representative who sponsored the constitutional amendment said, "Massachusetts will be forever known as the birthplace of homosexual marriage. From the Bay State to the Gay State. I had hoped that people of common sense, who understand what nature and marriage is all about, would prevent this from happening."

A lawyer who had represented the couples before the state high court said, "I hope what people see is that there are very committed couples from all walks of life in the commonwealth of Massachusetts who, in some cases, have been waiting decades to take legal responsibility for one another. This case has always been about real people and real families."

The archbishop of Boston said, "The creation of a right to same-sex marriage in the end will not strengthen the institution of marriage within our society but only weaken it, as marriage becomes only one lifestyle choice among many others."

Missourians were upset. Instead of limiting their reaction to words, they—and ten other states—passed an amendment to their constitution that banned same-sex marriage.

The President of the United States, George W. Bush, said, "Marriage is a sacred institution between a man and a woman. Today's decision ... violates this important principle. I will work with congressional leaders and others to do what is legally necessary to defend the sanctity of marriage."

During June's gay pride march in New York City, which snaked down Fifth Avenue, from the Upper East Side to the West Village, gay marriage was a dominant theme.

Some U.S. senators and representatives proposed a federal marriage amendment to the U.S. Constitution. It would define marriage as limited to a man and a woman.

Based on Bayles 2004; CNN 2004; Davey 2004; Healy 2004; Weitzstein 2004.

Objective Conditions and Subjective Concerns

Again: To Have a Social Problem, We Need *Both* Objective Conditions and Subjective Conditions

What is and is not a social problem when it comes to human sexuality takes us to the essence of social problems, to those principles that I introduced in the first chapter. You will recall from our discussion that objective conditions alone are not adequate to make something a social problem. So it is with homosexuality and the other topics we will discuss in this chapter. If we had only objective conditions—people who have sexual preference for members of their own sex, for example—we would have no social problem. You will recall that subjective concern is also essential—that there be a lot of people who don't like the objective condition and would like to see it changed.

Regardless of whether you are homosexual, heterosexual, or bisexual—and regardless of your own position on homosexuality—you are familiar with these subjective concerns. As recounted in the opening vignette, when the Massachusetts Supreme Court determined that same-sex marriage did not violate that state's constitution, it set off a flurry of expressions of subjective concerns. Although attitudes about homosexuality have softened in recent years (which we shall review shortly), there remain considerable numbers of upset people who want things changed.

Societies Channel Sexual Behavior

Our job in this chapter is to examine three human activities that are mired in controversy, more so, perhaps, than any social problem other than abortion. As we do so, it is important to stress a sociological principle that is fundamental to this chapter: As much as we might like it otherwise, *sex is never only a personal matter.* All societies control or channel human sexual behavior. A major way that human groups channel sexual behavior is through the social institution of marriage and family, which shapes people's ideas of right and wrong. Challenges to people's ideas of marriage and family are not taken lightly, as is evident with the issue of same-sex marriage.

Why Are Violations of Sexual Norms a Social Problem?

Because many people view the topics of this chapter in moral terms, it is also important to stress another point that was made in the first chapter: Sociology cannot make moral judgments. Sociology, however, is well-equipped to report on attitudes and social controversy—the concerns that make contemporary society so exciting. To understand the three social problems that make up this chapter, we shall apply at least one of the three theories to each. We shall apply conflict theory and symbolic interactionism to homosexuality, view prostitution through the lens of functionalism, and use symbolic interactionism to analyze pornography. As usual, we shall attempt to present fairly both the scientific evidence and the controversial positions involved.

Homosexuality

Let's begin by looking at sociological findings regarding issues that often are on people's minds when they talk about homosexuality. Despite strong social norms and socialization into heterosexuality, how do people become homosexuals? How many people are homosexuals? Do some people have sex with people of their own gender—and yet they are heterosexuals? With changing norms, how much opposition is there to homosexuality today?

BACKGROUND: GETTING THE LARGER PICTURE

Homosexual Behavior vs. Homosexuality

To place matters in perspective, we need to get the larger picture. Attitudes toward **homosexual behavior**—sexual *relations* between people of the same sex—vary widely around the world. One of the most startling attitudes—to Western ears—is that of the Keraki of New Guinea. During puberty rites, which are kept secret from females, each boy is initiated into sodomy (anal intercourse). The following year, the boy continues to play a passive role with older boys and unmarried men. After that, until he marries (a woman), he, too, sodomizes the younger boys (Ford and Beach 1972). Another group in New Guinea, the Sambia, believe that a boy will remain small and weak and never become a man if he does not ingest semen. To prevent this, all Sambian boys have oral sex with men, and their homosexual behavior is considered a passage to "masculinization." The boys go on to a heterosexual life of marriage and procreation (Gilmore 1990).

Attitudes also vary toward **homosexuality,** the sexual *preference* for people of one's own sex, but here cross-cultural attitudes are more consistent. No society in the world considers exclusive, or even predominant, homosexuality in adulthood to be the norm. As sociologist Arno Karlen (1978:241) summarized this point, "Like sanctions against incest, adult–child coitus, and rape, the sanction against *predominant adult* homosexuality is universal."

Possible Reasons for Negative Sanctions and Disapproving Attitudes

Why do these universal sanctions exist? From a functionalist viewpoint, the primary reason centers on the role that the family plays in human societies. Every culture expects adults to become parents, and all societies build the family around some form of mother, father, and children. To tolerate or approve general homosexual behavior would upset this fundamental biologically-based arrangement.

Attitudes in the U.S.

In recent years, Americans have become more tolerant about homosexuality. An example is the changing attitudes of college freshmen. Look at Figure 3-1, which is based on national samples and represents fairly accurately the attitudes of all college freshmen. As you can see, the attitudes of college freshmen held fairly constant until 1990, and since then made a sharp shift toward tolerance. As you can also see, the attitudes of women freshmen have consistently been more favorable than those expressed by the men. Despite this change, of all freshmen across the United States, one of five women and one of three men still want homosexual relations to be illegal.

Let's get a broader picture of U.S. attitudes. These survey results, shown in Table 3-1 on page 52, are also from a well-chosen national sample. From this table, you can see that 60 percent of Americans think that homosexual relations between consenting adults should be legal. Americans are still divided, however, and thirty-five percent want homosexual relations—even between consenting adults—to be illegal. From this table, you can sketch a profile of those who are most likely to support the legalization of homosexual relations: college-educated younger white women who live in a Western city or the suburbs, who make over $75,000 a year, and who are Democrats or Independents. Those most likely to want homosexual relations to be illegal are elderly black male high school graduates with low incomes who live in rural areas of the South and who vote Republican. Attitudes follow the expected age pattern, with the younger more likely to favor the legality of homosexual relations. As you can see, unlike college freshmen, the attitudes of men and women across the nation are almost identical.

Homosexuals and the Law

The social institutions of U.S. society have presumed the norm of **heterosexuality,** the sexual preference for persons of the opposite sex. For example, until 1960, *in all states,* even private, consensual sexual acts between adults of the same sex were illegal. In 2003, 12 states still had such laws on the books, but in that year, in *Lawrence et al. v. Texas,* the U.S. Supreme Court struck down the Texas law that made such sex illegal (CNN 2003). This decision applies to all states.

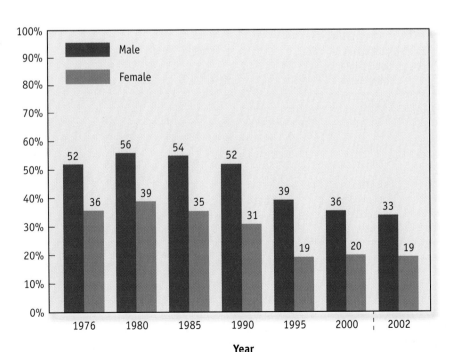

FIGURE 3-1 *What Do College Freshmen Say About Homosexual Relationships Being Illegal?*
The percentage of national samples of U.S. college students who agree with this statement: "It is important to have laws prohibiting homosexual relationships."

Source: *Sourcebook of Criminal Justice Statistics* 2002:Table 2.91.

TABLE 3-1 Attitudes Toward the Legality of Homosexual Relations

Question: "Do you think homosexual relations between consenting adults should or should not be legal?"

	LEGAL	NOT LEGAL	NO OPINION
NATIONAL	60%	35%	5%
SEX			
Female	60	35	5
Male	59	36	5
RACE			
White	60	35	5
Black	56	38	6
AGE			
18 to 29 years	72	26	2
30 to 49 years	65	31	4
50 to 64 years	56	40	4
50 years and older	49	44	7
65 years and older	39	51	10
EDUCATION			
College postgraduate	71	25	4
College graduate	71	26	3
Some college	64	31	5
High school graduate or less	49	46	5
INCOME			
Under $20,000	50	43	7
$20,000 to $29,999	53	44	3
$30,000 to $49,999	63	33	4
$50,000 to $74,999	58	38	4
$75,000 and over	72	23	5
URBAN/RURAL			
Urban area	65	29	6
Suburban area	64	32	4
Rural area	46	49	5
REGION			
West	73	23	4
East	65	30	5
Midwest	57	38	5
South	49	46	5
POLITICS			
Independent	64	31	5
Democrat	63	34	3
Republican	51	42	7

Source: *Sourcebook of Criminal Justice Statistics* 2003:Table 2.99.

Hate Crimes

Over the years, homosexuals have been the victims of violence because of their sexual orientation. Until 1990, however, there was no way of knowing the extent of their victimization. In that year, Congress passed the *Hate Crime Statistics Act,* which authorized the FBI to collect data on "crimes that manifest evidence of prejudice based on race, religion, ethnicity, and sexual orientation." Later, disability and national origin were added to this list. **Hate crimes** are not distinct crimes, but, rather, they are regular crimes such as assault that are motivated by dislike or hatred of the victim's characteristics. In this instance, the victim is chosen because he or she is a homosexual. Each year, about 1,600 homosexuals are the victims of hate crimes (*Statistical Abstract* 2003:Table 319). The actual total is larger, because not all victims file reports and not all police agencies report these data to the FBI.

Current Changes

Owing to the activities of gay liberation groups and the American Civil Liberties Union, accompanied by changing attitudes, homosexuals face less discrimination than they used to. The Civil Service Commission no longer denies federal employment to homosexuals. Similarly, such multinational giants as AT&T, GM, Ford, and IBM follow policies of not discriminating against homosexuals in hiring or promotion. San Francisco purposely recruits homosexuals as members of its police force. Homosexuals used to be easy targets of politicians who wanted to ingratiate themselves with voters and further their own political ambitions. Today, if a politician were to verbally attack homosexuals, it likely would be the end of that person's political career.

Such changes have not meant the end of open discrimination. The FBI and CIA, for example, will not hire known homosexuals. And although the Defense Department follows a "Don't Ask, Don't Tell" policy, soldiers who are discovered to be homosexual are discharged from the military. The Supreme Court has upheld this policy.

To understand homosexual–heterosexual relations, let's look at them through the lens of conflict theory.

You are now familiar with the two dimensions of social problems: objective conditions and subjective concerns. As symbolic interactionists stress, subjective concerns are matters of definition—how people view something. What symbols do you see in this photo that the demonstrators are using with the goal of changing subjective concerns?

HOMOSEXUALITY VIEWED THEORETICALLY: APPLYING CONFLICT THEORY

Political Activism

In reaction to the discrimination they experienced, homosexuals found that politics was the best way to forge social change. *Coming out of the closet,* that is, publicly asserting a homosexual identity, they marched in public demonstrations, campaigning for legal reform and demanding more social rights. From local campaigns in some cities, such as San Francisco and New York, homosexuals became active as a group in national politics. As a result, some politicians actively court the homosexual vote, and unlike the recent past, no politicians with serious ambitions can make them a target of their hostility.

Opposition

The advocacy of homosexuality as an alternative lifestyle, however, has generated opposition, making gay advocacy a hot issue in schools and in work settings. As homosexuals have publicized their demands, homosexuality has become a political and social issue. Major facets of this issue are summarized above in the Thinking Critically box on whether homosexuals should be declared a minority group.

An Uneasy Truce

Conflict is inevitable when opposing groups jockey for position. One demands greater power, and the other resists that demand. Out of conflict can come a shift in

Thinking Critically about Social Problems

SHOULD HOMOSEXUALS BE DECLARED A MINORITY GROUP?

This issue divides Americans. Many people feel strongly about it and land squarely on one side or the other. Where do your opinions fall? Why? Do you accept all the arguments of one of these positions? How does your own position differ?

THEY SHOULD

Homosexuals have been victims of hostility and discrimination, and they deserve the same legal protection as those given to other minority groups. Anyone who refuses to rent to someone because that person is a homosexual should face legal consequences. So should anyone who refuses to hire a homosexual who is qualified for a job—and that includes active duty in the military.

But the matter is more than avoiding and overcoming discrimination. Schools also have a duty to discuss homosexuality in order to reduce negative stereotypes and **homophobia** (fear and hatred of homosexuals). Children should be given the option of exploring their potential homosexual orientation within an accepting environment, not fed stereotypes and other negative images that make them ashamed of such desires.

In short, we are not asking for tolerance. Tolerance implies superiority on the part of those granting it. We demand that homosexual identity and sexual behavior be viewed as viable, legitimate, and normal as are heterosexual identity and sexual behavior.

THEY SHOULD NOT

Homosexuals are not a minority group, and it is inappropriate to award them special legal rights. Racial and ethnic minorities, and males and females, become members of a group through birth. They have no choice about belonging, nor does their membership imply any immoral behavior.

Homosexuals, in contrast, have chosen their lifestyle. They deserve no more legal protection for choosing to have sex with each other than does anybody else for their sexual preference. Does someone who prefers adultery deserve legal protection because of that preference? Even if some people are predisposed to homosexuality, is this any different from some people being predisposed to lying? We don't make lying an acceptable behavior and assign liars a minority status.

Anyone who believes that a homosexual lifestyle is immoral should not have to rent to homosexuals. Nor should churches be forced to ordain them, schools or other employers to hire them, or the military to accept them. Above all, children should not be encouraged to explore any so-called homosexual orientation.

power alignments and a reevaluation of thinking and positions. A common solution to keep the peace is for competing groups to make trade-offs, with each giving up something that it desires. Truces, however, can be uneasy, especially when they involve the coexistence of antithetical values. In such instances, conflict eventually resurfaces. All it takes is for one side to try to shift the terms of the uneasy and often unspoken alignment.

RESEARCH ON HOMOSEXUALITY

The Kinsey Research Let's turn now to a brief overview of sociological studies of homosexuality. Alfred Kinsey and his associates included homosexuality in their pathbreaking study *Sexual Behavior in the Human Male* (1948). To understand the Kinsey findings of more than a half century ago, keep in mind the distinction made earlier between homosexual behavior and homosexuality. Based on case histories of about 5,300 males, Kinsey found that 37 percent of U.S. males have at least one sexual experience with a same-sex partner that results in orgasm. Such experiences, however, do not make people homosexuals. As Kinsey pointed out, most of these homosexual behaviors are a form of experimentation, and almost all of these males go on to live heterosexual lives. Kinsey also concluded that about 4 percent of U.S. males are exclusively homosexual throughout life.

Kinsey's findings shocked the U.S. public and unleashed a storm of criticism in the academic community. The primary problem is that Kinsey used a biased sample, and there is no scientific way to generalize from his findings. Kinsey recruited some subjects from prisons and reform schools, whose inmates hardly represent the general population. He also interviewed only whites, and he had too high a percentage of men from the lower class (Himmelhoch and Fava 1955). Consequently, researchers no longer trust Kinsey's findings. In any scientific sense, they must be disregarded.

The Laumann Research In contrast, a team of researchers headed by sociologist Edward Laumann has carried out accurate research on U.S. sexual behavior (1994). Because Laumann interviewed a representative sample of the U.S. population, we can generalize his findings to the entire U.S. population. As you can see from Figure 3-2 on the next page, Laumann found that over a five-year period, 4.1 percent of U.S. men and 2.2 percent of U.S. women had sex with a same-sex partner. If the time period is extended to include all the previous years of their lives, these figures increase to 3.8 percent of the women and 7.1 percent of the men. This is a far cry from Kinsey's 37 percent for men.

As Figure 3-2 also shows, 1.4 percent of U.S. women and 2.8 percent of U.S. men identify themselves as homosexuals. These percentages are almost identical to those who report that they have had sex with a same-sex partner during the past year (1.3 percent of the women and 2.7 percent of the men). Even these figures may be slightly high, as the Laumann researchers counted as homosexuals people who identify themselves as bisexuals.

In the Spotlight on Research box on page 57, Laumann explains why he did his research, and the opposition that he had to overcome to do it.

Although Laumann's sampling technique is excellent, and this research gives us data from which we can generalize to the U.S. population, sociologists also like to gather qualitative data. Qualitative data allow us to analyze people's interactions and understand their perspectives. We are able to see how they put their worlds together—that concept we discussed in chapter 2, the social construction of reality.

The Humphreys Research To get qualitative information on homosexual behavior, sociologist Laud Humphreys devised an ingenious but widely criticized method. Knowing that some male homosexuals meet for impersonal sex in public restrooms ("tearooms," in the homosexual vernacular), Humphreys (1970) began hanging around these restrooms. He took the role of "watch queen," the one who gives warning when strangers approach, and observed

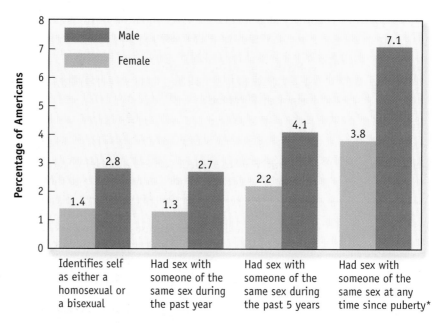

FIGURE 3-2 *Homosexual Identity and Sex with Someone of the Same Sex*

Source: Laumann et al. 1994:293–296.

*Note: Another form of this question yielded 4.3 percent for women and 9.1 percent for men.

what went on. He saw that these men used a system of gestures to initiate sex at the urinal and then moved to a toilet stall for fellatio (oral sex). Their quick, anonymous sex usually occurred without the exchange of a single word. Another sociologist, Edward Delph (1978), confirmed the silence that surrounds these sexual encounters.

Humphreys found something else that was surprising: Of the men he observed having tearoom sex, 38 percent were married. Humphreys wanted to find out why these married men engaged in homosexual behavior, and he managed to interview them. He found that the men identified themselves as heterosexuals, but they were frustrated sexually with their wives. In tearooms, they found a sexual outlet that did not threaten their emotional commitment to their wives, for it required neither socializing nor any kind of relationship. In essence, the tearooms functioned as a free house of prostitution, a place where they could obtain quick, oral sex at no charge. Sociologists Jay Corzine and Richard Kirby (1977) found similar homosexual behavior at truck stops: Heterosexual truckers have sex with homosexuals who search out partners at highway rest areas.

The Question of Research Ethics

You may have wondered how Humphreys knew that 38 percent of the men he observed having tearoom sex were married. What he did was to write down these men's license plate numbers and then trace their home addresses. He then had these men included in a health survey that his professors were conducting, and a year later he visited the men's homes, supposedly for the purpose of the medical study. For being deceptive, Humphreys met severe criticisms, both from other sociologists and even from the public. At first Humphreys vigorously defended himself, but in the second edition of his book (1975) he agreed that he should have identified himself as a researcher.

Situational Homosexual Behavior: The Prison

Certain places, such as prisons and boarding schools, induce **situational homosexual behavior,** that is, homosexual behavior by people who, if members of the opposite sex were available, would be involved in heterosexual relations. Let's look at a study of homosexual behavior in the state prison at Soledad, California. Sociologist George Kirkham (1971) found that the participants identified themselves as "queens," "punks," and "wolves."

Studying Sex in America

Edward Laumann, Dean of the Social Science Division at the University of Chicago, has done research on health, politics, power, status, and sex. Although he has pioneered theoretical work in how people form, maintain, and dissolve relationships, it is his research on sex that has received the most attention.

In the 1980s, when we were in the midst of an AIDS epidemic so vicious that the number of people with this disease was doubling every 10 months, I organized a workshop on AIDS and Society. As I listened to the presentations, I became convinced that there would be no magic bullet to stop this epidemic through immunization. To contain the spread of AIDS, people would have to change their behavior. Robert Michael, an economic demographer, and I concluded that we needed a national sex survey to document the sex practices of Americans. With this information, we could design ways to persuade people to take defensive measures.

Research into human sexual behavior is often considered "illegitimate," even by many social scientists. Despite this disapproval, we wanted the University of Chicago to pool its strengths in survey and sample design to conduct this national survey. John Gagnon, a sexologist, joined our research team. When the National Institutes of Health announced a search for research proposals to combat AIDS, we submitted our design for a national sex survey. We won that competition.

When *Science* magazine reported that our proposal was under review at the White House's Office of Management and the Budget, the *Washington Times* picked the story up with screaming headlines. Within a few days, a White Paper was circulating to every member of the House and Senate.

One objection was that sex reports normalize immoral sexual behavior, such as masturbation and anal and oral sex. Another was that the government has no business invading people's private lives, even if it is for reasons of the public's health. Michael and I were accused of being fronts for a cabal of homophiles who were attempting to legitimize gay sex.

Although the Senate Appropriations Committee recommended that our survey be funded, the House Appropriations Committee disagreed. For two years, we lobbied Congressional staffers, Senators, and Representatives for their support in funding the research, but with few results. Then Senator Jesse Helms submitted an amendment to an appropriations bill that transferred the funding that had been intended for our sex survey to a "say no to sex" campaign. The Senate voted 66 to 34 in favor of the amendment, giving me the dubious distinction of having Congress trying to stop my research.

With government funding cut off, we turned to private foundations. The Robert Wood Johnson, Henry Kaiser, Rockefeller, and McArthur foundations agreed to fund our research. To share the results of our survey with the scientific community, we wrote *The Social Organization of Sexuality*. This is a technical book, and as some have noted, it took the University of Chicago to take the fun out of sex.

We felt strongly that the public needed to know what we had discovered, and we wanted to have a hand in framing the public's understanding, not leave it to others. To do this, we arranged for Gini Kolata, a *New York Times* reporter who specializes in science and health news, to write a companion volume, *Sex in America*.

The men used "queen" to refer to an inmate who prefers male sexual partners. The queen, then, does not engage in situational homosexual behavior, for, in prison or out, "she" prefers male partners. To attract fellow prisoners, the queen exaggerates aspects of female sexuality. She may adopt a feminine nickname ("Peaches," "Dee-Dee"), tear the back pockets from tight prison denims to make them more form-fitting, use cosmetics made from medical and food supplies, and wear jewelry produced in hobby shops. The queen lets her hair grow as long as the guards allow and shows an exaggerated "swish" as she walks.

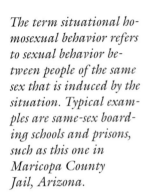

The term situational homosexual behavior refers to sexual behavior between people of the same sex that is induced by the situation. Typical examples are same-sex boarding schools and prisons, such as this one in Maricopa County Jail, Arizona.

When they first enter prison, most men find queens despicable. As the months pass, however, the queen evokes the memory and longing for women, and some change their mind. Some heterosexual men even enter into long-term relationships with queens. Their relationships resemble marriage, including an emotional relationship and the expectation of sexual fidelity. These relationships are brittle, though, for most queens are promiscuous. Some queens become the victims of prison pimps and are forced to prostitute themselves at the pimp's whim. Some are even sold to other pimps to settle debts. The queen is accorded some social status, for she is thought to be following her natural inclinations.

Next to the "rat," or informer, the "punk" has the least social status among prisoners. There are two types: "canteen punks," those who offer sex in exchange for candy, cigarettes, money, or personal favors, and "pressure punks," those who are pressured by threats or violence into giving sex to other men. Both types of punks are despised by prison inmates: canteen punks because they sacrifice their manhood to obtain goods or services, and pressure punks because they show weakness in the face of threats and violence.

How do men become pressure punks? Some are beaten and gang raped and then forced into this status for the rest of their prison term. Others are tricked into it. Some "fish" (a new inmate), unacquainted with prison ways, accept cigarettes, money, or help of some sort from an experienced inmate. Others are the victims of a rigged gambling game. In either case, if the fish cannot pay when the experienced inmate demands settlement of the debt, he is told that he must give sex as payment. At this point, the fish has just two choices—to submit or to fight. A fish who submits is marked as a punk from then on and must continue to provide sex for the rest of his prison term.

The prisoners' view of the "wolf" is different. Although the wolf has sex with punks, he does not lose his status as a "man." To remain a "man" and still engage in sex with other men, he presents an image of exaggerated toughness. Force and rape match this manly image that prisoners hold, and the more violence that surrounds the wolf's sexual acts, the more he is seen as masculine. He must also keep his sexual acts emotionless and impersonal. Some wolves "own" punks and prostitute them for cigarettes, drugs, or other favors.

Forming a Homosexual Identity

Heterosexual men who have sex with other men in prison prefer to have sex with women. After they leave prison, they do so. Once more, this reminds us of the distinction made earlier between homosexuality and homosexual behavior. But what do we know about the causes of homosexuality—the *preference* for someone of one's own sex?

Despite many theories and thousands of studies, we do not know the answer. Although it is possible that genetics in the form of DNA markers or the organization of the brain may underlie human sexual orientation, researchers have found no chemical, biological, or even psychological differences that distinguish homosexuals and heterosexuals (Hooker 1957, 1958; Masters and Johnson 1979; Paul et al. 1982; Hamer et al. 1993; LeVay 1993; Laumann 1994). Because of this, sociologists do not view homosexuality as the result of genetics, or even consider it to be due to certain types of family relations, such as an aloof, "weak" father and a close, "dominant" mother.

For reasons currently unknown, then, some people feel erotic desires for members of their own sex. Erotic desires are insufficient for people to label themselves homosexual, however, for many people who experience such desires continue to identify themselves as heterosexuals (cf., Laumann 1994). How, then, do people develop an *identity* as homosexual? Sociologist Vivienne Cass (1979) found that this transition centers on self-labeling. Utilizing case studies and symbolic interactionism, Cass identified six stages:

Six Stages in the Process of Developing a Homosexual Identity

1. *Identity confusion.* Finding his or her feelings or behaviors at odds with heterosexual orientations, the individual is confused and upset. He or she asks, "Who am I?" and replies *"My behavior or feelings could be called homosexual."*

2. *Identity comparison.* The individual begins to feel "different," as though he or she does not belong. He or she makes the first tentative commitment to a homosexual identity by saying, *"I may be a homosexual."*

3. *Identity tolerance.* The individual turns the self-image further away from a heterosexual identity and more toward a homosexual identity. The conclusion at this point is, *"I probably am a homosexual."*

4. *Identity acceptance.* The individual moves from tolerating a homosexual self-image to accepting a homosexual identity. After increasing contact with others who define themselves as homosexual, he or she concludes, *"I am a homosexual."*

5. *Identity pride.* The individual thinks of homosexuality as good and heterosexuality as bad. He or she makes a strong commitment to a homosexual group, which generates a firm sense of group identity. The individual may become politically active and thinks, *"I am a homosexual and proud of it."*

6. *Identity synthesis.* The individual decides that the "them and us" philosophy is inappropriate. He or she begins to feel much similarity with some heterosexuals—and much dissimilarity with some homosexuals. Although homosexuality remains essential to the individual's identity, it becomes merely one aspect of the self. The individual may say, *"I am a homosexual—but I am also a lot of other things in life."*

Self-Identities Are Not Fixed

In line with symbolic interactionism, Cass stresses that people construct their own self-images. Individuals who have begun to interpret their feelings and behavior in terms of homosexuality may stop at any stage. They may even move back toward a heterosexual identity. For example, in stage 1 when people consider the possibility that their behavior *could* be called homosexual, they can stop the behavior. They can also continue it, but define it as situational rather than as part of their sexual orientation. People in the third stage may feel positive about "probably" being homosexual and eagerly move to the fourth stage—or they may dislike this probability and move away from a homosexual identification. In metaphorical terms, people can continue the journey, get off the train at the station marked "Identification Stops Here," or get off at the station called "Return to Heterosexuality." To have begun the journey does not mean that people continue it to a final destination called "Homosexuality" (Bell et al. 1981).

Confirming Sexual Identities

When people are acquiring a sexual identity, they try to confirm that identity by associating with others who reinforce their budding identity. People who feel that they are heterosexual associate with heterosexuals and do "heterosexual things." Similarly, people who feel that they are homosexual associate with homosexuals and do "homosexual things." Both are confirming their developing identities. The heterosexual and homosexual worlds overlap, however, and the point at which they cross can present a challenge to fragile identities.

Challenging Sexual Identities

Although our sexual identity may be tenuous during childhood, over time it becomes more firmly rooted. By the time we are adults, we seldom question it. Not everyone's sexual identity is this firm, however. Apparently some homosexuals and heterosexuals never question their choice, but others have doubt about who they "really" are. As sociologist Rose Weitz (1991) found in her study of AIDS, some homosexuals are plagued with guilt, and AIDS can challenge their sexual identity. She found that some reaffirmed the social norms that condemn homosexual activities; asked their families, churches, and God to accept their apologies and to forgive them; and then asserted a "new self." Some even tried to convince others that this was their "real self" all along. To continue our earlier analogy, a few adult homosexuals get back on the train and take it to an earlier station in their sexual identity. Weitz also found that for some people whose identity as homosexual made them uneasy, AIDS was a catalyst that made them more comfortable with their identity. For them, the train stops at a station in which they embrace a homosexual identity.

In Sum

According to symbolic interactionism, identities, including one's sexual identity, are not fixed in nature or inherent in one's birth. Instead, we are born with an undirected sexual potential that becomes channeled by our experiences into a homosexual or heterosexual direction (or in other directions—bisexuality, bestiality, and various fetishes). A sexual identity does not unfold automatically from within—like an acorn that can become only an oak tree. Rather, sexual preferences are learned, and people acquire sexual identities to match.

DIFFERENCES BETWEEN MALE AND FEMALE HOMOSEXUALS

What differences have researchers found between male and female homosexuals? (The term for female homosexuals, **lesbian,** apparently first referred to the Greek island of Lesbos, home of the poet Sappho, who wrote lyric poetry celebrating the love of woman for woman.)

Incidence and Promiscuity

You already have seen that homosexuality is more common among males than females, a finding that is supported by all researchers who have reported on this matter. Let's see what other differences they have found. One of the most significant is that lesbians are more likely to seek lasting relationships, place greater value on emotional commitment and mutual fidelity, and shun the bar scene (Wolf 1979; Lowenstein 1980; Peplau and Amaro 1982). Consequently, although most male homosexuals have "cruised" (sought impersonal sex with strangers), fewer than 20 percent of lesbians have done so. As a result, lesbians tend to have fewer sexual partners than do male homosexuals.

Psychologist Alan Bell and sociologist Martin Weinberg (1978) interviewed about 1,500 homosexuals. They found that almost half of the white and one-third of the African-American homosexual males had at least 500 different sexual partners. About 28 percent of the white sample had more than 1,000 different partners. Although their sample is large, it is not representative of homosexuals, because their research focused heavily on bars and steam baths. In these settings, people are looking for sex, so the sample is skewed toward people who have many sexual partners. We need balancing studies of homosexuals who are committed to a partner. Bell and Weinberg's findings do, however, support other studies that indicate extensive promiscuity among male homosexuals.

When AIDS first appeared, it meant a death sentence. Shock and fear shook the homosexual community, and men reduced their number of sexual partners. After a cocktail of drugs to treat AIDS was developed, deaths plummeted. When it became apparent that people who were infected with HIV (the virus that causes AIDS) could live long lives, concerns dropped, and many male homosexuals started to practice less safe sex (Public Health 2002). The results of this change remain to be seen.

Why are there such substantial differences in promiscuity and commitment between male and female homosexuals? Symbolic interactionists would argue that the chief reason can be traced to differences in their socialization. Girls are more likely to learn to associate sex with emotional relationships, and like their heterosexual counterparts, lesbians tend to conform to this gender expectation. Similarly, boys tend to learn to separate sex from affection, to validate their self-images by how much sex they have, and to see fidelity as a restriction on their independence. In short, homosexuals reflect the broad-based gender expectations of our culture.

As stressed in chapter 1, there is no social problem that has only objective conditions. Like other social problems, then, homosexuality is a social problem because of subjective concerns. The two major concerns of heterosexuals are that it is immoral for people of the same sex to have sex with one another and that homosexuality poses a threat to the family. Americans, however, are divided on this issue, and some view homosexuality as a permissible alternative lifestyle. Like other social problems, homosexuality draws its share of extremists. Those on one side argue that homosexuals should be punished with legal and social sanctions, whereas extremists on the other side argue that homosexuality should be encouraged among our youth.

Why These Differences Between Male and Female Homosexuals?

As discussed in the text, attitudes toward prostitution vary widely among societies and in different historical periods. This 2,000-year-old depiction of a prostitute is in the Archeological Museum in Athens, Greece.

Prostitution

BACKGROUND: GETTING THE LARGER PICTURE

It is no accident that **prostitution,** the renting of one's body for sexual purposes, has been called "the world's oldest profession." Accounts of prostitution by both females and males reach back to the beginnings of recorded history. It exists in one form or another almost everywhere.

Attitudes toward prostitution vary immensely. The ancient inhabitants of the Mediterranean area, Asia Minor, West Africa, and southern India held an attitude that is startling to contemporary Westerners (Henriques 1966). There, prostitution was part of religion. It took place in the temple, as a type of service to their gods. In one form of **temple prostitution,** every woman was required to perform an act of prostitution before she could marry. In another, a woman was dedicated to the gods of the temple as a sacred prostitute—either for a specific time or, more commonly, for life. On a visit to India, I was surprised to find that in some villages temple prostitution still exists.

In ancient Greece, high-class prostitutes, called *hetairae,* were respected. Their portraits and statues were placed "in the temples and other public buildings by the side of meritorious generals and statesmen" (Henriques 1966:64).

**Attitudes Toward
Prostitution**

Today, in many Latin countries prostitution is seen as a necessary evil—something that keeps hot-blooded men away from the pure and innocent. Although many Mexicans, Italians, and South Americans may consider prostitution disgusting, they are also convinced that prostitutes indirectly protect the virtue of their own wives and daughters.

The attitudes of Americans toward the legalization of prostitution are shown in Table 3-2. This research reveals interesting profiles. Those most likely to favor the legalization of prostitution are white male college graduates with high incomes who live in the West. Those least likely to favor legal prostitution are black female high school graduates with low incomes who live in the Midwest. A surprise is that those who are between the ages of 50 to 64, usually a very conservative group, are the most likely to favor the legalization of prostitution.

How Many Prostitutes?

Although prostitution has flourished in the United States, no one knows how many prostitutes there are. Estimates range from about 100,000 to a half million (Winick and Kinsie 1971; Sheehy 1973; Pottêrat et al. 1990). Although a half million

TABLE 3-2 Attitudes Toward the Legalization of Prostitution
Question: "In your opinion, should prostitution involving adults aged 18 years of age and older be legal or illegal in your state?"

	LEGAL	ILLEGAL	DON'T KNOW/REFUSED
NATIONAL	26%	70%	4%
SEX			
Male	32%	63%	5%
Female	21%	77%	2%
RACE/ETHNICITY*			
White	27%	70%	3%
Black	20%	79%	1%
AGE			
18 to 29 years	25%	74%	1%
30 to 49 years	28%	68%	4%
50 to 64 years	32%	65%	3%
65 years and older	18%	77%	5%
EDUCATION			
College graduate	28%	69%	3%
High school	21%	76%	3%
INCOME			
$50,000 and over	33%	64%	3%
$30,000 to $49,999	26%	70%	4%
$20,000 to $29,999	27%	71%	2%
Under $20,000	18%	80%	2%
REGION			
East	28%	68%	4%
Midwest	20%	78%	2%
South	24%	75%	1%
West	34%	58%	8%

Source: *Sourcebook of Criminal Justice Statistics* 1997:table 2–99. Table dropped in later editions.
*Only these two groups are listed in the Source.

may seem surprisingly high, during the supposedly prudish Victorian period, prostitutes in London may have been 50 times as common—in proportion to the general population—as they are in the United States today.

Even if there is proportionately less prostitution today, prostitution is certainly alive and well. Some prostitutes have 400 customers a month (Forney et al. 1992), although the average prostitute probably engages in about 40 sexual acts a week (Sheehy 1973). If these estimates are anywhere near accurate—and we really don't know—in the United States there are between 3 million and 20 million acts of commercial sex per week. This comes to somewhere between 200 million and 1 billion a year.

Legal Prostitution

The only place in the United States where prostitution is legal is Nevada (Weitzer 2000). There, prostitutes are permitted to sell sex in all but five counties, including the urban counties where Reno, Las Vegas, and Lake Tahoe are located. In those urban counties, officials believe that legalized prostitution might drive away "family-type" gamblers. Illegal prostitution also thrives, as evidenced by police files on the thousands of prostitutes who have worked Las Vegas.

Changes in Prostitution

Prostitutes have kept up with the times. Even though the elaborately furnished "whorehouse" of bygone days is indeed bygone, massage parlors, call girls, and escort services have taken its place. Under cover of a legitimate service, "massage parlors" offer sex for sale. So do escort services: For a set fee a client arranges a date and privately negotiates the inclusion of sexual services. In Spain, "masseuses" make house calls. Their newspaper and magazine ads mention their qualifications, such as "19 years old, blue eyes, and just arrived from Germany." Such advertising also exists in Florida and several other states.

Another variation is corporate prostitution. In one version, a corporation hires prostitutes for its customers. A New York telephone company, for example, held what its executives called "pervert" conventions. In these week-long, raucous sessions, prostitutes provided sex for the company's suppliers (Carnevale 1990). In a second version, an employee of a corporation provides sex for clients of the firm. In the Issues in Social Problems box on page 64, one of my students explains how she became a corporate prostitute.

In short, we can note that prostitution changes along with other aspects of society and that it serves social functions—from playing a role in religious rituals to helping corporations remain competitive. In the following section, we shall examine the social functions of prostitution in more detail.

PROSTITUTION VIEWED THEORETICALLY: APPLYING FUNCTIONALISM

The Social Functions of Prostitution

On the most obvious level, prostitution flourishes because it satisfies sexual needs that are not met elsewhere. This, of course, is precisely why it can never be eliminated. In a classic article, sociologist Kingsley Davis (1937, 1966) concluded that prostitutes provide a sexual outlet for men who

1. Have difficulty in establishing sexual relationships (such as the disfigured or handicapped)
2. Cannot find long-term partners (such as travelers and sailors)
3. Have a broken relationship (such as the separated or divorced)
4. Want sexual gratification that they view as immoral—and is thus out of bounds for wives and girlfriends

Issues in Social Problems

ME, A PROSTITUTE?

Many women are initiated into prostitution over a period of time through a gradual step-by-step process, as illustrated by this account written by one of my students who wishes to remain anonymous. The account has been set according to the original paper, including typos and misspellings.

I am a average looking blond with blue eyes. I am a female of twenty years of age. My mother is a elementary school teacher with a doctorit degree. My father is the head of instramentation for a large oil company. He write books, makes movies and teaches around the world. I have one sibbling. She is 10 years old. My parents are very old fashioned. they are strickt with both my sister and I. We are Hard-Shell-Baptist, and attend church no-matter-what. They've instilled wonderful values in me. We live in the country on a farm (pleasure, we don't grow things). Our home is large and because both of my parents work we have a maid that comes three days a week to clean. I've always had to work around the house. Cooking meals, cleaning and doing farm chores such as, feeding the horses and cows, have always been a part of my dayly routine. Yet, there's never been anything I've ever done without. Anything that could be bought was automatically mine, just for the asking. Our entire family is close. We visit one another frequently and have get-togethers regularly.

I am from a family with an average annual income of over $100,000.00. My parents have never neglected me. No one has ever abused me. I've caused my share of trouble, but it was all jouvenile, never anything against the law of the state. I've never been a misfit. I was one of the "cool" kids. I was in with the "popular" crowd. I was in Student Government and Peer Leadership in High School. I was elected Snow Queen my junior year. I never had any problems with guys. There was always plenty around my house. I just could never get attached to guys my age, they came and they went . . . no big deal! I had a taste for older men even then.

When I was seventeen, I met a guy who was twenty-two. He was exciting and fun. He was my first love. He was also the first guy I'd ever had sex with. Kinky wouldn't even begin to explain him. We went out for about a year and a half. Through him I met Jesse. A gorgeous Spaniard, queer as a three dollar bill, but one of the nicest people you'll ever meet. Jesse is a "BIG" record promoter for a famous record corporation. We've been friends since the day we met. We call each other all the time and "dish" on guys.

I called Jesse up one day and asked if he'd get me tickets to go to a concert I wanted to see. He said sure as he had a million times before. Only this time he too had a request. He said, "I'm in a bit of a bind. I need someone to pick up a client and show him around town Friday!" "Cool!" I said. Jesse went on to explain, "You'll be given $200.00 to buy him dinner, go dancing, or whatever else he may want to do . . . what's left is yours to keep." "Wow, thats great," I exclaimed! I thought to myself, what could be better, a date in which we can do anything, the sky's the limit . . . you get payed for playing!!! What could possibly be better than that?

I made about $70. I had a wonderful time and so did the client. I told Jesse I loved being a escort and to fix me up as often as he liked. I was assigned many men after

Other researchers (Freund et al. 1991; Gemme 1993) have added that prostitutes provide a sexual outlet for men who

1. Desire quick sexual gratification without attachment
2. Are curious
3. Are sexually dissatisfied in marriage

The Functionalist Conclusion: Prostitution Is a Form of Social Control Over Male Sexuality

Although these observations may seem obvious, the conclusion that functionalists draw from them is not. They conclude that by meeting such needs prostitution functions as *a form of social control* over sexual behavior. By this, they mean that prostitution channels sexual desires away from unwilling partners to partners who are willing to satisfy them for a price. For example, some sexual deviants (whom prostitutes call "kinkies,"

that. I'd say a good 75% wanted to finish off their evenings with sex. Some even would get quite insistent. I asked Jesse what to do. Jesse said do what you want to do, guys will offer you their own money (as a write off to their own company as entertainment). To sleep with me, I thought. He said, "Do what you want to do, if you want the money, go for it! If you don't keep standing firm!" I told Jesse I couldn't do it. So, he began to filter my dates more so and more so. He was always careful not to set me up with the weirdo's or the real wild party hardy guys. I mostly got the married with three kids and a dog type from then on.

I worked at the pace of picking up $20–$100 per date, for about three months; about 60 guys total. Then I met with a client from Europe for the second time. He was a very attractive man of 40. His black hair was salted with a whitened silver. He was a family man. Though, as was the story with many of the men I escorted, he was having alot of problems with his wife. While sitting at a bar he whispered in my ear, "Would you please consider being with me tonight?" Knowing I'd turned him down the last time he was in town, he reached into his pocket for inspiration. $500.00 in crisp $100.00 bills he waved out like a fan and placed on the table. I looked at him and shook my head "No" I said. He put his hand on my arm and said, "How much do I have to offer you, $600, $700?" At this point I was getting pissed! In order to control my temper I flew off to the restroom in a rage. I remember standing at the sink, looking into the mirror, and thinking who in the hell does this man think he is!! I don't need his money! But still that much money, for sex?! ... how could it be? I went back to the table with thousands of thoughts running through my mind. He looked at me and said, "I'm sorry if I upset you, but, I'm willing to give you all the money I have with me, $1000 dollars. Hows that sound?" My initial thought was to slap the crap out of him, however, the things I could do with $1000 cash. I agreed and it wasn't hard. No commitments, no future to worry about, and no love to get in the way of habitions. I went home that night with 10 crisp $100 dollar bills and two $20's left over from the date, in my coat pocket. There's nothing to it. I can spend $100 on myself and stick the rest in a savings account. It's no biggy!

I told Jesse about it. I told him I couldn't believe how easy or how much money I made. He laughed and asked me if I had plans of ever doing this again. I said sure, it's no problem. He started throughing me that "kind" of clients. I made over $10,000 in the 4 mths to follow. Enough to buy me a new car. I never have made $1000 in a evening again but, it became a game to me. How high can you raise the bid? How much will it take to make this man make an offer straight up? How much teasing can you get buy with, without having him drop his attention?

I've worked more than 2 yrs. I've totally mellowed out of the games. If it looks good to me, and if I find the man attractive I'll do it. I've become very secure financially. I have multiple CD's, bonds and ect. I have three savings accounts and alot of money tied up in the stock market. My only regrets are I have to keep it a complete secret from everyone. My parents, who mean more to me than the world, my family, and even my dearest friends. I miss out on the average evryday social life of a college student. I have to lie to practically everyone I meet. But, nowhere will I find a job in which I can save as much money for my future. Or for that matter when I get out of college and get a respectable job in advertising, make that kind of money. But, my life will be back to a "normal" one. One in which I can be proud of, one which I can share with my friends and family, one in which I can make a "honest" living.

"weirdos," and "freaks") achieve sexual gratification by inflicting pain (**sadists**) or by having the prostitute inflict pain on them (**masochists**). Some clients want to be sexually humiliated, to be told by the prostitute that they are no good. Others combine the sex act with fantasy role playing; they may wear costumes, even diapers, or they might have sex in a coffin (Hall 1972; Millett 1973; Prus and Irini 1988).

These, however, are the unusual customers of prostitutes. Most clients (called "johns" or "tricks") are regular Joe Six-Packs—married, middle-aged men (Wells 1970; Freund et al. 1991). Why do married men patronize prostitutes? Perhaps the two most common reasons are that they find their wives sexually unreceptive, or they desire a sexual variety that their wives are unwilling to provide—especially "frenching" (fellatio or oral sex), apparently the act most requested of prostitutes (Melody 1969; Heyl 1979; Gemme 1993).

Functionalists, then, see prostitution as a means of controlling or channeling sexual behavior. Prostitutes meet the needs of the sexually unattached and of those who desire sexual acts that are not otherwise readily available to them. Prostitutes also provide access to sexual variety in a nonemotional and fleeting relationship. Furthermore, unlike dates, prostitutes do not threaten the male ego—it is unlikely that the john will be "turned down."

Symbiosis and the Sexual Black Market

Functionalists stress that when people demand a service that is not supplied by legitimate sources, a subterranean arrangement will develop to meet the need. The underground channeling of illegitimate services to clients, called a **black market,** is built on **symbiosis** (a mutually beneficial relationship). Those who purchase a service, those who provide it, and, often, those who are supposed to suppress it benefit from the illegal service. The clients of prostitutes purchase what they want; prostitutes work with a minimum of legal hassles (even calling their occasional fines the price of "licensing"); pimps and organized criminals earn untaxed income; and for a price, police who are "on the take" look the other way.

A Contrasting Feminist Conflict Perspective

Feminists provide an interpretation that contrasts with functionalism. Using a conflict framework, they stress that prostitution is one of the many ways that men exploit and degrade women. Men use prostitutes as objects for their own pleasure. Other men (pimps, police "on the take") exploit prostitutes for profit. The Global Glimpse box on the next page explores the exploitation of women in the Least Industrialized Nations.

RESEARCH ON PROSTITUTION

Types of Prostitutes

Besides masseuses and corporate prostitutes, other forms of prostitution also reflect modern society—from its patterns of employment to its electronic communications. Let's see what they are. (We shall discuss male prostitutes later.)

Call girls, the elite of the prostitutes, can be selective in choosing their customers, and they have steady, repeat business. They usually meet their customers at their own place or at the client's. To keep up with appointments, they use cell phones, pagers, fax machines, and e-mail. Some groups of call girls fly from city to city, where new customers await them (Campo-Flores 2002).

Convention prostitutes, as the name implies, specialize in conventions. These women pose as secretaries or sales agents and roam hotel lobbies, display rooms, and cocktail parties. Some develop strong opinions about which professionals spend the most money, and they try to concentrate on their conventions. In the symbiotic manner referred to earlier, the organizers of a convention may make arrangements for prostitutes to be available.

Apartment prostitutes rent an apartment and set up a business at which they work set hours. Some apartment prostitutes are married women who attempt to match their apartment hours to their husband's working hours. A husband who is ignorant of his wife's activities is likely to think that she has a regular job.

Stag party workers serve as topless waitresses or put on strip shows at stag parties, that is, parties for men only. They arrange to meet customers after the party or, sometimes, in a side room during the party.

Hotel prostitutes work out of a hotel and share their fees with the bell captain, desk clerk, or bellboys who steer johns to them (Reichert and Frey 1985; Prus and Irini 1988). Because this "added service" attracts male guests, the hotel sometimes provides their room free or at a cut rate.

House prostitutes work in a house of prostitution or "whorehouse." Although this form of prostitution has declined, during the 1800s and early 1900s almost all large

A Global Glimpse
THE PATRIOTIC PROSTITUTE

A new wrinkle in the history of prostitution is the "patriotic prostitute." Patriotic prostitutes are young women who are encouraged by their government to prostitute themselves to help the country's economy. Patriotic prostitution is part of global stratification, the division of the world's countries into "have" and "have-not" nations. Some have-nots, or Least Industrialized Nations, view their women as a cash crop to be exploited. They encourage prostitution to help pay interest on their national debt. A notorious example is Thailand, where in a country of 30 million females, between a half million and a million of them are prostitutes. About 20,000 are under the age of 15.

In some countries, government officials encourage prostitution by telling prostitutes that they are performing a service to their country. In South Korea, officials issue identification cards to prostitutes, which serve as hotel passes. In orientation sessions, they tell these young women, "Your carnal conversations with foreign tourists do not prostitute either yourself or the nation, but express your heroic patriotism."

With such an official blessing, "sex tourism" has become a global growth industry. Travel agencies in Germany advertise "trips to Thailand with erotic pleasures included in the price." Japan Air Lines hands out brochures that advertise the "charming attractions" of Kisaeng girls, advising men to fly JAL for "a night spent with a consummate Kisaeng girl dressed in a gorgeous Korean blouse and skirt."

The advertising, showing beautiful young women with "come hither" smiles, fails to mention the miserable slavery that underlies sex tourism. Some of the prostitutes were sold as children. Others are held in bondage while they pay off their families' debts. Some are even locked up to keep them from running away.

The enticing ads also leave out AIDS. In Nairobi, where about 10,000 prostitutes serve this thriving industry, perhaps half are infected with AIDS. Nor is the destruction of children mentioned. Although customers pay more for young girls and boys, especially for those who are advertised as virgins or "clean," the children are vulnerable to infection from lesions and injuries during intercourse. When they become too sick to service clients—or their disease becomes too noticeable—the children are thrown into the streets like so much rubbish.

Based on Gay 1985; Shaw 1987; Srisang 1989; Muecke 1992; Hornblower 1993; Beddoe et al. 2001; Hardy 2004; Leuchtag 2004.

U.S. cities and many small ones had brothels, which were located in an area known as the "red light district." By means of a red bulb shining from a window or house front, passersby were informed of the nature of the establishment.

Barbara Heyl, a sociologist who studied house prostitutes, reports that the women gather in the living room, the john makes his selection, and the woman then takes the john to a bedroom. The manager of the house (the "madam") keeps from 50 to 60 percent of the prostitute's earnings. Heyl reports that house prostitutes must learn how to persuade customers to spend more than they intend. She (1979:120) adds that this is especially difficult for the novice, "because the woman must learn to discuss sexual acts, whereas in her previous experience, sexual behavior and preferences had been negotiated non-verbally."

Bar girls, also known as "B-girls," wait in a bar for customers. Some pay or "tip" the bartender for being able to use the bar as their headquarters. Others hustle drinks (are friendly to bar patrons to get them to buy overpriced drinks) and receive a set fee for each drink they sell.

Streetwalkers have the lowest status among prostitutes. They also are the most frequently arrested. They are visible to the public, as they "work the street" in open view of police and customers. In some U.S. cities, streetwalkers are aggressive, hailing passing cars and opening the doors of cars that have stopped at traffic lights. Many are drug addicts who are also involved in larceny.

Another type of prostitute is known as *parking lot lizards.* These prostitutes frequent truck stops, moving from one truck to another in search of clients.

Male prostitutes who service women are known as "gigolos." In 1980, sociologist Ed Sagarin concluded that this "is an infrequent behavior, for which there is little demand and probably more folklore than reality." With changing sexual norms, women paying men for sex has apparently become more common. After *How Stella Got Her Groove Back,* a movie about a woman who rediscovered the joy of life with a Jamaican man half her age, appeared in 1998, more single women tourists came to Jamaica—especially to a beach area where older women "rent" young men ("Movie Spurs Jamaica Tourism"). We have reports, too, of young gigolos ("beach boys") in Bali. Some of them prefer Japanese clients, saying that these women are more generous than others (Beddoe et al. 2001).

Becoming a Prostitute

Researchers focus on prostitutes who are the most easily accessible—primarily the poor and those who have been arrested. (Those who get arrested also tend to be poor.) Prostitutes who come from higher social class backgrounds, such as my student, who is featured in the Issues in Social Problems box on pages 64–65, engage in forms of prostitution that make them less accessible to the police—and to sociologists. Keeping in mind this huge gap in the research, let's see why women become prostitutes.

The simplest answer to why someone becomes a prostitute is money—to make as much of it as easily as possible. This is an oversimplification, however, for running through the accounts that prostitutes give of their early home life are themes of emotional deprivation and sexual abuse (James and Meyerding 1977; Davis 1978; Williams and Kornblum 1985; Hodgson 1997). Sociologist Robert Gemme (1993), who interviewed Montreal street prostitutes, found that before they became prostitutes one-third had been raped and about half had been sexually abused. Sociologist James Hodgson (1997) found that money was not the motivation for very young prostitutes

Sociologists use several criteria to classify prostitutes, including the locations at which they solicit customers. Those dancers in the wild-west saloons, so celebrated in countless B movies, didn't make their money from dancing.

This photo illustrates how attitudes about prostitution vary around the world. These women in Amsterdam, registered with the government, receive the unemployment and social security benefits accorded other workers. The men in the foreground, who are walking along these canal-side buildings, are customers and tourists.

(ages 10 to 15). Instead, they were "in love" with a pimp, who, after seducing them, insisted they "turn tricks" to help out.

From the conflict perspective, this pattern of abuse is significant. Abused as children, when they had no power, most often by men, these women become locked into a way of life in which they continue to be victimized by men—by pimps who exploit their bodies for profit and by "johns" who use them for sexual pleasure.

The Three Stages in Becoming a Prostitute: 1. Drift

As you saw in the box "Me, a Prostitute?," becoming a prostitute is usually a gradual process. Nanette Davis, a symbolic interactionist who interviewed prostitutes in three correctional institutions in Minnesota, discovered that prostitutes go through three stages. In the first stage, they *drift* from casual sex to their first act of prostitution. "The 'drift' is a series of forks in the road where certain choices or events channel the young woman in a direction conducive to prostitution" (James and Davis 1982:348). Circumstances that may lead to drifting include a broken home, dropping out of school, pregnancy, drug use, and a juvenile record.

One event that sets up the drift into prostitution is having sex at a young age. On average, these women first had sex when they were 13½ (the youngest was age 7, the oldest 18). For about four years, the girls engaged in casual sex and then drifted to selling sex. One of Davis' informants described it this way:

I was going to school and I wanted to go to this dance the night after. I needed new clothes. I went out at ten o'clock and home at twelve. I had three tricks the first time, and fifteen dollars for every trick. (Davis 1978:206)

2. Transition

Davis calls the second stage *transitional deviance*. During this stage, which lasts an average of six months, girls experience **role ambivalence;** that is, they are not sure if they want to be a prostitute. They feel both attracted to and repulsed by prostitution. To help overcome their ambivalence, many try to **normalize** their acts; that is, they try to think of what they are doing as normal. For example, although they sell sex, they may call it something else. As one girl said:

I'm a person who likes to walk. There's nothing wrong with picking somebody up while you're walking. I always like walking around at night, and girls will be tempted. Girls like the offer. They like to see what a guy is going to say. (Davis 1978:203–209)

To "normalize" selling sex is to turn the deviance into a normal act. In effect, this girl is saying: "I'm just doing a normal thing, walking. It's the guy who makes the offer. If a girl is tempted—well, that's only natural, too."

3. Professionalization

Davis calls the third stage *professionalization*. During this stage, the girls no longer tell themselves that their behavior is normal, and they come to think of themselves as prostitutes. They begin to build their lives around this identity. They also defend their involvement in prostitution. Some sound as though they have read the functionalist perspective—they claim that they help wives by giving husbands a sexual outlet that reduces tensions in their marriage. Others, such as a madam who wrote a book about her life, say that prostitution helps to prevent rape. Note how closely what this madam says resembles the analysis of the functionalist Kingsley Davis:

As to my claim about performing a useful social service, every lusty, tourist-jammed town like San Francisco needs safety valves and outlets for its males. Shut down a town and the rape rate soars higher than an astronaut. (Stanford 1968:206–207)

From a symbolic interactionist framework, prostitutes eventually come full circle. They begin by defining their activities as normal, denying that they are prostituting themselves. Then, in this last stage, they again use normalization, acknowledging their prostitution but defining it as beneficial.

To see how young some prostitutes are (as well as how old), look at Table 3-3. The involvement of children in commercial sex is what especially upsets people. We shall return to this topic in the section on children and pornography.

The Pimp and the Prostitute: A Counterculture

Why would a woman rent her body, gamble on not being hurt by sadists, even risk death by AIDS, and then turn the money she makes over to a man? Let's see how the three sociological perspectives help explain this.

Functionalism looks at the services pimps provide. Presumably, pimps locate customers, try to screen out sadists, and bail the woman out of jail when she is arrested. In actuality, however, pimps are more likely to make the woman chase up her own customers, to be unconcerned if she is beaten by a john, and to be unavailable when she is arrested (Hodgson 1997). For this reason, we have to move beyond functionalism for an explanation.

The conflict perspective provides a different answer. Simply put, pimps have the power. They, not the prostitutes, control the streets. To control women, they use their greater physical strength, and they are ruthless. Consider what a former prostitute said:

I saw a girl walk into a bar and hand the pimp a $100 bill. He took it and burned it in her face and turned around and knocked her down on the floor and kicked her and said, "I told you, bitch, $200. I want $200, not $100." Now she's gotta go out again and make not another hundred, but two hundred. (Millett 1973:134)

TABLE 3-3 Arrests for Prostitution and Commercialized Sex, by Age

AGE	PERCENT	NUMBER
Under 15	.3	165
15–17	1.6	930
18–24	21.7	12,723
25–44	64.0	37,613
45–54	10.0	5,857
55–64	1.8	1,081
65 and older	.7	389
Total arrested:		58,758

Note: The source does not list prostitution separately, but includes them in a category called prostitution and commercialized vice. Consequently, the totals include a large proportion (48 percent) of males (Table 39 of the *UCR*).

Source: By the author. Based on *Uniform Crime Reports* 2002:Table 38.

The third answer is provided by symbolic interactionists, who attempt to attain a "view from within." Let's explore the insights provided by this perspective more fully. We need to begin by asking what a pimp means to a prostitute. To understand this, the typical background of prostitutes, which we discussed earlier, is significant, for being victimized as children makes them emotionally dependent, and pimps are experts at playing on this weakness. Many offer affection and tenderness. Others promise marriage, children, even a home in the suburbs after they have saved enough money from the woman's earnings. Pimps, however, are exploiters, and a pimp may be making the same promises to several women. He may tell each that she is the special one in his life, cautioning her not to tell the others so the two of them can use the earnings of the other women to fulfill their plans.

Pimps are unconcerned about the welfare of their women, except as it affects their earnings. The women are mere money machines, objects to be used or abused at will. The pimp's real interest is in the prestige he gets from other street males. His status depends on the number of women he controls in his "stable"; on how aloof he can remain from women while still making them bend to his will; and on his personal grooming, jewelry, cars, leisure, and free-spending ways.

Pimps and prostitutes form a **counterculture,** a **subculture** in which the values of the dominant culture are turned upside down. Listen to how things are turned on their head in the world of pimps and prostitutes. Anthropologists Christina and Richard Milner (1972), who studied this world, report that the women provide the income; the men spend it. The women work during the night and sleep during the day. The men don't work; they are conspicuous consumers. *Polygyny,* the union of one man with more than one woman, is the norm. The women can have sex with other men (not just the johns), and the pimps do not express jealousy. And when a woman gets pregnant, neither she nor her pimp cares who the father is.

Symbolic interactionists stress that to understand people we need to grasp their definitions of the situation. We need to see how their norms influence their behavior—just as our norms influence ours. When one takes an insider's view, the world looks like a different place—and it is. And that is the point, to see from within in order to understand human behavior—especially when it contradicts one's own standards and experiences.

Prostitution by teenage boys has become more open since sociologists first studied it in the 1950s. In some urban areas known as "meat racks," boy prostitutes gather in search of customers.

Homosexual Prostitution

Before we consider why prostitution is a social problem, let's turn to the selling and buying of sexual acts between people of the same sex. Homosexual prostitution often takes place in areas known as "meat racks," public settings such as street corners, parks, and bars. A study in Rome found that some homosexual prostitutes have 1,500 sexual partners a year (Gattari et al. 1992). A study in Chicago by sociologist David Luckenbill (1986) found that, like their female counterparts, male prostitutes also have a hierarchy. At the top are escort prostitutes, those who work for modeling or dating agencies. At the bottom are street hustlers, and at the middle are bar hustlers. The charge per trick goes up with each level.

Houses of Male Prostitution (rare)

Sociologist David Pittman (1971), who studied a house of male prostitution in St. Louis, found that the "madam" (a male) advertises for male models. When young men apply, he explains why he really wants to hire them. He photographs them nude and shows a catalog of his "models" to customers. With youth being so highly valued and customers insisting on a continuous supply of fresh bodies, these male prostitutes face intense pressure. Many turn to stimulant drugs, become depressed, and drink heavily. Their sexual performance flags, they lose customers, and are fired.

Boy Prostitutes

In a classic study from the 1960s, sociologist Albert Reiss, Jr. (1961) found that teenagers who were paid by homosexuals to receive oral sex managed to maintain a heterosexual identity. As you can imagine, this required an intricate balancing act. The boys accomplished this by (1) allowing no emotional involvement with the adult fellator, (2) making money the only purpose of the act (not sexual gratification, which they reserved for females), (3) tolerating no sexual act other than receiving fellatio, (4) never seeing a homosexual socially, and (5) openly having a girlfriend.

Prostitution by boys has become more open since Reiss studied it and probably more common as well (Cates and Markley 1992; Beddoe et al. 2001). Many of the boys are runaways from lower-class or welfare families. Some prostitute themselves to survive, others simply to have extra money. In some countries, such as Thailand, young boys are forced into prostitution. Many see the apparent increase in boy prostitution as a social problem in and of itself. A related problem is the frequency of AIDS among homosexual prostitutes.

Prostitution as a Social Problem

Why are there subjective concerns about prostitution? The primary concern is morality (Brace 1880:123–131). Some see prostitution as immoral because it involves sexual behavior between people who are not married to one another. Others see it as immoral because the sex is sold—and that for a price prostitutes engage in sexual acts. The second concern is that prostitution exploits women's bodies, degrades their spirit, and subjugates them to men. A third concern is that prostitution ruins "good" neighborhoods, depressing property values by bringing in unsavory characters and illegal activities such as drug dealing. A fourth concern is that prostitution is a crime. Victimless or not, prostitution is illegal, and that makes it part of a larger social problem. A fifth concern is that prostitution corrupts police and judges, uniting these "enforcers of morality" with pimps and madams; prostitution also feeds organized crime. Another subjective concern centers on spreading disease. AIDS has given this last concern special urgency. The final concern is aesthetic—the disgust people feel when they see used condoms and tissues left in public places, including schoolyards. In summary, subjective concerns about prostitution center on immorality, exploitation, property values, criminality, corruption of officials, the transmission of disease, and aesthetics.

We now consider another sexual behavior to which many also object.

Pornography

BACKGROUND: GETTING THE LARGER PICTURE

The Definition of Pornography

Originally, pornography referred to writings by prostitutes or to descriptions of the life of prostitutes. (*Porna* is Greek for "prostitute.") For our purposes, **pornography** may be defined as writings, pictures, or objects of a sexual nature that people object to as being filthy or immoral.

Pornography in Ancient Civilizations

Materials intended to cause sexual excitement go far back in history. Pornography abounded in the Roman Empire, as shown by excavations of the Mediterranean resort city of Pompeii, which was destroyed by an eruption of Mount Vesuvius in A.D. 79. There, archeologists uncovered brothels decorated with mosaics of men and women

Sex sells, and, with changing sexual norms, pornography has proliferated in the United States. With pornography offensive to most Americans, however, it is subject to more rigorous controls than other businesses. One form of social control used by many city officials is to segregate pornographic outlets, limiting them to specified areas of the city.

in sexual acts. The *Kama Sutra,* an Indian religious book dating from the eighth century after Christ, which is explicit about sex, includes suggestions on how prostitutes can please their customers (Henriques 1966).

Difficulties in Deciding What Is Pornographic

Deciding what is pornographic is difficult, for like beauty, pornography lies in the eye of the beholder. For example, are nude statues pornographic? Some think so. Are movies that depict sexual intercourse pornographic? More would probably say they are. Are movies or photos that depict oral sex pornographic? Again, probably a larger number would say yes. Are movies that show sex between an adult and a child or between a human and an animal pornographic? At this point, the rate of agreement would increase sharply.

Agreement on Legal Restrictions

On one matter, almost everyone agrees—pornography, whatever it is, should be restricted. As shown in Table 3-4, 56 percent of Americans think that the sale of pornography to teenagers should be banned, and another 38 percent would outlaw pornography altogether—a total of 94 percent who favor legal restrictions. Attitudes toward censorship follow broad social avenues. Those most likely to want to ban pornography for everyone are women, those with only a high school education, older people, and Protestants. Those least likely to want pornography to be illegal for everyone are men, African Americans, college graduates, people in their twenties, and Jews.

Pornography as Big Business

From its beginnings as an underground cottage industry, pornography has grown into an open and aggressive multibillion-dollar-a-year business. Behind today's pornog-

TABLE 3-4 Attitudes about the Distribution of Pornography

	SHOULD BE ILLEGAL FOR EVERYONE				SHOULD BE ILLEGAL ONLY FOR PEOPLES UNDER 18				SHOULD BE LEGAL FOR EVERYONE			
	1980	1990	2000	2002	1980	1990	2000	2002	1980	1990	2000	2002
NATIONAL	40%	41%	36%	38%	51%	52%	60%	56%	6%	6%	3%	5%
SEX												
Male	31%	33%	24%	31%	60%	59%	72%	62%	8%	6%	3%	7%
Female	47%	47%	45%	43%	45%	47%	51%	52%	5%	5%	3%	4%
RACE/ETHNICITY*												
White	41%	42%	36%	39%	52%	51%	60%	56%	6%	5%	3%	5%
African American	35%	34%	34%	32%	51%	57%	59%	60%	10%	7%	5%	6%
EDUCATION												
College	31%	36%	31%	34%	59%	57%	65%	61%	8%	7%	3%	4%
High School	42%	44%	41%	40%	52%	51%	55%	52%	5%	5%	3%	8%
AGE												
18–20	12%	17%	18%	29%	79%	65%	77%	59%	9%	13%	4%	12%
21–29	23%	29%	17%	17%	69%	67%	78%	75%	7%	3%	4%	8%
30–49	32%	36%	29%	32%	60%	60%	68%	64%	7%	4%	2%	4%
50 and over	40%	53%	52%	54%	50%	36%	43%	40%	8%	8%	4%	6%
RELIGION												
Protestant	45%	46%	44%	46%	48%	48%	53%	50%	5%	5%	2%	4%
Catholic	40%	39%	31%	34%	52%	56%	66%	61%	6%	4%	2%	4%
Jew	25%	25%	20%	19%	10%	59%	53%	79%	75%	20%	5%	2%
None	8%	22%	16%	21%	74%	66%	76%	68%	15%	9%	7%	11%

Source: *Sourcebook of Criminal Justice Statistics* 1992:Table 2–98; 2002:Table 2–97.
*Only these two groups are given in the sources; African American is listed as Black/other.

raphy lies an extensive network of people who profit from it: writers, publishers, actors, and filmmakers; owners of bookstores, video stores, theaters, and cable TV; corner newsstands and supermarket chains; and banks and financiers. To the extent that people use Internet Service Providers to view pornography, even AOL and CompuServe get their share. Like politics, pornography makes strange bedfellows.

PORNOGRAPHY VIEWED THEORETICALLY: APPLYING SYMBOLIC INTERACTIONISM

Roth *vs.* U.S.

The controversy about what is and is not pornographic—and what should be done about it—is one we have inherited from the past. One era's decisions may make little sense when viewed from a later historical perspective. In 1957, in the landmark *Roth vs. U.S.,* the U.S. Supreme Court ruled that materials are pornographic or obscene when

1. "Taken as a whole," the "dominant theme" appeals to "prurient interest" in sex.
2. The material violates "contemporary community standards."
3. The material is "utterly without redeeming social value."

Slippery Symbols and Muddled Meanings

Instead of settling anything, however, the key terms of the *Roth* decision (which are placed in quotes above) added fuel to the fire. *Prurient,* for example, means "lewd or impure." But what is lewd or impure to one person is not to another. The guidelines, which were supposed to clear up matters, merely muddied the waters. If the terms were clear, they were clear only to the Court.

As symbolic interactionists emphasize, all terms are empty of meaning until people determine for themselves what they mean. If two people watch the same movie containing nudity or sexual intercourse, one may see the beauty of art and the other the filth of pornography. What, then, does a phrase like "redeeming social value" mean? If an item contains explicit sexual content, where does it leave us if I decide that its other features have "redeeming social value," but you do not?

And so the war of symbols goes on. Some claim that certain materials violate "contemporary community standards," whereas others say that those same materials reflect community standards. Still others say there are no community standards! With the Internet, the matter has become even more complicated. Do those who exchange sexually explicit materials on the Internet form a community? Is the community where the materials were produced? Where they were downloaded?

California *vs.* Miller

After the *Roth* decision, prosecutors had difficulty obtaining convictions for pornography, and in 1973 the matter was brought again before the Supreme Court. In *California vs. Miller,* the Court tried to remove the ambiguities of its earlier decision. It kept the dominant "prurient" theme, said that "contemporary community standards" meant the local community, and eliminated the criterion of "redeeming social value" (Lewis and Peoples 1978:1071).

In the *Miller* decision, the Court acknowledged the central premise of symbolic interactionism, that the same thing can have different meanings to different people:

> Nothing in the First Amendment requires that a jury must consider hypothetical and unascertainable "national standards" when attempting to determine whether certain materials are obscene. . . .
>
> It is neither realistic nor constitutionally sound to read the First Amendment as requiring that the people of Maine or Mississippi accept public depiction of conduct found tolerable in Las Vegas or New York City. . . . (Lewis and Peoples 1978:1068)

Young *vs.* American Mini Theaters

The controversy continued, of course, because the description and depiction of sexual acts mean different things to different people. In communities where pornography symbolized filth and depravity to significant numbers of people (or to a number of influential people), pornography was either banned or restricted to outlets in designated areas. Pornographers vigorously resisted, and again the matter was brought before the Supreme Court. In 1976 (*Young vs. American Mini Theaters*) and 1986 (*Renton* case), the Court ruled that it was constitutional to restrict the location of adult movie theaters (Sitomer 1986).

Whose "Taste"?

Later, the Court ruled that "tasteful" nudity is permissible, such as in theater productions and art, but nudity is not allowable in "low-art" forms, such as striptease dancing (Heins 1991). Such a ruling brings us back to the original question, of course: Whose "taste" determines the matter? As conflict theorists would point out, it is not surprising that Supreme Court justices ruled that their own class-based preferences for nudity are not pornographic, but those of the lower classes are.

The Supreme Court has also ruled on a matter that especially angers people, the portrayal of sex with children. Pornographic magazines that depict children in sex acts with adults or with other children used to be easily accessible. Some of the children were as young as 4, but the most interest was focused on prepubescents from 8 to 10. The publications bore such titles as *Lollitots, More Lollitots,* and *Moppets* (Dunbar 1980).

As states passed strict laws and judges were willing to impose prison sentences, such magazines practically diappeared. Child pornography, however, did not disappear. It just went underground again and eventually surfaced on the Internet. There, people who are stimulated by child pornography meet online with others like themselves. They buy, sell, and swap files of children who have been forced, tricked, or bribed into sex acts. Although the photos that they exchange are illegal, the Web sites are located throughout the world and are difficult for law enforcement agents to track down.

It may get even harder to stop child porn. In 2002, in *Ashcroft v. Free Speech Coalition,* the U.S. Supreme Court ruled that because no child is involved it is unlawful to ban virtual child pornography, that is, computer-generated images of children in sex acts. Law enforcement officials feel that this ruling handicaps them because it is difficult to tell virtual images from the real thing. As a U.S. customs official said, "We're going to be forced to prove that every picture is a real child" (Sager et al. 2002).

In short, with people's perceptions and evaluations varying so widely, it has been almost impossible to pin down what pornography is. Today's changing technology has made the matter even murkier. Not only is the issue now whether an image is "obscene," but also if it is of a "real" child. It is obvious that this matter is far from decided and will remain a matter of controversy.

CONTROVERSY AND RESEARCH ON PORNOGRAPHY

The National Commission on Obscenity and Pornography

Pornography has become a controversial and emotional issue. The fear that pornography corrupts people so concerned Americans that in the 1960s President Johnson appointed a National Commission on Obscenity and Pornography. In 1970, the commission concluded that pornography affects some people more than others—that it stimulates the young more than the old, the college educated more than the less educated, the religiously inactive more than the religiously active, and the sexually experienced more than the sexually inexperienced. Unlike Kinsey (1953), who reported that erotic materials aroused males considerably more than females, the commission found that women and men are about equally aroused by watching pornography (Schmidt and Sigusch 1970).

The Meese Commission

Subjective concerns grew as pornography increased during the 1970s and 1980s. President Reagan asked the attorney general to appoint another commission to study the matter. The Meese Commission (1986:39) concluded

> the clinical and experimental evidence supports the conclusion that there is a causal relationship between exposure to sexually violent materials and an increase in aggressive behavior directed towards women. . . .

This, the Commission said, "will cause an increase in the level of sexual violence directed at women."

The commission's more specific findings (McManus 1986) include the following:

1. Of 411 sex offenders, the average had 336 victims.
2. Rape increases where pornography laws are liberalized.
3. Rapists are much more likely than nonoffenders to have been exposed as children to hard-core pornography.
4. Pornography makes rape seem "legitimate."
5. States with higher sales of pornography have higher rates of rape.
6. Males exposed to pornography that features sexual violence ("slasher films") become desensitized and see rape victims as "less injured and less worthy."

Is It Just Common Sense?

The commission (1986:39) also concluded that a "common-sense" approach makes the causal connection between pornography and sex crimes evident. But, as we saw in chapter 1, common sense and science are often a mismatch. It is precisely that jump from the evidence (the frequency of pornography among sex offenders) to the conclusion (pornography causes sex crimes) that was attacked when the commission published its report. Critics said that the commission was predisposed to see pornography as evil and as the cause of crime. Therefore, it misinterpreted the evidence and ignored studies that contradicted its preconceptions (Baron 1987; Brannigan 1987; Linz, Donnerstein, and Penrod 1987).

Causation vs. Correlation

Because neither the commission's report nor its rebuttals gives us final answers, we are still left with the thorny question, Does pornography *cause* sex crimes? Or are sex criminals, such as rapists and child molesters, just more likely to use pornography? There may be a cause/effect relationship, but researchers have been able to document only **correlations** (two or more things occurring together). For example, although sex offenders tend to use more pornography than do nonoffenders, not all sex criminals do so. In addition, noncriminals use pornography. Scientific proof (objective, consistent, verifiable) of a causal relationship, then, remains elusive.

More Controversy: The Danish and Japanese Experiences

To try to find answers, researchers examined the trend in sex crimes after Denmark legalized hard-core pornography in 1965 (Kutchinsy 1973). They found that sex offenses against children dropped. It is likely that some child molesters do not prefer children but, instead, take them as substitutes because they are unable to relate sexually to adults. For them, masturbating to pornography may provide another substitute. During the 1980s and 1990s, Japan, which had been hard-nosed about pornography, changed its practice, and hard-core pornography became common. Researchers studied trends in Japanese sex crimes, and they found that the number of rapes dropped (Diamond and Uchiyama 1999). It is difficult to determine cause and effect in these cases, however, as other factors may have been responsible for the changes.

What if pornography has different effects on different people? This is the conclusion that some researchers are making. It is difficult to classify people, but some men tend to be angry and aggressive, whereas others are more relaxed and "laid back." Some researchers are finding that pornography that portrays violence triggers sexual aggression against women among angry, aggressive men (Malamuth et al. 2000), but it has no such effect on the more relaxed men. We need more research to determine if this is so.

Science at Work

This is science at work. When a study is published, it enters what we might call the "court" of science, where it is judged by a jury of critical scientific peers. Researchers report their results, and other researchers meticulously examine those studies. They challenge the data and repeat the studies or reanalyze the original data and publish their own conclusions. Out of these investigations of social life and challenges of researchers' conclusions emerges knowledge that overcomes researchers' biases and either replaces or confirms our commonsense notions about social problems.

Some people find this rigorous and exacting process too slow. Feeling a pressing need to act, and convinced that severe consequences are at stake, they want to take a stand now. And based on their ideas about what is right and wrong and what they find offensive, they do take a stand.

The Feminist Position

For example, feminists are upset about how pornography portrays women. They are convinced that it teaches men to view women as "pieces of meat." Whether pornography causes sex crimes is not the point, they insist, for the degrading way that women are portrayed in pornography is part of their victimization in society. Some conclude that pornography—at least the type that shows violence against females—should be banned. The accompanying Thinking Critically about Social Problems box provides further information on this controversy among feminists.

There is no doubt that pornography does influence people. To think otherwise would be absurd. Sociologists Donal MacNamara and Edward Sagarin (1977:205) stated this point succinctly:

> To say that pornography cannot influence a person is to contend that books and the printed word, graphics, art, and slogans cannot move people and cause changes in their thoughts and hence their actions.

Safety Valve or Trigger?

The question, then, is not whether pornography influences people but, rather, how. Is the **safety valve theory** of pornography right? That is, does pornography protect society by providing the private release of sexual fantasies? Or is the **trigger theory** right? That is, does pornography trigger sexual offenses by stimulating sexual appetites, often for deviance and violence?

Unfortunately, researchers have been unable to settle the question of causation. Until they can, social activists—on whichever side of the issue—will continue to struggle for what they see as a better social world, based on their subjective concerns and not irrefutable evidence.

Social Policy

Now that homosexual acts in private between consenting adults are no longer illegal, the issue that remains centers on developing social policy to protect homosexuals from discrimination and to make certain that they have equality before the law. When it comes to prostitution and pornography, we still face issues of criminal acts. Let's look at these in some detail.

THE QUESTION OF MAKING CONSENSUAL BEHAVIOR ILLEGAL

Difficulties in Enforcing Laws Against Consensual Acts

Sociologists use the term **victimless crimes** to refer to illegal acts to which the participants consent. The crime has no victim because the people agree to do something with or for one another. A man pays a woman for sex; someone sells or buys pictures of adults involved in sexual acts—both may be illegal, but they occur with the consent of the people involved.

In most crimes, someone does something against the will of someone else. There is a victim and a perpetrator. When a victim reports a crime, the police know where and when it happened, and who the victim is. Without a victim, however, the police end up spending precious public resources attempting to determine that a crime occurred in the first place, and then prosecutors have difficulty in obtaining convictions because

Thinking Critically about Social Problems

SHOULD WE CENSOR VIOLENT PORNOGRAPHY?

As the following quotations indicate, feminists are divided on the issue of pornography. What do you think about these issues? Should pornography, especially that which shows sexual violence against women, be banned?

YES

The same people who defend pornography in the name of "sexual liberation" and freedom of speech, strenuously oppose all portrayals of Jewish or Third World men that are anti-Semitic or racist. Imagine the public outcry that would occur if there were special movie houses where viewers could see whites beating up Blacks, or Christians beating up Jews. But if it's called pornography and women are the victims, then you are seen as a prude to object.

—*Diana E. H. Russell, feminist researcher*

Clearly, with regard to computer pornography, new laws are needed that . . . send a clear message to producers and consumers of computer pornography that they will be liable for material which harms or degrades women and children.

—*Terry Gillespie, British feminist sociologist*

No

Despite the ugliness of a lot of pornography, despite the fact that I don't want to defend pictures of little girls being molested, I believe that censorship only springs back against the givers of culture—against authors, artists, and feminists, against anybody who wants to change society. Should censorship be imposed again, . . . feminists would be the first to suffer.

—*Erica Jong, feminist writer and poet*

As with Nazi rantings about Jews or racist trash spread by the Ku Klux Klan, speech graphically depicting the sexual humiliation and subordination of women is protected by the First Amendment because we have learned as a free people that it is impossible to censor speech we hate without imperiling the system of free expression upon which our political and social structure rests.

—*Harriet Pilpel, feminist attorney*

Based on Russell 1977; Blakely 1985; Gillespie 2000.

Demonstrations against pornography seem to have lessened. For the most part, opponents seem to have resigned themselves to what they see as inevitable social change. Certain aspects of pornography, especially the depiction of children, however, still arouse protest.

Victimless Crimes

the people involved consented to what took place. Unless there is a public outcry, both the public and the police prefer that law enforcement agents pursue criminals who have victims—thieves, muggers, rapists, and murderers.

Not all prostitution and pornography are victimless crimes, however. There can be force, coercion, or less than informed consent. If there is force, it is rape, a different matter entirely. If there is less than informed consent, there is also a victim. Child pornography, for example, is not a victimless crime. The children are not of age to give their consent, and child pornography often involves the abuse of adult authority. To deal adequately with social policy, we must separate such instances from those that involve full consent.

ALTERNATIVES TO MAKING CONSENSUAL BEHAVIOR ILLEGAL

Let's consider prostitution. Because prostitution is a commercial transaction—a business—some argue that it should be legalized. We license and tax businesses, so why should we exempt prostitution? Proponents of legalization point out that prostitution will persist and suggest that it is time for the state to regulate it. For pro and con arguments on legalizing prostitution, see the Thinking Critically box below.

Legalization of prostitution would eliminate bribes, a major source of police corruption. It also would free the police to concentrate on other areas of law enforcement. A major advantage of legalization is that the community can maintain control over the activity. It can determine zoning, licensing, taxation, and restrictions on age

Thinking Critically about Social Problems

SHOULD WE LEGALIZE PROSTITUTION?

YES

1. Prostitutes perform a service for society. They provide sex for people who otherwise cannot find sexual partners. They even help marriages by reducing sexual demands on wives.
2. To keep prostitution illegal is dysfunctional. It stigmatizes and marginalizes women who want to work as prostitutes. It also corrupts many police officers, who accept bribes to allow prostitutes to work. Some prostitution is run by organized crime, with women held in bondage. Legalization of prostitution will eliminate these problems.
3. If prostitution is declared a legal occupation, the government can regulate it. If the government licenses prostitutes, it can collect taxes and require prostitutes to have regular medical checkups. Prostitutes can be required to display a dated and signed medical certificate stating that they are free of sexually transmitted diseases.

No

1. Prostitution is immoral, and we should not legalize immoral activities. The foundation of society is the family, and we should take steps to strengthen the family, not tear it apart by approving sex as a commercial transaction outside the family.
2. The legalization of prostitution will not stop sexually transmitted diseases. For example, the HIV virus can be transmitted before the disease shows up in blood tests. Even though prostitutes are licensed, they will spread AIDS during this interval.
3. Prostitution degrades women. To legalize prostitution is to give the state's approval to their degradation. It also would affirm class oppression: Most prostitutes come from the working class and serve as objects to satisfy the sexual desires of men from more privileged classes.

participation. Licensing requirements for houses of prostitution or massage parlors, for example, could include mandatory health checks.

The Matter of Privacy

Central to deciding social policy is the issue of privacy. The argument is that if adults want to have sex in private, anyone may judge the morality of the act, but why should it concern the state? It may be a sin, but it should not be a crime. But there is another side to the privacy argument—the right of *privacy from* people who are involved in sexual acts. Those who find such activities morally repugnant should not have to see them. If the law were to permit these sexual acts, it should also prohibit street solicitation by prostitutes, sex in public places, and the display of sexual acts on the covers of magazines in supermarkets and other stores.

Segregation

To allow people to engage in these acts *and* to make it so that unwilling people do not have to view them, some suggest **segregation**—limiting these activities to specified areas. They also would insist on preventing blatancy in even those areas. For example, if prostitutes were segregated to a certain area of the city, they could advertise for customers through ads in newspapers or by a red light in an apartment window, but they could not walk the streets. Nor could pornographic outlets show sexually explicit marquees or posters. This would allow the patrons of prostitutes and the consumers of pornography to be able to carry out their consensual activities in semiprivate, while respecting the privacy of others from these activities.

The Matter of Children

The use of children in prostitution and pornography is an entirely different matter. Almost everyone feels that children should be protected from sexual exploitation. Their position is: If the purpose of the law is not to protect the least defenseless of our society, what is its purpose? As the Issues in Social Problems box below shows, private citizens can help to protect children from sexual victimization.

Issues in Social Problems

APPLYING SOCIOLOGY: TAKING BACK CHILDREN FROM THE NIGHT

Lois Lee isn't afraid to apply her sociological training to social problems. Lee did her master's thesis on the pimp–prostitute relationship and her doctoral dissertation on the social world of the prostitute. After receiving her Ph.D. in sociology from United States International University in 1981, Lee began to work with adult prostitutes. They told her, "You know, it's too late for you to help us, Lois. You've got to do something about these kids. We made a choice to be out here . . . a conscious decision. But these kids don't stand a chance."

Lee began by taking those kids, the teenagers who were prostituting themselves, into her home. In three years, she brought 250 home, where she lived with her husband and baby son. Lee then founded "Children of the Night," which reaches the kids by means of "a 24-hour hotline, a street outreach program, a walk-in crisis center, crisis intervention for medical or life-threatening situations,

family counseling, job placement, and foster home or group placement." By providing alternatives to prostitution and petty crime, Children of the Night has helped thousands of young runaways and prostitutes to get off the streets.

Lee's work has brought her national publicity and an award from the president. She credits her success to her sociological training, especially the sensitivities it gave her "to understand and move safely through intersecting deviant worlds, to relate positively to police and caretaking agencies while retaining a critical perspective, to know which game to play in which situation."

As Lee said during a CBS interview: "I know what the street rules are, I know what the pimp game is, I know what the con games are, and it's up to me to play that game correctly. . . . It's all sociology. That's why when people call me a social worker I always correct them."

Based on Buff 1987.

The Future of the Problem

With the rapid social change that engulfs us, it is difficult to peer far into the future. Assuming that a repressive dictatorship does not take over the political control of the United States, which would curtail civil rights and drive homosexuality, prostitution, and pornography underground, I foresee the following.

HOMOSEXUALITY AND THE FUTURE

Two Issues

Two primary issues are generating controversy. The first is the political struggle by homosexuals to be allowed legal marriage. This issue is likely to reach the U.S. Supreme Court, where the decision will be decided not according to the U.S. Constitution, which is silent on this matter, but by the politics of the justices who happen to make up the Court when the case comes before it. Obviously, then, the decision could go either way. The second issue also centers on a legal and social right: to serve as role models—to be openly homosexual and to occupy positions that mold the orientations of youth, such as public school teachers and scout leaders. The vast middle ground between those who espouse homosexuality and those who fear or despise it is likely to be occupied by those who believe that homosexuality should be discouraged but that homosexuals should not be oppressed.

PROSTITUTION AND THE FUTURE

Perhaps the easiest forecast in the entire book is this one: The demand for the services of prostitutes will continue. Always there will be sexually deprived people who want to patronize prostitutes, as well as those who want to pay for the "specialized sexual services" that prostitutes satisfy.

Although prostitution will continue to flourish, it will remain illegal in almost all areas of the United States. The police will overlook all but the most blatant acts both because they feel that they have better things to do and because many of them are convinced that sexual acts between consenting adults should be legal. We are likely to see an increase in the publicity given an aspect of prostitution that upsets both the public and the police, the prostitution of children. As the media give more publicity to prostituted children, subjective concerns among the public will grow. Spurred by the media, influential individuals will launch a campaign against the prostitution of children (and the exploitation of chil-

Elton John, one of the world's most famous entertainers, who has given concerts in 60 countries, used to keep his sexual preference at least semi-hidden. With changing sexual norms, John has been open about his 11-year relationship with David Furnish. In many ways, homosexual relationships are mirror images of heterosexual ones. The wealthy and famous almost always manage to have younger partners. John is 57; Furnish is 37.

dren in pornography), placing greater pressure on lawmakers. More laws will be passed. Most of them will have little effect.

PORNOGRAPHY AND THE FUTURE

Movement to the Mainstream

Changes in pornography are likely to be driven by two forces: technology and profits. As each new communication technology appears, pornography will be adapted to fit it. With the increased ease of producing and viewing moving images, as with digital video cameras and CD disks, more people will make their own "home porno flicks." Because pornography is so profitable, it is likely that the mainstream media will embrace it even more. Cable television, which offers subscribers XXX options, is likely to become even more explicit, perhaps even to broadcast live sex programs. As pornography goes more mainstream, the line between pornography and art will become even more blurred. It will become increasingly difficult to distinguish between pornography and regular Hollywood films. See the Technology and Social Problems box on electronic pornography below.

Potential Clashes

Some continuing clash between the pro- and antipornography forces is inevitable, for the values of these groups are contrary, and each desires to control the media. But pornography is now so entrenched in our society that it is likely that those who oppose pornography will limit themselves to an occasional statement decrying the fall of American values and then retreat into enclaves of people who agree with their views.

Technology and Social Problems
PORNOGRAPHY ON THE INTERNET

Pornography vividly illustrates one of the sociological principles discussed in this chapter—that people adapt their sexual behaviors to social change. It was not long after photography was invented that photographic pornography appeared. Today a major issue is pornography on the Internet.

What is the problem? Why can't people electronically exchange nude photos with one another if they want to? If that were the issue, there would be no problem. The real issue, however, is something quite different. What disturbs many people are the photos that show bondage, torture, rape, and bestiality (humans having sex with animals). Judging from the number of such sites, apparently a large number of people derive sexual excitement from such photos. To avoid legal prosecution, pornographers locate the sites that host such materials in countries with weak laws or enforcement, especially in Eastern Europe.

The Internet abounds with "news groups" (people who "meet" online to discuss some topic). No one is bothered about the news groups (or "chat rooms") that center on Roman architecture or rap music or turtle racing. But news groups that focus on how to torture women are another matter. So are those that focus on how to seduce children—or on the delights of having sex with preschoolers.

Any call for censorship raises the hackles of civil libertarians, who see all censorship as an attack on basic freedoms. Censorship, they say, is just the first step toward a totalitarian society. The extreme among them defend the right to display and exchange photos of children who are being sexually abused. But only the extremists. Most civil libertarians appear to reluctantly draw the line at child pornography, but they don't want the line drawn any further.

Granted that such news groups will be allowed to continue, the issue then is how to protect others from being exposed to them. For example, should school and public libraries be allowed to install Internet filters that screen out designated sites? One side insists that this violates the guarantee of the First Amendment's right of free speech, the other that it is only a reasonable precaution to protect children.

What do you think?

Based on Clausing 1998; Etzioni 1998; Kaplan 1998; Mendels 1998; O'Connell 1998; Locy and Biskupic 2003.

SUMMARY

1. All societies attempt to channel sexual behavior in ways they consider acceptable. When the violation of sexual norms is felt to be a threat to society, especially to the family, it is considered a social problem.

2. In applying conflict theory to *homosexuality*, we see that fundamental tensions exist between homosexuals and heterosexuals and that their adjustment to one another is uneasy. Symbolic interactionists have analyzed how a homosexual identity is learned through interaction with others. The process by which people take on a homosexual identity appears to involve six stages: identity confusion, comparison, tolerance, acceptance, pride, and finally synthesis.

3. From the lens of functionalism, we saw that *prostitution* persists because it serves social functions. From a functionalist standpoint, prostitutes service customers who are sexually dissatisfied or whose sexual desires are deviant, thereby relieving pressures that otherwise might be placed on people who are unwilling to participate. The three stages in becoming a prostitute are (1) the drifting period (drifting from casual sex into selling sex), (2) the ambivalent transition period, and (3) the professionalization period. Some young men who sell sex to men manipulate symbols to maintain heterosexual identities.

4. Most Americans agree that the distribution of *pornography* should be restricted. Women favor greater restrictions than do men. Deciding what is and is not pornographic has confused many, including the U.S. Supreme Court, which, in the tradition of symbolic interactionism, has ruled that what a community decides is pornographic is pornographic—for them.

5. Social scientists have been unable to determine the social effects of pornography. Feminists are concerned that, by dehumanizing women, pornography encourages men to see women as sexual objects to be manipulated and exploited. Social activists take action on the basis of their convictions, not on the basis of proof about causation.

6. *Victimless crimes* are illegal acts to which the participants consent. Prostitution and pornography are classified as victimless crimes by sociologists when adults are involved, but not when children participate, as they cannot give full consent. The suggestion that we legalize prostitution runs into huge opposition.

7. The interests of people who approve and disapprove of homosexuality, prostitution, and pornography are likely to continue to clash, but those who disapprove of them are likely to be fighting rearguard actions. Pornography, as it becomes adapted to technological advancements, will be more widely available than ever.

KEY TERMS

Black market   The underground channeling of illegitimate goods or services.

Correlation   Two or more things occurring together.

Counterculture   A subculture in which the values of the dominant culture are turned upside down.

Hate crimes   Crimes that are motivated by hostility based on race-ethnicity, religion, disability, national origin, or sexual orientation.

Heterosexuality   The sexual preference for people of the opposite sex.

Homosexual behavior Sexual relations between people of the same sex, regardless of their preference.

Homosexuality The sexual preference for people of one's own sex.

Lesbian A female homosexual.

Masochists People who receive sexual gratification by having pain inflicted on themselves. See also *Sadists*.

Normalization (of deviance) To think of one's norm violations as normal; a second meaning is *mainstreaming*, when acts previously defined as deviant or criminal become accepted.

Pornography Writings, pictures, or objects of a sexual nature that are considered filthy.

Prostitution The renting of one's body for sexual purposes.

Role ambivalence Feeling indecisive, or both positive and negative, about one's role.

Sadists People who receive sexual gratification by inflicting pain on others. See also *Masochists*.

Safety valve theory (of pornography) The view that pornography protects people by providing the private release of sexual fantasies. See also *Trigger theory*.

Segregation Confining an activity to specified geographical areas.

Situational homosexual behavior Homosexual behavior by someone who has a heterosexual identity; often occurs in same-sex settings such as prisons or boarding schools.

Subculture A group that is set apart from others by their distinctive values and other characteristics.

Symbiosis A mutually beneficial relationship.

Temple prostitution Prostitution that takes place in a temple, as a type of worship.

Trigger theory (of pornography) The view that pornography triggers sexual offenses by stimulating people's sexual appetite. See also *Safety valve theory*.

Victimless crime An illegal act to which the participants consent.

THINKING CRITICALLY ABOUT CHAPTER 3

1. This chapter began by stating that "a basic sociological principle is that sex is never only a personal matter." It goes on to explain that all societies control human sexual behavior. Why do you think this is true? What is it about sex that makes us inclined to control the sexual behavior of others? Be sure to base your explanation on group aspects of society, not on personality or individuals.

2. Do you think there should be a separate legal category called *hate crimes*? Explain. Does your answer depend on whether we refer to sexual orientation, race–ethnicity, or some other category?

3. What difference might it make for social policy if it is determined that homosexuality is either learned or genetic? Do you agree that this should make a difference? Why or why not?

Alcohol and Other Drugs

"DEBBIE! WHAT'S THIS?"

Seeing the familiar plastic bag, Debbie felt her face redden. Why hadn't she put it away as she always did? She swallowed, then burst out defiantly:

"My purse! You've got no business snooping in my purse!"

"I was just looking for a match—but I found a lot more! I never expected a daughter of mine to be a drug addict."

"Drug addict, huh? That's funny! Just because someone smokes grass doesn't mean she's a drug addict."

"Everybody knows marijuana is just the first step to the hard stuff, like heroin."

"Mom, it's you who's hooked. The first thing you do in the morning is light up a cigarette and have a cup of coffee. And after that you start popping Prozac."

"Don't you compare my medicine with your drugs. My doctor prescribes Prozac for my nerves."

"Okay, then what do you call your martinis? And I know why you dug in my purse for a match—it's because you're hooked on cigarettes."

"Don't you talk back to me, young lady. Ever since you started college you think you know it all. Just wait 'til your Dad gets home."

"Yeah, sure. Then you'll do the same thing you do every night—talk about it over a drink."

The Problem in Sociological Perspective

Just as Debbie's mother was shocked to discover that her daughter smoked marijuana, so hundreds of thousands of parents have had similar rude awakenings. Long an element of culture in the Far and Middle East, using drugs for pleasure has become common in the West: on college campuses, in the suburbs, and in the executive suite. One of the presidents of the United States even admitted to smoking marijuana—although, bringing laughter to millions, he said that he "didn't inhale."

Drug Use in Ancient Societies

The use of drugs has a long history. Over 4,000 years ago, a Chinese emperor recommended marijuana for "female weakness, gout, rheumatism, malaria, beriberi, constipation and absentmindedness" (Ray and Ksir 2003). About 2,500 years ago, the famous physician Hippocrates recommended mandrake, taken with a little wine, to relieve depression and anxiety (Blum et al. 1969). And about 500 years ago, when the Spanish Conquistadores landed in South America, they discovered that the natives chewed coca leaves for the stimulating effects of cocaine (DeRios and Smith 1977; Goode 1989).

Drug Abuse Defined

Just as drug use goes far back in history, so does **drug abuse**—using drugs in such a way that they harm one's health, impair one's physical or mental functioning, or interfere with one's social life. Noah, who is listed as the ninth descendant of Adam, was the first person in the historical record to get drunk. After the flood, he planted a vineyard, made wine from its first harvest, and drank himself into a stupor (Genesis 9). What is considered drug abuse, of course, depends on social norms, and you know how norms change from group to group. In one group, smoking marijuana just once can be considered drug abuse, whereas in another group smoking marijuana regularly might be considered just "more of the usual."

The Social History of Drugs

It is important to emphasize that *no drug is good or bad in and of itself* (Szasz 1975). If a drug is considered good or bad, this is simply a matter of social definition—how a group of people views the drug and reacts to it. And how perspectives

87

change. You are familiar with today's dominant view of tobacco—and the health warnings on cigarette packages. What a contrast with the 1940s and 1950s, when doctors used to recommend particular brands of cigarettes as good for people's health. I think you will find the ad for Camels rather different from today's ads.

The Failure of Punishment

But let's reach back a little further in tobacco's social history. When Christopher Columbus arrived on these shores, he found that Native Americans smoked something strange. This substance looked interesting, and he took it back with him to the Old World. Europeans tried it, and smoking tobacco became common. King James of England disliked this new habit, however, and in 1604 he wrote a pamphlet, warning his subjects that tobacco was "harmful to the brain, dangerous to the lungs" (Ray and Ksir 2003). Other rulers who viewed tobacco as evil went far beyond just issuing warnings. In 1634, the Czar of Russia ordered the noses of tobacco smokers slit. About the same time, the rulers of China and Turkey ordered tobacco smokers put to death; those in China faced decapitation (Goode 1989). All these antidrug campaigns failed.

It is interesting, too, that like many people today, King James was not one to let health concerns interfere with business. When tobacco growing became profitable, he declared its trade a royal monopoly (Ray and Ksir 2003). Today we have universities and foundations that tout their concern with social justice, but that can't resist the juicy dividends that tobacco stocks pay.

Although some people will risk their neck for a good smoke, others will do the same for the beverage that may or may not be good to the last drop. After coffee was introduced in Arabia in the 1500s, Islamic religious leaders became upset when people drank coffee to help them stay awake during long vigils. Thinking that coffee was intoxicating and, therefore, prohibited by the Koran, the religious leaders ordered coffee dealers beaten across the soles of their feet. These antidrug measures, too, failed (Brecher et al. 1972). A century later, in 1674, a group of Englishwomen wrote a pamphlet titled "The Women's Petition Against Coffee." They complained that their men were leaving "good old ale" in order to drink "base, black, thick, nasty, bitter, stinking, nauseous" coffee. Their real complaint? The coffee, they said, was making their men less active sexually (Meyer 1954).

Changing Social Definitions

The change in U.S. attitudes toward drugs has been extensive. I've already mentioned cigarettes, but consider this. In the 1800s, you could buy opium and morphine in drugstores, grocery stores, and general stores. If this were inconvenient, you could order these drugs by mail. Opium was advertised as a cure for diarrhea, colds, fever, teething, pelvic disorders, even athlete's foot and baldness (Inciardi 1986). Opium was so common that each year U.S. mothers fed their babies about 750,000 bottles of opium-laced syrup. To smoke cigarettes or drink alcohol was far more offensive than to use opium (Isbell 1969; Duster 1970; Brecher et al. 1972).

People project their fantasies and fears onto drugs. At one time, they may view a drug as a holy gift, but later define that same drug as part of a social problem. This drives home the point made in Chapter 1 about objective conditions and subjective concerns. It is not the *objective conditions* of drugs—such as whether or not they are harmful—that makes their use a social problem. Rather, it takes *subjective concerns*. As we saw with coffee and tobacco, what is considered normal drug use

If a drug is in high demand, passing a law will not stop that demand. The law merely drives the use of the drug underground, to a black market that connects users and suppliers in an intricate, illegal relationship. Although coffee is broadly socially acceptable today, in some societies it was once an illegal drug, with severe penalties attached to its possession and consumption.

at one point in history may be looked at as drug abuse at another time. Just as with abortion and prostitution, drugs are a part of social controversy. As with other social problems, people learn different views of drugs and line up on opposing sides of the issue.

In Sum: Objective Conditions and Subjective Concerns

In short, *whether a drug is considered good or bad depends not on objective conditions but on subjective concerns. Subjective concerns are not fixed, but they change over time. These concerns, and the views they generate, influence how people use and abuse drugs, whether a drug will be legal or illegal, and what social policies people want to adopt* (see Table 4-1 below). This is the central sociological principle of drug use and abuse, one that we shall stress over and over in this chapter.

The Scope of the Problem

"Mine" vs. "Yours"

Debbie, in our opening vignette, is like the other thirteen million Americans who have smoked marijuana during the past month (*Statistical Abstract* 2003:Tables 11, 201). To Debbie, marijuana isn't a drug. It's just something that makes her feel good and is "no big deal." On her part, Debbie's mother is like most Americans—she drinks coffee, alcohol, and colas, smokes cigarettes, and ingests a variety of substances that *she* has a hard time thinking of as drugs.

Drugs Defined

Like marijuana, alcohol and nicotine are drugs. To be a drug, a substance does not have to be sold in an alley or be exchanged furtively for money in a van. A **drug** is a substance that is taken to produce a change in one's bodily functions, behavior, emotions, thinking, or consciousness. *The essential difference among substances is not which substance people use, but whether a substance is socially acceptable or disapproved.* From this comes the clash in perspectives of people like Debbie and her mother.

Americans Are Pro-drug

Almost all Americans use drugs. We are born with the aid of drugs, and drugs ease our departure from life. We use drugs for sickness and for pleasure, to relieve anxiety, queasy stomachs, and headaches, and for all sorts of other pains and discomforts. As with alcohol, we take drugs to help us be sociable. And as with cigarettes, coffee, and colas, we take them routinely, unthinkingly, and habitually. (Yes, coffee, Coke, and Pepsi contain a drug. This drug, caffeine, is addictive, and some people "just can't get going" in the morning without their "fixes.") Far from being an antidrug society, we are actually highly prodrug.

Personal vs. Social Problem

Most of us take this kind of drug use for granted. To us, this is like eating popcorn or munching on potato chips. When drug use interferes with someone's health or how that person gets along in life, however, we begin to question it. But we consider this a *personal* problem. If large numbers of people become upset about a drug, however, and want to see something done about it, then that drug becomes part of a *social* problem. This, of course, takes us back to the main point with which we began this text: objective conditions and subjective concerns. As we consider two common drugs, nicotine and alcohol, note how much more important subjective concerns are than objective conditions.

TABLE 4-1 Legal Status and Use of Drugs

| | USE OF DRUGS | |
	LEGAL USE	ILLEGAL USE
Legal Drugs	a. Prescription b. Over the counter c. "Over the bar" and in vending machines	a. Forged prescriptions b. Black market sales of prescription drugs c. "After-hours" sales, "Underage" sales
Illegal Drugs	a. Marijuana prescribed for medical problems b. Cocaine for surgery	a. Crack, heroin, etc.

Source: By the author.

For generations, tobacco companies worked to get Americans hooked on nicotine. This ad from the 1950s urged people to give Camels a 30-day test, plenty of time to get people hooked on this drug. Nicotine's effects are deadly, but slow, and it may take 30 years or longer for nicotine to kill. During that time, the cigarette companies make huge profits from their victims. Nicotine, a legal drug, kills more people than the number who die from all illegal drugs combined.

Let's suppose that you are on your way to the airport to leave for a long-awaited vacation. You are listening to the radio and anticipating your arrival in sunny Hawaii. Suddenly, an announcer breaks into your reverie with a flash bulletin: Terrorists have hidden bombs aboard five jumbo jets scheduled for takeoff today. Each jet is going to crash. On each jet will be 200 passengers and crew, who will plummet from the skies, leaving a trail of agonizing screams as they meet their fiery destiny.

The announcer pauses, then adds: "The authorities have not been able to find the bombs. Because no one knows which flights will crash, all flights will depart on schedule."

What would you do? My guess is that you would turn your car around and go home. Adios to Hawaii's beaches, and hello to your own backyard.

Nicotine as a Social Problem

What does this have to do with nicotine? Nicotine—with its creeping emphysema and several types of cancer— kills about 400,000 Americans each year (Surgeon General 2003). This is the equivalent of five fully loaded jets, each carrying 200 passengers and 20 crew members, crashing each and very day. The crashes continue without letup, day after day, year after year. The passengers *know* that one of the jets will crash that day; yet they climb aboard anyway, thinking that it won't be *their* jet that crashes.

Obviously no one would get on a plane if this were the case. And if planes crashed like this, the government would stop the flights and fix the problem. Who in their right mind would take the risk that *their* plane would not be among those that crashed? Yet smokers do. They know that nicotine is lethal. They also know that smoking-related deaths are lingering and painful, a burden to both the victims and their families. Yet smokers continue to put this deadly poison to their lips, thinking that it won't be their plane that goes down.

Alcohol as a Social Problem

Alcohol, too, is far more dangerous than its broad social acceptability would imply. A dramatic example is motor vehicle accidents, which kill 42,000 Americans each year. Alcohol is a factor in 35 percent of these accidents, bringing the death toll for just these accidents to 15,000—about 41 a day (*Statistical Abstract* 2003:Table 1099). To continue our analogy, this is the equivalent of two jumbo jets, each loaded with 144 passengers and crew, crashing each and every week of the year.

As alcohol abuse ravages vital organs, the abusers of this drug become a burden to their families. Men are more likely to suffer the consequences of this drug, for most abusers of alcohol are men—about 2 or 3 men for each woman. In addition to the many health problems and deaths that come from alcohol abuse, like nicotine, this drug costs the nation billions of dollars a year in health care and in lost productivity.

Drug Addiction Defined

A serious problem with some drugs is **addiction,** or **drug dependence.** That is, people come to depend on the regular consumption of a drug to make it through the day. When people think of **drug addiction,** they are likely to think of addicts huddled in slum doorways, the dregs of society who seldom venture into daylight—unless it is to rob someone. Most people don't associate addiction with "good," middle-class neighborhoods and "solid citizens."

Nicotine Addiction

But let's look at drug addiction a little more closely. Although most people may think of heroin as the prime example of an addictive drug, I suggest that nicotine is the better example. I remember a next-door neighbor as he stood in his backyard, a lit cigarette in his hand, telling me about the operation in which the surgeon removed one of his lungs. I say "remember," because soon after our conversation he died from his addiction.

A major disease that comes from smoking is emphysema, which makes breathing increasingly difficult. Death eventually occurs from respiratory failure. You'd think that such a disease would be enough to make smokers quit, but chest specialists report that "even during the last months of their ordeal, when they must breathe oxygen intermittently instead of air, some of them go right on alternating cigarette smoke and oxygen" (Brecher et al. 1972:216).

Another example of nicotine's addictive power is Buerger's disease:

> In this disease the blood vessels become so constricted that circulation is impaired whenever nicotine enters the bloodstream. When gangrene sets in, at first a toe or two may have to be amputated. If the person continues to smoke, the foot may have to be amputated at the ankle, then the leg at the knee, and ultimately at the hip. Somewhere along this gruesome progression gangrene may also attack the other leg. Patients are told that if they will stop smoking, this horrible march of gangrene up their legs will be curbed. Yet surgeons report that some patients vigorously puff away in their hospital beds following even a second or third amputation (Brecher et al. 1972:216).

Avoiding Withdrawal

Why don't drug addicts just quit? People use drugs even under dire circumstances in order to avoid **withdrawal,** the intense distress—nausea, vomiting, aches and pains, nervousness, anxiety, and depression—they feel when they abstain from the drug. Withdrawal creates **craving,** an intense desire for the missed drug. Even after someone has kicked the habit, craving may last for months or even years. Craving is especially strong during times of emotional distress. Even years after breaking the physical habit, people may still experience an occasional desire for the drug. This is referred to as **psychological dependence.** (A personal note: After I quit smoking and no longer felt craving, I would have recurring dreams that I was smoking cigarettes. These dreams were so real that I would awaken abruptly in the middle of the night—feeling guilty for having fallen back into the habit.)

Looking at the Problem Theoretically

Why is it legal for people to use such lethal drugs as alcohol and nicotine, and yet people are put in prison for using milder drugs? This question points up how subjective concerns outweigh objective conditions, how the meanings we assign to drugs go far beyond their pharmaceutical characteristics. In order to understand the *social* significance of drugs, let's look at drugs through our three theoretical lenses.

SYMBOLIC INTERACTIONISM

Contrasting Definitions of Drugs

The meaning of a drug depends on who is considering it. A physician might perceive a drug as a tool to help patients; a drug dealer might view the same drug as a high-profit product; the police might see it as an evil substance to be stamped out; users might see it as the pathway to an adventure, a "high," or even a religious experience. Some users might view the drug as simply a mild diversion that can be done without, whereas others view it as an absolute necessity for getting through the day. The meaning of a drug, then, does not depend on the drug, but on how people interpret the drug.

The U.S. Temperance Movement as a Symbolic Crusade

As the Issues in Social Problems box on the next page stresses, alcohol has been associated with Americans from the time this country began. How, then, could this

Issues in Social Problems
THE PILGRIMS, BEER, AND THANKSGIVING

The *Mayflower* had completed its historic voyage. Now the Pilgrims faced the daunting task of settling the wilderness of the New World. They found the Indians friendly enough, but the harsh winter of 1620 was something else. Samoset, a tribesman, helped them survive that first threatening winter.

But beer also helped.

When winter hit, the colonists' buildings were still unfinished. To continue work on them, they had to brave the icy February winds as they ferried back and forth from the *Mayflower*. Life was becoming unbearable and death common from pneumonia, scurvy, and exposure.

Adding to their misery was the first beer crisis in the New World. It wasn't as though the Pilgrims lacked foresight. They were planners, and they had brought with them a large supply of beer. Like other Europeans, they distrusted water, and thought of alcohol as essential for good health. A stiff drink kept off chills and fevers, aided digestion, made work easier to bear, and warmed the body on cold nights. The Pilgrims considered nondrinkers to be "crank-brained."

But the trip had taken longer than expected, and so had their efforts at establishing a beachhead in the wilderness. They had run out of beer, and now they were forced to drink water. Seeing their plight, the captain of the *Mayflower* shared his own beer supplies with them. He could do this only so long, however, for he had to leave enough for his own crew to drink on the long journey back to England. Eventually, he had to stop sharing.

For the Pilgrims, the situation had become desperate. William Bradford, who became the governor of Plymouth, pleaded for just one "can" of beer. The captain of the *Mayflower* refused him. As the deaths mounted, however, the captain took pity on the Pilgrims. To alleviate their suffering, from his own supplies he gave beer "for them that hath need for it," particularly the sick.

With prayers, the help of Samoset, the *Mayflower*'s captain, and beer, the Pilgrims made it through that first bleak winter. And, unlike our grade school images, during their first Thanksgiving feast, the Pilgrims drank beer—and Samoset joined their merrymaking, for by this time he, too, had developed a taste for this frothy, heart-warming liquid.

Based on Lender and Martin 1982.

beverage ever have been outlawed, as it was in 1919—which then ushered in organized crime and the "speakeasies" that you may have seen in the old movies? In his account of the U.S. temperance movement, *Symbolic Crusade,* sociologist Joseph Gusfield (1963) focuses on alcohol as a symbol. He examines how abstinence (abstaining from alcohol) became associated with power and respectability.

The temperance movement, Gusfield says, was a response to social change. Anglo-Saxon Protestants had settled New England, and their customs and religion dominated the region. Then in the 1820s, millions of uneducated, poor immigrants poured in from Italy, Germany, and Ireland. These new immigrants brought with them customs that the educated and well-to-do New England "aristocracy" found alien—especially a different religion (Roman Catholicism) and the practice of drinking a lot of wine, beer, and spirits. The Anglo-Saxon Protestants despised these new immigrants, viewing them as ignorant, Catholic drunkards. As immigrants continued to pour in, the "aristocracy" gradually lost political power. They then began the temperance movement, reasoning that if they could not control the politics of the country, they at least could control its morals. The goal was to turn the new Americans into clean, sober, and godly people whose customs would reflect the moral leadership of New England.

Drinking and abstinence came to be two significant symbols, identifying people as members of one of two major groups. Abstinence, which was associated with morality and respectability, symbolized a hard worker, a person who was established and respectable. Drinking symbolized an unreliable drifter, an uneducated immigrant of questionable background. To abstain from alcohol became a requirement for anyone who strived for higher social standing.

As the United States grew even more urban, secular, and Roman Catholic, Protestants saw their power and values slipping even further away. They intensified their efforts to bring about laws that upheld temperance, and in 1919 they rejoiced when the Eighteenth Amendment to the Constitution was passed. Overnight, it became illegal for Americans to buy even a glass of beer. Prohibition, Gusfield says, marked the victory of middle-class, Protestant, rural values over working-class, Roman Catholic, urban values. But Prohibition was a failure. Like all other antidrug laws before it, Prohibition did not stop people from using the drug of their choice. Gradually, the anti-Catholic and antiurban forces weakened, and in 1933 the Eighteenth Amendment was repealed.

Changing Meanings: The Example of Marijuana

It is difficult for us today to see how emotionally charged the issue of drinking a glass of beer was. But this illustrates how our understanding of any drug must center on discovering the meanings that people attach to it. Many people view cocaine use as immoral, but for others it represents sophistication. Contrasting and changing meanings also surround marijuana. As long as marijuana was confined to "bohemian" or marginal groups, it posed no cultural threat. But in the 1960s, rebellious middle-class youth formed a subculture that was alien to their parents' world of hard work and straight living. To show their rejection of the middle-class world, they promoted marijuana and other psychedelic drugs. At that point, the meaning of marijuana changed, and a social problem was born—one that remains with us.

FUNCTIONALISM

Social Functions of Drugs

When functionalists study a drug, whether it be legal or illegal, they examine its functions and dysfunctions. Recreational drugs such as alcohol and marijuana "loosen" people up, or otherwise help remove tensions that interfere with sociability. These drugs are also functional for those who make money from growing, processing, distributing, and selling them. These same drugs are dysfunctional for people who abuse them. Similarly, prescription drugs are functional both for the medical profession and for the patients they serve. These drugs, too, are dysfunctional for those who abuse them.

A striking example of how prescription drugs are functional is their use with mental patients. In the 1950s, more than a half million Americans were locked in mental hospitals. Since then, our population has doubled, and if the rate of commitment had stayed the same, about a million Americans would be locked in asylums. But in the 1950s, psychiatrists began to prescribe mood-altering drugs (the psychopharmaceuticals), and in just a few years the number of patients confined to mental hospitals shrank by several hundred thousand. For these people, drugs were functional.

Dysfunctions of Drugs

Prescription drugs are also dysfunctional. Some psychiatrists use them to put patients in "pharmacological straitjackets." Instead of trying to find out what is wrong with the patient or with the patient's social environment, the physician takes the easier road and prescribes drugs. Such drug therapy exacts a price. "Doped up" patients become befuddled and lethargic. Some suffer neurological damage.

In short, drug use is dysfunctional when it interferes with people's physical or social functioning. As we saw in the example cited earlier of Buerger's disease, nicotine addiction provides a striking example of the dysfunction of a drug. Alcohol abuse is also dysfunctional, leaving behind a trail of impaired health, poverty, broken homes, and smashed dreams. Similarly, heroin, the barbiturates, and other addictive drugs create severe problems for addicts and their families and friends.

The dysfunctions of drugs extend far beyond the individual. Although difficult to measure, these large-scale costs involve drug-related crimes, such as burglaries and muggings, that are committed in order to support an addiction; unemployment;

medical costs due to illness and disease; the spread of AIDS among addicts who share needles; the harm suffered by people in automobile accidents; and the loss to society of a reservoir of human potential as people retreat into drugs.

Latent Functions of Drug Control

The history of drugs leads us to some unexpected twists and turns. The common-sense purpose of making a drug illegal, for example, is to deter the use of that drug. Making a drug illegal has a latent function, however—to strengthen the agencies that control that drug. Without these laws, some government agencies would go out of business. To protect their jobs, some bureaucrats are eager to define many more drugs as dangerous to the public's welfare. The more drugs that are illegal, the more secure their jobs.

The Example of Marijuana

Marijuana illustrates how making a drug illegal is functional for bureaucrats. In 1930, Harry Anslinger was appointed to head the Treasury Department's new Bureau of Narcotics. Congress cut his budget because the country was in the midst of the Great Depression. Marijuana was legal at this time, but Anslinger saw this drug as an opportunity to strengthen his faltering organization (Dickson 1968). Embarking on a campaign to pass a federal law against marijuana, Anslinger became a **moral entrepreneur,** a crusading reformer who wages battle to enforce his or her idea of morality. Anslinger received support from an unexpected source, the liquor interests who feared that marijuana might compete with alcohol (Rockwell 1972). With the help of this new ally, Anslinger was victorious, and Congress passed the Marijuana Tax Act in 1937. Anslinger's campaign to frighten people is recounted in the Issues in Social Problems box on the next page.

A Function for Some Can Be a Dysfunction for Others

The Marijuana Tax Act has been functional for the Bureau of Narcotics, which is still going strong. It has been dysfunctional, however, for the hundreds of thousands of Americans who have been caught in its enforcement web. When marijuana became popular with middle-class youth and it became impossible to enforce abstinence among millions of smokers, this did not stop the drug enforcers from searching out and arresting offenders. Drug use has kept them in business. This illustrates a central tenet of functional analysis: What is functional for some is dysfunctional for others.

CONFLICT THEORY

Drug Laws as Tools for Social Control

Common sense sometimes doesn't get us very far when it comes to drugs. As discussed in the Issues in Social Problems box on page 96, much more is involved in making a drug illegal than the harm done by that drug. We have to consider power. Some groups have the power to get laws passed to protect their interests; others don't. This takes us to the heart of the conflict perspective, how drugs are used as a political tool. If the use of a particular drug is common among some group, by making that drug illegal the state can unleash its police power against that group. In contrast, by keeping a drug legal, the state can protect favored groups that make money from a drug.

The Example of Marijuana

Let's look at how drug laws have been used as a political tool. In the 1920s, the United States was in the midst of an economic boom, and workers from Mexico were valued as a source of cheap labor. Then came the Great Depression of the 1930s. Suddenly, these same people were viewed as competitors for scarce jobs (Galliher and Walker 1977). Marijuana use was not popular in the United States, but it was among these workers. This presented an ideal opportunity for Anslinger, who began a campaign to label this unpopular group as dangerous drug abusers. In one of his many articles, Anslinger refers to "a hot tamale salesman pushing his cart about town . . . peddling marijuana cigarettes." The Marijuana Tax Act of 1937 became a political tool to drive unneeded Mexican workers back across the border (Helmer 1975).

The Example of Opium

Chinese immigrants were also on the receiving end of drug laws. In the 1800s, thousands of Chinese men came to the United States to help build the railroads. They brought opium with them, a legal drug at the time. When the railroad was completed,

Issues in Social Problems

SOCIOLOGY AND COMMON SENSE: LEGAL AND ILLEGAL DRUGS

COMMON SENSE

1. Common sense suggests that drugs that are illegal are harmful, whereas drugs that are legal are not harmful.

2. Common sense suggests that if a legal drug turns out to be addictive and is abused, it will be made illegal.

3. Common sense suggests that if a nonnarcotic has been classified mistakenly in the law as a narcotic, it will be reclassified and treated differently.

SOCIOLOGY

1. Drugs do not become illegal (or remain legal) on the basis of the social or personal injury they do. Drugs have a social history (pages 87–89, 110–112) that affects their legal classification. Making a drug illegal is a political process. Some interest groups have managed to get their viewpoints written into law.

2. Some addictive drugs are backed by well-financed interest groups, and these drugs remain legal. (See the examples of Valium, Xanax, and Prozac, p. 98.)

3. Marijuana was classified improperly as a narcotic in the 1937 Marijuana Tax Act. Although knowledge of this error is common, no interest group has been powerful enough to get this classification changed.

these workers were thrown into the job market. This coincided with a depression in the early 1870s and with a national financial panic in 1873. The men, who were willing to work cheaply, posed a threat to white workers, who beat, threatened, and killed them. In 1875, San Francisco and other West Coast cities began to prohibit opium dens. These laws did not target opium, but, rather, the Chinese men who threatened the jobs of the white working class (Morgan 1978). Even the U.S. Congress got into the act. In 1887, it passed a law that prohibited the importation of opium *by the Chinese* but not by white Americans (Szasz 1975).

Heroin, Too?

Conflict theorists also stress that politicians use drug laws to control what are called "the dangerous classes," those that produce rebels and revolutionaries. When oppressed people seek refuge in addictive drugs, their anger is diverted away from revolutionary impulses. Drugs, not social change, become their passion, the goal around which their life revolves.

Contrary to the impression that news reports sometimes give, that society is about to explode in a paroxysm of drug violence, from this perspective drugs such as heroin and crack stabilize society. They divert the attention and energy of the exploited away from their oppression, diluting their interest in social change. In addition, violence becomes directed toward members of their own community, not toward the ruling class. In this theoretical light, sociologist Andrew Karmen (1980:174) said that heroin users become too passive when nodding and too self-absorbed when they aren't high to fight for community control over the schools, to organize tenants for a rent strike, or to march on City Hall to demand decent jobs for all who want to work. Since narcotics pacify those who suffer most from mental and physical degradation, it's likely that some astute members of the ruling circles have decided its benefits outweigh its costs.

How Illegal Drugs Are Functional for the Powerful

One does not have to agree that society's elite masterminds the trade in heroin and crack cocaine to see that drugs can serve the interests of the powerful. An old ploy sometimes used by groups in power to protect their position is to focus attention on

Issues in Social Problems

MARIJUANA: ASSASSIN OF YOUTH

In his campaign to make marijuana illegal, Harry Anslinger used dramatic accounts and exaggeration. To frighten people, he wrote articles for popular magazines (Reasons 1974). In one of them, he tells this story:

There was this young girl. . . . Her story is typical. Some time before, this girl, like others of her age who attend our high schools, had heard the whispering of a secret which has gone the rounds of American youth. It promised a new thrill, the smoking of a type of cigarette which contained a "real kick." According to the whispers, this cigarette could accomplish wonderful reactions and with no harmful aftereffects. So the adventurous girl and a group of her friends gathered in an apartment, thrilled with the idea of doing "something different" in which there was "no harm." Then a friend produced a few cigarettes of the loosely rolled "homemade" type. They were passed from one to another of the young people, each taking a few puffs.

The results were weird. Some of the party went into paroxysms of laughter; every remark, no matter how silly, seemed excruciatingly funny. Others of mediocre musical ability became almost expert; the piano dinned constantly. Still others found themselves discussing weighty problems of youth with remarkable clarity. As one youngster expressed it, he "could see through stone walls." The girl danced without fatigue, and the night of unexplainable exhilaration seemed to stretch out as though it were a year long. Time, conscience, or consequences became too trivial for consideration.

Other parties followed, in which inhibitions vanished, conventional barriers departed, all at the command of this strange cigarette with its ropy, resinous odor. Finally there came a gathering at a time when the girl was behind in her studies and greatly worried. With every puff of the smoke the feeling of despondency lessened. Everything was going to be all right—at last. The girl was "floating" now, a term given to marijuana intoxication. Suddenly, in the midst of laughter and dancing, she thought of her school problems. Instantly they were solved. Without hesitancy, she walked to a window and leaped to her death. Thus can marijuana "solve" one's difficulties.

Here's another story that Anslinger told.

It was an unprovoked crime some years ago which brought the first realization that the age-old drug had gained a foothold in America. An entire family was murdered by a youthful addict in Florida. When officers arrived at the home they found the youth staggering about in a human slaughterhouse. With an ax he had killed his father, his mother, two brothers, and a sister. He seemed to be in a daze. . . . He had no recollection of having committed the multiple crime. The officers knew him ordinarily as a sane, rather quiet young man; now he was pitifully crazed. They sought the reason. The boy said he had been in the habit of smoking something which youthful friends called "muggles," a childish name for marijuana. . . .

[People need to be] told that addicts may often develop a delirious rage during which they are temporarily and violently insane, that this insanity may take the form of a desire for self-destruction or a persecution complex to be satisfied only by the commission of some heinous crime. (Anslinger and Cooper 1937)

If these stories didn't convince people, Anslinger had an ace up his sleeve. He said that this killer weed—his term—caused the loss of reproductive powers (Galliher and Walker 1977).

All things considered, it is little wonder that Anslinger's campaign resulted in Congress passing the Marijuana Tax Act in 1937.

Fingering the "Enemy" Behind "Bad" Drugs

some supposed threat posed by a disfavored group. This diverts attention from internal problems and makes people feel that they are all in the same boat—and that they had better bail together, because the boat is leaking.

Our history provides numerous examples of how those in power have used drugs to consolidate sentiment against disfavored groups. During the 1800s, Chinese opium dens were pictured as outposts of corruption and seduction. By World War I the "enemy" had changed, and German pharmaceutical firms and anarchists were supposedly smuggling heroin into this country. With the outbreak of World War II, Japan was identified as the power behind the narcotics trade. Then during the Cold War of the 1950s, the Soviet secret police were fingered as the sinister heroin supplier. During the Korean War,

China became the culprit. Then during the Vietnam War, North Vietnam and the National Liberation Front were singled as masterminds of the narcotics trade (Karmen 1980). Now that the Cold War is over, who will the government implicate as a new enemy supplier? Inevitably, it will be a group that is out of favor with the U.S. power elite.

In Sum

Each theory contributes a unique understanding of drugs as a social problem. Symbolic interactionists stress how drugs become powerful symbols that affect social life, as was the case with alcohol and the great drug experiment known as Prohibition. Functionalists examine the functions and dysfunctions of drug use: For example, some mental patients benefit from legal mood-altering drugs, but those same drugs impair the physical or social functioning of other patients. Conflict theorists examine drugs as part of a social order in which a privileged few are in control: Because drugs have been manipulated in the past for the purpose of enhancing power and control, this same process may underlie the heroin and cocaine trade today.

Research Findings

Everyone knows that the narcotics cause crime, destroy people's incentive to work, and devastate their health. But are these assumptions really true? In this section, we are going to report on some unusual research findings. But first, let's examine the medicalization of human problems, consider why the effects of a drug are not always the same, and present an overview of different types of drugs.

THE MEDICALIZATION OF HUMAN PROBLEMS

The King had a difficult time getting through the day—and the nights were no better. Middle age, unwelcome by almost everyone but especially dreaded by celebrities, had settled in, bringing a paunch and double chin that the Hollywood magazines ridiculed. To make matters worse, the breakup of his marriage had torn his only child from him. Throughout these ordeals, a longtime friend, Dr. George Nichopoulos, had been a great help. During the past 31 months he had prescribed 19,000 stimulants, depressants, and painkillers, some of which were highly addictive.

Now the King of Rock and Roll lay dead on his bathroom floor. The official report stated that Elvis Presley had died from heart disease. Other medical examiners claimed that his death could have resulted from the interaction of the many drugs in his system. Presley's body contained toxic levels of the sedative methaqualone, ten times more codeine than was needed for therapy, and low levels of ten other drugs: morphine, Demerol, and phenyltoloxamine (painkillers); amobarbital, phenobarbital, and amitriptyline (sedatives); pentobarbital (a sedative and sleep-inducer); Valmid and Placidyl (sleep-inducers); and Valium (a muscle relaxant).

At his trial for overprescribing, Dr. Nichopoulos testified that his drug plan for Presley called for drugs to reduce his appetite, drugs to stimulate his bowels, drugs to help him urinate, drugs to relieve itching, drugs to help dizziness, drugs to relieve pain, and drugs to help him relax. Dr. Nichopoulos was found not guilty.

Medicalizing Human Problems

Though extreme, Elvis Presley's death pinpoints one of today's major drug problems: *the legal abuse of legal drugs.* In the 1930s, the pharmaceutical industry began to manufacture psychoactive drugs. Since then, we have been gradually swept up in a drug revolution (Conrad 1975). Physicians now prescribe drugs for conditions that people used to assume were a normal part of life: anxiety and distress, feeling upset or uncertain, wrestling with perplexing problems, not fitting in, feeling dissatisfied. All of these have been redefined as medical problems. If the old attitude was that we all confront problems like these and we have to develop coping skills to deal with them, today's attitude is that such situations call for drugs. Sociologists call this **medicalizing human problems,** offering a medical "solution" for the problems that people confront in everyday life.

Valium

Valium (generic name diazepam) is a case in point. In the 1970s, Valium was touted as a solution for personal problems: This drug was so magical that physicians prescribed it not only to remove the "weariness" that housewives feel but also to relieve "anxiety and tension in parent–child relationships" (*Use and Misuse* 1980:395). Today's more popular drugs, Prozac, Xanax, and Zoloft, have similar capacities to help people get through everyday life. Doctors prescribe them for anxiety, irritability, sleeplessness, restlessness, inability to concentrate, and even a pounding heart. The serenity gained through popping pills is elusive, though.These drugs have side effects—from forgetfulness to suicidal thoughts. They are also addictive.

Xanax and Prozac

With so many people looking for an easy solution to life's problems (and who wouldn't want all of their problems to disappear by simply filling a prescription!), medicalizing problems of life has become big business. Xanax and Prozac each pull in over a *billion* dollars a year. Drug companies, physicians, and pharmacists all benefit by keeping the public believing that medicine is *the* way to cope with their problems.

Prescribing Drugs Turned Upside Down

This medicalizing of human problems has turned the order of medicine upside down. In many cases, it is no longer the doctors who do the prescribing but, rather, the patients. Here's how it works. Drug companies flood television and magazines with commercials for medications that you *cannot* buy over the counter. To get these drugs, you have to go to your doctor and tell him or her to prescribe them. This marketing strategy works. People see the commercials and imagine themselves living a happy, carefree life if they can just get their hands on Xanax, Prozac, or some other drug. Physicians don't want to lose business, so they write the prescriptions that their customers ask for. The doctors make money from writing—literally—billions of prescriptions. So do the pharmacists who eagerly fill them. And the drug companies laugh all the way to the bank.

Medicalizing Deviant Behavior:

Medicalizing human problems—to think of them not as normal aspects of daily life, but as a matter of "sickness"—has become so common that even children's rowdy behavior is now a "medical" problem. We used to say that children who disrupted their classroom were *unruly* and in need of discipline by parents and school. Now we call them *sick*—as though they have some sort of illness that medicine can cure.

1. Rowdy Kids

There is, of course, nothing new about teachers complaining that children are difficult to teach, or parents that it is difficult to control their children. What *is* new is for teachers and doctors *to turn behaviors into illnesses.* When a child's unacceptable behavior is given a name—perhaps **attention deficit-hyperactivity disorder** (ADHD) or **hyperkinesis** *(hyperactivity)*, it sounds as though the child *has* something. (The doctor or teacher looks solemnly at the alarmed parents and pronounces, "She *has* ADHD.") How frightening—and how untrue. What the child really has is a bogus "psychiatric disease" (Vatz 1994).

2. Political Dissenters

Just as unruly children are unacceptable to those in authority, so are political dissenters. And like teachers, politicians like to define dissenters as mentally disturbed so they can be given drugs to control their behavior. In the former Soviet Union, scholars, scientists, and artists who spoke out against the government were jailed in medical facilities and given "drug therapy." The same thing is happening in today's China (Muminovic 2002). The drugs produce disorganized thinking, which, in turn, "prove" that the dissenters are "crazy."

Functions of Medicalizing Human Behavior

The functions of medicalizing disruptive behavior—whether for writing articles that criticize the authorities or for disrupting the classroom—are obvious. The "drug therapy" helps Chinese authorities justify the arrest of dissenters. Most of the hundreds of thousands of U.S. children who take Ritalin for their "illness" sit still longer and appear to pay attention. The drug works so well that doctors are even prescribing Ritalin for toddlers who are going through their "terrible twos" (Kalb 2000). As you can see in these three cases, the drug is not really for the patient, but, rather, for the political authorities, the teachers, and the parents.

Dysfunctions of Medicalizing Human Behavior

There also are dysfunctions. Some schoolchildren get stuck with the label of mentally ill. Others suffer from brain damage, cancer, tics, lethargy, depression, and addiction from Ritalin (Breggin 1998). For the political dissenters in China, the dysfunction is more obvious, the loss of freedom. For the little kids who are medicalized to help *their parents* get through the "terrible twos," we don't yet have the results. They are likely to be equally as unpleasant.

The Appeal of Popping Pills

Because pills seem such a handy answer to problems that perplex us, medicalizing human problems has become a standard feature of contemporary life. If only we could find the perfect pill, our personal and social problems would disappear as we dip into the pharmacological wellspring of medical miracles.

THE EFFECTS OF DRUGS

Why Drug Experiences Differ

Why can the same drug affect two people differently? And why, when the same person takes the drug on different occasions, can its effects differ?

What someone experiences from a drug depends on three main factors (Ray and Ksir 2003). The first is the *drug*. Effects differ according to the amount of the drug, its quality, and how the drug is administered (smoked, shot into the bloodstream). The second is the *individual*. Effects can be different for users who are anxious, depressed, or relaxed. They also differ according to the individual's body weight and metabolism, and for reasons yet unknown, drugs affect men and women differently (Cimons 1999). The third factor is the *setting*, which can influence the individual's expectations or mind-set.

Conflict theorists point out how laws against drugs have been used as tools to control the oppressed classes. Laws against crack, like those against the use of opium, marijuana, and heroin, have served this purpose well. One reaction to oppression is to flee into addiction. Those who do so can harm themselves and their loved ones.

LSD (lysergic acid diethylamide) illustrates these factors beautifully. When people first began to use LSD, their psychotic reactions and suicides made headlines across the nation. These accounts then decreased, and eventually became rare. Sociologist Howard S. Becker (1967) concluded that the people who first took LSD thought that it might create panic—and they were likely to experience panic. As a subculture grew around LSD, it changed people's expectations—and their experiences. When people who had already used LSD introduced their friends to the drug, they told them what to expect. When first-time users saw strange colors, walls breathing, or felt a unity with plants, their "trip guides" assured them that this was normal, that it was temporary, and that they should relax and enjoy the sensations. As a result, negative LSD experiences dropped sharply.

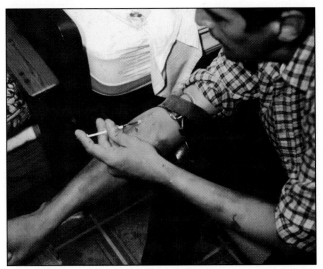

Expectations are especially important in regard to drugs that people use to alter their perception, to change their mood, or to make them more sociable—drugs that we shall now consider.

DRUG USE BY STUDENTS

Sociologists have studied drug use by high school and college students in detail. Let's look at some of their findings. We'll begin with Figure 4-1 on page 100, which is based on a sample so good that we can generalize these findings to all U.S. eighth graders and high school sophomores and seniors. As you can see, during the past month about half of all U.S. high school seniors drank alcohol. And almost one-third got drunk during this time.

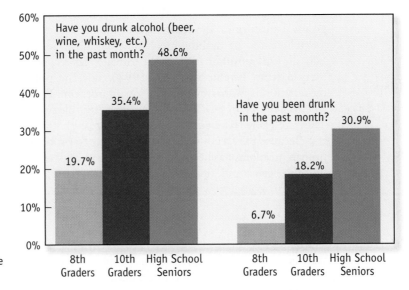

FIGURE 4-1 *Who Drinks Alcohol?*

Source: By the author. Based on Johnston et al. 2003b:Table 2; 2003a:Table 4-7.

Drug Use and College Plans

One of the more interesting findings of drug use by high school seniors is how significant college plans are. As you can see from Table 4-2, high school seniors who plan on going to four years of college use fewer drugs than those who don't have these plans. From this table, you can also see that underage drinking is common—as though you didn't know this. You may not have known, however, just how common marijuana smoking is among high school seniors. About 850,000 high school seniors smoked marijuana during the past month. About 250,000 of them went to school stoned—except for those who confine their *daily* marijuana smoking to the evenings. Even then, the effects would linger.

From High School to College

Look at Table 4-3 to get an overview of drug use by college students. Again, this sample is so good that we can generalize to *all* college students across the nation.

TABLE 4-2 What Drugs Do High School Seniors Use?
(in the last 30 days)

	TOTAL	SEX		COLLEGE PLANS	
		M	F	NONE OR LESS THAN 4 YEARS	4 YEARS
Alcohol	48.6%	52.3%	47.4%	53.0%	47.4%
Been Drunk	30.9%	34.3%	26.9%	31.7%	29.3%
Alcohol Daily	3.5%	5.3%	1.7%	4.8%	3.1%
Cigarettes	26.7%	27.4%	25.5%	37.5%	23.6%
Cigarettes Daily	16.9%	17.2%	16.1%	27.6%	13.8%
Marijuana	21.5%	25.3%	17.4%	27.0%	19.6%
Marijuana Daily	6.0%	8.7%	3.1%	10.3%	4.6%
Amphetamines	5.3%	5.3%	5.3%	8.1%	4.7%
Ecstasy	2.4%	2.6%	2.1%	3.3%	2.2%
Powder Cocaine	2.3%	2.7%	2.2%	3.4%	1.94%
Crack Cocaine	1.2%	1.4%	1.0%	3.41%	1.9%
LSD	0.7%	1.0%	0.4%	1.4%	0.5%
Heroin	0.5%	0.6%	0.4%	1.4%	0.3%

Source: By the author. Based on Johnston et al. 2003b:Table 4-7.

Three main findings stand out: First, you can see how college students maintain the patterns of drug use that they established in high school: Alcohol is the most commonly used drug, followed by nicotine and marijuana. The second pattern is one that shows up regularly in drug studies: Men use more illegal drugs than do women. Finally, note how college students avoid some drugs.

Objective Conditions Are Not Enough

These patterns are part of the objective conditions of drug use. They serve as a background factor, but they are not adequate to make a social problem. As you know, we also have to have subjective concerns. And those we have. With alcohol, subjective concerns center on alcoholism, underage drinking, drunk driving, and health consequences. Let's examine these concerns.

THE RECREATIONAL MOOD ELEVATORS

Patterns of Alcohol Consumption

Alcohol is America's first choice when it comes to drugs taken for sociability. Each year, the average American drinks 25 gallons of alcoholic beverages—about 21.7 gallons of beer, 2.0 gallons of wine, and 1.3 gallons of hard liquor (*Statistical Abstract* 2003:Table 216). The average drinker actually consumes about twice this amount, since about half—52 percent—of adult Americans do not drink alcoholic beverages. Yes, you read that right: The average drinker drinks about 50 gallons of alcohol a year. That's about a gallon a week.

Alcohol Consumption as a Social Problem

Of the approximately 100 million drinkers in the United States, about 10 million are considered **alcoholics,** people who have severe alcohol-related problems. Relatively few of them become derelicts and stand on street corners panhandling strangers. Rather, almost all—whether working or middle class—continue with their routines but have impaired social relationships. Their work and family life suffer the most.

Drunk Driving and Expectations of Gender

As noted earlier, each year about 15,000 Americans die in alcohol-related car and truck wrecks. Most of the drivers are young men, sloppy drunk. Why aren't just as many young women—or older Americans, for that matter—killed in vehicle accidents? The basic reason centers on what being a man means in our culture. Getting drunk is seen as *macho,* a way by which young men prove their budding masculinity (Snow and

TABLE 4-3 What Drugs Do Full-Time College Students Use? (In the past 30 days)			
	TOTAL	MEN	WOMEN
Alcohol	68.9%	70.2%	68.0%
Cigarettes	26.7%	30.0%	24.6%
Marijuana	19.7%	23.7%	17.2%
Amphetamines	3.0%	3.2%	2.8%
Cocaine			
Powder	1.6%	2.2%	1.2%
Crack	0.3%	0.1%	0.4%
Ecstasy (MDMA)	0.7%	0.9%	0.7%
LSD	0.2%	0.4%	0.1%
Heroin[1]	0.0%	0.0%	0.0%
DAILY USE			
Cigarettes	15.9%	16.6%	15.4%
Alcohol	5.0%	7.0%	3.7%
Marijuana	4.1%	5.7%	3.0%

[1]Certainly there are *some* college students who have used heroin in the past 30 days, but use of this drug is so rare that it does not register in this national survey of college students.
Source: By the author. Based on Johnston et al. 2003a:Tables 8-3, 8-4.

Cunningham 1985; Peele 1987). With driving after you've had "one too many" (or more than this) a symbol of male potency, the risk-taking of driving while drunk validates young men's still-developing sense of male identity.

My own experience as a member of U.S. culture confirms these ideas. I, too, had to prove my masculinity to my teenaged buddies by showing how much alcohol I could drink in an evening. Anyone who wouldn't do so would have been marked as a weenie. I still recall the approval of my friends—as well as some of the retching that followed. We live in a strange world, and somehow, sitting on a bathroom floor with your head hung over a toilet is masculine.

If getting drunk were equated with femininity, we would have a lot more young women drinking to excess. Based on my observations of high school students at drinking parties, we may be experiencing this process of cultural change at the moment. "Femininity" apparently is being redefined in more macho terms, and getting drunk is becoming more of the girl's rite of passage into womanhood. Granted that if this continues, and I expect it to, we can also anticipate an increase in the deaths of young women in car wrecks.

Health Consequences: Positive and Negative

To adequately understand any social problem, we need to know the best research results—whether or not those findings match what we want. When it comes to alcohol, we find both positive and negative consequences for health. Light-to-moderate drinking—one to two drinks a day, 5 or 6 days a week—has *positive* health consequences. Compared with people who don't drink alcohol at all, light-to-moderate drinkers have only one-third as many heart attacks (Rehm et al. 2003). Earlier studies reported on the positive effects of red wine. Although these results still hold, it turns out that it makes no difference if someone drinks red wine, white wine, beer, whiskey, or vodka. Regardless of the form it comes in, one to two drinks of alcohol a day is good for people's health.

Although the form that alcohol comes in is unimportant—for, whatever its form, alcohol apparently stimulates the production of the "good" cholesterol (HDL)—the *pattern* of drinking is important. One or two drinks a day are good for people's health, but *binge drinking* is harmful. Even though binge drinkers might average one or two drinks a day, consuming a lot of alcohol at one time increases the risk of sudden death from stroke and heart attacks (Rehm et al. 2003). Because binge drinking is especially prevalent on college campuses, this is a very significant statistic to the readers of this text.

Heavy drinking is also harmful. Heavy drinkers are more likely to have heart attacks and problems with their endocrine, metabolic, immune, and reproductive systems. They are more likely to come down with diabetes, epilepsy, and depression. They also run a higher risk of developing cancer of the tongue, mouth, liver, lungs, esophagus, larynx, stomach, colon, and rectum. For women, heavy drinking increases the risk of breast cancer (*Seventh Special Report* 1990; Rehm et al. 2003).

The Bill for Alcohol Abuse

Alcohol abuse is so extensive that each year a quarter of a million Americans are treated for this problem at substance abuse centers (*Statistical Abstract* 2003:Table 200). The bill for their treatment runs several billion dollars a year, which everyone, including abstainers, must pay. If we consider lost jobs, reduced productivity, alcohol-related crime, and social welfare, the total may run as high as $100 billion a year. This makes alcohol the most expensive of all drug abuse problems. Then, too, alcohol abuse brings costs that we can't measure in dollars—the spouse and family abuse, disturbed children, and shattered marriages.

Pregnancy and Childbirth

Embedded in this social problem is another problem, the use of drugs by pregnant women. Like other drugs, alcohol enters the fetus' circulatory system. Unlike the mother, however, a fetus cannot metabolize alcohol. When pregnant women drink, the alcohol becomes concentrated in the fetus' blood, raising its blood alcohol level to about *ten times* that of the mother's.

Fetal Alcohol Syndrome

The consequences of this abuse are anything but pleasant. Each year about 5,000 U.S. children of drinking mothers are born with a cluster of problems called **fetal alcohol syndrome.** These children are born addicted to alcohol, and for a week to six months they suffer painful withdrawal: They are irritable, their hearts beat irregularly, and some go into convulsions. But worse is the damage to their brains, which can impair their learning, memory, speech, and coordination. As you would expect, fetal alcohol syndrome is concentrated among groups that have higher rates of alcoholism. Apparently the hardest hit are Native Americans, whose rate of fetal alcohol syndrome is two to three times the national average ("Congress" 1994; Carroll 2000).

The Significance of How People Learn to Drink

Simply drinking alcohol, of course, does not lead to alcohol-related problems. Rather, social researchers have found that *how* one learns to drink is significant. Studies of groups that have low rates of alcoholism, such as Spaniards, Italians, Orthodox Jews, Greeks, Chinese, and Lebanese, indicate five keys to low-problem drinking (Hanson 1995).

- Drinking alcohol is a regular part of life.
- Alcohol is viewed as neutral—it is neither a poison nor a magical elixir.
- Drinking is not viewed as a sign of adulthood or virility.
- There is no tolerance for abusive drinking.
- Learning to drink starts early, and in the home. Parents provide role models of moderate (light, social, nonabusive) drinking.

Let's consider the opposite conditions, which lead to alcohol problems.

- Drinking alcohol is something special.
- Alcohol is either a horrible, sinful thing, or else a magical substance that has the capacity to make the world more pleasant.
- Drinking is a sign of being an adult.
- Getting drunk is approved.
- Sneaky drinking outside the home is how one learns to drink.

After Prohibition ended, Americans celebrated their freedom to again drink openly. This particular celebration—an international beer drinking contest—took place in Los Angeles. To have the contestants lie on their backs while participating may have proved convenient— after a winner was declared, it is likely that some contestants remained in this position.

Sound familiar? These five characteristics are an apt description of many adolescent subcultures.

Biological Causes

Some research supports a biological basis for alcoholism. Sons of alcoholic fathers run a higher risk than others of becoming alcoholics (Buck 1998), and twins share more drinking patterns than do nontwins (Prescott 2004). But we cannot rule out *social* reasons for these findings. Sons of alcoholic fathers, for example, may be following in the footsteps of alcoholic role models. As for twins, growing up in such similar environments is likely to produce all sorts of similar behaviors. It is possible, though, that biology makes a difference in how people's cells react to alcohol, predisposing some people to alcohol abuse. The evidence that links alcoholism to genes, however, is mixed, with findings contradicting one another.

Nicotine

Nicotine is the second most popular recreational drug in the United States. The Surgeon General has identified smoking as "the chief, single, avoidable cause of death in our society, and the most important health issue of our time" (Smith 1986). Tobacco is so harmful that "a nonsmoker has a better chance of reaching the age of 75 than a smoker has of reaching the age of 65" (Goode 1989)! The dollar cost is also high, about $28 billion a year in health care and another $43 billion in lost productivity. Yet the tobacco industry spends $10 billion a year to promote their products, mostly to convince young people that smoking is sexy and a fast road to growing up (American Lung 2003). Tobacco companies still target youth, but perhaps none so brazenly as the new company featured in the Global Glimpse box below.

These objective conditions of the extent of smoking and the amounts being spent to promote smoking among youth provoked extensive subjective concerns. These concerns gave birth to a strident, powerful antismoking campaign. Among the results are no-smoking sections in restaurants and a ban on smoking in offices, on domestic flights, and in government buildings. Despite an outcry, some states have even banned smok-

A Global Glimpse

TARGETING COLLEGE STUDENTS: FIRST DEATH, THEN SHAG

In the 1990s, the Enlightened Tobacco Company of England marketed a cigarette called Death. Death was sold in a black package emblazoned with a white skull-and-crossbones. This death logo was also stamped near the filter of each cigarette. Ads for Death were bordered in black, resembling funeral announcements.

The company said that people have the right to smoke—but they should be informed as to what they are doing to their bodies. Openly advertising death, they said, is better than half-truths, deceptions, and weaselly health warnings. In contrast, Americans know that the Surgeon General's warning, which appears on each package of cigarettes, cannot be true. After all, the happy, carefree young people who are smoking cigarettes in those thousands of ads wouldn't be happy and smiling if the product really were lethal.

Death cigarettes died, though. Perhaps confronting smokers with death isn't good for business after all.

The newest tobacco company in Great Britain is Shag. The company's slogan: "Have you had one lately?" To promote its brand, Shag gives out free samples of cigarettes to college students, along with free Shag brand condoms (Murray 2004).

Death and Shag—in a twisted way, sort of at opposite ends of one another. But no matter how you look at it, smoking kills. Death from smoking isn't merciful—like those who meet their end in quick, violent car crashes. Nicotine deaths are agonizing and slow—like those of people who are injured in car wrecks, who feel intense pain, and then linger with that pain for months before passing on.

ing in bars. Table 4-4 shows how effective this campaign has been. As you can see, at the height of addiction, *most* men smoked, as did one of three women. The decline has been precipitous, to one of four men and one of five women. Unfortunately, the lowest rate of smoking—among those age 65 and over—does not represent results from the antismoking campaign. Rather, by this age so many smokers have died that there aren't many smokers left alive to show up in a survey.

Figure 4-2 on page 106 also depicts the decrease in smoking since its height of popularity in the 1960s. In a strange twist of logic, the tobacco industry claims credit for this decline. They say it is evidence of their efforts "to deter youths from smoking" ("Frequent Tobacco Use" 1992)! For another view, see the Issues in Social Problems box on targeting kids and minorities on page 108.

The "Brown Plague"

Now that Americans are smoking less, the tobacco companies have turned to the Least Industrialized Nations to pursue easier victims and more profits. Because so many men in these countries already smoke, the companies have launched advertising campaigns that target women (Preidt 2003b). The global death toll of what is being called this century's *brown plague* is astonishing—about 5 million lives are lost a year. Most of the victims live in the Least Industrialized Nations (Preidt 2003a).

Health Costs and Legal Awards

Because the costs of caring for U.S. victims falls largely on the government in the form of higher Medicaid bills, in the 1990s the states sued the tobacco companies. In return for dropping their lawsuits, the states were awarded $209 billion from the cigarette manufacturers. This huge settlement, to be paid over 25 years, did not put a single cigarette company out of business. To cover their costs, cigarette manufacturers merely raised prices for their addicted smokers. The states are spending only about half of their award on health care. They are diverting the other half to a variety of projects, from fixing sidewalks to balancing state budgets ("GAO Delineates . . ." 2003).

TABLE 4-4 Cigarette Smoking by Sex and Age

	1965	1975	1985	1995	2001
BY SEX					
Male	52%	43%	33%	27%	25%
Female	34%	32%	28%	23%	21%
BY SEX AND AGE					
MALES					
18–24 years	54%	42%	28%	28%	30%
25–34 years	61%	51%	38%	31%	27%
35–44 years	58%	51%	38%	33%	27%
45–64 years	52%	43%	33%	27%	26%
65 and over	29%	25%	20%	14%	12%
FEMALES					
18–24 years	38%	34%	30%	22%	23%
25–34 years	44%	39%	32%	29%	23%
35–44 years	44%	40%	32%	27%	26%
45–64 years	32%	33%	30%	24%	21%
65 and over	10%	12%	14%	12%	9%

Source: By the author. Based on *Statistical Abstract* 1994:Table 212; 1997:Table 221; 1998:Table 238; 2003:Table 203.

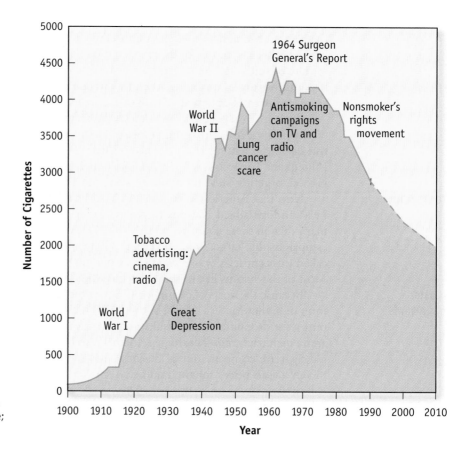

FIGURE 4-2   *Number of Cigarettes That Americans Age 18 and Older Smoke Each Year*

Source: By the author. Based on Economic Research Service, U.S. Department of Agriculture; projection by the author.

Marijuana

Trends in Smoking Marijuana

The third most popular recreational drug in the United States is marijuana. During the 1960s, marijuana was an underground drug smoked furtively by a few adventurous souls. By the 1970s, it was smoked by millions. Based on personal experience, I can add that this drug became so popular and semi- "out in the open" at this time that many professors smoked marijuana with their students. By 1979, one of three Americans (36 percent) age 18 to 25 smoked marijuana at least once a month (*Statistical Abstract* 1998:Table 237). The popularity of marijuana has dropped sharply since then, and today 16 percent of Americans of this age smoke marijuana this often (*Statistical Abstract* 2003:Table 201).

Schizoid Legal Reactions

The states' reaction to marijuana's surge in popularity during the 1960s and 1970s was schizophrenic. Alaska legalized possession of marijuana for personal consumption, but Nevada made the possession of even a single joint punishable by up to six years in prison (Goode 1989:30). Alaskans decided they had erred and revoked their law. So did Nevada, which swung in the other direction. In 2002, Nevada made the possession of up to one ounce of marijuana punishable by only fines, with no jail time allowed.

Although marijuana has declined in overall usage, it remains a popular drug. As I mentioned earlier, about 13 million Americans smoke marijuana. Figure 4-3 summarizes marijuana use among high school and college students. You can see that marijuana use peaks during the senior year in high school; during the college years, it holds fairly constant, with only a slight decline.

Health Implications: Positive or Negative

How does marijuana affect its users' health? Many assertions have been made—that marijuana impairs the body's immune system, reduces the male sex hormone

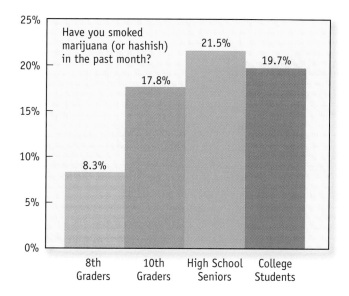

Have you smoked marijuana (or hashish) in the past month?

	8th Graders	10th Graders	High School Seniors	College Students
	8.3%	17.8%	21.5%	19.7%

FIGURE 4-3 *Who Smokes Marijuana?*

Source: By the author. Based on Johnston et al. 2003a:Table 8-4; 2003b:Table 4–7.

Medical Uses of Marijuana

The Amotivational Syndrome

Contrasting Reactions

testosterone, lowers fertility, damages chromosomes, and causes brain damage. Although widely heralded in the mass media when such studies first appeared, follow-up studies have not substantiated these findings. It is possible that, like cigarettes, heavy usage of marijuana can damage the lungs. At this point, though, unlike with alcohol and nicotine, we have no firm basis to conclude that marijuana either harms or helps people's health.

Smoking marijuana, however, impairs motor coordination, making it unsafe to smoke and run machinery, drive a vehicle, or fly a plane. People who are high on marijuana have less consciousness of external stimuli, such as red lights or stop signs (Carroll 2000). THC, the primary psychoactive agent in marijuana, remains in the body several days after smoking, although its lingering effects are not perceptible to the smoker. In one study, pilots who were tested 24 hours after they had smoked marijuana, when they no longer felt "high," showed deterioration in performing simulated landing maneuvers. Perhaps most telling is this finding: In a posthumous sample of 400 male drivers in California who had been killed in auto accidents, 37 percent had THC in their blood (Goode 1989:147). Obviously, it is not prudent to ride or to fly with someone who has smoked marijuana.

Research findings also show positive aspects of marijuana, such as relieving glaucoma and migraine headaches. Marijuana also helps to reduce the side effects of nausea and vomiting in patients who are undergoing chemotherapy. Marijuana also relieves "asthma, epilepsy, muscle spasticity, anxiety, depression, pain, reduced appetite, and withdrawal from alcohol and narcotics" (Carroll 2003). To uncover marijuana's positive and negative effects, we need further research, but in our conservative political climate such research is discouraged because of marijuana's social reputation.

On the negative side, marijuana is associated with an **amotivational syndrome.** People who smoke marijuana extensively may become lethargic, lose their concentration, and drift away from long-range plans. Researchers have found that marijuana smokers tend to receive poorer grades and are more likely to drop out of high school (Kleinman et al. 1987). That this is not just a correlation and that marijuana is the cause, however, has not been proven. The evidence for an amotivational syndrome consists mainly of impressions and anecdotes: "Before she smoked grass, Shirley had so many plans, but look at her now." Research on rhesus monkeys is intriguing: Monkeys that smoke are less motivated than nonsmoking monkeys to work for bananas. When researchers stop giving the monkeys marijuana, their motivation returns to normal after about nine months (Slikker 1992). Obviously, we need some solid research on humans.

As we have seen in other instances, we must approach "facts" with caution, for a look below the surface often yields a different view. A deeper look at the amotivational syndrome shows that, compared with their classmates, heavy marijuana smokers are more likely to come from broken homes, to drink more alcohol, to commit more delinquent acts, and to be involved in a subculture that places less value on academic achievement. In other words, it is difficult to separate cause and effect. Marijuana can be just "one element in a large and complex picture of interrelated problems and behaviors" (Kleinman et al. 1987; White 1991).

Marijuana certainly is an excellent example of the subjective nature of social problems. Until 1937, when the Marijuana Tax Act was passed, marijuana was an ingredient

Issues in Social Problems

TARGETING KIDS AND MINORITIES

Let's listen in on a conversation between Kent Reynolds, the CEO of a major tobacco company, and John Winston, director of sales.

"John, I want to show you something. My daughter brought this social problems text home from college. Look at this table on page 105."

"Yeah, that confirms our own studies. Our customer base is eroding. Too many people are believing those lies the (expletive deleted) antismokers are telling—cancer and all that. We've got to get the kids started earlier."

"What've you got in mind?"

"Well, if we could get the kids hooked—oops, I mean started . . . I was thinking about adding some flavor they like."

"Good idea. They've already added cherry to Skoal Long Cut. That's getting to a lot of kids. And they've been smart about it—keeping the nicotine down so the kids gradually get into it. Then they move on to Copenhagen after they're hooked—I mean, used to the taste. No one's done chocolate yet. That might work."

"Yeah. Kids love chocolate. If you okay it, we can test-market Chocolate Smokeless Tobacco. And, of course, chocolate-flavored cigarettes. And we might try butterscotch and raspberry. We'll make 'em all low-nicotine and low-tar."

"What about the minorities?"

"We're already loading *Ebony* with ads. My research department reported that one of eight pages of *Ebony*'s color ads go to cigarettes."

"Great. How about sponsoring cultural events, like a jazz festival?"

"Kool's already got that covered."

"Come to think of it, Parliament's already got that World Beat Concert Series, too."

"Yeah, but we're underwriting the Harlem Week Festival in New York City."

"And don't forget all the money we're using to buy—I mean, contribute—to the National Black Caucus of State Legislatures."

"And the United Negro College Fund and the National Urban League are already in our budget."

"Sometimes I wonder if all this money is paying off."

"Don't worry about that! You never see any of that antismoking propaganda in *Ebony*—and that's no coincidence."

"I've never even seen a copy. But I depend on you to know these things, John."

"Well, the real payoff is that African-American men are smoking more than the whites."

"What about the women?"

"Sorry. Despite everything we've done, they've got the lowest rate of smoking."

"We've got to do better, John"

"We will."

"But we've got to be careful. They're starting to blame us for blacks having higher rates of lung cancer and heart disease and stuff like that!"

"It's their soul food, Kent."

"Do you think we could target Latinos?"

"Marlboro's already got that pretty well covered. Remember those rodeos for Mexican Americans they sponsor in California?"

"That's right."

"And we're already buying off—I mean, contributing—all that money to the Hispanic Congressional Caucus and the National Association of Hispanic Journalists."

"How about the Native Americans, then? Maybe we're missing them."

"I think you've got something there. And the Chinese Americans, too. And then there's the Abyssinian Americans and the . . ."

in about thirty medical products (Carroll 2000). Physicians also prescribed marijuana as a medicine for a variety of conditions. No longer can they do so. Marijuana possession used to be legal for anyone, but now it is subject to some type of penalty in every state. At one point in our history, an Alabama judge even sentenced a man *to death* for selling marijuana (*New York Times* 1991). Reactions range from seeing marijuana as a threat to society to viewing it as a treatment for medical problems. Millions of users

Although the popularity of marijuana has declined, it remains a major drug of choice of young Americans. Because of legal bans on research, we know little of the health consequences of marijuana use, either positive or negative.

"But the perfect answer would be to bypass all that race and gender stuff and just target 3-year-olds of every background."

"I'll get to work on that right away. I know it can be done. Ninety percent of six-year-olds used to be able to match Joe Camel with Camel cigarettes. Too bad they can't use Joe any more." (laughs)

"Maybe we can make a kid's nicotine gum—just a little nicotine in the spearmint."

"Now you're talking."

"Yeah. And how about cute cutouts of our cigarette packs for the preschools—and maybe coloring books, too!"

"We can give them free colors in a flip-top box that looks exactly like our cigarette packs."

"Great idea! We can call 'm Kiddie Packs. Maybe we can wrap the colors in white paper."

"Too bad we can't include a cigarette lighter—but they're too young to handle fire."

That night both Kent and John enjoy peaceful sleep, dreaming of chocolate-flavored cigarettes, and butterscotch, and raspberry, and . . . .

Based on Johnson 1992; Freedman 1994; Pollay 1997; *Statistical Abstract* 2003:Table 203.

pay thousands of illegal distributors so they can smoke marijuana, and thousands of enforcement agents are collecting pay to oppose it.

The Social History of Cocaine

Cocaine, a fourth drug that is used for recreational purposes, helps us understand how a drug that is socially respectable can be transformed into a social problem. Lavishly praised by physicians in the late 1800s, cocaine was used throughout the United States, especially in patent medicines. Famous people, such as Sigmund Freud and Sir

Do you recognize this person? Many Americans run afoul of U.S. drug laws. This mug shot, taken by the sheriff's department of Kalamazoo, Michigan, in 1979, is of Tim Allen, who served two years in prison for dealing cocaine. Allen later became famous as the star and producer of the hit television program, Home Improvement.

Arthur Conan Doyle, the creator of Sherlock Holmes, swore that cocaine got their creative juices going. Yet by the end of the first decade of the twentieth century, cocaine had been transformed from a medicine and "pick-me-up" into a dangerous drug—much as Dr. Jekyll became Mr. Hyde (a story, by the way, that was written in three days by Robert Louis Stevenson while he was high on cocaine [Ashley 1975]). What caused this transformation?

We should note first that cocaine was never without controversy (Ashley 1975). When the Spaniards invaded Peru in the 1500s, they conquered a people who chewed coca leaves. The Spaniards attributed the drug's effects to the devil and rejected the use of cocaine as evil. During the 1800s, a turnaround occurred when Angelo Mariana, a French chemist, introduced a wine that contained the coca leaf extract. The Pope appreciated this wine and presented Mariana with a medal for his accomplishment (Ray and Ksir 2003). As cocaine became associated with respectable people, it became so popular that hundreds of thousands of Americans sipped cocaine as a "pick-me-up," for it had become an ingredient in Coca-Cola, a drink that took its name from the coca leaf.

Then came the drug's downfall. In the late 1800s, reporters began to link cocaine with the poor and with criminals—especially gunmen—whom they depicted as taking cocaine to get up their nerve to commit robberies (Ashley 1975). These news stories led to a public outcry, and in 1903 the Coca-Cola Company found it prudent to eliminate cocaine from its drink. Even today, however, Coca-Cola contains an extract from the coca leaf (Miller 1994). In the early 1900s, it was still legal to use cocaine in products, but it had to be listed as an ingredient. Then in 1914, the Harrison Act classified cocaine as a narcotic (an error, because cocaine is a stimulant) and specified penalties for selling this drug.

The Harrison Act paved the way to a black market in cocaine, one that still exists almost a hundred years after the passage of this law. This black market delivers cocaine effectively, for about 12 percent of Americans age 12 and over—about 30 million people—have used cocaine (*Statistical Abstract* 2003:Table 201). As we saw in Tables 4-2 and 4-3, in just the past month about 3 percent of all U.S. high school seniors and 2 percent of college students used cocaine in the form of powder or crack. Though snorting is the preferred method of use, smoking cocaine base, called *freebasing,* is also popular.

Popular and Medical Uses

Cocaine has two distinct uses, one medical and one popular. Surgeons apply cocaine as a local anesthetic and as a vasoconstrictor (a substance that reduces blood flow to the area to which it is applied). Cocaine is the medical profession's anesthetic of choice for surgery involving the nose, throat, larynx, and lower respiratory passages. The most common use of cocaine, however, is to obtain a high—feelings of well-being, optimism, confidence, competence, and energy. Cocaine also has a reputation as an aphrodisiac, for it is thought to create or heighten sexual desires, to increase sexual endurance, and to cure frigidity and impotence (Inciardi 1986:78–79).

Risks of Cocaine Use

Cocaine's high is intense. Those who become addicted to it report a craving so strong that "they will give up many of the things they value—money, possessions, relationships, jobs, and careers—in order to continue taking the drug" (Goode 1989:198–199). In the form of cocaine called *crack,* the pleasure is so intense it is akin to orgasm. The high, which lasts from 5 to 12 minutes, is followed by a "crash" that leaves its users irritable, depressed, nervous, or paranoid. Although crack is inexpensive, because its effects are short-lived it is costly to remain high. The desire for the intense pleasure is so great that some women rent their bodies for crack, and a new form of prostitute, the "crack whore," has emerged.

Cocaine has other dysfunctions. Perhaps the most dramatic are heart attacks, brain damage, and death (Kozel 1995, 1996; Julien 2001). The dysfunction that captures headlines and stimulates subjective concerns, though, is "crack babies." As with alcohol and nicotine, if a pregnant woman uses cocaine it enters the fetus' system. There, its concentration can equal or exceed that of the mother's. The cocaine can interfere with the normal development of the heart, brain, and other organs. It can also cause the brain to bleed (Julien 2001). In the attempt to prevent "crack babies," some authorities have developed the controversial social policy discussed in the Thinking Critically about Social Problems box.

Crack Cocaine   Crack can be produced easily in a home kitchen. With huge profits at stake, illegal drug entrepreneurs ("corner crack dealers") fight for territory ("turf") and customers. As a result, violence sometimes surrounds crack—coming from those who will do anything to get the drug and from those who will do anything to make money from the drug.

Following on the heels of intense publicity over violence associated with crack, in 1986 the U.S. Congress made crack dealing a federal offense and began giving higher penalties for crack than for powder cocaine. Because powder cocaine is more likely to be used by whites and crack by African Americans (Lewis 1996; Riley 1998), blacks charged racial discrimination. After eight years of prison sentences that were handed down primarily to African-American users, in *U.S. v. Ricky Davis* (1994) the U.S. District Court in Georgia declared that crack and cocaine are one and the same drug, and sentences imposed for the use of crack can be no heavier than those imposed for the use of powder cocaine.

Thinking Critically about Social Problems
ON PREGNANCY, DRUGS, AND JAIL

Consider the following court cases.

A pregnant woman in Washington, D.C., was charged with check forgery. The usual sentence for first-time offenders is probation. When the woman tested positive for cocaine, the judge sentenced her to prison, saying; "I'm going to keep her locked up until the baby's born."

A California woman who had taken street drugs was charged with child abuse after she delivered a brain-damaged baby who died soon after birth.

An Illinois woman was charged with manslaughter when her two-day-old infant died due to her cocaine use during pregnancy.

In Florida, a woman was convicted of two counts of delivering drugs to a minor. The prosecution alleged that the woman had passed cocaine to her newborn child through the umbilical cord after the baby was delivered but before the cord was cut.

FOR YOUR CONSIDERATION

Should judges jail a pregnant woman because she uses drugs such as cocaine that can harm her fetus? If so, because alcohol and nicotine can harm a fetus, should judges be permitted to jail pregnant women who smoke cigarettes or drink alcohol? If not, what's the difference?

Based on Broff 1989; Humphries et al. 1992; Pagelow 1992.

From this brief social history of cocaine, we can see that several principles are involved in determining a drug's social reputation:

Principles Underlying a Drug's Social Reputation

1. A drug's reputation is not based on objective conditions. It does not, for instance, derive from tests that reveal that drug A causes serious problems, drug B does not, and therefore drug A is banned and drug B permitted. If such a scientific approach characterized a drug's social history, alcohol would be banned, and marijuana would be available in grocery stores (Ashley 1975).
2. Like humans, drugs gain their reputation through the people and events with which they are associated.
3. Drugs that are associated with people or events generally considered respectable are likely to be defined as good and desirable; drugs associated with people or events generally considered disreputable are likely to be defined as bad and undesirable.
4. The reputation or social acceptability of drugs is not fixed but is subject to change.

THE HALLUCINOGENS

LSD

Perhaps the most famous of the hallucinogens is LSD (lysergic acid diethylamide). This drug was first synthesized by the Swiss chemist Albert Hoffman in 1938. Its psychoactive property was not discovered until 1943, when Hoffman accidentally inhaled a minute dose. He reported what happened to him:

> Last Friday, April 16, 1943, I was forced to stop my work in the laboratory in the middle of the afternoon and to go home, as I was seized by a peculiar restlessness associated with a sensation of mild dizziness. Having reached home, I lay down and sank in a kind of drunkenness which was not unpleasant and which was characterized by extreme activity of imagination. As I lay in a dazed condition with my eyes closed (I experienced daylight as disagreeably bright) there surged upon me an uninterrupted stream of fantastic images of extraordinary plasticity and vividness and accompanied by an intense, kaleidoscope-like play of colors. This condition gradually passed off after about two hours. (Hoffman 1968:184–185)

At first, LSD was thought to produce psychoses, and people avoided it. Then, in 1960, Harvard professor Timothy Leary began experimenting with LSD. Leary was fired for violating experimental guidelines and became a guru of the 1960s youth counterculture. He preached a message about how great LSD was, saying that everyone should experience changed consciousness and become nonconformist. Leary's slogan, "turn on, tune in, and drop out," struck a responsive chord with the youth of the time, and LSD use spread. This tasteless, odorless substance, an ounce of which contains 300,000 doses, reached its height of media attention in about 1967 and its peak of usage in about 1979 (Goode 1989:178–179). As we saw on Table 4-2 (page 100), about three-fourths of a percent of all high school seniors used LSD within the past month. Although this is a small percent, it totals about 20,000 high school seniors. The 0.2 percent of college students who used LSD in the past month equals about 30,000 students (*Statistical Abstract* 2003:Tables 246, 282).

Peyote and Mescaline

The use of peyote is an old custom on this continent, as Native Americans were using this cactus when Cortez arrived in the 1500s. It is now used legally in the United States only by members of the Native American church for religious purposes (Schaefer 2004). About twenty states forbid any use of peyote (Carroll 2000). Mescaline, which was synthesized from peyote in 1919, produces similar visual effects. Both peyote and mescaline have had famous proponents: Havelock Ellis (1897, 1902) was enthusiastic about peyote, and Aldous Huxley (1954) sang the praises of mescaline. In the 1960s and 1970s, anthropologist Carlos Castaneda (1968, 1971, 1974) popularized the use of peyote among a cultlike following. The drug always has a die-hard group of users, with occasional recruits.

Although some drugs are rejected, others become socially acceptable and are adapted into a group's culture. Mescaline (from peyote buttons) and psilocybin (from mushrooms) are a part of the culture of some Native-American Mexicans. Shown here is a huichol *(yarn painting), a standard art form among these groups.* Huicholes *reflect visions induced by these drugs.*

Psilocybin

The magic mushrooms of Mexico (*Psilocybe mexicana*) were also being used when Cortez arrived on these shores. Because they were associated with pagan rituals, Cortez launched a campaign against the mushrooms (as he had against peyote), driving their use underground. Not until the 1930s was it discovered that natives of southern Mexico were still using them. Their active ingredient is psilocybin, which was isolated by Albert Hoffman in 1958 and later synthesized. As with peyote, reports about this drug often contain a spiritual or religious emphasis (Ray and Ksir 2003).

PCP

PCP (phencyclidine hydrochloride), called *angel dust*, was synthesized in 1957 by Parke-Davis and sold as a painkiller. As people found out, it also produced hallucinations. Because it requires a minimum of equipment, PCP is often manufactured in home laboratories. Affecting the central nervous system, PCP makes it difficult to speak and usually brings on altered body image and feelings of unreality. Some users report euphoria and feelings of power, loneliness, or isolation; others experience numbness and feelings of dying (which is why PCP is also called "embalming fluid"). Higher dosages may result in loss of inhibition, disorientation, rage, convulsions, or coma (Crider 1986; Ray and Ksir 2003).

Ecstasy (MDMA, methylenedioxyamphetamine), a popular party drug, gives an euphoric rush like cocaine combined with some of the mind-expanding effects of the psychedelics. The 2.4 percent of high school seniors who have used Ecstasy in the past month come to about 67,000 students. Users report that Ecstasy relaxes them, increases empathy and feelings of intimacy, and enhances sensual experiences, such as making touching more pleasurable. Side effects for some users are mental confusion and anxiety. The main concern about this drug, though, is that it may be acting as a toxic substance and causing irreversible brain damage (Carroll 2000).

THE AMPHETAMINES AND BARBITURATES

The Amphetamines

The amphetamines—Benzedrine, Dexedrine, Methedrine, Desoxyn, Biphetamine, and Desamyl—go by such street names as "uppers," "pep pills," "bennies," "dexies," "speed," "meth," "crystal," and "ice" (Carroll 2000). Discovered in 1887, Benzedrine became popular in the 1920s in over-the-counter inhalers intended to dilate the bronchial tubes. Later Benzedrine was available by prescription in tablet form for hyperkinesis and, in 1939, as an appetite suppressant. During World War II, amphetamine was used to help soldiers stay awake. Also at this time, people began to soak the amphetamine from Benzedrine inhalers, and amphetamine abuse began. In the 1960s, "speed" (methamphetamine dissolved in liquid) began to be used by "speed freaks," who injected the drug, sometimes every two or three hours, for "runs" of three or four days. Each injection of this kind produces a "rush" or "flash," a sudden feeling of intense pleasure, followed by moderate feelings of euphoria.

Some users hallucinate, while others develop feelings of paranoia, or become hostile and aggressive—symptoms that have been called the *amphetamine psychosis* (Ray and Ksir 2003). Heavy amphetamine use is sometimes accompanied by behavioral fixations—in which activities are repeated over and over, such as counting the corn flakes in a box of cereal. Amphetamine withdrawal may bring outbursts of aggression, feelings of terror, and thoughts of suicide or homicide (Carroll 2000; Julien 2001).

The Barbiturates

In 1862, Dr. A. Bayer of Munich, Germany (the Bayer of aspirin fame), successfully combined urea with malonic acid and made a new compound, barbituric acid, from which over 2,500 derivations have been synthesized. Of these, phenobarbital (Luminal), amobarbital (Amytal), pentobarbital (Nembutal), and secobarbital (Seconal) are the best known. Medically, the barbiturates are used as an anesthetic and to treat anxiety, insomnia, and epilepsy. Used for nonmedical purposes, they provide an experience similar to alcohol. Regular barbiturate use leads to physical dependence. Withdrawal causes nausea, anxiety, sweating, dizziness, trembling, muscular twitching, and sometimes convulsions, coma, and death. Because the risk of death is higher for those who stop "cold turkey" (abruptly), physicians usually substitute a long-lasting barbiturate and then slowly withdraw it (Ray and Ksir 2003).

THE NARCOTICS

The Illegal Flower

Of the many flowers admired by Americans, one flower has a unique reputation. In 1901 it became illegal to import this flower, and in 1942 Americans could not even grow it without a license from the Secretary of the Treasury. This flower is so loathed by officials that in 1956 a federal law went into effect that (except for first convictions for possession) prohibited judges from suspending sentences, giving probation, or granting parole for flower-related offenses. This law also made execution possible for someone who sells derivatives of this flower to a person under age 18 (Ray and Ksir 2003).

What flower is this? It is the opium poppy. The derivative so feared and hated by some (and desired by others) is heroin. Figure 4-4 illustrates the process by which opium yields heroin.

Challenging Traditional Views: How Addictive Is Heroin?

The common view is that heroin is so addictive and the withdrawal pains so severe that addicts will do anything to avoid withdrawal. Note how the writer William Burroughs (1975:135) described his own addiction:

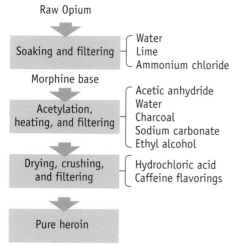

Raw Opium

↓

Soaking and filtering — Water
Lime
Ammonium chloride

Morphine base

↓

Acetylation,
heating, and filtering — Acetic anhydride
Water
Charcoal
Sodium carbonate
Ethyl alcohol

↓

Drying, crushing,
and filtering — Hydrochloric acid
Caffeine flavorings

↓

Pure heroin

FIGURE 4-4 *How Opium Is Converted into Heroin*

Source: By the author, based on *The Heroin Trail*, 1974, and "Opium Poppy Cultivation . . ." 2001.

Junk (heroin) yields a basic formula of . . . total need. . . . Beyond a certain frequency need knows absolutely no limit or control. In the words of total need: "Wouldn't you?" Yes you would. You would lie, cheat, inform on your friends, steal, do *anything* to satisfy total need. Because you would be in a state of total sickness, total possession, and not in a position to act in any other way. . . . A rabid dog can't choose but bite.

This is the conventional view of heroin addiction. When a team of sociologists headed by Bruce Johnson (1985) explored heroin addiction, however, they found something different. These researchers rented a storefront in a neighborhood in Harlem that had "the highest number of street-level heroin abusers in the country." They also rented another storefront in a similar area. The two neighborhoods were so well known for heroin dealing that they drew customers from around the region. To build repeat business, some dealers even used brand names: Tragic Magic, Black Death, and Dynamite. For two years, a research staff of former heroin users built rapport with 201 current users. Collecting day-to-day reports from these addicts, the researchers found that many heroin users are *not* physically addicted; for a period of time they use heroin once or twice a day, and then—without suffering withdrawal symptoms—they go for several days without the drug.

Use of heroin in Vietnam also supports these findings. About 14 percent of U.S. soldiers used heroin, and its potency was far stronger than any available back home. After the soldiers left the stress of the war and were reintegrated with family, friends, and work, the vast majority ceased using the drug. They had few, if any, noticeable physical problems. As the Assistant Secretary of Defense for Health and Environment said:

As functionalists stress, whenever laws are passed against a drug that is in high demand, a symbiotic black market springs up to meet that demand. Although it is illegal, cocaine is in high demand; the intricate black market that serves the demand stretches across continents. Shown here are 2,400 pounds of cocaine that were shipped from Colombia to the United States. The cocaine was seized in Baltimore, Maryland. The armed guard is a member of the Federal Drug Enforcement Agency.

Everything that I learned in medical school—that anyone who ever tried heroin was instantly, totally, and perpetually hooked—failed to prepare me for dealing with this situation. (Peele 1987:211)

Reconciling the Evidence

How can we reconcile such contradictory conclusions? Certainly William Burroughs' description of his own addiction to heroin (and similar reports by other users) is accurate. He did not make it up. At the same time, Johnson and his associates are also accurate. They did not make up their findings either. Other researchers have noted that some yuppies use heroin on an occasional basis (Spunt 2003), and some people use heroin at weekend parties without becoming addicted. Where does this leave us? From these mixed reports, it seems reasonable to conclude that heroin is addicting to some people, but not to others. Some people do become addicts and match the stereotypical profile. Others are able to use heroin on a recreational basis.

Both, then, may be right. With the evidence we have at this point, it would be inappropriate to side with either extreme. That is, it would not match research findings if we concluded that anyone can use heroin without getting addicted or that anyone who uses heroin gets addicted. We must await further research to find the key to this addiction.

The Dangers of Street Heroin

The primary danger of street heroin is that its users never know what their money is buying. No federal drug agency protects the consumer, and street heroin may be cut with substances that kill, or it may not be cut enough and thereby be potent enough to kill. Users may develop allergies to the quinine commonly used to cut heroin, or even to the heroin itself, and die from acute congestion and edema of the lungs. Some die so rapidly that the needle is still in their arm when they are found.

Fetal Narcotic Syndrome

As with alcohol and cocaine, pregnant women who use narcotics deliver babies that are addicted. Suffering from **fetal narcotic syndrome,** these newborns are pitiful. They have tremors, they are underweight and can't sleep right, and they vomit, sneeze, and frantically suck their tiny fists (*Drug Dependence in Pregnancy* 1979).

Do Narcotics Cause Crime?

Let's consider the questions with which we opened this section: Do the narcotics cause crime? Do they destroy people's health? And do the narcotics destroy people's incentive to work? Almost everyone knows the answer: Narcotics do cause crime, prevent people from working, and destroy health.

These assumptions seem to be supported by sociological research. Sociologists James Inciardi and Anne Pottieger (1994), who studied Miami crack users, found that the average crack user had committed 6,000 crimes in just the past three months! This astronomical number comes into somewhat better focus when we learn that 98 percent of their crimes were illegal drug sales. Similarly, sociologists Bruce Johnson, Kevin Anderson, and Eric Wish (1988), who interviewed 105 drug addicts, found that during just the past 24 hours these men had committed 46 robberies, 18 burglaries, and 41 thefts. Seventy-five percent of the $7,771 they netted went for drugs, and 25 percent for other items such as food. The average street addict commits 150 nondrug crimes a year and inflicts thousands of dollars of losses on victims (Johnson et al. 1985:185).

But here is the surprise: Narcotics are *not* the cause of these crimes. Narcotics do not make people unproductive citizens, or destroy their health. These three beliefs are myths. To see how this can be, consider physicians who become addicted to narcotics. They do *not* rob, burglarize, or prostitute themselves. Nor do they stop working. Nor does their health deteriorate more than usual (Winick 1961).

Why not? The answer is that physician addicts are able to divert narcotics from legal sources in order to obtain them for their own use. They do not have to scramble for money to purchase narcotics, and they can continue to work at their medical practice. With pure drugs cheap and readily obtainable, there is no need to prey on others. Nor do the new yuppie heroin users find a need to prey on others. They simply pay for their drug of choice from their earnings at work (Spunt 2003).

In and of themselves, then, the narcotics do not drive people to crime, make people stop working, or destroy their health. *Although such conditions are common among street addicts, they are not the consequence of narcotics.* Jerome Jaffe (1965:292), a physician who studied physician addicts, concluded

> The addict who is able to obtain an adequate supply of the drug through legitimate channels and has adequate funds, usually dresses properly, maintains his nutrition, and is able to discharge his social and occupational obligations with reasonable efficiency. He usually remains in good health, suffers little inconvenience, and is, in general, difficult to distinguish from other persons.

Crime as a Consequence of Laws, Addiction, and a Black Market

This point must be underscored. Narcotics do *not* cause the things we commonly associate with them. Rather, *the laws* that make these drugs illegal create a black market, handing over a monopoly to organized crime. The criminal underworld then commands the highest price possible, and *poor* addicts turn to crime to buy drugs. Physician addicts, in contrast, are not dependent on this black market. Yuppies, who use the black market in heroin, are able to afford the price. Both the physicians and yuppies are able to function in a comparatively normal fashion.

As we noted in the preceding chapter, making a product or service illegal will not stop it from being available. The law simply drives the transaction underground and makes a black market profitable. If tough laws are not the answer (recall the mutilation and the death penalty that once applied to tobacco use), then what is? Let's look at some alternatives.

Social Policy

Difficulties in Agreeing on Social Policy

Of all the social problems, developing adequate policies for drug use is one of the most difficult. Like abortion, this problem is surrounded by irreconcilable differences of opinion, strong emotions, prejudices, fear, and fuzzy thinking. It is also enveloped in contrasting moralities, subcultural values, and vested financial and personal interests. For just one example of the difficulty, perhaps impossibility, of any social policy being "adequate," see the Issues in Social Problems box on the next page. For another, consider this: The implications of the health findings on alcohol are that we should encourage light to moderate drinking, but discourage heavy drinking. Which of our high schools and colleges—or our churches and state governments—would promote such a policy? ("Okay, class, this is why you should drink a beer or two almost every day.")

Even trying to analyze the health consequences of drugs, poses a dilemma. As Oakley Ray (1998) put it:

> From a medical point of view *no drug is safe.* With some doses, modes of administration, and frequency of use, all drugs cause toxic effects and even death. It is equally true that at some doses, modes of administration, and frequency of use *all drugs are safe.* The concern here is whether a drug, used the way most people use it today, is physically harmful. From this position, alcohol and marijuana are relatively safe drugs the way most people use them. Nicotine, in contrast, is a very harmful drug, since the usual amount of cigarette smoking does increase the mortality rate. (Italics added.)

From a medical standpoint, then, no drug is safe and all drugs are safe.

The matter becomes even more complicated when we add the *social* dimension. That is, under what circumstances do drugs cause social harm? To answer this, a symbolic interactionist would want to know from whose point of view we are defining social harm. For example, the dispossessed of the inner city and the middle classes are bound to see things differently. Functionalists would want to know when drugs interfere with people reaching their goals or with the welfare of society—and that is difficult to determine. And conflict sociologists might want to know whether the so-called social harm were not actually a prelude to wide-scale social change.

Issues in Social Problems

JUST WHAT *CAN* YOU DO? THE LARRY MAHONEY CASE

"Larry Mahoney," said his friend, "wouldn't hurt anybody for the world." Another said that "since he was a little baby, he hasn't any meanness in him." Those are apt descriptions of this 34-year-old father from Kentucky. He is an all-around, pleasant, easygoing guy. How, then, could he have killed 24 teenagers and 3 adults?

It happened on a Saturday night in May. All Larry wanted was a good time, so he did what most of the "good old boys" of his town did: After a hard week at work at the chemical company, Larry headed for his favorite watering hole. There he met his friends, and he drank, and laughed, and drank some more. The time passed quickly, and Larry had to get home to his wife and children.

He climbed into his pickup truck and took off down the road. Things looked a little blurry, but they always did after his drinking sprees. This time, though, he didn't notice that he was going the wrong way on the interstate.

As if from nowhere, he saw a school bus headed toward him, and then he heard the sounds that he still can't shake—the loud crash of metal searing against metal, followed by piercing screams of agony as the bus with 27 passengers was engulfed in flames.

After he was charged with 27 counts of murder, Larry's friends came to his defense. Bobby Simmons, a gas station attendant, said, "It's a terrible mistake he made. But that boy ain't no murderer." Some families held bake sales and yard sales to raise money for his bail. Lillian Keef O'Banion, a widow in her eighties, put up the deed to her farm.

Chris Rogers, a farm worker, pinpointed the attitude in Carrollton, Kentucky, where Larry grew up and lived all his life, when he said, "Let's tell the truth about it. That could be you or me sitting in that jail. What he done ain't no different than what a lot of people in this town or anywhere else have done. To hear people on TV talk, you'd think Larry don't even feel bad about this. Let me tell you, he feels himself like he ought to be killed."

The national president of MADD (Mothers Against Drunk Driving), sickened at this support of Larry, said, "This was no accident. People intentionally drink, and they intentionally drive. I'm sick and tired of people sugar-coating murder."

A few miles south, on Interstate 71, where Larry Mahoney killed the 24 children and 3 adults, someone erected a white wooden cross and planted roses in the grassy median. Forty of the passengers on that church outing escaped with their lives, but they wonder why their friends had to die just because Larry Mahoney wanted a good time.

FOR YOUR CONSIDERATION

Mahoney served 10 years in the Kentucky state prison at La Grange. Do you think this was just? Instead of going to prison, do you think that he should have been fined and had his driver's license revoked? Or should he have been given the death sentence, as some prosecutors demanded? What do you think would have been appropriate?

Based on D. Johnson 1988.

The "Get-Tough" Policy

Get tough appears to be the dominant sentiment in the United States. To solve this problem, let's pass strict laws and put teeth in them. What is wrong with this visceral response? Remember the discussion at the beginning of this chapter about other societies in history? The ones that slit noses and cut off heads for smoking cigarettes or beat the soles of people's feet for drinking coffee? Even draconian measures don't work when people want drugs.

A War on Drugs

Back in the 1980s, President George Bush declared a "war on drugs." He ordered the Coast Guard, the Customs Service, the Border Patrol, the Immigration and Naturalization Service, and the Drug Enforcement Agency to stop illegal drugs from coming into the United States. The Pentagon even attempted to build a "'fence' of radar-equipped balloons" at the Mexican border (Fialka 1988). The result? Before this policy, a huge supply of drugs flowed into the United States. After this policy was put into effect, a huge supply of drugs flowed into the United States. In fact, the flow increased, so the price of heroin dropped, and its purity increased. So much for that war.

Why Can't We Just Lock Them All Up?

Some just shake their heads and say that if we can't stop the drugs from coming in, we at least can lock up the dealers and users. This is impossible: There are so many dealers and users that we don't have enough jails and prisons to lock them up. Consider these statistics: Several million Americans use cocaine each year, while other millions use heroin, hallucinogens, barbiturates, and inhalants. During just the past month, about 13 million Americans smoked marijuana. How could we possibly lock all of these people up? How many dealers does it take to supply just the marijuana smokers? If each dealer has 25 customers, there are a half million dealers.

Consider this: To build one prison cell costs about $100,000. To keep one inmate locked up for one year costs a minimum of $25,000. If we were going to lock up just the drug dealers, where would we get the money? If we put two dealers in a cell, a half million new cells would run $50 billion. It would then cost another $25 billion a year to keep those million people in prison.

I haven't even mentioned the fact that there are people waiting in line to take the place of dealers who are arrested. Get rid of one dealer, and two fight to take his or her place.

I think you get the idea.

Consider also that get-tough policies fuel black markets. They are fountains of profits for independent entrepreneurs and organized crime. We have seen the hard reality when we made drinking alcohol a criminal act. An underground network sprang up immediately to keep that drug supply going. It is no different with other drugs. When a drug is criminalized—whether alcohol, heroin, cocaine, or marijuana—people who want that drug buy it from an underground network. In the case of addictive drugs, to get their money, the poor who are addicted prey on others. The latent dysfunctions—bankrolling organized crime, more muggings, burglaries, theft, prostitution, and premature deaths—are worse than the original problem that the laws address.

Developing Reasonable Social Policy

With illegal drugs so popular and attitudes so divergent, how can we develop a reasonable social policy? As functionalists stress, we must anticipate the unintended consequences of social policy. To discourage cigarette smoking, let's suppose that we raise taxes, say, by $3 more a pack. If we did so, as intended, cigarette smoking would decline. An unintended consequence, however, would be that the crime of smuggling cigarettes from Mexico and Canada would jump. Even more serious, though, is that such a policy would have the *opposite* effect among teenagers, and more of them would start to smoke. I'm sure that you think I'm exaggerating, but this is just what happened when lawmakers in Canada raised cigarette taxes (Izumi 1997). The huge black market in cigarettes that sprang up made it easier for teenagers to obtain cigarettes.

Banning Advertising and Raising Taxes

An adequate social policy could begin by banning *all* advertising for drugs known to be harmful. Nicotine is certainly a case in point, and we can begin by banning all advertising for cigarettes and tobacco products. As it now is, when young people open magazines and newspapers, they are greeted by smiling, happy, healthy people, beckoning them to join their carefree lifestyle of pleasurable smoking.

Drug Education

An adequate social policy must also include drug education that is based on scientific studies. To build such a program, we must determine *both* the beneficial and harmful effects of drugs—and communicate those findings regardless of our biases. Our own values concerning "good" or "bad" drugs should have nothing to do with this. For example, we need scientific studies to determine the effects of marijuana. If marijuana is safer than tobacco, which appears to be the case, then, like it or not, we need to communicate that information. We cannot shy away from communicating either marijuana's good or bad effect because we have a bias for or against this drug.

Drug education must be *connected to the realities of the users*. Nonusers' ideas about morality and the risks of using drugs are not the same as those of users. For example, emphasizing violence as a consequence of PCP is ineffective if the users do not see violence as a problem. In the same way, stressing a milder consequence—that PCP produces a foggy, forgetful condition—can be effective if that is what the users experience and fear (Feldman 1985:5). To try to impose an outside reality onto users is to ensure failure.

Unintended Consequences of Drug Education

Drug education is a two-edged sword. On the one hand, students who are given information about drugs use drugs in greater moderation. On the other hand, giving them information piques their curiosity, and more students are likely to use drugs (Blum et al. 1976; Levine 1986). More drug use, but in greater moderation, is what we can expect from formal drug education programs. I stress formal, because an informal drug education program already exists—one that comes from the streets and is filled with misinformation. The alternative, no formal drug education, produces two extremes: more people not using drugs, but heavier use of drugs by others. In sum, although drug education stimulates interest in drugs, it also cuts down on their abuse. If the purpose of drug education is to decrease drug *use,* it is missing the mark; if its purpose is to decrease drug *abuse,* it is on target.

Dealing with Drug Addiction

We also need an adequate social policy to deal with drug addiction. We know that locking up addicted people fails, for upon release most of them go back to their drugs. A successful program cannot focus on addiction as though addicts live in a social vacuum. Any successful program must take into account the background factors of an addict's life. Addiction is often part of subcultural orientations and deprivations. These may include poverty, unemployment, dropping out of school, hopelessness, despair, and a bleak future. To reflect such life realities of drug abusers, we must develop multiple approaches.

People who become drug dependent have strong motivations to continue their drug use. Those addicted to nicotine have no difficulty obtaining their drug. Cigarettes are legally available and comparatively inexpensive. Tobacco crops are even subsidized by the Department of Agriculture. With the average cost of supporting a nicotine habit running about $1,000 to $1,500 a year, cigarette addicts do not mug, steal, or kill to obtain their drug. Heroin and cocaine, in contrast, are illegal, their cost considerably higher, and many users are involved in criminal activities.

Addicts as Patients

A successful drug addiction program, then, might include free or very cheap drugs. For example, heroin addicts could be prescribed heroin by physicians who would treat them as patients. As Arnold Trebach (1987:369) put it:

> The availability of prescribed heroin would mean that multitudes of addicts would be able to function as decent law-abiding citizens for the first time in years. Their health should be much improved because their drugs would be clean and measured in labeled dosages. The number of crimes they commit should drop dramatically. By implication, addicts to other narcotics, such as morphine and codeine, would also reap the same benefits. They would be eligible to receive maintenance doses of the drugs on which they are dependent. Hordes of potential crime victims would, accordingly, be denied the pleasure.

Such a policy would break the addicts' dependence on the black market, remove a major source of profit for organized crime, and eliminate the need for addicts to prey on others. If the program provided only such benefits, it would be a night-and-day improvement over the present situation, but it still would not break the social cycle on which addiction is based. To make a dent in addiction would require a three-pronged attack: counseling for personal problems, practical help in seeking and maintaining employment, and clinical services for those who want to end their addiction.

Methadone Maintenance

Methadone maintenance helps us to understand some of the problems of developing rational social policies for dealing with drug addiction. Methadone, a synthetic narcotic that is in itself addicting, was developed by the Germans during World War

II as a painkiller for wounded soldiers (Wren 1998). To help break addiction to heroin, methadone is given orally in medically supervised clinics. This transfers addiction from an illegal drug, heroin, to a legal drug, methadone.

What sense does it make to transfer someone's addiction from one narcotic to another? If we are going to supply drugs to addicts, why not simply give them the narcotic to which they already are addicted? Obviously, the answer goes back to the social reputation of drugs with which this chapter opened. The social equation is: The narcotic heroin is evil; the narcotic methadone is good.

Planning Versus Implementing

As conceived, the methadone maintenance program called for extensive support services from counseling agencies and from employers. For budgetary reasons, however, at most locations these elements were deemed inessential and were cut. Of the original plan, all that is left is its "bare-bones" function—the dispensing of methadone. This alerts us to a major danger of social policy: Politicians who fund a program may not see it in the same way as do the professionals who designed it. If politicians and bureaucrats scuttle essentials in order to cut costs, they dismantle the original program in all but name.

Basic Principles for Developing Successful Social Policy: The Example of Alcoholics Anonymous

Alcoholics Anonymous (AA) is a successful program whose principles can be applied to other drug problems. The main principle is that the program should be directed and staffed by people who have experienced the addiction themselves—and have overcome it. They know firsthand the orientations of the abusers, what they are going through, and how to talk their language on a "gut level."

Alcoholics Anonymous (AA) is a good example. Begun in 1935 in Akron, Ohio, by two alcoholics, AA is now a worldwide organization of 100,000 local groups, numbering about 2 million members in 150 countries ("AA Fact File," 2004). The essentials of Alcoholics Anonymous are summarized in what this group calls The Twelve Steps. To overcome addiction to alcohol, you must

1. Admit that you are powerless over alcohol and your life has become unmanageable.
2. Believe that a Power greater than yourself can help restore you to sanity.
3. Make a decision to turn your will and life over to God, as you understand Him.

Methadone maintenance is a controversial treatment for heroin addiction. At least, it passes for treatment. Methadone maintenance simply replaces an illegal narcotic with a legal one. "Treatment" consists of merely transferring addiction from one drug to another.

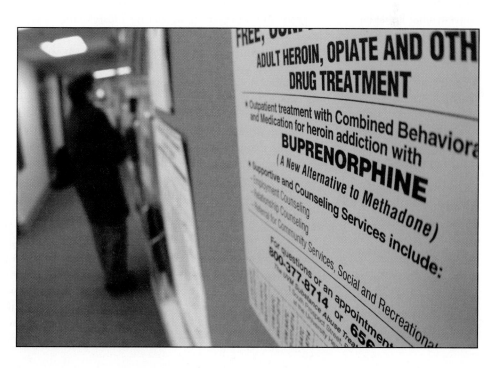

4. Make a moral inventory of yourself.
5. Admit to God, yourself, and another human being the exact nature of your wrongs.
6. Be ready to have God remove your defects of character.
7. Ask God to remove your shortcomings.
8. Make a list of all persons you have harmed and be willing to make amends.
9. Make such amends wherever possible, except where it will injure others.
10. Continue to take personal inventory and promptly admit wrongs.
11. Seek through prayer and meditation to improve your conscious contact with God, as you understand Him, praying for knowledge of His will for yourself and the power to carry it out.
12. Have a spiritual awakening as a result of these steps and try to carry this message to alcoholics and to practice these principles in all your affairs.

(*Source:* The Twelve Steps are reprinted with permission of Alcoholics Anonymous World Services, Inc. (A.A.W.S.) Permission to reprint the Twelve Steps does not mean that A.A.W.S. has reviewed or approved the contents of this publication, or that A.A.W.S. necessarily agrees with the views herein. A.A. is a program of recovery from alcoholism *only*—use of the Twelve Steps in connection with programs and activities which are patterned after A.A., but which address other problems, or in any other non-A.A. context, does not imply otherwise.)

To put these steps into practice, members meet weekly with others who have had alcohol problems or who are struggling to overcome them. From their fellow members, they draw encouragement to continue their abstinence. They also carry the telephone number of "someone who has been through it," whom they can call at any hour for personal support in handling a crisis without turning to alcohol.

Matching the Subculture of the Target Group

To be effective, a social policy must match the subculture of its target group. A policy must be geared to its age, race-ethnic, gender, and social class composition, as well as to its values, lifestyle, and problems (Crisp 1980). This means that programs for different groups must have different emphases. For example, a program that is successful with middle-class youth will fail if it is transferred without modification to inner-city youth.

Rewarding Conventional Behavior

As sociologists Charles Faupel and Carl Klockars (1987) stress, a rehabilitation program should offer an alternative lifestyle and reward conventional behavior. For this, the addict needs to be integrated into a community of people where "straight" values are dominant, including social networks that value employment and nonexploitive relationships.

A Controversy: Teaching Drug Use

A social policy that is designed to teach the "evil" of drug use is doomed to failure. As we have seen, ours is a drug-using society. It seems, then, that a rational goal would be to teach people to *use* drugs sensibly and thus to decrease the amount of drug *abuse*. This principle would apply to all drugs—not just to those that match *our* ideas of "good" drugs.

Matching Cultural Values

Social policies must also match general cultural values. A primary value in our culture is that people work productively. One reason that *some* drug use for pleasure is viewed negatively is the fear that individuals will drop out, live off the efforts of others, and not take care of themselves or contribute to society. Rehabilitation programs can address these concerns and encourage active participation in our economic system.

Another mainstream cultural value is individual rights. Applied to social policy, this value means the right of people to abuse their own body with drugs they choose to use. Regardless of how we may feel about the abuse, it seems that people have the right to consume substances that you and I may choose not to.

All Policies Are Controversial

As I said, developing adequate social policy for drug abuse is difficult. We all hold strong opinions about addicts and drugs. Owing to our backgrounds, all of us have biases. Because we see the world from different perspectives, no social policy can satisfy everyone, and all social policies are bound to displease many. I hold no illusions: The ones I suggest can meet no other fate.

The Future of the Problem

Broad Patterns of Drug Use

In light of the pro-drug orientation of Americans, we can expect drug use to remain high. Because drugs are subject to fads, as some drugs decrease in popularity, others will become more popular. As a young clientele rushes to the latest high, we can expect moral entrepreneurs to alarm the public, who will perceive use of the drug as a threat to mainstream values, with some even seeing it as a threat to society itself. Alarms over different drugs, then, will be sounded from time to time.

New Drugs

With advances in chemistry, a new generation of drugs will appear. Designed to work only on particular receptors of the brain, these drugs will be more precise in their effects. The market for these drugs will be high, as people prefer to take drugs to cope with the rigors of modern life than to work on their problems. This ready market will stimulate the demand for drugs and put even greater pressure on physicians to become "drug dispensers." For an example, see the Technology and Social Problems box below.

Drugs in the Workplace

Workers—blue-collar workers, office employees, and executives—will continue to use drugs on the job. Easier to conceal than a bottle of vodka, marijuana has become a favorite recreational drug used at work. We can expect continued controversy over blood tests and urinalysis by both workers and employers.

The Unholy Alliance

The social reputations of drugs will continue to affect people's lives. Some drugs will remain in disrepute, their users disgraced and stigmatized. From the standpoint of

Technology and Social Problems
VIAGRA ON THE INTERNET

When Viagra made its appearance on the drug scene in 1998, it quickly became the butt of jokes throughout the world. Designed to help men with erectile problems, Viagra is a marvel of technology. Viagra also quickly became an abused drug. It gained a reputation as a recreational aphrodisiac for men who had no penile dysfunctions, one that would enable them to prolong lovemaking. And for reasons I fail to understand, women, too, became abusers.

Viagra has become a gold mine for doctors, who "sell" prescriptions for $35 to $50, the price of an office visit. Some even sell this drug directly online so you can bypass the formality of visiting a doctor. If you do an Internet search for Viagra, sites appear that offer this drug. Clicking answers to questions replaces a medical examination. The site I visited to write this box had most answers already filled in. Of course, you are supposed to change those answers if they don't match your situation, but this question gives you an idea of how this so-called medical history is a sham:

Do you require a Pharmacist Consultation for this medication? Clicking Yes may delay your shipment while our Pharmacist attempts to contact you (eDrugstore.MD 2004).

Click the answers, fill in your credit card information, and you can pick your dosage and the number of pills that you want. The minimum cost, with shipping, is $85.99. For an additional charge, you can have Viagra delivered to your door the very next day.

If you don't want to bother filling out the few online questions, you might try your local junior high school. At some, the girls are selling Viagra to each other. Such a fun drug!

functionalism, we can expect drug enforcement agents, working with legislators and feeding the general public's fears through the news media, to keep many substances illegal. This will keep the black market profitable and will continue to produce drug crimes. The outcome will be a self-fulfilling prophecy, for the resulting crimes, especially the headline-producing violence, will continue to make the drug enforcement establishment vital for society. *Organized crime and drug enforcement agents, then, will remain reluctant symbiotic partners, sharing a mutual interest in keeping drugs illegal.*

The Easier Course

The social policies I have suggested are not likely to be part of our future. It is much easier not to figure out solutions, not to work with the disreputable who have become drug dependent, but simply to follow a knee-jerk, gut reaction of banning everything that is disliked. To join the "war on drugs" is politically expedient—and it means action, not a frustrating search for viable alternatives to our long history of failed get-tough policies.

The Hidden Threat in Social Policy

One final note. If we view ourselves as the "good" people and "them" as "evil strangers" in our midst (people who harm or who don't really belong in our society), then addicts and other drug abusers will continue to be treated harshly. We good people can turn a blind eye to what happens to them, for such views sever mutual identity, ultimately denying them even basic humanity. This approach impedes the development of adequate social policy, not only for drug abusers but also for the mentally ill and others who violate middle-class standards of behavior. From such attitudes flow totalitarianism, the curtailment of people's rights, and the treatment of others as subhumans—all for the sake of maintaining a middle-class view of the world. Lurking in the shadows of social policy, this threat needs to be brought into the light where it can be examined thoroughly.

SUMMARY

1. What constitutes *drug abuse* is a matter of definition. What is considered drug abuse at one time or in one society may be considered drug use at another time or in another society. From the historical record, we know that drug use and abuse are ancient.

2. Americans have a strong pro-drug orientation, although they consider some drugs to be disreputable, and those who use them to be part of a social problem. People generally consider the particular drugs that they use to be outside the realm of a social problem.

3. A major problem in drug abuse is *addiction*—becoming dependent on a drug so that in its absence one feels the stress of withdrawal. One of the most highly addicting drugs is nicotine. Heroin appears to be less addicting than previously thought.

4. Symbolic interactionists emphasize the social meanings of drugs. Prohibition, for example, has been analyzed as a symbolic crusade: As the old order lost political control, it attempted to dominate society morally by wrapping itself in abstinence (morality) and associating drunkenness (immorality) with the newcomers.

5. Applying functionalism: Legal drugs are functional for the medical profession, their patients, and those who manufacture and sell these drugs. Illegal drugs are also functional for their users, manufacturers (or growers), and distributors. The dysfunctions of drugs include misprescribing, arrest for breaking the law, and abuse that harms people physically and socially. A major latent function of illegal drugs is to support agents of social control.

6. Applying the conflict perspective: Drugs have been criminalized to maintain interests of people with access to power. Opium, for example, was made illegal in an attempt to overcome the economic threat that cheap Chinese labor posed to white workers. Similarly, marijuana legislation was a tool directed against the Mexican working class in the United States. Some see the heroin trade as a means of defusing revolutionary potential.

7. Applying the symbolic interaction perspective: Pharmaceutical companies, with the cooperation of the medical profession, play a central role in getting Americans to define drugs as a first choice to relieve the stresses of everyday life. Defining problems of living as medical matters, known as the *medicalization of human problems,* includes defining unruly children as sick and in need of medication.

8. The same drug has different effects on different people and on the same person at different times. These differences are due to characteristics of the drug, the individual who is taking it, and the setting in which it is taken. Especially significant are the user's expectations.

9. Of all the drugs that Americans use, nicotine causes the most harm. Alcohol abuse, which destroys vital body organs, also causes *fetal alcohol syndrome.* The social setting in which people learn to drink influences their chances of becoming a problem drinker. We need more studies to determine the effects of marijuana and other drugs. Cocaine's social history illustrates how a drug's reputation depends on the people with whom it is associated.

10. The narcotics are addicting but in and of themselves do not cause crime or destroy people's work incentive or health. Street addicts deal with a black market that demands exorbitant prices and motivates them to commit predatory crimes. Street addicts buy drugs whose purity is far from guaranteed—and suffer the consequences. Physician narcotic addicts, in contrast, maintain normal lives because they need not deal with a black market and are able to obtain pure drugs.

11. Developing an adequate social policy is difficult because drugs arouse strong emotions and biases. At a minimum, an adequate social policy would involve drug education that presents scientific findings honestly, whether they are favorable or unfavorable to any particular drug. It would also break the addicts' dependence on a black market and provide help for their multiple problems. Alcoholics Anonymous appears to be a model recovery program.

12. We can anticipate that the future will bring more use of drugs in the workplace, more effective products from pharmaceutical companies (which will further increase the demand for drugs), and social policies similar to those we now have: illegal status for drugs that are out of favor, stigmas for their users, and overflowing coffers for members of organized crime.

KEY TERMS

Addiction See *Drug addiction*.

Alcoholic Someone who has severe alcohol-related problems.

Amotivational syndrome The tendency for people who smoke marijuana extensively to become apathetic, lose their concentration, and become unable to carry out long-range plans.

Attention deficit-hyperactivity disorder See *Hyperkinesis*.

Craving An intense desire for a drug.

Drug A substance taken to change bodily functions, behavior, emotions, thinking, or consciousness.

Drug abuse Using drugs in such a way that they harm one's health, impair one's physical or mental functioning, or interfere with one's social life.

Drug addiction Depending on the regular consumption of a drug in order to make it through the day.

Drug dependence See *Drug addiction*.

Fetal alcohol syndrome A cluster of congenital problems caused by the alcohol consumption of the newborn's mother.

Fetal narcotic syndrome A cluster of congenital problems caused by narcotic use of the newborn's mother.

Hyperkinesis A term used to refer to a supposed medical condition that causes children not to pay attention and to disrupt classroom activities. Also known as hyperactivity, attention deficit disorder, and attention deficit-hyperactivity disorder (ADHD). See also *Medicalization of human problems*.

Medicalization of human problems To define the problems normally encountered in daily life as a matter of sickness, and therefore properly handled by the medical profession.

Methadone maintenance A program for heroin addicts in which the narcotic methadone is substituted for the narcotic heroin.

Moral entrepreneur A crusading reformer who wages battle to enforce his or her ideas of morality.

Psychological dependence The craving for a drug even though there no longer is a physical dependence on that drug.

Withdrawal The distress that accompanies abstention from a drug to which one is addicted.

THINKING CRITICALLY ABOUT CHAPTER 4

1. Which perspective—symbolic interactionism, functionalism, or conflict theory—do you think best explains drug policies in the United States? Why?

2. If women can be prosecuted for child abuse for taking drugs during pregnancy, does it follow that they should also be prosecuted for failure to attend prenatal classes or for not eating properly during pregnancy? How about for smoking cigarettes? Why or why not?

3. If you had the power to decide which drugs should be legal and which should not, what criteria would you use in making your decision?

CHAPTER 5

Violence in Society: Rape and Murder

THERE WASN'T MUCH FOR TEENAGERS to do in Littleton, Colorado. Not much happened in this quiet town of 35,000, a middle-class suburb southwest of Denver. To get attention, some of the high school kids wore black trench coats and black shirts with swastikas. They called themselves the Trenchcoat Mafia and threw around a few phrases in German.

"Just kids. They'll grow out of it," was the adults' typical response. "We all went through stages."

The Trenchcoat Mafia had their own table in the cafeteria and their group picture in the yearbook. The caption: "Who says we're different? Insanity's healthy. . . . Stay alive, stay different, stay crazy! Oh, and stay away from CREAM SODA!!"

Just another high school group: jocks, Goths, stoners, geeks, preppies, oddballs. Every school has some.

The jocks despised the Trenchcoat Mafia. They threw them into lockers and called them scumbags, faggots, and inbreeds. They threw rocks and bottles at them from passing cars.

Two seniors, Eric Harris and Dylan Klebold, honors students and members of the Trenchcoat Mafia, talked and dreamed about killing their classmates, especially the jocks. Eric even had his own Web page, where he named those he wanted to kill and how he wanted to kill them. As a class project, Eric and Dylan made a video in which they pretended to kill the classmates they didn't like. Just talk. But as the killings on *Doom*, the video game they loved, no longer satisfied, the boys hatched a plan for real killing. It was risky. Maybe they would survive, maybe not. But if not, they would go out in a blaze of glory. April 20, Hitler's birthday, would be perfect.

The carnage left Columbine High School seared into the national memory. TV viewers switched on their sets and found that a quiet Tuesday afternoon had been interrupted by stunning events. The drama was high as SWAT teams moved in and cautiously began to assess the situation. Bodies lay strewn on sidewalks. No one knew how many were dead inside the school. The nation watched transfixed as events unfolded.

As bombs went off and shots rang out, students ran in terror, hiding in closets and crawling under tables. Harris and Klebold went from room to room in search of victims. In the library, they found several students hiding under a table. "Do you believe in God?" asked one of the shooters. "Yes," replied Cassie Bernall. "There is no God," the gunman retorted, as he placed a gun against her head and squeezed the trigger.

Before the boys turned their guns on themselves, they killed twelve of their fellow students and one teacher. They wounded twenty-three students.

Based on Bai 1999; Gibbs 1999.

The Problem in Sociological Perspective

The Sociological Perspective on Violence

Violence, the use of force to injure people or to destroy their property, goes far beyond individual tendencies or what some might term "violent personalities." Violence involves society itself. Some societies encourage violence, whereas others discourage it. As a result, some societies have high rates of violence, and others have low rates. Sociologists, then, don't focus on personality or on individual tendencies. Rather, *the sociological question of violence is: What is it about a society that increases or decreases the likelihood of violence?* Throughout this chapter, we shall grapple with this central question.

Types of Violence

Sociologists divide violence into two major types: individual violence and group violence. **Individual** (or **personal**) **violence** consists of one person physically attacking others or destroying their property. **Group** (or **collective**) **violence** consists of two or more people doing these same things. Sociologists divide group violence into three types.

1. **Situational group violence** is unplanned and spontaneous, such as a brawl among hockey players. Something in the situation stimulates or triggers the violence.
2. **Organized group violence** is planned, but it is unauthorized, such as the school shooting in our opening vignette or acts committed by terrorists.
3. **Institutionalized group violence** is violence carried out by agents of the government, such as an army at war or the SWAT team responding to the shootings at Columbine High School.

Rape and murder, the focus of this chapter, usually takes the form of individual or group violence, depending on whether the victim is attacked by an individual or by a group. If soldiers execute men and rape women and girls after they take over a territory, it is institutionalized violence.

The Scope of the Problem

What makes violence a social problem?

Is Violence a Personal Problem or a Social Problem?

If two people get into a fight and end up in the hospital, that is their *personal* problem. The same is true if a woman, enraged at discovering her husband with a lover, shoots them to death. And the same is true if a man rapes a woman. Although these examples involve severe, bitter violence, they portray only objective conditions. To be a *social* problem, violence must also arouse widespread subjective concern. Many people must see the violence as reducing their quality of life and want something to be done about it.

The Subjective Dimension of Violence

Violence has become a social problem in the United States, but it is important to note that it is not the amount of violence (an objective condition) that makes violence a social problem. Rather, *subjective concerns* about violence are widespread. Parents worry about their kids walking to school. Women feel vulnerable as they get on elevators or as they walk alone at night from their classrooms to their cars. They feel relief when they get inside their cars—after they've shut and locked their car doors. As Table 5-1 shows, this fear is not spread evenly throughout society. As you can see, women

With our high rate of violence, feelings of vulnerability and fear are common. Fear is not distributed evenly throughout society, but is related to income, age, gender, and race-ethnicity. The reasons for these variables are discussed in the text.

TABLE 5-1 Are You Afraid to Walk Alone at Night in Your Own Neighborhood?

	2002		2000		1990		1980		1967	
	YES	NO	YES	NO	YES	NO	YES	NO	YES	NO
SEX										
Male	19	81	23	76	19	81	21	79	17	83
Female	47	52	52	47	58	41	60	39	55	44
RACE-ETHNICITY[1]										
White	30	70	36	61	39	60	42	58	36	63
Black/other	41	58	45	54	50	48	52	47	50	50
AGE										
18 to 20 years	41	59	40	58	43	57	45	54	38	62
21 to 29 years	30	70	41	58	33	65	41	59	40	59
30 to 49 years	27	72	36	63	38	62	39	60	34	66
50 years and older	37	63	41	58	48	51	47	52	43	56
EDUCATION[2]										
College	31	69	38	61	39	60	42	58	38	62
High school graduate	34	64	38	61	41	58	44	55	39	61
Less than high school graduate	32	67	44	54	51	48	42	57	30	59
INCOME										
$50,000 and over	22	76	28	71	NA	NA	NA	NA	NA	NA
$30,000 to $49,999	32	68	34	66	NA	NA	NA	NA	NA	NA
$20,000 to $29,999	37	62	42	58	NA	NA	NA	NA	NA	NA
Under $20,000	41	57	50	48	NA	NA	NA	NA	NA	NA
OCCUPATION										
Professional/business	31	69	34	65	36	63	42	58	37	63
Clerical/support	46	54	54	45	56	42	53	46	47	53
Manual/service	26	74	37	62	38	61	38	62	36	63
Farming/agriculture	25	75	31	69	28	72	15	82	18	82
REGION										
Northeast	35	65	37	62	40	59	47	53	34	66
Midwest	23	77	34	64	36	64	33	66	37	63
South	33	65	42	57	46	52	44	55	42	58
West	38	62	42	57	41	58	52	48	40	60
RELIGION										
Protestant	31	69	39	59	43	56	43	56	37	63
Catholic	35	65	41	58	38	61	45	55	43	56
Jewish	60	40	36	64	61	39	50	50	47	53
None	30	70	35	64	32	64	38	62	36	64
POLITICS										
Republican	30	70	33	66	41	58	41	57	35	65
Democrat	39	61	43	56	47	52	46	54	40	60
Independent	28	72	39	59	35	64	41	59	39	60

[1] These two categories were used when this research was first done in the 1960s. As inadequate as these categories are, researchers still use them.

[2] The question that interviewers asked nationally representative samples of Americans was: "Is there any area right around here—that is, within a mile—where you would be afraid to walk alone at night?" (This is really not just "your neighborhood," as the heading indicates.)

Source: *Sourcebook of Criminal Justice Statistics* 2002:Table 2–36.

are much more afraid than men of becoming victims of violent crime. As you can also see from this table, fear recedes as income increases—largely because people with higher incomes live in "better" (read, more affluent and less violent) neighborhoods. Some of these neighborhoods are even guarded by gates and sentries.

The Objective Dimension of Violence

From this table, you can also see that Americans aren't as afraid as they were a few years ago. As objective conditions have changed, so have subjective concerns: Crimes of violence have dropped, and today's streets are safer than they used to be.

Where does this place us today? Although fears have receded, they are still common. Are Americans overreacting to a small amount of violence that the media have blown out of proportion? Look at Figure 5-1. You can see that we still have a *lot* of violent crime. On average, ten women are raped every hour; every half minute one person tries to injure someone else (aggravated assault); and every half hour an American dies from such an attack (homicide or murder). In short, we are not talking about a fistfight here and there, an occasional rape, or isolated incidents of spouses turning on one another.

Different Groups Have Different Rates of Violence

From your knowledge of U.S. society, you know that social location makes a difference in people's chances of being a victim of violence But did you know that it made this much difference? African-American males are *seven* times more likely than white males to be murdered. Similarly, African-American females are more than *three* times as likely as white females to be homicide victims. Another major factor is age: Those least likely to be murdered are the elderly and children up to the age of 17; those most likely to be murdered are people in their twenties (*Statistical Abstract* 2003:Tables 310, 313).

Rates of Violence Also Vary by Country

Although the United States certainly has a lot of violence, as Table 5-2 on the next page shows, our rates are not the highest in the world. From this table, you can see that countries with a high murder rate do not necessarily have a high rape rate, and vice versa. Monaco provides the best example: no killings, but it has one of the highest rape rates. The United States, unfortunately, is high in both rape and murder.

A word of caution, however. Don't take the totals shown on these tables as "facts." A lot of errors go into them, and at best they merely *indicate* that one country has more or less violence than another. From what I have seen in traveling in some of these countries, much of their violence never gets officially recorded—and that includes the United States.

Rates versus Amounts

As you can see from Figure 5-2, violent crimes in the United States have undergone some remarkable changes. From the 1960s to 1991, not only did the amount of violence increase, but so did the **rate of violence,** the number of violent crimes for each 100,000 Americans. If over a 10-year period our population increases 20 percent and rape and murder also increase 20 percent, the rate would remain unchanged; al-

FIGURE 5-1 *The Clock of Violence*

These totals are U.S. national averages. Crimes do not occur with this regularity. As the text indicates, crimes vary by time of day and by seasons. The FBI also counts armed robbery as a violent crime, whether or not anyone is hurt during the crime. Armed robberies, occurring on average every 1.2 minutes, are included in the total.

Source: *FBI Uniform Crime Reports* 2002.

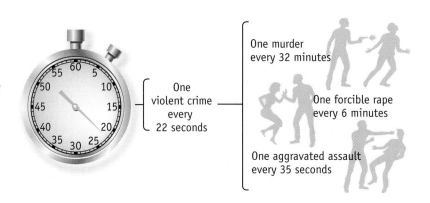

One violent crime every 22 seconds

One murder every 32 minutes

One forcible rape every 6 minutes

One aggravated assault every 35 seconds

TABLE 5-2 How Countries Compare in Murder and Rape

COUNTRY	MURDER RANK	MURDER RATE*	RAPE RANK	RAPE RATE*
Uganda	1	25.08	7	13.56
Bermuda	2	11.54	9	9.62
Luxembourg	3	11.18	3	29.71
Mexico	4	11.05	16	4.10
France	5	9.93	20	0.32
United States	6	9.07	6	23.72
Jamaica	7	8.24	4	29.72
Kuwait	8	5.84	5	24.65
Hungary	9	4.46	14	5.39
Hong Kong	10	2.64	18	1.54
Sweden	11	2.43	11	7.63
Austria	12	1.38	10	8.38
Korea	13	1.33	13	6.04
West Germany	14	1.26	8	11.35
Finland	15	1.20	12	6.93
Tunisia	16	1.01	1	46.03
Ireland	17	0.96	19	1.38
England and Wales	18	0.93	17	1.82
Denmark	19	0.65	15	4.83
Spain	20	.0.47	21	0.18
Monaco	21	0.00	2	37.50

*Rates reported per 100,000 people.
Source: Based on Archer and Gartner 1984.

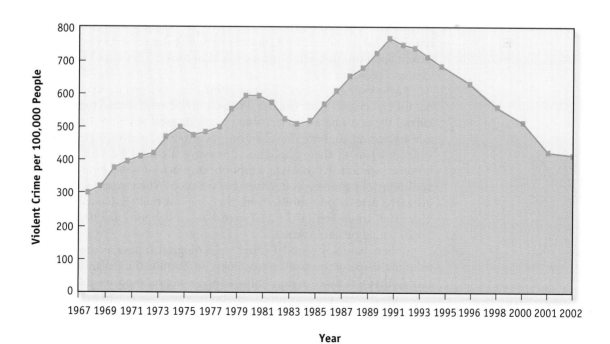

FIGURE 5-2   *The Rate of Violence*
Source: Various editions of *FBI Uniform Crime Reports,* including 1997, 2001, and 2003.

though there would be more rape and murder, the increase would simply have kept pace with the larger numbers of people. One's chances of being raped or murdered would be unchanged.

The Growth of Violence

As you can see from Figure 5-2, however, violent crimes far outpaced the U.S. population. In just 12 years, from 1968 to 1980, the rate of violent crimes *doubled*, soaring from 300 to 600 violent crimes per 100,000 people. This means that in 1980 one's chances of being a victim of violent crime were twice what they were in 1968. If the U.S. population had not increased by a single person, there still would have been twice as many violent crimes in 1980 than there were in 1968. As you can see, the rate then declined, and in 1984 it reached its low for the 1980s. The rate of violent crime then turned upward again, reaching its peak in 1990. Then the rate began to drop sharply, and today's rate of murder, rape, robbery, and aggravated assault is only about *half* of what it was in 1990. Despite the welcome decrease of these crimes, the rate of violent crime still remains higher than it was in 1968.

Our Current Decline Means More Violence Now Than in the Past

A common perception is that the United States is more dangerous than it used to be. Is this true? As you can see, this depends on what years you compare. Our streets are more dangerous today than they were in 1968—but they are much safer than they were in 1990.

Let's look at the theories that social scientists have developed to explain violence.

Looking at the Problem Theoretically

Before we look at violence from the perspectives that sociology offers, let's examine some of the theories developed in other academic disciplines.

NONSOCIOLOGICAL THEORIES

Theories Centering on Biological Factors

In the 1800s, Cesare Lombroso (1835–1909), an Italian physician, examined thousands of prisoners. He was struck by how different they looked than the regular people he knew. Lombroso (1911) concluded that violent people (and other criminals) are *atavistic;* that is, they are biological throwbacks to an earlier period when humanity was violent and primitive. His evidence was their looks: They have lower foreheads, larger ears, and receding chins.

Anthropologist Konrad Lorenz (1966) also saw evolution as the key to violence, but his explanation went like this. We humans, he said, are biologically ill-equipped for killing: We don't have claws, slashing teeth, or great strength. Because of this, we did not develop an inhibitory mechanism—as did dogs, wolves, and baboons—that stops violence when an enemy becomes submissive. Because we have a powerful intellect, however, we learned to make weapons. Our lack of a blocking mechanism and the availability of weapons produce terrible violence. When we are angry or wish to dominate, we destroy one another with the weapons that we have developed. As Lionel Tiger and Robin Fox (1971:210) remarked, if baboons had hand grenades, few baboons would be left in Africa.

Others have suggested a variety of biological factors as the cause of violence—from the shape of the skull (phrenology) to hormonal imbalance (endocrinology). A theory that was taken seriously for a time was proposed by anthropologist Earnest Hooton (1939), who concluded that body type is the key to understanding violence: Tall, thin men, he said, tend to be the killers, whereas short, heavy men are prone to sexual crimes. A more recent biological explanation of violence is the XYY chromosome theory: Most men have an X and a Y chromosome; some men, however, have an extra Y chromosome, which supposedly propels them toward violence. Some theorists who take the biological route base their explanations on human evolution. Those humans that survived were the violent ones, and these select few passed to their children genes that predispose us to violence. As a result, violence is part of our nature.

Psychologist John Dollard (1939), who also stressed that violence is built into our nature, proposed a **frustration-aggression** theory of violence. As you know, it is frustrating to strive for a goal and not to be able to reach it. Dollard conducted a series of experiments on how people relieve their frustration by striking out at others. Often we strike out in mild ways, such as telling someone off, but sometimes we strike out violently.

Psychological Theories

Some psychologists point to learning as the cause of violence. Following the lead of B. F. Skinner (1948, 1953, 1971), they stress that if someone is rewarded ("reinforced," as they call it), that person will tend to be violent again. The "reward" (or "reinforcement") can be any gain—consumables such as candy or food, or social symbols such as money, status, or even a smile. For a rapist, the reward can be sex and power. For a killer, the reward might be revenge, a sense of power, or satisfaction at exterminating an enemy. Other psychologists emphasize that violence is learned through **modeling,** copying another person's behavior. In a classic study, psychologists Albert Bandura and R. H. Walters (1963) found that children who see others hitting dolls or pounding on furniture tend to do the same things themselves. Children who have not seen this sort of behavior are less likely to perform it.

The Sociological Approach

Sociologists are not impressed by theories that look inside people, but they do acknowledge the value of explanations that stress factors in the environment, such as frustration-aggression and modeling. Rather than looking for violence-inducing characteristics *within* people, such as chromosomes and inhibitory mechanisms, sociologists focus on matters *outside* people. They examine how *social life* shapes and encourages—or discourages—violence. For example, in one society, violence may be channeled into approved forms, such as the social roles of warrior, boxer, or football player. Other societies may downplay violence and develop mechanisms to ensure that it rarely occurs.

Let's apply our three sociological perspectives to violence. In doing so, let's try to understand why males are more likely than females to be violent and why violence is higher among members of the working or lower classes.

SYMBOLIC INTERACTIONISM

Why do people kill? Consider what a detective on the Dallas police force said back in the 1960s:

> Murders result from little ol' arguments over nothing at all. . . . Tempers flare. A fight starts, and somebody gets stabbed or shot. I've worked on cases where the principals had been arguing over a 10 cent record on a juke box, or over a dollar gambling debt from a dice game. (Mulvihill et al. 1969:230)

Edwin Sutherland: Differential Association

This hasn't changed. People still kill over "little" things. Symbolic interactionists have developed two theories that help us to understand why. In the first, sociologist Edwin Sutherland (1947) stressed that people learn criminal behavior by interacting with others. In its simplest form, Sutherland's theory goes this way: People who associate with lawbreakers are more likely to learn to break the law than are people who associate with those who follow the law. To refer to this basic principle, Sutherland used the term **differential association**—that is, they are associating with different people or groups.

Although Sutherland developed his theory to explain lawbreaking, we can apply its five basic points to violence:

1. People learn violence by interacting with others, primarily in intimate relationships.
2. People learn not only techniques for doing violence but also attitudes, motives, drives, and rationalizations about violence.

3. People use violence because they learn more attitudes (or definitions) that are favorable to using violence than they learn attitudes (or definitions) that are unfavorable to using violence. (Sutherland called this an *excess of definitions*.)

4. The most significant interactions in which people learn violence are those that take place earliest in life and those that are the most frequent, last the longest, and are the most emotional or meaningful.

5. The mechanisms for learning violence are the same as those for learning anything else, including nonviolent or cooperative behavior.

Marvin Wolfgang: Subcultures of Violence

A second theory, **subcultural theory,** complements differential association. In a nutshell, this theory says that people who grow up in a subculture that approves of violent behavior have a high chance of learning to be violent. Sociologist Marvin Wolfgang wanted to know why the homicide rate was high among lower-class African-American males. In a classic study (1958), Wolfgang examined the murders that occurred in Philadelphia from 1948 through 1952. He also observed police interrogations.

Wolfgang found something significant: The lower-class African-American men whom he studied connected the willingness to be violent with honor and manliness. They viewed insults as challenges to their manliness, and violence as the appropriate response. Situations that others might perceive as trivial were *not* trivial to them. Anyone who backed down from a confrontation (even if it was about that dollar gambling debt quoted earlier) was seen as less than a real man. If he backed down, he risked being viewed as a "chicken" or a "girl"—and would be laughed at by others. With their "rep" at stake and "dissing" common, a self-fulfilling prophecy was set in motion: The young men carried weapons for both protection and as a symbol of their manliness. As a result, violence among these men is common.

Fitting the Theories Together

Differential association and subcultural theory fit together well. Subcultural theory stresses that violence is woven into the life of some groups, and differential association emphasizes that people in these groups learn that violence is a suitable response to many of the problems of life. To be "dissed" or insulted is not a trivial matter, even if it is over a minor gambling debt or a record on a jukebox. With one's reputation at stake, violence or the threat of violence is necessary to keep or enhance one's standing among peers. As sociologist Elijah Anderson (1990, 1999) documented, this equation of manliness and violence continues to be a feature of the everyday lives of African-American inner-city young men. This explanation goes a long way toward explaining their high homicide rates.

Other groups also connect manliness and violence. In her participant observation of Chicano gangs, sociologist Ruth Horowitz (1983) found that these young men also equate manliness and honor with violence. In the Spotlight on Research box on the next page, Horowitz shares insights that she gained from her research.

The situation is similar in the Mafia. Michael Franzese, a college-educated member of the Mafia, put it this way:

> If somebody were to dishonor my wife or my child, I would view it as something that I had to take into my own hands. I don't see why I have to go to the police. As a man, I would feel that it was an obligation that I had to take care of. And I would have to be prepared in my own mind to kill this guy. This is a basic principle. (Barnes and Shebar 1987)

Based on their research, symbolic interactionists stress how "manliness" or "masculinity" is associated with violence. As a result, we find more violence among males than females. Social class is also significant, for the working class incorporates more violence into its definitions of appropriate male behavior than do the middle and upper classes. As a result. year after year, across racial-ethnic lines and in every region of the United States, violence is more prevalent among males than females and among

Studying Violence among "The Lions"

When she was a graduate student at the University of Chicago, Ruth Horowitz (now Professor of Sociology at New York University) did a participant observation study of young people in a Chicano community in Chicago. Her purpose was not to understand violence, but to understand poverty. She wanted to see how the explanations of poverty that sociologists had developed matched what she observed in "real life."

Two major explanations of poverty are the culture of poverty and the social structure of poverty. According to the culture of poverty, poor people have different values than the middle class, and this is why they act as they do. According to the social structural perspective, the poor act as they do because, unlike middle-class people, they do not have the same opportunities to attend good schools or to obtain good jobs. Consequently, the poor turn to illegal opportunities, and crime becomes part of their life.

One afternoon, a month after meeting the "Lions" gang and shaking hands with all of them in the park, several 16 year-old young women introduced themselves. They asked me several questions about myself, and they were able to give me a definition of sociology. They told me about school and their trips around the city. Several of these women went on to college; others became pregnant and married. The life experience of siblings varied, too; some went to school and became white-collar workers,

while others ran afoul of the legal system and went to prison.

When I first began my research, the "Lions" were 15 to 17 years old, had guns, and did a lot of fighting. Some had after-school jobs and dressed in tuxedos for *quinceaneras* and weddings. In the streets, these same young men had developed a reputation by being tougher than other gangs. They would even seek opportunities to challenge others. At home and during most parties, in contrast, they were polite and conformed to strict rules of etiquette.

For seven years, I did participant observation with these youths. When I returned after a three year absence, many of the "Lions" were still hanging out together, but quite a few were working, had married, and had children. A few of the gang members attended college, and others remained in the street. One had been killed in a drug deal gone wrong. A major change was their relationship to violence. Instead of provoking incidents, now they responded only when someone challenged their reputations.

The two models of poverty did apply. Violence had been part of the culture they had learned, and a lack of opportunities did contribute to a sense of being left out. But there was more to it. Actual violence depended on how the "Lions" defined a particular situation. As sociologists phrase this: Violence was situational and constructed interactionally.

working-class males than males from higher social classes. Until the association between masculinity and violence is broken, you can expect these patterns to continue.

FUNCTIONALISM

Emile Durkheim: Asking the Sociological Question

Violence was one of the first social problems that sociologists studied. In the late 1800s, Emile Durkheim, the first university professor to be formally identified as a sociologist, examined the murder rates in Paris and the suicide rates in European countries (1897, 1904). He was struck by how stable these rates were. Year after year, the countries that had high rates of violence continued to have high rates, whereas those with low rates continued to have low rates. Durkheim found that a country's rate of violence is so consistent that he could use it to predict its future rate. He called this **normal violence**—the violence that a group normally (or usually) has.

Durkheim found this regularity to be a sociological puzzle. If murder or suicide rates represent the number of *individual* acts of killing, why is the rate in each society so consistent? Instead of a country's rate of murder or suicide being high (or low) year after year, why doesn't its rate fluctuate? Why isn't its rate high one year and low another? To solve this puzzle, Durkheim developed the *sociological perspective:* He concluded that the characteristics of a society regulate individual impulses and desires.

To appreciate Durkheim's conclusion, consider what life used to be like in farming communities. Children followed in their parents' footsteps and either worked in the village in which they were reared or farmed nearby land. They would spend their entire lives in a village where everyone knew one another. Their close bonds restrained whatever individual impulses they might have had to lash out violently, for how they followed the community's norms affected their social standing—and they needed the community to survive. Their close relationships (or high social integration, in Durkheim's term) kept the rate of violence low.

Now imagine that this same community is undergoing rapid social change. The society is industrializing, and the villagers are moving away to take low-paying, unskilled jobs in cities where they know few people. They live in the midst of strangers, where they face being fired by bosses who care about profits, not workers, and eviction by landlords who care more about collecting rent than about what happens to a family. Unlike the factors that promote cohesion in farming communities, these urban characteristics loosen social bonds. People feel fewer ties with one another, and the rules that used to apply no longer work. Durkheim gave the name **anomie** to such feelings of being unconnected and uprooted. Under these circumstances, no longer do impulses to violence have the constraints that they did in the village. As a result, the city is a more dangerous place.

Another functionalist, Robert Merton (1968), used anomie to explain crime in U.S. society. He developed what is called **strain theory.** Merton said that success—especially in the form of money or the possession of material goods—is a **cultural goal;** that is, this goal is held out for all Americans. Society also offers approved (or legitimate) ways to reach this goal, such as education and jobs. These are called **cultural means.** Socialization into the goal is remarkably successful, and almost all Americans learn to want money or material goods. The cultural (approved) means, however, are more limited. Those who find their way blocked are more likely to turn to illegitimate means, such as robbery and theft. The *strain* (or frustration and anxiety) that comes from blocked goals also motivates people to commit crimes of violence. Just as strain theory would predict, we find higher rates of violence among groups that experience higher blockage to financial success—the poor, African Americans, and Latinos.

Strain theory does not explain why some people whose goals are blocked are violent and others are not. We all face blocked goals, but few of us are violent. To answer this question, sociologist Walter Reckless (1973) developed **control theory** (also called **containment theory**). Other sociologists have expanded on these ideas (Gottfredson and Hirschi 1990; Burton et al. 1998). Reckless assumed that people have a natural tendency toward violence. He then asked what forms of social control overcome our natural inclinations. He theorized that two systems control our "pushes and pulls" toward violence. The first, *inner* containment, refers to our inner capacity to withstand pressures to be violent. The second, *outer* containment, refers to groups, such as family, friends, and the police, that divert us away from violence. The likelihood that we will be violent depends on the strength of these two control systems relative to our pushes and pulls toward violence. If our control systems are weaker than the pushes and pulls, we are violent. If they are stronger, we are not.

As you can see, this theory is so vague that it explains everything—and nothing. Consider differences in groups: If women are less violent, it must be because their systems of control are stronger than their pushes and pulls toward violence. If some ethnic group is more violent than another, it must be because its systems of control are weaker than the pushes and pulls that it experiences. It is the same for individuals: If John is violent and Mary is not, then John's controls are weaker than his pushes and pulls toward violence, but Mary's are stronger. When everything is vaguely answered, then nothing is answered.

CONFLICT THEORY

Violence Is Inherent in Society

Conflict theorists view violence as inherent in society. We can expect violence because groups are competing with each other for highly desired but limited resources. Although conflict may be hidden beneath surface cooperation and even goodwill, the true nature of human relationships is adversarial. When this basic nature emerges, violence often is the consequence.

Class Oppression Leads to Violence

The major division among people in our society is social class. Despite appearances to the contrary, say conflict theorists, the social classes find themselves on opposite sides of vital issues in life. The essential division is between those who own the means of production—the factories, the machines, and the capital (investment money)—and those who work for the owners (Marx and Engels 1848, 1906). The workers, who must struggle to put food on the table, pay rent, and buy clothing, are at the mercy of the owners, who make their decisions on the basis of profit, not the workers' welfare. For example, the owners can decide to close a factory and move the manufacturing or assembling process to Mexico or China. With low pay and the threat of unemployment hovering over them, the working class, both male and female, is the most likely to strike out violently at others.

And Gender Competition

The situation is particularly tense for working-class males. Traditionally, men of all social classes assumed the role of breadwinner. This role has always been threatened by capitalism's recurring boom and bust cycle, which makes working-class men expendable pawns in the capitalists' pursuit of profits. Today, men face another threat, women who are competing for the jobs that men have traditionally held. With their position in the family threatened and their economic security flimsy, working-class men commit more violent crimes than do either working-class women or men from higher social classes. And the most exploited—those who are confined to the inner city and whose breadwinner role is practically nonexistent—have the highest rates of desperate, violent striking out against others.

Probing Beneath the Surface

Conflict theorists also point out that if we look beneath the surface we will see that the capitalist class is actually *more* violent than the working class. Just as the wealthy own the means to produce wealth, so they control the police powers of the state, which they use to suppress riots and strikes at home and to send armies abroad to protect their markets and resources—to Vietnam, Grenada, Panama, Kuwait, Serbia, Afghanistan, Iraq, and so on. Thus, it is not violence itself but the *form* of violence that distinguishes the workers from the capitalists. The rich may not kill with their own hands, but their rape of the environment and their armies account for vastly more deaths.

IN SUM

Because violence is an universal characteristic of human societies, sociologists are interested in its causes. True to their calling, sociologists look for *social* causes. They want to know why some societies are more violent than others, as well as why some groups in the same society are more violent than others.

As stressed throughout this text, for there to be a social problem we need not only objective conditions but also widespread subjective concerns. Suicide is ordinarily viewed as a personal problem, not a social problem. For decades, there have been educational and publicity campaigns to try to arouse the subjective concerns necessary to make suicide a social problem. An example is the Jason Foundation's Teen Suicide awareness campaign, publicized here at a press conference featuring David Keith.

From a Personal to a Social Problem

Symbolic interactionists stress that each group has its own ideas and norms about violence. Some groups prefer indirect ways of handling disagreements, whereas other groups consider violence an appropriate response to many situations. To solve problems, the middle and upper social classes often turn to the legal system, which transcends personal confrontation. The lower classes, in contrast, are more likely to take matters in their own hands—and this breeds violence. Depending on the groups with which one associates (differential association), then, people have a greater or lesser chance of learning to be violent.

Functionalists emphasize that social conditions that strengthen social bonds decrease violence, and social conditions that produce *anomie* increase violence. Violence tends to be higher among groups whose access to culturally approved goals is blocked. The pushes and pulls toward violence that people experience, however, do not necessarily result in violence. The outcome depends on inner and outer controls.

Conflict theorists stress that class exploitation underlies violence. Members of the working class have higher rates of violence because they face more problems in life. Seldom is their violence directed against their oppressors, however, for the capitalists control the powers of the state and use them to protect their privileged positions. Instead of targeting their oppressors, workers almost always misdirect their violence, aiming it primarily against one another. Although the biased statistics produced by the state won't show this, the capitalists are more violent than are members of the working class, for their wars and destruction of the environment kill far more people.

Research Findings

As we review the research on violence, we will focus on rape and murder, the two most serious forms of violence. Because rape only recently emerged as a social problem, we pay particular attention to its natural history, especially to the role of feminists in changing our ideas about rape. (Most state laws label consensual intercourse between someone above the age of consent and someone below the age of consent **statutory rape.** Our topic is **forcible rape,** an entirely different matter, as no consent is involved.) After this, we turn our focus to murder in the United States. As we do so, we will examine the who, what, when, where, and why of the real-life "whodunits."

Rape

THE NATURAL HISTORY OF RAPE AS A SOCIAL PROBLEM

When I say that rape emerged only recently as a social problem, I do not mean that rape is new to the social scene. On the contrary, accounts of rape go back thousands of years to the Old Testament and Greek mythology. What is new is the perception of rape as a *social* rather than a personal problem and understanding rape as violence rather than passion. Let's see how this change took place.

As I have emphasized throughout this text, objective conditions are not sufficient for something to constitute a social problem. A social problem requires subjective concerns: A significant number of people (or a number of significant people) must be upset by the objective conditions. Subjective concerns about rape are common. Parents teach their children to avoid strangers. Women fear becoming a victim of rape. A special fear is the possibility that their car will break down. To combat their fears, women take defensive measures, such as avoiding certain areas of the city and carrying cell phones.

The Feminist Reconceptualization of Rape: From Passion to Power

The natural history of rape as a social problem began during the 1960s and 1970s, when Western women began to question the roles that they had been assigned, which revolved around husband, home, and children (Friedan 1963; Millett 1970). Many women began to see themselves less as individuals who were facing unique circumstances and more as members of a social group that faced similar situations. Feminists analyzed how society makes men dominant and women submissive. They stressed how females are taught to be supportive of males and to have lower educational and career aspirations.

Up to this time, the traditional view of rape dominated thinking. In this view, rape is considered a personal problem. It is an act driven by individual passion. Men are thought to have an overwhelming sex drive: When aroused, they can lose control and take women by force. Women must be careful not to arouse men's passions.

As feminists analyzed their situation, they began to perceive rape as a *social* rather than as a personal problem Feminists attacked the traditional view, saying that it blamed women for being raped. A woman must have acted provocatively or somehow excited the man, or he would not have lost control. If women would stop giving off the sexual cues that stimulate rape, the problem would go away. In a scathing rebuttal to this traditional view, Dorothy Hicks, a physician who treated rape victims in Miami, Florida, asked if an 80-year-old woman or a 4-month-old baby is particularly sexy (Luy 1977).

Feminists developed an entirely different perspective on rape. Rape, they said, is a form of violence, not an act of passion. Rape is one of the many ways by which men control women. Through rape and the fear of rape, men make women submissive and ensure their own dominance. The root of the problem, then, is the basic relationship between men and women.

This new view did not suggest that men deliberately use rape to frighten women into subservient positions. The process is much subtler. Men are taught "to associate power, dominance, strength, virility and superiority with masculinity, and submissiveness, passivity, weakness, and inferiority with femininity" (Scully 1990; Scully and Marolla 1985/2005). To equate masculinity with dominance and power teaches men that aggression is part of their sex role. By nature larger, taller, and stronger, and thus born for domination, no "real" man takes no for an answer. Besides, women say no when they don't really mean it, and, as some movies show, a woman's initial unwillingness may change as she is dazzled by a man's sexual advances (Reynolds 1976; Finkelhor and Yllo 1985, 1989).

As you can see, the new view of rape as dominance and violence contrasts sharply with the traditional view. As these ideas were accepted, they became part of the official response to rape, and many states renamed rape **criminal sexual assault.** This new view also helps make sense of previously incomprehensible findings. Some rapists, for example, beat their victims, even those who submit or those they already have raped. Other rapists threaten their victims with death and insert dirt, sticks, stones, and even shoes into their victims' vaginas.

THE SOCIAL PATTERNS OF RAPE

How Many Rapes Are Reported?

How common is rape in the United States? According to the FBI, 72,000 U.S. women are forcibly raped each year (*FBI Uniform Crime Reports* 2003:Table 15). This is the official total, the number of women who report this crime to the police. The actual total is *three times higher:* Each year, over 200,000 U.S. women are raped.

Solving the Question by Victimization Surveys

How do we know that forcible rape is three times higher than the official statistics? Twice a year, researchers conduct what is called *The National Crime Victimization Survey*. In this survey, they interview about 90,000 Americans in 45,000 households. The researchers ask about the crimes that have happened to them and whether they reported those crimes to the police. Only about 32 percent of victims report their rapes to the police (*Statistical Abstract* 2003:196).

Rape Is Not Random: It Follows Social Patterns

Rape follows predictable social patterns. These patterns show that rape is not the act of a few sick men from the lunatic fringe of society, but that rape is intimately linked with our culture (Schwendinger and Schwendinger 1983; Murnen et al. 2002; Scully and Marolla 1985/2005). Rape follows patterns of acquaintanceship, time, season, geography, sex, age, and race-ethnicity. A woman is more likely to be raped by someone she knows than by a stranger. Night is more dangerous than day, for two of three rapes occur between 6 P.M. and 6 A.M. The most dangerous hours are 8 P.M. to 2 A.M.; the safest, from 2 P.M. to 6 P.M. As Figure 5-3 shows, rapes are more likely to occur in summer than in winter. July and August are the peak months for rape, whereas the fewest rapes occur in December and February. Another pattern is the age of the victim. Although rape victims range from babies to the elderly, the typical victim is in her late teens, between 16 and 19 years of age (*Statistical Abstract* 2003:Tables 322, 323). About four out of five rapists use no weapon, depending instead on surprise, threats, and physical strength. When a weapon is used, it is most commonly a gun (*Sourcebook of Criminal Justice Statistics* 2003:Table 3.20).

A woman's chances of being raped vary tremendously from one state to another. Here is the extreme: Women in Alaska are more than four times as likely to be raped than are women in West Virginia or Vermont. From the Social Map on the next page, you can see which states are the safest and which are the most dangerous.

Rapists are not scattered randomly throughout society. Although women can rape men or other women, it is rare. Rape is almost exclusively a male crime, and primarily a crime of young men. Although only 10 percent of U.S. males are ages 17 to 23, they account for 33 percent of those who are arrested for rape (*Sourcebook of Criminal Justice Statistics* 2002:Table 4.7; *Statistical Abstract* 2003:Table 11). Similar findings hold true for race-ethnicity: Only about 12 percent of the U.S. male population is African American, but African-American males account for 35 percent of arrested

FIGURE 5-3 *Forcible Rape by Month*

Source: *FBI Uniform Crime Reports* 2003:Table 2.18.

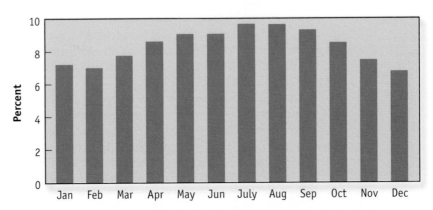

The Percentage of All Rapes That Occur Each Month

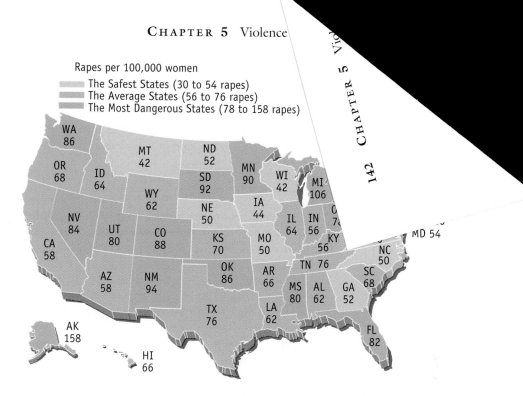

Rapes per 100,000 women
The Safest States (30 to 54 rapes)
The Average States (56 to 76 rapes)
The Most Dangerous States (78 to 158 rapes)

FIGURE 5-4 *Social Map: How Safe Is Your State? Rape in the United States*

Source: By the author, based on *Statistical Abstract* 2003:Table 307.

rapists (*Sourcebook of Criminal Justice Statistics* 2002:Table 4.10; *Statistical Abstract* 2003:Table 23).

Applying Our Three Theories

Why are African-American men overrepresented in rape statistics? For this, let's turn to two of our theories. First, according to *conflict theory,* the lower classes are oppressed—and, as we reviewed earlier, one reaction to oppression is violence. Compared with men from other social classes, lower-class men commit more forcible rapes. Because African Americans are overrepresented in the lower social classes, they would be disproportionately involved. We can look to *functionalism,* particularly strain theory, for a second explanation. Because African-American men often are blocked from legitimate avenues of attaining social status, their frustrations may lead them to turn against women inappropriately. As some have suggested, rape could be a way of establishing power in the face of socially imposed powerlessness (McNeely and Pope 1981).

Does Resistance Help Avoid Rape?

Is a woman more likely to be raped if she resists or if she gives up without a struggle? Sociologists Pauline Bart and Patricia O'Brien (1984, 1985) compared women who had been attacked. They found that the women who were raped generally had tried to plead with their attackers, whereas those who had been able to avoid being raped had resisted—they yelled, fled, or fought back. In general, the avoiders had focused on not being raped, whereas the raped women had focused on not being killed. Other studies support the finding that women who resist are less likely to be raped (Kleck and Sayles 1990; Zoucha-Jensen and Coyne 1993; Ullman 1998). Apparently the more strategies that a woman uses (scratching, biting, gouging, kicking, hitting, screaming, running), the greater her chances of avoiding rape (McIntyre, Myint, and Curtis 1979; Block and Skogan 1982).

Does Resistance Help Avoid Injury?

Yet, this matter is not so simple. Although a woman who resists her attacker is less likely to be raped, she apparently is more likely to be injured. This is what sociologist Sarah Ullman (1998) found in her study of rape victims in Chicago. Her finding is supported by an earlier government study of a million rape victims (*Sourcebook* 1991:Table 3-20). In a more recent study of 203,000 victims, about half report that fighting back helped them. However, about a fourth of the women who fought back said that their resistance only made their situation worse (*Sourcebook of Criminal Justice Statistics* 2003:Table 3.23).

How can we reconcile these findings? Not all rapists are the same. Fighting back scares some rapists away, while it only enrages other attackers, causing even more injuries. In addition, some rapists want their victims to struggle, for this excites them sexually. Unfortunately, a woman who is being attacked does not know what kind of rapist she is facing, and she cannot know what the results of her resistance will be. At this point, let's look at what kind of rapists there are.

PROFILING THE RAPIST

Ten Types of Rapists

The following summaries, worked out with Linda Henslin and based on studies of rapists who have been caught, profile ten "types" of rapists (Cohen et al. 1969; Hotchkiss 1978; Athens 1980; Hills 1980; Scully and Marolla 1985/2005). These profiles show that many motivations underlie rape, but we do not know the proportion of rapists within each type or what other types may exist.

The Woman Hater

At some point in his life, the *woman hater* was severely hurt by a woman who was significant to him. In many cases, this woman was his mother. This hurt inflicted an emotional wound and created a hatred of women. By sexually assaulting women, this man gains personal power. By degrading his victim and sometimes brutally assaulting her sexual organs, he retaliates for his festering wound.

The Sadist

Although the *sadist* may have no particular negative feelings toward women, he also beats his victims. He has learned to receive pleasure by hurting others, and women are merely handy outlets for him. By raping women, he combines the pleasure he receives from inflicting pain with the pleasure he receives from sex. Because he enjoys it when his victim begs, pleads, and shows fear, the sadist is likely to increase his sexual excitement by beating his victim before sexual penetration. He sometimes prolongs the pleasure by beating her during and after the rape.

The Generally Violence-Prone

For the *generally violence-prone* man, rape is just another act of violence. He sees the world as a violent affair. If he is going to get anything, he must wrest it from others using violent means—and that includes sex. Unlike the previous two types, his pleasure in rape is rooted in the sex rather than in the violence, and he uses only enough violence to make the woman submit. It is fine if he can accomplish the rape with threats, but if it requires injuring or killing the victim, so be it. Even though he may have abducted a total stranger, he believes that if she resists she deserves to be hurt because she is "holding out" on him.

The Revenge Rapist

The *revenge* rapist uses rape to get even with someone. His victim may be the person he is angry at, or she may be just a substitute for his real target. An example is a man who went to collect money that another man owed him. He thought, "I'm going to get it one way or another." When he found that the man was not home:

> I grabbed her and started beating the hell out of her. Then I committed the act. I knew what I was doing. I was mad. I could have stopped, but I didn't. I did it to get even with her and her husband. (Scully and Marolla 2005:54)

The Political Rapist

The *political* rapist also chooses his victim as a substitute for his enemy, but, in addition, he uses the rape to make a political statement. In *Soul on Ice* (1968), for example, Eldridge Cleaver recounts how he raped white women to "strike against the white establishment." Much of the raping done by soldiers during war is of this type. The soldiers are not motivated by a hatred of women or by sadism, but by hatred of the enemy. By raping "the enemy's women," they show contempt for the enemy and declare their own superiority. Probably every war has political rape, but an extreme example occurred in 1971 during the Bangladesh war for independence from Pakistan: The Pakistani army raped 200,000 Bangladeshi women (Russell 1979; Schwendinger and Schwendinger 1983).

The Walter Mitty

Generally passive and submissive, the *Walter Mitty* rapist has an unrealistic image of masculinity. He uses rape to bridge the gap between the way he perceives how men ought to be and the way he perceives himself. He fantasizes that his victims enjoy being raped—for he is an excellent sex partner. Carrying his fantasy one step farther, he sometimes calls his victim the next day, asking her how she enjoyed it and trying to make a date with her. He is unlikely to beat his victim, but he will use as much force as necessary to make her submit.

The Opportunist

Unlike the first six types of rapists, the *opportunist* does not set out to rape. Rather, he grabs an unexpected opportunity, which often occurs during a robbery or burglary. For example, one man drove to a local supermarket to find someone to rob. The first person to come along was a pregnant woman. As he was robbing her, threatening her with a knife, the woman was scared out of her wits and she blurted out that she would do anything if he didn't hurt her. At that point, he decided to force her to drive to a deserted area, where he raped her. He explained:

> I wasn't thinking about sex. But when she said she would do anything not to get hurt, probably because she was pregnant, I thought, "why not." (Scully and Marolla 2005:56)

The Date Rapist

Date rapists, also called *acquaintance rapists,* are the eighth type. Some of these rapists feel that they deserve sex because they have invested time and money in a date or sexual seduction; they are collecting a sexual "payoff" from their investment. Date rapists generally prefer to avoid violence. As the Issues in Social Problems box on page 146 shows, date rape involves many motivations other than "collecting" and consists of much more than a man being more insistent than he should. It is uncommon for date rapists to be reported to the police and, if reported, to be convicted (Kanin 2003). In a study of students at Texas A&M University, psychologists Charlene Muehlenhard and Melaney Linton (1987) found that date rape most commonly occurs not between couples who are on their first date, but between couples who have known each other about a year. This study is summarized in Table 5-3.

Please note that these findings do *not* represent all college students. This is a one-time measurement in one academic discipline at one college.

TABLE 5-3 Date Rape and Other Unwanted Sexual Acts Experienced by Undergraduates

The results of a survey of 380 women and 368 men enrolled in introductory psychology courses at Texas A&M University.

Percentages add up to more than 100 because often more than one unwanted sexual act occurred on the same date.

UNWANTED SEXUAL ACTIVITY	WOMEN WHO REPORTED THIS HAD HAPPENED TO THEM	MEN WHO REPORTED THEY HAD DONE THIS
	(%)	(%)
He kissed without tongue contact	3.7	2.2
He kissed with tongue contact	12.3	0.7
He touched/kissed her breasts through her clothes	24.7	7.3
He touched/kissed her breasts under her clothes	22.6	13.1
He touched her genitals through her clothes	28.8	15.3
He touched her genitals under her clothes	28.4	13.9
He performed oral sex on her	9.9	8.8
He forced her to touch his genitals through his clothes	2.9	0.7
He forced her to touch his genitals under his clothes	5.8	2.2
He forced her to perform oral sex on him	2.5	4.4
He forced her to have sexual intercourse	20.6	15.3

Source: Muehlenhard and Linton 1987:190.

The Recreational Rapist

A ninth type is the *recreational* rapist. For him, rape engenders male camaraderie, for he joins friends to participate collectively in a dangerous activity. As sociologists Diana Scully and Joseph Marolla (1985/2005) discovered in their interviews of imprisoned rapists, one man may make a date with a victim and then drive her to a predetermined location, where he and his friends rape her. One man said that this practice was so much a part of his group's weekend routine that they rented a house just for the purpose of recreational rape.

The Husband Rapist

The last type is the *husband* rapist. Contrary to common opinion, marital rape is real rape. It is not an innocuous event involving a husband who has simply become too insistent about having sex. After interviewing wives who had been raped, sociologists David Finkelhor and Kersti Yllo (1985, 1989) concluded that such an idea is a "sanitary stereotype." Marital rape can involve violence and sadism every bit as horrible as any that we have discussed. Some wives are forced to flee in terror for their lives and sanity.

REACTIONS TO RAPE

Let's look at what happens to the rape victim after her attack. We will focus first on her personal reactions and then on what some pinpoint as a social problem itself, how the criminal justice system treats rape victims.

Disbelief and Shock

Disbelief is the first reaction of a woman who finds herself confronted by a rapist (McIntyre et al. 1979). The event is so frightening and alien that most victims report they could not believe it was happening. Shock quickly follows.

Styles of Dealing with the Trauma

The trauma of rape does not end with the physical attack. The woman typically finds her self-concept shattered, her emotions wounded, her whole life disrupted. About half of rape victims deal with their trauma in an *expressive* style, venting their fear, anger, rage, and anxiety by crying and sobbing, or by restlessness and tenseness. The other half reacts in a *controlled* style, carefully masking their feelings behind a calm and composed exterior (Burgess and Holmstrom 1974).

Life and relationships are no longer the same. Doubt, distrust, and self-blame plague rape victims. Some feel guilty for having been alone in that place at that time. Others feel that they let themselves get in a compromising situation. If they didn't scream and fight back, that bothers them. They feel that there must have been something—*anything*—that they could have done—or not done—that might have changed the situation. I think you get the idea of how bottomless such self-accusations can be.

In addition to the nightmares, many victims become afraid—of being alone, of the dark, of walking on the street, or of doing such ordinary activities as shopping and driving. Anything that reminds them of the event—and they never know when something will set this off—can send them into anxiety and depression. The victim's personal relationships may also deteriorate, for it is not uncommon for the woman to feel less intimate and trusting and to withdraw emotionally. On top of this, a husband or boyfriend might wonder what "really" happened (Russell 1979).

The Trauma of Dealing with the Legal System

Although many police departments have grown sensitive to the plight of rape victims and have trained women officers to do the interviewing, the criminal justice system often adds to the victim's suffering (Madigan and Gamble 1991; Jordan 2001). Many police officers who arrive on the scene or at the hospital have little experience in dealing with rape victims. To conduct their investigation, they must ask detailed questions, some of a sexual nature. Some officers become embarrassed, others are insensitive, and still others are disbelieving. Some male officers even think that the woman "asked for it." Others don't believe it was rape if the woman doesn't have bruises and cuts. Some officers suspect that the victim is trying to use the police to "get even" with a boyfriend. Because some rape charges are bogus, this is a legitimate concern on

After feminists publicized their views about sexual violence, date rape became recognized as a special problem within the social problem of rape. Alcohol is often used by date rapists to lower the defenses of their victims. (This is not a photo of date rapists, but such "fun" activities involving alcohol often precede rape.)

the part of the police—but that concern comes across as suspicion of the victim. Just when the woman needs compassion the most, when her world has been turned upside down, she can find herself in the midst of suspicion and embarrassment, which engenders hostility and embarrassment on her part.

One victim gave this account of her experience with the police:

> They rushed me down to the housing cops who asked me questions like, "Was he your boyfriend?" "Did you know him?" Here I am, hysterical. I'm 12 years old, and I don't know these things even happen to people. Anyway, they took me to the precinct after that, and there about four detectives got me in the room and asked me how long was his penis—like I was supposed to measure it. Actually, they said, "How long was the instrument?" I thought they were referring to the knife—how was I supposed to know? That I could have told them 'cause I was sure enough lookin' at the knife. (Brownmiller 1975:365)

Even if a woman is fortunate enough to be questioned by sensitive, compassionate police officers who have been trained in rape investigations, this is just the beginning of her experience in the criminal justice system. In 44 percent of the reported rapes, the rapist is arrested (*Sourcebook of Criminal Justice Statistics* 2002:Table 4.19). The victim then faces a dilemma. If she fails to press charges, the rapist goes free—and he may well rape again. But if she prosecutes, she must recount her rape in detail, forcing her to face aspects of the criminal justice system that are designed to protect the accused. The woman must relive her attack, perhaps repeatedly, as she goes over the details with the prosecuting attorney. Then she must describe everything in a public courtroom in front of her rapist, his attorney, a judge, perhaps a jury, journalists, and even curiosity seekers. Here, the defense attorney may try to blacken her character, for in some states her prior sex life can still be examined on the witness stand. Everything she says can be challenged, and because the rape was so sudden and might have occurred in darkness, any fuzziness in her details presents an opening for the defense attorney. In the courtroom, the accuser can become the accused. As one rape victim said of her experience:

> I had heard other women say that the trial is the rape. It's no exaggeration. My trial was one of the dirtiest transcripts you could read. Even though I had been warned about the defense attorney, you wouldn't believe the things he asked me to describe. It was very humiliating. I don't understand it. It was like I was the defendant and he was the plaintiff. I wasn't on trial. I don't see where I did anything wrong. I screamed, I struggled. (Brownmiller 1975:36)

The "Legal Rape"

Many reasons underlie this second victimization, which some call the "legal rape" of the victim. Part of this is due to presumptions of innocence that are built into the judicial system. For justice to be served, if someone is accused of a crime, including rape, that person must have the right to question the accuser and to present a vigorous defense. In addition to this, there is a carryover of the traditional male view into the judicial system. From this perspective, women who go out alone at night or who go into bars are "asking for it"; men have a strong sex drive that is hard to control, and women provoke them sexually; some women—and they have no right to do this—change their minds just before sex, and then cry rape.

Homosexual Rape

To be complete, I need to mention homosexual rape. Although we have concentrated on the social problem of men raping women, men also rape other men. As noted in Chapter 3, this form of rape (along with forced prostitution) is common in our jails and prisons, with younger prisoners often being marked as victims. At the moment,

Issues in Social Problems
DATE (OR ACQUAINTANCE) RAPE

Carol had just turned 18, and it looked like her dreams had come true. It was only the beginning of her freshman year, and yet she had met Tom, the all-state quarterback. At Wiggins Watering Hole, the college bar, he had walked over to her table and made some crack about the English Comp professor. She had laughed, and the two had spent most of the evening talking.

When Tom asked to take her back to the dorm, Carol didn't hesitate. This was the man all the girls wanted to date! At the dorm, he said he would like to talk some more, so she signed him in. Once in the room, he began to kiss her. At first, the kisses felt good. But Tom was not about to stop with kissing. He forced her to the bed and, despite her protests, began to remove her clothing.

With his 240 pounds, and her 117, there wasn't much of a contest. Carol always wondered why she didn't cry out; she was asked this at the trial. This brutal end to her virginity also marked the end of her college career. Depressed and distrustful, Carol left college and moved back with her parents. After a hearing, the university suspended Tom for a few games. Tom then resumed his life as before. He still goes to Wiggins Watering Hole.

For Letitia, 27, the evening started out friendly enough. After a cozy dinner at her apartment, her boyfriend suggested that she lie down while he did the dishes. As she lay in bed, he walked in with a butcher knife. Her formerly tender lover bound and raped her. When it was over, he fell asleep.

The public has little understanding of date rape. Most seem to think that it involves a reluctant woman who needs a "push" to go along with what she really wants. A study at UCLA found that 54 percent of the men and 42 percent of the women believe that forced sexual intercourse can be permissible. At Auburn University, 61 percent of the men said that they had touched a woman sexually against her will.

Convictions for date rape are hard to get, and some prosecutors discourage women from bringing such charges. A social worker at a rape treatment center said, "Most people are very understanding if a stranger breaks into your house with a gun and rapes you, but if you say you made a date with the rapist, they always wonder how far you went before you said no."

Obviously, most people don't know Carol and Letitia.

What can be done? Campus antirape groups—preferably composed of both women and men—offer one remedy. Lectures and workshops can introduce incoming freshmen to the reality and perils of date rape. Well-publicized prosecutions can go a long way to cutting the risk, and antirape groups can encourage women to press charges and insist that prosecutors do their job. Student groups, composed of concerned students, both women and men, can pressure the college administration to react strongly to date rape. We know that "if there were a pattern of assaults on quarterbacks, universities would respond very quickly."

Based on Engelmayer 1983; Seligmann 1984.

however, people prefer to ignore these objective conditions. Until there is an outcry from the public or from authorities, by sociological definition we do not have a social problem. I anticipate that this will be one of the social problems of rape in the future, at which time we will look at our present attitudes as barbaric.

Murder

If Martians were to study the earth, they might find our fascination with murder bizarre. The Martians might report that murder has become a major form of U.S. entertainment, that every night Americans watch beatings, bombings, shootings, slashings, stabbings, strangulations, and other mayhem on television—with gruesome close-ups in living color.

As the text stresses, for rape victims the trial can be brutal. When Kobe Bryant was accused of rape, he was able to hire topnotch attorneys. With a ruling that the accuser's sexual past could be brought up, she stopped cooperating with authorities, and filed civil charges instead. Bryant, who admitted that he had sex with the woman, then stated that he understood how her "no" might actually have meant "no." Bryant is shown with his wife at a press conference after he was accused of rape.

THE SOCIAL PATTERNS OF MURDER

Real-Life "Whodunits"

THE WHO

One of the steps in establishing a social problem is agitation by concerned people, which arouses concern in many others. Through this process, rape became defined as a social problem. To alert students to potential danger, many campuses place posters in prominent spots.

A lot of campus rapes start here.

Whenever there's drinking or drugs, things can get out of hand. So it's no surprise that many campus rapes involve alcohol.

But you should know that under any circumstances, sex without the other person's consent is considered rape. A felony, punishable by prison. And drinking is no excuse.

That's why, when you party, it's good to know what your limits are. You see, a little sobering thought now can save you from a big problem later.

© 1990 Rape Treatment Center, Santa Monica Hospital

As any mystery reader knows, we must explore the who, what, when, where, and why of murder. Let's first examine the statistics so we can uncover the social patterns of murder. Then we can try to figure out the sociological "why" of those patterns.

Although most people's fears of murder center around strangers, of all violent crimes, murder is the *least* likely to be committed by a stranger. It also is the most likely to be solved. Look at Figure 5-5 on page 148 for a comparison of arrest rates by type of crime. Then look at Table 5-4 on page 149, which shows the relationships between victims and their killers. Strangers account for only about 25 percent of U.S. killings. Three out of four murder victims are killed by members of their family or by their lovers, friends, neighbors, or other acquaintances.

The "who" of U.S. murder follows the patterns of social class, sex, age, and race-ethnicity that we found when we examined the crime of rape. The poor are more likely to kill. So are younger people. Although only about 14 percent of the U.S. population are between the ages of 15 and 24, from this group come *half* of the killers (*FBI Uniform Crime Reports* 2003:Table 38; *Statistical Abstract* 2003:Table 11). Figure 5-6 on page 149 illustrates how much more likely males are to kill than females. Males kill 90 percent of everyone who is murdered in the United States. Although females make up 51 percent of the U.S. population, they commit only 10 percent of the murders. As you can see from Table 5-4 on page 149, spouse murders also follow this pattern; husbands are more than four times as likely to kill their wives than wives are to kill their husbands.

Similar startling differences mark African Americans and whites. Although African Americans make up only about 12 percent of the U.S. population, in 50 percent of the cases where the race-ethnicity of the killer is known, the murderer is an African American (*FBI Uniform Crime Reports* 2003:Table 2.6). From Table 5-5 on page 150, you can see that murder is overwhelmingly *intraracial;* 86 percent of white victims are killed by whites, and 93 percent of black victims are killed by blacks.

THE WHAT

Although people use a variety of weapons to commit murder, every year the number-one choice of Americans is the gun. As you can see from Figure 5-7 on page 151, all other weapons take a distant second place. Two obvious reasons that guns are the favorite choice for killing are that they are highly effective, and they are readily available in the United States. More subtle reasons are that men are the number-one killers, and guns are identified as masculine. Significant cultural stereotypes reinforce this image. For example, our culture romanticizes cowboys and hunters and bandits, who personify the union of guns, killing, and masculinity. To settle a quarrel, then, the U.S. male is much more likely to reach for a gun than, say, a kitchen knife or a bottle of poison.

THE WHEN

Like rape, murder is not evenly distributed across the seasons. July is consistently the highest month for murder, and February the lowest (*FBI Uniform Crime Reports* 2003:Table 2.3). Year after year, more murders occur during the last six months of the year. The FBI used to break killings down by day of the week, but they stopped doing this. When they did, they reported that nights were more dangerous than days, and weekends more dangerous than weekdays. The most dangerous time of the week was Saturday night, which, as sociologist Alex Thio (1978) observed back in the 1970s, may be why cheap handguns are called "Saturday night specials." It is likely that these patterns of more killings occurring at night and during weekends still hold.

The good news is that between 1991 and 2002 the U.S. murder rate plunged 43 percent, dropping from 9.8 killings per 100,000 Americans to just 5.6 (*FBI Uniform Crime Reports* 1992 and 2003:19). The bad news is that although the U.S. murder rate has declined so sharply, it remains one of the highest in the world. As with rape, the states vary tremendously in their individual rates, and where you live vitally affects your chances of being murdered. Here is the extreme: People in Louisiana are *sixteen* times

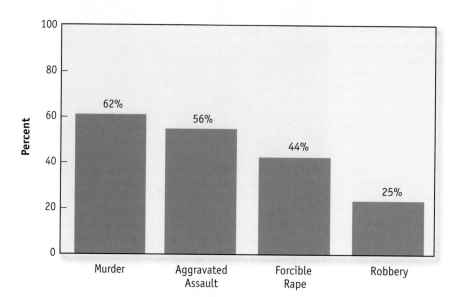

FIGURE 5-5 *Crimes Cleared by Arrest*

Source: By the author, based on *Sourcebook of Criminal Justice Statistics* 2002:Table 4.19.

TABLE 5-4 How Are Murder Victims Related to Their Killers?			
FAMILY	22.2%	ACQUAINTANCES	53.3%
Wife	7.5%	Girlfriend	5.5%
Son	3.0%	Friend	4.4%
Daughter	2.6%	Boyfriend	1.9%
Husband	1.7%	Neighbor	1.4%
Father	1.4%	Acquaintance, general	40.1%
Mother	1.4%		
Brother	1.1%	Strangers	24.5%
Sister	0.3%		
Other Family	3.4%		

Note: These relationships refer to cases in which the relationship between the killer and victim is known. In 46 percent of killings that relationship was not reported by the police.
Source: *FBI Uniform Crime Reports* 2003:Table 2.12.

more likely to be murdered than are people in North Dakota. Figure 5-8 on page 151 shows which states are the safest and the most dangerous.

THE WHERE

Most people think that your chances of getting murdered are greater in the city than in the country—and they are right. In large cities (those with populations over 250,000), 6.2 of every 100,000 people are murdered each year. In rural areas, the murder rate drops to 3.6 per 100,000 people. But even safer are the smaller cities. There, the murder rate drops to 3.2 per 100,000 people (*FBI Uniform Crime Reports* 2003:Table 2). Table 5-6 on page 152 shows how uneven the murder rate is among cities.

SOCIAL BASES OF THE SOCIAL PATTERNS

THE WHY

Why do these patterns exist? As we will see, they reflect our society. We do not know all the answers, and some are complicated, so let's begin with the simpler reasons.

Acquaintanceship

Most murder victims are killed by someone they know, because most murders are crimes of passion spurred by heated arguments. As many analysts have pointed out, we

FIGURE 5-6 *Killers and Their Victims*
Source: *FBI Uniform Crime Reports* 2003:Table 2.8.

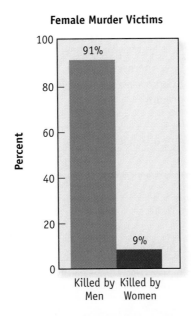

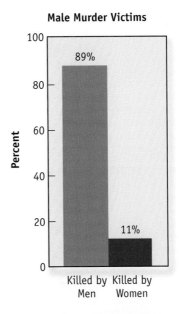

are much more likely to argue with people we know than with strangers. It is with people we know that we share money, property, and love—the things that fuel quarrels and sometimes lead to violent death.

Poverty

Why are murderers so likely to come from the most deprived groups of Americans? The three sociological perspectives help us to understand this pattern. *Conflict theorists,* who view the poor as oppressed people, see their high murder rates as the result of their poverty. As sociologist Elliott Currie (1985:160) put it:

> Brutal conditions breed brutal behavior. To believe otherwise requires us to argue that the experience of being confined to the mean and precarious depths of the American economy has *no* serious consequences for personal character or social behavior.

Because most murder victims of the killers who come from poverty are also usually poor, conflict theorists conclude that people in poverty are striking out at one another instead of at their oppressors.

Functionalists who work within strain theory point out that people experience a lot of stress when they are denied access to the approved means for attaining material success. People who feel greater stress are more likely to strike out at others. Functionalists who emphasize control theory point out that the poor have weaker internal and external controls to inhibit their desires to strike out at others. For example, the poor have less to lose if they are arrested or go to jail. Compared with people from higher social classes, the poor risk less because they are unlikely to own their homes, and their jobs pay relatively little and are already insecure. The poor also are less likely to have reputations at stake in voluntary organizations such as the Chamber of Commerce or professional associations.

The Meaning Behind Murder

To this, *symbolic interactionists* add that in some subcultures of the poor, police trouble can actually enhance people's reputation. Young males become more of a "man" if they are sent to "juvvie" (juvenile detention) or to jail. In some subcultures, the prison experience has become so common that young men expect to go there, just as young men in other social classes expect to go to college. Symbolic interactionists also stress that the social classes have distinct ways to resolve disputes. Middle-class people who have a grievance are likely to seek legal recourse, such as lawsuits. In contrast, poor people place less trust in the judicial system, and they are unable to afford lawyers. As a result, poor people are more likely to settle disagreements outside the law. Their direct confrontations more easily lead to heated words, physical assault, and death.

Some symbolic interactionists stress subcultural theory and differential association. In a subculture of poverty, to settle scores directly with an antagonist is a "macho" act. People are expected to stand up to others. They are admired for doing so and looked down on if they prove themselves to be "yellow" or "chicken." This applies to both males and females. People who grow up in this subculture are likely to learn to react violently to life's problems.

TABLE 5-5 Race-Ethnicity of Killers and Their Victims

		KILLERS	
		WHITE	BLACK
VICTIMS	White	86%	14%
	Black	7%	93%

Note: Does not include victims or killers whose race-ethnicity is unknown.
Source: By the author, based on *FBI Uniform Crime Reports 2003*:Table 2.8.

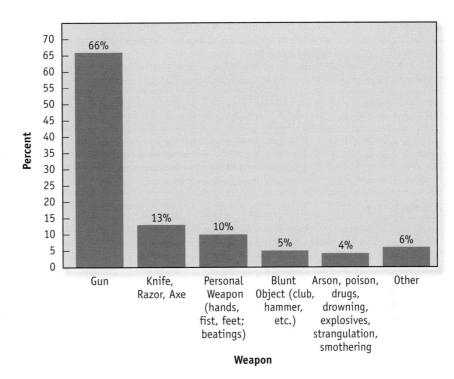

FIGURE 5-7 *American's Choice of Murder Weapons*

Source: By the author, based on *FBI Uniform Crime Reports* 2003:Table 2.10.

To trace the path by which people became involved in murder, Lonnie Athens, a symbolic interactionist, interviewed 58 prisoners. He found this general pattern: The killer considered some act that the victim did as intolerable. A spouse or lover might have refused sex or threatened to leave, or someone—whether a stranger or friend—spewed insults. The killer interpreted this situation as one that called for violence, often because this act threatened the killer's self-image or social standing among friends. Faced with this interpretation of the situation—intolerable conduct for which violence is the appropriate response—the individual killed.

FIGURE 5-8 *The "Where" of Murder*

Source: By the author, based on *FBI Uniform Crime Reports* 2003:Table 5.

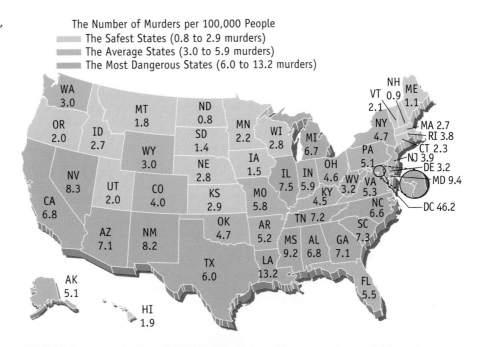

The Number of Murders per 100,000 People
- The Safest States (0.8 to 2.9 murders)
- The Average States (3.0 to 5.9 murders)
- The Most Dangerous States (6.0 to 13.2 murders)

A woman prisoner whom Athens (1980:36–37) interviewed said that a stranger at a party had accused her of cheating him of $20. The man kept insulting her and laughing at her:

> Then I told myself, "This man has got to go one way or another; I've just had enough of this (man) messing with me; I'm going to cut his dirty . . . throat." I went into my bedroom, got a $20 bill and my razor. I said to myself . . . "now he's hung himself," and I walked out of the bedroom. I went up to him with a big smile on my face. I held the $20 bill in my hand out in front of me and hid the razor in the other hand. Then I sat on his lap and said, "O.K., you're a fast dude; here's your $20 back." He said, "I'm glad that you are finally admitting it." I looked at him with a smile and said, "Let me seal it with a kiss" . . . and then I bent over like I was going to kiss him and started slicing up his throat.

Killing as a Manly Act

This last example notwithstanding, why do men kill more often than women? As we have seen, men are more likely to value violence. Men in poverty especially are likely to believe that a real man is tough—and toughness includes the willingness to be violent. One's standing in the group may depend on being known as "the kind of guy who can't be pushed around." Not to fight when insulted is cowardice, the worst quality a young man can show in certain subcultures.

As we saw earlier, among some groups killing is even associated with manliness, and spilling blood brings honor. In the Mafia, killing an enemy is the equivalent of courage: Killing is the measure of one's *capacity as a man*. There, "the more awesome and potent the victim, the more worthy and meritorious the killer" (Arlacchi 1980:113).

Symbolic interactionists stress that females are less likely to be socialized to be violent. Where males learn to associate masculinity with being tough, showing bravery, and being violent when it is necessary, most females learn less-violent ways of handling loss of face. The result of this socialization into gender is that *in every society around the world* men kill at a rate several times that of women (Daly and Wilson 1988; Chernoff and Simon 2000). (To be fair to other theorists, I need to point out that biological and evolutionary theorists point to this worldwide uniformity in the killing pattern as strong evidence for their theories of genetic inheritance.)

Why the Racial–Ethnic Differences?

Let's apply some of these social patterns to explain why African Americans kill at a higher rate than their proportion of the population. African Americans are more

TABLE 5-6 Murder: The Ten Safest and Most Dangerous U.S. Cities

	SAFEST			MOST DANGEROUS	
RANK	CITY	MURDERS PER 100,000 PEOPLE	RANK	CITY	MURDERS PER 100,000 PEOPLE
1	Honolulu, HI	2.3	1	New Orleans, LA	44.0
2	San Jose, CA	2.4	2	St. Louis, MO	42.6
3	Virginia Beach, VA	2.8	3	Detroit, MI	41.3
4	Saint Paul, MN	3.1	4	Washington, D.C.	40.4
5	El Paso, TX	3.5	5	Baltimore, MD	38.7
6	Raleigh, NC	3.6	6	Atlanta, GA	33.5
7	Colorado Springs, CO	3.8	7	Newark, NJ	32.6
8	Anchorage, AK	3.8	8	Memphis, TN	24.2
9	Austin, TX	3.9	9	Kansas City, MO	23.2
10	Portland, OR	3.9	10	Chicago, IL	22.9

Note: From data reported by police officials in cities over 250,000 people.
Source: By the author, based on *Statistical Abstract* 2003:Table 308.

More Americans are killed by guns than by any other weapon. Liberals blame the easy availability of guns, and they campaign to have the sale of guns banned. To this, conservatives reply, "Guns don't kill people; people do." The debate continues, as do efforts to ban or limit the sale of guns.

likely to be poor, and the subculture to which lower-class African-American males belong identifies masculinity with the willingness to defend oneself aggressively. Functionalists would add that African Americans are socialized to strive for the cultural goal of material success, but discrimination blocks many of them from reaching that goal through legitimate means. This increases their strain, leading to a higher rate of violent crime, most of which is directed against people nearby. A widespread pattern of racially segregated housing helps to account for the intraracial pattern of murder, the black-on-black violence.

What about violence that crosses racial lines? To explain interracial patterns, functionalists stress the connection between race-ethnicity and money. If a burglary, robbery, or mugging results in a killing across racial lines, it is more likely to involve poor African Americans robbing whites than poor whites robbing African Americans. Conflict theorists add that the oppression of African Americans by whites produces racial hatred that has many negative consequences, including deadly incidents of striking out against the dominant group. If African Americans were in the driver's seat of society and possessed vastly more wealth than whites, we would expect this pattern to be reversed.

To understand race-ethnicity and violence, we need to focus on another aspect of social class. In *The Declining Significance of Race*, William Julius Wilson (1978) analyzed how changing social events had an impact on the class divisions of African Americans. As racial barriers dropped, many African Americans joined the middle class as they were able to get more education and, with it, better jobs. Seizing their opportunity, they moved out of the ghetto and into more desirable areas of the city and suburbs. Left behind was an *underclass,* a group of people who were desperately poor and were plagued with social problems—high unemployment, many single mothers, and a lot of drug addiction, murder, robbery, and rape. As Wilson put it, this group "is increasingly isolated from mainstream patterns and norms of behavior." It is here that U.S. violence is concentrated.

Why the Temporal Patterns?

The timing of U.S. murder also reflects broader social patterns. During weekdays, when murders are less frequent, people are working and meeting personal and familial responsibilities. On weekends, when murders are more frequent, people are more likely to socialize in public and to drink more than usual. This increases the likelihood of quarrels, with the peak coming on the traditional "Saturday night out." The explanation for the seasonality of murder follows similar lines. Because people are more likely to get out of the house and socialize during warm weather, murder peaks during the summer and decreases during the winter. If you have ever spent time in the inner city, as I have, you are familiar with some of the "finer points" of that "summer socializing" that leads to murder: gambling, drinking, and boasting.

Why the Geographic Patterns?

Finally, the geography of murder intrigues sociologists. For more than a century, the South's murder rate has been higher than that of the rest of the country. This pattern is broadly evident in the Social Map you looked at earlier, on page 151. That the South has a higher murder rate year after year has led some researchers to conclude that there is a "southern subculture of violence" (Huff-Corzine et al. 1991). Southerners supposedly learn more violent ways of resolving their disagreements than do people reared in other regions of the United States. They take violence more for granted as a regular part of life, and more violent themes run through their music, their literature, and even their jokes. Apparently, southerners are more likely to own guns, to know how to shoot them, and to use guns during quarrels. Sociologists find these explanations suggestive, but not totally satisfactory (Doerner 1978; Messner 1983; Huff-Corzine et al. 1986). We need more creative thinking to establish an explanation that will be more broadly acceptable.

Before concluding this section, let's look at two patterns of murder that have gripped the public's attention: mass murder and serial murder.

Mass Murder

Mass murder is "the killing of four or more victims at one location, within one event" (Zawitz 1988). Examples are Richard Speck's murder of 8 nursing students in Chicago one July night in 1966; Charles Whitman's killing of 16 people in a sniper attack from a tower at the University of Texas that same year; James Huberty's shooting of 21 people at a McDonald's in 1984; the 87 deaths caused by Julio Gonzalez, who torched the Happy Land Social Club in the Bronx in 1991 because his girlfriend was dancing with someone else; George Hennard's shooting of 22 people at a Luby's Cafeteria in Killeen, Texas, in 1991; Colin Ferguson's shooting spree as he walked through a New York commuter train and methodically fired forty shots, in 1993, an incident that left 6 people dead; and the rash of school shootings that has so alarmed the public, such as the one described in our opening vignette. To my knowledge, only two woman have joined the list of mass murderers. In 1981, Priscilla Ford killed 6 people in Reno, Nevada, by deliberately driving her car onto a crowded sidewalk during a Thanksgiving Day parade. In Houston in 2001, Andrea Yates drowned her five small children in the family bathtub while her husband was at work.

When Timothy McVeigh blew up a federal building in Oklahoma City, Oklahoma, on April 19, 1995, 168 people died. This is the largest mass murder by a single individual in the history of the United States. (McVeigh may have been assisted by others, but, if so, only a small number of people were involved.) McVeigh's stunning number of victims was greatly overshadowed by the events of September 11, 2001, of course, which claimed about 3,000 lives. Nine-eleven was a special type of mass murder, for it involved many people making plans over a period of years, detailed financing, and the transportation and coordination of men from other countries. Although this act perfectly fits the definition of mass murder, it is so different from "typical" mass murder that it might be better thought of as an act of war. If we were to include war killings in this category, however, the picture would change abruptly. We will leave acts of war as a separate category.

Serial Murder

Serial murder is the killing of several victims in three or more separate events. The murders may occur over several days, weeks, or years (Zawitz 1988). The elapsed time between murders distinguishes serial killers from mass murderers. Here are some examples:

- Between 1962 and 1964, Albert De Salvo ("the Boston Strangler") raped and killed 13 women.
- During the 1960s and 1970s, Ted Bundy killed dozens of women in four states, bludgeoning, strangling, and sexually molesting them.

- In the late 1970s, John Wayne Gacy sexually molested and killed 33 young men in Chicago.
- During 1976 and 1977, David Berkowitz ("Son of Sam") murdered 6 people in New York City.
- Between 1979 and 1981, Wayne Williams killed 28 boys and young men in Atlanta (Levin and Fox 1985).
- In 1983, Henry Lee Lucas admitted to a killing rampage that left hundreds of victims strewn across the nation. Lucas may have killed only 5 or 10 people. Apparently, Lucas loved the attention he received for his confessions, and, to clear their books, the police urged him to confess to everything but the assassination of JFK. (Ressler and Shachtman 1992).
- During the 1980s and 1990s, the "Green River" killer left the bodies of prostitutes strewn around the countryside near Seattle, Washington. In 2003, Gary Ridgway, an automobile painter, was given 48 consecutive life sentences for killing 48 women.
- The serial killer with the most victims appears to be Harold Shipman, a quiet, unassuming physician in Manchester, England. From 1977 to 2000, he killed 230 to 275 of his elderly women patients. He gave the women lethal injections while making house calls.
- One of the most bizarre serial killers was Jeffrey Dahmer of Milwaukee. Not only did Dahmer kill young men, but he also had sex with their dead bodies and fried and ate parts of his victims. So he wouldn't go hungry, he kept body parts in his freezer.

Gary Leon Ridgway appeared in King County Superior Court in Seattle, Washington, in December, 2001, to plead not guilty on four counts of first-degree murder. Investigators linked Ridgway to the murders of up to 49 women and girls in Washington.

Almost all serial killers are men, but an occasional woman joins this list of infamy. In North Carolina in 1986, the husband of Blanche Taylor Moore was taken to the hospital with arsenic poisoning. He survived, but the ensuing investigation led to the exhumation of 6 bodies, including her father, her first husband, and a boyfriend. Arsenic was found in all of them. In 1987 and 1988, Dorothea Montalvo Puente, who operated a boarding house for senior citizens in Sacramento, killed 7 boarders. Her motive was to collect their Social Security checks. In Missouri, from 1986 to 1989, Faye Copeland and her husband killed 5 transient men. Aileen Wuornos hitchhiked along Florida's freeways and killed 7 middle-aged men after having sex with them. For this, she was executed.

I researched one of the first serial killings to attract the attention of the U.S. public. Fascinated by television reports, I went to Houston, where Dean Corll, with the aid of two teenage accomplices, had killed 27 boys. The 33-year-old had befriended Elmer Wayne Henley and David Brooks, two teenagers from broken homes. From 1971 to 1973, the boys picked up young hitchhikers and delivered them to Corll to rape and kill. Sometimes they even brought him their own neighbors and high school classmates.

My interviews confirmed what has become common knowledge about serial killers: They successfully lead double lives that catch their friends and family unaware. Henley's mother swore to me that her son was a good boy and couldn't possibly be guilty. Some of his high school friends told me the same thing. They stressed that he couldn't be involved in homosexual rape and murder because he was interested only in girls. I conducted my interviews in Henley's bedroom, and for proof Henley's friends pointed to a pair of girls' panties that were hanging in the room.

Mass murder is usually committed by men who relieve pressure by exploding in an outburst of killing. (Because several mass murders have been committed by postal employees at work, in the popular vernacular, this is known as "going postal.") Serial murderers, in contrast, are generally more methodical in their planning. Many of these killers are motivated by lust and are sexually aroused by killing. To refer to this, the FBI even uses the term "lust murder." As with Ted Bundy and Jeffrey Dahmer, some have sex with their dead victims. Bundy returned day after day to the countryside where he had left his victims to copulate with the corpse. Other serial killers, however, are more "garden variety," motivated by greed, like Dorothea Puente, who killed for money.

Have Mass and Serial Murders Become More Common?

Many assume that mass and serial murders are more common now than they used to be, but we do not know this. In the past, police departments had little communication with one another, and when killings occurred in different jurisdictions, it was difficult to connect separate killings. Today's more efficient investigative techniques make it easier for the police to conclude that a serial killer is operating in an area. Part of the perception that such killings have increased is also due to ignorance of our history: In our frontier past, serial killers went from ranch to ranch, and mass murderers wiped out entire villages of Native Americans.

Social Policy

Social policy on violence has three aspects: how to deal with offenders, how to deal with their victims, and how to prevent violence. Let's look at each.

DEALING WITH OFFENDERS

Two Extreme Positions:

Dealing with offenders brings us face to face with irreconcilable views. The extreme positions are held by the retributionist and the reformist.

The Retributionist

The **retributionist** focuses on the victims of violence. Seeing their suffering, retributionists argue that anyone who is violent deserves only punishment. Retributionists believe in an "eye for an eye and a tooth for a tooth." Matching violence with violence, they would castrate rapists and kill murderers. They rejoice in the streets when killers like Bundy and Gacy, who have tortured their victims before killing them, are executed.

The Reformist

The **reformist,** in contrast, directs our attention to the offenders. Reformists see violent offenders as victims themselves. Emotionally wounded through dysfunctional families, social inequality, or discrimination, assailants are venting their frustration and anger by striking out at others. Reformists want policies to help families function better and to provide offenders with psychiatric, medical, and social services. They see the ultimate solution as prevention—avoiding violence by helping families and changing the social structure to eliminate social inequality and discrimination.

The retributionist and reformist views are so far apart emotionally and intellectually that their proponents can hardly talk to one another. With their eyes on the offenders, the reformists plead for understanding and help in order to change people and social circumstances. With their eyes on the victims, the retributionists reply, "How would you feel if your daughter had been raped and tortured?" The two groups are not talking about the same thing at all.

Between the Extremes

Somewhere between these extremes are people who do not care why someone was violent (so they aren't concerned about social change); nor do they have a desire to repay offenders in kind. They simply want to get violent people off the streets and remove their threat to society. Their position is simple: Lock 'em up, and throw away the key.

Steps That Can Be Taken:

These strong emotional reactions and extreme positions make it difficult to develop sound social policy for dealing with rapists and murderers. In addition, much is unknown about the causes of violence, and precious little is known about how to prevent it. Realizing that there is no easy path and no simple truth, let's examine some steps that can be taken.

Letting Victims Determine the Penalty

First, why not let the victims of violent crimes determine the prison term of the offender? No law would need to be changed, because victims would choose within the sentencing limits already established by law. This approach, which would provide the victim with a sense of satisfaction and justice, has been tried by an occasional judge. In Minneapolis, a judge allowed a 65-year-old great-grandmother to determine the prison sentence of the 26-year-old man who raped her ("Minneapolis Judge" 1989).

Reducing the Penalty for Rape

Second, consider a legal change that might decrease rape. Paradoxically, we would *reduce* the penalty for rape. Because current penalties are so severe, many juries are more inclined to acquit a man than to subject him to what they consider an unreasonable penalty, such as life imprisonment. Reducing penalties might lead to *more* convictions, and because men who are convicted for rape tend to have committed rapes other than the ones they were charged with, this could reduce the number of rapes in our society.

Establishing Degrees of Rape

If we were to adopt this policy, we might establish degrees of rape similar to the degrees of murder. Degrees of rape would reflect the reality that some rapes cause more serious injuries than others. Laws might include sexual assault in the following categories:

> *First degree*—abduction that involves transporting the victim to another location and causing severe bodily injury
> *Second degree*—abduction with less bodily injury
> *Third degree*—no abduction but serious bodily injury
> *Fourth degree*—no abduction and little bodily injury
> *Fifth degree*—no abduction and no bodily injury

This suggestion can be improved upon. For example, some will feel that abduction is less important than serious bodily injury and may want to reverse the second and third degrees. In any event, I suggest that prison be mandatory for anyone convicted of rape, and that sentences be meted out according to injury. I also suggest that prosecutors enforce our current, severe kidnapping laws in all rape cases that involve abduction.

DEALING WITH VICTIMS

The second major issue is social policy for the victims of violence. For murder, there would seem to be no issue to deal with, for the victim is dead. The family of a murder victim, however, has also been victimized. Family members are deprived for life of a loved one—a father, a mother, a child, a brother, a sister, a wife, a husband. Their ties are severed, their lives disrupted, never to be put back the way they were. Then there are the victims of rape. They are emotionally scarred, sometimes for life. They must also bear medical expenses and deal with the loss of income from missed work. Their families, too, suffer anguish, frustration, and anger.

Victim Compensation

A basic responsibility of government is to protect its citizens from violence. If a government fails to provide basic safety, should its citizens have the right to be compensated for that failure? Although some might consider such an idea too innovative and utopian, it was first suggested by Hammurabi 4,000 years ago. Forty-four states do have

Issues in Social Problems
A BILL OF RIGHTS FOR RAPE VICTIMS

You have the right to be afraid. It is a healthy, normal reaction to a life-threatening situation.

You have the right to be angry. But try not to show it; it can cost you physical injury, perhaps your life.

You have the right to do whatever will save your life.

You have the right to expect sympathetic and compassionate treatment from police and other authorities. You are the injured party, and they need you for any criminal investigation.

You have the right to know the status of your case and the whereabouts of the perpetrator if he is caught.

You have the right to know the progress of the police investigation if the offender has not been caught.

You have the right to expect support, not blame, from the rest of society.

You have the right to expect your government to protect you from violent crime. When it fails, you have the right to be compensated for the physical, emotional, and economic losses you have suffered.

Based on Hanson, October 5, 1977.

---

programs to compensate victims of violent crime for both medical costs and lost earnings. For all the publicity they receive, however, one might think this policy is a state secret (Zawitz 1988).

Training Personnel

The treatment of rape victims in the criminal justice system is improving. More law enforcement personnel are trained to deal with sexual assault. Some police departments assign special investigators and full-time prosecutors to sexual assault cases. As the skills of these professionals improve, more rapists will be convicted. Given the gender-sensitive nature of these investigations, some hospitals train women physicians and other hospital staff to deal with female rape victims. Such steps should be encouraged. (See the Issues in Social Problems box on a bill of rights for rape victims above.)

Support Groups

For many victims, the trauma of violence lingers for years, and they need long-term counseling. Support groups that are run by victims of violent crimes can be especially effective. Such people have experienced the problems first hand, and they know how to reach out to others (Gilmartin-Zena 1985; Chesler et al. 1990; Gardner 1992).

PREVENTING VIOLENCE

Four Social Policies:

1. Long Prison Terms for Repeat Offenders

2. Gun Control: Fewer Guns or More Guns?

Social policy also needs to center on preventing violence. I suggest four social policies. First, some men commit a large number of rapes. Some rape several times a month until they are caught—which can take years. Long sentences for repeat offenders ("career rapists")—with little chance of parole—will prevent many women from being raped.

Second, is the matter of gun control. As we saw in Figure 5-7 on page 150, most murder victims die from gunshot wounds. Proponents of gun control argue that because most murders are crimes of passion, emotional outbursts would be less lethal if guns were not so easy to get. Some propose that we could reduce the U.S. murder rate by registering all guns and licensing gun owners. Opponents argue that gun ownership is a constitutional right that should not be removed because some people abuse guns.

The two extremes of gun control show why it is difficult to establish social policy and why this debate on gun control continues without letup. On the one side are those who want to abolish gun ownership altogether. They consider gun ownership as an anachronistic custom that has "no redeeming social value." On the other side are those who argue that Americans need *more* guns. They argue that if all law-abiding citizens had guns, few rapists and killers would break into our homes—and even fewer would survive if they did. They also argue that Americans have more guns now than ever before and that most states now allow people to carry concealed handguns in public—and that the rates of both murder and rape have dropped.

3. Research the Social Causes of Violence

Third, policy makers should support research to determine how our culture creates a climate for violence. Remember the sociological question that was posed at the beginning of this chapter: What in a society increases or decreases the likelihood of violence? Because sociologists do not assume that Americans are genetically more violent than most people in the world, the answer lies in our culture. Once we determine what those aspects of the culture are, we can change them. I suggest that researchers

1. Examine less-violent cultures to determine what factors minimize violence.
2. Determine how to help Americans channel aggression constructively.
3. Find ways to minimize antagonisms and increase respect between the sexes.
4. Identify effective ways to teach males that females are not appropriate outlets for their frustration or aggression.
5. To the degree that individual violence is based on economic inequality, develop programs to provide more opportunities for the disadvantaged.

4. Keep the Problem Before the Public

We also can apply a fundamental point stressed throughout this book, that social problems do not consist only of objective conditions but also depend on subjective concerns. As sociologists Lynda Holmstrom and Ann Burgess (1989) emphasized, issues sometimes leap into prominence and then fade from sight. This could happen with sexual violence. If we are to work toward effective solutions, we must keep this social problem before the public.

The Future of the Problem

Our History Indicates Continuing High Rates of Violence

Given our history, our rate of violence is destined to remain higher than that of most nations. From time to time, our rape and murder rates will decline, offering hope that some fundamental change is taking place, but these occurrences will be followed by increases in rape and murder. To attain a low and permanent rate of violence would require major structural changes in our society. Without these changes, high rates of violence will be with us until our society ends—and that ending may well be a violent one.

The Three Theoretical Perspectives Also Indicate a Continuation of High Violence

Viewing the future through the lens of our three theoretical perspectives supports this view. *Conflict theory* indicates that tensions will be an ongoing part of our society. Short of revolution (which has proven no panacea for any society), the wealthy will remain in control, and discrimination will continue. Thus, the poor, especially minorities that are poor, who suffer not only from poverty but also discrimination, will continue to show up disproportionately in the statistics on violence. The *functionalist* lens shows that violence works, not always, but often enough for it to be perpetuated: People do get revenge and other satisfactions from killing their enemies. Some rapists gain feelings of dominance, power, and sexual satisfaction through forcible rape. The *symbolic interactionist* lens focuses on violence as a cultural symbol that is held out as a means of resolving conflict. This is a potent symbol, for it combines violence, power, strength, and dominance with a sense of manliness. Violence, then, will continue, as men try to live up to this cultural image.

The Sociological Perspective Indicates the Need to Make Structural Changes

The *sociological* perspective of violence is essential to understanding our present and our future. Our high rate of violence is not caused by a high number of violent psychopaths. This social pattern is a product of our history and our current social structure. Inequalities that are built into our society underlie much of the violence that we experience. Into whatever future we project ourselves, without major structural change violence will remain part of our way of life. This understanding of the *social* basis of violence can become the key to changing basic relationships—and to focusing that change in a direction that decreases violence.

SUMMARY

1. Sociologists analyze how *violence* is rooted in society. How a society is organized—its social structure—increases or decreases its amount of violence.

2. Each society has a rate of violence that, without major social change, is fairly constant over time. Sociologists call this a society's *normal violence.*

3. Biologists, anthropologists, and psychologists have theories to account for violence. The sociological response is that whatever predispositions humans have toward violence are encouraged or inhibited by the society in which they live.

4. Symbolic interactionists use two theories to explain violence. The first, *differential association,* stresses that violence is learned in association with other people. The second, *subcultural theory,* emphasizes that some groups are more approving of violence than others. People who grow up or associate with groups that approve of violence are more likely to learn violence.

5. Functionalists stress that some people become dissociated from cultural norms. Durkheim used the term *anomie* to describe this uprooting and estrangement. Anomic individuals are more likely to rape and to kill. Merton's *strain theory* suggests that violence is an alternative path that some people choose when they find the *cultural means* (such as education and jobs) to reach *cultural goals* (such

as financial success) blocked. *Control or containment theory* suggests that the inner and outer control of rapists and murderers are weaker than their pushes and pulls to commit these acts.

6. Conflict theorists emphasize that the groups within a society compete for scarce resources. The major division is between those who own the means of production and those who do not. Those at the mercy of the owners have few resources, and they lash out violently—misdirecting their violence onto one another.

7. Feminists challenged the traditional view of rape as a personal problem, a crime of passion. Researchers now consider rape a social problem, a crime of violence rooted in the structure of relationships between men and women.

8. Rape and murder are not random, unpredictable acts. They are related to the larger social patterns of society: They reflect patterns of class, gender, age, race-ethnicity, timing, location, and acquaintanceship.

9. To prevent violence requires restructuring those aspects of society that foster violence. Without such restructuring, high rates of violence will continue. To determine a rational basis for social policy on these emotionally charged issues requires research on the social causes of violence.

10. Rape may fade from the public's mind as a social problem. To find workable solutions, we must keep this issue alive.

KEY TERMS

Anomie   Feeling estranged, uprooted, unanchored, normless—not knowing what rules to apply to the situations one faces.

Collective violence   See *Group violence.*

Containment theory   A functionalist theory that focuses on the pushes and pulls thought to cause people to commit criminal acts. Whether one commits a violent act depends on the relative strength of inner containment (controls within the individual) and on outer containment (controls outside the individual).

Control theory   See *Containment theory.*

Criminal sexual assault   A legal term that refers to sexual attacks, especially to attempted rape and forcible rape.

Cultural goal   A goal held out as legitimate for the members of a society. See also *Cultural means.*

Cultural means   The general, approved ways of reaching cultural goals. See also *Cultural goal.*

Differential association A symbolic interactionist theory that stresses how criminal behavior is learned. Applied to violence, it assumes that people learn to be violent in the same way that people learn to be cooperative. See also *Subcultural theory.*

Forcible rape Nonconsensual or forced sexual relations. See *Statutory rape.*

Frustration-aggression A psychological theory that stresses that aggression is likely when a goal is blocked.

Group violence A number of people attacking others or destroying their property.

Individual violence One person attacking another.

Institutionalized group violence Group violence that is carried out under the direction of legally constituted officials.

Mass murder Killing four or more people at one time in one location.

Modeling Copying another's behavior.

Normal violence The amount of violence that a group usually has.

Organized group violence Violence that some group planned and carried out, but the group was not authorized to do so.

Personal violence See *Individual violence.*

Rape See *Forcible rape.*

Rate of violence The number of violent acts per some measurement of population, usually per 100,000 people.

Reformist A social policy perspective oriented to helping offenders by changing either them or their environment. See *Retributionist.*

Retributionist A social policy perspective oriented to punishing offenders. See also *Reformist.*

Serial murder Killing several victims in three or more separate events.

Situational group violence Spontaneous group violence, such as a brawl among hockey players.

(The) sociological question of violence What is it about a society that increases or decreases the likelihood of violence?

Statutory rape Consensual sexual relations in which one person is under the legal age of consent. See also *Forcible rape.*

Strain theory A functionalist theory that stresses the adaptations that people make when they feel strain because their access to the cultural means to reach cultural goals is blocked.

Subcultural theory A symbolic interactionist theory that stresses a group's orientations: its distinctive norms, attitudes, values, beliefs, and behaviors. Applied to violence, people who grow up or associate with groups that have an orientation to violence will learn violent ways of handling life's problems. See also *Differential association.*

Violence The use of physical force to injure people or to destroy their property.

THINKING CRITICALLY ABOUT CHAPTER 5

1. Which five of the profiles or types of rapists that are discussed in this chapter (pp. 142–143) do you think are the most common? Explain your choices.

2. Do you think that retribution or reform is the more appropriate way of dealing with rapists and murderers? Explain.

3. Do you think that the government has a responsibility to provide compensation to victims of violent crime? Why or why not?

CHAPTER 6

Crime and Criminal Justice

WAS RECENTLY RELEASED FROM SOLITARY CONFINEMENT after being held therein for 37 months (months!). A silent system was imposed upon me and to even whisper to the man in the next cell resulted in being beaten by guards, sprayed with chemical mace, blackjacked, stomped and thrown into a strip-cell naked to sleep on a concrete floor without bedding, covering, wash basin or even toilet. The floor served as toilet and bed, and even there the silent system was enforced. . . . I have filed every writ possible against the administrative acts of brutality. The courts have all denied the petitions. Because of my refusal to let the thing die down. . . . I am the most hated prisoner in (this) penitentiary, and called a "hard-core incorrigible."

Maybe I am an incorrigible. . . . I know that thieves must be punished and I don't justify stealing, even though I am a thief myself. But now I don't think I will be a thief when I am released. No, I'm not that rehabilitated. It's just that I no longer think of becoming wealthy by stealing. I now think of killing—killing those who have beaten me and treated me as if I were a dog. I hope and pray for the sake of my own soul and future life of freedom that I am able to overcome the bitterness and hatred which eats daily at my soul.

—A letter from a prisoner in a state prison, as quoted in Zimbardo (1972).

The Problem in Sociological Perspective

What Is Crime?

What is crime? To help us understand its nature, let's look at the way one crime unfolded (Harlan 1988):

> On a Sunday morning in July, an undercover police officer entered a supermarket on Cape Cod. He purchased two cans of Del Monte whole-kernel corn and two cans of baby carrots.
> Corn and carrots were just the beginning of the crime wave.
> The following Sunday morning, undercover officers purchased Campbell's pork and beans and Progresso chicken-noodle soup. Then it was green beans. And more carrots.

What does selling vegetables have to do with crime? When he stood before the judge, unrepentant, and admitted that he had sold the canned goods, the owner of the store became a convicted criminal. He had violated Massachusetts "blue laws" that make it a crime to sell nonessential items on Sundays.

The Cultural Relativity of Crime

Your state may not have blue laws, but it does have merchandising laws. Consider, for example, the sale of alcohol as it relates to "closing hours." To sell whiskey, wine, or beer one minute before closing hour is legal; to sell them two minutes later is a crime.

These examples illustrate the essential nature of crime. **Crime** *is the violation of law.* Where there is no law, there is no crime. No activity is criminal in and of itself. Although we may agree that stealing, kidnapping, and rape are harmful and immoral, only law defines them as crimes.

This principle that law makes crime has many implications. One is that *crime is culturally relative;* that is, laws and crime vary from one society to another. Acts that are criminal in one place and time may be encouraged in other places and times. China gives us a nice example. Until almost the year 2000, making a profit was a crime in China.

"Profiteering," as it was called, was punishable by death, and violators of this law would be strung up in the public square as an example to others. Then Chinese officials decided that letting people make profits would stimulate their economy. The change has been so thorough that now Chinese capitalist are invited to join the communist party.

An act that at one point in time is considered criminal may at another point in time be considered a contribution to humanity. In the early 1900s, Margaret Sanger sent birth control information through the U.S. mail. Doing so was illegal, because such information was thought to injure the family and state. Sanger was indicted for mailing "obscene, lewd, and lascivious" materials. Today, in contrast, we consider the same act to be a service to an overpopulated world.

Travellers are sometimes surprised to find that an act taken for granted at home is a crime abroad, or that what is suppressed at home is taken for granted elsewhere. The cultural relativity of crime generates examples from the sublime to the ridiculous. Pork and alcohol are illegal in some Muslim societies, but there a man may take several wives as long as he can support them. How puzzling our beer-drinking, pork-chop-eating, monogamous society must seem to a Muslim!

The Political/Power Dimension of Crime

Recall the material on abortion in Chapter 1. Before 1973, abortion was a criminal act. After 1973, it was not. If the antiabortion groups amend the Constitution or the U.S. Supreme Court reverses its 1973 ruling, abortion will again become a crime. In short, determining which acts are criminal is a **political process**—a struggle among groups that have different interests and ideologies. As a result, each political system makes its own determination of what will be illegal.

Because law defines crime, a sociological analysis raises such questions as: Which groups in a society have the power to get their views written into the law? Why do the authorities pass laws against some behaviors but not against others? Why do some societies punish a behavior, while others ignore—or even encourage—it?

The Scope of the Problem

Two Parts to This Social Problem:

1. Crime

2. The Criminal Justice System

In considering crime as a social problem, we must also look at the **criminal justice system**—the agencies that respond to crime, including the police, courts, jails, and prisons. On the one hand, crime is a social problem when large numbers of people are upset about it, when they feel that crime threatens their security, peace, and quality of life. On the other hand, the criminal justice system is a social problem if people are upset about how it fails to prevent crime, or fails to rehabilitate offenders, or when it discriminates against certain groups of citizens. In this chapter, we will discuss these two intertwined parts of this social problem: crime and the criminal justice system.

CRIME AS A SOCIAL PROBLEM

How Extensive Is Crime?

How extensive is crime in the United States? We use two measurements. The first is the number of crimes. Each year Americans are the victims of about 16,000 murders, 95,000 forcible rapes, and ten million robberies, aggravated assaults, automobile thefts, and burglaries, (*FBI Uniform Crime Reports* 2003). The second measure is the **crime rate**—the number of crimes per some unit of the population, usually per 100,000 people. Figure 6-1 shows how the U.S. crime rate climbed during the 1960s and the 1970s. It peaked in 1980 and then declined until 1984, when it again turned upward. In 1991, crime began a long, steep drop.

This drop in crime is welcome news, and today U.S. society is almost as safe as it was in the 1960s. There is another side of the coin, however: The U.S. crime rate remains one of the highest in the world. Even with this huge drop, crime in the United

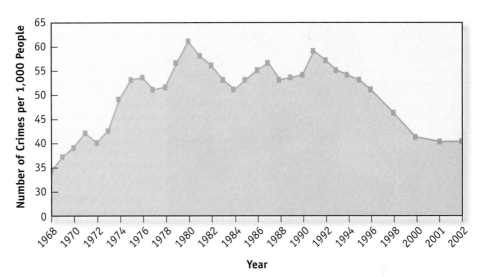

FIGURE 6-1   *The U.S. Crime Rate*

Source: By the author, based on reports of murder-manslaughter, forcible rape, robbery, aggravated assault, burglary, larceny-theft, and automobile theft; as contained in various editions of the *FBI Uniform Crime Reports,* including the 2003 edition.

States remains so high that each year 4 of every 100 Americans fall victim to one of the crimes shown in Figure 6-1 (*FBI Uniform Crime Reports* 2003:9).

Are There Societies Without Crime?

Although many societies have lower crime rates than ours, no society is without crime. As Durkheim (1897) pointed out, the very nature of crime makes it universal. Each society passes laws against behaviors that it considers a threat to its well-being. The behavior already exists. Passing a law does not eliminate the behavior; it just makes it illegal. When there are laws (or rules), there always will be criminals (or rule breakers). Thus no society or nation can ever be exempt from crime.

Subjective Concerns

As emphasized in previous chapters, an objective condition alone does not constitute a social problem. There must also be subjective concerns. People have to be upset about the condition and want something done about it. Just a few years ago, Americans considered crime to be the number one social problem facing the nation. As the crime rate dropped, so did Americans' fears of becoming a victim of violent criminals (*Sourcebook of Criminal Justice Statistics* 2002:Table 2.1). Americans are still concerned about their personal safety, however, and each urban resident knows which areas of the city to avoid. Women, who have greater concerns about becoming a crime victim, are especially careful at night.

THE CRIMINAL JUSTICE SYSTEM AS A SOCIAL PROBLEM

Example: Buddy, Gary, and Clyde

We cannot understand crime as a social problem without examining the system that deals with it. To see why, let's follow the case of Buddy Hudson, Gary Carson, and Clyde Johnson.

On a Saturday night, Buddy, a 19-year-old African American, teamed up with two whites, Gary, 34, and Clyde, 21, to rob a liquor store. The robbery netted them $1,590. After a week's spending spree, they tried their luck again, but this time a witness called the police. The three fled, but the police had a description of the men, and they were arrested.

To ensure that the courts would not throw the case out for violation of procedure, the arresting officers read the men the 1966 Miranda warning:

1. You have the right to remain silent.
2. If you do not remain silent, what you say can and will be used against you.
3. You have the right to be represented by a lawyer during questioning and thereafter.
4. If you cannot afford an attorney, the state will provide one at its expense.

Social control is necessary if society is to survive. Without social control, we all would be victims of the strongest and most ruthless, facing constant extortion, injury, or death. The problem is how to make the state subject to the will of the people, to prevent it from being the agent that extorts, injures, and kills.

The state did provide an attorney. His advice was to say nothing—to let him talk to the prosecuting attorney, who determines what crimes suspects will be charged with. After meeting with the prosecuting attorney, he reported back that the evidence was solid, and they would be charged with armed robbery, resisting arrest, and assault with a deadly weapon. They could go to prison for up to 60 years. He added that he could "cut a deal." He could get the charges of assault and resisting arrest dropped in return for a guilty plea to armed robbery. The prosecuting attorney would agree to a 3-to-5 (a minimum of three years and a maximum of five years in state prison).

Buddy, Gary, and Clyde figured that their attorney could do better. Clyde's mother put up $20,000 to secure her son's release on bond. Unable to raise bond money, Buddy and Gary remained in jail during the nine months it took for their case to come to trial (see the Issues in Social Problems box on being poor and going to jail, on the next page.) Just before the trial, Clyde pled guilty. Both the prosecuting and defense attorneys appeared surprised when the judge suspended Clyde's sentence and placed him on probation for five years. After their trial, Buddy and Gary were found guilty of armed robbery. (The other charges were thrown out for insufficient evidence.) The judge gave Gary a 6-to-10 and sentenced Buddy to a minimum of 15 years in prison.

A reporter asked about the differences in the sentences. The judge replied, "I have to show consideration for the defendant who cops a plea. It saves the court the expense of a trial" (Gaylin 1974:188–189). He added that Clyde had a job and that to send him to prison would serve no purpose. Keeping him at his job, however, would maximize his chances of being rehabilitated. When asked if he gave the longer sentence to Buddy because he was black, the judge, who was white, denied any racial bias. "That," he said, "is insulting. Race has nothing to do with this case. These are the facts: Although Gary Carson is older, he has fewer 'priors' (previous arrests). He doesn't need as stiff a sentence to teach him a lesson. Buddy's 'priors' tell me he's more dangerous." The judge added, "For people like you, I wish Buddy were white and Gary black." The reporter nodded, thinking that at this point, Buddy might have the same wish.

This case shows why our criminal justice system can be "more criminal than just."

Is the Criminal Justice System More Criminal Than Just?

1. Many of the poor spend months behind bars awaiting trial, while those with money buy their release with bonds.
2. Defense attorneys encourage **plea bargaining,** pleading guilty (whether or not one is guilty) in return for a lesser charge.
3. Judges dislike "unnecessary trials" and impose harsher sentences on those who insist on a trial (Newman 1966; Gaylin 1974).
4. Factors that have nothing to do with an offense affect sentencing, such as a defendant's age, employment, and the number of previous arrests. Even when the offense is the same, more lenient sentences are given to older defendants, those who have higher-status jobs, and those who have a better employment history.
5. The *number of adult arrests,* not the seriousness of previous charges, influences a sentence. Judges discount the type of charge because they know that in plea bargaining official charges often have little to do with the actual offense.

The Recidivism Rate

If the criminal justice system seeks to rehabilitate people, its **recidivism rate**—the percentage of people released from prison who are rearrested—shows how inadequate it is. As Table 6-1 on page 168 shows, within six years of their release about *half* of

Issues in Social Problems
YOU DON'T HAVE TO BE POOR TO GO TO JAIL—BUT IT HELPS

It isn't a crime to be poor, but it sure doesn't help when you're in trouble with the law. If you can't pay a fine, you go to jail.

"It's the only practical alternative," declares Woodrow Wilson, the judge in Bastrop, Louisiana. "Otherwise, some people would never be punished."

Every week people are ushered from Judge Wilson's courtroom to the city jail to pay their debts with days rather than dollars—or at least to wait until someone bails them out. Those with ready cash pay and leave.

This town isn't alone in how it handles indigent defendants. In rural areas especially, authorities routinely jail defendants who are unable to pay fines for minor crimes such as public drunkenness, bad checks, and speeding. They jail the poor even though it appears to violate U.S. Supreme Court rulings. Legal aid lawyers charge that the practice also damages the justice system, because defendants who have money get a better shake than those without. Still, indigent defendants keep winding up in jail.

Legal aid attorneys can't patrol all the courts, and most abuses occur in small, rural communities. The attorneys try to help people who are already in jail, but that can be slow. Roger Baruch, a prisoners-aid lawyer, recalls a man who spent six months in a Georgia jail because he couldn't pay traffic fines. By the time Mr. Baruch's group had filed the necessary papers, the man had been released.

Many judges and prosecutors claim not to know that such defendants are poor. "If they raised the issue, they wouldn't be put in jail," asserts an Aurora, Colorado, city attorney, "but I don't see that it's the responsibility of the court or the prosecutor to check out their ability to pay fines."

Officials in Monroe, Louisiana, about 20 miles south of Bastrop, hired a priest to evaluate defendants' finances. But he was let go because he sided with the poor too often.

Few believe that the problem ever will be solved. Mr. Baruch is one. He thinks that the practice is too deeply ingrained in Georgia's legal system.

"The so-called administration of justice is arbitrary and somewhat capricious," says Jackie Yeldell, a Bastrop attorney. "One thing is certain, though. You can be sure there aren't any wealthy persons in jail."

Based on Schmitt 1982.

---

former prisoners end up back in prison. If we include arrests and convictions beyond six years, the recidivism rate runs 85 to 90 percent (Blumstein and Cohen 1987). Despite going to prison several times, about 50 percent of inmates answer yes when asked, "Do you think you could do the same crime again without getting caught?" (Zawitz 1998).

The crime rate of former prisoners is much higher than their recidivism rate. Few are caught when they commit their first crime after being released from prison. Most commit many crimes before being arrested. Recall from Chapter 4, for example, that street addicts commit thousands of crimes in a single year.

Our judicial system, if it is to be judged by teaching people that crime does not pay, is a colossal failure: *The more often that someone has been put in prison, the greater that person's chances of going back to prison.* How can this be? There are many reasons, of course, but for just one recall our opening vignette: The treatment of that prisoner produced contempt and hatred, hardly the qualities we would recommend for bringing about law-abiding behavior.

Not only do prisons fail to rehabilitate, but also they are crime schools. People who have been declared unfit to live in normal society because they have committed crimes are housed together for years. One of their favorite topics of conversation is crime, and they boast to one another about all the crimes they've gotten away with. Here older, more experienced prisoners teach younger ones how to commit crimes. It

TABLE 6-1 Recidivism of U.S. Prisoners

	WITHIN SIX YEARS OF BEING RELEASED FROM PRISON, THIS PERCENTAGE OF PAROLEES WERE		
	REARRESTED	RECONVICTED	REINCARCERATED
All parolees	69%	53%	49%
SEX			
Men	70%	54%	50%
Women	52%	40%	36%
RACE/ETHNICITY			
White	64%	49%	45%
African American	76%	60%	56%
Latino	71%	50%	44%
Other	75%	65%	63%
EDUCATION			
Less than 12 years	71%	55%	51%
High school graduate	61%	46%	43%
Some college	48%	44%	31%
CRIME COMMITTED WHILE ON PAROLE			
Violent offenses	64%	43%	39%
Murder	70%	25%	22%
Robbery	64%	45%	40%
Assault	72%	51%	47%
Property offenses	73%	60%	56%
Burglary	73%	60%	56%
Forgery/fraud	74%	59%	56%
Larceny	71%	61%	55%
Drug crimes	49%	30%	25%

Source: Zawitz 1998a.

is, of course, an irony that the models for younger prisoners are criminals who have failed: *All* of them have been caught and are in prison. The irony appears to be lost on both teacher and student. Perhaps having such bad teachers is part of the reason for the high recidivism rate of former prisoners.

There is more to recidivism than such factors, of course; some of them will become apparent as we continue to examine crime and criminal justice as aspects of the same social problem.

Looking at the Problem Theoretically

As we saw in Chapter 5, each of the three theoretical perspectives provides different insight into the problem of criminal violence. We will now use these perspectives to look at property crime and the criminal justice system. We will use symbolic interactionism to examine the social class bias of police enforcement and to learn why we must view crime statistics with caution. Then, through a functionalist perspective, we will see how crime is an adaptation to a society's core values. Finally, using conflict theory, we will examine why the law comes down hardest on the poor who have stolen little, whereas it often is lenient toward the wealthy who have stolen much.

SYMBOLIC INTERACTIONISM

**The "Saints"
and the "Roughnecks"**

For two years, sociologist William Chambliss (1973/2005) observed two groups of adolescent lawbreakers in "Hanibal High School." He called one group the "saints." These were "promising young men, children of good, stable, white, upper-middle-class families, active in school affairs, good precollege students." Despite their background, however, the saints were some of the most delinquent boys in the school, "constantly occupied with truancy, drinking, wild driving, petty theft, and vandalism." Yet their teachers and families considered the boys "saints headed for success." Not one saint was ever arrested.

Chambliss also observed a second group of boys, whom he called the "roughnecks." Of the same age and race-ethnicity as the saints, and from the same high school, these boys also were delinquent, although they committed somewhat fewer criminal acts than the saints. Their teachers saw them as "roughnecks headed for serious trouble," and the police often dealt with them.

How Social Class Worked: Applying Symbolic Interactionism

1. Expectations and Perceptions

Why did the community perceive these boys so differently? Chambliss found that this was due to *social class*. As symbolic interactionists emphasize, social class vitally affects our perception and behavior. The saints came from respectable, middle-class families, the roughnecks from less-respectable, working-class families. These backgrounds led teachers and the authorities to expect good behavior from the saints but trouble from the roughnecks. And, like the rest of us, teachers and police saw what they expected to see.

2. Mobility and Visibility

The boys' social class also affected their *visibility*. The saints had automobiles, and they did their drinking and vandalism out of town. Without a car, the roughnecks hung around their own street corners, where their boisterous behavior drew the attention of police, confirming the idea that the community already had of them.

3. Interaction Styles

Social class also equipped the boys with distinct *styles of interaction*. When police or teachers questioned the saints, they were apologetic. They showed respect for authority, perhaps the most important factor in winning authorities' favor (Westley 1953; Piliavin and Briar 1964). Showing respect elicited a positive reaction from teachers and police, allowing the boys to escape school and legal problems. The roughnecks, in contrast, were "almost the polar opposite." When questioned, they were hostile. Even when they put on a veneer of respect, everyone could see through it. Consequently, teachers came down hard on the roughnecks, and the police were quick to interrogate and arrest them rather than to warn them.

Differential Association and Subcultures

The saints and the roughnecks illustrate the differential association and subcultural theories introduced in Chapter 5. Unlike nondelinquent groups, both the saints and the roughnecks were immersed in vandalism and theft. Despite their similarities in delinquent behavior, however, the saints and the roughnecks were reared in subcultures that have different orientations to life. The saints learned that college was their birthright; the roughnecks did not. The saints wanted good grades; the roughnecks didn't care. The saints learned middle-class politeness, which showed in their choice of words, tone of voice, and body language; the roughnecks did not. The reactions by authorities to these subcultural differences deeply affected the boys' lives.

The Significance of Labeling

Chambliss' research illustrates what sociologists call *labeling*, a practice that can set people on different courses in life. The labels "saint" and "roughneck," for example, carry different expectations. They affect people's perceptions and channel behavior in different directions. All but one of the saints went to college. One became a doctor, one a lawyer, one earned a Ph.D., and the others went into management. Two of the roughnecks won athletic scholarships and went to college. They became coaches. One roughneck became a bookie. Two dropped out of high school, became involved in separate killings, and were sentenced to prison. No one knows the whereabouts of the other. Although such distinctive events in life have many "causes," the boys lived up to the labels the community gave them.

Sociologists Irving Piliavin and Scott Briar (1964) also found how interaction affects outcomes with the police. Doing participant observation of the police at work, they observed these two cases:

> An 18-year-old white male was accused of statutory rape. The girl's father was prominent in local politics, and he insisted that the police take severe action. During questioning, the youth was polite and cooperative. He addressed the officers as "sir" and answered all questions. He also said that he wanted to marry the girl. The sergeant became sympathetic and decided to try to get the charges against the youth reduced or dropped.
>
> A 17-year-old white male was caught having sexual relations with a 15-year-old girl. When he was questioned, he answered with obvious disregard. The officers became irritated and angry. One officer accused the boy of being a "stud," interested only in sex, eating, and sleeping. He added that the young man "probably had knocked up half a dozen girls." The boy just gave back an impassive stare. The officers made out an arrest report and took him to juvenile hall.

Another Example of the Power of Symbols

Both young men had solid evidence against them, and the police faced political pressure to prosecute the 18-year-old. His politeness and cooperation, however, changed the officer's perception. His deference—his respect and regard for police authority—sent a powerful message that put the police on his side. The 17-year-old's demeanor sent a negative message and elicited negative reactions from the police.

Police Discretion

Symbolic interactionists emphasize how the police operate within a symbolic system as they administer the law. Their ideas of "typical" people—for example, of who is "safe" and who is "dangerous"—come alive during their work. The more a suspect matches their idea of a "typical" criminal, the more likely they are to arrest that person. **Police discretion,** deciding whether to arrest someone or to ignore a particular offense, is routine in police work.

Official Statistics Must Be Viewed with Caution

These examples illustrate why sociologists approach official crime statistics with caution. As noted in chapter 2, the "facts" of a social problem are not objective: A social "fact" is produced within a specific social context for a particular purpose. According to official statistics, working-class boys are much more delinquent than middle-class boys. Yet, as we have just seen, social class influences the reactions of the police, directly affecting *who shows up on those official statistics*. Similarly, as with Buddy, Gary, and Clyde, many factors affect how judges hand out sentences. Official statistics do not simply represent the "facts" of a society; they are biased social products.

Functionalism

Crime Is Natural and May Represent the Core Values of Society

Functionalists consider crime to be a natural part of society, not an aberration. They also view many crimes as a reaction to the core values of a society. Let's see how *conformity* to cultural values can generate crime. Specifically, why did sociologist Albert Cohen (1955) say that conformity to the "American way" creates crime?

Applying Strain Theory: How the Cultural Goal of Success Generates Crime

To see why, let's look at what sociologists Richard Cloward and Lloyd Ohlin (1960) identified as the crucial problem of the industrial societies: locating and training the most talented persons of every generation—whether born wealthy or poor—to fill the technical positions of society. These positions require ability and diligence. At birth, however, we cannot tell who has these traits. Therefore, society tries to motivate *everyone* to strive for success. Intense competition allows only the talented to emerge as victors. "Regardless of race, sex, or social class, success can be yours" becomes the motto—a cry that motivates people to compete intensely. Thus, by making success a universal goal—one that is not limited to the privileged, as in more highly stratified societies—industrial and postindustrial societies ensure their survival.

Merton: Five Adaptations to Social Goals

One result, however, is a lot of strain. Although almost everyone learns the goal of material success, not everyone has the same access to the approved means to reach that goal. Only so many high-paying positions exist, for example. To illustrate the ways that people react to this strain, sociologist Robert Merton developed the model that is illustrated in Table 6-2. (The *conformists* don't experience strain. They have access to approved ways to strive after success. People who experience strain make the other four adaptations.) The *innovators* accept the cultural goals, but they substitute other means of reaching them. An example is someone who decides to pursue wealth through fraud instead of through hard work. The *ritualists* give up on the goal, but they still keep active in culturally approved ways. An example is workers who no longer hope to get ahead, but who fulfill just enough requirements of the job to not get fired. The *retreatists* reject both the goal and the means; some, such as street addicts, retreat into drugs, others into a monastery or a convent. *Rebels* are convinced that society is corrupt and reject both the legitimate means and the goals. They also seek to replace the current social order with a new one.

Innovation is the adaptation that interests us. This is where crime comes in. Finding the legitimate means to the cultural goal of success blocked, and yet wanting that goal, innovators turn to *illegitimate* means. Buddy, Gary, and Clyde are examples. Thus, a high proportion of crime is a response to accepting the cultural goal, or, as Cohen said, "conformity to the American way."

An Explanation for the Property Crimes of the Poor:

1. Closed Access

Why do the poor commit so much property crime: burglary, theft, and robbery? Functionalists stress how the poor are bombarded with messages that urge them to want material success. Television portrays vivid images of middle-class lives, suggesting that full-fledged Americans can afford the goods and services portrayed in commercials and programs. Education is one of the main approved ways of reaching the goal of success, but the middle class runs the school system. There, the children of the poor are ill prepared for the bewildering world they confront, which conflicts so sharply with their background. Their grammar and swear words, their ideas of punctuality and neatness, their lack of paper-and-pencil skills—all differ from those of middle-class students. In addition, the schools that most poor children attend are inferior to the schools that educate children from higher social classes (Kozol 1999). These barriers create higher dropout rates among working-class students, blocking them from many legitimate avenues of financial success.

2. Open Access

Often, however, a different door opens to them, one that sociologists Richard Cloward and Lloyd Ohlin (1960) called **illegitimate opportunity structures.** These are opportunities woven into the texture of life in urban slums: robbery, burglary, selling drugs, prostitution, pimping, gambling, and other income-producing crimes or "hustles." The "hustler" or "player" becomes a model for others—glamorously successful, one of the few people around whose material success approximates the

TABLE 6-2 Merton's Typology of Individual Adaptation to Anomie

MODES OF ADAPTATION	CULTURE GOALS	INSTITUTIONALIZED MEANS
0. Conformity	+*	+
1. Innovation	+	–
2. Ritualism	–	+
3. Retreatism	–	–
4. Rebellion	±	±

*A + indicates acceptance, a – rejection, and a ± rejection of prevailing values and substitution of new values.
Source: Merton 1968: 194.

**And Crime
in Other Classes**

mainstream cultural stereotype. With these illegitimate opportunities beckoning, the poor are drawn into them in disproportionate numbers.

Functionalists know that the middle and upper classes are not free of crime, of course. They point out that *different* illegitimate opportunities are open to them, ones that make *different forms* of crime functional. For example, instead of pimping, burglary, or mugging, members of the middle and upper classes commit white-collar crime—tax evasion, bribery of public officials, advertising fraud, price fixing, and securities violations. Martha Stewart is a remarkable example. Stewart made over $1 billion dollars the day her company, Martha Stewart Omnimedia, went public on the New York Stock Exchange. Amidst charges of insider trading (trading stock on the basis of information gleaned from the "inside"), Stewart was forced to resign her position as head of the company she founded. Later, she served a few months in a "country club" prison. To put it mildly, the opportunities for crime that faced Martha Stewart were certainly different from the opportunities for crime faced by people who live in the inner city.

In Sum

In sum, conclude functionalists, a high crime rate is *inherent* in societies that socialize people of all social classes to desire material success, while limiting the legitimate means to that success. Although society expands people's desires by holding out limitless opportunities, many poor people find the legitimate avenues to success blocked. Many of them turn to illegitimate means.

**But Why Doesn't
Everyone Become
a Criminal?**

If many do, you might note, this also means that many do not. Why not? With the success motif so prevalent in society, and with the legitimate means to success limited, why doesn't everyone who finds his or her way blocked become a criminal?

Applying Control Theory:

To answer this, sociologists have developed control theory, focusing on controls that inhibit crime. *Inner* controls are what most of us mean by self-control. They include internalized morality, such as our ideas of right and wrong and our religious principles. They also include fears of punishment, feelings of integrity, the desire to be a "good" person, and the ability to defer gratification (Hirschi 1969; Rogers 1977; Heckathorn 1990; Oyserman and Markus 1990; Brownfield and Sorenson 1993). *Outer* controls include authorities such as the police, courts, and teachers, the potential damage to one's social standing and reputation, and the reactions of one's family.

Inner Controls

Outer Controls

The combination of inner and outer controls keeps most of us in line most of the time. Most of us use approved means to try to fulfill our culturally engendered desire for success. We will return to control theory in the section on juvenile delinquency.

The cartoonist indicates an essential principle that is highlighted by functionalists—that crime is functional for individuals and society.

(By permission of Johnny Hart & Creators Syndicate, Inc.)

CONFLICT THEORY

Crimes by the Elite Treated More Leniently

Two leading U.S. aerospace companies, Hughes Electronics and Boeing Satellite Systems, were accused of illegally exporting missile technology to China. The technology allowed China to improve its delivery system for nuclear weapons, placing the United States at risk. The two companies pleaded guilty and paid fines. No executives went to jail. (Gerth 2003)

Why This Distinction?

Have you ever wondered about such cases? By exporting the technology that can make China's missiles hit U.S. cities instead of ending up in the ocean, the top executives of Boeing and Hughes put us all at risk. Were these executives executed for treason? Were they sent to prison for the rest of their lives? Not all. They didn't spend even a single day in jail. The *companies* simply paid a fine out of their vast profits. The executives who committed this crime were chauffered back to their exclusive offices and homes in limousines. Yet other news reports tell us of young men or women from the lower class who are sent to prison for stealing a $5,000 automobile.

Power, Inequality, and Social Class

How can we have such inequitable results from a legal system that is supposed to provide "law, liberty, and justice for all"? Conflict theorists, who ask such questions about crime and criminal justice, stress that every society is marked by power and inequality. The most fundamental division of a capitalist society, they say, is between those who control the means of production and those who do not. Only a few people are in the buyer's seat and control the means of production. Most of us must sell our labor. Those who buy labor are called *the ruling class;* those who sell their labor are called *the working class.*

The Marginal Working Class

The working class consists of three major groups. In the first are the upper-level managers and professionals. Their positions are fairly secure, and the pay is good. In return for their security and comfort, managers and professionals show high loyalty to the ruling class and give strong support to the status quo. The second group consists of the stable working class. Most white-collar and blue-collar workers are members of this group. They get jobs, but the work is not as stable, and the pay is less. Their jobs, however, are adequate for survival. The third group is made up of the marginal working class, which receives the least of society's rewards. These people have shaky jobs, and their labor is in low demand. This group includes most of the unemployed, people who are on welfare, and those who live in the inner city. From the marginal working class (also called the "reserve army" of the unemployed) come most burglars, muggers, armed robbers, and car thieves.

The Law as a Tool of the Ruling Class

Conflict theorists emphasize that the law is not an impartial social institution that administers a code of justice shared by all. Rather, the law is controlled by the ruling class, which uses it to oppress the marginal working class and maintain their own privileges of power and wealth (Spitzer 1975; Jacobs 1978; Beirne and Quinney 1982). Because of this, the criminal justice system does not focus on the owners of corporations and the harm they do to the public through pollution, price manipulation, or unsafe products (Coleman 1989). Instead, the police and courts monitor the marginal working class: Members of this group show little loyalty to the ruling class and most revolutionaries come from this group. As a result, the law comes down hard on violators from the marginal working class.

Why Slaps on the Wrists for Crimes of the Powerful?

Violations by owners—the ruling class that controls the social order—cannot be totally ignored, however, for if their crimes become too flagrant, they might provoke an outcry among the working class and, ultimately, even revolution. To prevent this, as with the case of Martha Stewart, an occasional violation by the powerful is prosecuted. This stabilizes society by demonstrating that the criminal justice system applies to all. As we saw with Hughes and Boeing—whose top executives have strong connections with powerful political figures—the companies were only fined, and its

Sociologists have studied urban gangs since the 1920s. They have found that some of these gangs function as substitute families. They provide security and identity and are disproportionately made up of the poor.

executives went unpunished. The ruling class comes down hard on the property crimes of the working class, but it ordinarily ensures that lesser penalties are applied to its own versions of property crime.

Except for the rare prosecutions of the wealthy, such as Martha Stewart, which are held out to the public as proof of the fairness of the judicial system, few criminals from the wealthy classes appear in court. Most go before a state or federal agency (such as the Federal Trade Commission) that has no power to imprison. The FTC, headed by people of privilege, levies token fines. Most cases of illegal sales of stocks and bonds, price fixing, restraint of trade, and so on are handled within this less punitive system. In contrast, the property crimes of the working class are channeled into a court system that does imprison. Burglary, armed robbery, petty theft, and stealing automobiles threaten not only the sanctity of private property but also, if allowed to continue, the positions of the powerful.

In Sum
Conflict theorists stress this unique perspective for viewing the criminal justice system: The powerful use the legal system to control workers, mask injustice, and stabilize the social system. Law enforcement is not a system of justice, but a cultural device used by the powerful to carry out their policies and to keep themselves in power. This point comes out strongly in the Spotlight on Research box written by William Chambliss, a conflict theorist who has done research on criminal justice systems in different parts of the world.

Research Findings

To understand crime as a social problem, we'll first review research on five types of crime: juvenile delinquency, white-collar crime, professional crime, organized crime, and political crime. Then we'll look at research on the criminal justice system.

JUVENILE DELINQUENCY

The Origin of Juvenile Delinquency
With our views of life stages, it is difficult to grasp how different children used to be perceived. Earlier generations did not make the distinctions that we do. Children who broke the law used to be treated the same as adults. In the 1700s, girls as young as 13 were burned to death for their crimes, and 8- and 10-year-old boys were hanged for theirs (Blackstone 1899). When society industrialized in the 1800s, it was not only the adults but also the children who worked full-time in factories and mines. Some children operated machines 14 hours a day under miserable conditions for low pay. In the 1800s, society softened a bit, but age afforded neither an excuse for lawbreaking nor a protection from harsh penalties.

As industrialization progressed, international trade unions, founded in the 1800s, ushered in labor laws to protect children (Phelps 1939; Kuczynski 1946). At the same time, political and civic leaders recognized the need for an educated workforce. They also feared the influx of foreign values and looked on public education as a way to

SPOTLIGHT ON RESEARCH

My Personal Journey into Sociology

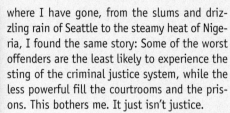

William Chambliss, who is Professor of Sociology at The George Washington University in Washington, D.C., became interested in criminology during his junior year in high school. That summer, he and a friend hitchhiked from Los Angeles to Walla Walla, Washington, where they worked with convicts picking peas. Chambliss got to know them and was fascinated to discover what the bank robbers, drug dealers, burglars, and thieves were planning to do when they were released from prison—commit more crimes.

After my experiences that summer, I knew that I wanted to be a criminologist. When I went to UCLA, I was exposed to sociology and criminology. There, I developed a passion for both that has never waned.

After college I was drafted into the Army and sent to Korea where I spent eighteen months as a special agent with the Counter Intelligence Corps. I was exposed to an immense amount of crime. But it was the crimes of the state and of the U.S. military that most interested me. They were the most egregious, not the crimes of the petty thieves and burglars or even what today we would call "terrorists." Between the pea fields of Walla Walla and the rice paddies of South Korea, I came to ponder what a short step it is from legitimacy to crime, from interrogation to torture, and from fighting soldiers to shooting and raping civilians.

Over the years, I have done research on organized crime, juvenile gangs, how laws are created, and economic crimes in U.S. cities. I have also studied crimes abroad: England, Sweden, Norway, Nigeria, Zambia, and Thailand. Everywhere I have gone, from the slums and drizzling rain of Seattle to the steamy heat of Nigeria, I found the same story: Some of the worst offenders are the least likely to experience the sting of the criminal justice system, while the less powerful fill the courtrooms and the prisons. This bothers me. It just isn't justice.

In one of my books, *Power, Politics and Crime* (Westview, 2001), I suggest these social policies:

1. Mandatory minimum sentences be abolished (including three-strikes laws), and, in general, the trend toward more severe punishments be reversed.
2. Crime statistics be gathered by agencies that are independent of law enforcement agencies.
3. Law enforcement agencies be put under civilian control.
4. The prosecuting attorney's office be depoliticized (removed from political influence or control).
5. Drugs be decriminalized. The primary reason for this is that the enforcement of anti-drug laws results in systemic bias against the poor and ethnic minorities.

My journey of discovery in criminology has exposed many shortcomings in the world we live in. It has also given me an opportunity to meet and work with wonderful people, some labeled criminals, others labeled heroes. Although I sometimes wish that "I didn't know now, what I didn't know then," more often I am eternally grateful for the opportunity to explore the world of crime and crime control and do what I can to help make it more equitable—which is its supposed purpose.

"Americanize" immigrants (Hellinger and Judd 1991). Mandatory education laws were passed, requiring all children to attend school, usually until they had completed the eighth grade or turned 16, whichever came first. Until this time, schooling had been a hit or miss affair: Some children went to school, but many did not.

These new laws on child labor and education were part of a significant perceptual shift. As views of children changed, teenagers came to be seen as a separate class of people—not as oldish children or youngish adults. To match this perceptual shift, new laws were passed that classified juveniles as a separate category in the criminal justice system (Platt 1969). This change in the law produced a new category of crime—**juvenile delinquency.** To separate children from adults, the first juvenile court was established in Illinois in 1899, which means that juvenile delinquency has been around for only a little over 100 years. Crimes by juveniles, of course, are nothing new—just the classification.

Extent of Juvenile Involvement in Crime

Some juvenile delinquency consists of **status crimes,** behaviors that are crimes if juveniles commit them, but not if adults do. Examples are curfew violations, underage drinking, and running away from home. Status crimes are not the primary social problem, for people are less concerned about them. It is the predatory crimes of violence that have upset people and have captured headlines.

Although 13- to 17-year-old boys make up only 3.7 percent of the U.S. population, they commit about 15 percent of the nation's **crimes against the person**—murder, forcible rape, robbery, and aggravated assault. This is about *four times* the number of violent crimes as would be proportionate to their segment of the population. This group also commits about a fourth of the nation's **property crimes**—burglary, larceny, motor vehicle theft, and arson (*FBI Uniform Crime Reports* 2003:Table 38; *Statistical Abstract* 2003:Table 11). This is *seven times* the number of property crimes that would be proportionate to their segment of the population.

Girls commit fewer crimes than boys, but they are closing the gap, which also alarms people. As you can see from Table 6-3, *far fewer* boys are arrested for property crimes now than 20 years ago, but 2 percent more girls are arrested for property crimes. For violent crimes, the contrast is even greater. Two percent fewer boys are arrested, but the number of girls who are arrested for violent crimes has soared by 81 percent. The change in what girls are arrested for is startling: A generation ago, their primary offenses were the status crimes of underage sex and running away from home. Today, over 10,000 girls are arrested each year for murder, robbery, and aggravated assault. Another 100,000 are arrested for larceny, theft, and arson.

The Delinquent Career

Sociologists have uncovered what they call the "delinquent career." Here are the patterns that Howard Snyder (1988) found when he studied the court records of 69,000 juvenile delinquents in Phoenix, Arizona:

1. After their first arrest, most youths (59 percent) never return to juvenile court.
2. The juveniles most likely to continue their delinquent behavior are those who are arrested a second time before age 16.

TABLE 6-3 Arrests of People Under Age 18

	NUMBER OF ARRESTS				PERCENTAGE OF ARRESTS		
	1981	2000	2002	PERCENT CHANGE	1981	2000	2002
PROPERTY CRIMES*							
Boys	398,924	218,816	206,052	−48%	81%	70%	68%
Girls	95,010	94,888	97,137	+2%	19%	30%	32%
					100%	100%	100%
VIOLENT CRIMES**							
Boys	47,415	48,169	46,528	−2%	89%	82%	82%
Girls	5,825	10,686	10,520	+81%	11%	18%	18%
					100%	100%	100%

*Property crimes are burglary, larceny-theft, motor vehicle theft, and arson.
**Violent crimes are murder, forcible rape, robbery, and aggravated assault.
Sources: By the author, based on *Sourcebook* 1993:Table 35; *FBI Uniform Crime Reports* 2000:Table 37; 2002:Table 37.

3. Juveniles who are charged with a violent crime (murder, rape, robbery, or aggravated assault) are likely to have committed many crimes.

4. The younger that juveniles are when they are first charged with a violent crime, the greater the likelihood that they will be charged later with a violent crime. (Those who are first charged at age 13 are *twice* as likely to be arrested for a later violent offense than those who are first charged at age 16.)

5. The juveniles who are the *most* likely to be rearrested are those whose first charge was burglary, truancy, motor vehicle theft, or robbery (see Figure 6-2).

6. The juveniles who are the *least* likely to be rearrested are those whose first charge was underage drinking, running away, or shoplifting.

7. Girls are much less likely to be rearrested than boys (29 percent versus 46 percent).

The Significance of Graduating from High School

You may have heard the parents of a boy who has gotten in trouble with the law say, "If only we can keep him in school, he'll have a chance. If he drops out, he's lost." Is this common observation—made by the parents of delinquent girls, too—correct? To find out, we would have to be able to compare the adult arrests of delinquents who complete high school with the adult arrests of delinquents who drop out. This is what Table 6-4 on page 178 does. As yu can see, when they are adults, delinquents who complete high school are only *half* as likely to be arrested as those who drop out of high school. The table also shows this remarkable finding: Children who are *not* delinquents who drop out of high school are *more* likely to be arrested as adults than delinquents who graduate from high school. The common observation is certainly correct.

Juvenile delinquents know that their crimes are condemned by society, yet they don't go around moaning, burdened by guilt. How do they avoid blaming themselves?

FIGURE 6-2 *Rearrest Based on the First Crime Juveniles Were Charged With*
Source: By the author, based on Juvenile Justice Bulletin, August 1988.

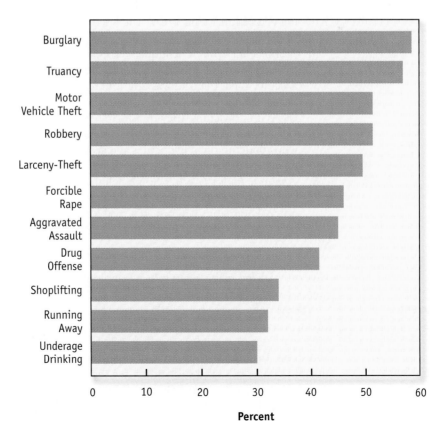

TABLE 6-4 High School Graduation, Delinquency, and Adult Arrests

	ARRESTED AS ADULTS	
	AFRICAN AMERICANS	WHITES
DELINQUENT IN HIGH SCHOOL		
Dropped out	47%	33%
Completed high school	24%	18%
NOT DELINQUENT IN HIGH SCHOOL		
Dropped out	30%	22%
Completed high school	16%	6%

Based on a longitudinal study of male Philadelphia high school students; no data for girls or other racial–ethnic groups.
Source: Rosen et al. 1991:Tables 2, 5.

Five Techniques of Neutralization

In a classic study, symbolic interactionists Gresham Sykes and David Matza (1957) uncovered five **techniques of neutralization** that delinquents use:

1. *Denial of responsibility.* Delinquents see themselves as propelled by social forces out of their control. Their unloving parents, bad companions, or bad neighborhood are the cause of their delinquency. By denying responsibility, they break the link between themselves and their acts. ("I'm just a billiard ball on the pool table of life.")
2. *Denial of injury.* Delinquents admit that their acts are illegal, but they deny that they hurt anyone. They call their vandalism "mischief," "pranks," or "just having a little fun." This breaks the link between themselves and the consequences of their acts.
3. *Denial of a victim.* If delinquents admit that they have done harm, they claim that the injury was not wrong "under the circumstances." The person they hurt was not a victim. What they did was "rightful retaliation." Vandalizing a school, for example, is revenge on unfair teachers; theft is a retaliation against crooked storekeepers. With no victims, they transform themselves from wrongdoers into avengers.
4. *Condemnation of the condemners.* Delinquents also take the offensive, calling those who condemn them hypocrites and accusing the police of being brutal or "on the take." By attacking others, they deflect attention away from their own behavior.
5. *Appeal to higher loyalties.* Some delinquents see themselves as torn between two incompatible expectations. The law pulls them one way, loyalty to friends another. The friends win out. If a rival gang hurts a friend, for example, retaliation is "more moral" than ignoring the injury.

These techniques allow delinquents to neutralize society's norms. Even if delinquents have internalized mainstream values—and not all have—these rationalizations let them commit crimes with a minimum of guilt or shame.

The Delinquent Subculture

Some delinquents have little to neutralize. They grow up in **delinquent subcultures,** where criminal activities are taken for granted. In these subcultures, they learn norms that support crime, as well as techniques for committing burglaries, robberies, and so on. In some of these subcultures, youths even learn to rape, kill, and terrorize. For an example of such a subculture, see the Thinking Critically box on the next page.

Why Do Only Some Youths from the Same Background Become Delinquent?

As this box illustrates, some children grow up surrounded by an illegitimate opportunity structure that offers a law-violating approach to the problems of life. Yet only some become delinquent. Why?

Thinking Critically about Social Problems

LORDS OF THE SLUMS

The Black Gangster Disciples rule this part of Chicago. Their insignia, a six-pointed star, marks the buildings. They prey on the single women who occupy more than 70 percent of the units in the Robert Taylor Homes and the Stateway Gardens. They store their drugs and guns in their apartments and turn the women into prisoners. Calling the police is not an option here.

Always tenuous, the balance of power has shifted. As the police drive by in unmarked cars, the warning whistles of young boys precede them. Other boys wait for the police to pass, then resume selling their drugs.

To be a good drug dealer you have to be hard. One resident tells how the leader of the Black Disciples came to her door looking for her son, who owed $300 for drugs. A Disciple member put a gun to her son's head. She paid.

He meant business. He killed a 66-year-old man for only $17.

One father told his 15-year-old son to leave the gang. The Disciples broke the man's arm.

At Rockwell Gardens, members of another gang, the Vice Lords, beat a 32-year-old man to death in full view of the tenants. When the police arrived, the leader of the Vice Lords sat on a kitchen chair in the basketball court, his soldiers at his side. His boys followed the police from door to door, staring at each tenant who dared to answer the knock.

Confident in their power, some gangs stage public events. One gang lieutenant has handed out dollar bills to children. Another has distributed more than a thousand pairs of sneakers. At one point, some of the city's top drug dealers and gang leaders got together to sponsor what they called "Players Picnic." They distributed flyers at the housing projects, hired a band, and gave away hot dogs and ribs.

The management and staff of the housing projects deny any knowledge of the Disciples. And not everyone thinks things are so bad. The Disciples guard the buildings at night, and some residents say the buildings are safer now than when the police controlled them.

FOR YOUR CONSIDERATION

Why has law enforcement failed in these housing projects? What principles discussed in this text could change this situation?

Based on Kotlowitz 1988.

Social Control Theory

For answers, let's first consider social control and then labeling theory. According to social control theory, three factors are involved: inner controls, outer controls, and the desire to commit a crime. When children grow up in the same neighborhood, the outer controls look similar. But as sociologist Joan Moore (1978) found in her classic study of three Chicano barrios (neighborhoods) in Los Angeles, the outer controls (the life situations) of youths in the same neighborhood can differ sharply. This, in turn, affects the youths' inner controls and their desire to commit criminal acts.

Inner Controls: Differences in Families

Moore used a variety of research techniques. She did participant observation of everyday barrio life, interviewed residents, and also hung out with former convicts. She found that the difference begins in the family. Despite their outward similarities, families in poor neighborhoods, like families everywhere, differ in their values and what they teach their children. Some parents are more oriented toward work and education. Teaching these values increases their children's inner controls and reduces their desire to commit crimes. These children strive to do better in school, and as teachers reward their efforts, their motivation to conform increases. For children who are reared in families where such traditional values are minimal, the criminally oriented peer group becomes more attractive. Because these children are not as oriented to work roles, gangs and crime become more enticing.

Outer Controls: Differences in Families

To better understand how significant outer controls are, consider extremes among families. Everyone knows that some families are rotten (in sociological terms, dysfunctional). Some parents sexually abuse their kids. Others physically and psychologically abuse their children. Abused children are likely to run away, for the streets look more appealing than what passed for a home. "On the run" these children do what they can to survive on the city's mean streets: They beg, steal, or sell their bodies. Compare such miserable situations with that of children who grow up in families where their parents love and nourish them emotionally. This common knowledge that home life has such far-reaching effects on children's likelihood to become delinquent is supported by an abundance of sociological research. Bill McCarthy and John Hagan (1992), for example, compared homeless adolescents in Toronto with youths who were still at home. It will come as no surprise to you that the homeless youths were more likely to have been abused physically and sexually by their parents, and that they were more likely to have committed crimes.

Labeling Theory: Consequence for Life

Labeling theorists stress the significance of a youth being labeled a delinquent. Such labeling can be a matter of sheer luck. I know a teenager who did the same things that his buddies did, but he happened to go home early one night. While everyone else "got busted" and became labeled a "delinquent," he did not. Also recall Chambliss' study of the "saints" and the "roughnecks," which illustrates how labels affect lower- and middle-class adolescents differently. Being labeled a troublemaker can set a youth apart and cause him or her to continue on the path to more trouble. In some instances, labels create a cloud of suspicion that cuts an adolescent off from conforming people and activities, channeling the individual in the direction of more violations.

In Sum

Using social control theory, we can gain a better idea of why in the same neighborhood only some youths become involved in criminal acts. Social control theory sensitizes us to differences in family values and to the significance of peer groups. Labeling theory helps to explain why some adolescents graduate from delinquency into adult crime. Social control and labeling theory also, of course, apply to crimes committed by adults. Let's look at some of those crimes.

WHITE-COLLAR CRIME

> After flashing photos of executives from Enron and Arthur Andersen on the television monitor, Jon Stewart, the anchor of *The Daily Show,* turned to the camera and shouted: "Why aren't all of you in jail? And not like white-guy jail—*jail* jail. With people by the weight room going, 'Mmmmm.'" (Leaf 2004)

When corporate scandals hit the news, we learn about top corporate executives who steal outrageous amounts of money. Occasionally, as with the bankruptcy of Enron, billions of dollars go unaccounted. For the most part—again, as conflict theorists say, with an occasional prosecution to teach us that the criminal justice system is impartial—corporate criminals go unpunished. Sociologist Edwin Sutherland (1949) coined the term **white-collar crime** for crimes "committed by people of respectable and high social status in the course of their occupation."

Their Cost

No one knows for sure how much white-collar crime costs the nation, but estimates place the bill at about $600 billion a year (McCain 2004). This is more than the cost of all street crime. Most white-collar crime never comes to the surface, but that which does can be enlightening. The most notorious example in recent years is the fraud at Enron, which cost stockholders more than $50 billion. Eleven thousand employees also suffered huge losses in their pensions. Bank robbers risk their lives for $10,000, but corporate executives manipulate computers and documents to make millions of illegal dollars for their corporations—or to rip off those same companies.

**Two Types
of White-Collar Crime:**

**1. Crimes Committed
on Behalf
of a Corporation**

**A Criminogenic
Corporate Culture**

**Example: The Case
of the Exploding Pinto**

The two major types of white-collar crime are those committed by employees *on behalf of* a corporation and those committed *against* a corporation. In crimes committed *on behalf of* a corporation, employees break the law in order to benefit their company. Examples include car manufacturers knowingly selling dangerous automobiles, drug companies faking test data so they can keep their drugs on the market, and corporations engaging in price fixing and tax dodging.

It is not uncommon for corporations listed on the major stock exchanges to produce a criminogenic (crime-causing) culture. The corporate culture revolves around not only corporate profits but also personal achievement and recognition. Pressures to increase profits and to climb the corporate ladder, combined with the insulation of executives from the consequences of their decisions, often lead to an "ethical numbness" or insensitivity (Hills 1987).

The corporate culture so dominates its members that even respectable people can end up calculating the cold-blooded deaths of others for profit. This is illustrated by the infamous "Pinto case." The Pinto was a car manufactured by Ford in the 1970s. After three young women in Indiana burned to death when their Pinto burst into flames following a rear-end crash, the Ford Motor Company was charged with reckless homicide (Strobel 1980; Fisse and Braithwaite 1987). No executives were charged, just Ford itself. It was alleged that Ford knew that in a rear-end collision the Pinto's gas tank could rupture, spew gas, and burn passengers to death (Dowie 1977, 1979). (Never mind how a corporation can know anything. The commonsense view is that it is people in the corporation who know things, and they who make criminal decisions. Common sense and the legal system, however, often walk different paths.)

Disclosed at the trial was heart-wrenching evidence that revealed the cold-blooded malice of Ford's executives. Installing a simple piece of plastic would have corrected the problem, at a cost of just $11 per car. The Ford executives faced a difficult decision—whether to pay the $11 or to sentence drivers and passengers to fiery deaths. Now, that is a real difficult choice—at least it was for these executives. The following memo shows their cost-benefit analysis—a comparison of what it would cost the company to make the change ("Costs") or to pay for the deaths ("Benefits," meaning the amount of benefits that would have to be paid). As you can see, the cost of installing the plastic was high ($137 million) compared to the amount of money that would have to be paid if they simply allowed people to die ($49.5 million). Their estimates turned out to be too low: Several hundred people burned to death, and many others were disfigured.

Ford's Internal Memo on the Pinto. "Benefits and Costs Relating to Fuel Leakage Associated with the Static Rollover Test Portion of FMVSS 208"

BENEFITS.

Savings: 180 burn deaths, 180 serious burn injuries, 2,100 burned vehicles.
Unit cost: $200,000 per death, $67,000 per injury, $700 per vehicle.
Total benefit: $180 \times (\$200,000) + 180 \times (\$67,000) + 2,100 \times (\$700) = \$49.5$ million.

COSTS.

Sales: 11 million cars, 1.5 million light trucks.
Unit cost: $11 per car, $11 per truck.
Total cost: $11,000,000 \times (\$11) + 1,500,000 \times (\$11) = \$137$ million.

Sources: Dowie 1977; Strobel 1980:286.

With the right lawyers and connections, people can get away with murder. Ford was acquitted. The company recalled its 1971–1976 Pintos for fuel tank modification and launched a publicity campaign to maintain an image of a "good" company. Ford executives claimed that the internal memo was misunderstood. They said that it "related to a proposed federal safety standard, and not to the design of the Pinto" (Fisse and Braithwaite 1987:253). Despite causing hundreds of deaths, no Ford executives were arrested or tried in court. They remained free, wealthy, and respected in their communities.

You might think that such a cold, brazen act would never be repeated by a U.S. automobile company. Unfortunately, such an expectation would be wrong. In 1998, a 13-year-old boy was burned to death when the gas tank of an Oldsmobile Cutlass station wagon ruptured. When GM was sued, a memo was discovered in which GM calculated the cost to fix the problem at just $4.50 per vehicle. GM also calculated the cost of lawsuits and figured these would average just $2.40 per car. Able to save an estimated $2.10 per car, GM did not fix the problem (Boot 1998).

The Pinto and Cutlass cases confirm the perspective of the conflict theorists: The powerful can and do manipulate our legal system. They can and do escape punishment for their crimes—including in these instances what I would call serial murder. Can you possibly imagine similar judicial results if poor people plotted to kill automobile executives? (For another example, see the photo on this page.)

The main crime *against* the corporation is employee theft, ranging from snitching company supplies to embezzling company funds. It also includes sabotage by disgruntled employees. To avoid tarnishing their public images with the disgrace of internal crime, most corporations deal privately with such offenders.

Stealing company secrets, such as formulas, manufacturing processes, or even marketing plans—and selling them to a competitor is a form of theft. A gray area emerges when one company hires a key employee of a competitor, who steals nothing but brings such vital knowledge to the new position. The employee is hired specifically because of this knowledge and commands a higher salary and often bonuses because of it. Because the knowledge is inside the individual's head, and no documents are stolen, this crime is difficult to prove.

Sociologist Donald Cressey, who produced a classic study of embezzlers, found that employees embezzle because they have an "unsharable financial problem"—overdue taxes, children's college costs, sometimes gambling losses. He (1953) also found that, like juvenile delinquents, embezzlers rationalize their crime. Many neutralize their behavior by thinking of their embezzling as a form of borrowing: Their theft is simply an unauthorized loan to tide them over in their financial emergency. Some think of themselves as having been cheated by their employers or having been taken advantage of in some way: The company deserves the embezzlement. Such techniques of neutralization let people violate the trust that their company placed in them and still consider themselves to be respectable, law-abiding citizens.

Cressey's findings are limited. Later research showed that not all embezzlers neutralize their crimes (Green 1993). Some just do it, without justifications (Benson 1985). Embezzlers also have many motivations, not just some unsharable financial problem. Some embezzlers are impulsive, others greedy (Nettler 1974). Some embezzle just to help with ordinary family bills. Motivations also change over the course of a long-term embezzlement. I knew an embezzler who headed a remote branch of a Spanish bank. After he embezzled a few thousand dollars for personal reasons, he saw it was so easy that he kept doing it even after he didn't need the money. When caught, his theft had amounted to millions.

The most costly crime against the corporation was the plundering of the U.S. savings and loan industry in the 1980s. Corporate officers, who had the trust of their depositors, looted their banks of billions of dollars. The total cost ran about $500 bil-

Example: The Case of the Exploding Cutlass

2. Crimes Committed Against a Corporation

The Example of Embezzlement: Cressey's Model

Exceptions to Cressey's Model

Example: The Case of the Disappearing Billions

Sociologists compute the costs of white-collar crime in dollar terms, but their analyses can make it sound as though white-collar crimes were a harmless nuisance. Perhaps most is. But some white-collar crime has horrible costs. Shown here is Patricia Anderson, who, with her four children, was burned when the gas tank of her 1979 Chevrolet Malibu exploded after a rear-end collision. One child's hand was burned off, and her ears burned to the bone. Outraged at the callousness of GM's conduct, the jury awarded these victims the staggering sum of $4.9 billion, the largest personal injury award in U.S. history. A judge later reduced the amount to $1.2 billion.

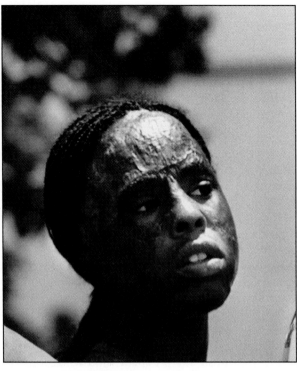

lion—$2,000 for every man, woman, and child in the country at that time (Kettl 1991; Newdorf 1991). Perhaps the most infamous culprit was Neil Bush, son of one president of the United States, the brother of another, and an officer of Silverado, a Colorado savings and loan. Bush helped bankrupt Silverado by approving $100 million in loans to a company in which he held secret interests (Tolchin 1991a).

Future generations will suffer from this looting. The interest alone is exorbitant. At 5 percent, a year's interest on an increase of $500 billion in the national debt would run $25 billion, at 10 percent, $50 billion. Because the government does not pay its debt but merely borrows more to keep up with the compounding interest, the $500 billion will double in a few years. As the late Senator Everett Dirkson once said, "A billion here and a billion there, and pretty soon you're talking about real money."

Changes in White-Collar Crime

Back in 1975, sociologist Rita Simon predicted that as more women worked outside the home they would become more involved in white-collar crime. This is just what happened. Like men, many women who join the corporate world are enticed by its opportunities for crime. Table 6-5 below tracks this change. The largest increase is in embezzlement, where women are now as likely as men to commit this crime. As you look at this table, you might notice how women's increase in white-collar crime parallels the rise in crime by female juveniles that we noted earlier (Table 6-3 on page 176).

Social Class Bias and White-Collar Crime

As noted in the quote that opened this section, white-collar criminals enjoy a privileged position within the criminal justice system. Because of their social position and ability to manipulate the law, few corporate criminals are punished. Some even get away with murder, as we saw with the automobile executives. When arrested, which is seldom,

TABLE 6-5 Arrests for White-Collar Crimes, by Sex

	1981		2000		2002	
	MALE	FEMALE	MALE	FEMALE	MALE	FEMALE
Embezzlement	70%	30%	50%	50%	50%	50%
Fraud	58%	42%	55%	45%	55%	45%
Forgery and counterfeiting	68%	32%	61%	39%	60%	40%
Fencing stolen property	88%	12%	83%	17%	82%	18%
Totals	71%	29%	62%	38%	61%	39%

Note: Not all these acts meet the definition of white-collar crime as developed by Sutherland. From the categories available in the source, however, these are as close as we can come.
Source: By the author, based on *FBI Uniform Crime Reports*, various editions, including 2003:Table 42.

white-collar criminals usually receive lenient sentences. Federal records (Carlson and Chaiken 1987) show that compared with street criminals, white-collar criminals are

1. More likely to have their cases dismissed by the prosecutor (40 percent versus 26 percent)
2. Less likely to have to put up bail (13 percent versus 37 percent)
3. More likely to get probation rather than jail (54 percent versus 40 percent)
4. More likely to get shorter sentences (29 months versus 50 months)

It seems fair to conclude that this is another example of the social class bias that operates in the criminal justice system. This bias also operates *among* white-collar criminals. Even though they have committed the same crime, executives who are higher up in the company generally are charged with lesser crimes and are given shorter sentences (Coleman 1989).

How rarely executives are convicted for their crimes and, if convicted, how unusual it is for them to serve even a single day in prison is revealed by a study of the 582 largest U.S. corporations. Sociologist Marshall Clinard (Clinard et al. 1979; Clinard 1990) found that criminal charges had been filed against 1,553 executives. Only 56 were convicted, giving them a better than 96 percent chance of avoiding conviction if arrested. Of this small number, 40 served no time in prison, and the 16 who did served a total of 597 days. Their average stay of 37 days each was about what the poor serve for disorderly conduct. Another way of looking at this same matter is to note that of 150,000 inmates in federal prisons, only 1,000 are white-collar criminals (Leaf 2004). Similarly, Neil Bush, the president's son who looted people's savings, had to pay a $50,000 fine—after friends of the president paid his legal fees (Tolchin 1991b; "Suit Settled" 1992). As sociologist Daniel Glaser (1978) observed, in a classic understatement, the criminal law has difficulty dealing with white-collar crime.

PROFESSIONAL CRIME

Crime as Work

Professional criminals are people who make their living from crime. The highly romanticized jewel thieves, safecrackers, and counterfeiters are examples of professional criminals. So are professional shoplifters, pickpockets, and fences—those who buy stolen goods for resale. Their activities, although illegal, are a form of work, and they pride themselves on their skills and successes.

The Criminal Subculture

In a classic study, Edwin Sutherland (1937) found that professional criminals organize their lives around their "work," much as people who work at legal jobs do. Professional thieves plan their work and may steal most every day of the year. They associate with like-minded people who share their values of loyalty, mutual aid, and scorn for the "straight world." They teach one another technical skills for committing crimes and avoiding detection.

Some of the criminal activities that Sutherland studied have declined. As people switched from cash to credit cards, pickpocketing faded, as did safecracking. As some forms of professional crime dwindle, however, others, such as identity fraud, increase. Thieves use computers at one location to hack into computers that may be thousands of miles away, even on different continents. As you can see from the Technology and Social Problems box on the next page, crime is keeping up with changing technology.

"Chop Shop"

Although its forms change, professional crime continues to be characterized by in-group loyalty, scorn for the values of the straight world, and pride in specialized skills. One of my students found these traits to be evident among the car thieves he studied for my undergraduate course in deviance. Based on the demand for parts, the owner of the "chop shop" ordered specific cars, paying set prices according to the make and model he wanted. He and his workers used acetylene torches and other tools to disassemble the cars. They sold the fenders, motors, transmissions, seats, doors, and so on

Technology and Social Problems
USING TECHNOLOGY TO COMMIT CRIME

The mathematics courses at the University of St. Petersburg were grueling, but like his classmates, Vladimir Levin hoped they would pay off. As Vladimir gained insight into how computer programs operate, he discovered a way to make his courses pay off handsomely.

Vladimir sat transfixed as he watched the numbers flash across his computer screen. He had hacked into a computer terminal at AO Saturn in St. Petersburg. With his programming know-how, he directed computers at Citibank in New Jersey to send money to bank accounts that he had opened in San Francisco, Holland, Finland, and Israel.

It had been a tense week for Levin. As the time drew near to execute his scheme, he had worried about all the things that could go wrong. But as he watched his computer screen, his face lit up. It was like hitting the jackpot in Las Vegas and watching the coins keep pouring out—only much more profitable. As Levin watched the totals grow, he smiled and started to relax. The numbers kept increasing, but he didn't want to be greedy so he called it quits at $12 million.

"Not a bad day's work," Levin thought. "The wonders of modern technology."

At their computers on the other end, Citibank officers didn't smile. They had spent vast amounts of money to make their computers impenetrable—the most protected in the nation, they were assured—and now some hacker had invaded them. Having their bank looted was bad enough, but they also didn't relish becoming a laughingstock: People began to joke about their full-page ads: "Call Citibank today and start using our PC banking service for free." It took a while to track down Levin and his accomplices, but with Citibank's determination and the cooperation of international police organizations, the culprits were apprehended.

Levin no longer needs his extensive mathematics background. In grade school he learned all the math he needs—how to subtract one day at a time from his prison sentence.

Based on "Citibank Thieves,"
St. Petersburg Press, 1995.

---

at standard rates to dealers in used auto parts. The small amount of metal that was left over was hauled away by an older man who sold it for scrap. Like small business owners across the country, the owner–manager of the "chop shop" carried a great deal of responsibility. He made the decisions, paid the rent on the shop, and had to meet the weekly payroll. Unlike "straight" employers, however, he arranged for a surreptitious supply of oxygen for the acetylene torches, paid wages in cash, and did not pay taxes.

Maintaining Solidarity

Solidarity among the team members of the "chop shop" helped them work together to perform their specialized functions. When they weren't working, the men socialized with one another. They drank together at the same tavern (which was frequented by other professional criminals), and they visited one another at home. By integrating their working and social lives, they minimized the intrusion of straight values, kept close tabs on one another, and reinforced ideas about the rightness and desirability of how they made their living.

Self-Definitions

Unlike amateurs, few professional criminals are troubled by their criminality. Crime is simply a way to make a buck. They see themselves as businesspeople, no different from clerks who sell shoddy merchandise or surgeons who perform unnecessary operations. Theirs is just another form of "making it" in U.S. society.

ORGANIZED CRIME

Independent Professional Crime vs. Organized Crime

The professional criminals we have discussed are independent operators. By contrast, participants in **organized crime** work in a local organization, which, in turn, is part of a national or international network. Not only do these professional criminals make their living from crime, but also they belong to interconnected criminal organizations.

Origin of the Mafia

In one sense, the Mafia is a myth. The myth is that a criminal organization developed in Sicily, moved to the United States, and now controls organized crime here. The Mafia does exist, and it did originate in Sicily. As *The Godfather* series depicts, the Sicilian government was weak, and local strongmen united to protect their families and communities from bandits. After establishing a private government, they also protected their communities from other strongmen—in return for regular tribute (Anderson 1965; Blok 1974; Catanzaro 1992). As politicians centralized the formal government, these men resisted and maintained their control over areas of Sicily. After the 1860s, they became known as the **Mafia.**

Maintaining Solidarity

The twin foundations of these private governments are the family and *omertá,* a vow of secrecy. Violators of *omertá* pay with their lives. These twin foundations are designed to ensure secrecy, solidarity, and separation from outsiders. To maintain close connections, the Mafia forges bonds through *village endogamy* (marriage between people from the same village) and *fictive kinship* (assigning obligations associated with close blood relatives to people who are not related; a godfather, for example, unites two families).

Non-Mafia Organized Crime

According to the Mafia myth, Sicilians introduced organized crime to the United States. New York City, however, has had organized crime for more than 150 years. It has been dominated by successive waves of ethnic immigrants—first the Irish, then the Jews, and only after that the Italians (Bell 1960). Today, organized crime in New York City is not dominated by any single ethnic group. It includes Sicilians and Italians, but also African Americans and Puerto Ricans. Miami has Cuban organized crime, and San Francisco and Los Angeles have Japanese organized crime (Wagman 1981). Russian mobsters are the new ethnic contender, arriving on the U.S. crime scene after the breakup of the Soviet empire in 1991. Some organized crime has no ethnic basis at all, such as outlaw motorcycle gangs, whose primary activity is dope dealing.

Transplantation of the Mafia to the United States

The Mafia myth, however, is valid in pinpointing an organization that is dominated by Americans of Sicilian–Italian descent, with connections across the United States and abroad. Transplanted to the United States, the various Mafias—and I emphasize the plural—continued their illegal activities among their own ethnic group. Prohibition provided the stimulus for these tightly knit organizations to expand. By the time Prohibition was repealed in 1933, the Mafias had become a power structure in major cities, especially Chicago and New York (Sykes 1978). The Mafias developed a **bureaucracy,** a hierarchy that has specialized personnel (gunmen, runners, executives, and others), departmentalization (narcotics, prostitution, loan sharking, and gambling), and an enforcement arm to keep profits flowing upward.

The Mafia as a Bureaucracy

Unlike most bureaucracies, the Mafias do not make public their organizational structures, but some cities appear to have the equivalent of a board of directors, a president and vice president, district managers with executive assistants, and, at the lowest level, soldiers who carry out the orders (Anderson 1965). In the Sicilian-American Mafia, about 5,000 members belong to about 24 "families" of 200 to 700 members each. These families are linked to each other by understandings and "treaties." The leaders of the most powerful families form

"Chop shops" operate all over the nation. Shown here are parts of a Jeep Cherokee that were recovered from a chop shop in Philadelphia, Pennsylvania. When my son's Jeep Cherokee was stolen, it never was found. Within a couple of days, I am sure, it, too, had been broken into its component parts, and they were on sale at several St. Louis locations.

a "commission" or "combine" to which weaker families pay deference (Cressey 1969; Riesel 1982a). The East Coast members call this structure the Mafia, or **cosa nostra** ("our thing").

Crime as Business

Crime is the Mafia's business, and they are successful. Despite the U.S. government's "war" against the Mafias—and a series of premature obituaries trumpeted in the media—the Mafias flourish. The Mafias—whether in their Sicilian, Colombian, or Russian versions—are the major importers and wholesalers of narcotics. They also run the main U.S. loan-sharking operations (making illegal loans at high rates of interest) and control some labor unions and in some areas the construction trade (Penn 1982; Riesel 1982b; Trust 1986). The Mafias have also infiltrated many legitimate businesses, such as the garment industry of New York City. Violence remains the way the Mafias do business—despite their public relations claims to the contrary.

Why the Mafia Has Been So Successful

Why has organized crime been so successful, despite efforts of the U.S. government? We can cite the following reasons (*Organized Crime* 1976):

1. Organized crime *is* organized. The more organized Mafias have a bureaucracy with full-time specialists in many criminal pursuits.
2. Organized crime provides illegal *services in high demand* (prostitution, gambling, and loan sharking)—"victimless crimes" in which no one complains to the police.
3. Organized crime wields influence through *political corruption*.
4. Organize crime uses *violence and intimidation* against victims and its own members.

Conflict theorists add a *fifth* reason—that organized crime serves the goals of the U.S. ruling class. According to sociologist David Simon (1981), the ruling class has used organized crime to keep labor from getting too organized or becoming too "radical." During the 1920s and the 1940s, periods of great labor unrest, corporations hired gangsters to break strikes and infiltrate unions, especially among autoworkers and longshoremen. Simon notes that during World War II, U.S. Navy Intelligence asked Mafia boss Charles "Lucky" Luciano to protect the New York docks from sabotage. Luciano, who was directing Mafia operations from prison, cooperated. Luciano also helped get the Sicilian Mafia to support the U.S. invasion of Sicily. As a reward, Luciano's prison sentence was commuted, and he was deported to Italy.

The Mafia and the U.S. Ruling Class

The allegations of Judith Campbell Exner add another dimension to the connection between the ruling class and the Mafia. Exner claimed to be a lover of President John F. Kennedy and of Sam Giancana, the head of the Chicago Mafia. She also claimed to have carried messages between them (Kelley 1988). Supposedly, Giancana delivered votes to Kennedy in key states and, at Kennedy's request, plotted the assassination of Fidel Castro. This connection has led to one of the many theories about Kennedy's assassination, that the mob assassinated Kennedy when he turned on them and directed his brother, Robert, head of the Justice Department, to pursue organized crime. These are only allegations, and there may be no substance to them (DiEugenio 1997).

Organized Crime as a Threat to the United States

Some sociologists emphasize that organized crime threatens the well-being of the United States. The most serious problem is not gambling, prostitution, loan sharking, and so on, but the corruption of our social institutions. With their many millions of untaxed dollars, the Mafias bribe police, judges, and politicians, subverting the institutions and organizations that deal with crime. Thus violence, bribery, and other forms of corruption work their way into the social system (Cressey 1969; Teresa 1973; Gosch and Hammer 1975; Ianni and Reuss-Ianni 1976; Gudkov 1980; Schwidrowski 1980). This leaves us with the frightening possibility that, as is the case in Russia today, much of our society could one day be controlled by organized crime.

Although it is certain that crime will continue, and along with it various versions of organized crime, the future of the Mafias, at least of the Sicilian-American version, is uncertain. In recent years, this Mafia has faced stiff competition from other groups,

Federal officials have made sharp inroads into organized crime. With the conviction of top mobsters, such as John Gotti, shown here, the government boasted that it had broken the Mafia. Any announcements of the Mafia's death, however, are a bit premature.

omertá has been weakened, and the FBI has successfully infiltrated this organization. With the police using more powerful electronic surveillance techniques and more mobsters willing to talk to avoid jail or to have their sentences reduced, the police have been successful in indicting and convicting even top Mafia bosses. One of these bosses, John Gotti (called "the Teflon don" because he had beaten so many criminal charges) captured the public's attention. Despite his crimes, which include murder, Gotti was romanticized and became a darling of the media. With the government's infiltration of this group, the Mafia appears to be in decline, but it is far too soon to sound its death knell. We will have to see how this group adapts to its changing situation.

POLITICAL CRIME

Two Types of Political Crime:

To Change or to Maintain the Social Order

Some conflict theorists view almost every crime as political—an act by the ruling class to oppress the working class, or an act of the working class to resist that oppression. I use the term **political crime** in a narrower sense—to describe crimes designed either to change or to maintain the social order. Crimes to *change the social order* include treason (the betrayal of one's country), sedition (rebellion, an attempt to overthrow the government), and such activities as resistance to the draft. The blowing up of a federal building in Oklahoma City by Timothy McVeigh and his conspirators is another example.

Crimes designed to *maintain the social order* include acts by the CIA: assassinations, manipulation of foreign governments, and illegal domestic surveillance. Political crimes include the illegal activities of President Richard Nixon and his aides during Watergate and probably the activities of President Ronald Reagan and Lt. Col. Oliver North to support the contras of Nicaragua. Some allege that political crime also includes using drug money to financee President Bill Clinton's campaign (Reed and Cummings 1994).

Although there is no end to conspiracy theories, which usually are difficult to impossible to prove, we do have ample evidence that U.S. politicians and bureaucrats order illegal acts. In some cases, illegal acts become a routine. Consider just one example: From the 1940s into the 1970s, the FBI committed thousands of burglaries and illegally opened and photographed tens of thousands of letters (Coleman 1995).

In summary, political crime illustrates clearly that social problems are a matter of definition rather than a collection of objective facts. Some people see the illegal activities of those who want to change the social order as a major social problem, but they excuse the political crimes of government officials as necessary for securing the domestic order. Others view the illegal acts of government officials as a major social problem, because these acts subvert the constitutional system that the officials are sworn to uphold. For still others, all political crime, whether designed to maintain or to change the social order, is a social problem simply because it is illegal.

THE CRIMINAL JUSTICE SYSTEM

Types of Crime and the Sting of the Criminal Justice System

Certain types of crime are easier to get away with than types of crime etc others. Least likely to be arrested are those who commit political crimes to maintain the status quo, for they are protected by the political system that they are supporting. Also running less risk are white-collar criminals who commit crimes in the name of a corporation and those at the top levels of organized crime. Respectability, wealth, power, and underlings insulate them. Probably the next safest are those who commit crimes against a corporation and professional criminals. Those in the first group are insulated by the corporation's desire to avoid negative publicity; those in the other group are protected by skill, by a criminal subculture, and by having minimal contact with the "straight" world. Those in organized crime who run the highest risk of arrest are "soldiers" who occupy the lowest level in the organization; they are considered expendable. Juvenile delinquents and others who commit street crimes run high risks of being apprehended. Because crimes that are designed to change the political system threaten the power elite, the state is probably the most efficient in dealing with this type of crime.

Plea Bargaining as Subversion of the Criminal Justice System

Keeping in mind, then, that the sting of the criminal justice system is not an equal threat to all, let's examine how this system operates. Buddy, Gary, and Clyde, whose defense attorney suggested that they plead guilty, represent in microcosm our criminal justice system. Prosecutors charge people with the most serious crimes possible, and then offer to accept a guilty plea to lesser offenses. Despite their constitutional obligation to *defend* their clients, public defense attorneys usually suggest to their clients that they plead guilty (Blumberg 1967; Maynard 1984). In *most* cases, what is supposed to be a trial becomes the perfunctory validation of pretrial agreements.

Plea bargaining has become so prevalent that *in the vast majority of cases people accused of a crime do not receive a trial*. On average, juries hear only *5 percent* of criminal cases (*Sourcebook of Criminal Justice Statistics* 2003:Table 5.43). Back in the 1960s, sociologist Abraham Blumberg explained that public defenders—regardless of their formal job description—develop "implicit understandings" about what their job *really* is: to be team players who produce "assembly-line justice" for the poor (Blumberg 1967). Today's situation remains unchanged. Of all the research that I have read on this topic, this statement has struck me as the most revealing: One public defender, in urging his client to accept a jail sentence, said, "Even if you're innocent, it's a good deal" (Penn 1985).

The criminal justice system is also slow and inefficient. Courtrooms are jammed and their hours in session short. Bureaucratic procedures wreck schedules. Police officers and other witnesses wait hours, even days, for cases to be called. Lawyers are

A common perception is that bias in the criminal justice system works only against African Americans and Latinos. Sociological studies, however, indicate that this bias goes in both directions and also favors these groups.

(© The New Yorker Collection 2000. David Sipress form cartoonbank.com. All Rights Reserved.)

"You look like this sketch of someone who's thinking about committing a crime."

expensive, and those assigned to the poor are overburdened. Rules for presenting evidence are complex. The result is that cases advance at a snail's pace. For those who plead guilty, the average time between arrest and sentencing is 10 months. For those who choose a jury trial, it is 14 months (*Sourcebook* 2003:Table 5.43). During this time, some innocent people remain locked behind bars, while some guilty people are released to commit more crimes while awaiting a distant trial.

The Public Defender as Team Player

Plea bargaining and the inefficiencies of the court system subvert the Sixth Amendment to the Constitution, which declares that "the accused shall enjoy the right to a speedy and public trial, by an impartial jury of the State and district wherein the crime shall have been committed." The poor do not receive a speedy trial. Indeed, most do not even receive a trial.

Is the Criminal Justice System Guilty of Racial Discrimination?

Let's discuss racial-ethnic discrimination in the criminal justice system. As you will recall, Buddy, the only African American in the trio, received the most severe sentence. The judge claimed that this was only because of Buddy's "priors." What is the answer?

Perhaps: The Prison Population

The issue is complicated, and sociologists differ in their conclusions. At first glance, the judicial system certainly seems to discriminate along racial-ethnic lines, especially when it comes to African Americans. Although African Americans make up about 12 percent of the U.S. population, 40 percent of jail inmates and 46 percent of inmates in prison are African Americans (*Sourcebook of Criminal Justice Statistics* 2003:Tables 6.16, 6.28). From Table 6-6 below, you can see that the percentage of African Americans on death row is over *three* times greater than you would expect from their percentage in the U.S. population. No other group makes up such a disproportionate share of prisoners or death row inmates. Perhaps no statement illustrates the impact of the criminal justice system on African Americans better than this one: "On any given day, almost one in three black men between the ages of 20–29 are in prison or jail, on probation or parole" (American Civil Liberties Union 1996).

No: "Priors" and Victimization Surveys

These data do not let us draw conclusions about bias, however, because they do not account for differences in crime among racial-ethnic groups. Sociologists have compared victimization studies (which contain no police bias) with the arrest rates of African Americans and white Americans for rape, robbery, and aggravated assault. They find that the

---

TABLE 6-6 Prisoners on Death Row, by Race-Ethnicity

RACE-ETHNICITY	NUMBER ON DEATH ROW	PERCENTAGE OF DEATH ROW INMATES	PERCENTAGE OF U.S. POPULATION	MORE (+) OR LESS (−) THAN WHAT YOU WOULD EXPECT FROM THE GROUP'S PERCENTAGE OF THE U.S. POPULATION[*]
White	1,596	45.6%	68.2%	−32%
African American	1,473	42.0%	12.2%	+248%
Latino	353	10.1%	13.5%	−24%
Native American	39	1.1%	0.8%	+39%
Asian American	41	1.2%	4.1%	−70%
Claim two or more races			1.2%	
Totals	3,503	100%	100%	

[*]This total is computed by dividing the difference between the group's percentage of the U.S. population and its percentage of death row inmates by its percentage of the U.S. population—after removing a presumptive equal proportionate share of the claim of two or more races.
Sources: By the author, based on *Statistical Abstract* 2002:Tables 36, 38, 1373; Bernstein and Bergman 2003; *Sourcebook of Criminal Justice Statistics* 2004:Table 6.77.

racial-ethnic makeup that victims report closely matches arrest rates (Hindelang 1978; Shim and DeBerry 1988; *Sourcebook of Criminal Justice Statistics* 2003:Tables 3.32, 4.10).

Yes: Police–Civilian Encounters

Yes: Two More Studies

Many sociologists, however, are convinced that the criminal justice system is biased against African Americans (Sellin 1928; Bullock 1961; Keil and Vito 1989; Bridges and Stern 1998). Sociologists Douglas Smith and Christy Visher (1981) trained civilians to ride with the police in Missouri, New York, and Florida. After observing almost 6,000 encounters between police and citizens, they concluded that the police are more likely to arrest African-American suspects. An examination of felony convictions in Florida showed that whites were more likely to have their cases dropped or to receive probation, and African Americans more likely to be convicted and to go to prison (Hale 1980). Sociologist Gary LaFree (1980), who examined court records in a midwestern community, found that African Americans who raped white women received more severe sentences than whites who raped white women.

Bias Works in Both Directions

Other studies show that bias works in *both* directions: Sometimes whites get more favorable treatment; at other times, minorities are treated more leniently. Consider these mixed findings: African Americans are given longer prison terms for rape and drugs, but whites receive longer sentences for murder (Butterfield 1999). Sociologist John Tinker (1981) found that Latinos in Fresno, California, were more likely than whites to have their charges dismissed, but if tried, they were more likely to go to prison. Sociologist Joan Petersilia (1983) found that minority suspects in California were more likely than whites to be released after arrest. If convicted of a felony, however, they were more likely to be given longer sentences. Petersilia, along with sociologists Stephen Klein and Susan Turner (1990), found that race did not make a difference in sentences for assault, robbery, burglary, theft, and forgery. For drug offenses, however, Latinos were more likely to be sent to prison.

Even Reverse Racism?

Sociologists Martha Myers and Susette Talarico (1986:246) found something even more surprising in Georgia—that whites are discriminated against:

> Where blacks are a substantial minority (24–49 percent), black and white offenders bear the brunt of greater punitiveness equally. Once blacks become a numerical majority, white offenders are at a distinct disadvantage. Put concretely, they are more likely than blacks to be imprisoned.

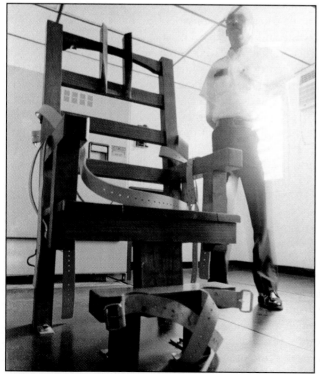

We also find mixed results when we look at how juvenile delinquents are handled in the courts. While they wait for a judge to hear their case, whites are more likely to be sent home, and blacks are more likely to be kept in juvenile hall. When they do receive a hearing, however, African Americans are more likely to have their cases dismissed (*Sourcebook* 1998:Table 5.77; 2003:Table 5.64).

At this point, then, we cannot conclude that the courts are biased for or against minorities or for or against whites. The evidence goes both ways.

Throughout history, many methods have been used to execute prisoners. Death by electrocution was supposedly an improvement over earlier methods. Shown here is the electric chair at Starke, Florida. After foot-long flames shot from the head of a prisoner being executed, the courts ordered this chair not to be used.

Federal prisons are known as the country clubs of the U.S. prison system. Alabama, in contrast, has some of the toughest prisons in the nation. As shown in this photo shot at Huntsville, to be sentenced to serve "hard labor" means exactly that.

Racial Bias in Capital Punishment

A look at **capital punishment** (the death penalty), however, shows that there at least used to be overwhelming racial bias, especially when it came to rape. No one has been executed for rape since 1967, but between 1930 and 1967, 455 U.S. prisoners were executed for rape. Forty-eight were whites; 455 were African Americans. Donald Partington (1965), a lawyer, examined all executions for rape and attempted rape in Virginia between 1908 and 1963. Convicted of these crimes were 2,798 men (56 percent whites and 44 percent African Americans). Forty-one men were executed for rape and 13 for attempted rape. *All were African Americans. Not one of the whites was executed.*

When judges used to give the death penalty for rape, what really made the difference was the race of the attacker *and* the race of the victim. In their study of rape and the death penalty in Georgia, sociologists Marvin Wolfgang and Marc Reidel (1975) found this: The best predictor of whether a man would be sentenced to death was knowing that the victim was white and the accused black.

The death penalty was so biased that in 1972 the Supreme Court ruled in *Furman v. Georgia* that it was being applied unconstitutionally. As Table 6-7 on page 192 shows, up to this point 3,896 prisoners had been executed. Fifty-three percent were African American, 46 percent white, and 1 percent Native American or Asian American. The states rewrote their laws, and in 1977 they again began to execute prisoners. As Table 6-7 shows, since then 65 percent of those put to death have been white and 35 percent African American.

Gender Bias in Capital Punishment

The death penalty apparently shows a strong gender bias: Of the 4,744 prisoners who have been executed since 1930, only 42 were women, a mere 0.9 percent. Since the death penalty was restored in 1976, 875 men have been executed, but only 10 women (*Statistical Abstract* 2005:Table 341). At present, 1.5 percent of prisoners on death row are women (*Sourcebook of Criminal Justice Statistics* 2003:Table 6.80). These totals could indicate bias in favor of women, but they could also reflect the relative frequency and severity of their crimes. We need more research to see what is really occurring.

Geographic Bias in Capital Punishment

We do know that geography makes a huge difference in a person's chances of being executed. As the Social Map on the next page shows, 13 states do not have the death penalty. As you can see from Table 6-8 on page 194, of the 37 states that do have the death penalty, some are much more willing to use it than others. This tendency is far more prevalent in the South. Texas held the record before the death penalty was abolished and does so once again. One of every three executions (35 percent) since 1977 has taken place in Texas.

TABLE 6-7 Prisoners Executed, by Race-Ethnicity

YEAR	WHITE		AFRICAN AMERICAN		NATIVE AMERICAN/ASIAN AMERICAN		TOTAL
	NUMBER	PERCENTAGE	NUMBER	PERCENTAGE	NUMBER	PERCENTAGE	
1930–34	371	48%	395	51%	10	1%	772
1935–39	456	51%	421	47%	14	2%	891
1940–44	276	43%	362	56%	7	1%	645
1945–49	214	33%	419	66%	6	1%	639
1950–54	201	49%	209	50%	3	1%	413
1955–59	135	44%	167	55%	2	1%	304
1960–64	90	50%	91	50%	0	0%	181
1965–69	8	80%	2	20%	0	0%	10
Totals before the death penalty was abolished							
	1,774	46%	2,080	53%	42	1%	3,896
1970–74	0	0%	0	0%	0	0%	0
1975–79	3	100%	0	0%	0	0%	3
1980–84	19	66%	10	34%	0	0%	29
1985–89	49	56%	39	44%	0	0%	88
1990–94	85	62%	50	36%	2	2%	137
1995–99	218	66%	114	34%	n/a	n/a	332
2000–03	194	69%	88	31%	n/a	n/a	282
Totals since the death penalty was reinstated							
	568	65%	301	35%	n/a	n/a	869

Note: Because this table does not include prisoners who were executed by the federal government, the total does not agree with that in Table 6-8. n/a—not available. Latinos are subsumed into the categories white and African American.
Sources: By the author, based on *Sourcebook of Criminal Justice Statistics* 1998:Table 6.88; 2000:Table 6.92; *Statistical Abstract of the United States* 2005:Table 341.

The Prison Experience: Internal Structure

Finally, let's look at the prison experience. Unlike Clyde, Buddy and Gary had to serve time. Prison turned out to be horrible. As with the prisoner whose letter opens this chapter, Buddy and Gary were offered no rehabilitation program. They and their fellow prisoners were locked away, forgotten by society—except when a riot riveted public attention. The warden was a political appointee, awarded his supposedly easy job

FIGURE 6-3 *Which States Have the Death Penalty?*
Source: By the author, based on Sourcebook of Criminal Justice Statistics 2003:Table 6.81.

TABLE 6-8 Number of Prisoners Executed, by Jurisdiction, 1930–2003

	NUMBER EXECUTED SENTENCE OF DEATH	
STATE	SINCE 1930	SINCE 1977
U.S. total	4,744	885
Texas	610	313
Georgia	400	34
New York	329	0
California	302	10
North Carolina	293	30
Florida	227	57
South Carolina	190	28
Virginia	181	89
Ohio	180	8
Alabama	163	28
Louisiana	160	27
Mississippi	160	6
Pennsylvania	155	3
Arkansas	143	25
Oklahoma	129	55
Missouri	123	61
Kentucky	105	2
Illinois	102	12
Tennessee	94	1
New Jersey	74	0
Maryland	71	3
Arizona	60	22
Washington	52	4
Indiana	48	11
Colorado	48	1
District of Columbia	40	0
West Virginia	40	0
Nevada	38	9
Federal system	36	3
Massachusetts	27	0
Delaware	25	13
Oregon	21	2
Connecticut	21	0
Utah	19	6
Iowa	18	0
Kansas	15	0
New Mexico	9	1
Montana	8	2
Wyoming	8	1
Nebraska	7	3
Idaho	4	1
Vermont	4	0
New Hampshire	1	0
South Dakota	1	0

Source: By the author, based on *Sourcebook of Criminal Justice Statistics* 2004:Table 6.81.

for party loyalty. As long as the prison remained "quiet," his job was secure. Buddy and Gary soon discovered that in return for the prisoners' cooperation in keeping the prison quiet, guards overlooked gambling, alcohol, drugs, even homosexual rape. To supplement their low salaries, guards smuggled in alcohol and drugs.

The Social Production of Brutality

Buddy and Gary were herded about like animals, forbidden to make even simple decisions. They were told when to work, what TV programs to watch, and when to sleep. Their letters were censored, their packages rifled, and their telephone conversations recorded. They expected these things, because they were prisoners. What they did not expect was the brutality and violence of the guards. As the prisoner in the opening vignette observed, violence could result from breaking a rule or even the suspicion of having broken one. Buddy and Gary concluded that the prison recruited sadists, for that is how they saw the guards. If they had taken a social problems course, however, they might have gained a different understanding of this brutal fact of prison life.

The Zimbardo Experiment

Philip Zimbardo, a social psychologist, conducted a fascinating experiment. Using paid volunteers, Zimbardo (1995) matched 24 college students on the basis of their education, race, and parents' social class. He randomly assigned one group as guards and the other as prisoners. Without warning, one night real police cars arrived at the homes of those who had been designated prisoners. They were "arrested," fingerprinted, and taken to the basement of the psychology building at Stanford University, which had been turned into a prison. Both "guards" and "prisoners" were given appropriate uniforms.

Subject to the arbitrary control of their captors, the prisoners felt a loss of personal identity. The guards, in contrast, felt an increase in social power and status. They also developed strong in-group loyalty. After several days, rumors of a prison rebellion spread. The guards reacted brutally, with about a third treating the prisoners as though they were subhuman. Things started to get out of hand, and after six days Zimbardo had to stop the experiment.

Zimbardo's experiment illustrates a fundamental sociological principle: The way society is structured and the groups to which we belong provide the bases for our orientations and how we act toward others. How a prison is organized is more important in determining how guards and prisoners act than are their individual personalities. As guards work in a prison, they come to see themselves as representatives of morality and the prisoners as enemies that need to be subdued, rather than as people who need to be helped. Their goal becomes upholding authority at all costs, even if this requires "justifiable" brutality. Eventually, the guards can come to see prisoners as "animals" who understand nothing but violence.

In Sum

Zimbardo's experiment created controversy in the scientific community. Some fellow social scientists accused Zimbardo of being cruel and irresponsible. The federal government responded with strict guidelines for research on human subjects, and it is not likely that similar experiments will be conducted again. Zimbardo's research, however, provides insight into what is wrong with our prisons, adding to our knowledge of why prisons fail to reduce crime.

If prisons are not the answer, what is?

Social Policy

Prevention

What is being done to solve these twin social problems of crime and the criminal justice system? We can never eliminate crime, but to the extent that we can prevent people from breaking the law, we can reduce the problem. Because street crime bothers Americans the most, and street crime is linked to poverty, the *best policy* would be to reduce poverty. Education is an effective way to reduce poverty because, on average, the farther that people go in school, the more they earn. In addition, as we saw on pgae 177, researchers have found a direct link between adult crime and dropping out of high school, so programs that help students graduate from high school would help to prevent crime.

Four Types of Policy for Lawbreakers:

We will, of course, always have criminals, so we need effective policies for dealing with them. There are four basic approaches: retribution, deterrence, rehabilitation, and incapacitation. Let's consider each.

1. Retribution

Retribution is punishing criminals to uphold collective values and to demonstrate that criminal behavior will not be tolerated. Proponents of retribution see offenders as morally responsible people whose violations of social norms have created a moral imbalance. To help restore the moral order, the punishment should fit the crime (Cohen 1940). An interesting form of retribution is *shaming*, which is discussed in the Thinking Critically box on the next page.

Restitution, making offenders compensate their victims, is a form of retribution. If people have stolen, for example, they need to pay the money back. Restitution is practical for property crimes, when the offender can repay the victim. It is less practical for unemployed offenders, although some judges require the unemployed to "work their debt off" in public projects.

Attempts to restore the "moral balance" are evident in the following examples of "making the punishment fit the crime":

Thinking Critically about Social Problems

PUBLIC SHAMING AS SOCIAL POLICY

"Shame on you!"

Do you remember those horrifying words from your childhood? If your childhood was like mine, you do. The words were accompanied by an index finger that pointed directly at me, while another index finger rubbed on top of it, seeming to send shame in my direction.

It was effective. I always felt bad when this happened. Even worse when I saw the looks of disgust on the faces of my parents or grandparents in response to my childish offense, whatever it may have been.

If you have read Nathaniel Hawthorne's *The Scarlet Letter*, you know about shaming. Hester Prynne, who committed adultery, a serious offense at the time, had to wear a red A on her clothing. For life, wherever she went, she was marked as a shameful adulteress.

Now judges are bringing back this old-fashioned device. Not the scarlet A, but its equivalent.

A judge has ordered thieves to wear a sandwich board saying, "I stole from this store," and to parade back and forth outside the stores they stole from.

A Texas judge ordered a piano teacher who pleaded guilty to molesting his young students to give away his prized $12,000 piano, not to play for 20 years, and to post a sign on the door of his home declaring himself a child molester.

Judges have ordered drunk drivers to put bright orange bumper stickers on their cars that say, "I am a convicted drunk driver. Report any erratic driving to the police."

As a response to prostitution, the Minneapolis police department has organized "shaming details." Prostitutes and their johns must stand handcuffed in front of citizens who let loose with "verbal stones," shouting things like, "You're the reason our children aren't safe in this neighborhood!"

Kansas City tried a different approach to prostitution. On "John TV" are shown the mug shots of men who have been arrested for trying to buy sex, and the women who have been arrested for selling it. Their names, birth dates, and hometowns are displayed prominently.

Does shaming work? No one knows if it reduces lawbreaking. But shaming certainly can be powerful. A woman convicted of welfare fraud was ordered to wear a sign in public that said, "I stole food from poor people." She chose to go to jail instead.

Even if shaming doesn't work, it does satisfy a strong urge to punish, to get even. In today's eager-to-punish climate, perhaps this purpose is enough. And perhaps it does help to restore a moral balance.

Examples are based on Gerlin 1994 and Belluck 1998.

Halfway houses, such as this one in Los Angeles, refer to a supervised environment in which residents live "half way" between freedom and being locked up in an institution. Residents set and enforce their own rules for living with one another. They also have limited freedom to come and go.

A Memphis judge invited victims to visit the thief's house and "steal" something back (Stevens 1992).

A Florida judge sentenced a white man who was convicted of harassing an interracial couple to work weekends at an African-American church.

A Texas judge ordered a "deadbeat dad" who had fathered 13 children to attend Planned Parenthood meetings (Gerlin 1994).

A judge in Ohio sentenced two men to dress in women's clothing and walk down Main Street for throwing beer bottles at a car and taunting a woman (Leinwand 2004).

Critics emphasize how difficult it is to decide that a crime merits a particular punishment and how inconsistent judges are in making those decisions. They also note that for crimes of violence, retribution might require unusual measures, such as castration for rapists—acts that courts may rule are unconstitutional. A California judge, for example, wanted to withhold AIDS treatment from a man who had raped two teenagers after he was released from prison for a previous rape (Farah 1995). Proponents reply that if retribution is the goal of punishment, the Constitution needs to be brought into line with the goal.

2. Deterrence

Deterrence aims to create fear by letting potential offenders know that they will be punished. Proponents view offenders as rational people who weigh the possible consequences of their actions: If someone is considering a crime and perceives that punishment is likely, that person will avoid the crime. Back in the 1970s, criminologist Ernest van den Haag (1975, 1983) proposed that we treat juveniles who commit violent crimes like adults ("adult crime, adult time"), abolish parole boards, and operate work programs for prisoners. With citizens demanding strong action, these attempts at deterrence have become popular.

Researchers have discovered two principles: First, the longer the interval between a crime and its punishment, the less the deterrence, or fear of the punishment. This underscores the need for the speedy trials guaranteed by the Constitution and for swift punishment for the guilty. Second, the more uncertain the penalty, the less the deterrence. The solution some have proposed is **uniform sentencing,** the same sentence for everyone convicted of the same crime.

Critics of deterrence point out that offenders are not always as rational about their crimes as proponents of deterrence suppose. Many lawbreakers simply do not weigh the consequences of their acts; or, if they do, they take the chance anyway, regardless of the consequences. For example, back in the 1700s, the punishment for picking pockets in England was hanging. When someone was being hung for picking pockets, pickpockets worked the crowd because the spectators, with their attention riveted on the gallows, made easy victims (Hibbert 1963).

When Good Intentions Go Awry: The Failure of "Scared Straight"

"Scared Straight" was once trumpeted by the mass media as a successful program of deterrence. In this program, delinquents went on prison tours, where inmates gave them a close-up view of prison life. Leering and shouting obscenities, they said they could hardly wait for the youths to be sent to prison so they could rape them. Those who operated the program reported that it kept 80 to 90 percent of the youths from further trouble with the law. Follow-up studies by sociologists, however, showed that the program had backfired. Criminologist James Finckenauer (1982) matched delinquents on the basis of their sex, race-ethnicity, age, and criminal acts. He then compared those who had been exposed to the scared-straight program (the experimental group) with delinquents who had not been exposed to it (the control group). Within six months, 41 percent of the experimental group but only 11 percent of the control group were again in trouble with the law.

How could this program backfire? It sounds so good. Finckenauer suggests that the boys were impressed by the macho performance of hypermasculine, in-charge men. (Let your imagination go a little here: You've probably seen photos or TV programs that show the tattoos and muscles that many men convicts display.) These are the type of powerful men that these boys want to be. Committing crimes after listening to these convicts was a way of showing their peers that this talk hadn't frightened them, and that they, too, were macho.

The failure of "scared straight" does not mean that programs of deterrence cannot work. It does, however, point up the need for sociological research. We cannot *assume* that a program is successful just because it sounds good, because it appeals to our common sense, or because its operators say that it works. If we are to develop sound social policy, we need solid research so we can evaluate programs. This point is underscored in the Thinking Critically box on "prison boot camps" on the next page.

3. Rehabilitation

The focus of **rehabilitation** is resocializing offenders, to help them become conforming citizens. Programs of rehabilitation include *probation,* returning offenders to the community under the supervision of a probation officer; *imprisonment* with the goal of teaching prisoners a trade or useful skills through high school or college courses; *parole,* releasing prisoners before they serve their full sentence, both as a reward for good behavior and as a threat (for, as in probation, if the court's rules are violated the convict goes back to prison to serve out the sentence); *furloughs,* freedom for a set time, such as a weekend, toward the end of the sentence, to let convicts adjust gradually to nonprison life; *halfway houses,* residences in which released convicts report to the authorities but supervise much of their own lives, such as household tasks, drinking, drugs, and curfews; and *honor farms* for prisoners who have shown good behavior, where supervision is less stringent and convicts can learn cooperative, responsible roles (Morash and Anderson 1978).

The Failure of Probation

The public is fed up with failed attempts at rehabilitation. Probation is especially offensive; the public perceives probation as an opportunity for felons to commit more crime. The public's perception is accurate; probation has failed. Figure 6-4 on page 200 summarizes what happened to 79,000 felons who were given probation. Within three years, 43 percent were rearrested for a violent crime (murder, rape, robbery, or aggravated assault) or a drug offense (Langan and Cunniff 1992). Another 19 percent had violated conditions of their probation.

The concept of probation is not unsound, however, although our implementation of it is. If probation were given to felons with the most promise, if they were provided with follow-up counseling, and if trained probation officers had small caseloads, it might work. As you have seen with the Scared Straight and boot camp programs, however, seemingly sound ideas can prove quite disappointing. To find out if these ideas work in practice, we would need sociological research.

Another approach is **diversion,** diverting offenders *away from* courts and jails. The goal is to keep offenders out of the criminal justice system—to shift them to community organizations or to funnel them into administrative hearings rather than to criminal trials. Diversionary programs aim to avoid stigmatizing offenders and to keep them out of the crime schools that go under the name of jails and prisons.

If rehabilitation programs were successful, almost everyone would favor them. The cost of rehabilitation would certainly be less than the price that criminals now exact from society—from the harm they cause their victims to the cost of supporting them in prison. The problem is that we do not know which rehabilitation programs work. The studies show conflicting results and do not inspire confidence.

Thinking Critically about Social Problems

SQUEEZE YOU LIKE A GRAPE

As they step out of the police cars into the Georgia countryside, a guard shouts into their faces, "You're nothing! You're nobody! You're fools! You're maggots!"

The youths look dumbfounded. Another guard shouts, "I don't like ya. I got no use for ya, and I don't care who ya are on the streets. This is hell's half acre, and I don't give a damn if ya get tossed outta here into prison. I promise ya, ya won't last five minutes before you're somebody's wife. Do ya know what that means, tough guys?"

The offenders are ages 17 to 25. Convicted of nonviolent crimes, they were given a choice of either one to five years in prison or 90 days of prison boot camp, followed by probation.

"You have to hit a mule between the eyes with a two-by-four to get his attention," explains a guard. "And that's what we do here." Within an hour of arriving, inmates are stripped of every sign of their previous life. Guards take their cigarettes and personal possessions. Their heads are shaved, and a white prison uniform with wide blue stripes replaces their jeans and T-shirts.

Inmates may not speak without permission. All responses must begin and end with "Sir." The lights go out at 10. Television watching is limited to one hour a day—only the news and PBS—all in black and white. No visitors are allowed for the first 45 days.

Inmates do hard physical labor. Up at 5 A.M., they cut grass with scythes and dig up tree trunks with shovels and pickaxes. If an inmate talks on the work crew without permission, he must do push-ups—or take the "chair position," unsupported, of course. Repeated violations mean being handcuffed and placed in a police car. Other inmates are made to watch as the violator is taken away to prison to serve the longer sentence.

Mississippi opened the first boot camp in 1985. Thirty-one states followed. Seven states opened camps for women.

The warden of this Georgia camp says, "They're not going to leave here any smarter, but we can provide some structure and discipline that they've never gotten. We can't fix the sociological problems that led to crime in the first place, but we can influence what they do next."

The sociologist, of course, replies, "Let's see the statistics. We need matched groups (offenders of the same background convicted of the same crimes) who go to prison and who go to boot camp. When we compare the rearrest rate of each group, we'll know if boot camps work."

Although we didn't get matched samples—for no one has done such rigorous studies—we now have measurements of those rearrest rates. They are not encouraging. Researchers compared the recidivism of juveniles who went through prisoner boot camps with the recidivism of juveniles who were sent to prison. They found nothing consistent. In some cases the recidivism rate of the juveniles who had gone to boot camp was lower, but in other cases it was higher. As a result, some states have shut down their boot camps and are sending their young offenders to traditional prisons.

Sources: Lamar 1986; Gest 1987; *Life,* July 1988:82–83; Morash and Rucker 1990; MacKenzie and Souryal 1995; Lohn 2005; Willing 2005.

4. Incapacitation

Consequently, the public clamors for **incapacitation,** removing offenders from circulation. The view of those who propose incapacitation is direct and to the point: Everything else has failed. We cannot change people who don't want to change, so let's get them off the street so they can no longer hurt people. Some offenders commit crime after crime ("career criminals"), so let's free ourselves of recidivists (DiIulio 1992). For a new form of incapacitation, see the Technology and Social Problems box on the next page.

Incapacitation has aroused considerable debate in sociology. Criminologist James Wilson (1975), who said repeatedly that incapacitation is the *only* solution that makes sense, advocated incapacitation in books, scholarly journals, and the popular media. Ernest van den Haag proposed "added incapacitation," increasing an individual's sentence each time that person is convicted. Some estimated that if everyone convicted of a serious offense were imprisoned for three years, our rate of serious crime would

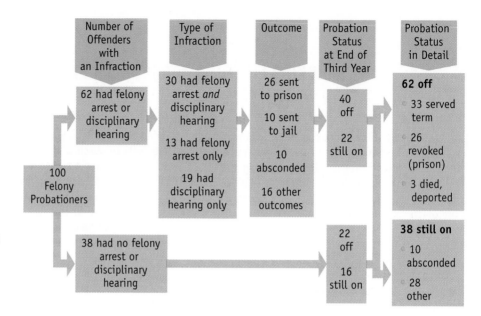

FIGURE 6-4 *The Failure of Probation*

Note: The numbers are percentages.

Source: Bureau of Justice.

drop by two-thirds (Shinnar and Shinnar 1975). Others estimated that such sentencing would reduce crime by only 3 or 4 percent (Greenberg 1975; Cohen 1978). Those who proposed incapacitation seem to be right. As we saw earlier, as judges gave out tougher sentences, the crime rate plummeted. Some sociologists, however, claim that the drop in the crime rate was due to other factors.

"Weed and Seed"

An innovative program is "weed and seed"—"weeding out" crime from targeted inner-city neighborhoods and then "seeding" them with economic and social programs (Eastland 1992). "Weed and seed" assumes that programs cannot be effective without public safety. The police patrol on foot to build rapport with the community and file federal charges against drug dealers and violent gang members (federal sentences are stiffer). Public schools, designated as safe havens, are kept open evenings and on Saturdays so adults can supervise homework and learn job skills themselves. In principle, "weed and seed" is sound, but as with other programs we have examined, we cannot depend on common sense. We need research to know if something works.

The Issue of Capital Punishment

The proponents of capital punishment argue that it is an appropriate retribution for heinous crimes, that it deters, and of course, that it incapacitates absolutely. Its critics argue that killing is never justified. They add that if capital punishment did deter, then states with the death penalty would have a lower homicide rate than those without it—but they don't. In fact, the states without the death penalty average a lower homicide rate (*Sociological Abstract* 2003:Table 119). Opponents also argue that the death penalty is capricious—jurors deliberate in secrecy and indulge their prejudices in recommending death—and that judges are irrational, merciful to some but not to others. They also stress that innocent people have been executed: The men released from death row because of new ways of testing DNA certainly back up this last argument.

Neither side convinces the other, and the data on whether the death penalty is effective are inconclusive. Nevertheless, the public demands that "something be done," and as Figure 6-5 shows, about two-thirds of Americans favor the death penalty. Figures 6-6 and 6-7 on page 202 show the increase in the number of prisoners sentenced to death and the numbers who have been executed.

Social Policy in Disarray

In sum, the United States has tried a variety of approaches to solve its crime problem. With little agreement on the basic purpose for the social response to crime (prevention, retribution, deterrence, rehabilitation, or incapacitation), our solutions are

Technology and Social Problems
USING TECHNOLOGY TO STOP CRIME

The idea was simple. "It's expensive to keep people in prison, and not everyone who is convicted of a crime should go to prison. Yet we need to keep tabs on offenders. How can we use technology to do this?"

Technology provides an effective device, an ankle bracelet that transmits a signal to a central monitor. A transmitter is strapped around the offender's ankle. If the offender leaves home, it breaks the signal and sets off an alarm at the monitoring station.

Able to transmit the location of an offender's whereabouts 24 hours a day, the ankle monitor not only is effective, but also it lowers costs. To keep a juvenile in custody runs about $100 a day, but the cost for home monitoring is just $10 a day. To keep an adult in prison runs about $75 a day; it's only $12 a day to use the ankle device. The costs include equipment and staff.

Some jurisdictions have even developed a pay-as-you go plan. Judges give adult clients a choice—go to jail or pay $12 a day for electronic monitoring. Not eligible are drug dealers, those who committed a violent crime, and those who used guns to commit their crime.

The ankle monitor is also suitable for probation and parole. Software can be programmed with an offender's work schedule and location. Probation officers can park outside a workplace to pick up a signal, but, better yet, failure to appear at work also sets off a signal. Probation officers check to make certain that it isn't a false call, then alert the police.

Hidden within this new technology is another benefit. Because electronic monitoring frees up prison cells, it allows courts to keep violent offenders in prison longer.

Victims of stalking get a special benefit. The software can be programmed to sound an alarm if an offender comes within a specified distance of a victim's home or workplace. Workers at the monitoring station warn the victim, who can leave the area.

The future of technology will soon make this tool seem primitive. Signaling devices will be implanted in felons' bodies. The implant will be connected electronically to the Global Positioning System, satellites that can track the precise location of any object. Software will be programmed with the offender's schedule—times and location of work or rehabilitation classes, even routes to and from work and restricted places in the community. If the individual deviates from the schedule, a computer will notify the police to make an arrest.

Technology is moving rapidly. We already have the capacity to insert devices in an offender's brain that can send pain if an individual deviates from scheduled activities. Soon we may be able to implant devices that will direct the individual's movements. This capacity to monitor and control people, of course, leads to the question of potential abuse by the government. Once authorities gain such power over felons, how do we keep them from turning it against the rest of us? Implants and the marvels of the Global Positioning System—what more could Big Brother ask to control its citizens?

Based on Campbell 1995, McGarigle 1997, "GPS Creates Global Jail" 1998, Knights 1999; Fitzpatrick 2004.

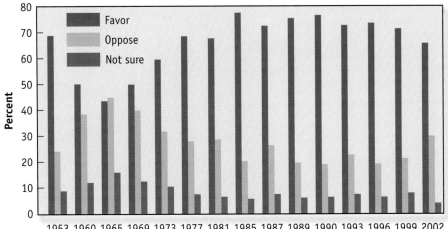

FIGURE 6-5 *Americans' Changing Attitudes Toward Capital Punishment Question: "Are you in favor of the death penalty for persons convicted of murder?"*

Source: By the author, based on Various editions of *Sourcebook of Criminal Justice Statistic,* including 2003:Table 2002:Table 2.48.

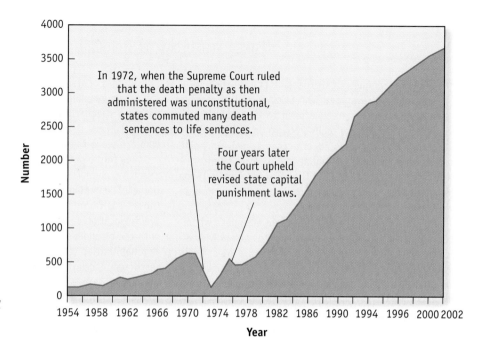

FIGURE 6-6   *Persons Under Sentence of Death*

Source: By the author, based on Greenfield 1991; Various editions of *Sourcebook of Criminal Justice Statistic; Statistical Abstract of the United States* 2003:Table 352.

piecemeal and in disarray. To have a rational social policy, we need to reform the criminal justice system. I suggest the following goals and guiding principles:

Suggested Goals and Principles for Reforming the Criminal Justice System

1. Clear laws based on the broadest possible consensus, rather than on the interests or moral concerns of small groups.
2. Swift, sure justice based on legal evidence presented in adversarial proceedings. (This would require eliminating plea bargaining and lengthy delays based on legal technicalities; it would guarantee a speedy trial for all who plead not guilty and require more courts, more judges, and longer working hours for judges.)
3. More rehabilitation programs, including diversion for most first offenders (who did not commit violent crimes) to try to incorporate them into the community.

FIGURE 6-7   *Persons Executed in the United States*

Source: Various editions of *Sourcebook of Criminal Justice Statistics; Statistical Abstract of the United States* 2003: Table 355.

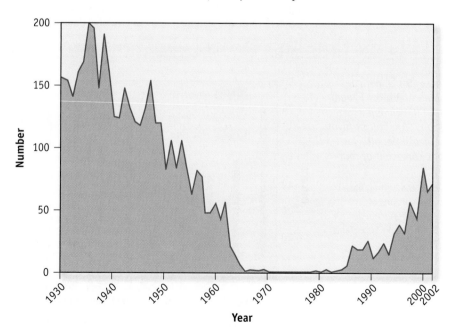

4. "Added incapacitation": Harsh penalties for repeat offenders, with the penalty becoming harsher each time a person is convicted.
5. Task forces to investigate organized crime and white-collar crime (with the provision that, for a specified time such as five years after they leave a task force, members cannot accept employment from the corporations they investigated).
6. Harsh penalties for people who are convicted of crime in the name of a corporation, including jail for executives, the forced sale of any division found guilty of crime, and huge fines to reduce the corporate profit motive (Liazos 1981).
7. Prison reform, including making the position of prison warden a civil service job, training prison guards rigorously and paying them well, allowing prisoners to have conjugal visits, and giving *to the nonviolent* the right to visit friends and family on the outside.
8. Unbiased research to determine what works and what doesn't work. In the ideal case, we would compare experimental and control groups. We certainly have the capacity to make such determinations, but we need cooperative politicians and other government officials to approve and fund such research.

The Future of the Problem

Gender

Will crime increase or decrease? The answer depends on the type of crime. Crime by women, for example, will probably increase as even more women leave traditional roles and enter domains that used to be occupied by men.

White-Collar Crime

We will be unable to tell whether white-collar crime is increasing or decreasing. If more white-collar crime is handled by the judicial system, it will *appear* to increase. Because we lack a baseline of white-collar crime from which to draw accurate comparisons, however, official statistics could show a doubling or even more in any given year, and we would still not know if this represented an increase or just a greater use of the judicial system.

Political Crime

The incidence of political crime will depend on political events. If we wage an extended, unpopular war, we could relive the political protests of the 1960s and 1970s. If we do have substantial illegal acts designed to change the political system, government officials may find the legal procedures too cumbersome to deal with and may, in turn, engage in illegal acts to protect a threatened political system.

Organized Crime

Organized crime will continue, taking different forms as social conditions change. If enforcement efforts that are directed against one part of organized crime, such as the Sicilian-American Mafia, succeed, that group will turn increasingly to legitimate businesses. The Mafia will not forsake crime, however, as illegal activities are the heart of its existence.

The Judicial System

The judicial system changes slowly. I anticipate that the criminal justice system will continue to focus on street crime, and that the crimes of the powerful will be largely overlooked or will be handled by civil agencies. I also anticipate an increase in a recent innovation in prisons—the hiring by states of private, for-profit businesses to build and operate prisons. Private firms now operate almost 200 prisons with over 120,000 inmates (*Sourcebook of Criminal Justice Statistics* 2000:Tables 1.92, 1.93; 2003:Table 1.102). This change is superficial, however, merely a switch in who is operating a prison. It does not affect the basic system.

The Need to Cut Crime at the Root

If we ever get serious about preventing the poor from being recruited to street crime, we must open the doors to legitimate ways of reaching success. This means that we must provide access to quality education and comprehensive job training. We must also create jobs that pay a living wage. People who have a high investment in the social system commit fewer crimes of violence. The greater their investment, the more they reject criminal norms. To change the social system in such a fundamental manner is a radical proposal, and unfortunately, crime will remain a serious social problem.

SUMMARY

1. Whether an act is a *crime* depends on the law, which, in turn, depends on power relationships in society.

2. Crime is universal, because all societies make rules against acts they consider undesirable. Laws turn these acts into crimes. Because laws differ, crime differs from one society to another and in the same society over time.

3. The social problem of crime has two parts: the crimes committed and the criminal justice system. Crime is a problem because people are upset about the threat to their lives, property, and well-being; the criminal justice system is a problem because people are upset about its failures and want something done about it.

4. The "saints" and the "roughnecks" illustrate how social class affects the perception and reactions of authorities, as well as how crime statistics are distorted.

5. Functionalists note that property crimes represent conformity to the goal of success but rejection of the approved means of achieving success. Just as some people have more access to legitimate opportunities, others have more access to *illegitimate opportunities*.

6. Conflict theorists regard the *criminal justice system* as a tool that the ruling class uses to mask injustice, control workers, and stabilize the social system. Law enforcement is a means that the elite use to maintain its dominance.

7. *Juvenile delinquents* use five major *neutralization techniques* to deflect society's norms: denial of responsibility, denial of injury, denial of a victim, condemning the condemners, and an appeal to higher loyalty.

8. *White-collar crime* is extensive but underreported. Corporations usually insulate white-collar criminals from the law, especially when the crimes benefit the corporation.

9. *Professional criminals* are people who make their living from crime. They have high in-group loyalty, scorn the "straight" world, and take pride in their specialized skills.

10. *Organized crime* is best represented by the Mafia, whose use of violence within a highly developed bureaucracy lies at the heart of its success.

11. *Political crime,* illegal activities intended to change the political system or to maintain it, ebbs and flows as political conditions change.

12. The criminal justice system fails to deliver justice because of overcrowded courts, *plea bargaining,* a team-player system that subverts public defense attorneys, possible racial-ethnic bias, and prisons that foster hostility and hatred.

13. Because our criminal justice system has no unifying philosophy with which to establish and evaluate social response to crime, our policies of social control are in disarray.

14. Crime in the future will depend on social change, including the role of women, social policies toward crime, and economic and political events.

15. To get at the root of this problem requires reform of the criminal justice system and a basic overhaul of our social institutions, especially changes that open more opportunities to the poor.

KEY TERMS

Bureaucracy   A highly structured hierarchy with specialized personnel.

Capital punishment   The death penalty.

Corporate crime   See *White-collar crime.*

Cosa nostra   The term by which East Coast mobsters refer to the Mafia. See *Mafia.*

Crime   Any act prohibited by law. What constitutes crime varies from one era to another and from one social group to another.

Crime against the person   An illegal act that results in physical harm, such as assault, murder, and rape.

Crime rates   The number of crimes per some unit of population, most commonly the number of crimes per 100,000 people.

Criminal justice system   The agencies that respond to crime, including the police, courts, jails, and prisons.

Delinquent subculture   A subculture whose members are oriented toward illegal acts.

Deterrence   The attempt to prevent crime by producing fear.

Diversion   Diverting offenders away from courts and jails to keep them out of the criminal justice system.

Illegitimate opportunity structure   The opportunity, built into one's environment, to learn and participate in illegal activities.

Incapacitation   A response to crime that focuses on removing offenders from circulation.

Juvenile delinquency   Illegal acts committed by minors.

Mafia   An organized crime group. The Sicilian-American version is bureaucratized with specialized personnel and departmentalization.

Neutralization   See *Techniques of neutralization.*
Organized crime   Organizations devoted to criminal activities.
Plea bargaining   Pleading guilty to a lesser crime in exchange for a reduced sentence.
Police discretion   The decisions that the police make about whether to overlook or to enforce a law.
Political crime   Illegal acts that are intended to alter or to maintain a political system.
Political process   A power struggle between interest groups and ideologies.
Professional criminals   People who earn their living from crime.
Property crime   Obtaining or destroying property illegally: burglary, theft, robbery, vandalism, and arson.
Recidivism rate   The percentage of people released from prison who are rearrested.
Rehabilitation   A response to crime that is designed to resocialize or reform offenders, so that they can become law-abiding citizens.
Restitution   A form of retribution by which offenders compensate their victims.
Retribution   A response to crime based on upholding moral values and restoring the moral balance upset by a criminal act. Making a thief repay what he or she stole is an example.
Status crimes   Acts such as curfew violations or running away from home that are crimes when committed by people of a designated status (for example, juveniles) but not when committed by others (for example, adults).
Techniques of neutralization   How people justify their norm-breaking activities, making their behaviors more acceptable to themselves and others.
Uniform sentencing   Giving the same sentence to everyone who is convicted of the same crime.
White-collar crime   Crime committed either against a business, agency, or corporation (such as embezzlement and fraud) or on behalf of the corporation (such as price fixing, fraudulent advertising, antitrust violations, and corporate tax evasion).

THINKING CRITICALLY ABOUT CHAPTER 6

1. Which of the three theoretical perspectives (symbolic interactionism, functionalism, or conflict theory) do you think does the best job of explaining the causes of crime? Why?
2. Which of the three perspectives (symbolic interactionism, functionalism, or conflict theory) do you think does the best job of explaining why white-collar criminals are treated differently from street criminals? Is your answer to this question different than your answer to Question #1? Explain.
3. Do you think that violent criminals should be treated differently from non-violent criminals in terms of punishment? Why or why not? Consider the case of the criminally negligent manufacturer whose product kills people but who has no actual contact with victims versus the street criminal who kills someone during a robbery.
4. Which of the four basic approaches for treating criminals (retribution, deterrence, rehabilitation, and incapacitation) do you think is the most appropriate? Why?

CHAPTER 7

Economic Problems:
Wealth and Poverty

At age 17, Julie Treadman faced more than her share of problems. Her boyfriend—her "first love"—had deserted her when she told him that she was pregnant. Exhausted and depressed, Julie had dropped out of high school. Now five months' pregnant, she wondered about her child's future.

When Julie had severe stomach pains, a neighbor called an ambulance, and she was rushed to Lutheran Hospital. When hospital administrators discovered that neither Julie nor her mother had money or credit, they refused her admission. Before they could transfer her to a public hospital for the poor, however, Julie gave birth to a stillborn baby.

This perplexed hospital administrators. They didn't want anyone around who could not pay their bills, but what could they do at this point? They quickly hit upon a Machiavelian solution: They ordered the ambulance driver to take Julie—dead baby, umbilical cord, and all—to the public hospital.

Based on an event in St. Louis, Missouri.

The Problem in Sociological Perspective

In this chapter, we examine economic problems facing our nation. Our primary focus will be on the unequal distribution of society's resources, especially as this produces the twin problems of wealth and poverty.

ECONOMIC SYSTEMS AND CHANGES

The Extremes of Social Class

The United States, where "all 'men' are created equal," has always had **social classes**— groups of people who occupy the same rung on the economic ladder. Where you are located on that ladder makes a vital difference for what life is like. We have the *working poor,* full-time workers who have to depend on food stamps to survive, and we also have Bill Gates, the richest man in the world, who spent $75 million for a house and $30 million for a Winslow Homer painting to decorate his living room. Most of us fall somewhere in between, of course—and not toward the Gates' end of the spectrum. In this chapter, we shall look at sociological research and theory on the rich and the poor, the powerful and the powerless. Let's start by considering how the economy affects all of us.

Capitalist Economies

The **economy** is not only money and jobs; it is the entire social institution that produces and distributes goods and services. How the economy functions affects the welfare of every individual, group, and community in the entire nation. At any given time, the U.S. economy is in a "boom," when everything seems to be percolating, or a "bust," when nothing seems to be going right. These "boom–bust" cycles plague **capitalist economies,** which are based on the private ownership of property and the investment of capital for the purpose of making a profit. Some students who are taking this course will graduate during a "boom" and will have their choice of jobs. Others, unfortunately, will graduate during a "bust," and even though they have earned bachelor's degrees, they will end up driving cabs, working in fast-food restaurants, or standing in unemployment lines.

Socialist Economies

Many nations, primarily eastern European countries under the domination of Russia, used to have **socialist economies;** the government owned the property, profit was

207

illegal, and government committees decided what items—from cars to toilet paper—would be produced, and where they would be distributed. The government also set the price for the items—taking into consideration neither the quality of the goods nor the demand for them. Everyone was guaranteed a job, and everyone worked for the government, which owned everything. Not only was everyone guaranteed a job, but also to miss work when you weren't sick was a crime.

Capitalist and Socialist Confrontations

The socialist and capitalist economies were almost mirror images of one anther. Capitalists believed that socialism was immoral, that socialism denied people the freedom of choice—including the right to choose where you were going to live and work. Socialists believed that capitalism was immoral, that capitalism put profit ahead of the welfare of people, and the poor were left to suffer. In what was known as the Cold War, proponents of each ideology viewed the other as a mortal enemy and threatened one another with nuclear destruction.

The Triumph of Capitalism

Production in the socialist countries was inefficient. Central committees decided what goods would be produced and how they would be distributed. Workers could not be fired; they could be jailed for not showing up for work, but not fired for producing less than others. Capitalism proved much more efficient, and the workers' standard of living in the capitalist countries grew. Workers in the socialist countries, in contrast, saw their living conditions decline, and they already were at a low level. As the Soviet economy deteriorated, in 1989 its leaders, under Mikhail Gorbachev, abandoned socialism and reluctantly turned to capitalism. Some attribute the fall of socialism to President Ronald Reagan, who outspent the Soviets on weapons and bankrupted their economy. No one knows for certain, and over the next century scholars will debate the reasons for the failure of socialism. The Soviet Union broke up into fifteen independent states, which followed Russia into the seductive pursuit of capitalism. China has maintained the façade of socialism, but it is well on its journey to capitalism. The Chinese are now encouraged to own property and to pursue profit.

At this stage in world history, then, capitalism has triumphed. The newly independent states that are traveling the road to capitalism, however, have encountered torturous economic problems. Russia has been thrown into such economic and political disarray that organized crime figures, mentioned in the last chapter, in cooperation with corrupt politicians and military, control a large part of the Russian economy. More than this: They assassinate politicians and honest business leaders who stand in their way, as well as journalists who threaten to expose them. Consequently, the security of Russia's nuclear weapons is in jeopardy, a matter to which we shall return in Chapter 15.

Foreign investment in Asia made its economies boom. The wealthy search for ways to display their status, such as by driving this antique car in Hong Kong.

As capitalism has come to dominate the globe (with the primary holdouts being China, North Korea, and Cuba), the leaders of the major capitalist countries have divided the world's nations into three primary trading blocs: North and South America, dominated by the United States; Europe, dominated by Germany; and Asia, dominated by Japan. To try to control capitalism's troublesome cycle of "booms" and "busts," the most powerful eight nations, known as G-8 (the Group of 8) hold an annual summit. There they decide ways to control the global markets. This organization used to be called G-7, until Russia was invited to join. Soon it will be called G-9, for China has now been invited to be an observer, the first step to becoming a partner in world domination.

Capitalism has the certainty of a "boom–bust" cycle matched by the uncertainty of not knowing when the

G-8 and Global Stratification

The "Boom–Bust" Cycle

Why Did Capitalism Triumph?

economy will switch from "boom" to "bust" and back again. To try to control this cycle, G-8 uses the International Monetary Fund, a world bank that lends to nations that are in economic trouble. The "boom–bust" cycle continues, however, and entire regions experience prosperity or poverty. In the 1990s, when the region dominated by Japan went into the "bust" part of the cycle and formerly booming factories in Thailand, Indonesia, and South Korea closed their doors, the value of these countries' currencies shrank, and capitalist leaders feared a global "bust." G-8 (then G-7) was able to pull this region out of the "bust," but now that we have global capitalism, the danger is that most of the world will be engulfed in these cycles.

The socialist economies had a primary advantage: the more even distribution of a country's resources. This resulted in guaranteed jobs for everyone (although the jobs paid little), a medical delivery system that reached almost everyone, and the elimination of hunger. With these benefits, why did capitalism win the war? The simple answer is that capitalism is more efficient at producing wealth. There certainly was greater equality in the socialist nations—almost everyone was poor. The capitalist countries are marked by tremendous **social inequality**—the unequal distribution of wealth, income, power, and other opportunities—but most people under capitalism have a high standard of living. Capitalism offers both the opportunity for economic success and individual freedoms. These features are so appealing that millions of people beat down the door to enter the United States, whether legally or illegally.

For some people, however, such as Julie Treadman in our opening vignette, the social inequality of a capitalist system has dire consequences. Because Julie couldn't pay, she was denied basic medical treatment and fundamental human dignity. Because this book is about social problems, not social opportunities, our focus is on the negative consequences of social inequality.

FOUR ECONOMIC PROBLEMS FACING THE UNITED STATES

Four Problems:

1. A Decline in Purchasing Power

Because the U.S. economy is essential to our well-being, it is important to try to understand the issues that affect its future direction. Let's look at four of the problems that spell future trouble.

The first is that people's **real income** (income adjusted for inflation) is stagnant. For 25 years, from the end of World War II until 1970, the real income of U.S. workers rose steadily. Even after you subtracted inflation from their paychecks, workers still had more money to spend. Since then, the paychecks of workers have continued to grow, but those paychecks have contained dollars without calories. That is, although paychecks show more and more dollars, making workers feel as though they are earning more than they used to, as Figure 7-1 on page 210 shows, the purchasing power of those dollars has not increased. The real income of today's. workers is about the same as it was in 1970. In short, the raises that U.S. workers have received over the past generation or so have been eaten up by inflation.

What has softened the blow for the average family is that more family members are working. In 1940, only 16 percent of wives worked for wages. Today about 70 percent of wives work for wages either full- or part-time (Davis and Robinson 1988; *Statistical Abstract* 2003:Table 597). Has adding this worker doubled the average family's income? Certainly the average family's income must have increased by at least half. Despite two incomes, however, after adjusting for inflation, the average household today brings in just 17 percent ($6,000) more a year than it did in 1980 ($42,000 versus $36,000) (*Statistical Abstract* 2003:Table 684). Think about this. Eleven million more wives work for wages now than in 1980, but the net gain to a family's income is only 17 percent (*Statistical Abstract* 2003:Table 597). This additional income is *before* the costs of child care, the second car that the job might require, the additional clothing, lunches, and so forth. After these costs are subtracted, one wonders if there has been any gain at all.

2. Taxes

The second major problem is taxes. Someone coined the term *Tax Freedom Day* to refer to the day when the average American has earned enough to pay his or her annual taxes. Politicians keep promising tax cuts, but they seldom deliver on that promise. Tax Freedom Day falls on April 11 (Tax Foundation 2004). On average, each of us must work for the government for over three months before we have a cent for our own needs!

3. Savings

Figure 7-2 illustrates the third major problem. The U.S. savings rate has dropped to a low not seen since the midst of the Great Depression of the 1930s. Americans save less than people in the other industrialized nations. Our drop in savings has significant consequences. It isn't just that the average family has less to draw on when that inevitable "rainy day" arrives. People's savings are put to work in the society; reduced savings mean that we have less money to invest in new plants and equipment, which may undermine our ability to compete in international trade or to increase our standard of living.

4. The National Debt

Fourth, we buy goods from other nations at such a frenzied pace that the United States has become the largest debtor nation in the world. When you add up what we pay for the products that we buy from other nations and what we receive for the products that we sell to those nations, each year we end up about $470 billion short (*Statistical Abstract* 2003:Table 1295). Year after year, these mountains of debt pile up, but this cannot continue indefinitely. Just as individuals must repay what they borrow or else get into financial trouble, so it is with nations. To finance the **national debt** (the total amount the U.S. government owes), we pay over $150 billion a year in interest (*Statistical Abstract* 2003:Table 476). This is money that we cannot use to build schools, colleges, and libraries, hire teachers, rebuild our cities, pay for medical services for the poor, operate Head Start programs, or pay for any other services to help improve our quality of life.

THE NATURE OF POVERTY

Three Types of Poverty:

1. Biological Poverty

With this broad background, let's analyze poverty. You might think that poverty would be easy to define, but its definition is neither simple nor obvious. There are three types of poverty. The first is **biological poverty,** which refers to starvation and malnutrition—

FIGURE 7-1 *Average Hourly Earnings, in Current and Constant Dollars*

Source: By the author, based on *Statistical Abstract* 1999:Table 698; 2003:Table 636.

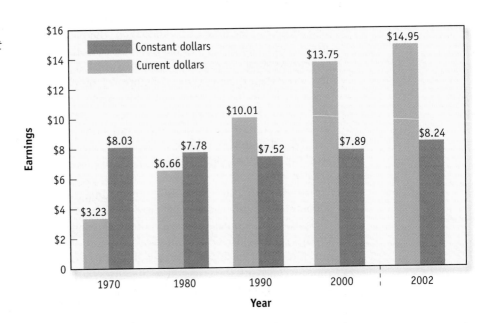

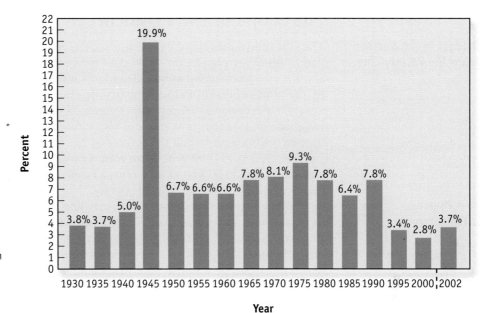

FIGURE 7-2 *How Much Do Americans Save?*

Sources: By the author, based on American Savings Education Council, 1999; *Statistical Abstract* 1990:Table 700; 1995:Table 710; 2003:Table 668.

to the starving children in Bangladesh and the Sudan whose pictures you see on TV. It also refers to housing and clothing so inadequate that people suffer from exposure. Our homeless endure biological poverty.

2. Relative Poverty

More common is **relative poverty.** This refers to people living below the standards of their society or group. Some relative poverty is serious, such as the Americans who try to get by on only half or even one-quarter of the average national income. On another level are members of country clubs who feel "poor" because they are among the few who don't have new Jaguars or Porsches. Relative poverty also exists on a world scale: What is poverty in the United States would mean comfortable living in India, where most people have little clothing and little food, and large families live in just a room or two.

3. Official Poverty

The United States and most other countries also have a third type of poverty. **Official poverty** refers to the income level at which people are eligible for welfare benefits. People below this **poverty line** are poor; those above it are not. The United States developed its definition of official poverty in 1962. The poor spent about one-third of their income on food, so the Social Security administration determined the poverty line by multiplying a low-level food budget by 3 (Fisher 1998). The U.S. government has kept this rough calculation, adjusting it annually to match the Consumer Price Index, the official gauge of inflation.

The Poverty Line Is Stuck in a Time Warp

Sociologists point out that this definition is stuck in a time warp. Sociologist William Julius Wilson (1992) and policy analyst Patricia Ruggles (1990, 1992) stress how food preferences and cooking patterns have changed since the 1960s, but not the government's definition of poverty. Poor people actually spend only about 20 percent of their incomes on food, so to determine a poverty line, we really ought to multiply their food budget by 5 instead of 3 (Uchitelle 2001). Sociologist Michael Katz (1989) also notes how unrealistic this definition is; it assumes that everyone is a careful shopper who cooks all the family meals at home and never has guests. Who lives like this? Nor does the poverty line account for different costs of living. It costs a bit more to live in Manhattan, New York, than it does in Manhattan, Kansas. Nevertheless, this is how the magical line is drawn to separate the poor from the nonpoor. Using this rock-bottom definition, let's look at official poverty in the United States.

The Scope of the Problem

Changes in the Number Below the Poverty Line

When the official definition of poverty was developed, about 40 million people—more than a fifth of the population—fell below the poverty line. In the early 1960s, President Johnson launched what he called the "war on poverty." With new welfare benefits and other programs, in just ten years the number of Americans below the official poverty line dropped to 13 percent, or about 25 million people. This dramatic reduction made it clear that poverty could be solved. Since then, however, little or no progress has been made, and the percentage has hovered between 12 and 15 percent. Currently, it is at 11.7 percent (*Statistical Abstract* 2003:Table 700). With our larger population, that 11.7 percent represents 35 million people, close to the same number who were poor before the "war on poverty."

Most Poverty Is Temporary

Most people who fall below the poverty line are not permanently poor. Most are poor only for short periods, such as when they are injured or sick, or during layoffs or slow seasons (such as in winter in the northern states, when there are few construction jobs). Although the U.S. total of poor people remains fairly constant from year to year, there is much change within it; each year millions of people rise above the poverty line, while millions of others fall below it.

Disagreements Over How Many People Are Poor

The poverty line, of course, is arbitrary in the first place, and the number of "poor" people can be reduced or increased at will by changing the official definition. Although some argue that the real number of poor is higher than the official measure, others claim it is less. They point out that when we figure income we don't count many benefits that people receive from antipoverty programs. We don't include Medicare, Medicaid, food stamps, and HUD vouchers (the amount the government pays in rent for poor families) as income.

Poverty as a Root of Other Social Problems

Although experts disagree about how many poor people there are, three facts stand out: Millions of Americans live in poverty; how poverty is defined has serious consequences, for the definition determines who will receive help and who will not; and poverty lies at the root of many of our other social problems. We have already seen the connection between poverty and prostitution, rape, murder, and alcoholism and other forms of drug addiction. In coming chapters, we shall see how poverty is related to other social problems such as racism, sickness, and abuse in the family.

SOCIAL INEQUALITY

The Tendency to Deny Social Inequality

Social inequality contradicts our ideals. A common way that Americans cope with this contradiction is to deny it. For example, when researchers ask people what class they belong to, most Americans—whether rich or poor—say that they are "middle class." An example of this tendency that has fascinated me is a statement made by Ann Getty, a former saleswoman who married an heir to the Getty oil fortune. She told an interviewer, "I lead a very ordinary life" (*New York Times,* Sept. 7, 1980). Her "ordinary life" included living in a San Francisco mansion and taking along her personal chef whenever she flew to Paris.

We know that all Americans are not equal, of course, and that the life chances of a waitress's daughter differ immensely from those of a son born to wealthy parents. We all know that the rich and politically connected pass advantages to their children. Because of this, we have social programs to help level the playing field. Affirmative action, as well as college scholarships and community colleges, are attempts to make opportunity more equal.

Structural Inequality

Such programs, however, run up against **structural inequality,** the inequality that is built into our economic and social institutions. Differences in wages are an exam-

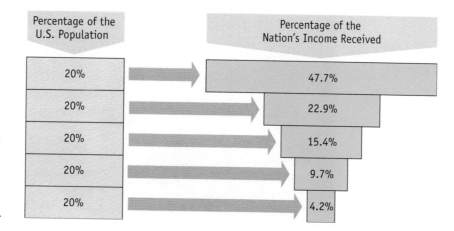

FIGURE 7-3 *How Is the Income of the United States Distributed?*

Source: By the author, based on *Statistical Abstract of the United States* 2003:Table 688.

ple. If a society has 100 million jobs and 30 million of them pay low wages, the job market has inequality built into it. Unemployment is another example. If a society has 107 million workers but only 100 million jobs, then 7 million workers will be unemployed, regardless of how hard they look for work. Job training programs will not solve this structural problem. The solution requires more jobs.

DISTRIBUTION OF INCOME AND WEALTH

How Income Inequality Has Increased

A major consequence of structural inequality is the vast inequality in the income of Americans. Look at Figure 7-3. The poorest fifth of Americans receives only 4.2 percent of the nation's income, whereas 47.7 percent of the country's entire income goes to the richest fifth. Despite numerous antipoverty programs, *income inequality today is greater than it was in the 1940s.* The poorest fifth of Americans now receive less of the nation's income than they did in the 1940s (a drop from 5.4 percent to 4.2 percent). The richest fifth receive more than ever (an increase from about 41 percent to 47.7 percent).

The Distribution of Wealth

Another way to view financial inequality is to look at the distribution of **wealth,** what people own—their property, savings, investments, and other economic assets. Americans are worth about $39 trillion, mostly in the form of real estate, corporate stock, and business assets (*Statistical Abstract* 2003:Table 710). As Figure 7-4 shows, one-tenth of U.S. families own 90 percent of all business assets in the United States. At the top of this group, wealth is incredibly concentrated. The richest 1 percent of Americans own about three-fourths of all business assets in the entire country (Beeghley 2004). This 1 percent virtually controls corporate America.

With $60 billion, the richest person in the United States—and the world—is Bill Gates, who dropped out of Harvard to cofound Microsoft Corp., the world's largest software company. (Gates's wealth fluctuates a few billion dollars up and a few billion

FIGURE 7-4 *How the Business Assets of the United States Are Distributed*

Note: The 10 percent of richest families also own 90 percent of all corporate bonds. For all corporate stock, the share of the richest 10 percent dips just a bit: They hold only 85 percent of this form of wealth. They also own 88 percent of all trust funds, 62 percent of all money market accounts, and 57 percent of all pension accounts.

Source: Beeghley 2004.

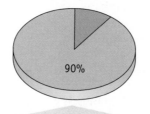

90% of all business assets in the United States...

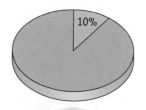

are owned by just 10% of U.S. families.

Poverty is much more than having little money. Poverty means the reduction of life's chances—including the greater likelihood of disease, death, and divorce. This photo was taken in Appalachia, a region where poverty persists generation after generation.

dollars down as the price of Microsoft stock changes.) Gates developed MS-DOS and Windows, two computer operating systems, and gets a licensing fee each time a computer that uses these systems is sold. He has now expanded into global communications.

How Much Is a Billion Dollars?

How much is a billion dollars? Because neither you nor I is likely to have a bank account this size, an illustration can help us grasp the enormity of a billion dollars—*one thousand million dollars:*

> Suppose you were born on the day Christ was born, that you are still alive today, and that you have been able to save money at the fantastic rate of one cent for every second that you lived—that is, 60 cents for every minute, $36 for every hour, or $864 for every day of your life during these past two thousand years. At that rate, it would take you *another* thousand years to save one billion dollars. (Shaffer 1986:00)

As research scientist James Smith said, "Wealth is a good thing, and everyone ought to have some" (Stafford et al. 1986–87:3). Then what is the problem? Part of the problem is that vast wealth brings vast power. Because owning 10 or 20 percent of a company's stock is enough to control it, the 1 percent of Americans who own nearly half of all corporate stock wields immense power over the economy. In their pursuit of even more wealth, this elite can move production to Mexico, India, or China, where labor is cheaper, closing down factories here and throwing thousands of people out of work. Most designer jeans, for example, are made in Korea or Hong Kong. The people in the United States who stand to lose their jobs—the workers—don't make these decisions, but they must live with the consequences.

The Problem with the Concentration of Wealth

How we define reality depends to a large extent on where we are located in the social class structure. The poorest fifth of Americans who today receive a smaller proportion of the nation's wealth than they did in the 1940s are not likely to have the view illustrated in this cartoon.

"The poor are getting poorer, but with the rich getting richer it all averages out in the long run."

Finally, because the rich can hire Washington lobbyists and pay for top financial advice, they perpetuate their advantages. They live in a world in which they are protected from unemployment, not being able to pay the rent, having the utilities cut off, the breakdown of the family car, injustice in the courts, and an unresponsive political system. Let's turn our attention to those who must cope with such things as part of their everyday lives.

THE EXTENT AND IMPACT OF POVERTY

As with other social problems, objective conditions alone are not enough to make poverty a social problem. Subjective concerns are also essential, and, actually, are more important. To see how this could be, consider the extremes: If poverty is extensive but few people are concerned about it, poverty is *not* a social problem. If a group has little poverty and many people want to do something about it, poverty *is* a social problem. Let's look at examples.

How Subjective Concerns Have Changed the Social Problem of Poverty

During the early years of the United States, *most* people were poor. Yet poverty was not considered to be a social problem. Life had always been like this, so *people assumed that poverty was part of the natural order.* As industrialization progressed, the nineteenth century produced an abundance of jobs and wealth. Poverty declined. But a mass migration of poor people to U.S. cities within the context of an increasing standard of living made the smaller amount of poverty more visible: Public leaders then declared poverty to be a social problem. As the immigrants were absorbed into the expanding workforce, once again poverty was lost from sight. Then came the Great Depression of the 1930s. As millions of people were thrown out of work, the ranks of the poor swelled. Poverty was then proclaimed to be the greatest problem facing the nation, and the government established emergency programs to reduce poverty. World War II and postwar prosperity diverted attention from poverty. Even though the objective conditions still existed, subjective concerns dropped. Hidden in out-of-the-way rural areas and isolated in urban slums, the poor remained invisible—and to most people, they were of little concern.

The War on Poverty

In 1960, President Kennedy tried to make poverty a campaign issue, but subjective concerns were not really aroused until Michael Harrington wrote *The Other America* in 1962. Rarely has a single volume of social science transformed people's consciousness as this one did. Harrington passionately argued that in the midst of "the affluent society," one-quarter of the nation lived in squalor. Policy makers read it, the media publicized it, and sociologists assigned it to their students. Within two years of the book's publication, President Johnson declared a "war on poverty." The federal government began a raft of programs for the poor: child-care services, Head Start, legal services, medical services, job training, subsidized housing, and community health centers. Then during the 1980s, deciding that big government, budget deficits, and the national debt were greater social problems, many programs were cut back. Some of them, however, were expanded. Head Start, for example, now reaches more children (900,000) than ever (*Statistical Abstract* 1996:Table 577; 2003:Table 572).

The "war on poverty" has been effective. As Figure 7-5 on page 216 shows, 22 percent of Americans had incomes below the official poverty line in 1960, but in just ten years this total dropped to 13 percent. The national average has held quite steady since then, hovering between 12 and 14 percent. It now is just 12 percent. National averages, however, cover up significant differences. To see what I mean, look at the poverty rates that are shown on Figures 7-5 and 7-6 on the next two pages.

The Impact of Poverty:

We'll return to racial-ethnic differences shortly, but first let's consider the impact of poverty. Being poor does not simply mean having less money and therefore going to fewer movies, buying fewer video games, and eating steak less often. Rather, people's economic circumstances envelop them, affecting profoundly every aspect of their

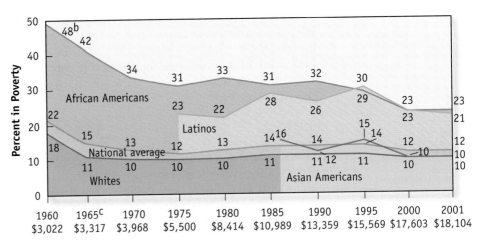

FIGURE 7-5 *Trends in U.S. Poverty: Percent Below the Poverty Line, by Race-Ethnicity[a]*

Source: By the author, based on *Statistical Abstract of the United* States 1992:Table 724; 2003:Tables 700, 702.

Notes:

[a]The poverty line shown here is a measure of poverty for an urban family of four. Native Americans are not included in the source. Measurement of poverty among Latinos did not begin until 1975, that of Asian Americans not until 1987.

[b]As the source excludes African Americans for 1960, data from 1959 are used for African Americans.

[c]As the source excludes 1965 data, 1966 data are used.

Housing

lives, including not only their housing, education, and jobs, but also their stress and well-being, health, justice, and even their marriages.

Most of the poor live in substandard housing. Many rent from landlords who neglect their buildings. The plumbing may not work. The heating system may break down in winter. Roaches and rats may run riot. And, unlike people who have a mortgage, paying rent does not build up equity in a home.

Education

Although public schools are supposed to give all children an equal opportunity to succeed, the poor are at a disadvantage. Because our schools are supported by property taxes, and property in poorer areas produces less taxes, the schools that the poor attend have smaller budgets and often outdated textbooks and inexperienced teachers who are paid less (Kozol 1999). This, of course, is common knowledge, and everyone knows how superior the schools are in the areas where the rich live.

Poverty affects people's chances of going to college. If you rank families from the poorest to the richest, as the family's income increases so does the likelihood that their children will go to college (Manski 1992–93; Reay et al. 2001). Similarly, the wealthier a family is, the more years of schooling that their children complete (Conley 2001). Most poor children who do go to college attend community colleges where many are funneled into vocational programs. In contrast, the children of the middle classes attend state universities and private colleges. The very wealthy even have exclusive high-school boarding schools for their children. The learning environments there include small classes and well-paid teachers (Persell et al. 1992). These students inherit a cozy social network: Their schools' college advisers are connected with the admissions officers of the nation's most elite colleges. These networks are so efficient that *half* of a private school's graduating class may be admitted to just Harvard, Yale, and Princeton (Cookson and Persell1985, 2005).

Employment

Unlike the career paths that are open to the children of the middle class and the rich, the low-paying jobs of the working poor lead nowhere. Because workers are often laid off from these dead-end jobs, their incomes, already low, are erratic. During unemployment, they have to cope with the complex bureaucracies of unemployment insurance, welfare, and other social programs that are designed to carry them along. Such experiences add to the stress of lives that are already filled with anxiety.

The poor are also given a different walk through the halls of justice. As discussed in Chapter 6, their life experiences make them more likely to commit robberies and assaults, crimes that are especially visible and for which offenders are punished severely. White-collar crime may be more pervasive and costly to society, but it is less visible and carries milder punishments. As mentioned in the previous chapter, when the poor are arrested, they lack the resources to hire good lawyers to defend themselves. Often, they cannot even post bail.

In short, wealth and income represent privileges—received or denied. The net result is a quality of life that goes right to the core of one's being. Job insecurity brings nightmares to the poor. Their jobs offer no pension plans and often no medical benefits. They live one paycheck away from eviction. If they get sick, they are laid off, and their job may not be there when they return to work. Among the stark repercussions: Those at the lower end of the income scale don't eat as well, they are more likely to have accidents at work and at home, their lives are shorter, and their children are more likely to die in infancy. And, like Julie Treadman in the opening vignette, they have less access to good medical care, which further jeopardizes their well-being.

Looking at the Problem Theoretically

As we saw in previous chapters, each of the theoretical perspectives gives a different view of a social problem. Let's look at poverty through these three lenses.

SYMBOLIC INTERACTIONISM

Andy, Sharon, and their two children live in a small house in a rural area. Andy farms sixty-five acres and works part-time in the local grocery store. Sharon works part-time as a cook at the Dew Drop Inn. Between their jobs and the farm, they make about $15,000 a year. They grow their own vegetables, and they fish in a nearby pond. Integrated into the community and with their basic needs satisfied, they don't think of themselves as poor. Neither do their friends and neighbors.

The Criminal Justice System

The Results of Social Inequality: Quality of Life

The Meanings of Social Inequality versus Official Definitions

FIGURE **7-6** *The Geography of U.S. Poverty*

Source: By the author, based on *Statistical Abstract of the United States* 2003:Table 699.

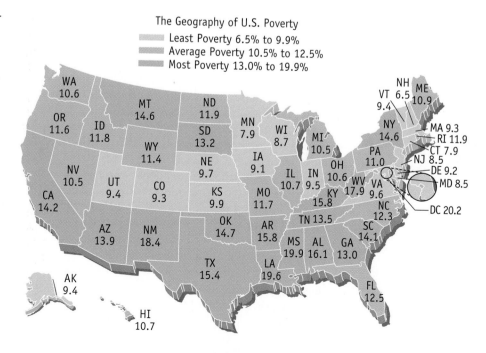

The Geography of U.S. Poverty
- Least Poverty 6.5% to 9.9%
- Average Poverty 10.5% to 12.5%
- Most Poverty 13.0% to 19.9%

Leslie attends a private college. Her parents pay her tuition, fees, books, rent, utilities, insurance, medical bills, and transportation. They also pay an average of $800 a month for "extras." Unlike many of her friends, Leslie has no sports car, and she complains about how hard it is to be poor. Her affluent friends feel sorry for her.

Keith, a struggling young actor, auditions often and works part-time as a waiter. He earns about $900 a month, which has to cover his rent, food, and all other expenses. To save money, he rooms with two other aspiring actors. "It's difficult to make it," he says, "but one day you'll see my name in lights." Keith sees himself as "struggling"—not poor. Nor do his actor friends think of him as poor.

Maria and her two children live in a housing project. Her rent is subsidized and cheap— $97 a month. Her welfare, Medicaid, and food stamps amount to $14,287 tax-free a year. Her two children attend school during the day, and she takes classes in English at a neighborhood church. Maria considers herself poor, and so do the government and her neighbors.

By the government's standards, all but Leslie are poor, and yet it is Leslie (and Maria) who *feel* poor. Why?

The Relativity of Poverty

Symbolic interactionists stress that to understand poverty we must focus on what poverty *means* to people. All of us try to evaluate where we are in life. To do so, we *compare* ourselves with others. In some rural areas, simple marginal living is the norm, but in Leslie's cosmopolitan circle people feel deprived if they cannot afford the latest upscale designer clothing from their favorite boutique. The meaning of poverty, then, is *relative:* What poverty is differs from group to group within the same society, as well as from culture to culture and from one era to the next.

Views of Poverty

To understand poverty, we must focus also on how the middle class view the poor. The dominant view might be that the poor are good people who are down on their luck and need a helping hand. Or they might view the poor as "no-goods" who refuse to work and are a drain on society's resources. Such differences in perception and meaning are significant, for they have a direct impact on social policy. Let's look at how views about poor people have changed.

Historical Changes in the Meaning of Poverty and Its Relationship to Social Action

The view of poverty in the early 1700s stands in marked contrast to today's perspective. At that time, Americans viewed poverty as God's will, and clergy preached that God put the poor on earth to provide an opportunity for the rest of us to express Christian charity (Rothman and Rothman 1972). Poverty was not viewed as a social problem, but as a personal problem. Poverty was considered to be an ordinary part of life that required compassion on the part of others.

The poor had been scattered among hundreds of villages along country roads. By the time of the American Revolution, however, the poor started to be concentrated in colonial cities such as Boston, Philadelphia, and New York City. Authorities set up welfare committees, and following the view of the time, the members of these committees distinguished between the deserving and undeserving poor. The deserving poor were the blind, the handicapped, and the deserted mothers. The undeserving poor were the beggars, peddlers, idlers, drifters, and prostitutes. At this point, the meaning of poverty changed. Poverty was no longer considered God's will, but it was something that happened to people who had character flaws.

As the United States industrialized and more people moved to the cities, the squalor bothered people of good intentions. Reformers launched campaigns to help the poor—and again the meaning of poverty changed. The reformers saw poverty as the product of corrupt cities. Urban temptations—alcohol, crime, and debauchery— held people in the bondage of poverty (Rothman and Rothman 1972).

Although we no longer believe that poverty is God's will, the idea that poverty ought not to exist—and the suspicion that it is due to the character of the poor—remain part of our symbolic heritage. We have vacillated between viewing the poor as worthy people who deserve our help and as worthless people who deserve nothing

Thinking Critically about Social Problems

WHY WE NEED THE POOR: HOW POVERTY HELPS SOCIETY

Most of us think of poverty in only negative terms: Poverty is undesirable, and we should get rid of it. Functionalists, in contrast, identify the functions of poverty, that is, the positive consequences that poverty has for society. Consider these twelve functions:

1. The poor ensure that society's dirty work gets done at low cost. Many factories, restaurants, farms, and hospitals could not survive in their present state without this underpaid workforce. If there weren't poor people, who would do the dirty jobs at low wages?

2. The poor create jobs for others. Think of the social workers and welfare agencies that serve the poor and, not incidentally, shield the rest of us from them. Most police officers would be without jobs if it weren't for the poor. And what would social workers do?

3. The poor serve as guinea pigs in medical experiments. The rest of us benefit from these advances in medicine. What would we do without those medicines?

4. The poor make the economy more efficient. They spend welfare money on leftover goods such as day-old bread and the many "seconds" produced by our factories. They also buy the furniture and cars that the rest of us discard. Where else would these undesirable items go if it weren't for the poor?

5. The poor make others wealthy. Many slum landlords, for example, would have to get jobs if it weren't for the poor. And what would the owners of the many liquor stores in the inner city do without the poor?

6. The poor help some people become upwardly mobile. Just above those who live in poverty are people who are striving to reach the fringes of the middle class. A good example is the people who run the many small grocery stores in the inner cities. Without the poor, they would have to close their doors.

7. The poor provide the frontline soldiers for war. They are the dispensable ones in the infantry who can be sacrificed during battle. (The Germans used to call them "cannon fodder.") Where else would we get the many people that we need to fill the "grunt" jobs in the armed services?

8. The poor stabilize our political system. Most poor people vote for Democrats, so to the degree that this party helps the U.S. political system, the poor contribute to that effort.

9. The poor provide entertainment. Their lives of despair are the story lines of countless novels, movies, and television program. News programs gain followers—and advertising revenue—by documenting the many murders and rapes committed by the poor. Some may disagree with this depiction, but to be shocked and frightened out of our ordinary lives by dramatic accounts of the lives of others is certainly one definition of entertainment.

10. The poor enrich our music. They have given us the blues, Negro spirituals, country music (from the Southern poor), and rock (the Beatles came from the slums of Liverpool). Without the poor having devastating experiences, the rest of us would have fewer tunes to hum.

11. The poor help motivate us. That there are "the projects," skid row, homeless shelters, and soup lines keeps us on our toes. We know that we had better get an education and work hard or else we could end up there. The poor have replaced the "bogeyman" of years past.

12. The poor also help our self-concept. They make us all feel superior.

By the time functionalists get through with their analysis, one wonders if society could actually exist without the poor.

Based on Gans 1971/2005.

but a kick in the pants. Symbolic interactionists make us aware that the meanings of poverty change as social conditions change.

FUNCTIONALISM

The Functionalist View of Social Inequality

In a classic essay in 1945, sociologists Kingsley Davis and Wilbert Moore developed the functionalist perspective on social inequality. Their argument was simple. Some tasks in

society are more important than others. These positions of responsibility require talented people who are willing to make a sacrifice to prepare for them. To attract such talented people, the positions must offer high income and prestige. Oil, for example, is vital to keeping the economy going, but to learn the advanced techniques to find oil or to manage oil fields takes years of training in geology. Consequently, geologists must be offered both a substantial salary and the respect of others. Anyone can wash dishes, so unskilled workers earn poverty wages at these jobs. Thus, disparities in income help society function.

The Social Functions of Poverty

Functionalists go beyond this by saying that poverty itself is functional for society. Sociologist Herbert Gans (1971/2005), a proponent of this perspective, points out that the poor make significant contributions to society's well-being. For a summary of this view, see the Thinking Critically box on the previous page. Functional theorists also analyze the dysfunctions of poverty, including alienation and despair, drug abuse, street crime, suicide, and mental illness. In the *Spotlight on Research* box below, Gans explains how he has struggled against arguments that victimize the poor.

SPOTLIGHT ON RESEARCH

Demonizing the Poor

Herbert Gans, Professor of Sociology at Columbia University, is a past president of the American Sociological Association. He has written extensively on urban poverty and anti-poverty policy.

Ever since the 1950s, sociologists have led poverty researchers in studying America's victimized and demonized poor—although they have not done nearly enough research on their victimizers and demonizers.

Perhaps because I am a refugee from Nazi Germany and came to the United States dirt-poor, a significant part of my teaching and research has been about poverty and anti-poverty policy. I have been concerned with the victimized and demonized, as well as the agencies and institutions that victimize and demonize the poor. In the early 1960s, I wrote *The Urban Villagers,* a book about a low-income neighborhood in Boston that was demonized as a slum, and about its residents who were victimized when their neighborhood was torn down.

Later in the 1960s, I wrote a good deal about poverty and antipoverty policy—what is today called public sociology. Along with other sociologists, I analyzed and criticized the "culture of poverty" arguments, which suggested that the poor practice a culture that helps to keep them poor and prevents their escaping from poverty. We argued that blaming the victims for their victimization diverted attention away from what really keeps them poor: the shortage of secure and decent paying jobs, the failures of the welfare program, as well as racism. Although their victimization resulted in depression and pathology, it was not a culture of poverty.

I returned to anti-poverty research in the late 1980s, when a new version of, and a new term for, the culture of poverty argument appeared. This time, the poor were demonized as an "underclass," an alleged stratum that existed under respectable society. This underclass was accused of such moral shortcomings as not wanting to work, turning to welfare or street crime instead, being promiscuous, and avoiding marriage.

My interest in victimizers and demonizers made me wonder who invented and spread the new blaming term. In 1995, I wrote *The War Against the Poor,* which identified its inventors. The book also described how journalists, social scientists, and political conservatives combined to use and popularize the term.

Since the late 1990s, when welfare reform and a boom in low-wage jobs enabled more poor people to work, their demonization has declined—at least for the moment. However, if enough working poor lose their jobs to a weak economy, they will surely be demonized again—with the same old arguments, but perhaps with another new term. Then sociologists must show once more that blaming the victims only makes it harder for the poor to escape from poverty.

CONFLICT THEORY

The Conflict View of Social Inequality

Conflict theorists view the functionalist argument as wrong-headed. To say that inequality comes from a basic social need to offer higher rewards to fill some positions is to justify the power of the wealthy and the deprivation of the poor. Social inequality, argue conflict theorists, comes from a basic struggle over limited resources. At any point in history, some group has gained control of society's resources, and that group uses its power to secure its gains and to exploit those who are weaker. The result is a social class system in which the wealthy pass advantages to their children, whereas the poor pass disadvantages to theirs.

Marx's General Theory of Social Class Relations

Karl Marx (1818–1883) was the first sociologist to develop a general theory of **social class** and class relations. He argued that social class depends on a single factor, the *means of production*—the tools, factories, land, and capital used to produce wealth (Marx 1867/1967; Marx and Engels 1848/1964). People either own the means of production (the capitalists, or *bourgeoisie*) or they work for those who do (the workers, or *proletariat*). The history of a society is best understood as a conflict between owners and workers, the wealthy and the poor. Because the capitalists are in power, they use the social institutions, such as a society's legal and political systems, to promote the interests of the owners and to control the workers.

The capitalists' control of the workers will not continue forever. The day will come when the workers will revolt. Workers will lose their **false class consciousness,** their mistaken idea that they are capitalists, or that they soon will soon start their own business and become wealthy. In its place will be *class consciousness,* the realization that they are all workers no matter what their status or occupation, whether it be garbage collector or college professor. With their eyes finally opened and with the realization of their common identity, the workers will seize the means of production and use them for the good of all. Thus poverty will be eliminated.

Modifications in Conflict Theory

Most sociologists acknowledge that Marx provided valuable insight into relationships between the powerful and the poor, but they find his class division, with only

Functionalists argue that the highest salaries go to the positions that perform the most important functions for society. Critics respond that if this were true then garbage collectors would be among the most highly paid members of society. The garbage collectors shown here, needless to say, do not receive the salaries and stock options awarded to CEOs.

owners and workers, inadequate for today's society. Erik Wright (1979, 1985) points out that many managers of corporations have little in common with office and factory workers. In fact, many top managers have more power than the stockholders they work for. Ralf Dahrendorf (1959, 1973) pointed to authority, not ownership, as the key dimension of social class.

Conflict theory comes in several versions. But no matter the form that it takes, conflict theorists always stress the relationship between those who have power and those who do not. The problems of the poor are due to their deprived position in a system of stratification, to their relative powerlessness and oppression.

IN SUM

The Contributions of Each Theory

Each of the three theoretical lenses provides us a unique understanding of wealth, poverty, and inequality. Focusing on the individual level, symbolic interactionists make us more sensitive to how social class works in our everyday lives. Symbolic interactionists explain, for example, why the amount of income that people have (objective measure) is not the same as the ways that people see themselves (relative poverty). Functionalists and conflict theorists look at the bigger picture. Where functionalists see inequality as originating from a broad social need to reward important positions, however, conflict theorists stress that poverty originates and is maintained in the means of production.

Research Findings

WHO ARE THE POOR?

A striking characteristic of poverty is how it is distributed. The poor are concentrated in the inner city and in rural areas such as Appalachia. The Social Map on page 216 shows the differences in poverty among the states. As you can see, the regional differences are striking.

Race/Ethnicity

As we saw in Figure 7-5 (page 216), poverty also follows lines of race-ethnicity: African Americans and Latinos are about twice as likely as whites to be poor. As you saw in that figure, Latinos and African Americans have about the same poverty rate, and for both groups this rate has dropped considerably in recent years. Latinos and African Americans are now about where the national average was in 1960. The drop in poverty among African Americans is especially striking. As Figure 7-5 shows, their poverty rate is now less than half of what it used to be.

Age

Poverty is also related to age. The poverty rate of children is one-third *higher* than that of adults. Overall, 11.7 percent of U.S. adults are poor, but 15.6 percent of children live in poverty (*Statistical Abstract* 2003:Tables 700, 701). Figure 7-7 shows how poverty among children mirrors the nation's racial-ethnic pattern: About one of eight or nine white and Asian American children lives in poverty, but for African American and Latino children it is about one of three or four. For any child to have to live in poverty is unfortunate, but such extensive poverty among children has severe implications for an entire generation of Latinos and African Americans.

Single-Parent Families

Why is poverty higher among children than adults? There is no single answer, but part of the explanation is that more women are heading families. If children are living with both parents, seldom are they poor. The rate of poverty jumps when it comes to single-parent families, especially when a family is headed by the mother. Today, as you can see from Figure 7-8, we have a lot more mother-headed families. The main reasons for this are our high divorce rate and an increase in births to single women.

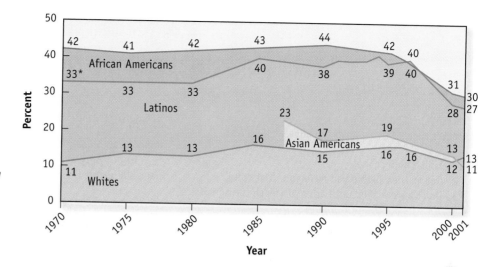

FIGURE 7-7 *U.S. Children in Poverty*

Source: By the author, based on *Statistical Abstract of the United States* 1994:Table 727; 2003:Table 701.

Life for a young unmarried mother can be brutal: She is not likely to receive much help from the father, she has a baby and herself to care for, and if she is unskilled and undereducated, how can she compete in the labor market? Similarly, a wife's income usually takes a nosedive after divorce: Child support often exists in name only: It is either unpaid or paid so irregularly that she can't count on it. And if a woman has been out of the workforce, her skills might be rusty. Consequently, compared with men, women and children are much more likely to be poor. Sociologists call this the **feminization of poverty**. (If you want to avoid poverty, see the Thinking Critically box on the next page.)

The Elderly

Poverty also used to plague the elderly, but, as mentioned in Chapter 2, their economic situation has improved. At 10 percent, the poverty rate of Americans over age 65 is now *lower* than that of the nation as a whole (*Statistical Abstract* 2003:Table 697). Social Security is the primary reason for the reduction in poverty among the elderly. This improvement shows that social legislation can work and that we can either allow a group to stay in poverty or not. We shall consider social policy later.

An Underclass to Do Society's Dirty Work?

Finally, there is the obvious pattern of low wages. People who earn the minimum wage are likely to be poor. I am not referring to college students who take minimum wage jobs while they are preparing for careers that pay well. Rather, the United States

FIGURE 7-8 *Growth in Families Headed by Women*

Note: Asian Americans include Pacific Islanders.

Sources: By the author, based on, for 1940, 1950, and 1960, U.S. Bureau of the Census, Current Population Reports, Series P-20, various numbers; for 1970, *Statistical Abstract* 1994:Table 71; for later years, *Statistical Abstract* 2003:Tables 44, 71.

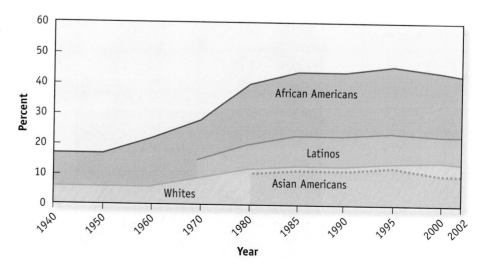

Thinking Critically about Social Problems
RULES FOR AVOIDING POVERTY

If you want to avoid poverty, follow three rules:

1. Finish high school.
2. Get married before you have your first child.
3. Don't have a child until after you reach the age of 20.

This message is being delivered to the black community by African-American leaders (Herbert 1998). Hugh Price, president of the National Urban League, and retired General Colin Powell say that 80 percent of African Americans who ignore these principles end up poor, but only 8 percent of those who follow them are poor. Although their statistics may not be exact, the rules are sound—and they apply to all racial-ethnic groups.

To not only avoid poverty but also to develop a financially secure life, I would like to add four more "rules":

1. Go to college.
2. Stay married.
3. Avoid alcoholism and any form of drug addiction.
4. Avoid credit card debt.

Poverty among people who follow these seven rules is practically nonexistent.

has an *underclass,* people who are locked into low-paying, dirty work. They do the "stoop labor" on farms and fill the sweatshops of our cities. Many work in the clothing industry's small factories or even at home, where they get paid a small amount for each piece of work they complete. Although there are no accurate counts, this underclass numbers several million.

In Sum

The patterns we have reviewed indicate that poverty is not a matter of people here or there being poor because they are lazy or stupid. Instead, poverty is a *structural* matter; that is, poverty is built into the social system and follows lines of age, gender, and race-ethnicity. Consequently, to understand poverty, sociologists examine features of the *social system:* discrimination, marriage and reproductive patterns, how welfare programs function, how the economy changes, and how an underclass is created and maintained. In later chapters, we shall discuss some of these patterns, but for now let's consider an analysis of poverty that has generated considerable controversy in sociology.

Poverty in the United States has become concentrated among women and children. Sociologists call this pattern the feminization of poverty. *Poverty is especially high among teenage mothers.*

IS THERE A CULTURE OF POVERTY?

We boast of vast achievement and of power,
Of human progress knowing no defeat,
Of strange new marvels every day and hour—
And here's the bread line in the wintry street!
BERTON BRALEY, "THE BREAD LINE"

Is there a culture of poverty, *a way of life that encourages poverty and is transmitted across generations? Most sociologists dislike this controversial theory because it seems to blame the victims of social arrangements. But see the caption for the cartoon on page 229.*

Poverty in the Midst of Plenty

How things have changed! A generation ago, Americans associated bread lines and soup kitchens with only the Great Depression, or perhaps with Charles Dickens' description of nineteenth-century London. But now the homeless are part of every major city across this rich land. Some are tucked out of sight. The blatant presence of others on our cities' sidewalks, ravaged by hunger and dressed in mismatched layers of out-of-date clothing, reveals the contrast between the American dream and its stark reality—between "us" and "them." Who are these homeless people, and how did they get that way? Some answers are provided on the next page in the Thinking Critically box on the homeless.

The homeless are only one segment of the "hard-core" poor. Where the urban hard-core poor live is easy to spot. Every major city has sections with filthy streets and neglected buildings, some boarded up, others burned out. Children and adults loiter on sidewalks and stoops, and the air may be filled with the stink of garbage or urine. Where the rural hard-core poor live is not so easy to spot. They are not as clustered together, and most are tucked away in tiny pockets.

A Limited Culture of Poverty

Based on participant observation and life histories, anthropologist Oscar Lewis (1959, 1966) concluded that the hard-core poor develop a way of life that traps them in poverty. He called this way of life the **culture of poverty.** When people conclude that they are never going to get out of poverty, they become fatalistic and passive. They develop low aspirations and think about the present, not the future. Perceiving a gulf between themselves and the mainstream, they feel inferior and insecure. They become self-destructive, as illustrated by their high rates of alcoholism, physical violence, and family abuse. Their lives become marked by broken marriages, desertion, wife beating, and single-parent households. Their way of life, this culture of poverty, makes it almost impossible for the hard-core poor to break out of poverty.

This is an interesting concept, but is it true? To find out, economist Patricia Ruggles examined national statistics. Her findings both challenge and support a culture of poverty. Contrary to popular belief, few people pass poverty on to the next generation: *Most children of the poor do not grow up to be poor.* Only about one in five persons who are poor as children are still poor when they are adults (Corcoran et al. 1985; Sawhill 1988; Ruggles 1989, 1990). But in support of a culture of poverty, Ruggles also found that about 1 percent of the U.S. population remains poor year in and year out. They were poor 20 years ago, and they are poor today. This group has three primary

Thinking Critically about Social Problems

BEING HOMELESS IN THE LAND OF THE AMERICAN DREAM

When I met Larry Rice, who runs a shelter for the homeless in St. Louis, Missouri, he said that as a sociologist I needed to know firsthand what was happening on our city streets. I resisted his "invitation," reluctant to leave my comfortable home and office to see who knows what. Then Larry hooked me: He offered to take me to Washington, D.C., where he promised that I would see people sleeping on sidewalk grates within view of the White House. Intrigued at the sight of such a contrast, I agreed to go with him, not knowing that it would change my own life.

When we arrived in Washington, it was bitter cold. It was December, and I saw what Rice had promised: sorrowful people huddled over the exhaust grates of federal buildings. Not all of the homeless survived that first night I was there. Freddy, who walked on crutches and had become a fixture in Georgetown, froze to death as he sought refuge from the cold in a telephone booth. I vividly recall looking at the telephone booth where Freddy's stiff body was found, still upright, futilely wrapped in a tattered piece of canvas. I went to Freddy's funeral and talked with his friends. To me, Freddy became a person, an individual, not just a faceless, nameless figure shrouded by city shadows.

This experience ignited my sociological curiosity. I was driven to find out more. I ended up visiting a dozen skid rows in the United States and Canada, sleeping in filthy shelters across North America. I interviewed the homeless in these shelters—and in back alleys and on street corners, in parks, and even in dumpsters. I became so troubled by what I experienced that for three months after I returned home I couldn't get through an entire night without waking up, startled by disturbed dreams.

One of the many things that impressed me was that there are many routes to homelessness. Here are the types of homeless people whom I met:

1. *"Push-outs":* These people have been pushed out of their homes. Two common types of "push-outs" are teenagers who have been kicked out by their parents and adults who have been evicted by landlords.
2. *Victims of environmental catastrophe:* This type really surprised me, but they, too, live on our streets. The catastrophes I came across ranged from fires to dioxin contamination.
3. *The mentally ill:* These people have been discharged from mental hospitals. They are given little or no treatment for their problems, and they are unable to care for themselves.
4. *The technologically dispossessed:* This group consists of unemployed workers whose work skills have become outmoded because of technological change.
5. *The technologically unqualified:* Unlike the technologically dispossessed, these unemployed workers never possessed technological qualifications.
6. *The elderly:* These people have neither savings nor family support; they are old, unemployable, and discarded.
7. *Runaways:* After fleeing intolerable situations, these boys and girls wander our streets.
8. *The demoralized:* After suffering some personal tragedy, these people have given up and retreated into despair. The most common catalyst to their demoralization was divorce.
9. *Alcoholics:* The old-fashioned skid-row wino is still out there.
10. *Ease addicts:* These people actually choose to be homeless. For them, homelessness is a form of "early retirement." They have no responsibilities to others, and they can do mostly as they please. Some of them, in their twenties, spend their days playing chess in the parks of San Francisco.
11. *Travel addicts:* These people also choose to be homeless. Addicted to wanderlust, they travel continuously. They even have their own name for themselves: "road dogs."
12. *Excitement addicts:* These people, among the younger of the homeless, enjoy the thrill of danger. They like the excitement that comes from "living on the edge." Being on the streets offers many "edge" opportunities.

As you can see, homelessness is far from being one-dimensional: People arrive on our city streets by many "routes." Note how different the "routes" are for the last three types (who are a minority of the homeless) compared with the first nine types, people who do not want to be homeless. From these findings, it should be obvious that, because there are many "causes" of homelessness, there can be no single solution to this social problem. We need multifaceted programs that are based on the various "routes" by which people travel to this dead-end destination.

characteristics: Most are African American, are unemployed, and live in female-headed households. About half are unmarried mothers with children.

How do we reconcile Ruggles's findings? The fairest conclusion seems to be this: Some people apparently do have a culture of poverty that perpetuates itself. These people learn behaviors that keep them poor, and they pass this way of life to their children. Because most people who are poor today will not be poor in just a few years, however, we can conclude that *most* poor people do not have such a culture.

WHO RULES AMERICA?

The Basic Question: Who Has the Power?

Conflict theorists stress that to understand society, we must understand who controls its scarce resources. Power, like wealth, is a scarce resource, and some people have much of it, whereas others have little or none. The possession of power is especially significant, because it determines who gets the lion's share of the other resources of society. Let's ask, then, who makes the big decisions in the United States?

Difficult to Answer in a Large, Modern, Complex Society

This question is not easy to answer. In the past, societies had a simpler organization. In feudal societies, the serfs formed a working class and the feudal lords an ownership class. The feudal lords controlled both the means of production and the political system. Today, in contrast, the owners of the means of production do not directly run the political system. In today's political state, connections with business are complex, with numerous, indirect lines running from one to the other. Let's see what answers sociologists have come up with.

The Power Elite/ Ruling Class

Sociologist C. Wright Mills (1959a) argued that a **power elite** rules the United States. With access to the center of political power, a tiny group makes the decisions that direct the country—and shake the world. As Figure 7-9 illustrates, the power elite consists of the top leaders of the largest corporations, the top commanders of the armed forces, and a few elite politicians—the president, his cabinet, and members of Congress who chair the major committees.

The Circulation of Elites

Mills stressed that the power elite is not a formal group. It meets neither in secret nor in public. In fact, some members may not think that they belong to it. But, structurally, it exists. The power elite consists of people whose interests have coalesced. As

FIGURE 7-9 *How Is Power Distributed in the United States? The Model Proposed by C. Wright Mills*
Source: Based on Mills 1959a.

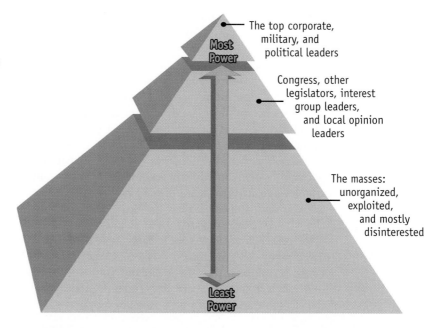

people move from top posts in business to government and back again, or from the military to management positions in the defense industry, the power elite gains cohesion. White House aides join powerful law firms. A law partner joins the president's cabinet or is appointed secretary of the treasury. The head of the treasury becomes the CEO of a leading bank or corporation. An air force colonel retires and heads the sales division of Boeing or McDonnell Douglas.

Shared Backgrounds and Interests

These people's shared interests and interlocking experiences in business and politics are sufficient to ensure that they think alike on major issues. But, in addition, these people come from similar backgrounds in which they have learned similar values and ways of looking at the world. Most are white Anglo-Saxon Protestants who have attended exclusive prep schools and Ivy League colleges. Many belong to the same private clubs and vacation at the same exclusive resorts. Some even hire the same bands for their daughters' debutante balls. They are united, then, by shared backgrounds, contacts, ideologies, values, and interests (Domhoff 1974, 1990, 2001).

Three Segments of the Power Elite

Mills said that the three groups that make up the power elite—the top political, military, and corporate leaders—are not equal in power. In identifying who was dominant, he did not point to the president, however, or even to the generals and admirals, but, rather, to the corporate heads. Because all three segments of the power elite view capitalism as essential to the welfare of the country, national policy centers around businesses interests. Making decisions that promote capitalism works to their mutual benefit.

The Ruling Class

Sociologist William Domhoff (1990, 1998, 2001) prefers to use the term "ruling class" instead of power elite. He studies the 1 percent of Americans who belong to the superrich, those so wealthy that *they are worth more than the entire bottom 90 percent of the nation* (Beeghley 2004). This 1 percent controls the nation's top corporations and foundations, even the boards that oversee our major universities. It also owns the major newspapers and magazines and radio and television stations. Members of this powerful group attempt, quite successfully, to shape the consciousness of the nation. It is no accident, says Domhoff, that from this group come most of the president's cabinet and top ambassadors.

An Informal Coalition

Conflict theorists stress that we should not think of the power elite or ruling class as a group that meets and makes specific decisions. Rather, with their interlocking economic and political interests and similar worldview, their behavior stems not from a grand conspiracy to control the country but from a mutual interest in solving the problems that face large businesses (Useem 1984). Able to ensure that the country adopts the social policies that it deems desirable—from fixing interest rates to sending troops abroad—this powerful group sets the economic and political conditions under which the rest of the country lives (Domhoff 1990).

The Pluralistic View

Not all sociologists agree with this view of a power elite that pulls the strings behind the scenes. *Pluralists* argue that social, economic, and political power is dispersed among many competing **interest groups,** such as unions, industries, professional associations, ecologists, hawks, doves, and the like. *No one group is in control,* they stress. Sociologist David Riesman and his colleagues (1951), who developed this *pluralist view of power,* maintained that the interests of the country's diverse groups frequently conflict, making a united policy or action impossible. Mills argued that members of the power elite settle important questions and differences among themselves, but the pluralists maintain that the country's many groups are divided by essential differences. Thus power is distributed among many competing interest groups (Kornhauser 1961; Marger 1987; Beeghley 2004).

Who Really Rules? The Dahl Study

The controversy between the pluralists and the sociologists who support the view of the power elite is long standing and unresolved. In 1961, sociologist Robert Dahl published a study on power in New Haven, Connecticut, the home of Yale University, which he felt proved that the power elite did not exist. Dahl found little overlap between the university's and town's social elites and little influence by either of them on the city's policies. Dahl's research became a classic in support of the pluralistic view of U.S. power.

The Domhoff Study

Sociologist William Domhoff (1978), who, as you have seen, supports the power elite view, decided to reanalyze Dahl's data and to collect more data for the same period. Contrary to Dahl, Domhoff found that Yale University, New Haven's businesses, and its other social institutions are interlocked extensively. Domhoff concluded that a power elite of corporate heads, bankers, social elites, and politicians shape New Haven's economy. He documented not only how the New Haven elite shapes local decisions but also how they are connected to national elites. Domhoff believes that each major city in the United States has such a power center and that lines run from these cities to the national power structure.

How about each industry? We have a study that has intriguing implications. When economists examined the relationships among the 72 U.S. companies that deal with low-level radioactive waste, they found intricate connections among the corporate directors. These companies are so bound together that the researchers conclude that they form a power bloc (Hayden et al. 2002). It is possible, and perhaps likely, that each type of industry in the United States has its own interlocking power structure. If so, and this has yet to be determined, the next question will be how the various blocs of power are related to each other and to the national power structure.

The Useem Study

The Moore Study

To see how extensively the corporate elite is tied together on a national level, sociologist Michael Useem (1979) examined the nation's 797 largest corporations. These corporations had 8,623 directors. Of these, 1,570 were directors in two or more of the corporations. Most of those who did not hold multiple positions in these largest corporations held directorships in smaller firms. In another study, sociologist Gwen Moore (1979) examined the 545 top positions in key U.S. institutions. They were clustered into 32 issue-oriented cliques (see Table 7-1). One core circle of 272 people was linked to almost all the smaller cliques. Moore (1979:689) concluded,

> the evidence examined here indicates that considerable integration exists among elites in all major sections of American society . . . . The existence of a central elite circle facilitates communication and interaction both within that large, diverse group and between its members and those in more specialized elite circles and cliques.

Useem and Moore concluded that there is a national interlocking power elite. Yet, because they were unable to study how decisions are made (for example, policy on the Middle East), their studies do not demonstrate that U.S. elites form a cohesive ruling group.

Is there a culture of wealth, *one that locks its members into wealth and privilege and is transmitted across generations? Sociologists have no difficulty in agreeing that such a culture (or, more accurately phrased, subculture) exists. We sociologists, like the rest of society, perceive through colored lenses, and a culture of wealth matches our bias in favor of the oppressed of society. As symbolic interactionists point out, it is impossible to perceive events except from some perspective. We use the research methods described in Chapter 1 to overcome our biases.*

"Actually, it's one giant organism connected by blood, genes, and a common source of old wealth."

TABLE 7-1 Members of the National Elite[*]

SECTOR	POSITION
Congress	Senators: members of the House of Representatives in the following categories: chairperson and ranking minority members of all House committees; all members of the Rules, Appropriations, and Ways and Means Committees.
Federal administration— political appointees	Secretaries, assistant secretaries, and general counsel of cabinet departments; heads and deputy heads of independent agencies.
Civil service	Two highest civil service grades from all cabinet departments and independent agencies.
Industrial corporation	Fortune 500 largest industrial corporations.
Nonindustrial corporation	Fortune 300 largest nonindustrial corporations.
Holders of large fortunes	Holders of fortunes worth at least $100 million.
Labor union	Presidents of unions with at least 50,000 members; officials of the AFL-CIO.
Political party	Members of Democratic and Republican National-Committees; state and city chairpersons of these parties.
Voluntary organization	Elected head and full-time director of various public-affairs organizations including professional societies, farmers' organizations, women's groups, religious organizations, civil rights organizations, and business groups.
Media	Editors of the largest circulation newspapers and public affairs periodicals; syndicated columnists and news executives; broadcasters and commentators of national networks.

[*]This table lists the politicians, civil servants, and industrialists who, according to one study, make up the national elite of the United States.

Source: From Gwen Moore, "The Structure of a National Elite Network," *American Sociological Review, 44,* October 1979:673–691. Copyright © 1979 by the American Sociological Association. Reprinted with the permission of the author and the American Sociological Association.

Is There a Culture of Wealth?

Although the question of a cohesive ruling group must remain open until we have more evidence, this brings us to another significant question: Does the culture of the elite—its set of institutions, customs, family ties, and connections—allow the rich and powerful to perpetuate their privileges? In other words, is there a **culture of wealth** that keeps people from falling down the social class structure, just as some claim that a culture of poverty makes it difficult for poor people to pull themselves up? Of course there is. The elite of any city, region, or nation—indeed of any group—tend to develop common sentiments and share similar values and goals. The sociological problem is not to determine whether this occurs but to discover how it operates.

Is the Concentration of Power a Problem?

That a culture of wealth exists, however, does not mean that the elite work together to rule the country. That is another matter entirely. Power and wealth do go together: Few poor people are powerful, and few powerful people are poor. Is the concentration of power and wealth a problem? The danger that many sociologists see is that it violates the democratic processes on which our country is premised. Interlocking interests by wealthy people in powerful positions can result in a few non-elected individuals being able to wield immense control over the country. One of the major needs in the study of social problems is more research on the relationship of wealth and power.

A Global Glimpse
KILLING KIDS FOR FUN AND PROFIT

What is childhood like in the Least Industrialized Nations? As in the United States, the answer depends primarily on who your parents are. If your parents are rich, childhood can be pleasant. If you are born into poverty but live where there is plenty to eat, life can still be good—although you will lack books, television, and education. But you probably won't miss them. If you live in a slum, however, life can be horrible, worse than in the slums of the Most Industrialized Nations. Let's look at the slums of Brazil.

You can take for granted alcoholism, drug abuse, child abuse, wife beating, a high crime rate, and not having enough food. Even in the inner cities of the Most Industrialized Nations, you would expect these things.

You might not expect the brutal conditions in which Brazilian slum (*favela*) children live. Poverty is so deep that children and adults swarm over garbage dumps to find enough decaying food to keep them alive. Sociologist Martha Huggins (1993) reports that the owners of these dumps hire armed guards to keep the poor out—so they can sell the garbage for pig food. The Brazilian police and death squads murder some of these children. Some associations of shop owners even put assassination teams on retainer and auction victims off to the lowest bidder! The going rate is a half month's salary—figured at the low Brazilian minimum wage.

Life is cheap in the Least Industrialized Nations—but death squads for children? To understand how this could possibly be, we need to note that Brazil has been politically unstable and has a long history of violence. With high poverty and a small middle class, mob violence and revolution always lurk just around the corner. The "dangerous classes," as they are known, threaten the status quo. Groups of homeless children, who have no jobs or prospects of getting work, roam the streets. To survive, these children clamber in and out of traffic to wash the windshields of cars that are stopped at red lights. They shine shoes, beg, steal, and sell their bodies.

These children annoy the "respectable" classes, who see them as trouble. Sometimes the children break into stores. They hurt business, for customers feel intimidated when they see poorly dressed adolescents clustered in front of a store. Some children even sell items that compete with the stores. Without social institutions to care for these children, one solution is to kill them. As Huggins notes, murder sends a clear message to the children, especially if it is accompanied by torture—gouging out the eyes, ripping open the chest, cutting off the genitals, raping the girls, and burning the victim's body.

FOR YOUR CONSIDERATION

Can the Most Industrialized Nations do anything about this situation? Or is it none of our business? Is it, though unfortunate, an internal affair for the Brazilians to handle?

INEQUALITY AND GLOBAL POVERTY

Why Are Some Nations Poor Year After Year?

Just as the United States is stratified into social classes, so the world's nations are stratified into rich and poor nations. The Most Industrialized Nations, which are wealthy, have **residual poverty,** or pockets of poverty. Most of the Least Industrialized Nations, in contrast, have **mass poverty:** Most of their citizens live on less than $1,000 a year. They are malnourished, are chronically ill, and die young. The Global Glimpse box above reports on the abysmal conditions of some children in nations that experience mass poverty.

Three Explanations:

Why are some nations poor year after year? Social scientists have proposed three answers. The first is that the rich nations exploit the poor nations. To obtain their raw materials, the more powerful nations used to invade and conquer weaker nations ("political colonialism"). Now they use **economic colonialism.** The Most Industrialized Nations import raw materials from the poor nations and give them industrial products in return. The Most Industrialized Nations dominate the market for food and raw materials. The poor nations must sell their food and natural resources—from bananas and

1. Economic Colonialism

coffee to tin and manganese—at prices so low that they are lucky to keep up with their expanding populations, much less pay their international debts and develop their own industrial capacity. As a result, these nations remain poor.

In this context, we might ask what would happen if one of the small, oil-rich nations were to gain control over the region's resources. If that nation could set oil prices, it could lead the Most Industrialized Nations by the nose. Would the Most Industrialized Nations allow this? The answer should be obvious. When Iraq made an attempt to dominate the Middle East, the result was the First Gulf War. At the time of that brief war, few Americans took the U.S. government's statements about "protecting Kuwait" at face value. Even the person on the street talked cynically about the bottom line being lower oil prices. During the Second Gulf War, on the heels of 9/11, such statements were not made as openly.

2. Interlocking Elites and Overlapping Circles of Power

A second answer as to why some nations remain poor is that their own power elite exploits them. Although these nations are dirt poor, each has a wealthy elite that lives a sophisticated, upper-class lifestyle in the major cities of its home country. This elite identifies with elites abroad and even sends its children to Oxford, the Sorbonne, or Harvard. The multinational corporations channel their investments through this local circle of power, which profits from exploiting its own country's resources. This local elite emulates the Most Industrialized Nations and builds laboratories and computer centers in the capital city. Such projects do not help the majority of their people, who continue to live in poverty in remote villages.

3. National Cultures of Poverty

A culture of poverty provides a third answer to why poverty continues in the Least Industrialized Nations (Landes 1998). (Oscar Lewis meant for this concept to apply to Latin American countries as well as to East Los Angeles or Appalachia.) As ambassador to India, John Kenneth Galbraith (1979), a social economist, observed what he described as a culture of fatalistic resignation, reinforced by religion. He pointed out that most of the world's poor eke out a living from the land. With barely enough to live on, they are reluctant to experiment with a different way to farm: If the attempt fails, it will lead to hunger or death. Their religion also teaches them to accept their lot in life as God's will and to look for rewards in the afterlife. Galbraith emphasized that the poor countries do not lack resources. Most have many untapped natural resources—most much greater than resource-starved Japan. Their weakness in world markets, however, combined with their fatalistic culture, makes it unlikely that they will rise from poverty.

These three reasons—economic colonialism, an exploiting local elite, and a culture of poverty—remain a matter of debate among social scientists. Perhaps each holds part of the truth. Rather than being exclusive, these three explanations may be complementary.

Social Policy

HISTORICAL CHANGES IN SOCIAL POLICY

Social Policies Depend on Assumptions of Cause

Our views of what causes a social problem influence the social policies that we favor. We reviewed how people's ideas about poverty changed: Poverty first was considered God's will, then was thought to result from character flaws, and then was attributed to the evils of the city. As these views changed, so did social policies. In colonial times, when poverty was thought to be God's will, it was a person's religious duty to shelter, feed, and clothe the poor. The poor were cared for on a personal, individual basis.

Historical Shifts in Views about Causes of Poverty and Matching Social Policy

During the American Revolution, when the poor were considered to be lazy and wayward people who needed discipline, Boston opened a workhouse. There the poor had to work until they showed that they had acquired self-discipline and appreciated hard work. Philadelphia Quakers took a gentler view and built almshouses that took in poor women and children. These social policies marked a departure from providing relief on an individual basis; instead, the government established institutionalized care of the poor (Nash 1979).

In the 1830s, when people believed that the squalor of cities caused poverty, they developed a policy that matched their belief. The logical solution was to take the poor away from the corrupting influence of the city. In the country, their sense of decency and order would be restored (Rothman 1971). This attempt failed because the institutions that were built for this purpose filled up and budgets were cut. The institutions became human warehouses of the worst sort.

To appreciate the attitudes of the time, consider this statement from Henry Ward Beecher, the most prominent clergyman of his day:

> It is said that a dollar a day is not enough for a wife and five or six children. No, not if the man smokes and drinks beer. . . . But is not a dollar a day enough to buy bread with? Water costs nothing, and a man who cannot live on bread and water is not fit to live. A family may live on good bread and water in the morning, water and bread at midday, and good water and bread at night. (quoted in Thayer 1997)

A dollar went a lot farther in those days, to be sure, and people did pump water freely from backyard wells. But to live on only bread and water?

During the Great Depression of the 1930s, the focus shifted to the masses of poor people whose problem was unemployment. At his 1937 Inaugural Address, President Franklin D. Roosevelt said,

> Millions of families are trying to live on incomes so meager that the pall of family disaster hangs over them day by day. . . . I see one-third of a nation ill-housed, ill-clad, ill-nourished. (quoted in Fisher 1998)

The Roosevelt administration created large-scale welfare for the unemployed, established massive work projects, and tried to revive the economy to create jobs. During World War II, the economy picked up and poverty declined sharply.

The less-visible and permanent kinds of poverty remained. As was described, the rediscovery of poverty in the 1960s led to new social policies based on the idea that the poor had been left behind during the country's rise to prosperity. Some programs provided education and training so the poor could get jobs. Other programs were based on the assumption that some of the poor, such as single mothers, children, and the elderly, needed to be subsidized.

The Essential Assumptions: Internal or External Causes

Views have shifted between attributing poverty to forces *within* a person (laziness, stupidity, evil) to attributing poverty to forces *outside* the person (God, evil cities, the economy). The implications for social policy that arise from these contrary assumptions are severe. Explanations of poverty that assume that causes lie within people lead to such policies as doing nothing (because no social policy will help) or even to sterilization. Explanations that are based on social causes spur programs of education, aid, social reform, job retraining, and stimulating the economy. Our cycles of social reform still reflect this duality of internal and external forces.

Although different generations define poverty differently, in each era the core issues remain: Who is responsible? and What shall we do about it?

THE FEMINIZATION OF POVERTY

The Poverty of Women and Children

The poverty that clusters around women and children is a special problem. To alleviate it, we can provide job training for women whose job skills are rusty or nonexistent. For many of these women to work requires child care facilities, and policies that promote child care will help. In addition, divorced mothers can be awarded child care that better reflects the father's earnings. In recent years, courts have done a better job of making sure that fathers pay child support, but they can still do a better job of enforcing support payments from fathers. It also seems reasonable that absent fathers, whether or not they were married to their children's mother, should support the children they fathered, rather than letting these children become the government's responsibility. Unfortunately, some unemployed fathers can pay little or nothing. Their own poverty is a related problem that must be solved.

PROGRESSIVE TAXATION

Taxation as Social Policy to Redistribute Wealth

A broader policy to help reduce inequality is **progressive taxation,** tax rates that progress (increase) with income. The federal and state governments tax wealthier people at higher rates and redistribute some of this money to the poor through welfare, Medicaid, housing subsidies, child care, and food stamps. Table 7-2 shows that as Americans earn more not only do they pay more dollars in taxes but also that they pay a larger percentage of their incomes in taxes.

Few wealthy people approve of the government taking their money in order to distribute it to the poor, and to retain more of their incomes they hire legal experts to find loopholes in the tax laws. A few wealthy individuals and corporations are so successful at finding loopholes that in some years they manage to pay no taxes. These are exceptional cases, however.

FOUR TYPES OF PUBLIC ASSISTANCE PROGRAMS

1. Social Insurance Programs

We can divide public assistance programs into four types. The first, social insurance programs such as unemployment compensation and Social Security, is designed to help those who help themselves. Money is deducted from paychecks, and workers draw on this pool when they need it. Few argue that workers who are laid off when an entire industry, such as steel or automobiles, is hit by recession don't deserve help.

2. Teaching Job Skills

The second type of program attempts to make the poor self-supporting so that they are no longer in need of social welfare. Most of these programs center around teaching job skills. This includes formal courses and on-the-job-training such as the Job Corps. Some programs stress personal grooming, punctuality, and politeness so that prospective workers can meet employer expectations.

TABLE 7-2 Income Taxes Paid by Americans

ADJUSTED GROSS INCOME	THE NUMBER OF RETURNS FILED	TAX PAID AS A PERCENTAGE OF ADJUSTED GROSS INCOME	APPROXIMATE TAX PAID IN DOLLARS	TOTAL AMOUNT PAID
Less than $5,000	13,950,000	4.5%	$261	$3,650,000,000
$5,000–$10,999	15,245,000	4.6%	$366	$5,580,000,000
$11,000–$18,999	19,087,000	6.5%	$980	$18,705,000,000
$19,000–$29,000	20,606,000	7.8%	$1,900	$32,000,000,000
$30,000–$39,999	13,548,000	8.9%	$3,100	$41,000,000,000
$40,000–$49,999	10,412,000	10.0%	$4,500	$46,000,000,000
$50,000–$74,999	17,076,000	11.2%	$7,000	$115,000,000,000
$75,000–$99,999	8,597,000	13.6%	$12,000	$99,000,000,000
$100,000–$199,999	8,083,000	17.3%	$23,000	$184,000,000,000
$200,000–$499,999	1,877,000	23.9%	$69,000	$147,000,000,000
$500,000–$999,999	396,000	28.3%	$192,000	$76,000,000,000
$1,000,000 or more	240,000	27.7%	$945,000	$226,000,000,000

Source: By the author, based on *Statistical Abstract* 2003:Table 491.

To keep people from starving and to stimulate the dormant economy during the Great Depression of the 1930s, the federal government began the Works Progress Administration (WPA). Men were put to work constructing public buildings, parks, and roads; women were put to work picking garden crops and canning food. Even artists were put to work. Shown here is a mural painted by WPA artists in the public school in Wilton, Connecticut. (By the way, every child in the United States sat at a desk like those shown here. The little hole in the upper right corner of each desk is an inkwell. Each student inserted a bottle of ink in which to dip his or her pen.)

3. Welfare

A third type of program is *welfare*—money, food, housing, and medical care that are given to people who have a low enough income. Here the distinction between the deserving and the undeserving is replaced by a humanitarian notion that people in severe need should be helped regardless of who is responsible. These programs, such as Temporary Assistance to Needy Families (TANF), food stamps, and public housing, generate controversy because people think that they encourage laziness and unwed motherhood. They also think that the people who receive this money really could work and take care of themselves. One consequence is a disparaging of people on welfare, the topic of the Issues in Social Problems box on the next page.

4. Workfare

A fourth type of program is *workfare*. Critics claim that welfare reduces people's incentive to work. They say, "Why will people work if they can get money free?" As U.S. welfare rolls swelled to 14 million people in the early 1990s, despite this being a period of prosperity, criticisms grew louder. The media gave high publicity to "welfare queens," "welfare Cadillacs," teenaged girls getting pregnant so they could get away from their parents, and women having more babies to get bigger welfare checks. As criticisms mounted, the federal government passed the 1996 *Personal Responsibility and Work Opportunity Reconciliation Act*. This law requires states to place a lifetime cap on welfare assistance and compels welfare recipients to look for work and to take available jobs. The maximum length of time that someone can collect welfare is five years. In some states, it is less. Unmarried teen parents must attend school and live at home or in some other adult-supervised setting.

Workfare was met with severe criticism ("It's just a way of throwing the poor into the streets"), but national welfare rolls plummeted. Overall, the number of Americans on welfare was cut by 60 percent (Caincian et al. 2003). This reduction occurred during the longest "boom" period in U.S. history, however. We know that recessions are

Issues in Social Problems
WELFARE: HOW TO RAVAGE THE SELF-CONCEPT

My husband left me shortly after I was diagnosed with multiple sclerosis. At the time, I had five children. My oldest child was 14, and my youngest was 7. My physician, believing I would be seriously disabled, helped get me on Social Security disability. The process took several months, and so it became necessary for me to go on public aid and food stamps.

By the time I needed to depend on my family in the face of a crisis, there weren't any resources left to draw on. My father had passed away and my mother was retired, living on a modest income based on Social Security and my father's pension. Isn't it funny how there is no social stigma attached to Social Security benefits for the elderly? People look at this money as an entitlement—"We worked for it." But people who have to depend on public aid for existence are looked at like vermin and accused of being lazy.

I can tell you from my own experience that a great deal of the lethargy that comes from long periods on welfare is due primarily to the attitudes of the people you have to come into contact with in these programs. I've been through the gamut: from rude, surly caseworkers at Public Aid, to patronizing nurses at the WIC [Women, Infants, and Children] clinic ("You have *how* many children?"), to the accusing tone of the food pantry workers when you have to go begging for a handout before the thirty-day time span has expired. After a while your dignity is gone, and you start to believe that you really are the disgusting human trash they all make you out to be.

Christine Hoffman, a student in the author's introductory sociology class.

inevitable, and, with them, unemployment. Critics are waiting to see what happens when this next "bust" period comes.

PRIVATE AGENCIES AND VOLUNTEER ORGANIZATIONS

Nongovernment Programs   When we think of aid for the poor, we generally think of the government. The United States also has thousands of volunteer organizations and private groups that work on their behalf. Because they work mainly with the desperate poor, who are tucked in out-of-the-way corners of our urban centers, their activities are largely invisible to most Americans. The soup kitchens of the inner city are run by volunteer organizations, most of them religious. The most well known of these organizations is the Salvation Army. In addition to its well-known soup kitchens and shelters for the homeless, the Salvation Army's efforts on behalf of the poor include alcohol counseling and job training. Perhaps the Salvation Army's tireless work to help the down-and-out is partially the reason for Congress's attempts to pass laws to fund religious charities. This effort has run into a roadblock of criticism, and as I write this, bills that would provide such funding are stalled in Congress.

The efforts of religious groups are well intentioned, and without them the social problem of poverty would be much worse. But the quality of what they do varies widely, as I discovered in my stays in the homeless shelters.

REGULATING THE POOR

Critics of welfare point to the grudging way in which welfare is administered and the humiliation that its recipients have to undergo. Our eligibility rules are complicated, with the result that many poor people fail to receive benefits. Welfare agents probe the private corners of poor people's lives. The rules and benefits are not uniform, and some states pay much less than others. After a set period of time, despite their continuing need or debilitating situation, people are kicked off welfare. Some of them end up on the streets.

Social Welfare Viewed from the Conflict Perspective: A Way to Control the Poor

To analyze social welfare, sociologists Frances Piven and Richard Cloward use conflict theory. They (1971, 1982, 1989, 1997) argue that capitalism needs unemployed, low-skilled, temporary workers to draw on when the economy is booming and that it can lay off when the economy slows. Welfare maintains this pool of workers at a minimal cost, keeping the poor alive until the next business expansion. Piven and Cloward support their assertion by documenting the changing rules of welfare: In times of high unemployment, when political disorder looms, welfare rules soften. In "boom" times, when those workers are needed, welfare rules are tightened. The purpose of welfare, these theorists conclude, is to control the unemployed, maintain social order, and provide capitalists a pool of cheap labor.

Following Piven and Cloward's analysis, we would conclude that it is no coincidence that the *Personal Responsibility and Work Opportunity Reconciliation Act* was passed during the longest "boom" in U.S. history. More workers were needed, and the federal government required states to tighten their rules for welfare eligibility. Some states even began to fingerprint applicants and to send investigators to their homes. The states also started to emphasize job training. New York City even changed the name of its locations from "welfare centers" to "job centers." Following this conflict analysis, then, it is reasonable to assume that the states will loosen their rules for welfare eligibility during the next recession so that the pool of marginal workers can survive until capitalists need them again.

GIVING THE POOR MORE MONEY

Eliminate poverty by giving poor people money so they are no longer poor. Who hasn't thought of this solution? It is so obvious. But what would happen if we did this?

The Income Maintenance Experiments

This is exactly what some social scientists wanted to know, and they convinced the government to go along with their plans. They developed what are known as the *income maintenance experiments*. Between 1975 and 1979, millions of dollars were given to thousands of poor people to find out what they would spend it on. Would they spend the money on liquor or food for the kids? Would they work less? How would the free money affect relations between husbands and wives?

The study was well done. Random samples of low-income people in Denver and Seattle were selected. Different subsamples were given different amounts of money. If people got jobs or earned more money, the amount they received was cut slowly. This was to help avoid the **welfare wall**—the disincentive to work that comes when the amount that people earn from working is not much more than what they get on welfare. The families were guaranteed this money for either three or five years—no matter how they spent the money—so they could change their living habits without worrying that the program might suddenly end.

What were the results? Some people did work less or drop out of the labor market. The reduction in work averaged 9 percent for husbands, 23 percent for wives, and 15 percent for female heads of households (West and Steiger 1980). The people who quit their jobs enjoyed the extra money and were glad to get away from poor paying, unpleasant jobs. Most people, however, continued to work as much as before.

Compared with control groups, the people in this program spent more on durable goods (cars, refrigerators, TVs) than they did on nondurable goods (food, entertainment) (Pozdena and Johnson 1979). They also bought more housewares and clothing (Johnson et al. 1979). In households headed by women, most of the new spending went for better housing. With the security that came from a regular income over several years, they also saved less and went into debt more—just like many families who are not poor.

One of the interesting consequences of this experiment was that it broke up marriages (a finding that has been challenged by some sociologists [Cain and Wissoker 1990]). Women who had been putting up with unhappy marriages found that their new source of income made it possible for them to leave their husbands. Congress was upset to learn of this and canceled the program because it did not want to encourage families to break up. Thus, the income maintenance experiments had some major and controversial effects on the lives of the poor. How you regard those effects depends on whether you think people should work regardless of the nature of the job, and whether you think they should keep their family together regardless of the nature of the marriage.

EDUCATION ACCOUNTS

How Could We Lose on This Proposal?

A promising proposal is *education accounts*. The government could establish a credit of, say, $35,000 for everyone at age 18 who graduates from high school (Haveman and Scholz 1994–95; Oliver and Shapiro 1995). This money (which would be adjusted annually for inflation) could be used only for education. Based on their background, abilities, and preferences, youths could choose from approved colleges and technical and vocational schools. The money would go for direct educational costs, such as tuition, books, and living expenses. Each youth would receive an annual statement of the value of the account.

An attractive aspect of this proposal, besides allowing individual choice, is that ultimately it would cost little or nothing: Such a program would reduce welfare and increase people's earning power *for their entire lives*. The additional taxes from those larger earnings could pay for the program. If any proposal is a "no-brainer," this one is. (Of course, I must admit that I have a bias toward encouraging people to go to college.)

PROVIDING JOBS

Philosophical Disagreement about How to Provide Jobs

Perhaps the most direct way to deal with poverty and to avoid the criticisms of those who don't want to give anything away is to provide jobs. President Roosevelt lifted millions out of poverty during the Great Depression by providing jobs building bridges, roads, parks, and public buildings. Creating jobs also has the benefit of stimulating the economy, for these workers spend the money that they earn. This, in turn, produces even more jobs. People who approve of job creation disagree violently, however, about how those jobs should be created. One group says that it is the government's responsibility to create jobs; the other insists that this is the role of private business.

Applying This Policy to the Urban Poor and to Women

This debate never will be resolved. Rather than becoming embroiled in it, let's note that regardless of the path we choose to get there, the important factor is that the jobs be available. Also important is that the jobs either provide a wage that lifts people out of poverty or else serve as a stepping-stone to jobs that will. Dead-end jobs that keep people in poverty do not meet the goal. And because good jobs are often in the suburbs, where they are inaccessible to the inner-city poor, we need to buttress this social policy by providing transportation that helps move the poor to the jobs. We also need to recognize that poverty clusters around women with children, so quality child care facilities also need to be made available.

The Future of the Problem

Two Voices

Poverty begs for a solution. The homeless, the rural poor, and those trapped in the inner cities can't be wished away. But no solution comes without a high price tag.

Some want vast programs that spend immense sums on the poor. They say, "Let's just do it, because it's right, and we can worry about the bill some other time." "Besides," they add, "if we can afford all those new weapons for the military, we can afford any programs that will help the poor." Others, in contrast, argue that we should establish effective programs to help the poor, but that it is not right to saddle future generations with our spending. They say that "If we can't pay for programs now, we can't afford them."

Muddling Along

Most Americans seem to find themselves between these positions—feeling that it is not right to have homeless people huddled over heating grates, or children's futures blocked because of their parents' poverty—but not knowing what to do about the situation. With the politicians and the public not seeing any clear solutions, and with the poor remaining disorganized and having little political clout, I anticipate that we shall continue to muddle along with our present programs. From time to time, there will be modifications, a little tinkering that gives the appearance of progress. Current tinkering includes limits on how long people can receive welfare and some modest job training programs.

It would be much more satisfying for you—and for me—if I were to see Utopia just around the corner: The government decides to eliminate poverty. Their solutions work, and everyone enjoys a decent standard of living. There are no more poor people. Everyone is prosperous and happy. But such a rosy future does not match reality.

The Coming Conflict

As conflict theorists stress, we will give the poor as little as is necessary to prevent our cities from going up in flames. When hundreds of thousands across the land reach the new time limits of welfare and are cut off from benefits, we don't know what will happen. If the times are prosperous, jobs will be available and problems will be averted. If our inner cities start to explode like a series of powder kegs across the United States—or even if the government faces such a threat—the choice will be to call out the National Guard to stop the burning and looting or to change the eligibility rules of welfare. Is there any question of the choice that would be made?

SUMMARY

1. There are several types of *poverty*. *Biological poverty* refers to starvation and malnutrition. *Official poverty* refers to falling below arbitrary standards set by the government. *Relative poverty* is feeling poor by comparison with others, although the individual may be objectively well off. Poverty follows lines of age, gender, and race-ethnicity.

2. Symbolic interactionists show how the meaning of income (for example, whether people see themselves as being rich or poor) differs from its objective measures. Functionalists emphasize that social inequality is a way of allocating talented people to demanding tasks and less-talented people to less-demanding tasks. Functionalists point out that although poverty may be dysfunctional for individuals, it is functional for society. Conflict theorists stress that those who win the struggle for society's limited resources oppress those who lose. They also stress that a *power elite* of top politicians and corporate and military leaders make society's big decisions. *Pluralists* disagree. They view society as made up of many groups that compete with one another in a marketplace of power and ideas.

3. Why do some people remain in poverty year after year? Some suggest that the reason is a *culture of poverty*, self-

defeating behaviors that parents pass on to their children. Most sociologists, however, view what is called the culture of poverty not as the *cause* of poverty, but instead as the *result* of poverty. Why do some countries remain in poverty year after year? Some suggest that this is due to a national culture of poverty. Others look to *economic colonialism* and exploitation by national elites.

4. Policies for dealing with poverty have been as diverse as the beliefs about its causes. In the seventeenth century, poverty was considered God's will, and it was a person's religious duty to help the poor. During the Great Depression, the poor were considered victims of economic conditions and were helped on a mass basis. Today, our welfare programs cause bitter debate. Rules have been tightened to make fewer people eligible for welfare and to "encourage" the poor to take jobs.

5. The future is likely to bring a continuation of our piecemeal welfare programs, with Americans continuing to be divided on the matter of the "deserving" and "undeserving" poor and to what extent they should be helped.

KEY TERMS

Biological poverty   Material deprivation so severe that it affects someone's biological functioning.

Capitalist economy   An economy based on the private ownership of the means of production, the pursuit of profit, and market competition. *See* Socialist economy.

Culture of poverty   Characteristics of the poor that help the poor stay poor. They include family violence, alcoholism, and low self-esteem.

Culture of wealth   Characteristics of the wealthy that help keep them from falling down the social class ladder.

Economic colonialism   One nation exploiting another nation's resources.

Economy   A society's system of producing and distributing goods and services.

False consciousness   Karl Marx's term for the workers' illusion that they are not oppressed; workers might think of themselves as entrepreneurs or investors, for example.

Feminization of poverty   The growth of poverty among women and children.

Interest groups   Groups organized around different interests (from the dairy industry to animal rights).

Mass poverty   Poverty so widespread that most people are poor.

National debt   The total amount that a nation owes; computed by adding its annual deficits and subtractings is annual surpluses

Official poverty   The level of income that a government recognizes as constituting poverty.

Poverty line   The official measure of poverty; calculated as three times a low-cost food budget.

Power elite   A small group of wealthy, powerful people who are said to make the major economic and political decisions in the United States. Also known as the *ruling class.*

Progressive tax   Tax rates that increase with income.

Real income   Income in constant dollars, that is, with inflation removed.

Relative poverty   Deprivation as measured by the standards of one's society and culture. On a personal level, people think of themselves as poor or not poor on the basis of their reference groups.

Residual poverty   Pockets of poverty in an otherwise affluent society.

Social class   A group of people who occupy the same rung on the economic ladder.

Social inequality   The unequal distribution of wealth, income, power, and other opportunities.

Socialist economy   An economy based on the public ownership of the means of production, central planning, and the distribution of goods without a profit motive. *See* Capitalist economy.

Structural inequality   Inequality that is built into social institutions.

Wealth   Savings, property, investments, income, and other economic assets.

Welfare wall   The disincentive to work when the income from working is not much more than the income from welfare.

THINKING CRITICALLY ABOUT CHAPTER 7

1. What is your reaction to Herbert Gans' observations on how poverty helps society? Do you think Gans is serious? (See the Thinking Critically box on page 219.)
2. Review the different rates of poverty by age, sex, geography, and race-ethnicity. Now explain them. To answer this question sociologically, you might want to first ask, "Why don't all groups have the same rate of poverty?"
3. A central debate in sociology has been whether the power elite or pluralist view is correct. Which do you think is right? Why?
4. What do you think can be done to solve the social problem of poverty?

CHAPTER 8

Race and Ethnic Relations

D AMN RIGHT I'M TEACHING VIOLENCE! It's about time somebody is telling you to get violent, whitey. You better start making dossiers, names, addresses, phone numbers, car license numbers on every damn Jew rabbi in this land.

—*William Potter Gale, a former colonel who served under General Douglas MacArthur in the Philippines in World War II*

Today we see the evil is coming out of government. To go out and shoot a Negro is foolish. It's not the Negro in the alley who's responsible for what's wrong with this country. It's the traitors in Washington.

—*Thomas Robb, publisher of "The Torch," a Klan newsletter*

Hitler is the reincarnation of the prophet Elijah. *Mein Kampf* is part of the Bible. The "terrible day of destruction" is coming.

—*Keith Gilbert, who started his own church, Restored Church of Jesus Christ, in Post Falls, Idaho*

The Klan called the mother of a white teenage girl who had been seen with black companions and warned her: "If you can't do anything about it, the Klan can, and will."

—*According to Bill McGlocklin, the Grand Kaliff of the Invisible Empire, Knights of the Ku Klux Klan in Denham Springs, Louisiana*

Outside Hayden Lake, Idaho, a neatly lettered sign—"Whites Only"—used to mark the entrance to the Church of Jesus Christ Christian. Members of the congregation carried rifles and wore Nazi swastikas. The group lost their property in a lawsuit. Richard Butler, the church's leader, argues that Jesus Christ was an Aryan, not a Jew, and Jews should be destroyed as the children of Satan. He keeps a photo of Adolf Hitler in his living room.

Based on King 1979; Starr 1985b; Murphy 1999.

The Problem in Sociological Perspective

Prejudice and discrimination are facts of life in the United States. Hostilities and tensions among racial and ethnic groups surface in street confrontations, disturbances in our schools, and the media-captivating activities of extremist groups such as those profiled in the opening vignette.

Discrimination as a Worldwide Problem

Prejudice and discrimination are common around the world. In northern Ireland, Protestants discriminate against Roman Catholics; in Israel, wealthier Jews, primarily of European descent, discriminate against poorer Jews of Asian and African backgrounds; in Japan, the Japanese discriminate against just about anyone who isn't Japanese, especially the Koreans and Ainu, who live there (Spivak 1980; Fields 1986; "Law Enacted . . ." 1997). In every society around the world, men discriminate against women.

Prejudice or Discrimination?

The difference between prejudice and discrimination is simple. **Prejudice** is an attitude—a prejudging of some sort. Usually the prejudging is negative, but it can be positive. **Discrimination,** in contrast, is an action. It refers to singling out a person or persons for unfair treatment. The unfair treatment can be based on almost anything. Discrimination is often based on appearance—age, race–ethnicity, sex, height, weight, or disability. Income and religious or political beliefs are other common reasons for discrimination.

Minority and Dominant Groups

When people are discriminated against because they belong to a group, they are called a minority. **Minorities,** as sociologist Louis Wirth (1945) defined them, are

242

groups of people who are singled out for unequal treatment on the basis of their physical or cultural characteristics and who regard themselves as objects of collective discrimination. Discrimination denies minorities full participation in their society.

"Minority" in this sense does not necessarily mean a *numerical* minority in a society. In colonial India, for example, a handful of British discriminated against millions of Indians, and in South Africa the black majority was relatively powerless, negatively stereotyped, and discriminated against. Although there are more women than men in each society, universally, men discriminate against women. Accordingly, sociologists refer to those who do the discriminating as the **dominant group;** this group has more power and privileges and higher social status.

The Origin of Minority Groups

What is the origin of minority groups? There are two origins: political expansion and migration. Some groups become minorities when a government expands its political boundaries. As anthropologists Charles Wagley and Marvin Harris (1958) pointed out, there are no minority groups in small tribal societies (except for females, whom we discuss in the next chapter). This is because everyone in tribal societies is "related"; they all speak the same language, practice the same customs, share similar values, and belong to the same physical stock. A second way that minority groups originate is through migration—when people who have different characteristics move into a political unit. The migration can be involuntary, as with Africans who were forcibly brought to the United States, or voluntary, as with Turks who chose to move to Germany for work.

Minorities come into existence, then, when people who have different customs, languages, values, or physical characteristics come under control of the same state organization. There, some groups who share physical and cultural traits discriminate against those who have different traits. The losers in this power struggle are forced into minority group status; the winners enjoy the higher status and greater privileges that their dominance brings.

Wagley and Harris noted that all minorities share these five characteristics:

Five Characteristics of Minority Groups

1. Their membership in a minority group is not voluntary but comes through birth.
2. Their physical or cultural traits are held in low esteem by the dominant group.
3. They are treated unequally by the dominant group.
4. They tend to feel strong group solidarity because of their physical or cultural traits—and the disadvantages that these traits bring.
5. They tend to marry within their group.

Because they possess similar cultural or physical traits, marry within the same group, and experience discrimination at the hands of a powerful group, a feeling of common identity often unites the members of a minority group. This identity (a sense of "we" versus "them") may be so strong that they feel that they share a common destiny. Despite such a sense of identity, shared experiences do not result in the same goals. Wirth (1945) identified four objectives of minority groups:

Four Objectives of Minority Groups

1. *Pluralism:* The group wants to live peacefully with the dominant group, but yet maintain its distinctive culture—the differences that set it apart and that are so important to its identity.
2. *Assimilation:* Focusing on the culture that they share with the dominant group, members of the minority group want to be absorbed into the larger society. They want to be treated as individuals, not as members of a separate group.
3. *Secession:* Wanting cultural and political independence, the minority seeks to separate itself nationally.
4. *Militancy:* Convinced of its own superiority, the minority wants a reversal in status and seeks to dominate the society.

Dominant groups also differ in their goals and attitudes toward minorities. Sociologists George Simpson and J. Milton Yinger identified six policies that dominant groups adopt. As you can see from Figure 8-1, these policies can parallel or oppose the aims of minorities. Let's examine these policies, beginning with the most humane.

Six Policies of Dominant Groups

1. *Pluralism.* **Pluralism** means that a dominant group permits or even encourages cultural differences. The United States' "hands-off" policy toward immigrant associations and foreign-language newspapers is an example of pluralism. (During times of war or terrorism, however, the government infiltrates and spies on immigrant associations.) Switzerland provides an outstanding example of successful pluralism: Although the French, Italian, German, and Romish Swiss have retained their separate languages and other customs, they live peacefully together in a political and economic unit. None of these groups is a minority.

2. *Assimilation.* **Assimilation** is an attempt to "eliminate" the minority by absorbing it into the mainstream culture. In its more severe form, *forced* assimilation, the dominant group bans the minority's religion, language, and other distinctive customs. In the former Soviet Union, the Russians treated Armenians this way. *Permissible* assimilation, in contrast, permits the minority to adopt the dominant group's patterns at its own speed. In the United States, cultural minorities have been expected to give up their differences, but racial minorities have been expected to maintain their physical differences by marrying within their own groups.

3. *Segregation.* Also known as *continued subjugation*, segregation is an attempt by the dominant group to keep a minority "in its place," that is, subservient and exploitable. When whites were in control of South Africa, they despised the blacks and their culture, but they found their presence necessary. As Simpson and Yinger (1972) put it, who else would do the hard work? To maintain their own dominance and social distance from the minority, this small group of whites used **apartheid** (uh-paŕ-tate), the forced segregation of blacks and whites in almost all spheres of life. Because of international sanctions, apartheid was dismantled.

4. *Internal colonialism.* This policy refers to exploiting the minority group's labor. Internal colonialism accompanies segregation and precedes the next two policies, population transfer and genocide.

5. *Population transfer.* In *direct* **population transfer,** the minority is forced to leave. This is what happened when King Ferdinand and Queen Isabella (who financed Columbus' voyage to North America) drove the Jews and Moors out of Spain and when the U.S. government forced Japanese Americans into camps during World War II. *Indirect population transfer* means making life so miserable for a

FIGURE 8-1 *Policies of Dominant Groups Toward Minority Groups*

Source: Henslin 2005; based on Simpson and Yinger 1972.

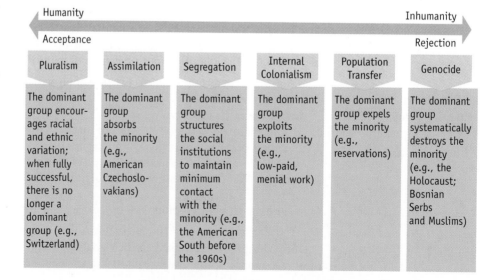

Pluralism	Assimilation	Segregation	Internal Colonialism	Population Transfer	Genocide
The dominant group encourages racial and ethnic variation; when fully successful, there is no longer a dominant group (e.g., Switzerland)	The dominant group absorbs the minority (e.g., American Czechoslovakians)	The dominant group structures the social institutions to maintain minimum contact with the minority (e.g., the American South before the 1960s)	The dominant group exploits the minority (e.g., low-paid, menial work)	The dominant group expels the minority (e.g., reservations)	The dominant group systematically destroys the minority (e.g., the Holocaust; Bosnian Serbs and Muslims)

Humanity ←——————————————————————→ Inhumanity

Acceptance ——— Rejection

minority that its members "choose" to leave. Facing the bitter conditions of czarist Russia, for example, millions of Jews made this "choice."

The Holocaust

6. *Genocide.* Hatred and greed can lead the dominant group to turn to a policy of extermination, or **genocide.** The most infamous example is the Holocaust, when the Nazis ran death camps to systematically kill minorities. Between 1933 and 1945 the Nazis slaughtered about 6 million Jews, a quarter of a million Gypsies, hundreds of thousands of Slavs, and unknown numbers of homosexuals, communists, people with disabilities, and mentally ill people whom Hitler did not consider "pure" enough to be part of his mythical Aryan race.

Hitler was convinced that **race**—the inherited physical characteristics that identify a group of people—was reality. He believed that a race called the Aryans was responsible for the cultural achievements of Europe. These tall, fair-skinned, mostly blond-haired people—a biologically superior "super race"—had a destiny: to establish a still higher culture, a new world order. To fulfill this destiny required forcing "inferior" races to perform tasks that were considered too lowly for the Aryans, avoiding the "racial contamination" that breeding with inferior races would engender, and isolating or destroying races that might endanger Aryan culture.

Although most people today find Hitler's ideas bizarre, in the 1930s both laypeople and the scientific community took such ideas seriously. Many biologists and anthropologists, for example, believed that some races were inherently superior to others. It is not surprising that these scientists always concluded that Caucasians were the superior race, for they themselves were Caucasian.

Race as a Social Reality vs. Race as Historical Myth

Ideas of racial superiority that justify one group's rule over another may be less popular today, but the idea of race remains a social reality. Almost everyone identifies with some "racial" group, classifies other people into "racial" groups, and treats them accordingly. Everyone has ideas, opinions, and attitudes on this topic, and these feelings and beliefs motivate their behavior. In this sense race remains very real.

In modern biology, however, pure race is a myth. People show so great a mixture of physical characteristics—skin color, hair texture, nose and head shapes, height, eye color, and so on—that no pure races can be substantiated. Instead, human characteristics flow endlessly into one another, and this melding makes any attempt to draw sharp lines arbitrary. Large groupings of humans, however, can be classified by blood type and gene frequencies. Depending on the criteria, biologists and anthropologists can develop arbitrary listings that contain any number of "races." Some scientists have classified humans into as few as two "races," others into as many as 2,000 (Montagu 1964). The Thinking Critically box on the next page illustrates just how arbitrary racial classifications are.

Because the idea of race is so embedded in our culture, race is a social reality that social scientists must confront. As sociologists deal with this topic, they often prefer to avoid a term so imprecise and sometimes provocative as *race*. Many, as I will

GROSSE POLITISCHE SCHAU IM BIBLIOTHEKSBAU DES DEUTSCHEN MUSEUMS ZU MÜNCHEN · AB 8. NOVEMBER 1937 · TÄGLICH GEÖFFNET VON 10-21 UHR

Before and during World War II, Adolf Hitler, the chancellor of Germany, was determined to create hatred of Jews. To do so, he harnessed the propaganda machine of the state, including schools, movies, radio, books, newspapers, magazines, and posters, such as the one shown here. This poster is an advertisement for the notorious anti-Semitic movie, The Eternal Jew, *which in 1937 was shown daily from 10 a.m. to 9 p.m. at the Munich Museum.*

Thinking Critically about Social Problems

CAN A PLANE RIDE CHANGE YOUR RACE?

According to common sense, our racial classifications represent biological differences. Sociologists, in contrast, stress that what we call races are *social* classifications, not biological categories.

Sociologists point out that *our "race" depends more on the society in which we live than on our biological characteristics.* For example, the racial categories that are common in the United States are merely one of *numerous* ways by which people around the world classify physical appearances. Although groups around the world use different categories, each group assumes that its categories are natural, merely a logical response to visible biology.

To better understand this essential sociological point—that race is more social than it is biological—consider this: In the United States, children who are born to the same parents are all of the same race. "What could be more natural?" Americans assume. But in Brazil, children who are born to the same parents may be of different races—if their appearances differ. "What could be more natural?" assume Brazilians.

Consider how Americans usually classify a child born to a "black" mother and a "white" father. Why do they usually say that the child is "black"? Wouldn't it be equally logical to classify the child as "white"? Similarly, if a child's grandmother is "black" but all her other ancestors are "white," the child is often considered "black." Yet she has much more "white blood" than "black blood." Why, then, is she considered "black"? Certainly not because of biology. Rather, such thinking is a legacy of slavery. Whites—in an attempt to preserve the "purity" of their "race" in the face of numerous children whose fathers were white slave masters and mothers were black slaves—classified anyone with even a "drop of black blood" as "not white."

Even a plane ride can change a person's race. In the city of Salvador in Brazil, people classify one another by the color of their skin and eyes, the breadth of their nose and lips, and the color and curliness of their hair. They use at least seven terms for what we call white and black. Consider again a U.S. child who has "white" and "black" parents. If she flies to Brazil, she is no longer "black"; she now belongs to one of their several "whiter" categories (Fish 1995).

On the flight just mentioned, did the girl's "race" actually change? Our common sense revolts at this, I know, but it actually did. We want to argue that because her biological characteristics remain unchanged, her race remains unchanged. This is because we think of race as biological, when *race is actually a label we use to describe perceived biological characteristics.* Simply put, the race we "are" depends on *where* we are—on who is doing the classifying.

"Racial" classifications are fluid, not fixed. You can see change occurring even now in those used in the United States. The category "multiracial," for example, indicates changing thought and perception. This change is picked up by the new category on U.S. census forms, "two or more races."

FOR YOUR CONSIDERATION

How would you ever explain to "Joe Six-Pack" the sociological point that race is more a social classification than a biological one? Can you come up with any arguments to refute this view? How do you think our racial-ethnic categories will change in the future?

Ethnicity

do in this chapter, use the term *ethnic* or *race-ethnic* group. Derived from the Greek word *ethnos*, meaning "people" or "nation," an **ethnic group** refers to people who identify with one another on the basis of their ancestry and cultural heritage. Their sense of belonging may center around unique physical characteristics, foods, dress, names, language, music, and religion. As we just saw, collective discrimination and intermarriage may also be significant factors.

The Scope of the Problem

Many ethnic groups with different histories, customs, and identities populate the United States. The largest groups are listed in Figure 8-2.

Immigration and Anglo/Conformity

U.S. immigrants, whatever their background, confronted **Anglo-conformity;** that is, they were expected to maintain English institutions (as modified by the American

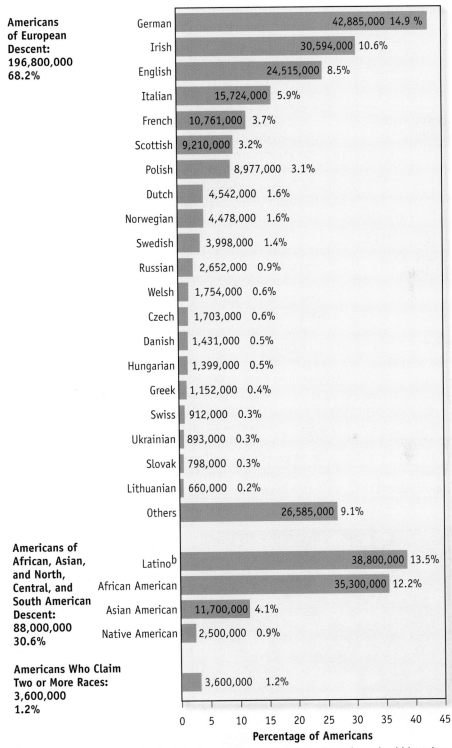

FIGURE 8-2 *U.S. Racial and Ethnic Groups*[a]

Source: By the author, based on *Statistical Abstract of the United States* 2002:Tables 36, 38, 1373; 2003:Table 43; Bernstein and Bergman 2003.

[a] Due to inconsistencies by the U.S. Census Bureau, the totals shown here should be taken as approximate.

[b] Most Latinos trace at least part of their ancestry to Europe.

The Melting Pot

Revolution), speak the English language, and adopt other Anglo-Saxon ways of life. The United States was supposedly destined to become a modified version of England. Many thought that the evolving society would become a **melting pot;** it would "melt" the European immigrants together into a new cultural and biological blend. As sociologist Milton Gordon (1964) put it, "the stocks and folkways of Europe [would be], figuratively speaking, indiscriminately mixed in the political pot of the emerging nation and melted together by the fires of American influence and interaction into a distinctly new type."

Ideological Myth vs. Reality

The melting pot became a reality for most European immigrants; most lost their specific ethnic identities and merged into a mainstream culture. Although individuals may identify themselves as "three-quarters German and one-quarter mixed Italian and Greek—with some English thrown in," they tend to think of themselves as "American." Some groups, however, have retained their unique cultures and ethnic identities. In recent years, large numbers of immigrants, especially those from Mexico, Cuba, Haiti, Vietnam, and India, have retained a strong ethnic identity.

Despite their desire to melt into U.S. culture, some non-Anglo Americans find the melting to be elusive. Differences in appearance evoke sterotypes, as Nazli Kibria, who did research on Asian Americans, explains in the Spotlight on Research box on the next page.

The concept of a melting pot also conceals as much as it reveals, for it referred to specific groups of Americans only. Americans of Anglo background never intended for non-Anglos to become part of a "biological mix." On the contrary, they wanted to enforce "racial" purity; they even passed laws prohibiting blacks and whites from marrying.

Prejudice and Stereotypes

Each new group of immigrants confronted prejudice, and new arrivals still do. Helping to keep prejudice alive are **stereotypes,** generalizations of what people are like. For example, the English immigrants despised the Irish immigrants who followed them, viewing them as dirty, lazy, untrustworthy drunkards. The Irish survived this stereotyping, became "respectable," and joined mainstream society. Minorities also hold stereotypes of the dominant group, and today whites and minorities hold debasing stereotypes of one another (Leonard and Locke 1993). As the Technology box on page 250 features, some people use the Internet to stir up hatred.

When Does a Social Problem Exist?

Prejudice, negative stereotypes, and discrimination are not necessarily social problems. Even if people are prejudiced against one another, diverse groups can coexist peacefully. A social problem exists when people get upset because prejudice and discrimination deprive minorities of the rights to which their citizenship entitles them. And if prejudice turns into hatred or conflict, ethnic relations are severely troubled.

As with other social problems, however, exactly what is problematic about ethnic relations depends on one's vantage point. As the chapter's opening vignette indicates, for members of the Ku Klux Klan and its sympathizers, minorities are the source of the social problem. These people think that minority group members who mix with the mainstream and prosper do so at the expense of whites.

Others are upset that prejudice and discrimination have thwarted the American ideal of equality of "life, liberty, and the pursuit of happiness." They see this failure of principles that the Constitution guarantees, along with the harm and tensions it

Underlying some aspects of U.S. race relations was the ideal that the United States would become a melting pot of the nations of the world. Sifted together, immigrants would become a new people. As discussed in the text, this ideal was more ideology than reality and did not apply to everyone.

SPOTLIGHT ON RESEARCH

Being a "Foreign" American

Nazli Kibria, Professor of Sociology at Boston University, did research on second-generation Chinese and Korean Americans. She explored their experience of being identified by others as "Asian." In this essay, she reports on how "racial identities" serve as markers (or signals) in everyday social encounters. These "markers" are based on how people perceive the physical characteristics of others.

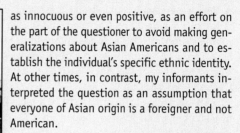

I use the term "second-generation Chinese and Korean Americans" to refer to people of Chinese and Korean ancestry who were born and-or from a young age reared in the United States. Based on their encounters with people of non-Asian origin, I explored the ways in which they experience the identity marker of "Asian race" in their daily lives.

In their everyday social encounters, non-Asian Americans often assume that Chinese and Korean Americans are "foreigners." With the perception of "Asian" often comes an image of an unassimilable alien—a presence that is fundamentally and unalterably outside of, if not diametrically opposite to, what is "American." Many of my informants said that they frequently were asked, "Where are you from?" While this question may be intended as an inquiry about one's regional origin in the United States (e.g., "Are you from Southern California?"), when asked of Asian Americans it is often meant as a question about nationality and ethnic origins. In fact, informants told me that if they answered the question in local terms (such as, "I'm from Boston"), the person often followed up with something like, "Yes, but where are you really from?"

My informants had several ways of responding to these queries. In some situations, they interpreted the question

as innocuous or even positive, as an effort on the part of the questioner to avoid making generalizations about Asian Americans and to establish the individual's specific ethnic identity. At other times, in contrast, my informants interpreted the question as an assumption that everyone of Asian origin is a foreigner and not American.

Among the strategies that my informants used to neutralize or at least to deflect the assumption of their foreignness were disidentifiers. To remove an identity of "foreignness" and provide an identity of "American," they used symbols, such as language, dress, demeanor, and even the people with whom they were seen or associated. Language was one of their main disidentifiers. During an encounter with strangers, they would deflect their presumed foreignness by speaking fluent and unaccented English. The need to use disidentifiers produced an awareness among my informants that for Asian Americans, the achievement and acceptance of an American identity requires vigilance and work.

Ascribing "foreignness" to second-generation Chinese and Korean Americans not only casts doubt upon their identity as Americans, but also it signals authentic ethnicity. That is, the dominant society assumes that second-generation Chinese and Korean Americans have ties to a community and culture that is either located or rooted outside the U.S. mainstream. These ties are assumed to be strong and genuine—authentic, rather than contrived or fake. My informants were especially aware of this assumption of ethnic authenticity when a non-Asian American would ask them to interpret Asian, Korean, or Chinese cultural practices, or in some other way to display their ethnic cultural knowledge.

**Numbers Fail
to Show the Significance
of Discrimination**

engenders, as the social problem of race–ethnic relations. This is how we shall look at the social problem of race–ethnic relations—as discrimination that hurts people.

The significance of discrimination goes far beyond any statistics about how many people are denied some particular benefit of society. Too often, we end up focusing on such cold numbers. Although numbers are important, what we often miss is how discrimination can touch all areas of its victims' lives. Because of discrimination, people often see themselves through the very lens that the dominant group uses to view them. They can come to deprecate ("put down") their own abilities, to think of themselves as less capable, less worthy, and, ultimately, as less human. Discrimination, in short, can detract from people's sense of being, the sense of their own humanity.

Technology and Social Problems
WHAT SHOULD WE DO ABOUT HATE SPEECH?

The Internet has proven a marvelous source of information. I personally am extremely pleased that the Internet developed, as I am now able to live and travel in other countries and still do what used to be called "library" research. Libraries, government agencies, and other sources lie at my fingertips—waiting to be accessed via telephone or satellite.

The Internet is also proving to be a remarkable source of misinformation. Anyone can put up a Web site and fill it with distortions of truth or with outright lies. People can nurse grudges, seek revenge for perceived wrongs, and fan hatred.

Such negative communications are upsetting, especially the hatred. Consider these statements:

Civil Rights come out of the barrel of a gun, and we mean to give the niggers and Jews all the civil rights they can handle. . . . Our security team will see that no live targets escape from the range. Any who refuse to run or can't for any reason will be fed to the dogs. The dogs appreciate a good feed as much as we do.
—*An invitation to a summer conference held by the Aryan Nations at Hayden Lake, Idaho. The group's founder, Richard Butler, is a former Lockheed executive. (Statements quoted in Murphy 1999)*

Who's pimping the world? The hairy hands of the Zionist. . . . The so-called Jew claims that there were six million in Nazi Germany. I am here today to tell you that there is absolutely no . . . evidence to substantiate, to prove that six million so-called Jews lost their lives in Nazi Germany. . . . Don't let no hooked-nose, bagel-eating, lox-eating, perpetrating-a-fraud so-called Jew who just crawled out of the ghettoes of Europe just a few days ago . . .
—*Statements of Khalid Abdul Muhammad, as quoted in Herbert 1998.*

Hatred knows no race-ethnic boundaries; the first statement was made by a white, the second by an African American.

Should we ban such statements—and punish their authors as lawbreakers? Should we allow such statements to be circulated as part of free speech, regardless of their inflammatory rhetoric, twisting of fact, prejudice, or hatred?

Canada has taken steps to ban hate speech. Ingrid Rimland of San Diego runs a Web site on which she sells anti-Semitic literature and publicizes the views of Ernst Zundel. Zundel, an immigrant from Germany who has lived in Canada 40 years, denies the Holocaust took place and preaches anti-Semitism. Canadian authorities accuse Zundel of controlling Rimland's Web site and have charged him under laws that prohibit the use of telephone lines to spread hate messages based on race, religion, or ethnic origin ("Canada Tries to . . ." 1998).

The technological solution may be a "hate filter" developed by human rights groups. When installed on a computer, this software blocks access to Web sites designed by those espousing intolerance: the Ku Klux Klan, skinheads, and neo-Nazis, as well as those that spew hatred for homosexuals or other groups.

Some say that in order to expose the ridiculousness of bad ideas, we should let them be viewed in the cold, hard light of day. Others take the position that censorship of even hatred is wrong; it is an attack on free speech and threatens us all. Still others say that hatred needs to be fought in any way it can, including passing new laws and using filters. What do you think?

Measures of Discrimination

Income

The Significance of Income

We don't have adequate measures of this more intimate aspect of discrimination, however, so we will have to concentrate on its surface manifestations. As we do so, keep in mind that for millions of Americans, discrimination is the central fact of their lives.

The first thing we can note is the highly visible area of economic well-being. As Table 8-1 shows, family incomes of African Americans, Latinos, and Native Americans are only 62 percent of the average income of white families. Measures of economic well-being—income, poverty, and unemployment—produce cold statistics. Behind these abstract measures are people whose lives are affected adversely. At issue is whether they can afford health care, nourishing food, and education—not whether they can afford

TABLE 8-1 Indicators of Relative Economic Well-Being

	FAMILY INCOME	
	MEDIAN FAMILY INCOME	PERCENTAGE OF WHITE INCOME
White	$51,224	
Asian American	$54,500	106%
Native American	$31,929*	62%
African American	$31,778	62%
Latino	$31,663	62%

	POVERTY	
	PERCENTAGE BELOW POVERTY	PERCENTAGE OF WHITE POVERTY
White	9.8%	
Asian American	10.8%	110%
Latino	22.8%	233%
African American	23.6%	241%
Native American	28.4%	290%

	EDUCATION	
	PERCENTAGE WHO HAVE COMPLETED COLLEGE	PERCENTAGE OF WHITE COLLEGE COMPLETION
White	26%	
Asian American	44%	169%
African American	17%	65%
Native American	13%	50%
Latino	11%	42%

*I doubt the accuracy of this total. It conflicts too greatly with the lower incomes for Native Americans that were reported in preceding years; it is suspiciously close to the incomes reported for African Americans and Latinos; and it does not account for the greater poverty of Native Americans. The explanation could be Indian casinos. If so, this would mask huge disparities among tribes.

Sources: By the author, based on *Statistical Abstract of the United States* 2002:Tables 36, 37, 38, 40, 771; *American Fact Finder* 2003:Tables GCT-P11, P12, P14.

a boat or a new car, or whether they can afford to vacation out of state—economic decisions that middle-class people might make.

A Matter of Life and Death

Such matters can even translate into life and death. Look at Table 8-2 on the next page. As you can see, an African-American baby has *more than twice* the chance of dying as does a white baby; the chances of a mother dying during childbirth are *three* times higher for African-American women. On average, African-American women die about five years younger than white women, African-American men six years younger than white men (*Statistical Abstract* 2003:Table 105). As measured by number of days sick, African Americans are not as healthy as whites. (Unfortunately, the source does not contain data for other race-ethnic groups.) In short, higher income provides better nutrition, housing, and medical care—and a longer life.

Education and Income

As you can also see from Table 8-1, the average family income of Asian Americans is higher than that of white families. As this table also shows, a much larger percentage of Asian Americans than any other group—including whites—has completed college and is equipped for the better jobs. This leads to the question of whether the lower family incomes of the other groups are due, not to discrimination, but to a lack of preparation to compete in the U.S. economic system. The issue is more complicated

TABLE 8-2 Health and Race-Ethnicity

	INFANT MORTALITY*	MATERNAL DEATHS*	LIFE EXPECTANCY
White	5.7	7.2	77.7
Black	14.0	24.7	72.2

*The rate is the number per 1,000. Infant mortality refers to the number of infants under 1 year old who die in a year per 1,000 live births. The sources do not provide data for other race-ethnic groups.
Source: By the author, based on *Statistical Abstract of the United States* 2003:Tables 105, 113.

than such a question would pose, however, for racial-ethnic discrimination runs through U.S. society. This means that we must also ask how discrimination leads to lack of preparation, which, in turn, leads to some groups ending up with less education.

Individual Discrimination

To understand the effects of discrimination, we need to move beyond thinking in terms of **individual discrimination,** one person treating another badly on the basis of race or ethnicity. Although this certainly creates problems, it primarily is a matter for the individuals to resolve. The law, however, may become involved if one person illegally withholds, say, employment or housing from someone on the basis of race-ethnicity.

Institutional Discrimination

Sociologists encourage us to move beyond individual situations and to think in broader terms. They point to **institutional discrimination** as the essence of the social problem. This is discrimination that is built into the social system that oppresses whole groups. For example, for generations whites denied African Americans the right to vote, join labor unions, work at higher-paying and more prestigious jobs, attend good schools, or receive care at decent hospitals. The group that controls most real estate sales in the United States, the National Association of Real Estate Boards (NAR), used to support racial discrimination as a *moral* act. Its 1924 code of ethics stated:

Example of Real Estate

> A Realtor should never be instrumental in introducing into a neighborhood . . . members of any race or nationality, or individuals whose presence will clearly be detrimental to property values in that neighborhood. (Newman et al. 1978:149)

The federal government had the same policy. To obtain loans from the Federal Housing Authority (FHA), developers of subdivisions had to exclude nonwhites (Valocchi 1994; Oliver and Shapiro 1995). Even after World War II, the FHA denied loans to anyone who would "unsettle a neighborhood." The FHA manual stated:

> If a neighborhood is to retain stability, it is necessary that properties shall continue to be occupied by the same social and racial classes. (Duster 1988:288)

Example of Mortgages

Times changed, and so did the federal government and the NAR. In 1950, under pressure, the NAR deleted the reference to race or nationality. The NAR continued to discriminate, however, and it was not until 1972 that the NAR adopted a pro-fair-housing position.

But where is institutional discrimination today? Laws and practices have so changed that this seems to be a thing of the past. Many aspects of institutional discrimination, as we have just seen with the NAR, are a thing of the past—but a study of 9,000 U.S. financial institutions shows that institutional discrimination is alive and well. Summarized in Figure 8-3, this study shows how discrimination is built into the social system. When bankers were shown these findings, they denied that they discriminated against anyone. They claimed that they gave whites more loans because they had better credit histories. To find out, the researchers went back to their data. They compared the late payments of applicants, even the loan size to their incomes. The results? When two applicants for a mortgage were identical in terms of debts, loan size relative to income, and even characteristics of the property they wanted to buy, African Americans and Latinos were 60 percent more likely to be rejected than whites (Thomas 1992; Passell 1996).

In 1990, the Federal Reserve Board gathered data on the lending practices of 9,300 financial institutions across the United States (Thomas 1992). As shown here, loan applicants who have the same income do not receive the same treatment. Note how much more likely banks are to turn down minorities.

This study illustrates institutional (or systemic) discrimination. The figures clearly indicate that being turned down for a mortgage is not simply a matter of an individual banker here and there discriminating, but, rather, constitutes a nationwide practice. Rejection by race or ethnicity prevails regardless of the individual's income or geographic area.

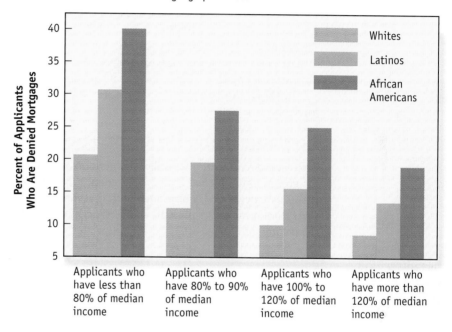

FIGURE 8-3 *Race-Ethnicity and Mortgages: An Example of Institutional Discrimination*

Discrimination Without Awareness: The Example of Heart Surgery

A fascinating aspect of institutional discrimination is that it can take place without racist intentions. *Discrimination can occur even when those who are doing the discriminating and those who are its objects are unaware of it.* Medical decisions provide an example. Researchers have found that white patients are more likely than either Latino or African-American patients to receive knee replacements (Skinner et al. 2003) and coronary bypass surgery (Smedley et al. 2003). Researchers don't yet know why or how race-ethnicity is a factor in making medical decisions. Even African-American physicians are more likely to give preventive care to white patients (Stolberg 2001). Discovering how interracial dynamics underlie medical decisions will be a fascinating area of future research.

Cultural Bias in I.Q. Testing

Another example of unintended discrimination is IQ testing. Some questions asked on these tests favor children from certain backgrounds (Knowles and Prewitt 1969). The following is a sample question from a standardized IQ test:

A symphony is to a composer as a book is to a(n) _____:
_____paper
_____sculptor
_____musician
_____author
_____man

What is discriminatory about this question? At first glance, it seems like an objective question that applies equally to everyone. Children from certain ethnic backgrounds, however, are more familiar with the concepts of symphonies, composers, sculptors, and musicians than are other children. This tilts the test in their favor. Those who make up the test do not intend to discriminate and are unaware that they are doing so.

If we turn matters around, perhaps the discriminatory nature of this question may become more apparent. Suppose that you were asked to take an IQ test that contained these questions:

If you throw the dice and "7" is showing on the top, what is facing down?

_____seven _____snake eyes _____box cars _____little Joes _____eleven

Which word is out of place here?

_____splib _____blood _____gray _____spook _____black

These questions, suggested by Adrian Dove (n.d.), a social worker in Watts, are slanted toward a nonwhite, lower-class experience. With these *particular* cultural biases, is it not obvious that children from some social backgrounds will perform better than others?

In Sum

In short, institutional discrimination is built into our social system. It operates throughout society—often with those involved unaware of it.

Looking at the Problem Theoretically

Prejudice, discrimination, hostility, and tensions characterize many relations between ethnic groups in the United States. To account for these negative features of life, social scientists have developed contrasting theoretical views. Although separately each of our three theoretical perspectives presents a limited perspective, taken together they bring more of the picture into focus.

SYMBOLIC INTERACTIONISM

The Role of Labels in Prejudicial Perception

"What's in a name?" asked Juliet. "That which we call a rose, by any other name would smell as sweet."

This may be true of roses, but in human relations words are not meaningless labels. The labels we learn color the way we see the world and influence what we experience.

Selective Perception

Symbolic interactionists stress that labels (such as stereotypes) affect prejudice by causing **selective perception.** Stereotypes lead us to see certain things and make us blind to others. They shape our perception, and we tend to look at the members of a group as though they all were alike. As Simpson and Yinger (1972) put it: We fit new experiences into old categories by selecting only those cues that harmonize with our prejudgment or stereotype.

Emotionally Charged Ethnic Labels

Racial and ethnic labels have special power over people. They are shorthand for emotionally laden stereotypes. "Nigger," for example, has numerous connotations. By no means is it neutral. This term is so loaded with negative emotions that television commentators won't quote it, using the phrase, "the N word," instead. Nor are "honky," "spic," "mick," "limey," "kraut," "dago," "wetback," or the many other words that people use to refer to members of ethnic groups neutral. The emotional impact of such words overpowers us, blocking out other kinds of realities about people (Allport 1954).

Socialization into Prejudice

Symbolic interactionists examine how we are socialized into prejudice and discrimination. No one is born with prejudice or with a desire to discriminate. Indeed, we are born without standards, values, or beliefs. But all children are born into particular families and ethnic groups. There they learn values, beliefs, and ways to perceive the world. If their group is prejudiced against another group, children learn to dislike that group and to perceive its members negatively. Similarly, if discrimination is common, children learn to practice it routinely.

Stereotypes and a Self-Fulfilling Prophecy

Stereotypes are powerful. They justify prejudice and discrimination. The negative stereotypes that characterize an ethnic group can legitimate the withholding of opportunities from its members and justify placing them into positions considered appropriate for people "like them." Stereotypes create a **self-fulfilling prophecy.** For example, if a stereotype defines members of ethnic group X as lazy, then it legitimizes keeping them out of jobs that require dedication, industry, and energy. If "appropriate" jobs are not available, members of ethnic group X are liable to be seen standing around street corners while members of ethnic groups Y and Z are working. Seeing members of Group X idle reinforces the original stereotype of laziness, whereas the basic discrimination that created the "laziness" passes unnoticed.

Labeling, Compartmentalization, and Genocide

Some ethnic labels are so powerful that they block out the morality that people learn early in life. In the 1960s and 1970s, for example, young U.S. men were sent to a small Asian nation where they were required to kill. Labels helped these young soldiers overcome their deeply rooted taboo against killing. Calling the Vietnamese "the enemy," "slopes," and "gooks" helped U.S. soldiers to perceive these people not as individuals but as members of an inferior group. The army bureaucracy adopted a similar strategy: Weekly it would release reports, not of *people* killed, but of what they called "body counts" and "kill ratios." Such labels help people **compartmentalize:** They allow people to separate negative acts from other aspects of their lives. This helps them to maintain feelings of goodness and self-respect, even when they do horrible things.

Dominant groups can be quite effective in using labels for this purpose. If they target some racial-ethnic group for slaughter, dehumanizing labels can relegate that group to a subhuman status. In this way, the people who are given the "dirty work" of killing are not killing "real" people. This helps them commit acts that are incompatible with their moral training and self-concept. Just as terms that dehumanized the Vietnamese helped U.S. soldiers commit acts that otherwise would have challenged their identities as moral people, so in the 1700s and 1800s white authorities and settlers labeled Native Americans "savages." Viewing Native Americans as something less than human, troops and settlers destroyed about 90 percent of the Native Americans (Garbarino 1976). The Boers, Dutch settlers in South Africa, characterized the native Hottentots as animals of the jungle and wiped them out. Holding similar views, British settlers in Tasmania hunted the local population for sport and even for dog food. Today, much as in earlier U.S. history, settlers (miners, ranchers, and loggers) in Brazil are wiping out Indian tribes as they seize their lands (Linden 1991; "Guardian of Brazil Indians . . ." 1997).

In Sum

Negative terms to describe a group of people, then, are dangerous, as they can lead to discriminatin and mass murder. Groups that build an identity around the hatred that can accompany such terms pose a special threat to society. In the Spotlight on Research box on the next page, Raphael Ezekiel discusses his research of such groups.

Symbolic interactionists examine how labels (or symbols) affect our relationships: how we learn ethnic labels, how we use labels to classify one another, how our classifications affect our perceptions and sort people out for different kinds of life experiences, how symbols of ethnicity change, and how symbols are used to justify discrimination and violence.

Like Hitler's Nazis, the Ku Klux Klan wants to create and fan hatred. Their original targets were blacks, Jews, and Roman Catholics. In recent years, they have given up on Roman Catholics, diminished their efforts against Jews, and now focus on African Americans. During the 1920s, the KKK was a potent political force in some states, especially Indiana. Although the Klan today is but a shell of its former self, groups that promulgate hatred, even though small, are dangerous to the health of a nation.

SPOTLIGHT ON RESEARCH

Studying Neo-Nazis and Klans

Rafael Ezekiel, a Senior Researcher with the Harvard School of Public Health, says that his interest in racism was stimulated by the contradictions he experienced as a child growing up with liberal, Northern, Jewish parents in a deeply racist East Texas town.

Dear students,

Jim Henslin asked me to write about my fieldwork. I got stuck, so I decided to interview myself.

Interviewer: What did you do, Professor?

Rafe: I spent three years hanging out with a neo-Nazi group in Detroit. After that, I interviewed national leaders from neo-Nazi groups and from Klans. I also went to their national and regional meetings. My book, *The Racist Mind*, comes from that work.

Interviewer: Did they know you were a Jew?

Rafe: I made sure they knew I was a Jew and opposed to racism. Good interviewing is interplay between you and your respondent—kind of a dance. That requires trust; trust requires openness and honesty.

Interviewer: But, then, why did they talk with you?

Rafe: Because I told them the truth—that I believe every person creates a life that makes sense to him or her, and my professional work is to go onto the turf of people whose lives seem unusual to most folk and let these people tell me, in their own words, the sense their lives make to them. That made sense to them.

Interviewer: Did you find anything out?

Rafe: Yeah. The leaders and members are real different. The leaders are men—this is essentially a male movement—force, macho, blood, all that. The leaders are not motivated primarily by hate or by racism. They are motivated primarily by hunger for power: Power is the goal; racism is the tool. To move a crowd by what they say. To scare a community by saying that they're coming. To fill the media with scare stories. A whole lot of this is theater—they provide the stimulus; we provide the fantasies.

There are always suckers whom you can recruit by talking racism. If you line up 100 white Americans, ranked by how much they fear and dislike African Americans, the big leaders wouldn't be at the head of the line—they'd be about 30 places back.

Interviewer: And the ordinary members?

Rafe: That's a whole different story. This is not a movement built on hate. It's a movement built on fear. When you talk with a member, talk honestly about his life—his, again—the emotion you sense under the surface is fear. The kids in the Detroit group felt, deep down, that their own lives might be snuffed out at any moment, like a candle in the wind.

Interviewer: Do you have any hints on how to do good fieldwork?

Rafe: Yeah. First, check yourself out—why are you doing this? What does it mean to you? Second, be real—with them, with yourself. Third, field notes. When you finish your interview and start home, roll the interview around in your mind. Don't analyze, just let it play in your mind. Like remembering a dream. Don't talk to anyone—no phoning—don't listen to the radio—just keep the interview rolling around. Go straight home and start writing. Write first pure emotion—primary process stuff—associations, feelings. What's going on inside you after this interview? What does it remind you of? Then write your secondary process stuff—what went on and what you think it means. Then, in terms of your project, where does this take you? Do you need more questions? Respondents? Finally, ask yourself: "So what?" What difference does it make to the world what you think you are understanding? As you write that, you will be writing much of your book.

FUNCTIONALISM

Why does ethnic discrimination persist in the United States? As you will recall, functionalists argue that the benefits of a social pattern (a characteristic of society) must be greater than its costs, or else that pattern would disappear. The benefits (or functions) of discrimination, then, must outweigh its costs (or dysfunctions). Let's see how this could be.

Functions of Past Ethnic Discriminations

It is easy to see the functions of past race-ethnic discrimination, how it directly benefitted the dominant group. Whites gained free land by killing Native Americans or by driving them west. Whites benefitted from owning slaves. (In Louisiana, free blacks also owned slaves.) They procured the labor free of charge, sold the cotton the slaves produced, and sold their labor as masons, carpenters, or factory workers. Slave labor allowed many owners to live a "genteel" life of leisure or to pursue art, education, and other "refinements."

A Legacy of Dysfunction

And today? The legacy of hatred that slavery bequeathed is a dysfunctional one. Urban riots, for example, exact a high cost—in property, lives, and heightened tension, hostility, hatred, and fear. It would appear that the high costs of discrimination would lead to its elimination. Because ethnic discrimination remains a fact of life in the United States, however, functionalists search for its benefits, or functions. Because ethnic discrimination was functional for the dominant group in the past, functionalists look for how today's dominant group benefits from discrimination.

Functions of Present Ethnic Discrimination

1. The "Dirty Work" of Society

Racial-ethnic stratification, the unequal distribution of a society's resources based on race or ethnicity, has three major functions. The first is to ensure that society's **dirty work** gets done. Sociologist Herbert Gans (2005) defines dirty work as society's "physically dirty or dangerous, temporary, dead-end and underpaid, undignified and menial jobs." Sociologist Emile Durkheim (1964, 1965) stressed that society needs a **division of labor,** people performing specialized tasks. Dirty work, such as garbage collection, is a necessary but disagreeable task within this division of labor.

Society can fill these jobs either by paying high wages to compensate for the work's unpleasantness and degradation or by forcing people to do them for low wages. To get society's dirty work done, then, it is functional to bar an ethnic group from higher positions. This ensures that the dirty work gets done and gets done cheaply.

When an ethnic group climbs the social class ladder, it leaves the dirty work behind. Because the dirty work still has to be done, other ethnic groups are recruited to perform those tasks. For example, many African Americans have moved into the middle class, and illegal aliens are doing much of the work they used to do. Mexicans who have entered the United States illegally, for example, have little control over their working conditions. They take jobs that practically no one else will do, often working long hours in crowded, dirty, sometimes dangerous conditions. And they work cheaply, for employers don't have to pay unemployment compensation, Social Security, hospitalization, overtime pay, disability compensation, or vacations.

Apart from what one could say about the inherent injustice of this situation, it is functional. The dirty work gets done, and *most* Americans benefit: They eat the produce that these undocumented workers pick and wear the clothing they make. The illegal immigrants also benefit: They earn far more than they would in Mexico. Their families, left in Mexico in desperate conditions, also benefit, as their relatives send them part of their earnings. Even the government of Mexico benefits, for the illegal immigration siphons off its more ambitious and dissatisfied citizens—who otherwise might direct their energies toward overthrowing an oppressive Mexican elite.

Boxing is another example of ethnic succession in dirty work. Boxing entertains sports fans and produces advertising revenues, but because of the harsh discipline it requires and the danger it entails, few are willing to box. Accordingly, most fighters come from ethnic groups that are largely blocked from more socially approved avenues of success. As a racial-ethnic group climbs the social class ladder, fewer of its members are willing to seek fame and fortune by boxing. The result is an "ethnic succession" in boxing (Weinberg and Arond 1952). As one group moves up the ladder, new fighters come from an ethnic group that is still struggling at the lower rungs of the ladder. In general, Irish boxers gave way to Germans, then to Italians, then to African Americans, who now are being rivaled by Latinos.

**2. Ethnocentrism
in the Dominant Group**

Another major function of ethnic inequality is **ethnocentrism,** a sense of group identity so strong that members of other groups are viewed as inferior. Ethnocentrism helps the dominant group justify its higher social positions and greater share of society's material rewards. They don't have to question why they get more than others or feel guilty about it, for aren't they superior? And aren't they performing the more responsible tasks that society requires?

**3. Ethnocentrism
in the Minority Group**

Ethnic stratification also produces ethnocentrism among minority group members. Their visible differences and the discrimination they face because of their distinctiveness create cohesion, a sense of identity with one another. Seeing that other ethnic groups have "made it" nourishes the hope that they, too, will succeed. This hope for the future strengthens the social system: It encourages minority groups to work hard, minimizes rebellion, and makes them willing to put up with demeaning circumstances—for the time being.

**Dysfunctions: Disrupting
Society and Denying
Individual Potential**

Ethnic discrimination is also dysfunctional; that is, it interferes with people's welfare and even the functioning of society. If an ethnic group becomes too alienated, it may disrupt society through strikes and riots. Another dysfunction is the destruction of human potential. Prejudice and discrimination can lower children's self-esteem, decreasing their capacity to compete in school and work. Because they confront discrimination, many minority children drop out of school and waste their potential in low-level jobs or street crime. Society is the loser, for it is denied the contributions that these youngsters could have made.

**To Analyze Functions
Is Not to Promote
Those Functions**

Functionalists are sometimes misunderstood: To identify social benefits that come from some negative behavior, such as discrimination, can be seen as promoting the behavior. The functionalists' main point, however, is that social characteristics persist only because they are functional. By analyzing the functions and dysfunctions of ethnic stratification, functionalists uncover some of the hidden consequences of institutional arrangements.

CONFLICT THEORY

What had seemed a personal hatred of me, an inexplicable refusal of southern whites to confront their own emotions, and a stubborn willingness of blacks to acquiesce, became the inevitable consequence of a ruthless system which kept itself alive and well by encouraging spite, competition, and the oppression of one group by another. Profit was the word: the cold and constant motive for the behavior, the contempt and despair I had seen. (Davis 1974)

With these words, Angela Davis, an African-American Marxist, recounted her new understanding of U.S. race and ethnic relations. What does she mean by this statement?

According to Marxist conflict theory, ethnic groups are pitted against one another in order to exploit workers and increase profit. It works this way:

**Extracting the Surplus
Value of Labor**

The United States is a **capitalist** society; that is, our economic system is based on investing capital with the goal of making a profit. Profit depends on selling items for more than they cost to produce. In conflict theory, this is called extracting the **surplus value of labor.** For example, if each item that a factory produces costs the owner of the factory $1 for materials; $1 for rent, utilities, and transportation; $1 for advertising, transportation, insurance, and the cost of borrowing money; and $1 for a worker to run a machine, the total cost of the item is $4. If the owner sells it for $5, he or she makes $1 profit. Conflict theorists say that the profit represents the surplus value of the labor used to produce the item.

**A Split-Labor Market
Lowers Wages**

Lower wages help investors and owners increase their profit. To keep wages low, capitalists use a **split-labor market;** that is, they weaken the bargaining power of workers by splitting them along racial, ethnic, or gender lines (Reich 1972, 1981; Shafir

1995; Bernstein 1996; Shafir and Peled 1998). If employers can keep workers fearful and distrustful of one another, they can prevent them from uniting to demand higher wages and more benefits.

The Reserve Labor Force

Capitalists also use people who are unemployed—the **reserve labor force**—in the same way. If all workers were employed, the high demand for labor would let workers insist on pay increases and better working conditions. If some people are unemployed, the owners have a pool of workers that they can dip into when they expand production or want to break a strike. When the economy contracts or when the strike is settled, these workers can be laid off to rejoin the unemployed, with no unsettling effects on society. Minority workers are ideal for this reserve labor force, because employers rely primarily on the more numerous white workers. In addition, white workers seldom object to what happens to members of minority groups, especially to the unemployed (Willhelm 1980).

Distorted Perception of the Self: False Class Consciousness

Workers are also held in check by **false class consciousness,** identifying themselves with employers. The common form is for workers to think that one day they will own their own business and be rich. False class consciousness prevents workers from seeing that their welfare is bound up with that of all workers, regardless of ethnicity or color. If workers identify with the property interests of capitalists instead of with their true working-class interests, they do not unite to bring about social change for the improvement of all workers. If white workers believe that their living standards will fall if minorities make economic gains, they can even feel that they have a stake in discrimination.

Distorted Perception of Others: The Enemy

The consequences of splitting labor in these ways are devastating, say conflict theorists. The system so distorts reality that it leads minorities and whites to view one another as enemies, able to gain some advantage for itself only at the expense of the other. The system encourages enmity. Whites might come to think of themselves as moral, hardworking taxpayers and view the competing minority as lazy and sexually promiscuous, as people who swell the welfare rolls and have to be supported by the taxes that the whites pay. The minority, in turn, might view whites as ruthless, untrustworthy, hate-mongering hypocrites. Such perceptions can encourage minority group members to strike out at people whom they view as their oppressors. Such attempts, however, are usually misdirected at their own neighbors. Whites and minority group members fail to see that the other is an essential part of their own class interests. The reality is that they both have a common enemy, the wealthy, who, to line their own purses, use ethnic divisions and hatred to oppress both.

Concessions Made in Order to Defuse

Riots and other violence that result from this situation sometimes put pressure on the social system. When the elite feel threatened, they try to defuse the bomb that might disrupt their power. They often use concessions, giving a little here and there, whatever seems necessary to quiet the workers. They may increase welfare benefits, assign token representation on committees, offer government aid to reconstruct the inner cities—or build swimming pools and gyms or even offer "night basketball." From the conflict perspective, these acts are not intended to change anything, only to protect the privileged position of the powerful.

An End to Discrimination?

Racial and ethnic antagonisms, then, divide the working class and strengthen capitalists. A racist environment not only deflects working-class hostilities, but also it prevents working-class consensus, the solidarity that would allow workers to challenge the control of the United States by the wealthy who own the means of production. Ethnic discrimination will end only when white and minority workers see that they both are oppressed. Losing their false class consciousness, workers of all groups will see the true source of their oppression, unite, and create a new social order in which they will receive the full value of their labor. With the new racial-ethnic harmony, society will no longer have minority and dominant groups.

IN SUM

The Theories Working Together

None of the three theoretical perspectives has an exclusive claim to truth. Each presents a particular truth. Each focuses on selected aspects of ethnic relations, emphasizing those aspects above any other. Symbolic interactionists alert us to the powerful role of labels in defining human relations: Labels are a lens through which people see themselves and other ethnic groups. When those labels are demeaning, they help people discriminate with a clear conscience. Functionalists turn our attention not only to the dysfunctions of racial-ethnic discrimination, but also to its benefits—its role in the division of labor, and the consequences of the ethnocentrism that it produces. Conflict theorists stress how prejudice and discrimination destroy worker solidarity, help hold down wages, and increase the profits of capitalists. Each theoretical lens, then, produces a unique understanding of race-ethnic relations. Combined, these perspectives provide greater understanding of race–ethnic discrimination than does any one of them alone.

Research Findings

As you saw on Figure 8-2 on page 247, whites make up 68 percent of the overall U.S. population, minorities 31 percent (African Americans 12 percent, Latinos 14 percent, Asian Americans 4 percent, and Native Americans 1 percent). About 1 percent of Americans claim two or more races. These groups that make up the United States are far from evenly distributed across the nation. As the Social Map below shows, the states' distribution of these groups seldom comes close to the national average. This is because minority groups tend to be clustered in regions. The extreme distributions are represented by Maine and Vermont, which have only 3 percent minority, and Hawaii, where minorities outnumber Anglos 76 percent to 24 percent.

What major problems do minority groups in the United States face? How do the groups differ from one another? How is their relationship to the dominant group changing? What strategies are minority groups using to bring about social change? To answer

FIGURE 8-4 *The Distribution of Dominant and Minority Groups in the United States*

Source: By the author, based on *Statistical Abstract of the United States* 2002:Table 22.

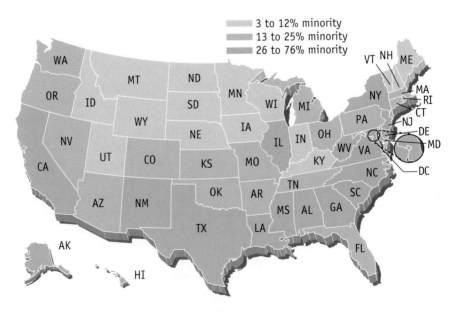

Note: This Social Map indicates how unevenly U.S. minority groups are distributed.

these questions, we shall present an overview of the four largest minority groups in the United States: Native Americans, Latinos, African Americans, and Asian Americans.

NATIVE AMERICANS

Numbers

When Columbus arrived on the shores of the "New World," the Native American population was about 5 million (Thornton 1987). Reaching a low of a quarter of a million around 1900, Native Americans now number about 2.5 million (*Statistical Abstract* 2003:Table 43). This includes Eskimos and Aleuts. Native Americans belong to more than 500 tribes (O'Hare 1992).

Early Relations

At first, relations between the European settlers and the Native Americans were peaceful. American (and Canadian) authorities even encouraged marriage between whites and Native Americans. In 1784, Patrick Henry introduced a bill in the Virginia House of Delegates to offer tax relief, free education, and cash bonuses to whites and Indians who intermarried (Kaplan 1990). As more Europeans arrived, they began a relentless push westward. Native Americans stood in the way of this expansion, and the Europeans began a policy of genocide.

From Genocide to Containment

As part of this policy (which they called "pacification"), the U.S. Cavalry slaughtered tens of thousands of Native Americans. When the cavalry butchered the huge herds of buffalo on which the Great Plains Indians depended, many thousands more died from malnutrition and disease. Because the Native Americans had no immunity to the European diseases, apparently more of them died from smallpox, measles, and the flu than from bullets (Kitano 1974; Dobyns 1983; Schaefer 2004).

In reading the accounts of this period, I am struck by the barbarity of the Anglos. One of the most grisly acts was the distribution of blankets contaminated with smallpox. The blankets were presented as a peace offering. Another was the Trail of Tears, which took place after the government changed its policy from genocide to population transfer and began to relocate Native Americans to specified areas called "reservations." The Trail of Tears was a forced march from the Carolinas and Georgia to Oklahoma, a journey of a thousand miles. Fifteen thousand Cherokees were forced to make this midwinter march in light clothing. Those who fell exhausted, mostly elderly and children, were left to die. Four thousand Cherokees perished.

Because each tribe was a nation, the U.S. government made treaties with the tribes. These treaties, ratified by the U.S. Senate, granted the Native Americans specified lands forever. The treaties often were broken when Anglo settlers demanded more Indian land and natural resources. In 1874, for instance, when gold was discovered in South Dakota's Black Hills, Anglos flooded those reservation lands. The cavalry supported the settlers, resulting in the well-known defeat of "General" (actually, Lt. Colonel) Custer at Little Big Horn in 1876 (Churchill and Vander Wall 1990). The symbolic end to Native American resistance may have been the 1890 massacre at Wounded Knee, South Dakota, where the cavalry murdered 300 (out of 350) Native American men, women, and children (Kitano 1974; Olson et al. 1997).

Stereotypes to Justify Inhumane Acts

As noted earlier, people use stereotypes and labels to justify their inhumane acts. These ways of perceiving help to keep their acts from conflicting with favorable definitions of the self. So it was with the U.S. Indian policy. Anglos viewed Native Americans as stupid, lying, thieving, murdering, pagan "savages" (Simpson and Yinger 1972). Killing a dangerous savage was seen as making the world a safer place for civilized people. The victors who wrote our history texts labeled whites as "pioneers,"

History Written by the Victors

not "invaders"; their military successes were "victories" but those of the Native Americans "massacres"; the seizure of Native American lands was called "settling the land," and the Native Americans' defense of their homelands against overwhelming numbers was not "courageous" but "treacherous" (Josephy 1970; Henslin 2005).

Continuing Effects

The government's attempt to destroy the Native Americans' way of life and relocate Native Americans on reservations still has negative effects today. Table 8-1 on page 251 shows how Native Americans rank on indicators of economic well-being. Their rate of completing college is low, and their rate of poverty is *three* times that of whites, the highest of any other group. Their life expectancy is also about eight to ten years less than that of the nation as a whole: One in four Native Americans dies before the age of 25, compared with the national average of one in seven. Their suicide rate is double the national average, and their rate of alcoholism runs perhaps five times that of the nation (Snipp and Sorkin 1986; O'Hare 1992). It seems fair to conclude that Native American life in the dominant Anglo society is far from satisfying.

The Reservation and Education

Why do so few Native Americans finish college? In the 1960s, anthropologists Murray and Rosalie Wax (1964, 1965, 1967, 1971) came up with answers that still apply. They found that a huge cultural gap separates the children's home and school life: Most Native American parents teach their children to be independent; at school they are rewarded for being dependent on their teachers. Most Native American parents teach their children not to embarrass their peers; their teachers expect them to correct one another in public. Geared to urban Anglo values, the schools prepare Native American children for a life that most will never lead. Because the school system, which is based on the values of the dominant group, denigrates Native American culture and teaches concepts that are largely irrelevant to reservation life, many parents feel alienated from it and refuse to visit their children's schools. The teachers, alienated by the rejection of their well-intended efforts, avoid the homes of their students.

Dead center in this conflict of values between the schools and the reservation are the children. Torn between home and school, their choice generally goes to the family and tribe. Lacking motivation to do well in school, they drop out. As the Waxes expressed it, the deck is so stacked against Native American children that they are, in effect, pushed out of school. Their continuing low rate of college graduation indicates little change in these contrasting orientations that were documented in the 1960s.

Changing Relations and Native American Activism

Native Americans can be called the invisible minority. Because a third of Native Americans live on remote reservations and half in just four states—Oklahoma, California, Arizona, and New Mexico—most Americans are hardly aware of their presence (O'Hare 1992). In addition, for the past 100 years or so, seldom have Native Americans made headlines by disrupting the Anglo-dominated society that they have refused to join. Today's conflicts are primarily legal. They center on the Native Americans trying to enforce the treaties they made with the United States. Minor legal skirmishes have centered on maintaining traditional fishing and hunting rights. Major legal battles are being fought over the Native Americans' demand for the waters of the Arkansas, Colorado, San Juan, and Rio Grande rivers—which were guaranteed by treaty. What most upsets Anglos, however, are the lawsuits that Native Americans have filed to reclaim millions of acres of land ranging from New England to the Southwest. By treaty, Congress guaranteed these lands to Native American tribes "in perpetuity."

The Treaties: Backed by the Full Faith and Honor of the U.S. Government

The federal government's primary legal strategy has been to obstruct the justice system by postponement. In some instances, legal cases are never heard, for those who filed the motion die and others lose interest as proceedings drag on for years, sometimes for generations. Some tribes, however, have won their legal battles. Blue Lake of New Mexico, a heavily forested area sacred to the Taos tribe, has been returned to them. Alaskan Native Americans, primarily the Inuits and Aleuts, were awarded a cash settlement of nearly $1 billion and legal title to 40 million acres. Other tribes have received smaller settlements.

The Continuing Battle Over Land

Because real estate is so significant for the country's welfare, and clouded titles interfere with basic commerce, Anglos in the affected areas are upset—and understandably so. In the state of New York, clouded titles have even made it difficult for owners to sell their land, even though it has been in their family for 200 years (Olson 2002). Some whites have hit upon a legal strategy that goes straight to the jugular—trying to strip Native Americans of their legal status as separate nations and remove their immunity to lawsuits. So far, such attempts have been rebuffed (Anderson and Moller 1998).

Tribal Casinos

Based on their status as separate nations, Native Americans in some states have the legal right to operate gambling casinos. One small tribe, the Mdewakanton Dakota in Minnesota, has struck it rich. Its casino near Minneapolis–St. Paul nets over $600,000 a year for *each* man, woman, and child of the 270-member tribe (Farney 1998). The Oneida tribe of New York, consisting of just a few hundred families, used to live in trailers on 32 acres. Now they employ 3,000 people in their casino, hotels, convention center, gasoline stations, and restaurants. Anglo neighbors have grown resentful of the tribe's new affluence (Dao 1999). Native Americans being wealthy, much less having an income higher than the national average, is an exception, of course, as is evident from the data we reviewed in Table 8-1 on page 251.

The Right to Self-Determination

Native Americans insist on the right to self-determination—to remain unassimilated in Anglo culture and to run their own affairs as separate peoples. Native Americans had no overarching term for the many tribes that inhabited North and South America. The term *Indian* was given to them by Columbus, who mistakenly thought that he had landed in India. The name stuck, and many Native Americans still use it to refer to themselves (Shively 1999). The term *Native American* was also made up by Anglos. Thinking of the 500 culturally distinct tribes as "one people," then, is an Anglo way of viewing matters. The tribes see themselves as many nations, many peoples.

These separate identities have served the dominant Anglos well, for they have not had to face a united Native American population. Perhaps, then, the most significant change in this aspect of ethnic relations is the development of **pan-Indianism.** Moving beyond identification with only a particular tribe, some Native Americans emphasize common elements that run through their cultures. They are trying to utilize these cultural themes to build a united self-identification and to work toward the welfare of all Native Americans. If effective, national Native American organizations will develop. They can help force the courts to act on the many Native American lawsuits, file hundreds or thousands of more lawsuits, and develop self-help measures that center around Native American values. Pan-Indianism, however, is a controversial issue among Native Americans. Some reject it in favor of ethnic diversity, preferring to stress the many Native American histories, languages, and even musical styles (Rolo n.d.).

Native Americans are the "invisible minority" in the United States. About half live out of sight on isolated reservations. With few exceptions, Native Americans have met oppression with silence, withdrawal, and legal claims. Shown here is one of the instances in which they have broken that silence, a protest that the Cleveland Indians use Native Americans as their mascot.

LATINOS (HISPANICS)

Numbers and Countries of Origin

The largest ethnic group in the United States is Latinos (or Hispanics), people who trace their origins to the Spanish-speaking countries of Latin America and to Spain. Like Native Americans, few Latinos think of themselves as a single people. They consider themselves Americans of Mexican origin, Americans of Cuban origin, and so on. Most do not identify readily with the terms *Latino* or *Hispanic*. They consider such a grouping to be artificial, and so it is. It is important to stress that *Latino* and *Hispanic* do not refer to a race, but to *ethnic* groups. Latinos may identify themselves as African American, white, or Native American (Salas 1996; Diaz-Calderon 1996, 1997).

In addition to 25 million Chicanos (those whose country of origin is Mexico), Latinos include about 3 million Puerto Ricans, 1 million Cuban-Americans, and 5 million people from Central and South America (*Statistical Abstract* 2003:Table 46). Although most Chicanos live in the Southwest, most Latinos from Puerto Rico live in New York City, and those from Cuba in the Miami area of Florida.

Officially tallied at 39 million, the number of Latinos in the United States is probably several million higher. Although most Latinos are U.S. citizens, millions have entered the country illegally. Most illegal immigrants are from Mexico. Each year, one and a half million Mexicans are apprehended at the Mexican border and returned to Mexico (*Statistical Abstract* 2003:Table 37). Some illegal immigrants come to the United States for temporary work and then return home. Most do not. In 1986, the federal government passed the Immigration Reform and Control Act, which permitted illegal immigrants to apply for U.S. citizenship. Over 3 million people applied, the vast majority from Mexico (Espenshade 1990). To understand better the reasons behind this vast subterranean migration, see the Issues in Social Problems box on the next page.

Geographic Distribution

Although there are vast stretches of Middle America in which no Latinos can be found, the United States has more Latinos than Canada has Canadians. As Figure 8-5 shows, two-thirds of Latinos are concentrated in just four states—California, Texas, Florida, and New York. Latinos have recently become the largest minority group in the United States, and they are bringing seismic changes to some areas, such as Florida's Dade County, which contains Miami. With its prominent Latino presence, especially with regard to the amount of Spanish that is spoken, Miami is being called "the capital of South America."

The Spanish Language

The factor that clearly distinguishes Latinos from other U.S. minorities is the Spanish language. Although not all Latinos speak Spanish, most do. About 28 million Latinos speak Spanish at home. About half cannot speak English or can do so only with difficulty (*Statistical Abstract* 2003:Table 56). Being fluent only in Spanish in a society where English is the dominant language is a severe obstacle to getting a good job.

In some areas, teachers used to punish children who spoke Spanish at school. Despite the 1848 Treaty of Hidalgo, which ended the Mexican War and guarantees Mexicans the right to maintain their culture, from 1855 until 1968 California banned teaching in any language other than English. In a 1974 decision (*Lau v. Nichols*), the U.S. Supreme Court ruled that to use only English to teach students who cannot understand English violated their civil rights. This decision, which paved the way for bilingual instruction for Spanish-speaking children, resulted from a lawsuit by Chinese students who wanted to receive instruction in Chinese (Vidal 1977; Lopez 1980).

The growing use of Spanish has become a social issue. Senator S. I. Hayakawa of Hawaii initiated an "English-only" movement in 1981. Supporters of this movement have succeeded in getting 26 states to pass a law declaring English their official language (Schaeffer 2004).

FIGURE 8-5 *Geographic Distribution of the Latino Population*

Source: By the author, based on *Statistical Abstract of the United States* 2002:Table 23.

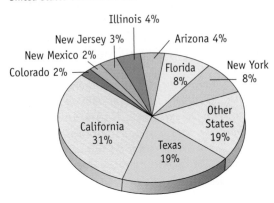

Issues in Social Problems
THE ILLEGAL TRAVEL GUIDE

Manuel was a drinking buddy of Jose's, a man I had met in Colima, Mexico. At 45, Manuel was friendly, outgoing, and enterprising.

Manuel had lived in the United States for seven years and spoke fluent English. Preferring his home town in Colima, where he palled around with his childhood friends, Manuel always seemed to have money and free time.

When Manuel invited me to go on a business trip with him, I accepted. I never could figure out how he made his living and how he could afford a car, a luxury that none of his friends had. As we traveled from one remote village to another, Manuel would sell used clothing that he had heaped in the back of his older-model Ford station wagon.

At one stop, Manuel took me into a dirt-floored, thatched-roof hut. While chickens ran in and out, Manuel whispered to a slender man of about 23. The poverty was overwhelming. Juan, as his name turned out to be, had a partial grade school education. He also had a wife, four hungry children under the age of 5, and two pigs—his main food supply. Although eager to work, Juan had no job, for there was simply no work available in this remote village.

As we were drinking a Coke, the national beverage of Mexico's poor, Manuel explained to me that he was not only selling clothing—he was also lining up migrants to the United States. For $200 he would take a man to the border and introduce him to a "wolf," who, for another $200 would surreptitiously make a night crossing into the promised land.

When I saw the hope in Juan's face, I knew nothing would stop him. He was borrowing every cent he could from every relative to scrape the $400 together. He would make the trip, although he risked losing everything if apprehended, for wealth beckoned on the other side. He knew people who had been there and spoke glowingly of its opportunities. Manuel, of course, stoked the fires of hope.

Looking up from the children playing on the dirt floor with the chickens pecking about them, I saw a man who loved his family. In order to make the desperate bid for a better life, he would suffer their enforced absence, as well as the uncertainties of a foreign culture whose language he did not know.

Juan opened his billfold, took something out, and slowly handed it to me. I looked at it curiously. I felt tears as I saw the tenderness with which he handled this piece of paper. It was his passport to the land of opportunity: a Social Security card made out in his name, sent by a friend who had already made the trip and who was waiting for Juan.

It was then that I realized that the thousands of Manuels scurrying about Mexico and the millions of Juans they were transporting could never be stopped, for only the United States could fulfill their dream of a better life.

Deprivation

Latinos fare poorly on the indicators of quality of life shown in Table 8-1 on page 251. They are more than twice as likely as Anglos to be poor. Their median income is only three-fifths that of Anglos, their unemployment rate is more than double that of Anglos, and only one of nine is a college graduate. At *every* level of education, whether it be a high school diploma or a doctorate, whites earn more (*Statistical Abstract* 1996:Table 244; 2003:Table 230). In response to their position in U.S. society, some Latinos have begun a movement that rejects assimilation and emphasizes the maintenance of Latino culture.

Political Power

Despite their numbers, Latinos hold only a tiny fraction of elected offices. Because of their huge numbers, we might expect 13 or 14 of the 100 U.S. senators to be Latino. *None* are. Of the 435 representatives, 19 are Latino. Overall, of the 500,000 elected public officials in the United States, only 4,400 are Latino (*Statistical Abstract* 2003:Tables 407, 418). Yet, compared with the past, even this small number represents substantial gains in the political system.

It is likely that Latinos soon will play a larger role in U.S. politics, perhaps one day even beyond their overall numbers. This is because they are concentrated in four states that hold one fourth of the 538 electoral votes: California (54), New York (33), Texas (32), and Florida (25). Already, presidents have seen the political wisdom of appoint-

Immigrants from Central America don't arrive with a Latino identity. They identify themselves, rather, as Salvadorans, Hondurans, Guatemalans, and so on. As this photo illustrates, their identity may broaden to Central American. The umbrella terms, Latino and Hispanic, were invented by Anglos, who lump immigrants who speak Spanish together. As Spanish-speaking immigrants assimilate, they may come to adopt these encompassing terms and establish a broader identity.

Internal Divisions

ing Latinos to major positions, such as U.S. Secretary of Transportation and Secretary of Health, Education, and Welfare. In addition to their ritual kissing of babies, presidential candidates now ritually utter a few Spanish phrases.

The potential political power of Latinos has not been realized because of severe divisions of national origin and social class. These distinctions nourish disunity and create disagreements about social and economic policy. As mentioned, Latinos do not think of themselves as a single people, and national origin is highly significant. People from Puerto Rico, for example, feel little sense of unity with people from Mexico. It is similarly the case with those from Venezuela, Colombia, or El Salvador. Latinos from rural and urban areas also have different cultural traditions and political views.

Social class divisions also obstruct united action. Like people of other ethnic backgrounds, Latinos are divided by education and income. In some cases, even when they come from the same country, the differences in their backgrounds are severe. Most of the half million Cubans who fled their homeland after Fidel Castro came to power in 1959 were well-educated, financially comfortable professionals or businesspeople. The 100,000 "boat people" who arrived twenty years later, however, were mainly lower-class refugees to whom the earlier arrivals would hardly have spoken in Cuba. The earlier arrivals have prospered in Florida and control many businesses and financial institutions: They feel vast divisions between themselves and more recent immigrants.

AFRICAN AMERICANS

It was 1955, in Montgomery, Alabama. As specified by law, whites took the front seats of the bus, while blacks went to the back. As the bus filled up, blacks had to give up their seats to whites.

When Rosa Parks, a 42-year-old African-American woman and secretary of the Montgomery NAACP, was told she would have to stand so white folks could sit, she refused. She sat there stubbornly while the bus driver fumed and whites felt insulted. Blacks, observing from the back of the bus, also wondered what she was doing.

Mrs. Parks was arrested. Instead of passing as an incident of little importance, her arrest touched off mass demonstrations, led 50,000 blacks to boycott the city's buses for a year, and thrust an otherwise unknown preacher who had majored in sociology at Morehouse College in Atlanta, Georgia, onto the stage of history.

Dr. Martin Luther King, Jr., who was later murdered in Memphis, Tennessee, organized car pools and preached nonviolence. Incensed at this radical organizer and at the stirrings in the normally compliant black community, the segregationists also put their beliefs into practice—by bombing homes and dynamiting churches.

The segregation of whites and African Americans was not limited to the Deep South. This 1939 photo was taken in Oklahoma City, Oklahoma. Memories of such conditions are still vivid in the minds of some older Americans.

American Apartheid

In the 1950s, the South was still practicing apartheid. African Americans, then called Negroes or colored, were not allowed to stay at hotels or to eat in restaurants that whites patronized. They even had to use separate toilets and water fountains. It was only a few years earlier, in 1944, that the U.S. Supreme Court had decided that African Americans could vote in the southern primaries. Just one year earlier, in 1954, the Court had ruled that African Americans had the legal right to attend public schools with whites (Carroll and Noble 1977; Polenberg 1980). Not until 1967 would the Court strike down the last of the laws (in Virginia and South Carolina) prohibiting marriage between blacks and whites (O'Hare 1992).

The King Strategy

In order to break down institutional barriers, King led African Americans in a strategy called **civil disobedience,** deliberately but peacefully disobeying laws that are considered unjust. Inspired by Mahatma Gandhi, who had played a crucial role in winning India's independence from Great Britain, King (1958) based his strategy on these principles:

1. Active, nonviolent resistance to evil
2. Not seeking to defeat or humiliate opponents, but seeking instead to win their friendship and understanding
3. Attacking the forces of evil rather than the people who are doing the evil
4. Being willing to accept suffering without retaliating
5. Refusing to hate the opponent
6. Acting with the conviction that the universe is on the side of justice

No overnight success followed, but the barriers did come down. In 1964 Congress passed the Civil Rights Act, making it illegal to discriminate in hotels, theaters, and other public places. Then, in 1965, the Voting Rights Act banned the literacy and other discriminatory tests that had been used to keep African Americans from voting.

Rising Expectations and Violence

Encouraged by such gains, African Americans experienced **rising expectations;** that is, they expected better conditions to follow right away. The lives of poor African Americans, however, changed little, if at all. Frustrations built, finally exploding in Watts in 1965, when residents of this central Los Angeles ghetto took to the streets in the first of the "urban revolts." The violence, which occurred despite the protests of Dr. King, precipitated a white backlash that threatened the interracial coalition that King had spearheaded. Congress refused to enact civil rights legislation in both 1967 and 1968. When King was assassinated on April 4, 1968, ghettos across the nation erupted in fiery violence. Under threat of the destruction of the nation's cities, Congress reluctantly passed the sweeping Civil Rights Act of 1968.

Leadership Following King's Assassination

After King's death, black militants rushed in to fill the leadership void. Like King, they emphasized black unity and pride in black identity. But, unlike King, some of them saw violent confrontation as the way to gain equality. Flashed across the nation's television screens were images of the Black Panthers, brandishing rifles and parading in public in military-style uniforms. The statements and acts of militants stirred up fear and hostility among whites. As a result, the militants lost their most forceful leaders. The police assassinated some in nighttime raids, shooting the leaders to death in their beds. Others were co-opted, bought off with job titles and government paychecks.

The leadership fragmented. It even disagreed about basic purposes, some arguing for secession from the United States, others for total integration. Leaders also disagreed about methods, some wanting violent confrontation, others peaceful protest. Integration and political action won. A more moderate approach replaced militancy, and even the Black Panthers switched to community organizing, providing breakfasts for schoolchildren, and running for political office. Lacking a charismatic leader, the momentum that had propelled the struggle for equality faded.

Political Gains

Change came in political representation. On the positive side, the mayors of many large U.S. cities are African American, and of 435 representatives, 39 are African American. On the negative side, of the 50 U.S. senators, *only one* is African American (*Statistical Abstract* 2003:Table 408; 2004 election results). Because African Americans, who number 35 million, make up about 12 percent of the population, we would expect about 12 African American senators. Although far from equitable, compared with the past this change in political representation represents substantial gains in the U.S. political system.

School Integration and "White Flight"

An elusive goal is an integrated public school system. In one of the ironies of race relations, the pathbreaking 1954 Supreme Court decision to integrate U.S. schools led to the schools becoming even more segregated. Following the 1954 decision, whites fled the cities and relocated in all-white suburbs. Others remained in the city but opened all-white private schools. In Atlanta, Georgia, for example, "white flight" changed the school system from 55 percent white to 90 percent black (Stevens 1980). As white flight continued, most schools of the major U.S. cities became primarily African American. With such an unanticipated result of the 1954 decision, in 1986 courts across the nation began to rule against desegregation plans. The result of these court actions has been the same as the 1954 ruling: even greater segregation (Frankenberg and Lee 2002).

African Americans, however, have made strong gains in education. The percentage of African-American high school graduates who attend college increased from 43 percent in 1980 to 62 percent in 1998. Since then, however, the numbers have moved backward, and today 55 percent of African Americans who graduate from high school go to college (*Statistical Abstract* 2003:Table 275). The reasons for this decline are uncertain, but it is ominous. To continue their hard-won economic gains, African Americans must reverse this decline: It is the college graduates who enter the better-paying positions and join the middle class. Because African Americans are more likely than whites to drop out of high school and now less likely to attend college than just a few years ago, a smaller proportion of African Americans will be prepared to compete for the better jobs.

An Ominous Change

Race or Social Class?

The overall changes are stunning when one realizes that in the 1950s whites were still forcing African Americans into "black-only" areas—and the law stood on their side. With the progress that African Americans have made in education, employment, politics, and legislation, the question has been raised whether race still underlies the relations between African Americans and whites. Some sociologists have suggested that, rather than race, the significant factor has become social class.

This view is supported by an event in Westland, Michigan, where African Americans banded together to keep out whites as neighbors. Annapolis Park is a subdivision of expensive homes that are inhabited by African Americans. The city council voted to allow the construction of a trailer park near the neighborhood. Objections to the trailer park, in which whites would live, were based on social class, not race. As one Annapolis Park home-owner said: "Let's face it. These are going to be lower-class whites. You wouldn't want a $15,000 home next to your place, would you?" (Associated Press, February 5, 1981).

Sociologist William Wilson (1978) put the matter this way: "Race relations in America have undergone fundamental changes in recent years, so much so that the life chances of individual blacks have more to do with their economic class position than with their day-to-day encounters with whites." Wilson uses the term **social class** to refer to "any group of people who have more or less similar goods, services, or skills to offer for income in a given economic order and who therefore receive similar financial remuneration in the market-place." He says that the changes have been so great that social class, not race, is what most determines African Americans' **life chances**—their quality of life and experiences. Neither Wilson nor any other sociologists denies that race is significant in life, just that social class is more significant.

Two Worlds of Experience

Wilson (1978, 1987) also points out that social class now separates African Americans into two groups—those with money and those without. Official statistics support this. Most African Americans are not poor. The African American middle class has expanded so greatly that it now holds three times the proportion of African Americans than it did in 1940. One of every three African American families makes more than $50,000 a year. Yet there is another side to the income statistics: One of every seven African American families makes less than $10,000 a year (*Statistical Abstract* 2003:Table 39). These figures indicate a division of African Americans into the "haves" and the "have-not" and, with it, two contrasting worlds.

One world consists of the middle class. These people work at jobs that offer advancement, earn good incomes and benefits, and live in middle-class suburbs or in exclusive areas of the city. They face little crime, and their children, who go to better schools, are motivated to go to college and prepare for good jobs. Not sociologically surprising, their orientations follow their middle-class experiences and middle-class lifestyles. They represent and believe in the "American dream." The second world consists of those who are stuck in poverty in the inner city. They confront violent crime daily; attend terrible schools; face dead-end jobs or welfare; and feel despair, as well as either apathy or hostility. The aspirations and values of these two groups have little in common.

Many sociologists take hearty exception to the idea that social class has replaced racial oppression. They say that this analysis misses the vital element—discrimination—that still underlies the relative deprivation of African Americans. They emphasize that at *all* levels of work—whether among factory workers, managers, or supervisors—an income gap separates African Americans and whites. They point out that without exception whites are on top. They also point out that at every level of education, whether it be a high school diploma or a doctorate, whites earn more (*Statistical Abstract* 1996:Table 244; 2003:Table 230). Both Wilson and his critics agree that an African American child's chance of growing up poor is much greater than that of a white child. In Wilson's view, however, social class, not racial-ethnic discrimination, is mainly responsible for perpetuating this situation.

Toward an Integration of the Positions

It seems fair to conclude that each position is partly correct, that each pinpoints part of today's reality. It is likely that both discrimination and a disadvantaged social class position make their relative contributions: Those who are poor face far fewer opportunities and much greater discrimination; those who enjoy an advantaged class position face much greater opportunities and considerably less discrimination.

ASIAN AMERICANS

World War II

It was a quiet Sunday morning, the seventh of December, 1941, a day destined to live in infamy, as President Roosevelt was later to say.

In 1942, Japanese Americans were considered a threat to the security of the United States. They were taken from their homes and moved to internment camps in the Arizona desert. Children were tagged so they wouldn't get lost in transit.

Exclusionary Policies

At dawn, waves of Japanese bombers began an attack on Pearl Harbor, a U.S. naval station in Oahu, Hawaii. The Japanese pilots found the U.S. Pacific Fleet anchored and unprepared for battle. The Americans were sitting ducks.

In response, the United States declared war on Japan, entering World War II and leaving no American untouched. Some left home to battle overseas; others left their farms to work in factories that supported the war effort. All lived with the rationing of food, gasoline, sugar, coffee, and other essentials.

This event touched Americans of Japanese descent in a special way. Just as waves of planes had rolled over Pearl Harbor, so waves of suspicion and hostility rolled over the 110,000 Japanese Americans who called the United States "home." Overnight, Japanese Americans became the most detested racial-ethnic group in the country (Daniels 1975). Many Americans feared that Japan would invade the United States and that Japanese Americans would sabotage military installations on the West Coast. Although not a single Japanese American committed even one act of sabotage, on February 1, 1942, President Franklin Roosevelt signed Executive Order 9066, authorizing the removal of any people considered threats to military areas. All people on the West Coast who were *one-eighth* Japanese or more were jailed in detention centers called "relocation camps." These people were charged with no crime; they were neither indicted nor tried. Having some Japanese ancestry was sufficient reason to be put in prison.

This was not the first time that Asian Americans had met discrimination. For years, differences in appearance and lifestyle had prompted Americans of European background to discriminate against Americans of Asian ancestry. Lured by gold strikes in the West and ready jobs for unskilled labor, about 200,000 Chinese immigrated between 1850 and 1880. There was a rush to unite the West with the East, and the Chinese were put to work building the East-West railroad. Although 90 percent of Central Pacific's labor force was Chinese, when the famous golden spike was driven at Promontory, Utah, in 1869 to mark the joining of the Union Pacific and the Central Pacific railroads, white workers prevented the Chinese from being present (Hsu 1971). After the railroad was finished, many Chinese settled in the West. To intimidate their new competition, white workers formed mobs and vigilante groups.

As fears of "alien genes and germs" grew, legislators passed anti-Chinese laws (Schrieke 1936). In 1850, the California legislature passed the *Foreign Miner's Act*, levying a special tax on Chinese (and Latinos) of $20 a month—at a time when wages were a dollar a day. The Chief Justice of the California Supreme Court ruled that Chinese could not testify against whites in court (Carlson and Colburn 1972). In 1882 Congress passed the *Chinese Exclusion Act*, suspending all Chinese immigration for 10 years. Four years later, the Statue of Liberty was dedicated. The tired, the poor, and the huddled masses it was to welcome obviously did not include the Chinese.

FIGURE 8-6 *The Country of Origin of Asian Americans*

Source: By the author, based on *Statistical Abstract of the United States* 2003:Table 23.

**Four Stages
in the Development
of "Chinatowns"**

These exclusionary practices led Chinese immigrants to form segregated communities called "Chinatowns." Four stages were involved in their development (Yuan 1963). The first was *involuntary segregation:* Discrimination forced the immigrants into separate living areas. The second was *defensive insulation:* The immigrants banded together for mutual help. The third was *voluntary segregation:* They chose to remain in the segregated community because that was where their friends and relatives lived, it avoided language difficulties, and it allowed them to follow their customs and religion (Buddhism), which were strange to the dominant group. The final stage, now in process, is *gradual assimilation:* As they become acculturated, individuals move out of Chinatown and adopt even more mainstream customs.

"Spillover Bigotry"

When the Japanese began to immigrate, they met spillover bigotry that had been directed against the Chinese. They also confronted discriminatory laws. Even the U.S. Constitution became a tool that was used against them. Initially a document that allowed only whites to be citizens, the Constitution was amended in the 1860s to include African Americans (Amott and Matthaei 1991). Because Asians had not been named in the amendments, the Supreme Court ruled that this prohibited them from becoming citizens (Schaefer 1979). Seeing their opportunity, California authorities passed the *1913 Alien Land Act,* prohibiting anyone who was ineligible for citizenship from owning land. (Most Native Americans were not granted citizenship in their own land until 1924; the Chinese gained citizenship in 1943, but for those born in Japan the exclusion remained until 1952.)

**Divisions Among
Asian Americans**

Contrary to stereotypes that prevail in our society, the 12 million Asian Americans are diverse peoples. As you can see from Figure 8-6 on page 270, they came from many different lands. As a result, Asian Americans are divided by many cultural heritages, including different languages and religions. Most Asian Americans live in the western states, one of three in California (*Statistical Abstract* 2003:Table 21). The two largest groups of Asian Americans, those of Chinese and Filipino descent, are concentrated in Los Angeles, San Francisco, Honolulu, and New York City. The third largest group, those of Asian Indian descent, is the most geographically dispersed.

As you can see, the category of Asian American lumps a lot of different groups together. As a result, any "average" that is computed for this group can conceal a lot of differences. The "average" poverty of Asian Americans, for example, is 11 percent. But if we look more closely, we find that poverty differs remarkably according to country of origin: Poverty is the greatest among the Cambodians, Hmong, and Laotians, and least among Japanese Americans (Lee 1998). Many of the Chinese who live in the urban settlements known as "Chinatowns" face the usual problems of ghetto poverty: poor health, high suicide, poor working conditions, and bad housing.

**Why Have Asian
Americans Been
So Successful?**

One general conclusion that we can make, with the caution I just indicated, is that most Asian Americans are remarkably successful. As Table 8-1 shows, the median family income of Asian Americans outstrips the incomes of all other groups, including that of whites. Researchers have found that the general economic success of Asian Americans is due to three main factors: family life, educational achievement, and assimilation into the mainstream culture.

1. Family Life

The divorce rate of Asian Americans is low, less than half the rate of whites (Reeves and Bennett 2003). One result is that of all racial-ethnic groups, including whites, Asian American children are the most likely to grow up with two parents. They are also the least likely to be born to a single mother (Lee 1998). Most Asian American children grow up in closely knit families where they are socialized into values that stimulate cohesiveness and high motivation to succeed (Bell 1991). Within a framework of strict limits and constraints, they are taught self-discipline, thrift, and industry (Suzuki 1985). This early socialization provides strong impetus for the next two factors.

**2. Educational
Achievement**

The second factor is educational achievement. As you saw on Table 8-1 on page 251, Asian Americans are the most likely of any group to complete college. Their rate of completing college is four times that of Latinos, three times that of Native Americans, more than twice that of African Americans, and more than half again as much as that of whites. This achievement in education opens doors to the professions and managerial positions.

3. Assimilation

Assimilation, the third factor, is indicated by several measures. Asian Americans have the highest intermarriage rate of any minority group: About two of five marry someone of another racial-ethnic group. Asian Americans are also the most likely to live in integrated neighborhoods (Lee 1998). Japanese Americans, the financially most successful of Asian Americans, are the most assimilated (Bell 1991). About 75 percent say that their best friend is not a Japanese American.

And Politics

Asian Americans are becoming more prominent in politics. With 60 percent of its citizens being Asian American, Hawaii has elected Asian American governors and sent several Asian American senators to Washington (Lee 1998; *Statistical Abstract* 2003:Table 408). The first Asian American governor outside of Hawaii is Gary Locke, who in 1996 was elected governor of Washington, a state in which Asian Americans make up less than 6 percent of the population. Locke was reelected in 2000, and chose not to run in 2004.

Social Policy

Although the goal of a unified society is laudable, the attempt to use our social institutions to reshape everyone into an Anglo mold does not work. Accordingly, it seems reasonable for social policy to center around the twin goals of encouraging cultural pluralism and preventing ethnic discrimination. Let's look at these.

ENCOURAGING CULTURAL PLURALISM

Encouraging Pride and Appreciation

The first goal of social policy, encouraging cultural pluralism, would be based on "cultural integrity"; that is, it would encourage pride and appreciation of ethnic cultures. Here are possible specifics:

1. Establishing national, state, and local "cultural centers" that feature a group's heritage
2. Holding "ethnic appreciation days" in the public schools, where ethnic customs, dress, dances, history, and food would be featured
3. Teaching history (and all courses with an historical emphasis) in ways that recognize the contributions of the many groups that make up the United States
4. Teaching foreign languages in our public schools, from grade school through high school. Starting so early, all students could learn two foreign languages

The first two suggestions are easy to implement, and they can go a long way toward encouraging appreciation of cultural differences and pride in one's own heritage. Granted the segregation of our urban schools, for the second strategy to be more effective, it should include cultural exchanges among our public and private schools. The last two, which are more extensive, could accomplish the same purposes. Note the emphasis on the public school system. It is here that our young people, the most malleable of our citizens, receive extensive training and are most likely to come into close contact with different ethnic groups.

Appreciation, but Not Retreat

Cultural pluralism does *not* mean a retreat by minority groups into their ethnic culture. Like members of the dominant group, members of minority groups need to be prepared to compete within the dominant Anglo institutions. Although children of minority groups should be encouraged to retain and to take pride in their rich heritage, like the children of the dominant group, they need to become proficient at English and other basic skills. The school system is uniquely situated to equip them with these tools. Without them, members of minority groups find themselves at a severe disadvantage in meeting their number-one need—competing with Anglos for jobs, especially well-paying positions that offer advancement.

PREVENTING ETHNIC DISCRIMINATION

Legal Enforcement

The second social policy, preventing ethnic discrimination, involves using the law to ensure that ethnic minorities are not discriminated against in jobs, housing, education, or any other areas of life that pertain to all citizens. This requires that our local, state, and federal governments be watchdogs. *The Civil Rights Act of 1964,* which forbids discrimination by race, color, creed, national origin, and sex, must be enforced. This law covers unions, employment agencies, and, as amended in 1972, all businesses with 15 or more employees. This law also prohibits discrimination in voting, public accommodations, all federally supported programs such as road construction, and federally supported institutions such as colleges and hospitals. Preventing ethnic discrimination also means funding the Equal Employment Opportunity Commission (EEOC), the organization that is empowered to investigate complaints of discrimination and to recommend action to the Department of Justice.

Tuition Vouchers

As noted, "white flight" was a common reaction to the forced integration of the public school system. U.S. parents have the right to send their children to any schools they can afford, and this right needs to be protected. Although controversial, there is an effective solution to white flight. If education vouchers in the amount of the average cost per student in a district's schools were given to each student, their parents could choose any school they wished, private or public. Some voucher programs already exist, but none as generous as what I am suggesting. For vouchers to help overcome racial–ethnic discrimination, all schools, of course, must be open to students of any race-ethnic background.

THE DILEMMA OF AFFIRMATIVE ACTION

The *Bakke* Case

The Civil Rights Act of 1964 created a dilemma: how to make up for past discrimination without creating new discrimination. The first dispute to catch the public's attention was the precedent-setting *Bakke* case (Sindler 1978). In 1972 and again in 1973, Allen Bakke was denied admission to the medical school of the University of California at Davis. Bakke sued when he learned that the school had admitted African Americans, Asian Americans, and Chicanos who had scored lower than he had on the entrance exam and who had lower grade point averages than his. Bakke argued that had he been a member of a minority group he would have been admitted. In other words, the university was racist—it had discriminated against him because he was white. The U.S. Supreme Court ruled that the Davis medical school had to admit Bakke because it was illegal to use quotas for minorities.

Inconsistency and Controversy

Following the *Bakke* case, the U.S. Supreme Court handed down a series of inconsistent rulings. It ruled that colleges cannot use quotas to determine whom they admit, but they can use race as a factor to create a diverse student body (Walsh 1996). In a 1989 precedent-setting *City of Richmond* decision, the Court ruled that state and local governments "must almost always avoid racial quotas" in awarding construction contracts. "Almost always" means that it might be okay, but then again it might not, which left everyone confused about where and when and in what ways preferential treatment is or is not constitutional.

The national debate continued, with few fond of affirmative action, but no one seeing alternatives to erase the consequences of past discrimination. Then during the 1990s, the tide turned against affirmative action, with a series of rulings by circuit courts and the U.S. Supreme Court. Perhaps the most significant development was *Proposition 209,* a 1996 amendment to the California state constitution that banned race and gender preferences in hiring and in college admissions. Despite

The Basic Dilemma

appeals by a coalition of civil rights groups, the U.S. Supreme court upheld the California law.

Another significant ruling was made in 2003. White applicants who had been denied admission to the University of Michigan claimed that they had been discriminated against because members of underrepresented minority groups had been given extra points just for being a member of the group. The Court's ruling was ambiguous. The Court ruled that the goal of racial diversity is laudable and that universities can give minorities an edge in admissions, but they cannot use an automatic system to do so. Race can be a "plus factor," but in the Court's words, there must be "a meaningful individualized review of applicants."

Such a murky message leaves university officials—and, by extension, those in business and other public and private agencies—scratching their heads. Trying to bring about racial-ethnic diversity is constitutional, but using quotas and mechanical systems is not. With the Court providing no specific guidelines and its University of Michigan ruling open to interpretation, we obviously have not yet heard the final word from the U.S. Supreme Court on this topic.

PRINCIPLES FOR IMPROVING ETHNIC RELATIONS

Four Sound Principles

Social policies should follow sound sociological principles. The principles developed by social psychologist Gordon Allport (Pettigrew 1976), which are based on experimental evidence, can provide a basic map for developing social policy:

1. Ethnic groups should possess equal status in the situation. The occupants of interethnic housing, for example, should have similar incomes.
2. People in interethnic contact should be seeking the same goals. Parents from different ethnic backgrounds, for example, can work together to improve their children's school.
3. To attain their goals, the groups must pull together. (Allport calls this cooperative dependence.) For example, to improve an integrated school system, voters from different ethnic groups must vote for a bond proposal.
4. Authority, law, and custom should support interaction among the groups. If authorities stand behind school integration, for example, positive interaction among the ethnic groups is more likely.

The Future of the Problem

Ethnic relations are constantly changing. Most Americans today reject many patterns of discrimination that were once taken for granted. Although huge gaps still remain between our ideals of equality and the reality of race–ethnic relations, the United States has moved toward greater equality.

From Apartheid to Integration

Before World War II, the U.S. government supported apartheid. The war caused the dislocation of ethnic groups, and U.S. society was never the same. One such dislocation was the migration of hundreds of thousands of African Americans to the North to work in the war industries. After the war, the federal government moved gradually from apartheid to a policy of integration and social equality. This broke many of the institutional barriers that had been directed against minorities. I can see no way that those barriers will ever be reestablished.

Controversy Over Affirmative Action

Stubborn barriers to equality do remain, however, and ethnic relations are haunted by them, as well as by the consequences of past discrimination. Affirmative action was designed to overcome these barriers, but, as you have seen, it has come under heavy attack. By their very nature, court rulings will disappoint one side or the other when two sides hold incompatible philosophical positions. This is inevitable, but inconsistent and vague court rulings leave people confused. With effective mechanisms to remedy inequalities yet to be developed, the proper role of affirmative action in a multicultural society is likely to remain center stage for quite some time.

Jobs

The major battlefield for racial-ethnic equality will be jobs. The outcome of this struggle is of fundamental importance because access to good jobs determines so much of people's quality of life. Two issues will be central to the outcome, the removal of remaining structural barriers and the preparation of workers. The dismantling of barriers is likely to be a very slow process. Preparation of workers depends on education.

Education

For most Americans, education holds the key to the future. Those who receive the better education will get the better jobs and enjoy the more satisfying lifestyles. Any group that receives less schooling than the national average faces severe disadvantages in our technological society. Granted this principle, then, as Table 8-1 on page 251 shows, the future looks brightest for Asian Americans and whites, much less bright for African Americans, and the worst for Native Americans and Latinos. The decline in the percentage of African-American high school graduates who go to college is especially ominous and must be addressed. Obviously, policies that produce greater educational achievement among minority groups need to be developed.

A Permanent Underclass?

A disturbing possibility is that we now have a permanent **underclass** (Wilson 1978, 1987), an alienated group, especially in the inner cities. This group has little education, lives primarily in single-parent families, has high rates of violent crime, drug abuse, disease, births to single mothers, and death by murder. Its norms are self-defeating, if the goal is to succeed in mainstream society.

A Tragic Cycle

Unless ways are found to reach this group, which was left behind as many residents of the inner city moved into middle-class jobs and middle-class neighborhoods, the tragic cycle will perpetuate itself. The children who are born in those conditions will be fated to repeat their parents' lives. A primary structural factor that makes this sorry possibility likely is that most jobs are located in the suburbs. Those who live in the urban ghettos lack the means of transportation to reach those jobs and the financial ability to move closer to them.

Collective Violence

These conditions carry severe implications for society as a whole. If large groups of people remain isolated from mainstream society, receive a meager education, can't get jobs, and are denied even proper police protection, a spark could ignite collective violence. With little being done about the problems of our inner cities, it is likely that there will be sparks. More riots, then, are likely, and at some point we will see a repeat of the 1992 riots in Los Angeles.

Bitter Divisions?

Militants, whether from a minority group or the dominant group, are an unpredictable factor in future racial-ethnic relations. Although ethnic pride is laudable—as I indicated in the social policy section, ethnic pride should be encouraged—some people mistake ethnic pride and hatred of others. Any group—of any race or ethnicity—that preaches hatred creates divisions among racial-ethnic groups. The resurgence of the Ku Klux Klan, though involving only a handful of people, shows an alarming potential of violence. I anticipate that the occasional outbursts of such groups, though dramatic, will be limited mainly to headline grabbing and will pose no serious threat to the future.

Social Action and the Great Divide

In 1944, Gunnar Myrdal (1898–1987), a sociologist from Sweden, wrote that the United States was caught between two major forces. In his classic *An American Dilemma,* Myrdal contrasted the "American creed," as expressed in Christian ethics and the Declaration of Independence, with the un-Christian and undemocratic behavior he observed. Myrdal was confident that Americans would resolve the dilemma in favor of the higher values of the American creed, rather than the lower ones of discrimination and prejudice. Conditions are much better today than they were in the 1940s—but the dilemma that Myrdal identified remains.

Valleys of hatred and despair will follow peaks of goodwill and high hopes. We have seen this in the past, and the future will bring more of the same. Although as individuals we have little power or influence, our actions, collectively, are significant. Ultimately, it is these actions that give shape to race-ethnic relations. None of us can overcome structural barriers, yet, together, we can dismantle them. I do not mean to sound Pollyannaish, but as C. Wright Mills realized, we can at least ask how we can help to create a more positive future.

SUMMARY

1. *Discrimination* occurs worldwide, as *ethnic groups* living in the same society struggle for dominance. *Dominant groups* develop ideologies and *stereotypes* to support their dominance.

2. *Minority groups* share five characteristics: unequal treatment, distinctive traits, solidarity, membership by birth, and marriage within their own group. Minority groups have four objectives: *pluralism, assimilation, secession,* and *militancy.* Five objectives of dominant groups are *assimilation, pluralism, population transfer,* continued subjugation, and *genocide.*

3. Although the idea of *race* greatly affects human behavior, biologically speaking, no human group represents a "pure race."

4. Race–ethnic discrimination is a life-and-death matter, affecting both the quality of life and mortality rates.

5. *Individual discrimination* consists of overt acts by individuals. *Institutional discrimination* is discrimination that is built into the social system.

6. Symbolic interactionists focus on how symbols of race and ethnicity divide people and affect their behavior, particularly how they affect perception, sort people into different life experiences, and justify discrimination and violence. Functionalists analyze functions of discrimination, such as fostering *ethnocentrism* and ensuring that society's *dirty work* gets done. They also analyze its dysfunctions, such

as destroying human potential. Marxist conflict theorists stress that ethnic divisions among workers help capitalists control workers and increase their profits..

7. Race–ethnic discrimination in the United States is especially severe for Native Americans, Latinos, and African Americans. Members of these groups have less education, higher unemployment, lower incomes, and higher rates of poverty than Anglos and Asian Americans. The pressures that these groups have placed on white-controlled social institutions have forced social change. Asian Americans have made the most social and economic gains—primarily through assimilation and family values that stress hard work, thrift, and education.

8. Major cleavages along social class lines divide U.S. ethnic groups. Some sociologists argue that *social class* has become more significant than race-ethnicity in determining an individual's *life chances.*

9. Social policies to encourage cultural pluralism and prevent race–ethnic discrimination were suggested. Groups that attain the most education have the brightest future. The major battlefield is jobs. Dilemmas over affirmative action continue.

10. With the creation of an *underclass,* we can expect urban riots. In no foreseeable future will *prejudice* and discrimination be eliminated. The storm cloud on the horizon is the resurgence of groups that preach division and hatred.

KEY TERMS

Anglo-conformity Requiring or expecting everyone in the United States to adopt Anglo culture, the customs inherited from English settlers.

Apartheid The enforced segregation of people on the basis of their perceived race or ethnicity.

Assimilation The absorption of a minority group into the mainstream culture.

Capitalism An economic system that is based on investing capital to make a profit.

Civil disobedience Deliberately but peacefully disobeying laws that are considered unjust.

Compartmentalize To keep separate in one's mind feelings, attitudes, and behaviors that are incompatible with one another or that threaten the self-concept.

Dirty work The tasks in society that few people want.

Discrimination The act of singling people out for unfair treatment.

Division of labor People performing different sets of specialized tasks.

Dominant group The group that has more power, privilege, and social status and that discriminates against a minority group.

Ethnic group A group of people who identify with one another on the basis of their ancestry and cultural heritage.

Ethnocentrism A strong identity with one's own group, causing one to think of other groups as inferior.

False class consciousness Workers identifying with the wealthy (employers, owners, investors) instead of with other workers.

Genocide Killing an entire people.

Individual discrimination Discrimination by one person against another.

Institutional discrimination Discrimination that is built into the social system.

Life chances What one may expect to get out of life (because of the conditions of the group into which one is born).

Melting pot The expectation that the European immigrants to the United States would "melt" or blend together, that is, interact, intermarry, and form a cultural and biological blend.

Militancy Seeking to dominate society (in Wirth's terminology).

Minority group A group of people who, on the basis of physical or cultural characteristics, are singled out for unequal treatment and who regard themselves as objects of discrimination.

Pan-Indianism Moving beyond tribal identification to work for the welfare of all Native Americans.

Pluralism Different ethnic groups living peacefully with one another, while maintaining their distinctiveness and tolerating differences in others.

Population transfer A minority relocating within a society or leaving the society altogether. In *direct* transfer, the minority is forcibly moved; in *indirect* transfer, the dominant group makes life so miserable for the members of a minority group that they "choose" to leave.

Prejudice An attitude whereby one prejudges others, usually negatively.

Race Inherited physical characteristics that visibly identify a group of people.

Racial-ethnic stratification Society divided along race–ethnic lines; the unequal distribution of resources on the basis of race or ethnicity.

Reserve labor force The unemployed, who can be called to work during periods of labor strife or economic expansion. Also called *reserve labor army*.

Rising expectations The belief that better conditions will come soon. Rising expectations develop when institutionalized barriers begin to fall; if conditions do not immediately change, frustration builds, sometimes resulting in group violence.

Secession Withdrawing from a society to establish one's own nation.

Selective perception Seeing only certain things, while being blind to others.

Self-fulfilling prophecy A prediction or expectation about how things will be that brings about the situation that was predicted or expected.

Social class A group of people who find themselves on about the same rung of the economic ladder; they have similar education, types of work, and income.

Split-labor market Workers who are split along lines of race, ethnicity, or gender.

Stereotype A belief that consists of generalizations of what people are like.

Surplus value of labor If an item sells for more than it cost to produce, that profit (or extra amount, or surplus value) is said to exist because of the value of the labor that went into producing the item.

Underclass Alienated people who live primarily in the inner cities; they have little education, high rates of unemployment, female-headed families, welfare dependency, violent crimes, drug abuse, disease, births to single women, and death by murder.

THINKING CRITICALLY ABOUT CHAPTER 8

1. On page 243 is a list of five characteristics that all minority groups share. Pick any minority group in the United States and give examples of how these five characteristics apply to that group.

2. On page 243 is a list of four objectives of minority groups. Explain how each objective applies to Latinos, to African Americans, to Asian Americans, and to Native Americans. Do these groups emphasize these objectives in the same way? If not, why do you think there are differences?

3. Which of the six policies of dominant groups that Simpson and Yinger identify (pp. 244–245) do you think that Anglos are directing toward African Americans? Toward Native Americans? Toward Asian Americans? Toward Latinos?

4. What is your attitude toward the laws against hate speech? Do you think that these laws should be eliminated (on the basis that they violate the constitutional guarantee of the right of free speech)? Or do you think that they should be strengthened and enforced? Explain.

5. Which of the three sociological perspectives (symbolic interactionism, functionalism, or conflict theory) do you think best explains why prejudice and discrimination exist in the United States? Explain.

CHAPTER 9

Sex Discrimination

OUTSIDE THE DELIVERY ROOM OF A Delhi hospital, the expectant mother's family keeps vigil, her husband smoking and playing cards with the men, the women knitting and recalling their own deliveries.

When the nurse brings the news, everyone falls silent. Faces drop—the newborn is a girl. Some relatives console the father; others curse the mother.

This scene is familiar in India. The birth of a son is seen as a gift from God; the birth of a daughter, at best, a disappointment.

This attitude persists, especially in India's tradition-locked villages. As a result, many girls face hardships and even early death.

Female infanticide is not uncommon, although specific instances are seldom documented. Authorities leave such sensitive family matters alone.

"Strangling baby girls at birth might be a thing of the past," says Promilla Kapur, a sociologist who specializes in the problems of Indian women. "However, what used to be done in a fairly crude manner is still often achieved indirectly."

A female infant can be deprived of milk or ignored if she falls sick. The male child gets the most nourishing food and preferential treatment from his mother.

The Indian girl stands little chance of earning money for her family. In Hindu society almost all women are expected to remain at home with their family. Jobs for women, especially uneducated women, are few . . . and most Indian women are uneducated.

Based on Chacko 1977.

The Problem in Sociological Perspective

You can see how important the sex of a child is in India. Parents on the edge of survival despair at the birth of a girl, for she must be fed and clothed but can contribute little to the family's income. They rejoice at the birth of a boy, for his birth signals the arrival of a child who can help sustain them in their old age.

Women as a Minority Group

Although the Indian situation is extreme, *sex is the major sorting device in every society in the world*. In our own society, men are paid more for the same work, and they dominate politics and public life. As noted in the last chapter, a minority is a group that experiences discrimination. Even though females make up 50.9 percent of the U.S. population (*Statistical Abstract* 2003:Table 12), sociologists consider women to be a minority group because of their position relative to men, the dominant group.

The Development of Sexism as a Social Problem

Sociologists have not always referred to women as a minority group. This came about only gradually, as they began to note parallels between the social positions of women and men and those of African Americans and whites. In 1944 Gunnar Myrdal, a Swedish sociologist who studied U.S. race relations, mentioned the parallels in *An American Dilemma*. He also noted the historical connection: The legal status of African-American slaves was derived from the legal status accorded to women and children in the seventeenth century, whose lives were controlled by the male heads of family. In 1951 an American sociologist, Helen Hacker, was the first to apply the term *minority* to women. Noting that discrimination against women "takes the form of being barred from certain activities or, if admitted, being treated unequally," Hacker said that women were marginal to a society that was dominated by men.

When men do an activity that is normally assigned to women, the prestige of that position increases. Why are the "great" chefs of the world men (with few exceptions, such as was Julia Child)? Shown here is Emeril Lagasse, an eminent television chef. Does his food taste better because it has been cooked by a man?

Is Male Dominance Universal?

The Sexual Stratification of Work

Just as the perception of sociologists was changing, so was that of women, who began to challenge the traditional relations between the sexes. Many came to see themselves not as *individuals* who had less status than men, but as a *group* of people who were discriminated against. During the 1960s and 1970s, women discussed and publicized their grievances with being second-class citizens in a society that was dominated by men. Subjective concerns grew as large numbers of women in the United States and around the world concluded that something needed to be done. This changed the relative positions of women and men from being simply an objective condition of society to a social problem. Sociologists then began to take this issue seriously, and they started to investigate **sexism,** the belief that one sex is innately superior to the other, and the discrimination that results from that belief.

Many things have changed since this earlier period of unrest and agitation, so let's see how extensive this problem is today.

The Scope of the Problem

When did sexism begin? Some social scientists, such as anthropologist Marvin Harris (1977:46), claim that men's domination of society "has been in continuous existence throughout virtually the entire globe from the earliest times to the present." After reviewing the evidence, historian and feminist Gerda Lerner (1986:31) agreed, saying that "there is not a single society known where women-as-a-group have decision-making power over men (as a group)." She also concluded that horticultural and hunting-and-gathering societies had the least gender discrimination, that in those societies women contributed about 60 percent of the group's total food.

Conclusions of universal domination by men make some social analysts apprehensive: If people think that men have always dominated every society around the world, perhaps they will conclude that this behavior is innate. They might then use this conclusion to justify dominating women today. This nature–nurture controversy is summarized in the Issues in Social Problems box on pages 282–283. There you will also see that some researchers question the universality of male dominance.

Don't women presidents, prime ministers, and monarchs disprove the universal domination of society by men? Sociologists point out that these are *individual* women in positions of power, not examples of women-as-a-group in control of a society. Those societies, too, are dominated by men, for men hold almost all the key positions. After extensive effort to close this gender gap, Sweden comes closest to exhibiting political equality between the sexes: Forty-five percent of its cabinet ministers and 45 percent of its parliament are women ("Women in the Riksdag" 2003).

Every society stratifies its members by sex; that is, they single out males and females for different activities. Around the world, for example, most work is **sex-typed,** associated with one sex or the other. Does this mean that anatomy requires that men and women be assigned particular work? In 1937, anthropologist George Murdock reviewed information on 324 societies. He found that what is considered "male" or "female" work differs from one society to another. For example, in some societies the care of cattle is women's work; in others, it is men's work. The only exception was metalworking, which was universally men's work. Three pursuits—making weapons, pursuing sea mammals, and hunting—were almost always men's work, but there were exceptions. No specific work was universally assigned to women. Making clothing, cooking, carrying water, and grinding grain were commonly women's work, but not always. Biology, then, is not an occupational destiny.

What does this have to do with sexism? That one society assigns an activity to men while another assigns it to women could be taken as a type of equality. Social scientists, however, discovered this: *Universally, men's activities are always given greater prestige.* Whatever work is assigned to men, that work is considered superior (Linton 1936; Rosaldo 1974). If taking care of cattle is men's work, then cattle care is thought to be important and carries high prestige. If taking care of cattle is women's work, however, it is considered less important and carries less prestige. To cite an example closer to home, when delivering babies was "women's work," the responsibility of midwives, it was given low prestige. But when men took over this job (despite opposition from women), its prestige shot up (Ehrenreich and English 1973). *It is the sex that is associated with the work that provides its prestige, not the work itself.*

Major Areas of Sex Discrimination

Sexism pervades every society in the world, and it touches almost every aspect of our social life. In her classic 1951 article, Helen Hacker, analyzing the situation at that time, listed these areas of discrimination against U.S. women:

1. *Political and Legal.* Women are often barred from jury duty and public office.
2. *Education.* Professional schools, such as architecture and medicine, apply quotas for women; there, women's participation is limited.
3. *Economic.* Women are usually relegated to monotonous work that falls under the supervision of men, for which they get unequal pay, promotion, and responsibility.
4. *Social.* Women are permitted less freedom of movement, fewer deviations in dress, speech, and manners, and a narrower range of personality expression.

Hacker also described how the three major roles of a female—sister–daughter, wife, and mother—fit this pattern of discrimination. She said that a sister does more housework than her brother, a wife is expected to subordinate her interests to those of her husband, and a mother bears the stigma for an illegitimate child.

Sex discrimination has changed so drastically since Hacker did her analysis that her description sounds as though she were speaking about another society—and in a sociological sense she was. Women are no longer barred from jury duty and public office, nor do they face quotas in professional schools. On a couple of significant levels, however, Hacker's analysis remains remarkably current. Feminists still struggle against unequal treatment in jobs, politics, and in informal social life.

Looking at the Problem Theoretically

Why are societies sexist? Let's apply our three theoretical lenses to see what contrasting perspectives emerge.

SYMBOLIC INTERACTIONISM

Sex and Gender

We must distinguish between two terms. When we consider how males and females differ, we usually think first of **sex,** the different *biological* equipment of males and females. Then we might think about **gender,** how we express our "maleness" or "femaleness." Symbolic interactionists stress that sex is biological, and gender is learned, or social.

Socialization into Sex Roles

Symbolic interactionists study how we are socialized into **gender roles,** the attitudes and behaviors that are expected of boys and men because they are males and of girls and women because they are females. Each society has ideas that some activities are "male" and others "female." To enforce these ideas requires that a society's

Issues in Social Problems

THE NATURE–NURTURE CONTROVERSY: BIOLOGY VERSUS CULTURE

What causes differences between men and women? Answers that are commonly given in discussions from cocktail parties to locker rooms fall into either biological or cultural explanations. So do the answers given by the experts. Most but not all sociologists favor the cultural side. Here are the basic arguments among sociologists.

CULTURE IS THE ANSWER

For sociologist Cynthia Fuchs Epstein (1986, 1988, 1989), the answer lies solely in social factors, especially socialization and social control. Here is her argument:

1. The anthropological record shows more equality between the sexes in the past than we had thought. In earlier societies, women, as well as men, hunted small game, devised tools for hunting, and gathered food. Studies of today's hunting and gathering societies show that "both women's and men's roles have been broader and less rigid than those created by stereotypes. For example, the Agta and Mbuti are clearly egalitarian . . ." This proves that "societies exist in which women are not subordinate to men. Anthropologists who study them claim that there is a separate but equal status of women at this level of development."

2. Not biology but rigidly enforced social arrangements determine the types of work that women and men do in each society. Few people can escape these arrangements to perform work outside their allotted range. Informal customs and formal systems of laws enforce this gender inequality of work, which serves the interests of males. Once these socially constructed barriers are removed, women can and do exhibit the same work habits as men.

3. The human behaviors that biology "causes" are only those that involve reproduction or differences in body structure. These differences are relevant for only a few activities, "such as playing basketball or crawling through a small space."

4. Female crime rates, which are rising, indicate that the aggressiveness that often is considered a biologically dictated male behavior is related to social not biological factors. When social conditions permit, such as with women attorneys, females also exhibit "adversarial, assertive, and dominant behavior." Not incidentally, their "dominant behavior" also shows up in their challenging the biased views about human nature that men scholars have proposed.

In short, not "women's incompetence or inability to read a legal brief, to perform brain surgery, [or] to predict a bull market," but social factors—socialization, gender discrimination, and other forms of social control—are responsible for differences in the behavior of women and

institutions work together. The result is so effective that people feel shame if mismatching occurs in their own behavior and insulted and angry if they see it in others. In the short space we have, I can indicate only a few of the elements involved in this orchestration of a society's institutions.

The process begins *before* birth (Henslin 2005). The expectant parents mentally project their child's participation into activities that are sex-typed. The father may see himself teaching his son how to play baseball; the mother may imagine dressing her daughter in frilly dresses and hearing people say how cute she looks.

Sex as a Master Trait

When their child is born, the parents announce its sex to the world. Through cards, telephone calls, and e-mail, they proclaim: "It's a girl!" or "It's a boy!" Even the newspapers report this momentous event. And momentous it is, for *in every society of the world the announcement launches people into their single most significant life-shaping circumstance*. Sex is a **master trait,** cutting across all other identities in life. Whatever else we may be, we always are a male or a female.

men. Arguments that assign "an evolutionary and genetic basis" to explain gender differences in social status "rest on a dubious structure of inappropriate, highly selective, and poor data, oversimplification in logic and inappropriate inferences by use of analogy."

BIOLOGY IS THE ANSWER

Sociologist Steven Goldberg (1974, 1986, 1989) finds it astonishing that anyone should doubt "the presence of core-deep differences between men and women, differences of temperament and emotion we call masculinity and femininity." He argues that inborn differences, not the environment, "give masculine and feminine direction to the emotions and behavior of men and women." Here is his argument:

1. The anthropological record shows that all societies for which evidence exists are (or were) **patriarchies** (societies in which men dominate women). Stories about **matriarchies** (societies in which women dominate men) are myths.
2. In all societies, past and present, the highest statuses are associated with males. All of them are ruled "by hierarchies overwhelmingly dominated by men."
3. The reason for this one-way dominance of societies is that males "have a lower threshold for the elicitation of dominance behavior . . . a greater tendency to exhibit whatever behavior is necessary in any environment to attain dominance in hierarchies and

male–female encounters and relationships." Males are more willing "to sacrifice the rewards of other motivations—the desire for affection, health, family life, safety, relaxation, vacation and the like—in order to attain dominance and status."
4. Just as a six-foot woman does not prove that women's height is due to social factors, so an exceptional individual, such as a highly achieving and dominant woman, does not refute "the physiological roots of behavior."

In short, only one interpretation of why every society, from the Pygmies to the Swedes, associates dominance and attainment with males is valid. Male dominance of society is "an inevitable resolution of the psychophysiological reality." Socialization and social institutions merely *reflect*—and sometimes exaggerate—inborn tendencies. Any interpretation other than inborn differences is "wrong-headed, ignorant, tendentious, internally illogical, discordant with the evidence, and implausible in the extreme." The argument that males are more aggressive because they have been socialized that way is equivalent to claiming that men can grow moustaches because boys have been socialized that way.

To acknowledge this reality is *not* to condone or defend discrimination against women. Whether one approves what societies have done with these biological differences is not the point. The point is that biology leads males and females to different behaviors and attitudes—regardless of how we feel about this or wish it were different.

Cast onto the stage of life with an assigned role to play, we spend much of our childhood and young adulthood learning what our role requires. Throughout the world, parents are the first "significant others" to teach children this role. The specifics vary from one society to another, but in our society parents begin by using pink and blue, colors that have been imbued with gender-role significance. Parents continue to coach us in our expected roles for longer than most of us want their help.

Subconscious Socialization

A classic study by psychologists Susan Goldberg and Michael Lewis (1969) indicates that parents also teach gender roles subconsciously, that is, without being aware that they are doing so. Goldberg and Lewis recruited mothers of six-month-olds to come into their laboratory so they could observe the development of their children. They also observed how the mothers interacted with their babies, although the mothers didn't know this. They found that the mothers kept their girls closer to them, and they touched and spoke more to them than to their sons. By the time

"Sex brought us together, but gender drove us apart."

The distinction between sex and gender that sociologists have drawn is gradually becoming part of public consciousness.

Stereotypes Become Reality

In Sum

Two Functionalist Theories of the Origin of Male Dominance:

1. Strength, Bravery, Warriors, and Rewards

the children were 13 months old, the girls were more reluctant than the boys to leave their mothers. During play, they remained closer to their mothers and returned to them sooner and more often than the boys did.

Goldberg and Lewis then surrounded each mother with colorful toys and placed her child on the other side of a small barrier. The girls cried and motioned for help more than the boys did; the boys tried to climb over or go around the barrier more than the girls did. The researchers concluded that without knowing it, the mothers had rewarded their daughters for being passive and dependent and their sons for being active and independent.

The Goldberg-Lewis study is difficult to interpret. Were these differences brought about by the mother's behavior, as the researchers suggest? Or did the researchers observe biological differences that were showing up at the age of 13 months? In short, were the mothers responding to differences in their children (the boys wanting to get down and play more, and the girls wanting to be hugged more), or were the mothers creating those differences? We don't yet have enough evidence to draw a firm conclusion.

In childhood, boys are generally allowed to be more active and to express more independence. Preschool boys, for example, are given more freedom to roam farther from home than their preschool sisters. They are also allowed to participate in more rough-and-tumble play—even to get dirtier and to be more defiant (Henslin 2005). Again, we face the same problem. Are the parents and teachers creating these differences in behavior? Or are the children responding to biological predispositions?

Most symbolic interactionists assume that the differences are learned. They emphasize that stereotypes tend to become reality. If males are considered to be aggressive and dominant and a person knows that he is male, he tends to fulfill those expectations by being aggressive and dominant. If females are considered to be passive and submissive and a person knows that she is female, she tends to fulfill those expectations. Not everyone follows the script, but so many do that most members of a society see "clearly" why *their particular stereotypes* represent what biology "really" is.

Symbolic interactionists emphasize that every society uses symbols of male and female to sort its members into separate groups. This process starts within the family and is reinforced by other social institutions. As a result, males and females acquire different ideas of themselves and of one another. As children, all of us learn the meanings that our society associates with the sexes. These symbols then become an essential part of how we picture life—an image that forces an interpretation of the world into "proper" activities for males and females.

FUNCTIONALISM

If male dominance is universal, or even nearly universal, how did it come about? Although the origins of sexism are lost in history, functionalists have two theories to account for it.

The first theory was proposed by anthropologist Marvin Harris (1977). He said that male dominance is universal because it is based on two universal conditions: (1)

social—the necessity to survive warfare, and (2) biological—differences in the physical strength of men and women. Harris's controversial explanation goes like this: In prehistoric times, humans lived in small groups. Because each group was threatened by others, it had to recruit people who would fight in hand-to-hand combat. People feared injury and death, so the recruiting wasn't easy. To coax people into bravery, groups developed rewards and punishments. Because an average woman is only 85 percent the size of an average man and has only two-thirds his strength, men were better at hand-to-hand combat. Men became the warriors—and females became their reward—for both their sex and their labor. Some groups allowed only men who had faced an enemy in combat to marry. Even today, in some tribal groups such as the Barabaig of Tanzania, women are a reward for men who show bravery (Aposporos 2004).

Because some women are stronger than some men, to exclude all women from combat might seem irrational. But if women were to be the chief inducement to get men to fight, this was necessary. To make the system work, men had to be trained from birth for combat, and women had to be trained from birth to give in to men.

According to this explanation, the reward for male bravery came at the expense of females. In almost all band and village societies, men assigned the "drudge work" to women—weeding, seed grinding, fetching water and firewood, doing the routine cooking, and even carrying household possessions during moves. Because men preferred to avoid these onerous tasks—and could if they had one or more wives—women were an excellent bait to induce men to bravery.

2. Pregnancy, Childbirth, and Infancy

The second theory is based on human reproduction (Lerner 1986; Hope and Stover 1987; Friedl 1990). It also goes back to early human history. Life used to be short, and women gave birth to many children. Because only women get pregnant, carry a child for nine months, give birth, and nurse, for a considerable part of their lives women were limited in what they could do. To survive, an infant needed a nursing mother. With a child at her breast or in her womb and one on her hip or on her back, a woman was physically encumbered. Thus women everywhere took on the tasks associated with the home and child care, while men took over hunting large animals and other tasks that required more speed and longer absence from the base camp (Huber 1990).

The result was that men took over. Men made and controlled the weapons used for hunting and warfare. They left the camp to hunt animals, returning triumphantly with prey. Leaving the camp, they also made contact with other tribes and accumulated possessions in trade. Men also gained prestige by returning with prisoners from warfare. In contrast, little prestige was given to the routine activities of women, who didn't do such triumphant things and were not seen as risking their lives for the group. The men's weapons, their items of trade, and the knowledge they gained from their contacts with other groups became sources of power.

The result was fundamental change in the relations of the sexes. As women became subject to the decisions of men, men justified their dominance. They developed ideas that biology imbues manhood with superiority. Men also shrouded many of their activities in secrecy and formed elaborate rules and rituals to avoid "contamination" by females.

In Sum

If either of these theories is true, the *origin* of male dominance is rooted in both social and biological factors. The *maintenance* of male dominance, however, is purely social; it is a perpetuation of millennia-old patterns. When tribal societies developed into larger groups and hand-to-hand combat and hunting dangerous animals ceased to be routine, men, enjoying what they had, held on to their privilege and power. With their dominance rooted in ancient custom, and reluctant to abandon their privileged position, men use cultural devices to control women. For an example, see the Global Glimpse box on the next page on female circumcision.

A Global Glimpse

FEMALE CIRCUMCISION

Female circumcision is common in parts of Africa, Malaysia, and Indonesia. This custom, often called female genital mutilation by Westerners, is also known as clitoral excision, clitoridectomy, infibulation, and labiadectomy, depending on how much of the vagina is removed. Worldwide, between 100 million and 200 million women have been circumcised. In Egypt, 97 percent of the women have been circumcised (Boyle et al. 2001).

In some cultures only the girl's clitoris is cut off; in other groups the clitoris, the labia majora, and the labia minora are removed. The Nubia in the Sudan cut away most of the girl's genitalia, then sew together the remaining outer edges with silk or catgut, so that as the wound heals the vagina fuses together. They leave a small opening—the size of a matchstick—for urine and menstrual fluids. In East Africa the vaginal opening is not sutured shut, but the clitoris and both sets of labia are cut off.

Among most groups, the surgery takes place when the girls are between the ages of 4 and 8. In some cultures, it occurs seven to ten days after birth; in others, not until girls reach adolescence. Because the surgery is often done without anesthesia, the pain is so excruciating that adults must hold the girl down. In urban areas, physicians sometimes perform the operation; in rural areas, a neighborhood woman usually does it.

Female circumcision can cause shock, pain, bleeding, infection, infertility, and death. Ongoing complications include vaginal spasms, painful intercourse, and lack of orgasms. The tiny opening makes urination and menstruation difficult. Frequent urinary tract infections result because urine and menstrual flow build up behind the opening.

When the woman marries, the opening is surgically enlarged to permit sexual intercourse. In some groups, this is the husband's responsibility. Before a woman gives birth, the opening is enlarged further. After birth, the vagina is again sutured shut, a cycle of surgically closing and opening that begins anew with each birth.

One woman, circumcised at 12, described her experience this way:

"Lie down there," the excisor suddenly said to me, pointing to a mat stretched out on the ground. No sooner had I laid down than I felt my frail thin legs tightly grasped by heavy hands and pulled wide apart. I lifted my head. Two women on each side of me pinned me to the ground. My arms were also immobilized. Suddenly I felt some strange substance being spread over my genital area. I would have given anything at that moment to be a thousand miles away; then a shooting pain brought me back to reality. . . . I underwent the ablation of the labia minor and then of the clitoris. The operation seemed to go on forever. . . . I was in the throes of agony, torn apart both physically and psychologically. It was the rule that girls of my age did not weep in this situation. I broke the rule. I reacted immediately with tears and screams of pain. . . . Never have I felt such excruciating pain!

[After the operation] they forced me, not only to walk back to join the other girls who had already been excised, but to dance with them. I was doing my best . . . then I fainted. It was a month before I was completely healed. . . . When I was better, everyone mocked me, as I hadn't been brave, they said. (Walker and Parmar 1993:107–108)

What are the reasons for this custom? Some groups believe that it enhances female fertility. Others think that it reduces female sexual desire, making it more likely that a woman will be a virgin when she marries and, afterward, remain faithful to her husband. Feminists, who call female circumcision "ritual torture to control female sexuality," point out that men dominate the societies that practice it.

Change is coming. The first ladies of four countries—Burkina Faso, Guinea, Mali, and Nigeria—have condemned the practice (Lacey 2003). In Kenya, two girls obtained a court order to stop their father from having them circumcised. Their community was shocked, but an attorney reminded the court that Kenya had signed human rights agreements.

What do you think?

Based on Mahran 1978, 1981; Ebomoyi 1987; Lightfoot-Klein 1989; Merwine 1993; Walker and Parmar 1993; Chalkey 1997 Boyle et al. 2001; Lacey 2003.

Conflict Theory

Power, Privilege, and Resources

Conflict theorists provide a contrasting view of sexism. For background, consider these principles: Power yields privilege. In every society, the powerful enjoy the best resources available. Their privileged lifestyles encourage them to feel that they are superior beings. Consequently, the powerful clothe themselves with ideologies that justify their position, cling tenaciously to their privilege, and utilize the social institutions to maintain their power.

As a group, men are no exception to these principles. They, too, cling to their positions, cultivate images of female inferiority to justify their greater privilege, and use economic and legal weapons against women. As Helen Hacker (1951) put it:

> In the wake of the Industrial Revolution, as women acquired industrial, business, and professional skills, they increasingly sought employment in competition with men. Men were quick to perceive them as a rival group and made use of economic, legal, and ideological weapons to eliminate or reduce their competition. They excluded women from the trade unions, made contracts with employers to prevent their hiring women, passed laws restricting the employment of married women, caricatured the working woman, and carried on ceaseless propaganda to return women to the home or keep them there.

The Struggle for Equality

Now that greater sexual equality is a part of U.S. life, it is easy to lose sight of the prolonged and bitter struggle by which women gained their rights. In the 1800s, females were under the legal control of a man, either a father or a husband, and possessed no legal or social right to self-determination. Women could not vote, make legal contracts, testify in court, hold property in their own name, or even spend their own wages (which by law belonged to the husband). To secure these rights, women had to confront men and the social institutions that men dominated. Men first denied women the right to speak in public, spat upon those who did, slapped their faces, tripped them, pelted them with burning cigar stubs, and hurled obscenities at them. Despite the opposition, leaders of the women's movement persisted. They chained themselves to the iron grillwork of public buildings and went on talking while the police sawed them loose. If arrested, these women would go on hunger strikes in jail.

In 1916, feminists (then called *suffragists*) formed the National Women's Party. In January, 1917, they formed a picket line around the White House. After the women had protested for six months, authorities had them arrested. The women refused to pay their fines, and judges sent hundreds to prison, including Lucy Burns and Alice Paul, leaders of these demonstrations. Their treatment in jail illustrates how seriously these women had threatened male privilege:

> The guards from the male prison fell upon us. I saw Miss Lincoln, a slight young girl, thrown to the floor. Mrs. Nolan, a delicate old lady of seventy-three, was mastered by two men. . . . Whittaker (the Superintendent) in the center of the room directed the whole attack, inciting the guards to every brutality. Two men brought in Dorothy Day, twisting her arms above her head. Suddenly they lifted her and brought her body down twice over the back of an iron bench. The bed broke Mrs. Nolan's fall, but Mrs. Cosu hit the wall. They had been there a few minutes when Mrs. Lewis, all doubled over like a sack of flour, was thrown in. Her head struck the iron bed and she fell to the floor senseless. As for Lucy Burns, they handcuffed her wrists and fastened the handcuffs over her head to the cell door. (Cowley 1969:13)

Universally, children imitate the adults around them. This process of modeling or role playing helps children prepare for roles that they will play as adults. Here, schoolchildren pretend to be doctors at the Kids' City mall in Mexico City.

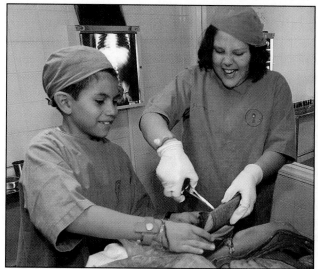

Today it is difficult to imagine U.S. women being treated this way for trying to gain rights that men already possess. The early suffragists were persistent and outspoken, however, and they used bold tactics to force a historical shift in the balance of power.

Since those days, there has been no overt conflict between men and women as a group (Hacker 1951). Today women face more subtle discrimination, including hidden quotas, jokes, glass ceilings, and the "purely personal preference" that men occupy the more responsible positions. Women still press for a greater share of society's power, but the struggle has changed. Women today pressure lawmakers, compete for positions in good colleges and graduate schools, and fight obstacles that inhibit advancement at work, including sexual harassment.

In Sum

From the conflict perspective, social equality is gained only by forcing men to yield—for men as a class do not willingly cede their control of society's institutions. Let's examine that struggle, pausing first to consider again the question of natural differences between the sexes.

Research Findings

THE QUESTION OF NATURAL DIFFERENCES BETWEEN THE SEXES

Are There Natural Differences?

Apart from obvious physical differences between males and females, what are the natural differences between the sexes? Is one sex innately more intelligent? More aggressive? Dominant? Protective? Nurturing? Tender? Loving? Passive?

Four Approaches in Studying this Question:

1. Studies of Children

The difficulty of separating culture from biology has plagued researchers in their attempt to answer such intriguing questions. Because each society places males and females on different roads in life, the society in which they are reared shapes any innate differences that may exist. To untangle this knotty problem, researchers have taken four approaches. The *first* focuses on children. If girls and boys show consistent differences at early ages, biology may be at work. In testing for differences, researchers have found that girls generally score higher than boys on verbal skills (Goleman 1987). Most girls begin to speak earlier than boys and are quicker to talk in short sentences and then to use longer sentences. They read earlier and do better in grammar, spelling, and word fluency. Boys, in contrast, tend to do better on spatial tasks (Bardwick 1971).

Test results in mathematics have provided a puzzle for researchers. When boys and girls are compared nationally, boys always outperform girls. This holds true if we compare their overall scores, or if we compare the scores of those who have taken specific courses: general math, algebra, geometry, or calculus (*Digest of Education Statistics* 2001:Table 126). Year after year, boys also score considerably higher in math on the SATs (college entrance tests). In 1967, boys scored 40 points higher; in 2002, it was 34 points higher (*Statistical Abstract* 2003:Table 264).

Do such differences reflect innate abilities? Some researchers think so. For fifteen years, psychologist and feminist Camillia Benbow searched for an environmental explanation. Gradually, she ruled out all possibilities and reluctantly concluded that these results are due to "a basic biological difference between the sexes in brain functions" (Goleman 1987).

Other social scientists insist that cultural factors explain such differences. To explain girls' higher verbal performance, they point to three social causes: (1) girls identify more with their mothers (who are themselves more verbal), (2) both mothers and fathers hold and speak to their daughters more than to their sons, and (3) little girls' games are more linguistic than boys' games (Bardwick 1971). As Carole Whitehurst

(1977:36) put it: "All *apparent sex* differences in intelligence *may* be explained by early learning and continual reinforcement."

This likely is true of verbal differences. In 1967 girls outscored boys on the verbal portion of the SATs, but in 1975 boys outscored girls, and boys have held the lead ever since (*Statistical Abstract* 2003:Table 264). The explanation must be environmental, for certainly there was no switch in male–female brain functions during this time. What that environmental explanation is, however, eludes us. During this same time, in no year have girls outperformed boys in mathematics, and biological explanations are excellent candidates for this consistent difference. If girls catch up or take the lead in mathematics, as boys did in verbal scores, this would be strong evidence of environmental causes.

Boys and girls also show differences in aggression. As Judith Bardwick (1971) pointed out, from early childhood to adulthood males tend to be more active and extraverted, females more passive and introverted. Again, the question is: Does this mean that males are innately more "aggressive" than females? Some researchers point to cultural factors. Parents may subtly (or less subtly) encourage their sons to be aggressive, believing that "sticking up for your rights," "showing you're not a sissy," and so on, are signs of masculinity. Parents also may express pleasure when their daughters are less demanding and more compliant—traits considered feminine. From infancy on, then, parents mold their children into cultural stereotypes of masculinity and femininity. But, to be fair, this does not rule out biology. Parents may be responding to biological differences, and even reinforcing them.

2. Cross-Cultural Studies

A *second* approach researchers have taken is to compare men and women cross-culturally. We reviewed this approach in the box on the nature–nurture controversy (pages 282–283). There we saw that researchers fail to agree on the meaning of anthropological findings.

3. Studies of Animals

The *third* approach researchers have taken to separate innate biological factors from cultural molding has been to observe monkeys. The findings about aggression are noteworthy, for differences show up early and consistently: "Within a month after birth, male rhesus monkeys are wrestling, pushing, biting, and tugging, while the female monkeys are beginning to act shy, turning their heads away when challenged to a fight by young males" (Bardwick 1971:91). Bardwick adds,

> The males quickly surpass the females in the rate of achieving independence from their mothers (helped by the way the mothers punish their sons more, pay less attention to them, and hold and carry them less). The males had higher general activity levels, did more biting, pushing, shoving, yanking, grabbing, and jerking. They also did more thumbsucking and more manipulation of their genitals.

We must always be cautious when drawing conclusions about humans from animal research, of course. To understate the matter, humans are not monkeys. Aggression, however, is related to the level of male hormones (Bardwick 1971; LeVay 1993), a matter that we shall now consider.

4. The Vietnam Veterans' Study

The *fourth* and most recent approach is intriguing. In 1985, the U.S. government began a health study of Vietnam veterans. To be certain the study was representative, the researchers chose a random sample of 4,462 men. Among the data they collected was a measurement of testosterone for each veteran. Until this time, research on testosterone and human behavior was based on very small samples. Now, unexpectedly, sociologists had a large random sample, one that is turning out to hold surprising clues about human behavior.

When the veterans with higher levels of testosterone were boys, they were more likely to get in trouble with parents and teachers and to become delinquents. As adults, they are more likely to use hard drugs, to get into fights, to end up in lower-status jobs, and to have more sexual partners. Not surprisingly, this history makes them less appealing candidates for marriage, and they are less likely to marry. Those who do marry are less likely to share problems with their wives. They also are more likely to have affairs, to hit their wives, and, it follows, to get divorced (Dabbs and Morris 1990; Booth and Dabbs 1993).

The Vietnam veterans study does *not* leave us with biology as the sole basis for behavior, however. Not all men who have high testosterone levels get in trouble with the law, do poorly in school, or mistreat their wives. A chief difference, in fact, is social class. High-testosterone men from higher social classes are less likely to be involved in antisocial behaviors than are high-testosterone men from lower social classes (Dabbs and Morris 1990). Social factors (socialization, life goals, self-definitions), then, also must play a part. Uncovering the social factors and discovering how they work in combination with biological factors such as testosterone will be of high sociological interest.

Perhaps a Combination of Biology and Culture

From our current evidence, we can conclude that *if* biology provides males and females with differences in temperament, personality, or predispositions in behavior, culture overrides those differences. It shapes people into the types of men and women that predominate in a particular society. Because people wear cultural blinders that mask the workings of their culture, people in each culture consider the characteristics that are implanted into their males and females to be overwhelming evidence of the "natural" differences between the sexes.

In the years to come, unraveling the influences of socialization and biology should prove to be an exciting—and controversial—area of sociological research. One level of research will be to determine if there are behaviors that are due only to biology. The second will be to discover how social factors modify biology. The third will be, in sociologist Janet Chafetz's (1990:30) phrase, to determine how "different" becomes translated into "unequal."

Research and Ideology

At this point, we have no final answer to the question of natural differences between the sexes in aggression, nurturing, forms of intelligence, and so on. Some researchers are convinced they are innate, others that they are learned. Like other areas of science, we must examine the data with an open mind, not try to make the evidence fit ideologies that favor either biology or culture. Unfortunately, research in this area of human behavior has become emotionally charged, and to draw conclusions on one side or the other indicates to some that one is "faithful" or "unfaithful" to an ideology. This, of course, is not science. One would hope that data, not ideology, will one day answer this question once and for all.

Let's examine inequality between the sexes, with a focus on U.S. society.

DISCRIMINATION IN EVERYDAY LIFE

Routine Sexism

Leaning against the water cooler, two men—both minor executives—are nursing cups of coffee, discussing last Sunday's Giants game, postponing the moment when they have to go back to work.

A vice president hears them talking about sports. Does he send them back to their desks? Probably not. Being a man, he is likely to join in the conversation and prove that he is "one of the boys," feigning an interest in football that he may not share at all. These men—all men in the office—are his troops, his comrades-in-arms.

Now, assume that two women are standing by the water cooler discussing whatever you please: clothes, work, the glass ceiling, any subject except football or some other sport. The same vice president sees them and wonders whether it is worth the trouble to complain that they are standing around gabbing when they should be working. "Don't they know," he will ask, in the words of a million men, "that this is an office?" (Korda 1973:20–21, paraphrased)

**Feminine
Terms as Insults**

In everyday life, women routinely encounter antagonistic attitudes from men. Women find their interests, attitudes, and contributions devalued. Masculinity is highly valued; it represents success and strength. Femininity is devalued; it is perceived as failure and weakness. Such attitudes are not new. During World War II, a team of researchers headed by sociologist Samuel Stouffer studied the motivation of combat soldiers. Out of this research came a sociological classic, *The American Soldier.* Stouffer and his colleagues reported (1949:132) that officers used feminine terms as insults to motivate soldiers:

> To fail to measure up as a soldier in courage and endurance was to risk the charge of not being a man. ("Whatsa matter, bud—got lace on your drawers?")

A generation later, during the Vietnam war, officers still used accusations of femininity to motivate soldiers. Drill sergeants would mock their troops by saying, "Can't hack it, little girls?" (Eisenhart 1975). This practice continues. In the Marines, the worst insult to male recruits is to compare their performance to a woman's (Gilham 1989). Male soldiers who show hesitation during maneuvers are mocked by others, who call them girls (Miller 2005).

Sociologists have observed this same behavior in sports. Douglas Foley (2006) heard ex-football players tell high school boys who had a bad game that they were "wearing skirts." Jean Stockard and Miriam Johnson (1980) heard boys playing basketball shout to boys who missed a basket, "You play like a woman." You've probably heard things like this yourself.

Inequality in Talk

Most people dismiss such remarks as insignificant: "That's just people talking." Such remarks, however, as Stockard and Johnson point out, are part of a general devaluation of women. They reveal a derogatory attitude that women face in everyday life. To make this idea clearer, Stockard and Johnson point out that: "There is no comparable phenomenon among women, for young girls do not insult each other by calling each other 'man.'" Conversations between men and women also mirror their relative positions of power in society. When men and women are talking, men are more likely to interrupt conversations and to control changes in topics (West and Garcia 1988; Smith-Lovin and Brody 1989; Tannen 1990, 2005). Even in college, men interrupt their instructors more often than women do. If their instructor is a woman, they interrupt even more often (Brooks 1982).

**Devaluation Underlies
Discrimination**

Sociologist Carol Whitehurst (1977:8–9) summarized the routine devaluation and discrimination that women face in everyday life:

> Women often are made the butt of jokes and are ridiculed, particularly for their efforts in behalf of women and women's rights. Their complaints and reports of mistreatment often are dismissed, treated lightly or even derisively. A woman often is not treated as if her opinions carry equal weight to those of a man, even if she has equal professional status. . . . When [men] . . . respond to a woman's complaint with "You're so cute when you get mad," it should be perfectly obvious that women are not being taken seriously, but are being considered on a level with children or idiots.

Although we are seeing changes in male–female relationships, the devaluation of women continues to be a background feature of social life. As Whitehurst says, this devaluation is important because it underlies all other forms of oppression.

DISCRIMINATION IN EDUCATION

**The Past: Wombs
Dominate the Mind**

Let's first take a glimpse at the past. About a century ago, leading educators claimed that women's mental life was dominated by their wombs. Dr. Edward Clarke, for example, a member of Harvard University's medical faculty, warned that education and study posed dangers for women. He wrote,

A girl upon whom Nature, for a limited period and for a definite purpose, imposes so great a physiological task, will not have as much power left for the tasks of school, as the boy of whom Nature requires less at the corresponding epoch. (Andersen 1988:35)

Clarke added that to preserve their fragile health, women should study only one-third as much as men—and not study at all during menstruation.

In some countries, women are still discriminated against in education. Table 9-1 provides a glimpse of how education is disproportionately reserved for boys in Africa and Asia. In 21 of the world's countries, girls make up less than 45 percent of secondary school students. From Table 9-1, you can see that seventeen of those countries are located in Africa, three in Asia, and that one (Turkey) straddles Asia and Europe.

The Present:

Clarke's quote reminds us how tremendously times have changed in the United States. Today, there are *two million* more women in college than there are men (*Statistical Abstract* 2003:Tables 280). The gap has grown so great that men may need special scholarships, remedial help, retention programs, and boosts of every sort. These enrollments may indicate that we are glimpsing the beginning of a fundamental change in this social problem. Following the basic model of social problems that I have stressed throughout this text, at this point we have only an objective condition. If enough people become upset about this condition, however, we will have another dimension to the social problem of sexual discrimination.

Sports

With the numbers of women in college, how can anyone say that there is discrimination against women in education? We certainly have to look more deeply for it than we used to, but U.S. education still contains strong elements of sexism. Some of it shows up in school sports: Boys become the football players, and girls join the drill team, drum majorettes, and pep squads (Foley 2006). As Carol Whitehurst (1977) put it, "The boys perform, the girls cheer." It is difficult to imagine girls playing a sport, with boys sitting on the sidelines with bated breath, eagerly jumping to their feet and even into the air when a girl makes a great play.

Consequences for Vocational Choice

Apart from this rather visible and interesting demonstration, in college we see what sociologists call *gender tracking;* that is, women and men tend to cluster in different specialties. Women earn 87 percent of bachelor's degrees in library "science," for example, whereas men earn 95 percent of bachelor's degrees in military "science." Similarly, women dominate home economics and men dominate engineering (*Statistical Abstract* 2003:Table 301). It is socialization—rather than any presumed innate characteristics—that channels males and females into sex-linked educational paths.

The Masculinity of the College Experience

Another factor is significant. When they enter college, most students face a man's world. Not only are most of their professors men, but they study mostly men authors in their literature courses, discuss the thinking of men in their philosophy courses, and read almost exclusively about famous men in their history courses. The social sciences, including sociology, also concentrate on the contributions of men. How this affects the orientations of women and men students is unknown at the moment, but it certainly has to be significant. From the reactions shared with me by men students who have taken courses in gender studies taught by women who have immersed them in a "women's world of thought," the impact is profound. For the men, it was upsetting. When something is gradual and taken for granted, such as the "men's world of thought," the impact is just as severe, but not as apparent.

Example of the Sciences

Although women now outnumber men in college and earn 55 percent of all bachelor's degrees, between the bachelor's and the doctorate something happens. Look at Table 9-2 on page 294, which gives us a snapshot of doctoral programs in the sciences. You can see how aspirations (enrollment) and accomplishments (doctorates conferred) are sex linked. In five of these doctoral programs men outnumber women, and in three women outnumber men (in two by a very small margin). In *all* of them, however, women are less likely to complete the doctorate.

THE MASS MEDIA

The mass media help to shape gender roles. The media give messages to children—and to the rest of us—that certain behaviors are considered "right" for boys and other behaviors "right" for girls. They also give messages about the "proper" relationships between men and women. To get some insight into how this occurs, we will look first at children's books, then at television, music, video games, and advertising.

Children's Books

Children's picture books have been a major focus of sociologists. It is easy to see that illustrated books for children are more than just entertainment; little children learn about the world from the pictures they see and the stories read to them. What the pictures show girls and boys doing becomes part of their view of what is "right."

When sociologists first examined children's picture books in the 1970s, they found that it was unusual for a girl to be the main character. Almost all the books featured boys, men, and even male animals. The girls, when pictured at all, were passive and doll-like, whereas the boys were active and adventuresome. While the boys did things that required independence and self-confidence, most girls were shown trying to help their brothers and fathers (Weitzman et al. 1972). Feminists protested these stereotypes and even formed their own companies to publish books that showed girls as leaders, as active and independent.

The result of these efforts, as well as that of the changed role of women in society, is that children's books now have about an equal number of boy and girl characters. Girls are also now depicted in a variety of nontraditional activities. Researchers find, however, that males are seldom depicted as caring for the children or doing grocery shopping, and they never are seen doing housework (Gooden and Gooden 2001). As gender roles continue to change, I assume that this, too, will change.

Television

More powerful than picture books is television, both because of its moving images and the number of hours that children watch television. In the cartoons that so fascinate young children, males outnumber females, giving the message that boys are more important than girls. A children's TV show that ran from 1987 to 1996, *Teenage Mutant Ninja Turtles,* captures the situation. The original turtles were Michelangelo, Leonardo, Raphael, and Donatello—named after men artists whose accomplishments have been admired for centuries. A female turtle was added. Her name? Venus de Milo. The female turtle was named not for a person, but for a statue that is world famous for its curvaceous and ample breasts. She never did anything. And, how could she—she has no head or arms ("Getting the Message" 1997).

Adult television reinforces stereotypes of gender, age, and sexuality. On prime time, male characters outnumber female characters, and men are more likely to be portrayed in higher-status positions (Glascock 2001). Starting at age 30, fewer and fewer women are shown, and about 9 out of 10 women on prime time are below the age of 46. Older women practically disappear from television. (Gerbner 1998). Women are depicted as losing their sexual attractiveness earlier than men. Men are portrayed as aging more gracefully, with their sexual attractiveness lasting longer.

Body image is part of gender roles, and television is effective in teaching us what we "should" look like.

PERCENTAGE	COUNTRY
32	Benin
36	Equatorial Guinea
37	Cambodia
38	Djibouti
38	Ethiopia
38	Niger
39	Burkina Faso
39	Eritrea
39	Mozambique
40	Senegal
41	Gambia
41	Laos
41	Nepal
41	Papua New Guinea
42	Burundi
42	Congo
42	Turkey
43	Mauritania
44	Angola
44	Malawi
44	Zambia

TABLE 9-1 Of Students Enrolled in Secondary School, What Percentage Are Girls?

Source: By the author, based on U.S. Agency for International Development, 2004.

TABLE 9-2 Doctorates in Science, by Sex

FIELD	STUDENTS ENROLLED IN DOCTORAL PROGRAMS		DOCTORATES CONFERRED		COMPLETION RATIO* (HIGHER OR LOWER THAN EXPECTED)	
	WOMEN	MEN	WOMEN	MEN	WOMEN	MEN
Agriculture	42%	58%	29%	71%	−31	+22
Mathematics	35%	65%	25%	75%	−29	+15
Engineering	20%	80%	16%	84%	−25	+5
Computer sciences	29%	71%	16%	84%	−44	+18
Social sciences	51%	49%	43%	57%	−16	+16
Biological sciences	52%	48%	46%	55%	−12	+15
Physical sciences	30%	70%	24%	76%	−20	+9
Psychology	72%	28%	67%	33%	−7	+18

*The formula for the completion ratio is X minus Y divided by Y, where X is the doctorates conferred and Y is the proportion enrolled in a program.
Source: By the author, based on *Statistical Abstract of the United States* 2002:Tables 769, 771.

Sociologists who studied situation comedies found that most female characters are below average in weight. They are also portrayed as dieting and as having a drive to be slender. Viewers not only learn that thinness is desirable, but also, compared with average women in the population, they learn a "distorted and unrealistic picture of women's bodies" (Fouts and Burggraf 1999).

Televised sports news maintains traditional stereotypes. Sociologists who studied the content of televised sports news in Los Angeles found that women athletes rarely receive coverage (Messner et al. 2003). When they do, they are sometimes trivialized by focusing on humorous events in women's sports or by turning the woman athlete into a sexual object. Newscasters even manage to emphasize breasts and bras and to engage in locker-room humor.

At the same time, stereotypes are being broken. On comedies, women are more aggressive verbally than men (Glascock 2001). Buffy the Vampire Slayer saves her classmates from Evil, while, with tongue in cheek, the Powerpuff Girls are touted as "the most elite kindergarten crime-fighting force ever assembled." Perhaps the most stereotype-breaking of all is *Xena, Warrior Princess,* a television series imported from New Zealand. Portrayed as super dominant, Xena overcomes all obstacles and defeats all foes—whether men or women.

Role models are important for what we aspire to, what we become, and how we evaluate ourselves. Shown here is Jennifer Lopez with some young women who are modeling her line of clothing.

Feminists have protested the degradation of women, including the exposure of the female body to sell products. The resulting change, however, has not been a decrease in the number of such ads. Instead, we now have ads that explicitly display the male body to sell products. This is a form of equality, although not the one that was intended.

Music

There are so many kinds (genres) of music that it is difficult to summarize their content accurately. In many songs for teens and preteens, the listeners learn that boys should dominate male–female relationships. A common message for girls is that they should be sexy, passive, and dependent—and that they can control boys by manipulating the boys' sexual impulses. In music videos, females are most often only background ornaments for the dominant males. Some rap groups glorify male sexual aggression and revel in humiliating women. In Country-Western songs, which have become so popular, the common message is that men are aggressive and dominant, whereas women are passive and dependent. These men do have a tender side, however: They cry into their beers after their cheating women have left them. But, never mind, some honky-tonk woman is waiting to revel in her dominant man.

Video Games

More than any other medium, video games give the message that women are not important: Male characters outnumber female characters seven to one (Beasley and Standley 2002). Matching the depictions of sex roles in the other media, video women show more skin than do video men.

Advertising

Advertising is an insidious propaganda machine for a male supremacist society. It spews out images of women as sex mates, housekeepers, mothers, and menial workers—images that perhaps reflect the true status of most women in society, but which also make it increasingly difficult for women to break out of the sexist stereotypes that imprison them (Komisar 1971:304).

This observation from the 1970s reminds us that little has changed in advertising. Although fewer women are now depicted as "housekeepers, mothers, and menial workers," television advertising continues to reinforce stereotypical gender roles. Commercials aimed at children are more likely to show girls as cooperative and boys as aggressive. They are also more likely to show girls at home and boys at other locations (Larson 2001). Men are portrayed in higher status positions (Coltrane and Messineo 2000). Women make most purchases, they are underrepresented as primary characters, and they are shown primarily as supportive counterparts to men (Ganahal et al. 2003).

Fighting Back

The use of the female body—especially exposed breasts—to sell products also continues. Feminists have fought back. In one campaign, they spray-painted their own lines to billboards (Rakow 1992). One billboard featured a Fiat with a woman reclining on its roof saying, "It's so practical, Darling," Feminists added the spray-painted line, "When I'm not lying on cars, I'm a brain surgeon."

Such resistance, as you know from the average 1,600 ads that pummel you each day (Draper 1986), has had little impact. The major change with how bodies are depicted in advertising is that the male body has become more prominent. More than ever, parts of the male body are also selected for exposure and for irrelevant associations with products.

In Sum

The essential point is that the mass media—children's books, television, music, video games, and advertising—influence us. They shape the images that we hold of the way people "ought" to be, and we tend to see one another as men and women through those images. Mostly subtle and beneath our level of awareness, these images channel our behavior, becoming part of the means by which men maintain their dominance in social life. This includes politics, to which we now turn.

THE WORLD OF POLITICS

Why Don't Women Dominate Politics?

Politics provides an excellent illustration of the relative position of men and women in the United States. As Figure 9-1 shows, women are vastly underrepresented in political decision making. In fact, the higher the office, the fewer the women. Only a handful of women have been governors or mayors of large cities. Despite the political gains women have made in recent elections, since 1789, over 1,800 men have served in the U.S. Senate, but only 35 women have served, including the 14 current senators. Not until 1992 was the first African American woman (Carol Moseley-Braun) elected to the Senate. No Latina or Asian American woman has yet been elected to the Senate (National Women's Political Caucus 1998; *Statistical Abstract* 2003:Table 408).

But why is it men who wield political power at all levels? About *8 million* more women than men are of voting age, and more women than men vote in our national elections (*Statistical Abstract* 2003:Table 419). So why don't women take political control of the nation?

Socialization

A good part of the reason for women's underrepresentation is socialization. As we have seen, our social institutions help to socialize females into dependency. This leads to the following syllogism: Politics is a form of dominance; dominance is masculine; therefore, politics is "unfeminine." This perception imposes severe restraints on women's recruitment, participation, and performance.

Professions, Perceptions, Positions, and Power

Other significant reasons center on sex roles and the relative positions of men and women. First, women are underrepresented in law and business, the careers from which most politicians come. Further, most women do not perceive themselves as a class of people who need political action to overcome domination. Most women also find the irreg-

FIGURE 9-1 *Who Controls U.S. Politics?*
Sources: By the author, based on *Statistical Abstract of the United States* 2003:Tables 408, 413, 415; National Governors' Association 2004; Election results 2004.

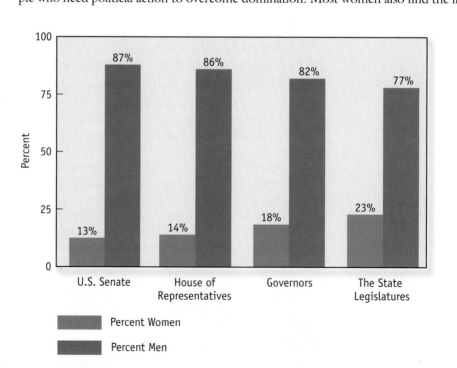

ular hours that running for elective office requires incompatible with being a mother. Fathers, in contrast, whose ordinary roles are more likely to take them away from the home, do not feel this same conflict. Women are also less likely to have a supportive spouse who will play an unassuming background role while providing child care, encouragement, and voter appeal. Finally, men prefer to keep their power and have been reluctant to bring women into decision-making roles or to regard them as viable candidates.

Changes

Recent social change, however, means that we can expect more women to win political office. More women are going into law and business, where they are doing more traveling and making statewide and national contacts. Increasingly, child care has become the responsibility of both parents. A main concern of many party leaders today is not the sex but the "winnability" of a candidate. This generation, then, is likely to see a fundamental change in women's political participation—and a woman occupying the Oval Office.

THE WORLD OF WORK

Trends in Women's Participation in the World of Work

Year after year, more women enter the world of paid employment. Table 9-3 documents this trend for the United States. We can see that, with one exception, for more than 100 years the number of U.S. women who are employed outside the home has increased consistently. The exception is the period immediately following World War II. By 1945, 38 percent of women were in the labor force, working in factory and office jobs while the men fought in World War II. As you can see, this rate dropped after the men came home from the war and reclaimed these jobs.

TABLE 9-3 Women in the Civilian Labor Force

YEAR	NUMBER	AS A PERCENTAGE OF ALL WORKERS	PERCENTAGE OF WOMEN IN THE LABOR FORCE	PERCENTAGE OF WOMEN NOT IN THE LABOR FORCE
1890	4,000,000	17	18	82
1900	5,000,000	18	20	80
1920	8,000,000	20	23	77
1930	10,000,000	22	24	76
1940	14,000,000	25	29	71
1945	19,000,000	36	38	62
1950	18,000,000	30	34	66
1955	21,000,000	32	34	66
1960	23,000,000	33	36	64
1965	26,000,000	35	37	63
1970	32,000,000	37	41	59
1975	37,000,000	39	42	58
1980	45,000,000	42	48	52
1985	51,000,000	44	50	50
1990	57,000,000	45	54	46
1995	61,000,000	46	56	44
2000	63,000,000	46	60	40
2002	67,000,000	47	60	40
2010*	76,000,000	48	60	40

Note: Pre-1940 figures include women 14 and over; figures for 1940 and after are for women 16 and over.
*Indicates estimate by the U.S. Dept. of Labor.
Sources: *1969 Handbook on Women Workers* 1969:10; *Manpower Report to the President* 1971:203, 205; Mills and Palumbo 1980:6, 45; *U.S. Bureau of the Census,* various years; *Statistical Abstract* 2003:Table 588.

The percentage of the population age 16 and over that is in the labor force at least part-time is known as the **labor force participation rate.** For women, the watershed year was 1985. In that year, for the first time in U.S. history, 50 percent of all women were employed outside the home. Today, close to half of all U.S. workers are women. As the Social Map shows, the percentage of women working for wages differs by state. The rate ranges from 49 percent in West Virginia to 71 percent in Minnesota.

The world of work is no exception to the general pattern of discrimination against women. Women come up against an "old boy's network," social contacts that keep jobs, promotions, and opportunities circulating among men. To overcome this exclusion, some women professionals have developed a "new girls' network." They pass opportunities among one another, purposefully excluding men in order to help the careers of women.

The Gender Gap in Earnings

But we need more than anecdotes to pinpoint discrimination at work. We need hard numbers, and the most precise figure is the *gender gap* in wages. At all ages and at all levels of education, the average man is paid more than the average woman. Considering all jobs in the nation, and looking at only full-time, year-round workers, women average only 67 *percent* of what men earn (*Statistical Abstract* 2003:Table 695). Until the 1980s, women's earnings hovered between 58 and 60 percent of men's, which means that to be paid two-thirds of what men make is an improvement! The European nations also have a gender gap in pay, but only Portugal has a gap as great as that of the United States (Clarke 2001).

Figure 9-3 gives us a snapshot of how powerfully gender affects earnings. If men and women have the same education, the average man earns much more than the average woman. This is true of all occupations and all levels of education. This gender gap in pay translates into an astounding lifetime total: *Between the ages of 25 and 65, the average man who graduates from college earns about a million dollars ($1,050,000) more than the average woman who graduates from college.*

Explaining the Pay Gap

Why do we have a pay gap between women and men? Could it exist because of the type of work that men and women do? Women are more likely to work at lower-paid

Figure 9-2 *Social Map: How Likely Are Women to Work for Wages?*

Note: Refers to women who are 16 years old and over who work for wages at least part-time in the civilian labor force; commonly called the *labor force participation rate.*

Source: By the author, based on *Statistical Abstract of the United States* 2003:Table 592.

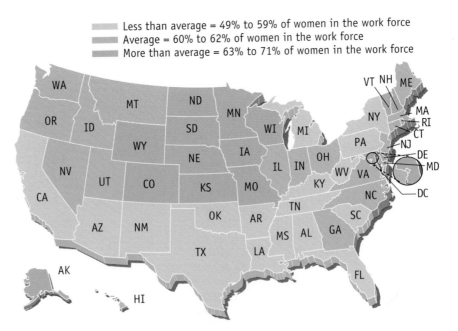

Less than average = 49% to 59% of women in the work force
Average = 60% to 62% of women in the work force
More than average = 63% to 71% of women in the work force

Note: Refers to women who are 16 years old and over who work for wages at least part time in the civilian labor force; commonly called the *labor force participation rate.*

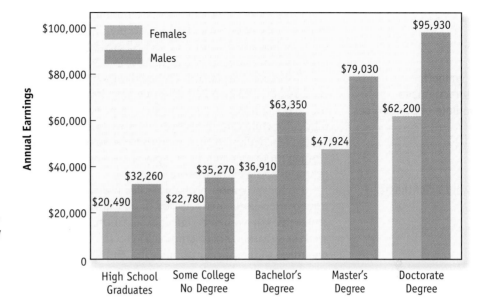

FIGURE 9-3 *How Much Will You Earn? Cash Penalties and Rewards for Being Male or Female*

Source: By the author, based on *Statistical Abstract* of the United States 2003:Table 230.

jobs, such as clerical work. They make up 98 percent of all secretaries, stenographers, and typists. Or does this gap exist because women professionals, such as physicians, typically put in fewer hours than men (Steinhauer 1999b)? Researchers checked such factors, and found that they account for about half the pay gap (Kemp 1990). The balance, they conclude, is due to gender discrimination.

How does gender discrimination work to create such a gap in income? Economists Rex Fuller and Richard Schoenberger (1991) help us understand how this comes about. They examined the starting salaries of 230 business majors at the University of Wisconsin, of whom 47 percent were women. They found that the women's starting salaries averaged 11 percent ($1,737) less than those of the men.

Were the women less qualified? Did they have lower grades? Or fewer internships? If so, they deserved lower salaries. To find out, Fuller and Schoenberger compared the men's and women's college records. What they uncovered can best be described as *deep* gender discrimination: The *women* had earned higher grades and done more internships. In other words, women had to have higher qualifications than men in order to be offered lower salaries!

What happened after these graduates were on the job? Did their bosses realize that the recruiters had made a mistake, so that after a while these initial salary differences were wiped out? On the contrary. The gender gap grew. In four years, the women were earning 14 percent ($3,615) less than the men.

Sociologically, it seems fair to conclude that "maleness" is so valued by employers that they pay hard cash for it—a conclusion that applies to other industrialized nations as well (Rosenfeld and Kalleberg 1990; Sorensen 1990; Shellenbarger 1995).

WHY IS OUR WORKFORCE SEGREGATED BY SEX?

Two Explanations:

1. Conflict Theory: A Dual Labor Market

Two explanations compete for why our labor force is segregated by sex (Blau 1975; MacKinnon 1979). The first is based on conflict theory. As we saw in chapter 7, Marxist conflict theory emphasizes how a pool of low-paid labor helps capitalists. They draw on those workers during periods of economic expansion, then lay them off when the economy slows down. The result is a **dual labor market**—better-paid workers who are employed regularly coupled with temporary, marginal, low-paid workers. Women are not singled out because they are women, nor are African Americans and Latinos singled out because of who they are. All are singled out for the underpaid and underutilized pool of marginal labor because, as minorities, they are relatively powerless.

2. Symbolic Interactionism: The Role of Stereotypes

The second explanation is based on symbolic interaction (MacKinnon 1979). Because men *perceive* women as less capable, less productive, and ultimately, less profitable, they pay them less. Aiding this stereotype is childbirth and women's greater responsibilities for child care: Employers view women as more dedicated than men to the family and less dedicated than men to the firm. With these perceptions, employers assign women more menial jobs and pay them less, while they assign men more responsible positions and pay them more.

Toward a Synthesis

Each explanation probably holds part of the answer. Women do confront structural barriers in the marketplace, and industries do profit from marginal pools of labor. Stereotypes of women do affect expectations and payoffs. Whatever the factors that created the situation, sex discrimination tends to be self-perpetuating. And, we might add, regardless of their personal opinions, employers generally will pay the least they can.

A controversial suggestion to help women adapt to this structural barrier is discussed in the Thinking Critically box on the next page.

SEXUAL HARASSMENT

Another form of sex discrimination that women face is **sexual harassment,** using one's position to make unwanted sexual demands. If power is unequal, the less-powerful person is less able to ward off such demands. The most vulnerable women are those who lack job alternatives.

The Individualistic View

The traditional view of sexual harassment makes it a *personal* matter of sexual attraction. A man gets interested in a woman and makes an advance; the woman accepts, rejects, or says "maybe." Perhaps her body language even "signals" that she *wants* to be approached sexually. There are always sexual attractions between men and women; some just happen to take place at work. These are events between individuals and are not a *social* problem.

The Structural View

Catharine MacKinnon (1979), the attorney and professor who wrote the classic book on sexual harassment, changed our thinking. MacKinnon rejected this traditional view. She argued that sexual harassment is a *structural* matter (built into the marketplace). She noted that women generally occupy an inferior status in boss–worker relations. She also said that the emphasis on women as sex objects at work encourages sexual harassment. Often women are hired because of their sexual attributes, although this precondition usually is hidden under the requirement that the newly hired be young, "attractive" women who can make a "good appearance" to the public. In short, sexual harassment begins with hiring procedures that judge women on factors other than their job qualifications (Silverman 1981).

From Personal Problem to Social Problem

Although this view is accepted widely now, when MacKinnon did her analysis, this view was new and controversial. Until 1976, sexual harassment was literally unspeakable—because it had no name." Until then, the traditional view dominated, and women considered unwanted sexual advances as something that happened to them as individuals. They did not draw a connection between those advances and their lower position in the marketplace. As women's liberation groups raised awareness of the *group* basis of these objective conditions, women gradually concluded that the sexual advances by men in more powerful positions at work were part of a general problem. As more women came to the same conclusion—and became upset about it and demanded that something be done—sexual harassment as a *social* problem was born. To catch a glimpse of how this definitional process is occurring in Japan, see the Global Glimpse box on page 303.

SUMMARY

1. Although females make up 50.9 percent of the U.S. population, men discriminate against them. Consequently, sociologists refer to men as a dominant group and women as a minority group.

2. Every society sex types occupations. That is, in all societies of the world, some work is thought suitable for men and other work appropriate for women. There is no inherent biological connection between work and its assignment to women or men, for "women's work" of one society may be "men's work" in another. In all societies, "men's work" is given greater prestige than "women's work."

3. Symbolic interactionists examine *gender* (masculinity and femininity), looking at how each society socializes the sexes into its ideas of what men and women ought to be like. Socialization includes learning *sexism,* the belief that one sex is innately superior to the other and the discriminatory practices that result from that belief.

4. Functionalists theorize that sexual discrimination is based on the need of early human groups to engage in hand-to-hand combat. Men had the physical advantage but needed to be motivated to become warriors. Women, offered as inducements for men to fight, were assigned the drudge work of society. A second functionalist explanation is that because women were physically encumbered through childbearing and nursing, men became dominant as they took control of warfare and trade.

5. Conflict theorists emphasize that the rights that U.S. women enjoy came out of a power struggle with men. The confrontations and violence between the sexes in the late 1800s and early 1900s have been replaced by legal pressure and economic and educational competition.

6. Given the inextricability of nature and nurture, we do not know the extent to which natural differences exist between the sexes. Both genetics and socialization can explain females' earlier proficiency in verbal skills and males' greater aggressiveness and abilities at mathematics. The door to biological explanations in sociology has been pried open a bit by the studies of Vietnam veterans.

7. Women confront discrimination in most of life, including a belittling attitude from men. The educational system and the mass media generally support existing gender roles. Although women outnumber men voters, men dominate politics; women tend to see politics as incompatible with femininity and motherhood.

8. Women often work at jobs that pay less and that offer less advancement. They also confront *sexual harassment* at work. As more women have moved into power positions at work, men, too, experience sexual harassment.

9. All social policies to deal with sex discrimination have ideological implications. Different groups of women propose antithetical social policies.

10. In the future, even larger numbers of women will be employed outside the home. This will continue to change power relationships at home and break down traditional stereotypes. The direction of the future is toward greater equality between the sexes.

KEY TERMS

Dual labor market   A pool of employees divided into two main segments, regularly employed and better-paid workers and low-paid temporary workers.

Gender   How we express our "maleness" or "femaleness." Refers to socialization or culture. Commonly called femininity or masculinity. See also *Sex.*

Gender roles   The behaviors and attitudes expected of males and females.

Labor force participation rate   The proportion of the population 16 years and older that is in the labor force.

Master trait   A trait considered so important that it overrides an individual's other characteristics. One's sex is an example.

Matriarchy   A society in which women as a group dominate men as a group.

Patriarchy   A society in which men as a group dominate women as a group.

Sex   The physical identity of a person as male or female. Refers to biology. See also *Gender.*

Sex-typing   Associating something with one sex or the other. "Men's work" and "women's work" are examples of sex-typing of occupations.

Sexism   The belief that one sex is innately superior to the other and the discrimination that supports such a belief.

Sexual harassment   The use of one's position to make unwanted sexual demands on someone.

THINKING CRITICALLY ABOUT CHAPTER 9

1. List ten examples of sexism in the United States. In what ways would your list be different if you had written it ten years ago? In what ways do you think it will be different if you were to write it ten years from now?

2. Which of the three theoretical perspectives (symbolic interactionism, functionalism, or conflict theory) do you think best explains sexism in the United States? Why?

3. In what ways do you think that gender roles are accented or reduced in cyberspace? How do you think that cyberspace will change gender roles?

4. What are the main changes that you see occurring in gender roles? Give examples. Why do you think that we are experiencing these changes?

CHAPTER 10

Medical Care:
Physical and Mental Illness

To PREPARE FOR THE BIRTH OF their first child, Kathie Persall and her husband, Hank, read books and articles about childbirth and took childbirth classes together. Unexpectedly at 5 o'clock one morning, the protective "bag of waters" that surrounds the fetus broke.

By 10 A.M., Kathie was on the maternity ward, hooked up to an electronic fetal monitor (EFM) and an intravenous feeding tube. Kathie was informed that the hospital had a rule that to prevent infection, delivery must take place within 24 hours after the waters break. At 11 A.M. the resident physician (not her own doctor) said that Kathie's labor would be speeded up by Pitocin, a powerful drug.

Kathie's sister, Carol, knew that inducing labor can lead to Caesarean section. She urged Hank to get Kathie off Pitocin, but Kathie and Hank felt that they couldn't tell the doctor what to do. By evening, doctors decided that Kathie's cervix was not dilating rapidly enough. They increased the Pitocin. One nurse thought that the flow of Pitocin looked blocked. She wiggled the bottle, and a large dose sped through Kathie's veins. Kathie writhed in pain as a massive contraction took over her body. Five or ten minutes later, when the contraction ended, the baby's heartbeat had dropped from 160 to 40 beats per minute.

The doctor rushed in, cut off the Pitocin, and gave Kathie another drug to stop the contraction. He said the situation had turned into an emergency, and Kathie had to have a Caesarean. Hank, who had been trying to comfort Kathie, protested. The doctor insisted that Kathie and Hank sign a consent form in case a Caesarean became necessary. On the form, Hank and Kathie read the long list of things that could go wrong. They did not want to sign it, but how could they resist? Moreover, Kathie was in pain and exhausted.

At midnight, the doctor told Kathie that a Caesarean was necessary because she had dilated only 5 centimeters in 13 hours of labor and would need another 13 hours to dilate enough to have a vaginal birth. Kathie knew it was wrong to assume that just because the first 5 centimeters had taken 13 hours that the next would take as long. Nevertheless, she felt overpowered, and at 1:10 A.M. Kathie went into surgery.

When the baby was born, Kathie was vomiting too severely from the anesthetic to even look at her new son. It took Kathie seven weeks to recover physically from the Caesarean surgery. She was left with a disfiguring scar, but this was nothing compared with her anger at the doctors, the hospital, and the medical procedures that had created the need for surgery.

The Problem in Sociological Perspective

More Than Biology

In Chapter 6, we focused on the twin problems of crime and the criminal justice system that is set up to deal with crime. When considering the topic of medical care, we again need to focus on twin problems: illness and the medical care system that is set up to deal with illness. Unlike a medical approach to illness, which focuses on the origin and development of disease, the sociological approach examines how *social* factors affect health.

Subjective concerns about this medical problem run high. As Table 10-1 shows, the U.S. public sees health care as the fifth most pressing social problem that it wants the government to solve. Health care even outranks education, poverty, and crime as problems for the government to address.

TABLE 10-1 The Most Important Problems Facing the Nation

RANK	PROBLEM	PERCENT WHO RANK IT NUMBER ONE OR TWO
1.	Economy*	44
2.	War**	38
3.	Terrorism***	13
4.	International Problems	8
5.	Health Care	5
6.	Education	4
7.	Ethics	4
8.	Budget deficit	3
9.	Poverty	3
10.	Crime	2

A random sample of Americans was asked: "What do you think are the two most important issues for the government to address?"
*The Economy (general) and unemployment.
**War and international tensions.
***Terrorism and national security.
Source: By the author, based on *Sourcebook of Criminal Justice Statistics* 2004:Table 2.1.

THE SOCIAL NATURE OF HEALTH AND ILLNESS

Most of us think of illness in biological terms, but much more is involved. What is considered health or illness depends on cultural ideas. This may seem strange. Isn't fever, for example, always a sign of illness? Not always. Many people dismiss a low-grade fever as "just a little temperature." Whether a fever is considered a sign of illness depends on how high it is and how long it lasts. Even then, interpretations of what fever means and how to treat it differ—even among medical authorities.

Changing Ideas About Disease: The Example of Black Lung Disease

Ideas about health and illness are not fixed. Years ago, coal miners reluctantly accepted lung cancer as an almost inevitable consequence of their job. They knew that longtime workers became short of breath and coughed up blood, and they even wrote folk songs about "black lung." Eventually the workers concluded that their symptoms constituted a disease and that they did not have to put up with it. Their unions had to fight not only management, as you would expect, but also a medical profession that refused to acknowledge coal mining as the cause of this disease. The result of these subjective concerns and the social struggle over them was a new understanding, not just of black lung disease but also of how the environment can create disease (Smith 1987).

Effects of Industrialization

The social nature of disease is also apparent when we consider industrialization. When the United States industrialized and became more affluent, heart disease became our number-one killer. Eating richer foods and getting less exercise increased heart attacks. The pursuit of pleasure leads to many diseases, including gonorrhea, syphilis, AIDS, and of course, the whole rack of diseases that we reviewed in Chapter 4 that come from addiction to cigarettes and alcohol.

Iatrogenesis

Another example of the social nature of illness is **iatrogenesis,** injuries caused by medical care. This is what happened when the nurse jiggled Kathie's bottle of Pitocin and the baby's heartbeat plummeted. Iatrogenesis is not trivial. Each year, between 44,000 and 98,000 Americans die at the hands of doctors. *If the number of Americans who are killed by medical errors were an official classification of death, it would rank as one of the top ten leading causes of death* (Steinhauer and Fessenden 2001). The discussion on medical incompetence in the Thinking Critically box on the next page focuses on another aspect of iatrogenesis.

Thinking Critically about Social Problems
Medical Incompetence

Most physicians are competent, but all physicians make mistakes. Most of us could accept this statement. The following statement, however, may be more controversial: Some physicians are so incompetent that they should not practice medicine. And you may find this one even more controversial: Some of the most incompetent physicians are so admired by their medical colleagues that they are promoted to the leadership of their state medical associations.

I once would have thought that the last two statements could not possibly be true. Then I studied suicide in Missouri. Poring over the coroner's records, I was struck by one decision that a person who had been shot several times may have committed suicide. Then I read about a father in Warren, Ohio, who was convinced that his 20-year-old daughter, found dead in a field seven miles from her home, had not committed suicide. For 17 years, he kept the case alive. Finally her former boyfriend was charged with strangling her.

When it became apparent that the coroner had missed "obvious" clues to the cause of the woman's death—"suspicious marks" on her neck—the sheriff's department investigated the coroner. Among their findings were these rulings that this physician had made:

• Suicide—the man had been run over with a bulldozer and shot

• Suicide—an inmate was found hanged on his knees with toilet paper stuffed in his mouth
• Death by carbon monoxide from a lawn mower—the lawn mower didn't work
• Death by carbon monoxide—no carbon monoxide was found in the person's blood

This coroner had served as president of the Ohio State Medical Association three years before his exposure.

Makes you wonder, doesn't it?

There are other types of medical blunders. A woman entered a New York City hospital because of a problem with her lungs: Her surgeon did a hysterectomy. In another hospital, a doctor removed the wrong kidney—leaving the cancerous one intact. In yet another hospital, a woman awoke from surgery to find that her surgeon had removed the wrong breast. In a Tampa hospital, a respiratory technician was supposed to disconnect a man from a ventilator. The technician disconnected the wrong patient. He died an hour later.

I trust that these surgeons and the respiratory technician will not be promoted. But that coroner did become president of the state medical association. . . .

What do you think?

Based on an AP release, February 12, 1995; Steinhauer 2001; Steinhauer and Fessenden 2001.

Organizational Rules

The way pregnancy is handled by physicians also highlights the *social* nature of health and illness. Physicians have defined a natural process (pregnancy and birth) as something that requires fetal monitors and powerful drugs. They also define a woman as "ill" if she does not deliver within 24 hours after her water breaks. This arbitrary definition of "illness" is imposed on a natural process in which some women deliver a baby in one hour, but others not for 48 hours or longer.

The Social Organization of Medicine as a Source of Problems

This takes us to the second part of this social problem, the social organization of medicine. Let's consider costs, Caesarean births, and quality of medical care.

Soaring Costs

As we all know, it is expensive to visit a doctor. It wasn't always so. To see how the cost of medical treatment has soared, look at Figure 10-1. In 1970, the nation's medical bill was $75 billion, but by 2005 it had exploded to $1.9 trillion, *25 times higher.*

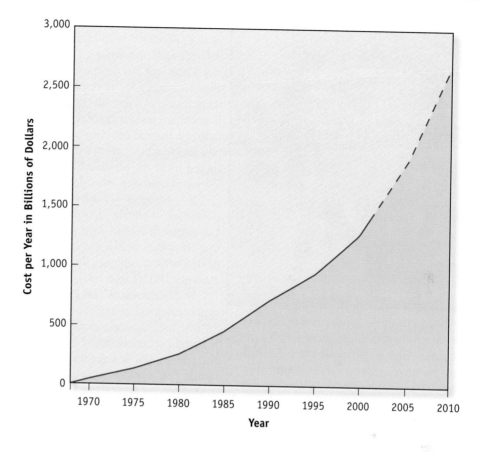

FIGURE 10-1 *The Nation's Medical Bill: Soaring Costs*

Note: The broken line represents estimates by the U.S. Centers for Medicare and Medicaid Services.

Source: By the author, based on *Statistical Abstract of the United States* 2003:Table 127.

During this time, the cost of the average goods we buy increased almost five times. If medical costs had increased at the same rate as the average inflation, our nation's annual medical bill would be $350 billion, just one fifth of what it is now.

Reasons for Rising Costs

Why did the nation's medical bill explode? A major factor is the growing number of older people, who require more medical treatment than others. Three aspects of the social organization of medical care also contributed: the development of expensive technology accompanied by the patients' demand for the latest treatment; a preoccupation with last-minute heroic intervention rather than with prevention; and the view that medical care is a commodity to be sold for a profit.

"Fee-for-Service"

Medicine for profit is called a *fee-for-service system.* This means that physicians collect a fee for each service they perform. Fee-for-service means that, just like mechanics and plumbers, the more services that physicians sell, the higher their profit. Consider our opening vignette: Do you think that Kathie's physician created a crisis so that a Caesarean would be "required" and she could earn a larger fee? It is unlikely. But some physicians really are that crass, and they perform unnecessary surgery to increase their profits. As shown in Figure 10-2 on page 316, in 1970 about 1 of 19 babies was delivered by Caesarean section. Now the total is 1 of every 4.

The Example of Caesarean Sections

Are U.S. women less healthy than they used to be, and therefore less able to deliver babies naturally? After all, today's rate of Caesarean delivery is *four* times higher than it used to be, and there has to be an explanation for this dramatic change. As there is no reason to make the assumption that today's women are less healthy, we must draw the conclusion that the increase in Caesarean deliveries has something to do with the medical profession. This conclusion is supported by the finding that the percentage of

Part of our changing health consciousness includes changing attitudes toward people with disabilities—and the attitudes of the disabled toward themselves. Shown here is Franz Nietlispach of Switzerland as he breaks the finish line tape of the 102nd Boston Marathon in the men's wheelchair division.

A Two-Class System of Health Care

Caesarean sections in some hospitals is *five* times that in other hospitals (Kilborn 1998). Regardless of a hospital's rate, *most* Caesarean deliveries are unnecessary.

Then why do we have so many Caesarean deliveries? Being able to charge a lot more certainly motivates doctors to encourage them. But this is just part of the picture. Many doctors want to deliver babies this way because this allows them to be *in control* of the delivery. Instead of being called at midnight or 3 A.M., the doctor can decide when babies will be born. Because these births are designed to fit the physician's schedule, more births now occur on Tuesdays than any other day of the week.

You probably will not be surprised to learn that the income of obstetricians ("baby doctors") jumped as they performed more Caesarean deliveries. You might be surprised, however, to learn that their income has increased so much that, with the exception of surgeons, it is higher than other medical specialties (*Statistical Abstract* 2003:Table 166).

Today's medical care crisis has its roots in the rise of specialized medicine that began around 1900 (Stevens 1971; Rosenberg 1987). Specialization moved medical care from the home to the hospital and encouraged a fascination with the latest medicines and techniques. Because specialized medicine is based on advanced training in research, it centers around medical schools. Because doctors prefer to practice near these schools, physicians are clustered around cities with medical schools or research hospitals, whereas the inner cities and rural areas have a shortage of doctors.

With health care viewed as a commodity rather than a right, the United States has developed a **two-class system of medical care:** One kind of medical care goes to those who can pay, and another kind goes to those who cannot. Julie Treadman, who was featured in the opening vignette of Chapter 7 (page 207), was at the lower end of this two-tier system; she was refused admission to one hospital and transferred with her dead baby to another. Because we treat health care as a commodity to be sold to the highest bidder, our medical care ranges from the finest in the world at major universities

FIGURE 10-2 *The Growth in Caesarean Births*

Source: By the author, based on *Statistical Abstract of the United States* 1990:Tables 88, 89; 2000:Table 90; 2003:Table 96.

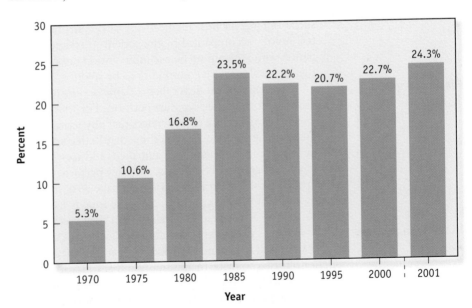

to that provided by an underground network of unlicensed, foreign-trained physicians who can barely understand their patients and who have flunked their U.S. exams.

The Scope of the Problem

ILLNESS AS A SOCIAL PROBLEM

The Nation's Health

How much illness is there in the United States? The answer depends on how we measure illness. One practical measure is the number of days that illness prevents people from carrying out their normal activities. For the average American, it is 15 days per year. As Table 10-2 below shows, however, those days are not spread evenly throughout the population. They are higher for females and the elderly, and they are somewhat higher for African Americans. For the poor, they are almost *triple* those of higher-income Americans.

Measures of Health:

A key measure of a nation's health is life expectancy at birth. In the United States, this measure has been rising for over a century, and it now stands at about 75 years for males and 81 years for females (*Statistical Abstract* 2003:Table 105). These are overall averages, but as with so many other conditions in our society, life expectancy is related to income: Those who have more money live longer. Men who have a family income of $25,000 or more live six to seven years longer than men whose family incomes is less than $10,000 (Pamuck 1998).

1. Life Expectancy

2. Infant Mortality

There is no question that women are the biologically stronger sex. From the beginning of life, more male fetuses than female fetuses are not healthy and abort naturally (called spontaneous abortion). At birth, girls have a better survival rate, and in every society of the world, women live longer than men. For every U.S. man who makes it to age 75, almost two U.S. women have survived. Yet U.S. women see doctors more often, averaging four visits a year compared to three for men (*Statistical Abstract* 2003:Table 167). Do women get sick more often than men? Or are men less likely to admit they are ill because illness does not fit some macho image? No one is sure.

While our life expectancy has been rising, our infant mortality rate has been falling. The *infant mortality rate* (of each thousand babies, the number who die before their first birthday) is one of the most accurate measures of a group's health conditions: It reflects the quality of nutrition, the health of mothers and babies, and the quality of health care. In 1960, the U.S. rate was 26 deaths per 1,000 births. Now it is just 6.8 per 1,000 (*Statistical Abstract* 1990:Table 110; 2003:Table 114). As the Social Map on the next page shows, infant deaths are not distributed evenly across the United States. The range is very broad, from just 3.8 in New Hampshire to *three* times that rate, 10.7, in Delaware. Note how the states with the highest death rates cluster in the South, whereas those with the lowest rates cluster in the West. This, again, shows the *social* basis of health, illness, and even death.

TABLE 10-2 Number of Days Americans Are So Sick That They Cut Down on Their Activities for More than Half a Day

SEX	
Males	12
Females	17
AGE	
Under 65	12
65 and over	31
RACE-ETHNICITY*	
White	14
African American	16
FAMILY INCOME	
Under $10,000	28
$10,000 to $20,000	21
$20,000 to $35,000	13
Over $35,000	10

*Only these racial-ethnic groups are listed in the source.
Source: By the author, based on *Statistical Abstract* 2000:Table 211.

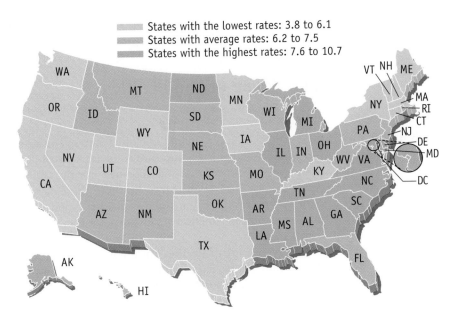

States with the lowest rates: 3.8 to 6.1
States with average rates: 6.2 to 7.5
States with the highest rates: 7.6 to 10.7

FIGURE 10-3   *The Geography of Death: Infant Mortality Rates*
Source: By the author, based on *Statistical Abstract of the United States* 2003:Table 114.

Health Crisis vs. Health-Care Crisis

The Social Basis of Physical Health

How the United States Compares

Considering that our life expectancy is increasing and our infant mortality is decreasing, we can conclude that the United States has no *health* crisis. (It does have a *health-care* crisis, however, which we shall discuss.) There are health problems, to be sure, and some are severe—cancer, AIDS, suicide, and physical problems from drug abuse. Tremendous battles have been won against most infectious diseases, and many people survive cancer and AIDS. Overall, the nation's health has been improving.

All of the Least Industrialized Nations have a worse infant mortality rate and a shorter life expectancy than we do (*Statistical Abstract* 2003:Table 1326). Life expectancy in some of these nations is less than 50 years, and infant mortality rates run 15 to 20 times higher than ours. That life expectancy and infant mortality improve with industrialization is another example of how *social* conditions affect the *biology* of health.

Since our infant mortality rate has improved so well, why is it a cause for concern? Let's compare our rates with those of other nations. Figure 10-4 shows some of the nations that have a *better* record of saving babies than we do. The cold numbers in this figure translate into needless deaths. If our rate were the same as Japan's, 5 of every 10 of the 27,000 U.S. infants who die each year would live (*Statistical Abstract* 2003:Table 113). Why can't we be as effective as Japan? Right now we aren't, and this means that an additional 13,000 children die each year. Our overall life expectancy (males and females combined) of 77.8 years is also less than the life expectancy in most of the nations shown on Figure 10-4. (The exceptions are Cuba, Czech Republic, and Portugal.) Japan, with a life expectancy of 80.8 years, holds the world record.

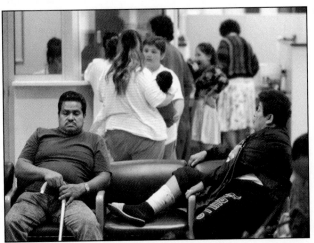

In the United States, medicine is a commodity to be sold. The result is a two-tier system of medical care—one for those who can pay, another for those who cannot. Shown here is a waiting room for the poor. If the waiting room gets too crowded, these patients may have to return another day.

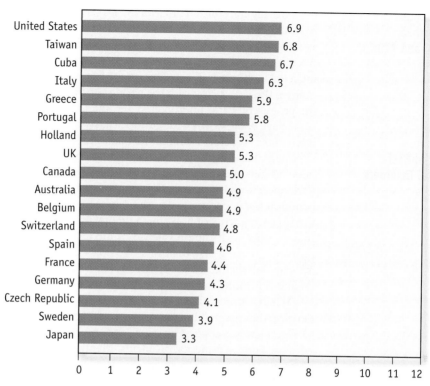

FIGURE 10-4 *Infant Mortality Rates*

Source: By the author, based on *Statistical Abstract of the United States* 1998:Table 1345; 2003:Table 1326.

Note: For some reason, Sweden and Switzerland were dropped from later years of the source. I assume that Norway, too, has a lower rate than the United States.

Why Are U.S. Rates Worse?

Why are infant mortality and life expectancy rates better in these other industrialized nations? The usual explanation is the poverty of many Americans: To live on the edge of survival simply is not good for people's health. As we saw in Table 10-2 on page 317, poor people are sick more often. They also experience more stress, have more emotional problems, suffer more accidents and violence, and don't eat as well. Poverty lies at the root of many health problems, and our advances in medical care are not reaching the poor to the same extent that they are reaching those who are better off.

Poverty vs. Lifestyle?

Although poverty is important, lifestyle is even more significant. Sociologist Ruben Rumbaut and geographer John Weeks (1994) were puzzled to find that poor immigrant women in California had a lower infant mortality rate than U.S.-born California women who were better off financially. Despite their much higher rates of poverty, unemployment, and welfare, Vietnamese and Cambodian refugees had lower infant mortality rates. Rumbaut and Weeks found that there was a *social* basis for these differences. The U.S.-born women gained more weight during pregnancy and were more likely to have abused drugs, including alcohol. Another reason was that the U.S.-born women were more likely to have a "surgically scarred uterus" from abortion. The immigrant women had fewer abortions.

Refugees

It is difficult to overstate the importance of lifestyle in determining health and illness, for *lifestyle is the major cause of illness and death.* To mention the most obvious: Overeating and lack of exercise lead to heart attacks and stroke. So does smoking, which also causes cancer. We reviewed the effects of smoking and alcohol abuse in Chapter 4, so we don't need to repeat anything but the bottom line here: Smoking and the heavy consumption of alcohol harm essential body organs and are part of the *social* nature of physical illness.

The Examples of Gonorrhea, Syphilis, and AIDS

Sexually transmitted diseases (STDs) are another example of how lifestyle is related to health. To state the obvious: Singles who practice abstinence run zero risk of STDs, as do couples who have sex exclusively with one another. All others are at risk, with the risk increasing with the amount of promiscuity and with unprotected sex. As with catching a cold, chance is also an important factor—being in the wrong place at the wrong time (in this case, being with the wrong person at the wrong time). Although the greater the promiscuity and unprotected sex, the greater the chances of contracting an STD, some have come down with gonorrhea, syphilis, and even AIDS from their first sexual intercourse. We shall examine the relationship of AIDS and lifestyle later.

The Social Basis of Mental Disorders

Mental illness, too, has a social nature. Some researchers conclude that mental illness has become more common because people today experience higher stress and have fewer social supports. We simply don't know, however, if mental illness is more common today because we have no base lines to compare. That is, we don't have any firm measurements of how much mental illness there used to be, so we can't compare that number with the prevalence of mental illness today. Actually, the measurement problem is even worse than this: We don't even know how much mental illness there is today—all such totals are speculations. We can dispense with the argument that mental illness is more common today, as there is no way of knowing.

Whatever mental illness is—and this is a matter of dispute, with some experts even denying that mental illness exists—we do know that it has a strong social basis (Szasz 1961). That is, people who experience more stress are more likely to also experience what are known as mental problems. Mental problems, of course, would be part of the objective conditions of a social problem. Where is the *social* part, the subjective concerns, that makes mental illness a *social* problem? This is the focus of the Issues in Social Problems box on pages 322–323. From this box, you can see why even the intensely personal act of suicide can be part of a *social* problem.

Problems with Mental Health Care Delivery

Just as problems of physical illness have two parts—the diseases and the medical delivery system—so do problems of mental illness. Let's look at how the medical delivery system is part of this problem:

> Standing among the police, I watched as the elderly nude man, looking confused, struggled to put on his clothing. The man had ripped the wires out of the homeless shelter's main electrical box and then, with the police in pursuit, had run from one darkened room to another.
>
> I asked the officers where they were going to take the man, and they replied, "To Malcolm Bliss" (the state hospital). When I commented, "I guess he'll be there for quite a while," an officer replied, "Probably for just a day or two. We picked him up last week—he was crawling under cars at a traffic light—and they let him out in two days."

A Two-Tier System

The police explained that to be admitted as a long-term patient one must be a danger to others or to oneself. Visualizing this old man crawling under cars in traffic and risking electrocution by ripping out electrical wires with his bare hands, I marveled at the definition of "danger" that the psychiatrists must be using.

Here in front of me, the two-tier medical system was stripped of its coverings. A middle-class or wealthy person would have received different treatment. Of course, such a person would not be in a shelter for the homeless in the first place.

Deinstitutionalization

Back in the 1970s, state mental hospitals discharged tens of thousands of seriously disturbed patients. The idea behind **deinstitutionalization,** as these discharges were called, was that these people could lead more normal lives in the community than they could in mental hospitals. The plan was to support them with medications and community mental health services. To save money, however, few of the planned community centers were ever built. Most patients were simply abandoned on the streets to fend for themselves. They did the best they could—living in fleabag hotels when they could afford it or in bus stations or cardboard boxes in back alleys. A few were sent back to mental hospitals when no one around could tolerate them; but most were left to wander the streets, no matter how bizarre their behavior.

The unfeeling, cruel way that deinstitutionalization was carried out is illustrated by what occurred in Austin, Texas. Patients from the state mental hospital were loaded in a van and driven to Houston (so they wouldn't bother Austin residents). There they were dumped at the Greyhound bus station on skid row (Karlen and Burgower 1985).

Problems with Physical Health Services

At the center of our social problem of illness and medical care is this contradiction: We live in an age of *chronic* disorders (that is, they are lingering and ongoing), but our medical services are geared for *acute* illnesses (those that have a sudden onset, a sharp rise, and a short duration). Our approach to cancer, heart disease, and other chronic disorders is heroic, hospital based, and expensive. Open-heart surgery is dramatic, but prevention is much more effective. We could save untold suffering and lives through public health measures that increase exercise and reduce pollution, smoking, and alcohol abuse. Such efforts, however, account for only a small fraction of what we spend on heroic measures to deal with health problems *after* people are stricken with them.

Feeding the Cost Spiral

This emphasis on "heroic medicine" is expensive. Intervening at advanced stages of a disease requires costly technical equipment, rare drugs, medical teams, and highly trained specialists. Patients who have serious illnesses want the best care, and the medical world has taught us that "the best" means complex, technical, and expensive. By promoting exotic "cures," companies that manufacture medical equipment and drugs feed this surge in cost.

Emergency Rooms

Another problem is that this age of specialists and hospital care has led to a shortage of primary-care doctors who treat routine problems. Consequently, for their basic medical needs some patients go to hospital emergency rooms, which stay open day and night and do not require an appointment. These services, however, are more expensive than office care; treating a fever or a splinter runs three to five times more. Insurance companies have rebelled at using hospital emergency rooms as doctors' offices and refuse to pay for such treatment. Patients now have to prove that their visit to an emergency room was an emergency.

No National Plan or Rational System

Health care remains a commodity to be purchased, not a citizen's right, however, and people without cash, a credit card, or a medical card are out of luck. Despite feeble pretensions to the contrary, profits, not health care, are the engine that drives the U.S. health-care system. One consequence is that the United States is the only industrialized nation without a national health insurance plan.

Where the Doctors Are

One final problem with the medical delivery system is the uneven distribution of medical services. Some areas have an abundance of physicians; in others, it is difficult to find a doctor. With its one doctor for every 275 residents, Beverly Hills represents one extreme. Just down the road is Bell Gardens, where poor people live. They have one doctor for every 27,000 residents, worse even than Haiti (Olivo 1999). The national distribution of physicians is shown on the Social Map on page 324. The distribution of doctors among the states is so uneven that Massachusetts has 419 doctors for every 100,000 residents, whereas Idaho has less than half that, just 156 doctors for every 100,000 residents.

Looking at the Problem Theoretically

SYMBOLIC INTERACTIONISM

Giving Meaning to Symptoms

Symbolic interactionists study how people use language and other symbols to define social reality. As an example, we all self-diagnose; that is, we figure out what our symptoms mean. Should we go to bed, call a doctor, or just carry on? People from different social classes and subcultures make these decisions differently. For example, lower-class people

Issues In Social Problems

SUICIDE: THE MAKING AND UNMAKING OF A SOCIAL PROBLEM

Suicide—deliberately drawing a razor blade across one's arteries, putting a gun in one's mouth and pulling the trigger, or swallowing a lethal dose of pills—chills the imagination. As sociologist Emile Durkheim (1897/1951) documented more than 100 years ago, suicide is more than individual inclination or a sign of personal problems. Suicide, concluded Durkheim, is based on *social* conditions. Durkheim drew this conclusion when he noticed that countries have different suicide rates, and that year after year a country's rate remains about the same. Look at Figure 10-6. From one year to the next, these rates show little change. You can expect about 31,000 Americans to kill themselves this year, and the next year, and the year after that (*Statistical Abstract* 1994:Table 125; 2003:Table 117).

From Figure 10-5, you can also see that men have a higher suicide rate. In the United States at least, many more women than men attempt suicide, but more men succeed at it. This is often interpreted as meaning that the women's attempts are more a "cry for help," whereas the men are more serious about accomplishing the act. This is likely true, but there is also another factor: Men are more likely to use guns to kill themselves, whereas women are more likely to take pills. Guns obviously allow less time to change one's mind or to allow someone to intervene.

Suicide illustrates the making and unmaking of a social problem. Around 1960, mental health professionals began to publicize the idea that suicide was a national problem. There were no major changes in objective conditions at this time, but subjective concerns had grown. The National Institute of Mental Health (NIMH) took these new subjective concerns to heart and began to finance an innovative idea—suicide prevention centers. The idea of swift intervention when people contemplate or attempt suicide was appealing, and across the nation suicide prevention centers were established to conquer what had become a social problem.

The suicide prevention centers failed. The suicide rate didn't budge. For example, today suicide is the third most common cause of death of U.S. 15-to-24-year-olds, about the same as it was back then (*Statistical Abstract* 2003:Table 117).

To prevent suicide, the major problem is not detecting suicidal intent, but managing patients who are known to be suicidal. This is difficult. Psychiatrists receive inadequate training in how to treat suicidal patients. Sometimes, they even contribute to their patient's suicide through a pattern of engagement and abandonment. The therapist initially responds to a suicidal patient with sympathy and concern, and the troubled individual begins to depend on the therapist as a helper. As treatment continues, the patient becomes not only more dependent but also more demanding. Disliking this pressure, the therapist pulls back, calls the intense dependency "infantile regression," and becomes less accessible just when the patient is most vulnerable. Feeling abandoned, the patient commits suicide (Light 1973).

These treatment failures and the lack of new techniques kept the suicide prevention centers from fulfilling their optimistic promise. Gradually, suicide as a social problem faded from the limelight. The government reduced its funding, and most of the suicide prevention centers closed. Some kept their doors open by broadening their focus to general crisis intervention.

Suicide illustrates how social problems are socially constructed. As Figure 10-5 shows, our suicide rate is not exceptional. Compared with other industrialized nations, our rate falls in the lower middle. Today's suicide rate is also about the same as it used to be. (The overall rate, males and females combined, was 12.5 in 1960 and also 12.5 in 1990. Since then, for reasons unknown we have had a significant decline, and the overall rate today is 10.7 [*Statistical Abstract* 2003:Table 115.]) Back then, suicide became a social

---

are more likely to regard back pain as part of life, middle-class people to view it as a health problem that needs to be treated. Similarly, to many people cold or flu symptoms indicate a visit to the doctor to "get a shot," whereas to adherents of alternative medicine these same symptoms indicate a need for drinking more water and taking more vitamin C and other antioxidants.

The Political Basis of Illness

Just as social classes and subcultural groups perceive health and illness differently, so groups compete to get their view of health accepted. This, in turn, changes the way we view "reality." For example, through the years the American Psychiatric Association listed homosexuality as a mental illness and had specialists who treated it. Homosexuals objected

problem because of political activity: Mental health professionals and government officials used the mass media to arouse the public. There was a public outcry about the "epidemic" of suicide, and suicide prevention centers were invented. Today we take our rate for granted, and no longer consider suicide a pressing social problem.

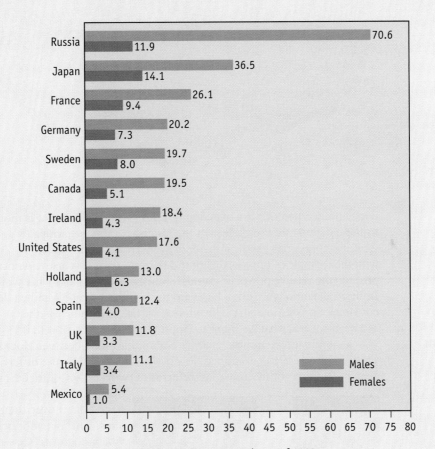

Note: The rate is per 100,000 people, as of 2003.

FIGURE 10-5   *International Suicide Rates*
Note: The rate is per 100,000 people, as of 2003.
Source: By the author, based on "Suicide Rates" 2004.

How Definitions Affect Perceptions

at being defined as ill, and through lobbying and intense political pressure succeeded in getting the APA to drop homosexuality as a mental illness. Establishing definitions is a two-way street: Just as medicine and psychiatry can declassify a behavior that had been considered an illness, so they can declare other behaviors to be illnesses. Asserting that alcohol abuse is a disease (not "drunkenness") is an example, as is defining children's unruly behavior as a symptom of "attention deficit disorder" (see Chapter 4).

Definitions of health and illness have an impact on how we see the world and on our behavior. If alcohol abuse is defined as a disease, we perceive an alcohol abuser as sick, but if it is defined as drunkenness, we perceive an alcohol abuser as a drunkard. These are

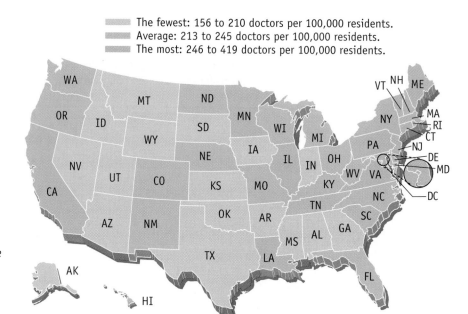

The fewest: 156 to 210 doctors per 100,000 residents.
Average: 213 to 245 doctors per 100,000 residents.
The most: 246 to 419 doctors per 100,000 residents.

FIGURE 10-6 *Where the Doctors Are*

Source: By the author, based on *Statistical Abstract of the United States* 2003:Table 163.

two entirely different ways of defining reality. The response that is thought appropriate to these definitions also differs: In the instance of disease, sympathy and help might be viewed as appropriate; in the instance of drunkenness, condemnation or humor. As we saw with the example of homosexuality and the American Psychiatric Association, a political process (the relative power of groups) sometimes determines what symbols we will use. In short, definitions are not inherent in the behavior; symbols, rather, develop out of social interaction of some sort. The symbols we use determine whether we view something as a problem and what we think are appropriate ways to deal with it.

Symbolic interactionists analyze communications between doctors and patients. Eliot Freidson (1961) examined how patients and doctors use different frames of reference. Patients come from a **lay referral network,** a set of friends, relatives, neighbors, and co-workers with whom they have talked over their medical problems. This network helps them decide which doctor to see—or even whether to see a doctor at all. In this lay referral network, a physician's knowledge is considered important, but so is the physician's personality. People want someone who shows an interest in them; they don't want to be a faceless patient. Also important is the amount of confidence that the doctor exhibits. People also want to be sure they won't come away empty-handed: They want to get a shot or a prescription, not just advice to get more rest or to go on a diet.

The physician, in contrast, uses a **professional referral network,** made up of other physicians and medical professionals. Here the meaning of

Why the Definitions of Physicians and Patients Clash

The homeless have become a common sight in our major cities. Sociologists have documented the major avenues to homelessness, one of which is mental illness. Almost all the homeless are in need of medical attention, but few of their physical and mental needs are being met.

"doing doctoring" is different, for medical schools put the emphasis on organs, symptoms, and diseases apart from the person. Sympathy for the patient and understanding an illness from the patient's point of view are less important to doctors than determining what and why some organ is malfunctioning and prescribing appropriate treatment (Haas and Shaffir 1993; Conrad 1995).

One consequence of the professional referral network is that some doctors treat patients not as persons, but as objects with sick organs, a process referred to as **depersonalization.** Patients detest being depersonalized, for it strips away their humanity. To doctors who see patients as objects, the psychological and aesthetic costs of procedures are of little importance. This is what happened with Kathie Persall's Caesarean surgery, and it is one reason that midwifery has reemerged as an appealing alternative (Weitz and Sullivan 1986). Another consequence of depersonalization is a tendency for patients to sue their physicians, for depersonalization breaks a social bond between patient and physician. The threat of malpractice suits, in turn, has produced **defensive medicine;** that is, physicians order lab tests and consultations that may not be needed, in order to leave a "paper trail" that shows they did everything reasonable in case they are sued.

Problems in Communication

These different backgrounds and expectations of physicians and patients lead to problems in communication. In an age of specialized medicine characterized by brief encounters between people from different walks in life, doctors often fail to tend to the personal or emotional side of health problems. Their long, strange-sounding words often baffle patients:

> When Mrs. J., a 47-year-old Queens schoolteacher, was told in a routine examination that she had a "uterine fibroid" and needed a hysterectomy (removal of the uterus), the only thing she could think of was "tumor." She asked the doctor if it was cancerous, and he frightened her more by saying, "Sometimes when we go in we find them to be cancerous." Fearing cancer of the uterus, she consulted two other physicians and learned that the fibroid was small, common in middle-aged women, and soon likely to shrink on its own as she went into menopause. (Larned 1977:195–196)

On the lighter side, one patient was unhappy after being put on a low-salt diet. As if that weren't bad enough, when she was hospitalized she was further dismayed to find that she was also put on a low-sodium diet (Silver 1979:4).

FUNCTIONALISM

The Basic Question: Who Benefits?

Functionalists assume that customs or social institutions persist only if they fulfill social needs. The functionalist perspective, then, raises some interesting questions. Whose needs are met by a health care system that is hospital based and oriented toward acute illnesses? Who benefits from allowing environmental diseases to flourish? What are the benefits of depersonalizing patients such as Kathie Persall, of making childbirth a rigorous medical procedure?

How the Medical Profession Benefits

Let's start with the obvious: It is difficult for doctors to make money from healthy people. Patients who get well quickly also mean less profits. But an expensive, hospital-based system oriented toward acute illness—now that's a dream come true. Everyone—physicians, medical suppliers, hospitals, and drug companies—makes money from giving patients intensive care. Each year, about one of every eight Americans is admitted to a hospital and stays an average of six days (*Statistical Abstract* 2003:Table 173). The average daily cost is shown in Figure 10-7 on page 326. This figure illustrates the skyrocketing costs of medical care better than words can say.

In our fee-for-service system, doctors sell their services. The more services they sell and the higher price they charge, the more they earn. One result is unnecessary surgery, such as the Caesarean surgeries mentioned earlier (see Figure 10-2 on page

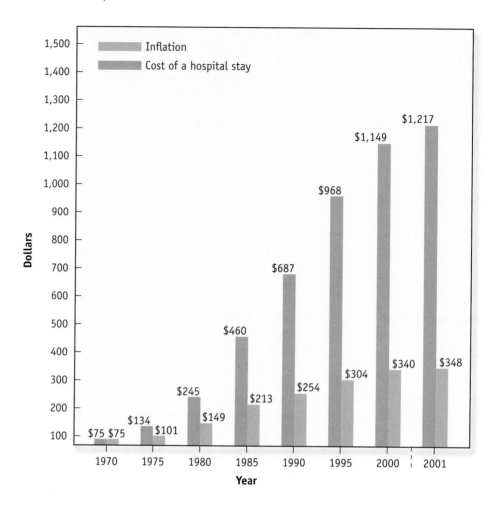

FIGURE 10-7 *How Much Does It Cost to Stay in the Hospital? One Day's Cost Compared to Inflation*

Source: By the author, based on *Statistical Abstract of the United States* 1998:Table 137; 2003:Table 171.

316). Another example is hysterectomies, which we will review in the section on conflict theory.

How Patients Benefit

Physicians, nurses, and investors in the U.S. health-care industry, then, benefit from our fee-for-service system. Patients benefit, too, however, for this system lets them shop around. They can choose which doctor to see and what service to purchase. That this system is functional for patients is indicated by our rising life expectancy and our decreasing infant mortality.

A Self-Correcting System

There are problems, of course, but functionalists point out that the system is self-correcting. For example, although the medical system is oriented to acute illnesses, after environmental health problems were recognized as serious, the government passed antipollution laws and formed the Environmental Protection Agency (EPA). Medical schools also responded, developing training programs in environmental medicine. Likewise, runaway costs have led to cost controls: HMOs (discussed later), new forms of medical care such as outpatient surgery, and limitations on the number of days Medicare and Medicaid pay for hospitalization. In short, functionalists regard health care as a system that responds to the shifting needs of the nation.

Global Functions and Dysfunctions

Functionalists also analyze functions and dysfunctions of medicine on a global level. Exporting Western medicine to the Least Industrialized Nations provides an excellent example. The vaccines, immunizations, and medicines sent to these nations were functional: They reduced those nations' death rates. But they were also dysfunctional: They allowed their populations to surge. The populations grew so fast that they outpaced the nations' ability to grow food, leading to mass starvation and political upheaval.

CONFLICT THEORY

The Basic View of Conflict Theorists

Conflict theorists shake their heads in disbelief when they hear anyone refer to the U.S. medical system as self-correcting. They view our patterns of illness and health care as the outcome of clashes between interest groups—which the most powerful have won. They argue that the poor are sicker than others because they have lost the struggle for the better income, education, food, housing, jobs, and medical services.

How Conflict Theorists See Medicare and Medicaid

What about Medicaid, which benefits the poor? Conflict theorists see this program, too, as the result of conflict. A groundswell of resentment about the treatment of the poor forced politicians to do something. Sentiment toward socialized medicine had grown, and the American Medical Association (AMA) campaigned to preserve the fee-for-service system. Medicaid was a Band-Aid designed to prevent the profit system from being replaced with socialized medicine. To consider, as functionalists would, that Medicaid was passed because health care providers saw that the poor needed free medical services is naive. It ignores the millions of dollars that the AMA spent lobbying to *prevent* this federally funded health insurance for the poor from becoming a reality.

Competing Interests of Doctors and Patients

Conflict theorists also take a different view of doctor-patient relationships. A Marxist conflict perspective emphasizes how patients and doctors form two classes in regard to the means of production of medicine—those who control it and those who receive it. Physicians want to maximize their income, whereas patients want to get well with the least expense. To reach their goal, physicians try to maintain power by controlling their interactions with patients. Their common failure to explain procedures or diagnoses is no accident; it is a way of keeping the oppressed class of patients ignorant and dependent (Waitzkin and Waterman 1974). This is also why doctors often prolong a patient's uncertainty about a problem or its treatment. Alienation of patient and physician, like that of owner and worker, is an inevitable part of a system in which the interests of the one oppose those of the other.

The Exploitation of Women

Sociologists who have done participant observation of the practice of medicine report a bias *against* women's reproductive organs. Sociologist Sue Fisher (1986), for example, was surprised to hear surgeons recommend total hysterectomy (the removal of both the uterus and the ovaries) even when no cancer was present. She found that men doctors regard the uterus and ovaries as a "potentially disease-producing" organ—and useless and unnecessary after the childbearing years. Some surgeons routinely recommend this profitable operation for every woman who has finished bearing children.

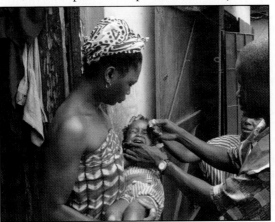

When Western medicine was exported to the Least Industrialized Nations, life expectancy there increased dramatically. One reason was the sharp drop in the death rate of children. Shown here are medical workers in Nigeria as they deliver medical services to a low-rent district.

Most of the 600,000 hysterectomies performed each year in the United States are unnecessary (Broder et al. 2000). It is no wonder that feminists refer to hysterectomies as a "war on the womb" (Fisher 1986).

Many surgeons look at hysterectomies as a virtual money machine. To increase their profits, surgeons drum up business by "selling" the operation. Here is how one resident explained it to sociologist Diana Scully (1994):

You have to look for your surgical procedures; you have to go after patients. Because no one is crazy enough to come and say, "Hey, here I am. I want you to operate on me." You have to sometimes convince the patient that she is really sick—if she is, of course [laughs], and that she is better off with a surgical procedure.

One way that surgeons convince a woman to "buy" the operation they are offering for sale is to say that her fibroids *might* turn into cancer. This statement is often sufficient, for it frightens the woman, who can picture herself lying in a casket, her tearful family inconsolable after the loss of their wife and mother. What the surgeon does *not* say is the rest of the truth—that the fibroids probably will not turn into cancer and that several nonsurgical treatments are available.

The Larger Picture:
The Exploitation
of Illness

From a Marxist conflict perspective, the entire medical system is an industry whose goals are profit and power. To reach these goals, its practitioners exploit sick people (Reynolds 1973). Marxists argue that their perspective best explains why medical care for the rich is so much better than that for the poor: Health care is *not* the goal of the U.S. medical system; the goal is profit for those who practice it. Physicians are businesspeople, patients are customers, and health care is the commodity they sell. Health care is like cars: Some people can afford new convertibles, whereas others can afford only old junkers. The government pays an increasing proportion of the nation's health-care bill because government in a capitalist society perpetuates and underwrites the interests of capitalist industries—including medicine. Conflict theorists argue that health care should be a right of *all* citizens, and that people's illnesses and diseases should never be exploited for profit.

Research Findings

After a brief overview of physical health problems in the United States, we will concentrate on social inequalities of health and health care. We will discuss inequalities by age, race–ethnicity, and social class, examine our two-class system of medicine, and consider how health insurance creates its own inequalities. Finally, we will discuss social inequalities in mental illness.

AN OVERVIEW OF PHYSICAL HEALTH PROBLEMS

Historical Changes
in Health Problems

Figure 10-8, which compares today's ten leading causes of death with those of 1900, makes the *social* nature of death evident. As you can see, only six of the ten leading causes of death are the same. Most of today's top killers—heart attacks, cancer, lung diseases, accidents, suicide, and homicide—are caused by people's behavior or by environmental pollution. Homicide is a sign of changing times—and changing health problems. During the 1990s, murder edged into the top ten. It is still there, the tenth leading cause of death in the United States. These changes in leading causes of death over the past hundred years reinforce the point made earlier about how health and illness are related to lifestyle and the environment.

A Reduction
of Infectious Diseases

Figure 10-8 also reveals how significant infectious diseases used to be. Pneumonia was the number one killer, with tuberculosis (TB) close behind. Every family also feared polio, whooping cough, German measles, smallpox, and diphtheria. Then, during the first half of the twentieth century, these diseases receded, death rates plummeted, and life expectancy rose from 47 years to over 70. What happened?

Why This Decline?

The usual answer is that modern medicine wiped out these diseases. I do not want to detract from the real accomplishments of modern medicine, for most of us know someone who would not be alive today if it weren't for bypass surgery or some organ transplant. And drugs have played a significant role in treating some diseases, such as syphilis, bacterial pneumonia, and hypertension. Some vaccinations, too, such as the one for polio, have reduced deaths dramatically.

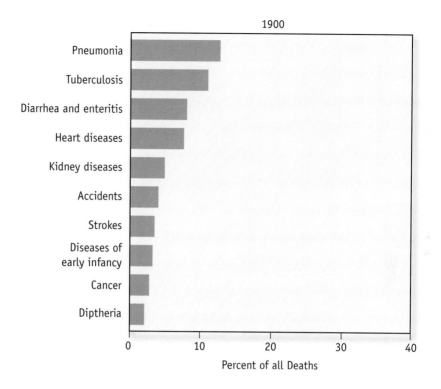

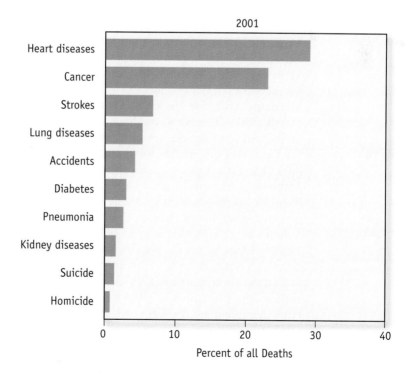

FIGURE 10-8   *The Ten Leading Causes of Death in the United States*

Sources: By the author, based on Rockett 1994; *Statistical Abstract* 2003:Tables 118, 119.

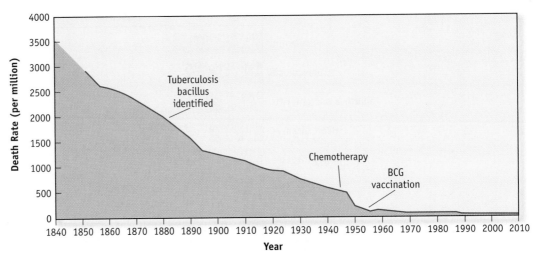

FIGURE 10-9　*The "Conquest" of Tuberculosis*
Tuberculosis used to be one of the greatest killers. Many people believe that modern medicine "conquered" TB with the discovery of streptomycin in 1947 and a vaccine in 1954. In fact, the death rate for TB had been declining steadily for almost 100 years before these discoveries. Many other infectious diseases "conquered" by modern medicine follow a similar pattern.

Source: McKeown 1980; *Statistical Abstract of the United States* 2003:Table 116. Totals from 2002 to 2010 are the author's estimate.

Most of the infectious killers of the nineteenth century, however, had been declining for decades *before* antibiotics, immunizations, or specific drugs had been developed (McKeown 1980). Although medical myth has it that new drugs and vaccinations conquered TB in the 1950s, as Figure 10-9 shows, TB had been declining since the 1800s. If modern medicine did not conquer the infectious diseases so feared by earlier generations of Americans, what did? The answer is not dramatic: cleaner public water supplies and improved social and economic conditions. Infectious killers declined as people became healthier and stronger from cleaner water, better and more food, and better housing.

The Return of TB　　Infectious diseases, however, have a way of fighting back. They can go underground and develop new strains that are resistant to known drugs and vaccines. The Technology box on the next page discusses worldwide implications of this problem. Even TB has resurfaced with deadly strains. More people around the world die of TB now than when the vaccine was discovered (Garrett 1999). Some strains have become resistant to *all* known treatment (Altman 1992a; Specter 1992). Health officials in New York City so fear the possibility of an outbreak of tuberculosis that they order the arrest of TB patients who refuse treatment or who terminate care before their course of treatment is completed. They lock these patients in hospital rooms where guards sit at their door every hour of every day (Specter 1992). TB patients in other states who refuse treatment are also being arrested (Colarossi 2001).

The most feared infectious disease today, however, is AIDS. Let's look at how this disease is related to behavior.

HOW DISEASE IS RELATED TO BEHAVIOR AND ENVIRONMENT: THE CASE OF AIDS

The Social Basis of AIDS　　AIDS is an excellent example of the relationship between behavior, environment, and disease. This disease was first noted in male homosexuals. One person, Gaetan Dugas, an airline steward from Canada, played a key role in its rapid transmission, for he or

Technology and Social Problems
SUPERBUGS IN THE GLOBAL VILLAGE

The retired detective came down with a fever, and he didn't want to eat, wash, or get dressed. His daughter took him to the hospital. He died a few hours later.

The outcome was not too unusual for a 79-year-old. But what happened next was. When a lab analyzed a vial of his blood, the doctor could hardly believe the results. Nothing would kill the staph infection in the deceased's blood, not even vancomycin, the antibiotic of last resort.

Japan reported another case, and others cropped up in France and England. Tests showed that the strains from these cases were not related to one another, and so far a worldwide outbreak of infections that are immune to every type of antibiotic has been avoided. Apparently the detective's strain of staph was buried with him.

But it is just a matter of time. At some spot in the world, someone else will come down with a germ that is resistant to every antibiotic. With global travel, in just a matter of days that strain will spread throughout the global village.

The signs grow more ominous. A bacteria resistant to vancomycin showed up in chicken feed. No one knows how this happened, but the fear is that something like this will happen again, and that it will be transmitted to chickens, then mutate to humans (Grady 1999).

Following the discovery of penicillin in the 1940s came a series of effective microbe killers. By the 1970s, more than 100 antibiotics sat on pharmacy shelves. The war against microbes had been won, or so the medical industry thought. Researchers relaxed and stopped developing new antibiotics. Promising new drugs, already in development, were even canceled as superfluous.

In the presence of antibiotics, the weak germs die off, but strong ones can mutate, survive, and proliferate. This is especially likely to happen if people do not complete the full course of their medical treatment and stop taking a drug when they feel better. The more that antibiotics are used and misused, the more that drug-resistant bugs proliferate (Amábile-Cuevas 2003).

Are antibiotics misused? The Institute of Medicine reports that 20 to 50 percent of the 145 million prescriptions given to U.S. outpatients each year are unnecessary. The same goes for the 190 million doses of antibiotics given to hospital patients.

We all carry staphylococcus germs on our skin and nostrils. There they are harmless, but they wait for a chance to infect us through scrapes and cuts and surgical incisions. If our current, relatively mild staph germs are replaced by a mutant, virulent strain, simple cuts and scrapes could become mortal wounds. A sore throat could be fatal. Many patients who go to hospitals for routine surgery will be carried out in coffins (Stolberg 1998b).

This threat has broken through the apathy of the medical industry. Pharmaceutical firms are searching for the next generation of antibiotics to fight the next generation of microbes. The race is close. If we win and are able to develop new antibiotics in time to prevent a global epidemic, will we then repeat this process—overprescribing, not completing the course of treatments—with the microbes again mutating and developing resistance to the new drugs?

Granted the notable folly of much of human behavior (and the institutional factors that promote it—especially a medical establishment eager for profits), I am certain that this will happen. A sage once said that those who do not study history are doomed to repeat it. I would add that although we study history, and even know its lessons, in some instances we set ourselves on a course determined to repeat it. This is one.

one of his sex partners had sex with 40 of the first 248 AIDS cases reported in the United States (Shilts 1987). The disease then hit another group whose lifestyle also encouraged its transmission—intravenous drug users who shared needles. The third of the groups that were the hardest hit represents an environmental risk: Hemophiliacs, who need regular blood transfusions, were exposed to the disease through contaminated blood. Lifestyle was also central to how the disease entered the general population; the bridge was prostitutes who had sex with intravenous drug users and with bisexual and heterosexual men. Lifestyle and environment continue to be significant:

AIDS is more common among drug users who share needles and among people who have multiple sexual partners.

AIDS is a global epidemic, with millions of people around the world infected. Of all regions in the world, sub-Saharan Africa has been hit the worst. There, AIDS is the leading cause of death. The primary reason that AIDS is so common in this region is the common practice of men having unprotected sex with prostitutes. In some African countries, AIDS is expected to wipe out half the teenagers. Hardest hit is Botswana, where two of every five adults are infected with AIDS (United Nations 2002).

The situation is quite different in the United States, where a combination of drugs, called protease inhibitors, has dropped AIDS deaths from a high of 50,000 in 1995 to under 14,000 now (*Statistical Abstract* 1998:Table 144; 2003:Table 117). The new drugs—at a cost of $20,000 per year per patient—prevent people who are infected with the HIV virus from developing full-blown AIDS and keep those who have the disease from dieing from infections (such as the flu or pneumonia) that used to kill people who had AIDS. New infections have also dropped to a third of what they were. Figure 10-10 shows how AIDS is related to race-ethnicity. The reason that these groups have different rates of AIDS is not genetic. No racial-ethnic group is more susceptible to AIDS because of biological factors. Rather, the reason is *social*, especially not using condoms and drug users sharing needles.

The HIV virus mutates rapidly, and medical researchers fear that the protease inhibitors may prove to be only a stopgap measure. Some newly infected patients have contracted strains of HIV that are resistant to anti H.I.V. drugs (Santora and Altman 2005). If drug-resistant strains become widespread, as is likely, the epidemic could surge again. Several new drugs, however, hold the promise of taking over where the protease inhibitors leave off.

Although African Americans make up just 12 percent of the U.S. population, they account for about *half* of all new HIV infections. A combination of reasons underlies this startling statistic. The first is cultural-behavioral: a disbelief that it can happen, a distrust of doctors, a reluctance to talk about AIDS, lack of knowledge about its transmission, higher-than-average use of injected drugs, and reluctance to use condoms. The second is organizational: Most money for HIV prevention has bypassed African Americans, going instead to AIDS organizations with roots in the gay community (Stolberg 1998a).

FIGURE 10-10

Source: By the author, based on Centers for Disease Control 2004.

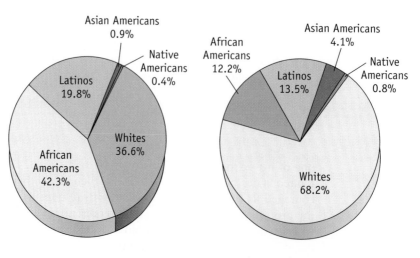

Percentage of AIDS Cases   **Percentage of U.S. Population**

SOCIAL INEQUALITIES IN PHYSICAL ILLNESS

Poverty and Health

Let's look more closely at the social inequalities that underlie the U.S. health picture. From earlier chapters, it should not surprise you to learn that economic factors largely determine who will be healthy and who will be sick. Poor children, for example, are more likely to be undernourished or to lack a balanced diet. As a result, they are more vulnerable to disease. As we saw in Table 10-2 (on page 318), the poorer people are, the sicker they are. Even their death rates are higher.

This takes us to the heart of the matter. *Social* inequality—the essential factor that underlies our patterns of disease and death—is seldom considered a problem for our health-care system to deal with. Instead, our system focuses on acute health problems, patches people up, and sends them back to the same environment from which they came.

Occupational Health Problems

Occupational health hazards are also distributed unequally in society. For example, the workers in manufacturing plants, not the managers, are more likely to be exposed to dangerous working conditions and toxic chemicals. Some chemicals merely irritate the skin; others cause skin cancer or attack vital body organs. Carbon monoxide, mercury, and uranium destroy the kidneys; the ethers, chlorines, and the heavy metals invade the nervous system.

Machinery and equipment also can be harmful to health. The noise level of some factories causes hearing loss—for workers (bosses are usually sheltered behind protective partitions or located in quieter buildings). Arc welding, lasers, and radar all produce radiation and damage the eyes. Increasingly considered a social problem, occupational illnesses will receive more attention in the future.

Paying the Bill: Inflation, Insurance, and Medicaid

Looking at who pays the medical bill helps to expose social inequalities of health care. Before today's patchwork insurance coverage, there were private hospitals and clinics for those who could pay (considered "the worthy") and public facilities for those who could not (considered "the unworthy") (Rosenberg 1987). Because medical students need patients to practice on and public hospitals provided them, some public facilities were affiliated with medical schools. The medical care at these facilities was often superior. On the whole, however, with lower salaries, worse working conditions, and outdated equipment, public hospitals attracted the less-qualified doctors and nurses. Iatrogenesis, injuries caused by medical care, was common, including death due to a low level of medical knowledge and incompetent physicians.

Before World War II, professional health care was still fairly primitive. Most health care took place at home, and doctors made house calls to supplement and direct home health care. Hospitals, which were considered a last resort, were feared places. They were known as "the place where people go to die."

After World War II, medical technology improved, and the costs of treating illness increased. Many middle-class people who had serious health problems found that they could no longer afford hospital care. Coupled with the desire of physicians and hospital owners to increase their income, this problem led to the creation of medical and hospitalization insurance. The idea spread, and such insurance eventually became a standard benefit for business and government employees. As a result, most working-class and middle-class people who had steady jobs received medical care. The poor were still left out in the cold, with only charity to take care of the worst cases.

Unanticipated Consequences

Those who suffered the most health problems, the poor and the elderly, were passed over. In 1966, Congress tried to remedy this sorry situation by passing Medicaid for the poor and Medicare for the elderly. Neither is comprehensive or generous, but overnight these plans provided medical coverage for millions who needed it the worst. Because these programs did not control what health providers could charge, however, the cost of medical care rose rapidly. Soon people's out-of-pocket expenses were as much as they had been before the government began these programs.

As functionalists stress, human actions have unanticipated consequences. One of Medicaid's was that it undermined public hospitals. City and county officials figured that because the poor now had medical insurance, they no longer needed free facilities. Eager to save money, many cities and counties closed their public hospitals and clinics. This left many of the poor in the lurch; because Medicaid's rates were low, many doctors and private hospitals refused to accept Medicaid patients. The working poor have been especially hard hit—their income is so low that they cannot afford to buy insurance, but not so low that they qualify for Medicaid. Fifteen percent of the nation, or about 41 million people, have no health insurance (*Statistical Abstract* 2003:Table 152).

Race-Ethnicity and Insurance

Lack of medical insurance highlights the racial-ethnic inequalities that run through U.S. society. Because African Americans and Latinos have a larger proportion of working poor, they are more likely to lack medical insurance. Whereas 14 percent of whites are not covered by insurance, the rate for African Americans is 19 percent, and for Latinos 33 percent (*Statistical Abstract* 2003:Table 152).

SOCIAL INEQUALITIES IN MENTAL ILLNESS

Social Class and Mental Health: Consistent Findings

Do some social classes have more emotional problems than others? This intriguing question has a consistent answer. Since 1939, sociologists have found that people's emotional well-being gets worse as you go down the social class ladder. Those in the lower social classes are more likely to be depressed, anxious, nervous, and have phobias. (In sociological parlance, this is known as an "inverse correlation between mental problems and social class.") This finding has been confirmed in numerous studies (Faris and Dunham 1939; Srole et al. 1978; Lundberg 1991; Starfield et al. 2002).

The Midtown Manhattan Project

The term *mental illness* is so imprecise, however, that we have to be suspicious of what is being measured. For example, experts disagree about when to apply labels such as "schizophrenic" or "depressive." To overcome this problem, in 1978 sociologist Leo Srole and his colleagues at Columbia University did a study that became a classic in sociology: the Midtown Manhattan Project. The Srole team developed its own scale of symptoms, trained its own interviewers, and then interviewed a representative sample of New Yorkers. As shown in Figure 10-11, like both earlier and later studies, these researchers found that the poor have considerably more emotional problems.

Four Explanations of the Greater Emotional Problems of the Lower Classes

Why do the poor suffer more mental disorders than people in other classes? According to the *drift hypothesis*, people with emotional difficulties tend to be less successful in life, so they drift from higher-income families down into the lower classes (Fox

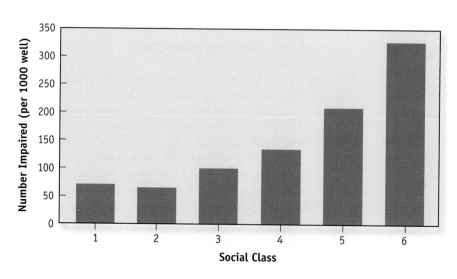

FIGURE 10-11 *Social Class and Mental Problems* Results of the Srole study of mental health problems among adults. Number 1 is the wealthiest, number 6 the poorest.

Source: From Leo Srole et al., *Mental Health in the Metropolis: The Midtown Manhattan Study.* Copyright © 1978 by Leo Srole. Reprinted with the permission of Esther Srole.

1990). According to the *genetic hypothesis,* genes cause schizophrenia, manic depression, and other severe disorders, and the poor are more likely to have these genes. Why should this be? The answer is provided by the drift hypothesis: Even if these genes once were distributed evenly among the social classes, many of the people who have these genes would drift downward, leaving a disproportionate number of poor families with these traits.

The genetic explanation for the most severe disorders, such as schizophrenia and manic depression, is influential in the medical community. But since the family that rears the child is usually the biological family, it is difficult to separate genetic influences from the effects of socialization. To try to do so, researchers have studied identical twins who have been reared in different families. They report that if one of the twins has schizophrenia the likelihood of the second twin having this illness is so high that it proves the genetic hypothesis. Social psychologist Leon Kamin (1981), however, who reviewed the data that "prove" that a recessive gene causes schizophrenia, found so many methodological problems that he concluded the research is worthless.

According to a third explanation, the *socialization hypothesis,* children who are reared by disturbed parents are more likely to learn pathological ways of coping with the world. They are less equipped to deal with the challenges of education and career. People in the higher classes who are reared in such homes drift to the lower classes, whereas lower-class children from such homes remain in the lower class.

Sociologists prefer an explanation called the *environmental hypothesis.* Here the focus is on how the environments of the social classes differ. Let's rephrase the basic finding that the lower classes have more "mental illnesses": Another way to say this is that people in the social classes that are better off financially are happier, less depressed, less filled with anxiety, and less phobic (that is, they have fewer fears). In short, they are "mentally healthier." And why shouldn't they be? For them, life is better—less "nasty, brutal, and short." People who are in the middle classes and above have better job security, finances, physical health, medical care, and marriages. Not only do they have greater security at the present time (not absolute security, of course, but much greater security than the poor have), but they also have hope for the future. They realistically plan and look forward to a larger house, better cars, exotic vacations, their children's college, and a relaxing, enjoyable retirement. Of course, sociologists say, their mental health is better. Why would anyone expect anything less?

Compare this situation with the stress-filled package that comes with poverty: jobs that can quit on you anytime, low wages, unpaid bills, trouble paying the rent, and insistent bill collectors; more divorce, alcoholism, and violence; and greater vulnerability to crime combined with worse physical health and less access to good medical care. Such conditions certainly deal severe blows to people's emotional well-being.

To be fair (and my bias as a cultural sociologist certainly shows up here), as with some of the materials we covered in the preceding chapter, until we have more evidence environment versus heredity must remain an open question.

Therapies in Health Care   In order to understand how mental health services are related to social inequality, let's consider types of therapy and health-care institutions. In **individual psychotherapy,** a therapist listens and tries to guide the patient toward a resolution of emotional problems. A type of psychotherapy is **psychoanalysis,** which Sigmund Freud pioneered as a way to uncover the subconscious motives, fantasies, and fears that shape people's neurotic behavior. The patient meets an analyst several times a week and talks about whatever comes to mind, while the analyst listens for hidden patterns, particularly those that reveal unresolved conflicts from early childhood. More common is **short-term directive therapy,** in which a counselor focuses on current situations to help clients understand their problems. In **group therapy,** a group of patients, with the guidance of a therapist, helps each other to cope with their problems.

A form of Western medicine is talk therapy; that is, troubled individuals talk to a counselor or therapist about their problems. One form of talk therapy is group therapy; a group of individuals talk about their problems in counselor-led sessions. Despite its cost, there is no evidence that talk therapy is any more effective than talking to a friend or neighbor.

Drug therapy, the use of tranquilizers, antidepressants, and antipsychotic drugs to relieve people's problems and help them cope with life, is another option. As with Prozac (discussed in Chapter 4), some of these drugs have serious side effects. Drug therapy is often criticized for being a way to treat the symptoms of troubled people without getting at their underlying problems.

In some cases, especially depression, **electroconvulsive therapy (ECT)** (also known as electroshock therapy) is used. Wires are attached to either side of a patient's skull, and low-voltage electric shocks are sent repeatedly through the brain. A side effect is memory loss. I used to be an orderly at Renard Hospital in St. Louis, a private mental hospital affiliated with Washington University Medical School. Occasionally, I held patients down during ECT treatment. I vividly recall how they convulsed wildly as the electricity coursed through their brains, and how disoriented they were afterward.

Again—the Ability to Pay

The type of therapy that a troubled person is likely to receive does not depend on the person's problems, but on the person's ability to pay. People who have money and good insurance are more likely to be guided through their problems with **talk therapy**—psychotherapy, group therapy, and so on. "Talk" therapy is expensive, and it would be a rare instance in which a poor and uninsured person receives it. The poor and uninsured are likely to receive no help at all, but when they do receive help, they are likely to be given drug therapy, which has been called a "pharmaceutical straitjacket." (The drugs given in mental hospitals make patients drowsy, lethargic, and easier to handle. They also often make them confused.)

A Surprising Statement

It is difficult, however, to say that these patterns of therapy and social class represent inequality: *We do not know which therapies work.* Costly psychoanalysis may be no more effective than drug therapy or even no therapy at all. Psychoanalysis may even be less effective. Consequently, we cannot say whether the poor are receiving worse—or better—treatment for their emotional problems. The rigorous studies that demonstrate the effectiveness of therapy are yet to be done. An emerging type of therapy, described in the Technology and Social Problems box on the next page, is also likely to remain unexamined and unproven.

A Two-Tier System

Health-care facilities for treating mental illness used to parallel the facilities for treating physical problems: public hospitals for the poor and private hospitals or office visits for the affluent. The state and county hospitals had so many patients and so little money that thousands of patients languished in back wards, where they were driven

Technology and Social Problems
CYBERBABBLE, CYBERSHRINKS, AND CYBERSHAMS

The effectiveness of "talk therapy" is questionable. Talking to a friend or clergy (or your mother-in-law, for that matter) may be as effective (or ineffective) as psychotherapy. Talking, in other words, may be helpful regardless of who the listener is—or it may not be helpful. We just don't know. It certainly is more pleasant to talk to a supportive, sympathetic, and understanding listener than to someone who challenges what you say—but even which type of listener is more effective in helping with problems has not been demonstrated.

E-mail therapy has now made its appearance; patient and therapist send e-mail back and forth. Some therapists and patients use chat rooms. Others add video links so they can see each other. Some therapists offer a one-shot deal for a flat rate. Some sell their virtual couches by the minute, others by the month (Cohen 1997).

Cybertherapy offers an advantage that the telephone does not: Time zones make no difference. Patients who are traveling around the world can zap off an e-mail whenever they like without waking the therapist in the middle of the night.

Cyberbabble is being taken seriously and likely will develop into a full-fledged form of counseling. The American Psychological Association is setting up guidelines, and California requires that insurance companies pay for online therapy (Cohen 1997). Therapists are establishing ethical guidelines (King and Poulos 1999). And the sign of acceptance: Some universities are setting up programs

of virtual counseling. The one at Duke University, called the Virtual Reality Program, recruits patients by saying that this type of therapy is more efficient, easier to schedule, and more confidential. In the Duke program, the patients actually come to a university office, where they use computer simulations. The therapist, says an online ad for the program, can treat people who have a fear of flying by having the patient "repeatedly land the virtual airplane."

We have just entered the age of virtual therapy, barely able to envision its future. One form that is being developed is fascinating. In computer-enhanced therapy, the therapist and patient will engage in discussions through computer-animated characters that represent themselves. From a supply of images, the patient will choose his or her appearance, as well as the appearance of the therapist and the online setting where their session takes place. The online, animated characters will then talk to one another. Supposedly, this format reduces embarrassment for patients, encouraging them to talk about unflattering problems and feelings (Onion 2004). I might add that it will also allow the therapist to express emotions—remaining in private, the therapist can show shock, take offense, or even laugh at the patient—all without the patient being the wiser.

Does cyberbabble work? No one knows. But, then, no one knows if other forms of therapy work either. So the therapists might as well collect fees this way as any other. And in most forms, the cybershrink doesn't even have to leave home or have patients drop by. Quite a deal.

as crazy by the disturbed people around them and the stark rooms they called home as they were by their own inner turmoil. Few received anything that could be called treatment.

With deinstitutionalization, described earlier in this chapter, the population of state and county mental hospitals shriveled. Although such places now offer short-term treatment and outpatient services, they still warehouse chronic patients who cannot cope in other environments.

How Nursing Homes Replaced Mental Hospitals

As with physical illness, the type of payment that is available shapes what happens in the care of mental patients. Medicare allowed the states to transfer the cost of treating the poor to the federal government. Because many of these patients were elderly and qualified for nursing homes, some nursing homes became what psychiatrists Fritz Redlich and Stephen Kellert (1978) called decentralized back wards. People who would have been placed in mental hospitals under previous practices now are placed in nursing homes. The primary force behind this change was not an improvement in therapy, but Medicare legislation.

In Sum

In conclusion, social inequalities in the treatment of mental problems continue, but today far more services are available over a wide range of facilities. As with physical illness, the working poor are less likely to receive mental health services.

Social Policy

Forces Pushing Up Costs

We have reviewed conditions that have pushed up the cost of health care. The fee-for-service system encourages physicians to sell specialized services and to get patients to come back for visits. Doctors who are paid for every office visit, whether a visit is necessary or not, tend to encourage visits rather than dissuade them or to practice preventive medicine. Focusing on acute problems is also profitable for hospitals. With depersonalization breaking bonds between physician and patient, and living in a litigious society, many patients look for reasons to sue. Malpractice insurance is expensive, and it further drives up the cost of medical care. Concentrating on disease intervention is more expensive and less effective than prevention. Let's look at policies that address these basic forces.

BEING PAID TO STAY HEALTHY

Getting Rebates

Some employers give their workers a rebate for staying healthy—or at least for staying away from doctors. In return for a higher insurance deductible, such as $1,500 a year, employees who spend less than the deductible are paid the difference between the $1,500 and what they spend. Workers who spend only $100 collect $1,400, which is a nice bonus. Where this program has been tried, employee health costs go down. As one teacher said, "Before, I kind of overdid it. Now I feel I have an investment in my own health."

PREPAID MEDICAL CARE

HMOs

In the best-known type of prepaid medical care, the **health maintenance organization (HMO),** a medical corporation (sometimes owned by physicians) bids to take care of the health needs of a business' employees. The business pays a monthly fee for each employee. If the health care of an employee runs more than this fee, the medical corporation loses money; if it costs less, it makes money. Because the medical corporation receives no more than this fee, its directors are motivated to reduce medical costs.

Patients demand—and doctors like to deliver—high-tech care. There is something glamorous about the latest technology. Such technology, however, has driven up the cost of medical care, and, as I found out from personal experience, a week's stay in a hospital can now run over $50,000. HMOs represent an attempt to hold medical costs in check.

Doctors are paid salaries, but they can receive bonuses if they reduce patient costs. The doctors try to strike a balance between ignoring trivial and self-limiting symptoms and giving good health care. They are also motivated to treat medical problems before they become serious and their remedy grows expensive. Where fee-for-service doctors are happy to charge $45 each time a patient runs to them with the sniffles and will hold their hands for a few minutes and prescribe the same medication that is available over the counter, HMO doctors don't feel the same way about the matter.

Because the doctors make more money if patients stay well, they encourage preventive care, such as immunizations, well-baby checkups, mammograms, and physicals. They urge patients to adopt a lifestyle that improves health, one based on better diet, exercise, rest, and avoiding the abuse of drugs, including alcohol. Unnecessary tests, surgery, and hospital admissions represent costs to the physicians and medical corporation, so they avoid them. For the same reason, they also minimize the length of hospital stays. The reduction in costs can be dramatic, as HMO patients have less surgery and hospitalization than fee-for-service patients (Ward 1991; Cuffel et al. 1999).

A Conflict of Interest

As you read this description of HMOs, you may have perceived the built-in conflict of interest. The physicians face a dilemma: profits or patient care? An unintended consequence of avoiding hospitalizing patients and conducting expensive tests or treatments is that HMO doctors withhold some *necessary* treatments, tests, and hospitalizations. For example, a woman I know was sent home from the hospital even though she was still bleeding from her surgery. If she had remained longer, she would have used up more than her "share" of allotted costs and eaten into the corporation's profits. This would not have happened to a fee-for-service patient who could afford to pay for the health care.

Limiting Doctors

Physicians are chafing at HMOs. Their two major concerns are loss of autonomy and reduced quality of health care. Doctors have to call their HMO for permission to give certain treatments. This puts the HMOs in the position of dictating to doctors what treatment they can give their patients (McGinley 1999). ("You can do that if you want, but we won't pay for it.") Some HMOs even determine how many patients the doctors must see each day. One HMO, for example, insisted that its physicians see eight patients an hour, limiting them to 7½ minutes per visit. This did not leave the doctors enough time for completing paperwork, analyzing lab results, and, of course, for calling HMO officials to get approval for treatments (Greenhouse 1999).

Problems with HMOs have made the news. A mother tried to get her HMO doctor to refer her toddler to a specialist because of a persistent ear infection. She succeeded—after a year (Kilborn 1998). A physician recalls how he fought with his HMO for three hours to get permission to do a procedure. The HMO officials kept refusing, even though the woman was coughing up life-threatening amounts of blood (Steinhauer 1999a). The doctor of the acquaintance I mentioned (the one who was sent home from the hospital still bleeding) may have wanted her to remain until she was well, but could not receive approval from the HMO he was working for.

PHYSICIAN ASSISTANTS

Delegating Responsibility

Another strategy for controlling costs is to use *physician assistants*. Half to three-quarters of all the problems that are dealt with in a typical doctor's office are medically trivial. Physician assistants and nurses can provide much of this medical care and educate patients with chronic disorders. To delegate routine and time-consuming responsibilities to assistants makes more sense than making sure that everyone who has the sniffles is seen by a physician whose job requires twenty-three years of education and commands one of the highest salaries of any occupation.

Conflict with Doctors

The use of physician assistants has led to an in-house rivalry, however, and the first volleys in a battle over turf have been fired. Physician assistants must work under the supervision of physicians, but they don't like doctors breathing down their necks. They want to be able to give more independent care, but their efforts at establishing greater autonomy have been met with hostility from doctors (Aston and Foubister 1998). At this point, the attitude of the medical profession is, "If they want to do more, they can go to medical school."

TRAINING PHYSICIANS

Closing the Gender Gap

Medical schools graduate about 15,000 physicians a year, the same now as they did in 1980 (*Statistical Abstract* 2003:Table 303). As Figure 10-12 shows, a startling change has occurred in the gender makeup of those graduates: In 1960, only 6 percent of medical school graduates were women. Today, women make up almost half of the nation's medical school graduates.

Will Gender Change Make a Difference?

It is doubtful that this change in gender will have any significant effect on how medicine is practiced. The medical delivery system is in place, the characteristics we reviewed are firm, and gender is mostly irrelevant. Women doctors are as likely as men doctors to be generous or greedy, patient or profit oriented, in favor of heroic medicine or preventive medicine. They, too, will prefer fee-for-service medicine and will be just as likely to avoid the poor and to set up practices where they make more money. Such orientations are consequences of core values in the general society and of those passed on in medical schools. Gender does not make someone lean in one direction or the other.

Breaking a Monopoly and Getting Medical Care to the Poor by Purposefully Overproducing Doctors

A social policy that might reduce costs and help get doctors to the poor, where they are needed the most, would be to overproduce physicians. The government could encourage the opening of new medical schools. It could either finance them, or, if turned over to investors, offer tax breaks. I suggest that we modify a system that Mexico has. In return for spending a specified amount of time in areas where there is a doctor shortage, students could go to college and medical school free of charge. They would also be paid a monthly salary. I suggest the new physicians be required to give four years back for the eight that they spend in college and medical training. These graduates would not be given their final certification until they completed those four years.

FIGURE 10-12 *M.D. Degrees, by Sex*

Source: By the author, based on *Statistical Abstract of the United States* 1994:Table 295; 2003:Table 303.

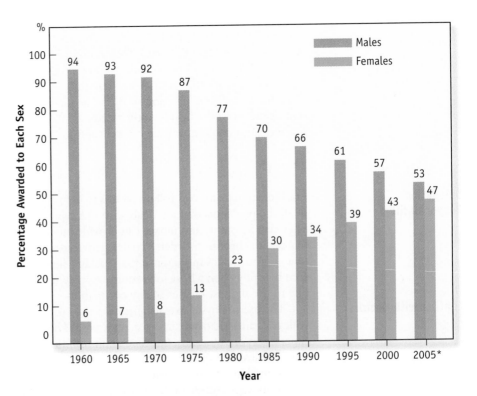

Note: Asterisk indicates the author's estimate.

During these years of service, the government would pay for their medical malpractice insurance and pay them a salary equal to the average U.S. wage.

Not only would such a program help to get doctors to the areas where the need is the greatest, but also it would increase competition among doctors. Currently, the American Medical Association stifles competition by limiting the number of medical graduates. If more doctors graduated, patients would have a greater choice of physicians. As competition among doctors grew, doctors would likely reduce their prices, and the rise in medical costs would slow. The waiting period in doctors' offices would also lessen as overcrowding and overscheduling decreased. If patients have more choice, some of the more incompetent physicians should be driven out of medicine. Communities that have not been able to lure a physician to their town should be able to recruit physicians.

The outcry of physicians to such a proposal would be loud, for their income would drop as prices for their services fell. The physicians' labor union (or more accurately, their business organization), the American Medical Association, would mobilize to fight such a proposal. By controlling the nation's medical schools, the AMA limits the supply of physicians, guaranteeing high medical costs. An oversupply is not in the interest of this powerful monopoly.

OUTREACH SERVICES

Home Health Care

Because hospitalization is expensive and many hospital stays are unnecessary, they are being replaced with outreach services whenever possible. **Home health care,** for example, is less expensive and often more humane than care that is available in nursing homes and hospitals. Many elderly people are put in nursing homes not because they are ill but because they can no longer live independently at home. Home health care lets them remain at home, in the environment they are used to and that they prefer. On the negative side, home health care encourages profiteering. For instance, a home health care company may pay its workers $12 an hour to care for the homebound, yet charge Medicare $25 an hour and pocket the difference.

Community Health Care

Outreach programs for the mentally ill can be improved. We can provide ex-mental patients the community care that was supposed to accompany deinstitutionalization. The need is great, as anyone who takes time to talk to the homeless can attest. Group homes and supervised apartments can be established for the mentally disturbed, the mentally handicapped, and the chronically ill who have difficulty living in the community on their own.

The "Worthy" versus the "Unworthy"

Such programs are costly, of course, but cost is not the primary obstacle. If we refer to a "worthy" group, such as wounded veterans, hardly anyone objects. But if we suggest establishing such services for the homeless, who are viewed as "unworthy," the objections are never-ending. I suggest that it is not the cost, but the beneficiaries, that are people's concern.

PREVENTIVE MEDICINE

Preventable Deaths

Half of all deaths of Americans are preventable. (Preventable is a strange term to use in this context, I know, but it is the standard term. It would be more accurate to say that these deaths are postponable, as each of these people would die eventually.) The two main causes of preventable deaths are deaths from smoking (435,000 a year) and deaths from improper diet and lack of exercise (400,000 deaths a year) (Mokdad et al. 2004). As subjective concerns and greater knowledge about health have increased— and because it senses profit—the AMA has begun to stress preventive medicine.

**Three Types
of Prevention**

Preventive medicine sounds ideal as a way to ensure good health and reduce medical costs, but how do you put it into practice? Health planners distinguish among three types of prevention. **Primary prevention,** such as improved nutrition and childhood vaccinations, keeps a disease from occurring in the first place. **Secondary prevention,** such as self-examination for breast cancer, involves detecting a disease before it comes to the attention of a physician. **Tertiary prevention** is not very different from medical care. It means to prevent further damage from an already existing disease. Examples are controlling pneumonia so that it does not lead to death and maintaining a diabetic on insulin.

Lifestyle

Primary prevention is promising because with proper nutrition, exercise, and not smoking, people can avoid many diseases. For example, only about 15 percent of people who get lung cancer are nonsmokers. A diet rich in beta-carotene, raw fruits and vegetables, and vitamin E supplements reduces the risk of cancer. Wheat bran, canola oil, soy milk, cantaloupe, avocados, olive oil, and green vegetables such as cabbage also appear to reduce the risk. And those leafy green vegetables that are hardly anyone's favorite—broccoli, brussels sprouts, and spinach—also seem to fight cancer (Sugimura 2002).

Bovine Growth Hormones

Studies on the effects of milk on health show mixed results. Some studies indicate that milk can reduce cancer (Cho et al. 2004), whereas other research indicates that milk might increase the risk of cancer (Mayne et al. 1995). If milk does increase the risk of cancer, this could be due to the pesticides and herbicides in the cows' fodder, or even from the hormones that cows are given to promote their growth. Some researchers claim that bovine growth hormones pave the way for cancer by inhibiting the body's natural cancer fighters (Epstein 2001). Some researchers also accuse Monsanto, a global corporate giant that produces bovine growth hormones, of caring more about profits than people's health. To this some reply with a yawn, "Big surprise."

Immunizations

Childhood immunizations, too, are effective techniques of primary prevention. Not only do immunizations save lives but also they save vast sums that would have been spent on medical care. Yet about one of ten U.S. children has not been immunized against measles, mumps, diphtheria, hepatitis, and polio (*Statistical Abstract* 2003:Table 191). In many rural and poor areas, the figure is worse.

**Drug Abuse
and Homicide**

Although not usually thought of as preventive medicine, no program would be complete unless it also focuses on preventing drug abuse and homicide. From what we learned in Chapters 4 and 5, to reduce drug abuse is to prevent many serious health problems. Such programs could prevent the untimely deaths of many inner-city youths. In addition, drug abuse prevention programs that are directed against smoking and alcohol abuse could save hundreds of thousands of middle-class lives. Drug abuse programs, then, are one way to improve the nation's health.

**Taking a Back Seat
to Heroic Intervention**

Preventive medicine is quiet and unassuming. It often is obscured by the drama of open-heart surgery, screaming ambulances, and doctors and nurses rushing about in emergency rooms. If you take care of your body and manage to stay well, no one thinks much about it. Become seriously ill, however, and people jump to attention. Preventing something from happening means that you never see it happen. In fact, this is what most people want—not to get sick. Yet most people only talk about this goal, and few are willing to work to reach it. Although entire communities could reduce their risk of heart disease, unhealthy habits such as fatty foods, booze, and the boob tube are much more appealing to most of us than are vegetables, fruit juices, and aerobic exercise.

**A Growing
Medical Problem**

Something disturbing is happening in the United States, and it does not bode well for our health:

In Cape Canaveral, Florida, while waiting for a space shot, I struck up a conversation with a British couple in their twenties. As we chatted while awaiting the delayed launch, I asked them what they thought about the United States. They looked at each other in that know-

More Americans are overweight today than ever before in the history of the United States. The likely causes are a surplus of income, an abundance of food, less physically active occupations (a reduction in farming), more leisure, and more sedentary lifestyles (television watching), accompanied by more sugary foods and a custom called "snacking." Being overweight produces a variety of health problems, from weakened knee joints to heart attacks.

ing way that couples do, and asked if I really wanted to know. I said I did. They replied, hesitatingly, that they had never seen so many fat people in their lives.

When a friend from Spain visited me, he commented on the things that struck him as different. He was surprised to see people living in metal houses (no mobile homes in Spain). He also asked why there were so many fat Americans.

Are these valid perceptions, or just some twisted ethnocentric observations by foreigners? I wish I could say that the perceptions aren't true, but the statistics bear them out. Americans are getting fatter, much fatter. In 1980, one of four Americans was overweight. By 1990, the percentage of overweight Americans had jumped to one of three. Now, incredibly, it is *over half* (58 percent) (*Statistical Abstract* 1998:Table 242; 2003:Table 209).

Perhaps we should just shrug our shoulders and say, "So what?" Is this generalized fatness anything more than someone's idea of how much we should weigh? It is a great deal more. Fat is more life threatening to Americans than AIDS or even alcohol abuse. Health experts estimate that 300,000 U.S. adults die each year of fat-related causes (Tarmann 2002). Fat people are more likely than thin people to have strokes (Bonow and Eckel 2003), to suffer heart attacks (Kenchaiah et al. 2002), and to come down with diabetes (Troiano 2002). And compared with thinner people, when people who are overweight come down with these health problems, they are more likely to die (Calle et al. 2003).

This increase in the weight of Americans, so apparent to people from other cultures, flies in the face of what we know about preventing health problems. Our knowledge has gone one way, but our lifestyles another. For example, the average American drinks 49 gallons of soft drinks a year—more sugared, caffeinated, and carbonated water with harmful chemicals than milk and fruit and vegetable juices combined (*Statistical Abstract* 2003:Table 216). Because this lifestyle is firmly ingrained—and continuously reinforced by appealing advertising—it is more difficult to implement preventive medicine than it is to continue the less-effective but more-dramatic medical procedures. To put this in plain English, most people apparently prefer to go to a doctor to be treated for health problems than to exercise and eat healthier.

To see how severely lifestyle can affect people's health on a national basis, read the *Spotlight on Research* box on page 347.

HUMANIZING HEALTH CARE

What Is Depersonalization?

Depersonalization is a problem in medicine. What do people mean when they complain about it? People object that they are treated as things, not as people with feelings and personal needs. For Kathie Persall, depersonalization was based on a hospital policy that governed induced labor and caesarean sections—a policy that ignored her desires. When one psychiatrist says to another, "I have a paranoid schiz on Ward 5," or an OB/GYN doctor says to the nurse, "There's a pelvic in Room 3," she is depersonalizing the patient (Henslin and Biggs 2005). Without their knowledge or consent, some people are even used as guinea pigs to see if a new medicine works.

Examples of Depersonalization

Sociologists who have studied depersonalization in public clinics note how the poor not only have to wait for hours to be seen, but aren't even given normal eye

A Global Glimpse

HEALTH CARE IN SWEDEN, RUSSIA, AND CHINA

To better understand our own medical system, it helps to examine health care in other nations. Sweden, Russia, and China illustrate contrasting themes in health care around the world, helping us to place the U.S. medical system in cultural perspective (Henslin 2005).

HEALTH CARE IN THE MOST INDUSTRIALIZED NATIONS: SWEDEN

Sweden has the most comprehensive health care system in the world. National health insurance, which is financed by contributions from the state and employers, covers all Swedish citizens and alien residents. The government pays most physicians a salary to treat patients, but 5 percent work full-time in private practice (Swedish Institute 1990). Except for a small consultation fee, medical and dental treatment by these government-paid doctors is free. The state also pays most of the charges of private physicians. The government reimburses travel expenses for patients and for the parents of a hospitalized child. Only minimal fees are charged for prescriptions and hospitalization.

Medical treatment is just one component of Sweden's broad system of social welfare. For example, people who are sick or who must stay home with sick children receive 90 percent of their salaries. Swedes are given parental leave at the birth of a child and when a child is sick. They also are guaranteed a pension.

Sweden's socialized medicine is inefficient. Swedes have not solved the twin problems of getting rid of waiting lines and motivating physicians to work hard. Because medical personnel know exactly how much their pay will be, regardless how many patients they see, they are not productive. When reporters visited Sweden's largest hospital on a weekday morning, when 80 of 120 surgeons were on duty, they found 19 of 24 operating rooms idle. Their photos of empty operating rooms—at a time when there was a one- to two-year waiting period for hip replacements and cataract operations—provoked a public outcry (Bergström 1992). The waiting list for cataract surgery has grown to 30,000 Swedes—in a population of 9 million ("Swedish Health Care . . ." 2002). If the same rate of Americans were waiting for surgery, the U.S. line would be 600,000 people long.

Swedish lawmakers decided that to improve efficiency they need to abandon the socialized model, and they are gradually turning the health-care system over to the private sector. The government has already sold some hospitals to private companies ("Social Darwinism . . ." 2001).

We don't yet know what the Swedish medical system will look like by the time this transition is complete.

HEALTH CARE IN THE INDUSTRIALIZING NATIONS: RUSSIA

Russia's medical system is in tatters. Under the communists, Russia had established a system that made free health care available to most people. Doctors would even visit patients at their homes (Gaufberg 2004). Like the rest of the nation's production, the health-care system was centralized. The state owned the medical schools and determined how many doctors would be trained in what specialties. The state paid medical salaries, which it set, and determined where doctors would practice. Physicians were poorly trained, had low prestige, and earned less than bus drivers.

Under Russia's fitful transition to capitalism, its health-care system has deteriorated, and the health of the population has declined. An example is Moscow's ambulance system. It used to be efficient—dial 03, and an ambulance would arrive within minutes. When Russia turned to capitalism in 1991, ambulances sometimes took eight hours to arrive because the drivers were using the ambulances as freelance cabs, and they kept emergency cases waiting (Field 1998). Since then, ambulance service has improved, especially in Moscow (Gaufberg 2004).

The only hospitals comparable to those of the United States are reserved for the elite (Light 1992; Gaufberg 2004). In the rest, conditions are deplorable. To be assured of care, some patients bring their own linens, medicines, and syringes with them to the hospital. Doctors are paid about $35 a month and may go unpaid for six months at a time (Paddock 1999). In some hospitals, surgeons resharpen scalpels until they break. Some even use razor blades for surgery (Donelson 1992). Outdated and broken equipment is not replaced. Some doctors face the choice of operating without anesthetic or not operating at all (Paddock 1999). Physicians are paid so little that in order to have food, they grow potatoes. They walk to work because they cannot afford the equivalent of a dime to take a bus (Goldberg and Kishkovsky 2000).

The bright spot is that physicians continue to work despite their low status and miserable pay. Many are motivated by idealism and the desire to help, coupled with the hope that things will get better. A second bright spot is that some doctors are making the transition to private practice, which could be the beginning of a new medical system built on the rubble of the old (Goldberg and Kishkovsky 2000).

In the meantime, Russia's medical system remains broken. Perhaps no event more pinpoints the disarray than this:

Three patients lay unconscious in the intensive care unit, kept alive only by the Siberian hospital's life support system. Two were elderly; one was 39.

On Wednesday, the hospital received a telegram from the local power company: "You haven't paid your bill for five years. You owe us $94,931. Pay up, or we'll shut off your electricity." The next morning, at 6 A.M., the company shut off the power. Forty minutes later, all three patients were dead. (Paddock 1999)

The years of environmental degradation under the communists have also taken their toll. Serious birth defects have jumped to four times the U.S. rate. A likely culprit is radiation pollution from decades of nuclear irresponsibility (Spector 1995). Perhaps the single best indicator of the deterioration of health is the drop in life expectancy that began in the 1960s (Cockerham 1997). As shown in Table 10-3, the health of Russians is closer to that of China than to the Most Industrialized Nations. Life expectancy is not only a medical issue, but also a barometer of a society's health.

HEALTH CARE IN THE LEAST INDUSTRIALIZED NATIONS: CHINA

Because this nation of 1.2 billion people has a vast shortage of trained physicians, hospitals, and medicine, most Chinese see "barefoot doctors," people who have only a rudimentary knowledge of medicine, are paid low wages, and travel from village to village. Physicians are employees of the government, and the government owns all the country's medical facilities. With its emphases on medicinal herbs and acupuncture, Chinese medicine differs from that of the West. Although Westerners have scoffed at the Chinese approach, some have changed their minds, and on a limited basis, medicinal herbs and acupuncture are used in the United States.

Like Russia, China has begun the journey to capitalism. As part of this transition, Chinese authorities have decided that profits must be part of the medical system. The central government has withdrawn financing from its system of local health centers (Beech 2004). Patients are now expected to pay for their medical treatment; if they cannot pay, most go untreated. A hospital stay can now cost several hundred yuan, when the average monthly wage is 200 yuan. Some physicians take extra jobs because they cannot survive on their meager salaries. Some surgeons also demand payment before they will operate, as with the surgeons who, arms scrubbed and held high in the air, refused to enter the operating room until the patient's relatives had stuffed their pockets with cash (Sampson 1992).

At this point in its transition, China's medical system has deteriorated so greatly that the World Health Organization ranked it 144 of 191 nations. WHO ranked the medical care system of Bangladesh higher (Beech 2004).

FOR YOUR CONSIDERATION

No nation has discovered the perfect medical system, and every country faces a medical crisis of "too much demand at too great a cost" (Moore and Winslow 1993). In what ways would you say that the U.S. medical system is superior—and inferior—to each of these systems? Would you prefer to be treated within one of them rather than in the U.S. system? Why or why not? Short of socializing medicine, which goes against the values of Americans, how do you think the U.S. medical system can overcome the deficiencies reviewed in this chapter—and maintain its strengths?

TABLE 10-3 Indicators of Health

	SWEDEN	UNITED STATES	RUSSIA	CHINA
Life expectancy	79.2	77.3	67.3	71.6
Infant mortality[a]	3.9	6.8	20.1	28.1
Birthrate[b]	11.7	14.2	9.4	16.0
Death rate	10.8	8.7	13.9	6.7
Health costs as a percent of gross domestic product	8.6	12.9	2.3	NA

[a]Per 1,000 live births.
[b]Per 1,000 population.
NA = Not available.
Source: By the author, based on Field 1998; *Statistical Abstract of the United States* 1998:Tables 1345, 1348; 2002:Table 1312.

How to Repersonalize Medical Treatment

contact. Nurses address them by number and don't look in their direction when they respond. If they aren't able to see a doctor that day, it's just one of those things. After all, what do poor people have to do that's important, anyway?

Sociologist Jan Howard and her assistants (1975), who made such observations, also make policy recommendations for repersonalizing health care. This must begin in medical training, Howard stressed. Medical students need to be taught the *inherent worth* of patients—the view that each individual is valuable and deserves personal attention. Physicians and nurses also need to learn *holism*, the view that a person's body, feelings, attitudes, and actions are intertwined and should not be segregated into separate organ systems for the convenience of clinicians. Howard also notes how waiting rooms can be made more humane by having adequate lighting, comfortable seats, appropriate reading materials, warm decor, convenient bathrooms, and noninstitutional furniture arrangements.

Until physicians make more money by giving holistic treatment, this change is not going to come about. The present orientation of physicians would have to be challenged by patients going elsewhere for more personalized medical care. With the control of the medical establishment by the American Medical Association, patients simply have few options.

SELF-CARE GROUPS

The Goals, Their Potential and Resistance

One reaction to the high costs of health care and the depersonalization of patients is the emergence of self-care groups. Some of these groups stand in sharp conflict with the medical profession; others are begun, promoted, or even supervised by medical professionals. The goals of self-care groups are to maintain health, prevent disease, and do self-diagnosis, medication, and treatment. Diabetics, heart attack victims, cancer patients, people who have had breast surgery, smokers, alcoholics, and people who suffer from rheumatism, arthritis, AIDS, disabilities, mental illnesses, and genetic problems have formed groups to help each other. They discuss new developments in their diseases or problems, encourage one another to take preventive measures, and support one another emotionally. Few physicians encourage self-care groups. Almost all continue to focus on acute care. From a conflict perspective, one could say that self-care groups threaten medical profits and control, for many of their suggestions bypass physicians.

In Sum

The policy ideas discussed here focus on two major problems of health and medical care: high costs and the general lack of preventive medicine. The aim of these policies is to move health care away from the hospital and back to changes in lifestyle. These policies offer low technology and inexpensive alternatives to highly technological and costly medical care. For a comparative context to evaluate the U.S. medical system and the policies discussed here, see the Global Glimpse box on pages 344–345.

The Future of the Problem

TECHNOLOGY

"Pushes for Technology"

As we look to the future, the first significant trend is more technology. Medical technology will continue to develop, and patients will continue to demand cutting edge technology when their lives are threatened—regardless of the cost. Cost is a factor only when the emergency is over and the bills arrive.

Technology Has Led to Severe Ethical Dilemmas

Out of these technological advances have arisen ethical problems that plague medical professionals and laypeople alike. If people can be kept alive artificially, must doctors keep them alive? Does "brain dead" really mean "dead"? If so, should physicians

SPOTLIGHT ON RESEARCH

Solving a Health Mystery

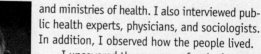

William Cockerham, Professor of Sociology at the University of Alabama at Birmingham, studies international aspects of health. He has done research on health and lifestyles in Russia and Eastern Europe, and he is doing similar research in Japan.

In the mid-1990s, I attended a medical sociology conference in Vienna. Sociologists from the former socialist countries in Eastern Europe reported that their countries were in the midst of a health crisis. They said that men were dying prematurely, and that the life expectancy for women had either declined or stagnated. What was striking about their presentations and in the discussions that followed was that no one could explain why this was occurring. That in peacetime an entire group of industrialized societies was experiencing a prolonged deterioration in the health of the population was unexpected.

The lack of an explanation for this crisis presented an intriguing research question. The killer turned out to be an increase in heart disease that had begun in the mid-1960s. A review of the evidence showed that infectious diseases, environmental pollution, and poor medical care were not enough to cause this surge in mortality. A clue that social factors were important was the fact that the rise in death rates was not universal. Heart disease differed by gender, age, urban-rural locale, education, and region. The group most affected was middle-aged, urban men who did manual work.

We now knew the "what" and the "who," but not the "why." To discover the "why," I traveled to Russia and Eastern Europe. There, I collected data from clinics, hospitals, and ministries of health. I also interviewed public health experts, physicians, and sociologists. In addition, I observed how the people lived.

I uncovered three reasons for the increase in premature deaths. The first was policy failures: the failure to address the increase in heart disease and to adopt measures to lower smoking and drinking. The second seemed to be stress, which had increased with the collapse of communism: Workers had lost jobs and state benefits, such as housing and food subsidies. In addition, inflation had made their money worth less, driving down the value of their pensions and salaries. The third—and the primary reason—turned out to be unhealthy lifestyles. Heavy drinking and smoking and lack of exercise characterized the people who died prematurely from heart disease. To say "heavy" drinking is an understatement: Russian adult males, who comprise 25% of the population, drink 90% of the alcohol consumed in a country that averages 14 gallons per person annually.

I did not have enough data, however, to determine conclusively that stress—which has a well-established connection to heart disease—was especially important. A grant from the European Union provided funds to survey 18,000 people in eight countries of the former Soviet Union. This survey showed that women actually are more stressed than men. While stress undoubtedly makes the women's lives less pleasant and has consequences for their health, it is not killing enough of them prematurely to come close to the mortality rates of the men. As bad as the situation may be for the women, the key to explaining the health crisis ultimately lies in the men's behavior.

be allowed to remove "body parts" from people who (only because of machines) are still breathing? In some hospitals, they already do so. Should medical researchers be allowed to test dangerous drugs on these people, because, after all, they are "really" dead? They already do this in some hospitals. Another controversy, **euthanasia,** is discussed in the Thinking Critically box on the next page.

How the Internet Is Affecting Medicine

The Internet is helping to give some control back to patients. People who have rare diseases, for example, can participate in discussion groups on the Net. Although people don't meet personally in this new type of self-care group, they share their experiences and knowledge with one another. Physicians are concerned. Not only do they feel threatened because they are no longer the sole possessors of esoteric knowledge

Thinking Critically about Social Problems
SHOULD DOCTORS BE ALLOWED TO KILL PATIENTS?

Euthanasia is a hot topic among both medical professionals and the lay public. Articles on euthanasia appear regularly in the print media and on television, designed, some say, to provide information or, as others claim, to subtly condition the U.S. public to accept it.

Except for the name, this is a true story:

> Bill Simpson, in his seventies, had battled leukemia for years. After his spleen was removed, he developed an abdominal abscess. It took another operation to drain it. A week later, the abscess filled, and required more surgery. Again the abscess returned. Simpson began to go in and out of consciousness. His brother-in-law suggested euthanasia. The surgeon injected a lethal dose of morphine into Simpson's intravenous feeding tubes.

At a medical conference in which euthanasia was discussed, a cancer specialist who had treated thousands of patients, announced that he had kept count of the patients who had asked him to help them die. "There were 127 men and women," he said. Then he added, "And I saw to it that 25 of them got their wish." Thousands of other physicians have done the same (Nuland 1995).

When a doctor ends a patient's life, such as by injecting a lethal drug, it is called *active euthanasia*. To withhold life support (nutrients or liquids) is called *passive euthanasia*. To remove life support, such as disconnecting a patient from oxygen falls somewhere in between. The result, of course, is the same.

Two images seem to dominate the public's ideas of euthanasia: One is of an individual devastated by chronic pain. The doctor mercifully helps to end that pain by performing euthanasia. The second is of a brain-dead individual—a human vegetable—who lies in a hospital bed, kept alive only by machines. How accurate are these images?

We have the example of Holland. There, euthanasia is legal. Incredibly, in about 1,000 cases a year, physicians kill their patients without the patients' express consent. In one instance, a doctor ended the life of a nun because he thought she would have wanted him to but was afraid to ask because it was against her religion. In another case, a physician ended the life of a patient with breast cancer who said that she did *not* want euthanasia. In the doctor's words, "It could have taken another week before she died. I needed this bed" (Hendin 1997, 2000).

Some Dutch are concerned that they could be euthanized if they have a medical emergency. They carry "passports" that instruct medical personnel that they wish to live. Most Dutch, however, support euthanasia. Many carry another "passport," one that instructs medical personnel to carry out euthanasia (Shapiro 1997).

In 1997, Oregon became the only U.S. state where medically assisted suicide is legal. During the next six years, doctors reported that they helped 171 people kill themselves. Little is known about the background of those who were assisted in their deaths. In Michigan, Dr. Jack Kevorkian, a pathologist (he didn't treat patients—he studied diseased tissues) decided that regardless of laws, he had the right to help people commit suicide. He did, 120 times. And he taunted authorities. He sometimes left bodies in vans and dropped them off at hospitals. Kevorkian provided the poison, as well as a "death machine" that he developed to administer the poison. He watched while patients pulled the lever that released the drugs, but he never touched that lever.

Michigan prosecutors tried Kevorkian for murder four times, but juries refused to convict him. Then Kevorkian went too far. He played a videotape on national television, showing him giving a lethal injection to a man who was dying from Lou Gehrig's disease. Prosecutors put Kevorkian on trial again. He was convicted of second-degree murder and was sentenced to 10 to 25 years in prison.

FOR YOUR CONSIDERATION

If Kevorkian had lived in Oregon, he could have killed people any time they asked him to do so. But not in Michigan—or in any of the other states. Do you think Michigan or Oregon is right? Why? What do you think the future will hold? Will we go the way of Oregon or Michigan?

Finally, as is evident in Holland, physician-assisted deaths have a way of expanding. In addition to what is reported here, Dutch doctors also kill newborn babies who have serious birth defects (Smith 1999). Their justification is that these children would not have "quality of life." Would you support this?

on rare disease and treatment of common disorders, but also they fear that misinformation may be circulated. Medical experiments may also be contaminated: By sharing information on the Internet, some patients are able to determine whether they are receiving an experimental drug or a *placebo*, a substance that is designed to look like a medicine but that has no medical value (Bulkeley 1995).

REDIRECTING MEDICINE

The Carlson Predictions

In the 1970s, Rick Carlson (1975) drew a bleak picture of the future. In the year 2000, he foresaw a more complex and stressful society, a larger aging population with incurable degenerative diseases, and more illnesses resulting from lifestyle and environmental deterioration. Carlson held out little hope that our medical system would turn to preventive medicine and work on overcoming the environmental and lifestyle causes of illness. He concluded that poverty would not be cured and that the poor would continue to have more illnesses than the affluent. He was right on all counts.

The Potential

Carlson argued, however, that we can change our health-care system, transforming it into a much better system for meeting our medical problems. His ideas are worth repeating. An effective system would include these elements:

First, it would teach people *to demand better health rather than more medicine*. To do this, people must be aware that their health is largely their own responsibility. Such a program would require more research on self-health care and disease prevention. Some physicians would continue to provide acute and emergency care, but others would be retrained in preventive and environmental medicine. The infirm aged would be cared for in residential complexes that are humane and pleasant, such as those in Denmark and Sweden. Funds saved from spending less on acute and emergency medical care should go to programs that feature accident prevention, food safety, occupational safety, nutrition, and exercise. Efforts would be made to reduce the stresses of modern life by designing more relaxing work environments in offices and schools; building hiking and bike paths, tennis courts, and parks in our communities; and reducing noise pollution.

Why the Potential Is Unlikely to Be Realized

The potential for improving the general health of our people is immense. A focus on preventive medicine, however, runs counter to what both the public and the medical profession expect—heroic intervention in acute cases. This cultural orientation makes it unlikely that we will redirect our focus to improving general health through prevention.

SUMMARY

1. What people consider to be health and illness varies with culture and social class. Far from being based solely on biological factors, what people consider a health problem is also based on *social* factors.

2. Industrialization brought better health, but with it also came an increase in some health problems—cancer, heart disease, drug addiction, and other chronic illnesses caused by lifestyle, general aging, and environmental pollution. AIDS illustrates the relationship among behavior, environment, and disease. Physical and emotional problems are more common among the poor. To explain the relationship between social class and mental illness, sociolo-

gists prefer environmental explanations rather than genetic ones.

3. The U.S. medical system is centered on specialized, hospital-based, and heroic intervention. A fee-for-service system increases cost. In preventive medicine, the emphasis would be on changing people's lifestyles and environment.

4. Social inequalities in medical and mental health services stem largely from the way we pay medical bills. In our fee-for-service system, health care is not a right but a commodity sold to the highest bidder. The United States has a *two-class system of medical care*—public clinics and poorer

treatment for the poor and private clinics and better treatment for the more affluent.

5. Two policies designed to control medical costs are to pay patients to stay healthy and to pay doctors not to treat patients unnecessarily. HMOs are a form of prepaid health practices that give successful bidders a fixed amount of money to attend to the health needs of a group of people. Medical services and tests come directly off the corporate bottom line, leading to a conflict of interest in treating patients. On the other hand, if HMOs let their patients become too sick, it costs more than if they catch problems early.

6. The medical profession may respond to changing patterns of illness by adapting its approach so that the focus changes from acute problems to chronic problems and to problems caused by lifestyle and environmental pollution. If so, the emphasis will be on preventive medicine—better health habits, a healthier environment, and education designed to teach people how to take care of themselves and to manage their illnesses.

Key Terms

Defensive medicine   Medical practices performed by physicians to protect themselves in the event of a malpractice lawsuit.

Deinstitutionalization   A policy developed in the 1960s of discharging patients from state and county mental hospitals into the community, where they were supposed to receive community-based services.

Depersonalization   Treating patients as things, rather than as individuals.

Drug therapy   The use of drugs such as tranquilizers and antidepressants to treat emotional problems.

Electroconvulsive therapy (ECT)   A treatment for emotional problems in which a low-voltage electric current is passed through the brain. Also known as electroshock therapy.

Euthanasia   Mercy killing.

Group therapy   A treatment for emotional problems in which members of the group talk about how they interact with others and help each other to cope with their problems.

Health maintenance organization (HMO)   A comprehensive prepaid health-care organization designed to reduce costs by minimizing unnecessary medical services.

Home health care   Organized health services for people who are living at home with chronic or disabling diseases.

Iatrogenesis   Illnesses or other health problems caused by medical care.

Individual psychotherapy   Treatment for emotional problems. A therapist listens and tries to guide the client toward a resolution of those problems.

Lay referral network   Friends and relatives from whom sick people get suggestions about what to do about their illnesses. See also *Professional referral network*.

Primary prevention   Measures that keep a disease from occurring, such as vaccinations. See also *Secondary prevention, Tertiary prevention*.

Professional referral network   The health-care professionals that physicians use to evaluate their work. See also *Lay referral network*.

Psychoanalysis   A treatment for emotional problems created by Sigmund Freud; the goal is to uncover subconscious motives, fantasies, and fears by having patients speak about whatever comes to mind.

Secondary prevention   Early detection and precautions that keep a disease from getting worse.

Short-term directive therapy   A treatment for emotional problems in which a therapist actively tries to solve the client's problems.

Talk therapy   Treatments of emotional problems that are based on "talking" (psychotherapy, group therapy, etc.).

Tertiary prevention   Medical care of an existing disease aimed at preventing further damage.

Two-class (or two-tier) system of medical care   A medical delivery system in which the poor receive one type of medical care and the affluent another.

THINKING CRITICALLY ABOUT CHAPTER 10

1. If you were asked, "What do you think are the two most important issues in health care for the government to address?" what would your answer be?

2. What do you think the government's role should be in medical care? Why?

3. What political, economic, or other social factors do you think contribute to the United States being the only industrialized country that doesn't have a national health-care system?

4. Why do you think women live longer than men?

5. Which of the perspectives (symbolic interactionism, functionalism, or conflict theory) do you think best explains health-care problems in the United States? Explain.

The Changing Family

NANCY AND ANTOINE WERE PLEASED. Their four-year-old daughter, Janelle, had been accepted at Rainbow Gardens Preschool in Manhattan Beach, California, a prosperous suburb of Los Angeles. The preschool came highly recommended by their close friends, whose son was attending the school. With Nancy's promotion and Antoine's new job, schedules had become more difficult, and Rainbow Gardens was able to handle their need for more flexible hours.

At first Janelle loved preschool. She would happily leave Nancy or Antoine, whoever drove her, for the pleasures of her little friends and the gentle care of loving teachers. Then, gradually, almost imperceptibly, a change came over her. At first, Janelle became reluctant to leave her parents. Then she began to whimper in the mornings when they were getting her ready. And lately she had begun to have nightmares, waking up crying and screaming several times a week, something she had never done. The counselor they took Janelle to said it was nothing to worry about; all kids go through things like this from time to time. Janelle was just going through a "developmental adjustment," and she would be just fine in a little while.

When allegations of sexual abuse of three-, four-, and five-year-olds at Rainbow Gardens made headlines, it was devastating to parents around the nation. The unthinkable had become real. Had it happened at their preschool, too—with their child? But for Nancy and Antoine, it was more than a nagging question. Overnight, Janelle's nightmares, her crying, and her bed-wetting took on new meaning. The gentle teachers, so affectionate with the children, child molesters? Janelle undressed, photographed, forced to commit sexual acts with adults, and threatened with the death of her puppy if she told?

Nancy and Antoine don't know. It is either this or simply a "developmental adjustment." Now it is Nancy's and Antoine's turn for nightmares.

The Problem in Sociological Perspective

"Nightmare at Rainbow Gardens" could be the title of a horror movie, a real-life one for some parents. Each year, some unknown number of children is abused sexually at day-care centers. Back in the 1980s, a kind of hysteria swept the country. Rumors spread that day-care centers were packed with child molesters. Some teachers were tried and convicted, sometimes on flimsy evidence (Rabinowitz 2004). A Massachusetts man served 18 years in prison before his pleas of innocence were finally acknowledged. Despite the hysteria, some children are abused at day school, a frightening prospect for parents. Why aren't the children home safe with their families? Why are 5 million U.S. children entrusted to the care of strangers in a new social institution called day care (*Statistical Abstract* 2003:Table 577)?

The Family Is Engulfed in Change

Day care—and its risks—is part of a sea of change that has swept our society, engulfing families and forcing them to adjust. For the family, change is nothing new. As the basic social institution (also called the basic building block of society), the family always feels changes that occur in other parts of society.

Effects of Industrialization on the Family:

The most significant event to affect the family was the industrial revolution. Because its consequences were so severe and because they continue to affect family life today, let's explore its significance. Before industrialization, economic survival was perilous. Almost everyone worked at home. The entire family was involved, both the parents and their children. When industrialization moved production to factories, it vitally affected family life:

1. Removing the Father from the Home

1. Men left home to work in factories. This opened a major gap between the husband–father and other family members. For most of the day they now lived different lives, one at work and the others at home. Husband and wife no longer shared activities during their working hours. Separated from the household, the husband–father's orientation to life changed.

2. Children: From Economic Assets to Economic Liabilities

2. Industrialization turned children from an economic asset into an economic liability. When production was farm based, children contributed to their family's survival—from milking the cows to working in the fields. In some of the first factories, children still worked alongside adults. As we saw in Chapter 6, however, the movement to "save" children ended their employment. Although children could no longer bring home a paycheck, they still consumed much of the family's limited resources. Children became nonproductive and expensive.

3. Increased Education

3. Industrialization brought a demand for more education. As children spent more years in school, they became dependent on their parents longer. Their prolonged education and longer dependency made children even more expensive.

4. A Lower Birthrate

4. The discovery of vulcanized rubber during the 1840s made large-scale production of the condom possible. With further refinements in design and manufacture in the 1920s, the condom allowed couples to limit the number of their children (Douvan 1980; Laslett 1980). Because children had become nonproductive and expensive, the birthrate plunged. Today, our birthrate is the lowest in our history, and it is expected to fall still further. (See Figure 11-1.)

FIGURE 11-1 *U.S. Birthrate, 1890–2050*

Source: By the author, based on *Statistical Abstract of the United States,* various editions and 2001:Table 4.

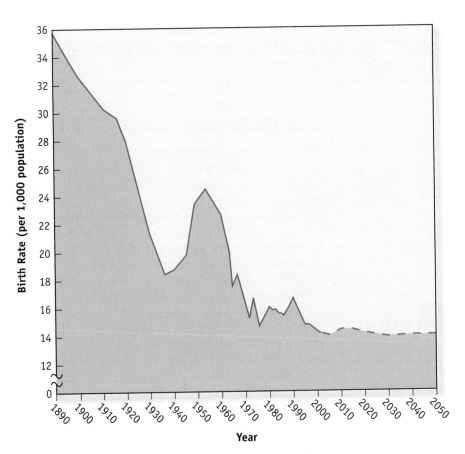

Year

Note: Broken line indicates U.S. government projections.

5. From Rural to Urban

5. Industrialization changed people's settlement patterns. Until about 100 years ago, almost everyone in the world lived in the country. As production moved to factories, workers moved where the work was. Housing in the city was expensive, and people reduced the size of their families even more.

6. Loss of Functions

6. As industrialization continued, other institutions grew stronger and stripped the family of many of its traditional functions, such as producing food, educating the young, providing recreation, and nursing the old and sick.

7. Change in Women's Roles

7. Industrialization changed women's roles. The wife–mother had been responsible for basic food production (milk, butter, eggs, vegetables), preparation (baking and cooking), and storage (canning, salting). She also made, washed, ironed, and mended the family's clothing, cleaned the house, and took care of the children, the sick, and the elderly. As her functions were reduced, she increasingly became an "emotional provider"; that is, the wife–mother was expected to be the stable counterpoint to the husband's pressures at work and to lavish attention on a diminishing number of children.

8. Greater Equality

8. Industrialization brought greater equality to the family. As traditional roles changed, so did feelings about how things "ought to be" between husband and wife and between parents and children. This gradual change did not happen without struggle, for men were reluctant to give up their more privileged positions. Indeed, the struggle over equality (or authority) is still a primary source of marital tension.

9. More Divorce

9. Industrialization increased divorce. Before industrialization, divorce was rare. But with the changes just outlined, especially the reduced functions of the family and the lower birthrate, marriages became fragile.

10. Longer Lives and More Intergenerational Ties

10. Industrialization improved health and brought longer lives. One consequence is that today's grandparents are more likely to be alive and to participate in the lives of their grandchildren than at any time in history (Bengtson et al. 1990). It is even becoming more common for grandparents to rear their grandchildren.

11. The "Quiet Revolution"

The family is always adjusting to changes that are taking place in society. As ideas of masculinity change, for example, behaviors that once were not acceptable for men come to be thought of as normal. After those changes become standard, a current generation may have difficulty understanding why such behaviors ever threatened men's sense of "masculinity."

11. The changes continue. One of the most fundamental changes ever to affect the family—women leaving home to take paid employment—is having a major impact on this generation. This trend began with the industrial revolution. With but a single interruption—at the end of World War II, when millions of women left the jobs they had taken in the war industries—it has continued without letup.

What is new is the extent of the change: In the 1980s, for the first time in history, more than half of married women worked for wages at least part-time outside the home. Today about 61 percent do (*Statistical Abstract* 2003:Table 595).

That so many married women work for wages reinforces most of the trends we have discussed, especially changes in husband–wife roles, divorce, and the birthrate. It also complicates rearing children, which some consider *the* social problem of today's family. Because the movement of wives and mothers from the home is part of a gradual historical trend, and yet is so fundamental—forcing change in all family relationships—it sometimes is called the *quiet revolution.*

In Sum

The family is always in transition. Just as the family adapted to large-scale social events that began centuries ago, so it adapts to today's current events. The family is not an independent unit, and to survive it must adapt to what is happening in society. Because the family provides for the economic well-being of its members, as with industrialization of years past, the family is especially sensitive to economic changes.

The Scope of the Problem

Personal Troubles, or Social Problems?

Because the family is always adapting to changes in society, what makes those adaptations a social problem? Sociologist C. Wright Mills (1959b) phrased it well. He said that when an individual here and there gets divorced, we have a **personal trouble.** If divorce is widespread, however, it is a sign that there is a problem with the *structure* of marriage. In other words, individual divorce is a *personal* trouble, but widespread personal troubles indicate a *social* problem. As we have seen throughout this text, however, objective conditions are only part of the picture. By themselves, objective conditions are not adequate to make a social problem: We also need subjective concerns—and we certainly have them when it comes to the contemporary family.

Indicators That the American Family Is in Trouble

Let's consider indicators that the family is in trouble. If you mention this to someone, usually the first thing to pop into their minds is divorce. As Figure 11-2 shows, perceptions that divorce has become more common are true. In 2000, there were 4.6 times more divorced Americans than in 1970. (Because of rounding, on the figure this looks like there are 5 times as many.) During this time, the population increased only 38 percent. Another way to look at the trend in divorce is to compare the number of Americans who are getting married with the number who are getting divorced. As Figure 11-3 shows, for every two couples getting married, another couple is having their marriage declared null and void.

Is Divorce a Sign of Weakness or Strength?

We can interpret divorce statistics in different ways. Some see our increase in divorce in a positive light: More divorce means that families are becoming *stronger.* How could

Figure 11-2 *How Many Millions of Americans Are Divorced?*

Source: By the author, based on *Statistical Abstract of the United States* 1989:Table 50; 2003:Table 61.

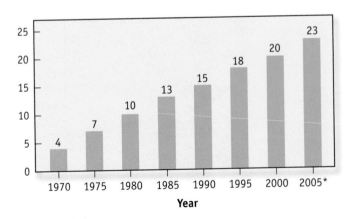

Note: Asterisk indicates the author's estimate.

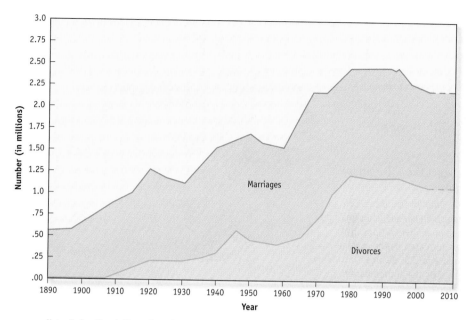

FIGURE 11-3 *American Marriage, American Divorce*

Source: By the author, based on *Statistical Abstract of the United States,* various years, and 1998:Table 92; "Births, Marriages . . ." 2004.

Note: Broken lines indicate the author's estimates.

anyone interpret divorce this way? Here's the thinking: No longer willing to put up with miserable marriages, men and women terminate them. They then look for new partners, and most end up with more satisfying marriages. Even if this interpretation is not correct, Figure 11-3 does show something positive about divorce. After rising for about 80 years, U.S. divorces peaked in 1980, held steady for about 15 years, made a slight decline, and have been holding at this slightly lower level since then. The ratio of one divorce for every two marriages has held steady. Individual states, however, differ considerably from these national statistics. As the Social Map on page 358 shows, divorce is considerably less—or greater—in some states than in others.

Divorce involves things that we can't put numbers on—the hopes and dreams of millions of adults crushed, shattered, and transformed into bitterness and rancor. Although people are concerned about the couples involved, they see them as adults who make their choices—and their mistakes. What really concerns people are the *children* of divorcing parents. Each year, the lives of about 1 million children are disrupted by divorce (Cherlin 2002). These children are filled with unsettling fears of the future as their parents break up. Divorce is so extensive that, as Figure 11-5A on page 358 shows, only about 3 of 4 U.S. children live with both parents.

Few adults enter into divorce lightly. The decision to divorce is usually painful, preceded by years of dissatisfaction and unhappiness. Couples who divorce find themselves on an emotional roller-coaster, filled with fears and anxiety about an uncertain future (Weissbourd 1996). They can feel as though they are being torn apart, that their identities are being shredded. No longer can they depend on many of the identity markers that had become part of their stability in life.

The Children of Divorce

During this process, the children find themselves in a no-win situation. If their quarreling parents remain together, the children are vulnerable to anxiety and depression (Jekielek 1998). If their parents divorce, the children are also subject to anxiety and depression. For most children, divorce also means a reduced standard of living (Grella 1990). For some, it means poverty.

The Slowing Rate of Remarriage

The pattern of remarriage has changed rapidly. In the 1960s, a third of divorced women remarried during the *first* year after their divorce. Within two years, half had

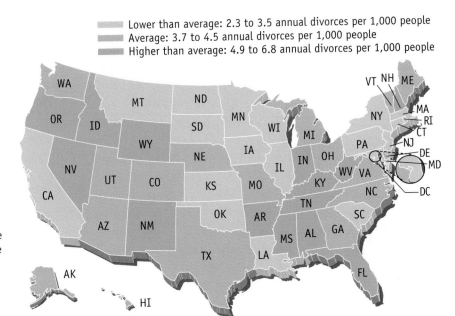

Lower than average: 2.3 to 3.5 annual divorces per 1,000 people
Average: 3.7 to 4.5 annual divorces per 1,000 people
Higher than average: 4.9 to 6.8 annual divorces per 1,000 people

FIGURE 11-4 *Variations in Divorce*

Note: Data for California, Colorado, Indiana, and Louisiana, based on earlier editions, have been decreased by the average decrease in U.S. divorce.

Source: By the author, based on *Statistical Abstract of the United States* earlier editions and 2002:Table 111.

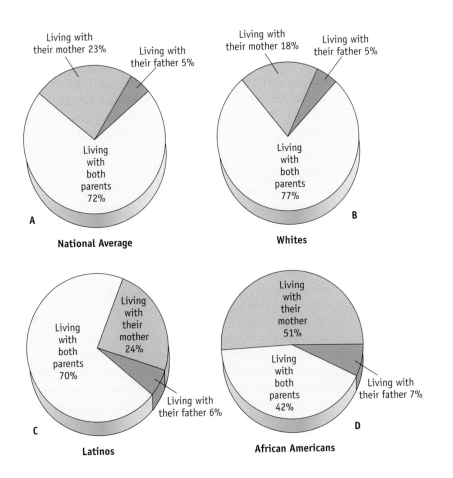

FIGURE 11-5 *Where Do U.S. Children Live?*

Source: By the author, based on *Statistical Abstract of the United States* 2001:Table 70.

Living with their mother 23%
Living with their father 5%
Living with both parents 72%
A **National Average**

Living with their mother 18%
Living with their father 5%
Living with both parents 77%
B **Whites**

Living with their mother 24%
Living with both parents 70%
Living with their father 6%
C **Latinos**

Living with their mother 51%
Living with both parents 42%
Living with their father 7%
D **African Americans**

Note: Only these groups are listed in the source.

Despite the best efforts of single parents, their children are more likely to drop out of school, to get in trouble with the police, and to end up in poverty. A special problem is the relationship of children to absent fathers. In the typical case, the father maintains contact with his children for a short period after the divorce and then reduces his contact as his interests become focused on a new woman. Often, her children replace his own. Sociologists call this pattern serial fatherhood.

remarried (*Statistical Abstract* 1998:Table 161). Today, women take a longer time to remarry, and half of women who divorce never do marry again (Bramlett and Mosher 2002). Figure 11-6 illustrates how significant race-ethnicity is in determining whether women remarry. (Comparable data are not available for men.) Some take this change as a negative sign, an indication that people distrust marriage more than they used to and are, therefore, more hesitant to marry. This could be, but it also could mean that people are more selective than they used to be. Perhaps they are even making wiser choices. No one knows for sure.

Figure 11-7 on page 360 summarizes a statistic about U.S. families that has greatly upset people. Each year, more than 1 million babies are born to unmarried mothers. This is one-third (34 percent) of all U.S. babies (*Statistical Abstract* 2003:Table 92). This rate is sharply higher from our past: It is *six* times higher than it was in 1940, *three* times higher than it was in 1970 and about *double* what it was in 1980.

As we have seen throughout this text, social problems often follow lines of race and ethnicity. You can see this in matters of the family also. As Figure 11-7 shows, the proportion of births to single women differs markedly among racial-ethnic groups. To look at the extremes, the proportion of births to unmarried Asian American women is less than one-fourth what it is among African American women. From Figure 11-5, you can see that when children live with just one parent it is likely to be the mother.

FIGURE 11-6 *The Probability That Divorced Women Will Remarry in Five Years*
Source: By the author, based on Bramlett and Mosher 2002.

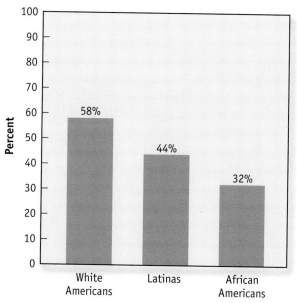

Note: The source excludes other groups and men.

Births to Single Women

This is true regardless of the child's race-ethnicity. From this figure, you can also see that an African American child is the least likely to be living with both parents.

Births to single women, and divorce, can be looked at as individual matters, of course, and they are. When multiplied by millions, though, their consequences reverberate throughout society. The primary problem is that the children of single and divorced parents are denied benefits that children in two-parent families take for granted, especially having their father as a male role model. Millions of boys and girls have to learn the male role from mothers, boyfriends, television, and the streets. This is especially hard on boys, who often end up with grossly inadequate substitutes. With high rates of divorce and births to single women, *15 million* children live without fathers at home. Another *3 million* live without their mothers (*Statistical Abstract* 2003:Table 71). As always, overall statistics conceal significant variations. The Social Map shows how the states compare in the percentage of families that are headed by single parents.

One-Parent Families

Being reared by only one parent has a significant impact on children. Sociologists may argue (as they do) about cause and effect, that this or that is not proven and could be due to something else, but every year of every decade children who come from mother-headed families are more likely to drop out of school and get in trouble with the law. This statistic applies to every region of the country and to every racial-ethnic group. There just are no exceptions. I know of no other group in which children reared by both parents are more likely to drop out of school or to get into trouble with the law.

The absence of the father is proposed by some as the major explanation for some of the problems we analyzed in other chapters. The higher a group's rate of mother-headed families, for example, the higher is that group's rate of violent crimes. Such a statistic says nothing about the individual child, of course. Although children from mother-headed homes are more likely to drop out of school and get in trouble with the law, any particular child may grow up to become an artist, an astronaut, or (and what can you expect of this author!) a sociologist. But, *on average*, which is what sociologists deal with, the absence of a father is more likely to lead to such problems.

FIGURE 11-7 *Of All Births, What Percentage Are to Single Women?*

Source: By the author, based on *Statistical Abstract of the United States* 1992:Table 87; 1998:Table 100; 2003:Table 84.

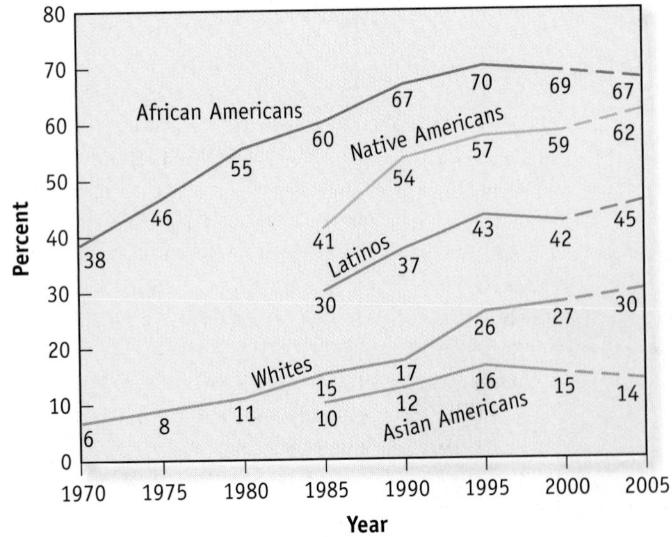

We don't understand the mechanisms by which this occurs, and as much as we would like it to be otherwise, on average, a mother by herself does not do the same job of rearing children that a mother and father do together. On a personal note, let me add that it was difficult for my wife and myself to guide a son through the turbulence of adolescence. To counteract the effects of peer groups required countless discussions, and even our combined efforts were at times barely sufficient for this shared task. But for so many, the burden falls on just one parent, who finds it too much to cope with.

Sociologist Travis Hirschi (Pope 1988:117–118) says that, all else being equal, one parent is probably sufficient. The problem, he says, is that rarely is all else equal:

The single parent (usually a woman) must devote a good deal to support and maintenance activities that are at least to some extent shared in the two parent family. Further, she must do so in the absence of psychological or social support. As a result, she is less able to devote time to

Note: Broken lines indicate the author's estimates. The source does not provide data for other groups.

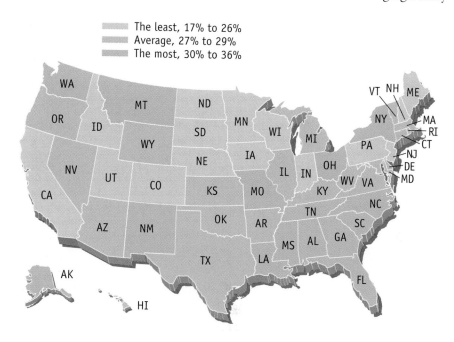

The least, 17% to 26%
Average, 27% to 29%
The most, 30% to 36%

FIGURE 11-8 *Families Headed by Single Parents*
Source: By the author, based on "Kids Count Data Sheet" 2004.

monitoring and punishment, and is more likely to be involved in negative, abusive contacts with her children.

One-parent families are not limited to fatherless families, of course. Our three million motherless households also present tremendous obstacles to fathers who rear children alone. How should a single father teach female roles to his daughter? Whether man or woman, the single parent must try to be both mother and father, which, if not impossible, is certainly a formidable task. (We don't have enough studies on the consequences of father-headed families.)

Life for single mothers is usually filled with difficulties. In the typical case, these mothers are younger, have little education, and have an inadequate income. Although their resources are highly limited, their responsibilities are great.

The essential problem appears to be defective discipline—in either direction, excessive leniency or excessive control (Pope 1988). To find the proper balance is difficult for any family, but more difficult for one parent to achieve than for two.

As always, it is difficult to determine cause and effect, and sociologists are especially good at complicating explanations by adding more data. In this case, when we add cross-cultural data, we see that explanations based around father absence are not adequate. Look at Figure 11-9, which compares births to single women in ten Most Industrialized Nations. Four of these nations have a rate higher than ours.

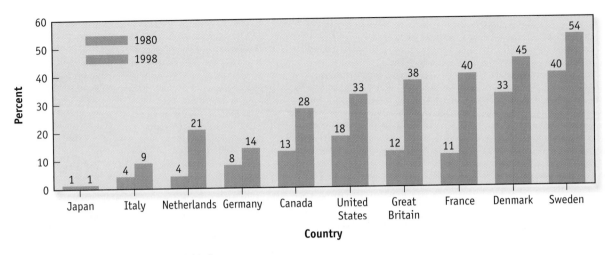

*Note: As a percentage of all births.

FIGURE 11-9 *The Increase in Births to Single Women in the Most Industrialized Nations**
Source: By the author, based on *Statistical Abstract* 2001:Table 1331.

Yet in none of them is the rate of juvenile delinquency or violent crimes as high as ours. Therefore, something else also has to be at work. That "something else" is the culture within which one-parent families live—family support systems, subcultures of violence, access to guns, and views of life. Sociologists have *not* unraveled this thorny problem.

Although some might disagree that divorce, a slowing rate of remarriage, births to single women, and families headed by one parent indicate a social problem, no one disputes that runaway children offer dramatic evidence that something is drastically wrong with many U.S. families. No central agency keeps track of runaways, so we lack firm figures. The media often say that one million children run away from home each year, but that is simply a round number used to gain the public's attention. Whatever the total, each year about 100,000 children are arrested on charges of running away from home (*Sourcebook of Criminal Justice Statistics*, 2003:Table 4.6). Runaways certainly are not fleeing happy homes. They are trying to escape from intolerable situations—incest, beatings, and other debilitating family conditions.

Runaways and "Pushouts"

The streets are tough, and survival is precarious. Runaways (and "pushouts," children who have been shoved out by parents who no longer want them) often fall into the hands of predators, making their already bruised lives even more desperate. As adults who work with runaway children observe: "Their alternative to starvation is to steal or to turn to the only thing they have—their bodies. Most get involved in prostitution and pornography when they tire of sleeping in doorways, have no money and no place to go."

Family Violence

Violence is another indication of family problems. Police and welfare workers know the scene all too well: the battered child, wife, husband, parent, or even grandparent. Sixty thousand people are arrested each year for family violence (*Sourcebook of Criminal Justice Statistics*, 2003:Table 4.6). Sociologists Suzanne Steinmetz and Murray Straus (1974; Straus 1992) stress that it would be hard to find a group or institution in the United States in which violence is more of an everyday occurrence than the family. They add that we have seen only the tip of the iceberg.

The Family Is Not Disintegrating

Problems of violence, divorce, runaways, and so on indicate severe problems in the U.S. family. They do *not* indicate, however, that the family is disintegrating. Although the contemporary family is in trouble, as a social institution it will endure its present crisis. Despite family problems, humans have found no satisfactory substitute for the family, and millions of people report that their needs for intimacy and sense of identity and belonging are met within marriage and family. In this text, however, we examine *problems,* not the joys of marriage and family. At this point, we will turn our theoretical lenses on these problems.

Looking at the Problem Theoretically

Basic Concepts

For most of us, the family is our major support system. Our family nourishes and protects us when we are young. It gives us security and love and shapes our personality. Sociologists call the family that rears us our **family of orientation** because it introduces us to the world and teaches us ways to cope with life. As a result, most of us try to establish stability, identity, and intimacy through marriage. When we marry, we form what is called a **family of procreation.**

Despite the high value we place on marriage and family and the many benefits they give us, divorce has become common. Why? Sociologists have used their three theoretical lenses to examine how divorce is related to changes in society. As always, each lens yields a unique interpretation, but, as you will see, in this case the theoretical contribution of each dovetails neatly with the others.

SYMBOLIC INTERACTIONISM

Why Has Divorce Increased?

To explain why our divorce rate is so high, symbolic interactionists examine what people expect out of marriage. In 1933, sociologist William Ogburn noted that personality was becoming more important as people chose a husband or wife. A few years later, in 1945, sociologists Ernest Burgess and Harvey Locke observed that affection,

Equality is a goal with which most of us agree in principle. Because we all perceive reality from particular corners in life, however, putting "equality" into practice is problematic: What some see as gaining equality, others view as a demand for privileges. For one group to gain equality, then, some other group might undergo a reduction in privileges. Shown here is one example of this problem.

**Changing Ideas
of Marital Satisfaction**

understanding, and compatibility were becoming more central to marriage. These sociologists had documented a major change: Society had become more complex and impersonal, and increasingly people were looking for marriage to satisfy their needs for intimacy.

**An Overloaded
Institution**

These trends have escalated. Society has grown more impersonal, and today husbands and wives expect even greater emotional satisfaction from one another. We have come to see marriage as a solution to the tensions produced by our problem-ridden society (Lasch 1977), and we are likely to expect our spouse to meet most of our personality and emotional needs. Because these expectations place a heavy burden on marriage, often more than it can carry, sociologists say that marriage and family have become an *overloaded institution*.

Ideas of Love

Our idea of love encourages us to expect marriage to deliver too much. To Americans, love carries ideas of total happiness. If we are "truly in love," we will be satisfied emotionally and, somehow, enjoy a continuous emotional high. For Americans, love has become *the* reason for marriage. The idea of love motivates people to marry, but the unrealistic expectations associated with our idea of love set people up for disappointment. When dissatisfactions arise in marriage, as they inevitably do, spouses tend to blame one another, believing the other to have somehow failed them. Their engulfment in the symbol of love blinds them to the unreality of their expectations. In effect, our culture's lesson is that we should base a lifelong relationship on a temporary emotional state.

Ideas about Children

Ideas about children have undergone an historical shift so profound that the customs of earlier generations seem strange to us. This change, too, has deeply affected the family. In medieval society, children were seen as miniature adults (Aries 1962). With no sharp separation between their worlds, adults and children mixed freely with one another. At about age 7, boys became apprentices in some occupation, whereas girls of this age learned the homemaking duties that were associated with their cultural role. These practices don't make sense to us. We consider age 7 to be a tender phase of early childhood. In short, from being viewed as miniature adults, children have been culturally transformed into impressionable, vulnerable, and innocent beings.

One of the traditional functions of marriage, although not mentioned in the text, was to maintain racial-ethnic and even religious lines. In Minnesota, for example, even though both were white, a marriage between a Swedish Lutheran and a German Lutheran upset the respective families. Marriage between a Lutheran and a Roman Catholic horrified them. To cross what was called the "color line" was unthinkable, a violation of a more. Today's situation is vastly different, as illustrated in this photo.

Ideas about Parenting

Ideas about children—what they are like and what we can expect of them—lie at the root of what we expect of parents. Three generations ago, until about 1940, U.S. children "became adults" when they graduated from eighth grade and took a job. Because we now view children as more vulnerable and we expect them to be dependent much longer, we expect parents to give their children greater protection and to nurture them for many more years. We even expect parents to help their children achieve "self-development" so they can "reach their potential." As the tasks associated with child rearing have expanded, and as the expected emotional ties between parents and children have become more intense, the family has been thrust into even greater "emotional overload."

Changing Marital Roles

The past is being wiped away as change also sweeps over traditional ideas of the "right" way to be a wife or a husband. It used to be that everyone (including the neighbors and in-laws) expected husbands to assume the role of breadwinner. It was his responsibility to provide for the family. If he did that well, he was considered a good father. Those same neighbors and in-laws expected the wife to stay home, to take care of the house and children, and to attend to the personal needs of her husband. If she did those things well, she was considered a good wife. Traditional roles—whatever their faults, and there were many—provided clear-cut guidelines for behavior. Newlyweds knew what to expect of one another—because they, too, held these same ideas—and neither they nor their friends and relatives questioned those basic expectations. No longer.

Today's newlyweds are expected to work out their own roles. Although this gives them a great deal of freedom and flexibility, it also produces a major source of tension and disagreement. A couple's ideas might not mesh. They may disagree over whether the wife should be career oriented, or to what extent, and over how to divide responsibilities for the home and children. Because guidelines are still unclear, couples face a role vacuum that can create discontent. How can you fulfill adequately your marital role if you can't agree on what goes into that role?

Collectively, then, these fundamental changes in the meaning of marriage—our ideas about love, children, parenthood, and the roles of husband and wife—put tremendous pressure on spouses and provide a strong push toward divorce. These changes have created the "emotional overload" mentioned earlier. We expect marriage to provide unlimited emotional satisfaction, something that it just cannot deliver.

Perception of Alternatives

While these fundamental changes were taking place, another change also occurred that affected marriage deeply. More women were taking jobs outside the home, and this, too, changed people's ideas about marriage. As wives earned paychecks of their own, they began to perceive alternatives to putting up with unhappy marriages. Symbolic interactionists consider the *perception of alternatives* as an essential first step to making divorce possible.

Changed Attitudes Toward Divorce

It is difficult for us to grasp how seriously divorce was once taken. Divorce used to represent failure, irresponsibility, and immorality. Divorced people were social outcasts. They were suspected of all sorts of evil things and disinvited as dinner guests. As divorce became more common, its meaning changed: Divorce was transformed from being a symbol of failure to one of self-fulfillment, of opportunity rather than shame. This symbolic leap became one more push toward divorce. When being a divorced person carried a stigma, divorce was held in check. As divorce became a sign of personal change and development, the stage was set for widespread divorce.

Legal Changes

The law also used to hold divorce in check, for divorce was granted only on rigorous grounds. In some states, such as New York, to obtain a divorce required that one spouse prove that the other had committed adultery. This proof required witnesses and a trial. As people's ideas about divorce changed, the laws against it were relaxed. Today, in most states, "incompatibility," as vague as that term is, is adequate for divorce.

Couples can work out their own "no-fault" divorce, and judges "compatibly" divorce them. In Florida, the couple can sign papers in a lawyer's office, and they don't even have to appear in court. Such legal changes have further reduced the stigma attached to divorce, which, in turn, has contributed to the divorce rate.

Are These Changes Good or Bad?

Are these changes good or bad? Symbolic interactionists take the position that nothing is good or bad in and of itself. They view "goodness" and "badness" as value judgments. Thus, different groups evaluate divorce differently. Depending on its assumptions, one group is alarmed at changes in divorce, sex roles, ideas of what children are, and so on, whereas another group looks at these same changes and feels pleased that the family is evolving. Symbolic interactionists can't say which view, if either, is correct, for symbolic interactionism provides no framework to make value judgments about anything.

In Sum

To explain why divorce increased, symbolic interactionists analyze how the symbols associated with the family have changed. They stress that symbols both reflect and create reality. That is, symbols not only represent people's ideas, but those same symbols also influence people's behaviors and ideas. Although symbolic interactionists can analyze social change, they cannot pass judgment on it.

FUNCTIONALISM

When functionalists analyze social change, they look at how change in one part of a social system affects its other parts. Earlier, in "The Problem in Sociological Perspective," pages 353–355, we examined the impact of industrialization and urbanization on the family. We saw, for example, how the birthrate fell as children became more dependent, unproductive, and costly.

Seven Traditional Functions of the Family:

Functionalists have identified seven traditional functions of the family. They point out that around the world the family provides

1. Economic production
2. Socialization of children
3. Care of the aged
4. Care of the sick and injured
5. Recreation
6. Sexual control of family members
7. Reproduction

1. Economic Production

Let's see how the industrial revolution and urbanization have affected these seven traditional functions of the family and how this is related to divorce. Before industrialization, the family was an economic team; for survival, its members were forced to cooperate. *Moving production from home to factory disrupted this team.* This isolated the husband–father from the daily activities of the family, separated the wife–mother from the production of income, and made older children, who went to work for wages, less dependent on their family.

2. Socialization of Children

While economic production was changing, the government was growing larger, more centralized, and more powerful. One consequence was that the government began to undermine family functions. For example, lawmakers passed mandatory education laws, making it illegal for parents not to send their children to school. Parents faced fines and jail sentences if they did not put their children in the government's care. In this way, the government took over much of the responsibility for socializing children.

3 and 4. Care of the Aged and Sick

Care of the sick and aged took a similar course. Before industrialization, there were few trained physicians, and medicine had been a family matter. As medical schools developed, along with hospitals and drugs, medicine came under government control. Gradually medical care shifted from the family to medical specialists. It was similarly the case with care of the aged. As the central government expanded and its agencies multiplied, care of the aged, too, became a government obligation.

5. Recreation

As industrialization progressed, the country became more affluent. The family's disposable income increased, and businesses sprang up to compete for that income. Entertainment and "fun" had consisted primarily of home-based activities—card games, parlor and barn dances, sleigh rides, and so on. As family-centered activities gave way to public-centered paid events, the family lost much of its recreational function.

6. Control of Sexuality

The family had also controlled the sexuality of its members, but even this changed. Sexual relations in marriage were the only ones that were viewed as legitimate; sexual relations outside marriage—even between a couple that was going to get married—were considered immoral. Although this was only an ideal, and marriage never enjoyed a monopoly on sexual relations, the "sexual revolution" opened many alternatives to marital sex. Consequently, to understate the matter, marital control over sexuality is considerably weaker than it used to be.

7. Reproduction

At first glance, the seventh function, reproduction, appears to remain solidly in the family's domain. Yet even this vital and seemingly inviolable function of the family is not going unchallenged. Recall Figures 11-7 and 11-9 (on pages 360 and 363). These figures indicate how giving birth outside marriage has become much more common. In the United States, one-third of reproduction has moved away from the traditional family unit of husband and wife. In addition, married women can get abortions without informing their husband, and teenagers can obtain birth control and, in most states, abortions without parental consent. Buttressed by laws and government funding, then, a good deal of control over reproduction has been removed from the family.

Can reproduction be removed even farther from the family? Some envision a future in which women, single or married, homosexual or heterosexual, order semen to match their specifications: sex, race-ethnicity, height, hair color, eye color, body type, even intelligence, personality traits, and musical, artistic, poetic, and sports ability (Bagne 1992). Sociologist Judith Lorber (1980:527) proposed a system of "professional breeders":

> A system of completely professional breeders and child rearers could be conducted with the best of modern technology—fertility drugs for multiple births, sperm banks, embryo transfers, and uterine implants to expand the gene pool and so on. Professional breeders could be paid top salaries, like today's athletes, for the 15–20 years of their prime childbearing time. Those who were impregnated could live in well-run dormitories, with excellent physical care, food, and entertainment.

We are caught in the middle—between the past and the mind-boggling, technologically driven future. Although we can speculate, none of us knows the specifics of that future. Perhaps Lorber's vision may come about—although such a future could usher in a *1984 Big Brother* or a Hitleresque *Lebensraum*.

In Sum

The family, then, has lost many of its traditional functions, and other functions are under assault. From a functionalist perspective, such changes have weakened the family unit. The fewer functions that family members have in common, the fewer are their "ties that bind." As these bonds have weakened, the family has become more fragile. Divorce, then, became more common—the inevitable consequence of eroded functions in a context of greater social strain.

CONFLICT THEORY

Conflict theorists point us in a different direction. They stress that marriage and family reflect a basic social inequality of men and women. In general, men control, dominate, and exploit women, and marriage is one of the means by which they do this.

Traditional Male-Female Relationships Represent Inequality and Exploitation

Historically, men have dominated women. The home was a place where women served their fathers, husbands, and brothers. Men decided whom their daughters would marry—often on the basis of the benefits that they themselves would derive, such as gaining favor with more powerful men. A common example is kings forging alliances with other kings by giving their daughters in marriage. Both custom and the law allowed men to discipline not only their children, but also their wives. A husband could spank his wife—if she "needed" it. Even beating a wife was considered permissible if she became rebellious or had an affair. In some areas, killing an unfaithful wife was within the community's norms.

Reflections Today

Our own forms of marriage and family reflect these millennia-old patterns of power. One of the most striking examples is the traditional U.S. wedding ceremony. While the mother sits passively on the side, the father walks down the aisle with his daughter and "gives" her to her husband. This is but a pale reflection of the power men once wielded—when fathers were able to choose their daughters' husbands—but it is a reflection nonetheless.

Marriage as an Arena for a Continuing Historical Struggle

Although men's power has eroded severely, inequality between men and women remains, making marriage an arena for this ongoing struggle between the sexes. This, say conflict theorists, is the key to understanding today's family problems. In individual marriages, historical causes drop from sight. As husbands and wives argue and fight, they don't view their personal problems as rooted in broad historical change. They experience personal disagreements with their spouse, not something historical or in the abstract. At the root of personal marital disagreements, however, stress conflict theorists, lies this historical struggle between men and women over rights, obligations, and privileges.

As industrialization progressed, women's roles changed. As their experiences expanded beyond home, church, and neighbors, they came to resent arrangements that they had taken for granted. Housework became one of these sources of resentment. Sociologist Arlie Hochschild (Hochschild and Manning 1995) points out that even today, most wives, after returning home from an eight-hour shift of work-for-wages, put in a "second shift" doing cooking, cleaning, and child care. In two-paycheck families, wives average 15 hours more work each week than their husbands. The cumulative total is incredible: Over a year, wives work an *extra month of twenty-four hour days*. Husbands resist attempts to reduce their power, and wives resent their husband's reluctance to share responsibilities. Within the intimacy of the family, then, this basic historical struggle is being played out. At times, this competition between the sexes breaks into open conflict, taking the forms of spouse battering and child abuse.

Consciousness of Oppression

This analysis may fly in the face of your own experience. Many wives do not *feel* oppressed, and some husbands feel that *they* are oppressed. A woman who does not feel oppression, say conflict theorists, is blind to her real situation and may be suffering from false consciousness. A man who feels oppressed, however, may be expressing social reality, for the social system oppresses both males and females. The difference, however, is that although society may torment both sexes, society is the creation of men and reflects their reality (de Beauvoir 1953).

Power, Perception, and Behavior

This unequal balance of power has caused men and women to experience dating and marriage differently. Women who expected their life to revolve around being a wife and mother, looked for security in a husband. Such women are more anxious than men about dating, finding a mate, and the quality of family life (Greer 1972). Men, who found their basic security outside marriage at work, were less concerned about the outcome of dating and their marital relationship. In these traditional orientations, most women invest more time and effort in making the marriage work and are more dependent on its outcome (Firestone 1970). Women who are more career oriented are less dependent on marriage for their status and welfare in life. Their relationship to their husbands reflects their changed historical situation.

The 1950s marked a watershed era in U.S. middle-class families. As millions of soldiers returned home from World War II, their millions of wives and girlfriends left the war industries and returned to the home. Freed from economic pursuits, the wife was expected to focus her efforts exclusively on the home. With more free time, she was expected to put more effort into nurturing the children, even to help them "develop their potential," a new concept in parenting. This historical period is bathed in images that characterized only a minority of families, images that form a mythical lens through which we view that "ideal" period of family life.

In Sum: Divorce as a Sign of Changing Power

In short, conflict theorists stress that marriage and family reflect fundamental, historical relationships between men and women. Divorce reveals the basic conflict that is inherent in family life, the social inequalities that pit husband and wife against one another. Higher divorce rates are not a sign that the family is weakening but, rather, that women are making headway in their historical struggle with men.

Research Findings

Let's look at major characteristics of marriage and family today: age at first marriage, cohabitation, remaining single, childlessness, family violence, sexual abuse, and abandonment of the elderly. Then let's consider whether these characteristics indicate the death of the family.

COHABITATION AND THE CHANGING AGE AT FIRST MARRIAGE

Changes in Age at First Marriage

From 1890 to 1950, Americans married at younger and younger ages. By 1950, U.S. brides were younger than at any time in our history: The typical bride had just left her teens. By 1970, the grooms were also the youngest since the U.S. government kept records. After plateauing for a about twenty years, there was an abrupt reversal, and *today's average first-time bride and groom are older than at any time in U.S. history.*

Cohabitation

Why this reversal? Figure 11-10 on the next page holds the answer. Look at the sharp increase in the number of unmarried couples who are **cohabiting,** living together

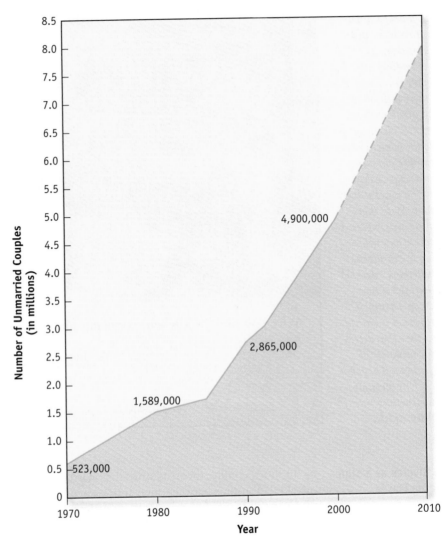

FIGURE 11-10
Cohabitation in the United States

Source: By the author, based on *Statistical Abstract of the United States* 1985:Table 54; 2003:Table 69.

Note: Broken line is the author's estimate.

in a sexual relationship. Sociologists estimate that if cohabitation had not grown like this, the average age at first marriage would probably show little change.

It is not that most cohabitants are opposed to marriage. They are opposed, rather, to marriage for themselves at this time. For a variety of reasons, they do not feel that they are ready to handle the commitments and responsibilities of marriage. Although attracted to one another and wanting more than to be just "going together," many couples fear that their relationship isn't solid enough for marriage. They feel that they might develop this commitment, however, while they cohabit. Finances are also a major concern. Some couples fear that marriage will tie them down financially, but cohabitation doesn't require this same commitment. Marriage is also supposed to be a declaration of financial independence, and for many young people, especially college students, cohabitation keeps them eligible for support from their parents. For some, of course, cohabitation is simply a way to enjoy regular sex with a dependable partner minus the hassles of dating.

The Increasing Number of Single Americans

So many Americans have postponed their wedding day that the percentage of single young people has surged. The percentage of women age 25 to 29 who are single today is almost *four* times higher than it was in 1970 (only 11 percent unmarried in

1970 compared with 40 percent today). The percentage of single men of this age group has jumped almost *three* times (19 percent unmarried in 1970 and 54 percent today) (*Statistical Abstract* 1993:Table 52; 1998:Table 62; 2003:Table 63).

Remaining Single

Few people look at being single as a permanent alternative to marriage. Some do, however, and as sociologist Peter Stein (1992) found, those who plan on remaining single all their lives still feel a strong need for intimacy, sharing, and continuity. To attain these satisfactions, which marriage and family ordinarily provide, the permanent singles cultivate a network of people who feel as they do about marriage. Through these friendships, they satisfy their needs for intimacy.

CHILDLESSNESS

Pressures to Have Children

Although most married women give birth, about one of five (19 percent) does not (DeOilos and Kapinus 2002). Childlessness has grown so fast that this is *twice* what it was 20 years ago. As sociologist Charlene Miall (1986) found, infertile couples feel stigmatized because it goes against cultural expectations to have children. These couples maneuver defensively, tiptoeing around topics that involve children in their conversations with friends, relatives, and fellow workers. They even select friends who are comfortable with childlessness.

The Process of Remaining Childless

Even fewer couples *choose* to remain childless. Sociologist Jean Veevers (1973, 1980) found that of 52 wives who had been married at least five years and had deliberately never given birth, about a third had made an agreement with their husbands before they married not to have children. In fact, they had sought husbands who would agree to remain, in their terms, child free. For them, not bearing children was not a problem.

About two-thirds of the wives that Veevers studied, however, had planned to have children, but something happened. These women had gone through four stages. First, they postponed the decision to get pregnant while they worked toward a specific goal, such as graduating from college or buying a house. Then they shifted their postponement to a vague future, a "sometime" that never seemed to arrive. In the third stage, they decided that not having kids wasn't so bad, that they might want to remain childless. Finally, in the fourth stage, they viewed their childlessness as a permanent rather than a temporary state.

The Stigma

All the wives who decided to remain childless felt stigmatized. Friends and relatives put pressure on them to bear children and made negative comments because they weren't pregnant. These pressures peaked during their third and fourth years of marriage, then decreased after they were married for five or six years. To help cope, the couples talked about what Veevers calls their "mythical child," the one that they would adopt "one day." Few couples, however, made an effort to contact a child placement agency, and none of those who did followed up their initial contact. The "mythical child" helped the couples to adjust, for it made their childlessness seem temporary. Talking about adoption affirmed to themselves and others that they were "normal" people who like children. Even after the wives became too old to bear children, adoption remained a symbol that held open the possibility of socially altering biological facts.

The "Mythical" Child

FAMILY VIOLENCE

The middle-aged man, an alcoholic, pushed the frail 70-year-old woman to the floor when she refused to give him money. She sprawled there, stunned and helpless, while he screamed insults. When the police arrived, the woman was concerned about protecting her attacker. She didn't want him to be arrested. He was her son.

This was not the first—or last—time that this woman would be victimized by her son. Parent abuse is but one form of family violence that researchers and the general public are discussing.

The wife is the usual victim of marital violence. Violence can begin over "nothing," little disagreements that are part of all marriages. Some men, however, view violence as a legitimate way to express their frustrations. Husbands who are violent are likely to have been reared in homes in which their own fathers were violent, a process sociologists call the "cultural transmission of violence."

Murray Straus heads the Family Violence Research Program at the University of New Hampshire. He and fellow sociologists Susan Steinmetz and Richard Gelles have studied this cruel irony—that the social group we most often look to for intimacy and love is sometimes characterized by cruelty and violence. To determine the amount and types of violence in U.S. homes, they interviewed nationally representative samples of couples. Their questions about acts of intentional physical injury ranged from slapping, pushing, kicking, biting, and beating to attacking with a knife or gun (Straus et al. 1980; Straus and Gelles 1988; Straus 1992).

Here is one of the most startling aspects of their research: The FBI reports violence in numbers per 100,000 people, but violence among family members is so common that these researchers reported incidents per 100 people. They found that each year, 16 of every 100 spouses physically attack their husband or wife. This is 1 spouse out of every 6! To my knowledge, no other violent crime even approaches this rate.

Because most couples (84 percent) were not violent during the past year and most violence is mild (such as slapping), some dismiss these figures. To this, Straus and Gelles (1988) reply (paraphrased):

> Let's suppose we are talking about a university. Would anyone say that there wasn't much of a problem because, after all, 84 percent of the faculty didn't hit a student last year? Or would anyone argue that this isn't significant because, after all, most episodes were just slapping, rather than punching or beating up?

Violence among spouses, whatever its forms, is a topic of research by sociologists. Sometimes sociologists become interested in a social problem because of personal experience with it. This is how it was for sociologist Kathleen Ferraro, who shares her experiences in the *Spotlight on Research* box on the next page.

Compared with their parents, children are even more violent. During the year preceding the interview, two-thirds of the children had attacked a brother or sister. Most had shoved or thrown things, but one-third had kicked or bitten a sibling. In rare instances, the attack involved a knife or gun. Straus suggests that these totals are severe underestimates.

Equality Between the Sexes?

This surprises some people, but in marital violence, husbands and wives are about equally as likely to attack one another (Gelles 1980; Straus 1980, 1992). It is a different matter, however, when we look at the *effects* of violence. Then sexual equality vanishes. As Straus points out, even though she may cast the first coffeepot, he usually casts the last and most damaging blow. Because most men are bigger and stronger than their wives, women are at a disadvantage in this literal battle of the sexes, and more women than men need medical attention. And when one spouse kills another, four times out of five the wife is the victim (*FBI Uniform Crime Report* 2003:Table 2.7).

Violence and Social Class

When it comes to social class and violence, you might hear someone say, "Violence occurs in all social classes." This statement is true, because, like everything except poverty, all social classes have some of it. But such a statement hides much more than it reveals. Like everything else, including money, violence is not distributed equally among the classes. Violence follows well-worn "social channels," which makes spouses in some social classes much more likely to be abusers—or victims—than others. The highest rates of violence (Gelles 1980) are found among

Families with low incomes
Blue-collar workers

SPOTLIGHT ON RESEARCH

Intimate Partner Violence

Kathleen Ferraro, Professor of Sociology at Northern Arizona University, wanted to be a sociologist from the time she was twelve. She never imagined, though, that her research would focus on "intimate partner violence," because she never knew that this existed.

I found out about "intimate partner violence" at age twenty-three when I married my first husband. He went to high school with me, and came from a well-respected family. He was a naturalist, a bird-watcher, did not drink or use drugs, and showed no violent tendencies. After we exchanged vows, however, he changed almost immediately, displaying the "power and control" tactics that have become common knowledge today. He monitored my movements, eating, clothing, friends, money, make-up, and language. If I challenged his commands, he slapped or kicked me or pushed me down. I left him on these occasions, staying with other graduate students at Arizona State University, but I had no way to understand what was happening. My husband always convinced me to return. He stalked and threatened to kill me—even in front of police officers—but my faculty mentor, Albert J. Mayer, and friends hid me until my father-in-law came to take my husband back to our home town on the other side of the country. I obtained a single party, no-fault divorce, and never saw him again.

These events took place in 1974 and 1975, before the battered women's movement transformed public understanding of "domestic violence." In a graduate class on social deviance, Erdwin Pfuhl required us to write a paper on a form of deviance with which we had personal experience. I could not think of anything. While I waited outside

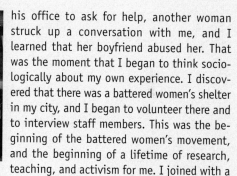

his office to ask for help, another woman struck up a conversation with me, and I learned that her boyfriend abused her. That was the moment that I began to think sociologically about my own experience. I discovered that there was a battered women's shelter in my city, and I began to volunteer there and to interview staff members. This was the beginning of the battered women's movement, and the beginning of a lifetime of research, teaching, and activism for me. I joined with a group of people to establish another shelter, and that is where I conducted the interviews and ethnographic work for my dissertation, *Battered Women and the Shelter Movement,* and for the *Social Problems* article, "How Women Experience Battering: The Process of Victimization."

The women taught me how difficult it is to make sense of violence and emotional abuse that comes from a person they love and believe loves them. The rationalizations the women used to understand what was happening to them were similar to those used by people who commit crimes: the "techniques of neutralization" described by Gresham Sykes and David Matza (reviewed in Chapter 6 in this text). For women at the shelter, these techniques included: denial of victimization, denial of the victimizer, denial of injury, denial of options, appeal to higher loyalties, and the salvation ethic. Because of fear, lack of resources, and institutional failure to respond to battering, the women found escape from violent relationships to be difficult and precarious. Leaving an abuser does not necessarily end the violence, and leaving is often the most dangerous time for women.

Families in which the husband is unemployed
Families with above-average numbers of children
People with less education
Individuals who have no religious affiliation
People under 30

Poverty as a Key

Poverty is the key to understanding the first five of these findings. Poverty opens only some of the doors, however, for, as you can see, age and religion are also factors. Although family violence occurs in all social classes, blue-collar spouses, especially husbands, are considerably more violent than white-collar spouses. The researchers suggest that this is because blue-collar husbands experience more stress than their white-collar counterparts. Although this might be true, we can also apply symbolic interactionism. Blue-collar men belong to a broad subculture in which violence tends to be viewed as an expression of "manliness."

Alcohol as a Key

Sociologists Glenda Kantor and Murray Straus (1987) also found another key: alcohol. Based on a national probability sample, they found a direct relationship between alcohol consumption and wife battering; that is, the more a husband drinks, the more likely he is to beat his wife. The lowest rates of violence against wives are by husbands who do not drink, the highest among those who go on binges.

The Social Heredity of Violence

Straus, Gelles, and Steinmetz also discovered what they call the *social heredity of violence*. By this term, they mean that children learn from their parents that violence is a solution to problems. After the children grow up and marry, they apply this lesson. As Figure 11-11 shows, the more violence that people experience during their teen years, the more likely they are to be violent after they marry. As these researchers (1980:113) explain Figure 11-11: "Those with scores of zero are the people whose parents did not hit them and did not hit each other. At the other extreme are people with scores of 9. They are the people whose parents frequently hit them when they were teenagers and whose parents were frequently violent with each other." The researchers drive home this point by saying:

> When one member of a couple had experienced the double whammy of being hit as a child and observing his or her parents hitting each other, there was a one in three chance that at least one act of violence had occurred during the year of the study!

Why does a woman remain with a husband who abuses her? This question has intrigued members of the public and sociologists alike. Researchers have studied many samples of women, and they have found remarkably consistent answers. Findings from one of these studies are featured in the Issues in the Social Problems box on the next page.

Some wives, of course, leave their husbands after the first blow and never return. Others remain, but after being brutalized for years, they kill their husbands. Wife beating has become a controversial defense for wives who have killed their husbands. For example, Cindy Hudo, a 21-year-old mother of two in Charleston, South Carolina, was charged with the murder of her husband, Buba. Here is what she said:

> I start in the car and I get down the road and I see Buba walking, and he's real mad. I just look at him. So, I pull over, you know, and I'm trying, you know—"I didn't know to pick you up. You know, I'm sorry." And he didn't even say nothing to me. He just started hitting on me. And that's all I wanted to do, was just get home, because I was just self-conscious. I don't want nobody to see him hitting me, because I didn't want him to look bad. I had to go to work in a half-hour, because I was working a double-shift. And he told me I had forty minutes to get all my furniture out of the house and get my clothes and be out or he was going to throw them out.
>
> And I was sitting there, because I could talk him down. You know, because I didn't want to leave him. I just talked to him. I said, "Buba, I don't want to leave." I said, "This is my house." And then he told me . . . (unclear) my kids. And I said, "No, you're not taking my kids from me. That's too much." And so I said, "Just let me leave. Just let me take the kids. And, you know I'll go, and you know, I won't keep the

FIGURE 11-11 *How Is Marital Violence Related to the Family Violence That Teenagers Experience?*

Source: From Murray A. Straus, Richard J. Gelles, and Suzanne K. Steinmetz. *Behind Closed Doors: Violence in the American Family* (Garden City, NY: Doubleday, 1980), p. 112. Copyright © 1980 by Murray A. Straus and Richard J. Gelles. Reprinted with permission.

Husband-to-wife violence rate during the survey year
Wife-to-husband violence rate during the survey year

Percent

Amount of Family Violence Experienced as a Teenager

Issues in Social Problems

"WHY DOESN'T SHE JUST LEAVE?" THE DILEMMA OF ABUSED WOMEN

"Why would she ever put up with violence?" is a question on everyone's mind. From the outside, it looks so easy. Just pack up and leave. "I know I wouldn't put up with anything like that."

Yet this is not what typically happens. Women tend to stay with their men after they are abused. Some stay only a short while, to be sure, but others remain in abusive situations for years. Why?

Sociologist Ann Goetting (2001) asked this question, too. To get the answer, she interviewed women who had made the break. Goetting wanted to find out what it was that set them apart. How were these women able to leave, when so many can't seem to? She found that:

1. They had a positive self-concept.

Simply put, they believed that they deserved better.

2. They broke with traditional values.

They did not believe that a wife had to stay with her husband no matter what.

3. They found adequate finances.

For some this was easy, but for others it was not. To accumulate enough money to move out, some of the women saved for years, putting away just a little each week.

4. They had supportive family and friends.

A support network served as a source of encouragement to help them rescue themselves.

If you take the opposite of these four characteristics, you have the answer to why some women put up with abuse: They don't think they deserve anything better; they believe it is their duty to stay; they don't think they can make it financially; and they lack a supportive network. These four factors are not of equal importance for all women, of course. For some, the lack of finances is the most significant, whereas for others it is their low self-concept. For all, the supportive network—or the lack of one—plays a significant role.

FOR YOUR CONSIDERATION

On the basis of these findings, what would you say to a woman whose husband or partner is abusing her? How do you think battered women's shelters fit into this explanation? What other parts of this puzzle can you think of—such as the role of love?

kids from you or nothing like that." And he said, "I'm going to take them and you're getting out."

[Buba then loaded a shotgun, pointed it at Cindy, and said:] "The only way you're going to get out of this is if you kill me and I'll—I'll kill you." [Buba then gave the shotgun to Cindy and] just turned around and walked right down the hall, because he knew I wouldn't do nothing. And I just sat there a minute. And I don't know what happened. I just, you know, I went to the bedroom and I seen him laying there and I just shot him. He moved. I shot him again because I thought he was going to get up again. . . .

I loved him too much. And I just wanted to help him. ("20/20," October 18, 1979)

Although Cindy had shot and killed her husband, who at the time was unarmed and unresisting, a jury acquitted her on the basis that she was a battered wife.

As with Cindy Hudo, in a few celebrated cases wife battering as a defense for homicide has worked, and wives have been acquitted for killing their husband. No matter how understandable the desire to kill may be under conditions of extreme duress, brutality, and fear, this defense raises nagging questions about justifying the killing of spouses.

SEXUAL ABUSE IN THE FAMILY

Marital Rape

**How Common
Is Marital Rape?**

How common is marital rape? This area of human behavior is shrouded in secrecy, making it difficult to gather information. Sociologists David Finkelhor and Kersti Yllo (1985, 1989), however, broke through that shroud. They interviewed 330 women in a representative sample of the Boston metropolitan area. Ten percent of the women reported that their husbands had used physical force to compel them to have sex. Based on another sampling technique from which we can generalize, sociologist Diana Russell (1980) estimates that 12 percent of married women have been raped by their husbands. If 10 to 12 percent are even close to being accurate, we are talking about five or six million married women who have suffered this form of sexual abuse.

**Three Types
of Marital Rape**

From interviews with 50 women who had been raped by their husbands, Finkelhor and Yllo found three types of sexual assault in marriage:

1. *Nonbattering rape.* In about 40 percent of the cases, the husband sexually assaulted his wife without intending to do physical harm. The attack was usually preceded by a conflict over sex, such as the husband feeling insulted when his wife refused to have sex.
2. *Battering rape.* In about 48 percent of the cases, the husband intentionally inflicted physical pain during the sexual assault. He was retaliating for some supposed wrongdoing on his wife's part.
3. *Perverted rape.* In these instances, about 6 percent, the husband seemed to be sexually aroused by the violence. These husbands forced their wives to submit to unusual sexual acts. (The remaining 6 percent contain elements of more than one type.)

Effects of Marital Rape

How did the rapes affect the wives? The short-term effects were anger accompanied by grief, despair, shame, and a feeling of "dirtiness." The most common long-term effect was the woman's inability to trust intimate relationships or to function sexually.

**The Timing
of Marital Rape**

Marital rape most often occurs during separation or when a marriage is breaking up. In rare instances, however, husbands rape their wives throughout marriage. One woman, for example, had endured marital rape for twenty-four years—her marriage only ended when her husband divorced her!

**Why Do Some Women Put
Up with Marital Rape?**

Although most women quickly leave a marriage after being raped by their husbands, some remain. Why? The answer appears to be similar to why women who are physically but *not* sexually abused remain with their husbands. They are afraid to leave. They fear they do not have the skills to make it on their own. They don't have a supportive network. Or, they have children, and with their low self-esteem, they feel they cannot survive without their husbands.

Incest

Another area that sociologists have investigated is **incest**—forbidden sexual relations between relatives, such as brothers and sisters or parents and children. Sexual relations between siblings or with one's own children are condemned almost universally. If a social group allows incest, it is for specific categories of people, and often under limited circumstances. Examples include Thonga lion hunters of East Africa, who may have sex with their daughters on the night before a big hunt, and brother–sister marriages among the Egyptian pharaohs and the Incas of Peru (La Barre 1954; Beals and Hoijer 1965). Apart from such rare exceptions, incest is viewed as abhorrent, sinful, or unnatural. Revelations of incest are met with repugnance, and incest is one of the few issues on which most Americans strongly agree.

With such strong condemnation, incest should be rare, but is it? Sociologist Diana Russell (1986) interviewed a probability sample (from which we can generalize) of 930 women in San Francisco. She found that before these women turned age 18, 16 percent had been victims of incest. Before you conclude that 16 percent of all the women you know or meet have been victims of incest, you need to know that Russell's definition of incest was curiously broad. Not only did her definition include sexual relations with a relative, but also it included unwanted kisses. Russell found that in only 5 of 100 cases were the police informed. Although this study does not reflect common assumptions about what incest is, we can conclude that incest is much more common than the numbers that are officially reported.

Who Are the Offenders?

Who are the offenders? Russell found that the most common offenders are uncles, followed by first cousins, then fathers (biological, adoptive, step, and foster), brothers, and finally other relatives from brothers-in-law to stepgrandfathers. In Russell's sample, incest between mother and son was rare, a finding confirmed by other researchers (Lester 1972).

Effects on Victims

Incest creates enormous burdens for its victims (Bartoi and Kinder 1998; Lewin 1998). Susan Forward, a psychotherapist who was herself a victim of incest, reports:

> I understand incest not only as a psychotherapist but as a victim. When I was fifteen my father's playful seductiveness turned into highly sexualized fondling. This is a difficult admission for me to make, but even more painful is the fact that I enjoyed my father's attentions.
>
> I felt enormously guilty about my participation in the incest, as if I had been responsible. I know now I was not. It was my father's responsibility as an adult and as a parent to prevent sexual contact between us, but I didn't understand that at the time.
>
> I also felt guilty about competing with my mother—who was only thirty-three and very attractive.
>
> I was flattered by my father's attraction to me, and his caresses felt good, but after several months my guilt became too great. I somehow found the courage to tell him to stop, and he did. The psychological damage, however, had already been done.
>
> As my guilt feelings accumulated, my self-image deteriorated. I felt like a "bad girl." I began to punish myself [sub]consciously, most prominently by marrying an unloving man instead of pursuing the acting career I had dreamed of since I was five. Later, when my children were in school, I finally got a job on a television series. Good jobs followed and success was within my grasp. But my guilt still fought me on a [sub]conscious level, telling me that I didn't deserve success. So I allowed myself—[sub]consciously, of course, to become overweight and matronly at twenty-eight. My acting career stagnated. My marriage was a mess. I was desperately unhappy. Yet I had absolutely no idea that there was any connection between what my father had done to me and the problems in my life. (Forward and Buck 1978:1)

The "Pro-Incest Lobby"

Marital rape is often viewed as a case of the husband being a little too insistent and the wife a little too reticent. Marital rape, however, can be every bit as brutal as a rape by strangers.

A tiny minority takes the position that incest is not a problem. The problem, they say, is the *attitude* toward incest. If the attitude were different and incest were allowed, no one would have a problem. This small "pro-incest lobby," sometimes called the "new permissivists," claims that the state should not pass laws against incest because such laws are based on outdated biblical ideas. People who have this view argue that prohibiting incest chills affectionate relationships of sexual love that can bind people to one another (De Mott 1980).

If the pro-incest lobby ever were to succeed in removing what has been called the "last taboo," the change certainly would affect family life—and, as most would say, devastatingly. The chances of this happening range from impossible to remote.

OLD AGE AND WIDOWHOOD

Problems of Adjustment

In contrast with our past, most Americans today survive to old age. Old age brings many problems of adjustment, especially the need to adjust to deteriorating health, the death of loved ones, and the knowledge of one's own impending death. When the elderly retire (or disengage from their usual productive roles, as sociologists put it), their social worth can be challenged. They may even face subtle and less-subtle accusations of being parasites—of robbing younger workers by bankrupting the Social Security system.

The Family as Buffer

The family stands as a buffer between the individual and outside forces. Families that function well give their members a sense of belonging and personal worth. Most adults thrive on the love and understanding that they find within their family. For the elderly, this is especially important: Not only is the family their chief source of identity but also their place in the family stands in sharp contrast to the negative stereotypes by which the elderly are portrayed in the general society.

From Extended to Nuclear Family

Several generations ago, Americans lived in **extended families;** that is, other relatives, perhaps a grandmother or an uncle, lived with the parents and their children. During this agrarian period, the aged, who owned the land, could maintain positions of authority, gradually relinquishing control while easing younger family members into responsible roles. Although we cannot be sure, the transition to old age may have been smoother and perhaps less painful than today. We have to be careful about picturing a rosy past of that never was, however. Even if individuals were located within a larger family unit, their adjustment to deteriorating health, the death of loved ones, and the knowledge that they, too, would soon die could not have been easy.

Unlike the situation in the past, the "older generation" no longer lives with their adult children, and the **nuclear family,** consisting of parents and children, has become our dominant family form. This living arrangement has led to stereotypes of relationships between adult children and their parents. A common image is of people living in dispersed family units, with the elderly living alienated and isolated from the ungrateful children they reared. Abandoned and embittered, the elderly eventually live out their last years in nursing homes.

The Myth of Family Abandonment

We noted in Chapter 2 that such imagery is far from the truth. A team of sociologists who studied the residents of Muncie, Indiana, found that the elderly maintain contact with their adult children (Caplow et al. 1982). National studies show that 56 percent of Americans age 65 and over are still living with their spouse. Another 13 percent live with other people, and 31 percent live alone (*Statistical Abstract* 2003:Table 64).

Intimacy at a Distance

Sociologist Elaine Brody (1978) reported that abandonment of the elderly is about as true as the illusion of a golden past in which the whole family lived idyllically on a farm, joyfully meeting each other's every need. She says that in the United States both the elderly and the young *prefer* to live apart. The elderly prefer to live near, but not with, their children—described as "intimacy at a distance."

Sociologist Suzanne Steinmetz (1988) reports that parents and their adult children who live together tend to get on one another's nerves. The elderly appear to be acting on a good "sixth sense," then, when they want to live near, but not with, their children. Far from abandoning their aged parents, children remain key figures in their support system (Bengtson et al. 1991).

The Institutionalized Elderly

As was discussed in Chapter 2, the 4 percent of the aged who live in nursing homes are *not* typical of older people (*Statistical Abstract* 2003:Tables 11, 185). Most need help with bathing (97 percent), dressing (88 percent), and even going to the toilet (58 percent). Most are in wheelchairs; or else they use walkers to get around. Seven out of ten can no longer manage money or take care of their personal possessions. Most of them even need help to use the telephone (*Statistical Abstract* 2003:Table 185).

Nursing home residents, then, confirm common stereotypes about the elderly. These certainly are not a healthy group, but remember that nursing home residents do not represent elderly people in general. On the contrary, *most* elderly Americans enjoy good health and the company of their family and friends.

Although most of the elderly who end up in nursing homes do not have families to take care of them, some do. Contrary to stereotypes, the elderly people who have families have not been "dumped" by ungrateful children. As Elaine Brody reported (1978:20–21):

> Prior to institutionalization, most families have endured severe personal, social, and economic stress in attempting to avoid admission [to a nursing home]; it is typically the last, not the first, resort; and the decision is made reluctantly. The "well" spouse usually is in advanced old age. The adult children are often approaching or engaged in the aging phase of life with attendant age-related stresses and often are subjected to competing demands from ill spouses or their own children.

Adjustment to Widowhood

Even for people who enjoy good health and family relationships in their older years, death comes eventually. When death ends a marriage, the survivor is forced to face life without the partner who had become such an essential part of life. In the midst of disrupted family relationships and the loss of social roles, the widowed face three main problems: loneliness, anxiety, and money (Hiltz 1989).

Sociologist Robert Atchley (1975) studied retired schoolteachers and retired employees of a telephone company who were in their 70s. He found that the widowers generally did better than the widows. The men were more likely to be active in organizations, to have more contact with friends, and to be less anxious. The key, Atchley found, was money. The men were more secure financially, which made them less anxious about life. Atchley also found a surprising variable—the ability to afford a car. Those who had cars, whether widows or widowers, got out of the house more, participated in more group activities, and visited their friends more often. The mobility that a car offered was *the* key factor in reducing social isolation, loneliness, and anxiety.

Atchley's findings can be summarized as a principle that runs through social life: In general, the more adequate their income, the better that people adjust to whatever challenges they face.

THE DEATH OF THE FAMILY?

A Picture of Decline?

Marriage is doomed. Our high divorce rate shows that it is no longer a viable social institution. The many problems that we have reviewed in this chapter signal the end of the contemporary family. As Figure 11-10 (on page 370) shows, *nine times* more couples are cohabiting today than in the 1970s. If this trend continues, eventually most people will live together, not marry. Table 11-1 also illustrates why the family is dying: The average household has been *shrinking*, indicating that there is little left of the family. Then, too, there is that interesting statistic that we reviewed, that one-third of U.S. children are born to unmarried mothers. As more unmarried women bear children, marriage will become a quaint custom reserved for a few traditionals.

Are such proclamations of the death of the family true? Let's look at sociological research.

The truth is that marriage flourishes. Although young Americans are taking longer to say "I do," they are still taking those vows. As you can see from Figure

TABLE 11-1 Average Size of U.S. Households

1960	1970	1980	1990	2000	2002
3.3	3.1	2.8	2.6	2.6	2.6

Source: By the author, based on *Statistical Abstract of the United States* 1991:Table 61; 1994:Table 70; 2003:Table 66.

11-12 on page 381, by the time they reach age 26 or 27, one half of all women are married. For men, that halfway mark hits at about age 29. Then comes a rush to the altar: By the end of their thirties, just one of seven women and one of five men remain unmarried. Overall, about 96 percent of Americans marry—perhaps the *highest* percentage in our history.

Other sociological research also indicates that the U.S. family is not disintegrating. Muncie, Indiana, is one of the most thoroughly researched of U.S. cities. In the 1920s and 1930s, sociologists Robert and Helen Lynd (1929, 1937) analyzed family life in this middle-American city, which they called "Middletown." In the 1980s, other sociologists went back to Muncie to find out if the family had declined during those 50 years. To see if it had, they checked the rates of suicide, mental breakdown, and domestic violence.

The Highest Marriage Rate in History
The "Middletown" Research

To their surprise, Theodore Caplow and his fellow researchers (1982) found that these problems were *less* frequent in Middletown than they had been two generations earlier. They also found that people are not living in isolated nuclear families, as some stereotypes indicate. Rather, the nuclear families are embedded in larger kin networks, where people find economic support and satisfying personal relationships. Most parents and their grown children keep in close touch. Perhaps these researchers' most surprising finding was that marriage had become more vibrant. Marriage in the 1920s was shallower; husbands and wives didn't talk as much with one another. Now that male and female roles are less segregated, husbands and wives talk things over more—and they are *more satisfied* with marriage. Caplow concludes that "for most of their members most of the time, Middletown's composite families provide a safe and comfortable niche in a hazardous world." *The idea that the family has declined is a "sociological myth."*

Yes, but . . .
Changes, but No Collapse

Despite such a rosy assessment, in this chapter you've seen some of the problems that U.S. families are struggling against. These challenges are severe. As I stressed earlier, the family always has been in transition, but recent transitions are startling. Figure 11-13 on page 382 shows that only a quarter of U.S. households consists of a married couple with their children, about the same as the number of Americans who live alone. Only 52 percent of all U.S. households are made up of married couples, with or without children. Don't interpret the category—"Married couple, no children"—as meaning childless couples. Married couples who have never had children are included in this category, to be sure, but most of these couples are "empty nesters": Their children have grown and left home.

Table 11-2 is another way of summarizing some of the vast changes that are engulfing the family. Note especially the increase in the number of children who are living with only one parent and the increase in cohabitation.

What shall we make of these contradictory findings? We can conclude that the changes and problems that the family is experiencing are not signs of its collapse. Despite divorce, cohabitation, births to unmarried women, family violence, and forces that pull people apart and even make them flee, for most people family life remains attractive: Americans are marrying at about their highest rate in history, and most divorced people eventually remarry, although more slowly than before. Some sociological research even documents areas of family life

"Money can't buy happiness" is an old saying. But it is not true. Money does buy happiness. Compared with poor people, wealthier people are more satisfied with life—and more optimistic about the future. Their health is better, they live longer, and even their marriages last longer.

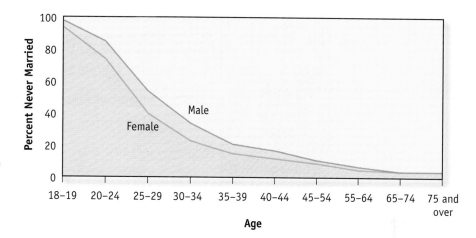

FIGURE 11-12 *The Percentage of Americans Who Have Never Married*

Source: By the author, based on *Statistical Abstract of the United States* 2003:Table 63.

that have improved over the years, especially more satisfying interaction between husbands and wives.

Social Policy

The Family Besieged by Professionals

Social policy for the family is mired in controversy, for every policy steps on someone's toes. In *Haven in a Heartless World* (1977), social historian Christopher Lasch said that people are looking to the family as a refuge of love and decency in a cruel and heartless world. The family, however, often cannot provide these comforts because it has been besieged by professionals—doctors, social workers, and teachers. These practitioners have attempted to enlarge their own professional domains at the expense of the family. Under the guise of helping, they have stripped the family of some of its functions, eroding its capacity to provide protective intimacy.

What did Lasch mean? One example is professionals who claim to be experts in sexual adjustment. They write books and magazine articles about what sexual relations be-

TABLE 11-2 How U.S. Families Are Changing

	1970	1980	1990	2000	2002	CHANGE SINCE 1970
Marriages performed	2,159,000	2,390,0000	2,448,000	2,200,000	2,200,000	+ 1.9%
Divorces granted	708,000	1,189,000	1,175,000	1,100,000	1,100,000	+55%
Married couples	47,500,000	52,300,000	56,300,000	56,497,000	57,915,000	+22%
Unmarried couples (cohabitants)	523,000	1,589,000	2,856,000	4,900,000	5,100,000*	+975%
Persons living alone	10,851,000	18,296,000	23,000,000	28,724,000	28,775,000	+265%
Married couples with children at home	25,541,000	24,961,000	24,537,000	25,248,000	25,791,000	+1%
Children living with both parents	58,926,000	48,294,000	46,658,000	47,013,000	47,100,000	−20%
Children living with one parent	8,230,000	11,528,000	16,624,000	16,391,000	16,421,000	+200%
Average size of household	3.3	2.8	2.6	2.6	2.6	−21%
Married woman who are employed	18,000,000	24,000,000	30,000,000	35,146,000	35,400,000	+197%

*Author's estimate.

Source: By the author, based on U.S. Department of Commerce and *Statistical Abstract of the United States* 1992:Tables 49, 52, 56, 60, 62, 66, 67, 68, 69, 73, 127, 134, 619; 2001:Table 59; 2003:Tables 66, 69, 71, 74, 596.

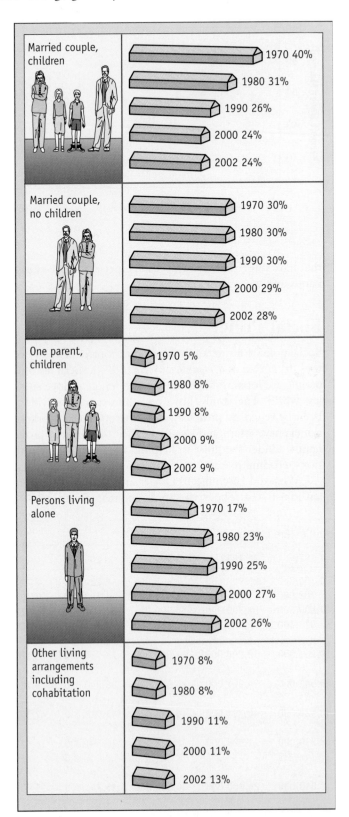

FIGURE 11-13   *What Are Americans' Living Arrangements?*

Source: By the author, based on *Statistical Abstract of the United States* 2003:Table 66.

tween husband and wife "ought" to be like. These self-styled experts appear on radio and television, where they proclaim their expertise. As a result, husbands and wives feel less able to work out their own sexual problems, for only "sexual experts" have the "real" answers. Another group of professionals stakes claim to child rearing. They profess to know the correct method for rearing children, making parents worry that, as mere laypersons, they might be damaging their children through clumsy, improper parenting. Husbands and wives, then, look to "professionals," who intrude into these traditionally private areas of family life.

In short, Lasch says, we are on a road that leads to a "therapeutic society," one in which "experts" claim that all problems are their domain. "Public concern" by "experts" about the plight of the family—publicized on television and radio, in magazines and books—masks what is really happening—taking away the family's authority and placing the family under control of outside influences. The situation is even worse than this, Lasch says, for contrary to popular opinion, "experts" have *not* benefited the family. Instead, they have marketed their services and products and established self-serving miniempires.

Professionals have reacted bitterly to this attack on their skills, accomplishments, and motives. They deny that they have self-serving motives and that they intrude into family life, undermine its authority, and reduce its "self-sufficiency" (Joffe 1978). The troubled family needs them, they reply.

The Dilemma of Family Policy: Taking Sides

Lasch's denunciations expose a core dilemma. Any social policy for the family finds itself on one side or the other of issues that divide fair-minded people who have the best interests of the family at heart. For example, consider what seems to be a neutral matter, making financial aid available to troubled families. One side suggests that such a policy would aid the family; another side, however, sees it as an attack on family self-sufficiency; it discourages families from looking out for themselves, making them further dependent on "Big Brother."

The Battleground of Definitions: Intervention or Interference?

Another example is Hillary Rodham Clinton's book, *It Takes a Village: And Other Lessons Children Teach Us.* Clinton's declared purpose was to make the public aware of the need of community involvement in child care. Yet the book set off a storm of controversy: It alarmed some people, who viewed the book as a rallying cry for the state to intrude on the family, to eventually take child rearing away from parents.

How Values Underlie Policy

Almost all policy falls on one side or the other of this explosive issue. Suppose that parents tell their 14-year-old girl that she cannot have sex because premarital sex is wrong. The daughter faces a dilemma. She is afraid that if she does not have sex with her boyfriend, he will date more cooperative girls. She also is "in love," and she wants to please her boyfriend. The girl goes to a family planning clinic and tells them her plight. Counselors encourage her to assert herself against domineering and old-fashioned parents. They assure her that she can come to them for a free and confidential abortion if she becomes pregnant. They also offer her a Norplant.

Who is "right" in this example? As symbolic interactionists stress, our understanding of what "ought" to be depends on our values. As sociologist Carole Joffe (1978), who originated this example, said: From one perspective, the decision of a teenager to seek out adequate contraception is a step forward in "liberation." From another standpoint, of course, to talk about "adequate" contraception is to prejudge the issue. From this perspective, this example does not represent a step toward "liberation," but, rather, an intrusion on family privacy.

Each Family Member Has a Different Experience and View

We face divisive issues, then, when it comes to family social policy. In this context, it is important to emphasize the symbolic interactionist position—that different family members experience family life differently. Arrangements that some family members find comfortable and satisfying, others find oppressive (Joffe 1978). As the Thinking Critically box on children's rights on the next page highlights, an issue that pervades family policy is that helping some family members harms others. What is government intervention to some is government interference to others. Both sides agree, however, that the young and defenseless need to be protected from physical and psychological harm and exploitation, as well as from anything that deprives them of their health and well-being. But even here, a basic dilemma plagues social policy: encouraging families to be responsible and independent versus protecting individuals within the family (Chilman 1988). How do we protect individuals without a "Big Brother" to watch over every family's shoulder?

Thinking Critically about Social Problems
CHILDREN'S RIGHTS

In 1943, the U.S. Supreme Court determined that a cardinal principle of U.S. law is that "the custody, care, and nurture of the child reside in the parents." This decision usually has been interpreted to mean that parents have a total right to decide matters concerning the welfare of their children, with the state intervening only to stop abuse or neglect. [Go to the next column.]

TO PROTECT CHILDREN FROM DOMINEERING PARENTS, WE MUST STRENGTHEN CHILDREN'S RIGHTS.

In the journal *Human Rights,* Patricia Wald (1974) wrote that a "very young child" has the right "to be consulted and informed about critical decisions in his life, and (the) right to be represented in those decisions." To protect the child from the "consequences of unilateral parental actions . . . the child's interests deserve representation by an independent advocate before a neutral decision maker."

Wald also suggested that communities provide runaway shelters (or homes) for children under 16 who do not want to return home. "Parents would have no right to forcibly take their children away from such homes," she proposed. A child ought to be able to seek legal advice to redress grievances against his or her family. Some say that children should be able to sue their parents for poor child rearing.

These proposals are designed to balance a system that currently favors the parents at the expense of children. For example, as things now stand, if parents want to take a job out of town, they do. The child has no choice in the matter and simply has to move with them. This is a "crucial decision that affects the child's life": If the parents move, the child has to leave friends and attend a new school. The child should have the right to "an independent advocate to argue his or her case before a neutral decision maker." If the child does not want to go and the parents insist on moving, the independent advocate should be able to remove the child from the family.

Americans, however, are divided over the rights that parents should have over their children. The central question is: At what point does the authority of the state supersede the authority of parents? When does the privacy of the family take precedence over the concern of well-intentioned outsiders? Let's look at the major arguments.

TO PROTECT FAMILIES FROM "BIG BROTHER," WE MUST STRENGTHEN PARENTS' RIGHTS.

The threat to children's well-being does not come from parents but from an increasingly intrusive government. To assure the rights of fathers and mothers to parent their own children, Phyllis Schlafly (1979) proposed The Family Protection Act. This Act would guarantee that:

1. Parents have the right to visit public school classrooms and school functions.
2. Parents can review textbooks before public schools adopt them.
3. No federal funding will be given for courses that encourage children to rethink the values that their parents have taught them, courses often called "values clarification" and "behavior modification."
4. Parents must give their consent for their children to enroll in courses about religion or "ethics," and can keep their children out of such courses that they find offensive.
5. Parents must give consent for unmarried minors to get contraceptives or an abortion and must be informed if their child is treated for a venereal disease.
6. If a child's "right to self-expression" conflicts with the parents' "right to educate or discipline," in the absence of compelling evidence of parental unfitness, the courts must rule in favor of the parents.

The Issue of Poverty

Apart from certain family problems, such as marital rape and child abuse, many sociologists see poverty as the root of family troubles. Some sociologists suggest that a guaranteed family income is the best solution to family poverty. Others see the solution as a robust economy with full employment. To this, we might add educational opportunities open to all. Income, jobs, and education would not solve all the family's problems, especially, say conflict theorists, those that are rooted in sexist-power orientations. They would, however, go a long way to solving many of them.

The Future of the Problem

The Sea of Social Change

Social change is the hallmark of our society. Seemingly overnight, familiar landmarks are torn down and replaced by a strip mall or by another of an endless series of fast-food outlets. Computers recognize your speech, type your message, and check your grammar; devices connected to the Global Positioning System announce your location, even guide you through traffic in a strange city. On the Internet, type something in English, and it can be translated instantly into German or Spanish or any major language before being transmitted to someone in a distant part of the world. (It comes out garbled, but that will change.) Soon you'll be able to have one telephone number that will stay with you for life and will be valid throughout the world. Change is so rapid and extensive that parents and children live in different worlds—so much so that grown children who are visiting their parents after an absence of months or even years often find that after the first hour or two they have little left to talk about.

Future Shock

The speed, extent, and intensity of today's social change are mind-boggling. We barely get used to one idea, object, or relationship when another overpowers it—and us. Alvin Toffler (1971) called this dizzying barrage of change to which we have no leisure or opportunity to adjust future shock. **Future shock** is the vertigo, the confusion, the disorientation that we experience when our familiar world is transformed.

The U.S. family is experiencing future shock. It has already had to adapt to large-scale social change, for industrialization and urbanization left little untouched. Now computers are changing the worlds of work, education, recreation, and entertainment. Parents and children e-mail one another from office, school, and home, giving brief updates on changing plans. Because the family is continuing to adapt to changing social conditions, its future is unclear. But let's venture into these uncharted waters.

Changes We Can Expect

The lofty goals of love and marriage are established firmly in our culture, and love will continue to be the "proper" basis for marriage. People will also continue to marry at a rate close to what we now have. The age at first marriage will continue upward a while longer, then stabilize. Cohabitation will continue to increase for another decade, and then gradually level off. The proportion of married women who are employed outside the home will continue to increase, eventually plateauing at about 75 to 80 percent. Marriage will become even more oriented around companionship. With this orientation coupled with more wives working outside the home, husbands and wives will develop more equal relationships. Marriage will remain brittle, and the United States will continue to have one of the highest divorce rates in the world. Day care will become more common for children of working parents (see the Issues box on the next page). Whether you interpret such changes as good, bad, or indifferent depends, of course, on your values.

The Ideological Struggle

The struggle by ideologically committed groups to control the family will intensify. Family policy will mirror these contrasting ideologies. With their incompatible views of right, justice, and the good life, oppositional groups will continue to try to make family policy conform to their own vision of reality. Regardless of who wins in the short term, this competition of ideas and values will continue. The future looks exciting, the outcome uncertain. This struggle is not theoretical or abstract: Much of your own family life hangs in the balance.

Issues in Social Problems
WHAT DOES DAY CARE COST A COMPANY?

Suppose that you are the president of Union Bank in Monterey, California. Some of your employees have asked you to provide a day-care center. You would like to do so, but you can't spend stockholders' money on day care simply because you think it is a nice idea. You have to know the bottom line.

"Find out what it would cost us to have a day-care center," the manager told Sandra Burud, a social science researcher. At first, determining costs may sound fairly easy. You simply add the cost of the facilities and personnel, and you have the answer. But what you want to know is the *net* cost. After all, day care is supposed to benefit the company. Will the benefits be greater or less than the cost? How much in either direction?

Now the problem becomes difficult. How can you accurately estimate changes that the day care center will make in employee turnover? This, in turn, will change interview costs, hiring bonuses, and job advertisements. Then, too, you have to try to measure productive time lost while an employee is on maternity leave or is job hunting, while a job goes unfilled, or while a new employee is learning the ropes. Employee turnover is costly: Merck Pharmaceuticals has determined that during their first fourteen months on the job new employees cost the company five months of work. Some costs are impossible to measure, such as poor morale and loss of reputation with the community if a lot of employees quit. In fact, Burud decided that she couldn't put numbers on these variables and had to skip them.

In the midst of such uncertainties, Union Bank decided to go ahead and open a day-care center. This cost the bank $105,000. Then Burud compared 87 employees who used the center with a control group of 105 employees who didn't use the center. She found that employee turnover among the center's users was 2 percent; among the control group, it was 10 percent. Employees who used the center were also absent an average of two days a year less than the control group. Their maternity leaves were also one week shorter.

The bottom line? After subtracting its costs of running the day-care center, the bank saved $232,000.

Should you, the president, have your bank open a day-care center? Now, that is an easy decision.

Such companies as Marriott Hotels have paid attention to the bottom-line results of corporate day care and have opened their own centers. Other companies, such as Levi Strauss and AT&T, subsidize their employees' child care.

Based on Solomon 1988; Shellenbarger 1994.

SUMMARY

1. The family is always adjusting to social change. One of the most significant effects of the industrial revolution was the removal of economic production from the household.

2. Whether change within the family is perceived as a social problem or as merely a form of adaptation depends on people's values. Indicators that many see as evidence of a social problem are divorce, runaway children, births to single women, one-parent families, and violence and sexual abuse in the family.

3. In analyzing why the divorce rate is high, symbolic interactionists stress the changing ideas of sex roles and expectations of marriage; functionalists, the declining functions of the family; and conflict theorists, a changing distribution of power in the family.

4. The average age at first marriage declined from 1890 to about 1950, then began to increase in about 1970. Today, the average age at first marriage is about the highest in our history. The primary reason is *cohabitation*. As many people postpone marriage, a growing proportion of the young remain single.

5. Married couples without children remain childless because of infertility, the decision not to have children, or the continuous postponement of children until childlessness becomes inevitable. Childless couples face a stigma.

6. Physical violence between family members is common. Although wives initiate about as much violence as husbands, they are injured more often. People reared in violent homes are more likely to be violent to their own spouses and children. Incest and marital rape are more frequent than commonly supposed.

7. That the elderly are abandoned by their families is a myth: Most adult children and their parents keep in close touch.

The elderly prefer to live near their children, but not with them, a preference called "intimacy at a distance." Widowhood appears to be easier for men than women; this is not due to gender—rather, those who are better off financially adjust better to the death of a spouse.

8. The family is far from doomed, and is much healthier than most imagine. More Americans are marrying today than ever. The "Middletown" studies indicate that today's husbands and wives are more satisfied with married life than married couples were 50 years ago.

9. Social policy on the family is controversial because it pits individual rights against government intervention. Some even accuse "family professionals" of expanding their domain at the expense of the family.

10. These trends are likely to continue: increases in cohabitation, age at first marriage, two-paycheck families, day care, and marital equality. Groups that are concerned about the family differ in their ideas about the way the family "should" be, and it remains to be seen which groups will be most influential in determining social policy.

KEY TERMS

Cohabitation A couple who are living together in a sexual relationship outside marriage.

Extended family A family in which other relatives, such as the "older generation" or unmarried aunts and uncles, live with the parents and their children.

Family of orientation The family into which people are born and from which they receive their basic orientations to life.

Family of procreation The family that is formed by marriage and that generally results in procreation, or the birth of children.

Future shock The confusion or disorientation that accompanies rapid social change.

Incest Forbidden sexual relations between relatives, such as brothers and sisters or parents and children.

Nuclear family A family that consists of a husband, wife, and their children.

Personal trouble A problem that an individual experiences. If this trouble is widespread and enough people become concerned about it, it is a social problem. Examples are unemployment and divorce.

THINKING CRITICALLY ABOUT CHAPTER 11

1. What do you consider to be the three greatest benefits and the three greatest downsides of the changes in the composition of U.S. families? Do you think that these changes are bringing more negatives or positives? Explain.

2. Which perspective (symbolic interactionism, functionalism, or conflict theory) do you think does a better job of explaining the changes that are taking place in U.S. families? Explain.

3. Rank the seven traditional functions of the family according to how important you think they are today. Explain your rankings.

4. With the huge increase in cohabitation, the high divorce rate, the number of runaways, and the extent of abuse in families, how can the author not conclude that marriage is doomed? Explain.

CHAPTER 12

Urban Problems

KELLIE MOISER WAS A 17-YEAR-OLD high school student who worked part time at the corner ice-cream store. Since she was a little girl, Kellie had dreamed of becoming a model. Kellie's mother encouraged her dream, hoping that it would be a way out of the ghetto.

But Kellie never got the chance.

Michael Hagan, 23, also lived in the slums of south-central Los Angeles. He likes Olde English "800" Malt Liquor, especially when he smokes PCP.

He also likes guns.

And a little blood doesn't bother him, either.

One Monday evening, Hagan was on a binge with other members of his gang, when they decided to go after a rival gang. They piled into an old Buick and sped toward enemy turf. There they spotted four teenagers, two boys and two girls.

The teenagers were not gang members. They were just kids who had gone out for ice cream. When they saw the gun, they ran. Kellie didn't run fast enough. Hagan methodically pumped fifteen slugs into her, six into her back.

The cops took the killing in stride. For them, it was just one more in an endless stream of murders that occur in this part of the city. They didn't have much to go on, witnesses clammed up, and the detectives had other priorities.

Kellie's mother didn't have much to go on, either, but she set out to solve her daughter's murder. Out of a fury born of grief, she stormed the streets in search of the killers. She even barged into local drug houses. The word got around, and a sympathetic inmate in the county jail sent her a letter telling her the name of the shooter.

Kellie's mother shook her head in disbelief when she found out who had killed her daughter. She said, "I knew these gang members when they were just babies. Now look at them. They've turned into killers."

Hagan, the shooter, says, "Jail ain't bad. To me, life ain't much better on the streets than in jail. I can live here; no problem."

"The gang is your family," Hagan explains. "If you're a Crip, I fight for you, no matter what the odds. If you're the enemy, it's do or die."

Hagan adds, "If I had a son, I'd give him a choice: Either he can go to school and be a goody-goody, or he can hit the streets."

Hagan smiles broadly as he adds, "I done did something, and I'm known. I consider myself Public Enemy Number 1."

Based on Hull 1987.

The Problem in Sociological Perspective

Hagan is part of the American nightmare—the unsafe streets, the drive-by shootings, the senseless killings, without conscience, that destroy those who are trying to build a future. Before we get to Hagan, however, let's look at the history of cities.

The Global Urban Movement

Two hundred years ago, almost everyone in the world lived in rural areas. Only 3 percent lived in towns of 5,000 or more (Hauser and Schnore 1965). By 1900, the total of city dwellers was up to 13 or 14 percent. Today, about half of the entire world lives in cities (Massey 2001).

In its early years, the United States, too, was almost exclusively rural. In 1800, only about 6 of 100 Americans lived in towns of 2,500 or more. As Figure 12-1 shows, cities became increasingly popular as places to live, and by around 1920 half of Americans lived in cities. Today, 4 of every 5 Americans do, but as illustrated by the Social Map on page 391, urbanization differs considerably from state to state.

389

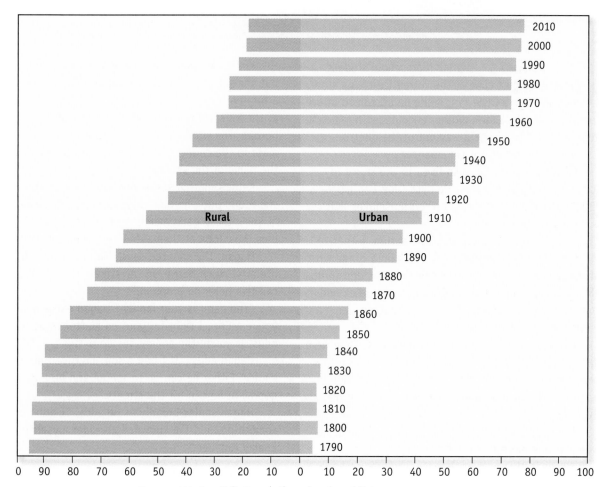

FIGURE 12-1   *U.S. Population, Rural and Urban*

Source: By the author, based on *U.S. Bureau of the Census; Statistical Abstract of the United States* 2003:Table 30. The projections from 2000 to 2010 are by the author.

The Evolution of Cities

Although the speed and extent of today's urbanization are new to the world scene, cities are not. Somewhere between 6000 and 8000 B.C., people may have built cities with massive walls, such as biblically famous Jericho (Homblin 1973). Some, however, think that cities originated later, in conjunction with the invention of writing. For certain, by 3500 B.C. there were cities in several parts of the world. They appeared first in Mesopotamia, then in the Nile, Indus, and Yellow River valleys, around the Mediterranean, in West Africa, Central America, and the Andes (Fischer 1976).

Agriculture was the key to the development of cities. Only when people produce a surplus of food are some people able to stop farming and gather in cities to pursue other occupations. A **city,** in fact, can be defined as a large number of people who live in one place and do not produce their own food. As agricultural techniques become more efficient, they spur urban development. During the fourth millennium B.C., the plow was invented: As this invention spread, the resulting agricultural surplus stimulated the development of towns and cities across wide areas of the world.

Early plows, although a great improvement on the digging sticks that had been used, were primitive, and for the next five thousand years, the food surplus was only enough to allow a small minority of the world's population to live in urban areas. Then

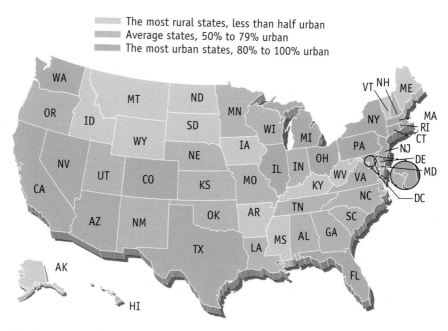

The most rural states, less than half urban
Average states, 50% to 79% urban
The most urban states, 80% to 100% urban

FIGURE 12-2 *How Urban Is Your State?*

Source: By the author, based on *Statistical Abstract of the United States* 2002:Table 29.

Note: The most urban state is New Jersey; the source reports that it is 100 percent urban. The most rural state is nearby Vermont, where 72 percent live in rural areas.

came the Industrial Revolution of the 1700s and 1800s, which sparked the urban revolution that we are still experiencing. The Industrial Revolution stimulated not only the invention of mechanical means of farming, which brought food in abundance, but also mechanical means of transportation and communication. These allow people, resources, and products to be moved efficiently—essential factors on which the modern city depends.

Cities as Solutions

In and of themselves, cities are not problems, so why is this a topic in a social problems text? Cites are actually designed to solve problems, to make life better by transcending the limitations of farm and village. Cities offer the hope of a better life, of gaining work, education, and other advantages. With these benefits, cities are growing around the world. As discussed in the Global Glimpse box on page 393, people in the Least Industrialized Nations are deserting their rural way of life and flocking to urban areas for just these reasons.

Table 12-1 on the next page lists the world's ten largest cities. Only four of these megacities are in the Most Industrialized Nations, and they are growing slower than those in the Least Industrialized Nations. In fifteen years, New York City, Osaka, and Los Angeles are expected to drop off this list. Of the many cities in the Most Industrialized Nations, only Tokyo will remain as one of the world's ten largest cities. Tokyo will still be the world's largest city, but it will be followed by Bombay, Lagos, Shanghai, Jakarta, São Paulo, Karachi, Beijing, Dhaka, and Mexico City (*United Nations Demographic Yearbook* 1997).

Cities as Problems

In the next section, we'll survey the scope of urban problems, but first I want to stress that this central context underlies many of those problems: Cities have a difficult time meeting people's needs for **community,** a feeling of belonging, the sense that others care what happens to you and that you can depend on the people around you. Some people do find community in the city, but others find alienation, and they live in isolation and fear. Some people, like Hagan, even band together to create fear, making the city, for many, a miserable place to live.

TABLE 12-1 The World's Ten Largest Cities

RANK	CITY	COUNTRY	POPULATION 2000	REMARKS
1	Tokyo	Japan	33,900,000	incl. Yokohama, Kawasaki
2	Mexico City	Mexico	22,500,000	incl. Nezahualcóyotl, Ecatepec, Naucalpan
3	Seoul	South Korea	21,900,000	incl. Bucheon, Goyang, Incheon, Seongnam
4	New York	USA	21,750,000	incl. Newark, Paterson
5	São Paulo	Brazil	19,900,000	incl. Guarulhos
6	Bombay	India	19.200,000	incl. Kalyan, Thane, Ulhasnagar
7	Delhi	India	18,700,000	incl. Faridabad, Ghaziabad
8	Los Angeles	USA	17,600,000	incl. Riverside, Anaheim
9	Osaka	Japan	16,750,000	incl. Kobe, Kyoto
10	Jakarta	Indonesia	16,650,000	incl. Bekasi, Bogor, Depok, Tangerang

Source: By the author, based on Brinkhoff 2004.

The Scope of the Problem

An Antiurban Bias

Thinking of the city as a source of problems is nothing new. In 1780, Thomas Jefferson said that cities were "pestilential to the morals, the health, and the liberties of man." Jefferson (1977) added that cities contribute to the good government of a nation about as much as sores contribute to the strength of the body. The other extreme is an image that many Americans carry of rural life as the serene source of virtue, an agrarian paradise where life is innocent, simple, and happy (Hadden and Barton 1973). The cold brutality of urban life—the Hagans wandering the streets in search of victims—makes people long for something better. The bottom line of attitudes is a deep ambivalence: People dream of fleeing the city to find safety and security in a simpler life, yet they remain fascinated with the city, seeking it for work, cultural attractions, and diversions.

An Ambivalence

This ambivalence toward the city—its threat and its allure—will be woven throughout this chapter as we examine major problems that face our cities.

What Is Urban About Urban Problems?

In one sense, almost all social problems are "urban." Because most Americans live in cities, poverty, crime, unemployment, divorce, drug addiction, violence, and so forth are concentrated in cities. None of these problems is urban by nature, however, because these problems can—and do—occur everywhere. Aside from their greater frequency in cities, there is little that is specifically urban about such problems.

In two senses, however, there are *urban* problems. First, city life *increases* social problems. For example, the *rates* of burglary, robbery, suicide, alcoholism, and rape are *higher* in cities than in rural areas. Why should this be? Why do cities increase such behaviors and even produce people like Hagan? Or, conversely, why do rural areas diminish them? We will return to this question, for it is central to understanding urban problems.

Second, the United States is facing an *urban crisis*. U.S. cities have areas that almost everyone fears and avoids. There, amidst burned out and boarded-up buildings, addicts and the unemployed slouch on apartment steps. Drug dealers openly work "their" street corners, a lucrative turf that they defend by violence. Hagans prowl the filthy streets, mugging and raping and killing. Anyone who enters these areas is at peril—even the police. There are other indications of an urban crisis. During economic downturns, some cities shorten the school year because they cannot meet the payroll. Some slash library and garbage collection budgets and even reduce police and fire protection. Across the nation the middle class has rushed to the suburbs, abandoning the inner city to the poor, a flight that has impoverished the city. Another problem is **urban sprawl;** as cities expand, they invade the countryside, devouring farmland, leaving in

A Global Glimpse

WHY CITY SLUMS ARE BETTER THAN THE COUNTRY: THE RUSH TO THE CITIES OF THE LEAST INDUSTRIALIZED NATIONS

Thoughts of the Least Industrialized Nations often bring images of people tending animals or harvesting crops, enjoying a peaceful life in the green countryside or along babbling brooks. Such images no longer represent the reality that most people in the Least Industrial Nations face—if ever they did. The rural poor of these countries are flocking to the cities at such a rate that, as we saw in Table 12-1, the Least Industrialized Nations now contain most of the world's largest cities. In the Most Industrialized Nations, industrialization generally preceded urbanization, but in the Least Industrialized Nations *urbanization is preceding industrialization.* These cities cannot support their swelling populations.

The settlement patterns are also different in these cities. When rural migrants and immigrants move to U.S. cities, they usually settle in deteriorating housing near the city's center. The wealthy reside in suburbs and luxurious city enclaves. Migrants to cities of the Least Industrialized Nations, in contrast, establish illegal squatter settlements outside the city. There they build shacks from scrap boards, cardboard, and bits of corrugated metal. Even flattened tin cans are scavenged for building material. The squatters enjoy no city facilities—roads, public transportation, water, sewers, or garbage pickup. After thousands of squatters have settled an area, the city reluctantly acknowledges their right to live there and adds bus service and minimal water lines. Hundreds of people use a single spigot. About *5 million* of Mexico City's residents live in such squalid conditions, with hundreds of thousands more pouring in each year.

Why this rush to live in the city under such miserable conditions? At its core are the "push" factors that arise from a breakdown of traditional rural life. With a safer water supply and the importation of modern medicine, the death rate in rural areas dropped. As a result, their populations multiplied, and no longer is there enough land to divide up among children. Without land, there is hunger. People are deeply dissatisfied with the resulting hardscrabble character of rural life. Then, too, there are the "pull" factors that draw people to the cities—jobs, schools, housing, and even a more stimulating life.

At the bottom of a ravine near Mexico City is a dismal bunch of shacks. Some of the parents have 14 children.

"We used to live up there," Señora Gonzalez gestured toward the mountain, "in those caves. Our only hope was one day to have a place to live. And now we do." She smiled with pride at the jerry-built shacks . . . each one had a collection of flowers planted in tin cans. "One day, we hope to extend the water pipes and drainage—perhaps even pave. . . ."

And what was the name of her community? Señora Gonzalez beamed. "Esperanza!" (McDowell 1984:172)

Esperanza is the Spanish word for hope. This is what lies behind the rush to these cities—the hope of a better life. And this is why the rush won't slow down. In 1930, only one Latin American city had over a million people—now fifty do! The world's cities are growing by one million people each week (Brockerhoff 2000).

Will the Least Industrialized Nations adjust to this vast migration? They have no choice. Authorities in Brazil, Guatemala, Venezuela, and other countries have sent in the police and even the army to evict the settlers. It doesn't work. This just leads to violence, and the settlers keep streaming in. The adjustments will be painful. The infrastructure (roads, water, sewers, electricity, and so on) must be built, but these poor countries don't have the resources to build them. As the desperate rural poor flock to the cities, the problems will worsen.

Do you see any solutions?

its place asphalt and buildings. The term **urban crisis** refers to this cluster of interrelated urban problems.

Looking at the Problem Theoretically

As usual, our three theoretical perspectives yield contrasting insights. As we apply symbolic interactionism to the inner city, we will glimpse the "slum's" social organization, which ordinarily remains invisible to outsiders. Using functionalism will make visible the zones of activity that develop as a city expands. Finally, from the conflict perspective, we will see how class conflict creates urban problems.

SYMBOLIC INTERACTIONISM

Symbolic Interactionists Provide an Insider's View of Social Life, Including Slums

If Americans are ambivalent about the city, they are not so when it comes to the inner city. Most fear them, and everyone avoids them. Most middle-class Americans shake their heads and say that they can't understand why anyone would live "like that."

These are outsider's views. Symbolic interactionists try to see how life looks to the people who live it. They try to discover the meanings that people give to their experiences, how they feel about their situation, and how they cope with their problems. As symbolic interactionists study the worlds of the urban poor, they try not to impose their own values or views on others. This approach to understanding urban life is called the **Chicago school of sociology,** because it represents the approach used by the sociology department of the University of Chicago in the 1920s and 1930s. This department produced classic studies of urban life. In 1923 Nels Anderson wrote *The Hobo,* followed in 1927 by Frederic Thrasher's *The Gang.* In 1929 Harvey Zorbaugh's *The Gold Coast and the Slum* contrasted the poor and the rich in Chicago. Then, in 1932, Paul Cressey published *Taxi-Dance Hall,* about women who made their living by dancing with men. Making the city their sociological laboratory, these sociologists, as others have done since, focused mostly on the lives of the poor.

The Chicago School of Sociology

The contrasts of the city—its many groups with their distinctive ways of life—fascinated sociologists at Chicago. They were impressed with how people of different backgrounds develop unique subcultures and live in separate areas of the city. As Louis Wirth (1938) said, the city is made up of "a mosaic of social worlds." Sociologists today also find these social worlds fascinatingly different, and they remain topics of sociological research. These smaller social worlds that urban people live in have unique codes and understandings of social life. These distinctive customs make it easy for people from different areas to misunderstand one another.

Whyte's Study

In this tradition, sociologist William Foote Whyte did participant observation in an inner city for two or three years. In the classic book that he wrote to recount his experiences, *Street Corner Society* (1943, 1995), Whyte explains that what may look to outsiders to be disorganized is, in fact, a tightly knit way of life. By participating in the residents' lives—hanging around the street corner with "the boys," going to dances, bowling, playing baseball—Whyte was able to identify the various types of people who lived there. The young men separated themselves into two main groups: the college boys, who were upward bound, and the corner boys, who remained in their old neighborhood. Each group was further subdivided into smaller worlds, such as the group of young men whom Whyte met each evening. Other major groups were the racketeers and politicians. Each group had its own statuses, its own norms, and its own ways of controlling its members.

Suttles's Study

Thirty years later, sociologist Gerald Suttles did participant observation in an inner city of Chicago. He found social statuses and forms of communication equally as complex as those Whyte had uncovered among the Italians he studied. Suttles documents how African Americans, Puerto Ricans, Chicanos, and Italians, although sharing the same physical space, have their own forms of communication. One group's customary ways of expressing itself—its distinctive language, gestures, and clothing—are often offensive to members of another group. How people make eye contact is an example. Here's what Suttles (1968:66–67) says:

Whites say that Negroes will not look them in the eye. The Negroes counter by saying the whites are impolite and try to "cow" people by staring at them. . . . The most subtle accounts are those which describe almost entirely nonverbal encounters: "When I went over to the Negro nurse, she didn't even look up," "I'd go again (to an Italian restaurant) but they really stare you down," "I can understand why those guys (older Italians) can't half speak English, but why they gotta eyeball everybody walk past?"

Within each area of the city, different groups stake out a unique existence. They develop their own ways to express themselves, live by their own codes, and evaluate their members accordingly. Although these background assumptions unite a group's members, they hinder communication with others. This creates hostility among the diverse groups that compose the urban mosaic. As the quote from Suttles shows, these differences lead to suspicion and misunderstanding. They can even lead to death.

Anderson's Studies

Sociologist Elijah Anderson did participant observation in yet another Chicago slum. He, too, emphasizes how you cannot understand a group of people unless you see the world as they see it. Focusing on Jelly's, a bar and liquor store in an African-American area, Anderson (1978) explains the intricate boundaries between "us" and "them." He found three main groups at Jelly's:

The regulars. These men see and present themselves as hard-working. They subscribe to mainstream values, are proud of their involvement in families, and have aspirations of getting ahead. Their values can be summed up with the single word *decency*—working regularly and treating other people right.

The wineheads. These men neither value work, nor do they work regularly. Their main concern is getting enough money to buy wine. They beg from others and have low status.

The hoodlums. These men pride themselves on "being tough" and having access to easy money. Few work regularly. They are involved in petty theft, stickups, burglaries, and fencing stolen property. The other men at Jelly's do not trust them, nor do they trust one another.

When Anderson (1990, 1995) was hired as a sociologist at the University of Pennsylvania, he moved into what he calls the Village-Norton, a neighborhood in Philadelphia that was being "gentrified"; that is, more affluent people were moving into the area and rehabilitating its buildings. **Gentrification** creates tensions because it raises property values, taxes, and rents, forcing the poorer residents to move to lower-rent areas. Although the area begins to look prettier, the poor resent the invasion of their neighborhood and do not benefit from it.

The Village-Norton bordered an African-American ghetto, and tension between residents of the two areas was high. Both African-American and white residents viewed with suspicion any unknown African American who was on the streets of the Village-Norton. Eye contact was a significant source of tension. Whites were afraid to look too long at African Americans that they didn't know, fearing that their look might be interpreted as an invitation to interact. To avoid this problem, whites either pretended not to see African Americans or else they looked right through them without speaking. Used to more outgoing interaction, many African Americans found this behavior offensive. The truce was uneasy, and only after people lived in the area for a while did they learn the norms that reduce tension and allow the two groups to coexist. In the *Spotlight on Research* box on the next page, Anderson discusses the "code of the street."

In Sum

Within any area of the city, groups stake out territory, establish social boundaries between themselves and others, and work out a sense of identity and belonging. This is no less true of the residents of the inner city. If you look beyond the run-down buildings, you find intricate patterns of social behavior. People there, like people everywhere, interact on the basis of background assumptions and within social networks of associations and friendships. The assumptions, codes, and norms of inner-city residents, however, often differ sharply from those of the middle class.

Symbolic interactionists also remind us that the poor do not experience urban problems in the abstract. They encounter specific problems. For example, the poor do

SPOTLIGHT ON RESEARCH

The Code of the Street

While a graduate student at the University of Chicago, Elijah Anderson began to study the men who hung around a Southside bar named Jelly's. As an outsider, he drew attention the first time he entered the bar, but after ordering a drink, the curiosity of others seemed temporarily satisfied. It was here where Anderson, now Professor of Sociology at the University of Pennsylvania, learned about the social world of the urban ghetto and the "code of the street."

Of all the problems that beset the inner-city poor black community, none is more pressing than that of interpersonal violence and aggression. Violence wreaks havoc with the lives of community residents and increasingly spills over into downtown and residential middle-class areas. The inclination to violence springs from the circumstances of life among the ghetto poor: the lack of jobs that pay a living wage, the stigma of race, the fallout from rampant drug use and drug trafficking, and the resulting alienation and lack of hope for the future.

Out of this pervasive despair has evolved a street culture. This code of the street consists of informal rules that govern behavior in public, including violence. By regulating the use of violence, the code allows those who are inclined to aggression to precipitate violent encounters in an approved way.

At the heart of the code is the issue of respect—of being treated "right," or granted the deference that one deserves. In the street culture, especially among young people, respect is viewed almost as an external entity. It is hard-won but easily lost, and so must be guarded constantly. By his appearance—including his clothing, demeanor, and way of moving—a man feels that he possesses a measure of respect and that he can avoid "being bothered" in public. If he is bothered, not only may he be in physical danger, but also he has been disgraced or "dissed" (disrespected).

The code of the street is a cultural adaptation to the profound sense of alienation from mainstream society and its institutions that many poor inner-city black people feel. This includes their lack of confidence in the police and the judicial system. When called, the police may not respond, which is one reason that many residents feel that they must be prepared to defend themselves and their loved ones against those who are inclined to aggression. Thus the person who is believed capable of "taking care of himself" is accorded respect.

The code of the street has emerged as a result of the breakdown or weaknesses of civil law in the most distressed inner-city communities. It is a survival strategy that centers on reputation, respect, retribution, and retaliation. When people rely on themselves and their reputation for protection, we have a situation that leads to high rates of violence. A legacy of institutionalized racism, joblessness, and alienation suffuses distressed inner-city neighborhoods and exacerbates these conditions.

---

not experience the *concept* of urban decay. Rather, they deal with cutbacks in city services; buses that run late or not at all; factories that move to Mexico and wipe out their jobs overnight; and killers like Hagan who stalk their neighborhood, hallways, and elevators. In short, symbolic interactionists focus on how people make sense of their experiences as they attempt to cope with urban life.

FUNCTIONALISM

Burgess's Theory of Concentric Zones

The University of Chicago also produced urban studies that reflect the functionalist perspective. One of the main studies was done by sociologist Ernest Burgess, who analyzed how cities grow. As Figure 12-3 illustrates, he located five zones, each with distinct functions. Burgess visualized the city as expanding outward from its center, the central business district (Zone I). Zone II, which encircles the downtown area, con-

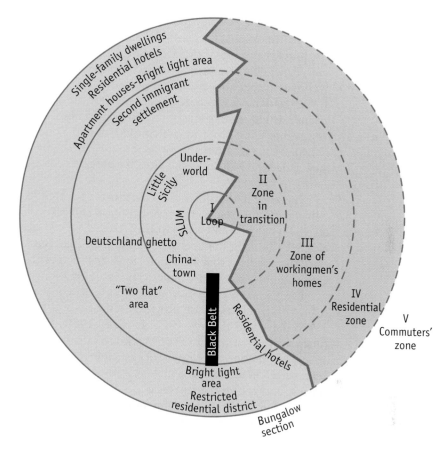

FIGURE 12-3 *Burgess's Concentric Zone Theory of the Growth of the City*

Source: From Ernest W. Burgess. "The Growth of the City: An Introduction to a Research Project" in *The City*. Robert E. Park, Ernest W. Burgess, and Roderick D. McKenzie, eds. Chicago: University of Chicago Press, 1925. (Pages 47–62 in the 1967 edition). Reprinted with the permission of the University of Chicago Press.

Note: On the right side of this figure are the concentric zones that flow from the central business district as a city expands. The left side shows the city of Chicago in 1925. The jagged vertical line represents the shore of Lake Erie.

tains the city's slums. To escape the slum, skilled and thrifty workers move to Zone III. Zone IV contains better apartments, residential hotels, single-family dwellings, and gated communities where the wealthy live. Still farther out, beyond the city limits, is Zone V, a commuter zone of suburbs or satellite cities.

Burgess intended his **concentric zone theory** to represent the "tendencies of any town or city to expand radially from its central business district." He noted, however, that no "city fits perfectly this ideal scheme." Some cities face physical obstacles such as lakes or rivers that make their expansion depart from this model. As Burgess also noted, businesses deviate from this model when they locate in outlying zones. This was in 1925. Burgess didn't know it, but he was seeing the beginning of a major shift that led to today's suburban shopping malls, strung like beads around the city. This shift has been so strong that malls today account for most of the country's retail sales.

Mobility as an Essential Characteristic of Cities

This classic model of urban growth helps us understand urban problems. Burgess stressed that city dwellers are always on the move. In addition to commuting for work, school, shopping, and recreation, they move into better zones when they can afford to. This creates an **invasion–succession cycle,** one group moving into an area that is already occupied by people who have different characteristics. The invasion creates antagonisms between the groups: The one resents displacement; the other feels unwelcome. Although Burgess did his analysis a long time ago, the process continues. Today, however, people not only move outward, away from the city center, but, now that we have gentrification, also *toward* it.

Social Problems and the Zone in Transition

Burgess also noted that the most mobile areas have the most severe social problems. This is because these areas lack a sense of community, they have fewer controls over one another's behavior, and they suffer from *anomie* or alienation. As Burgess put it, high mobility leads to demoralization, which is accompanied by promiscuity, vice, juvenile delinquency, gangs, crime, poverty, and the breakup of families. Mobility and its accompanying problems are concentrated in Zone II, which Burgess called a *zone in transition*. He said that here we find the city's "poverty, degradation, and disease," the "underworlds of crime and vice." In Burgess's colorful phrase, this zone is "the purgatory of lost souls."

The zone in transition also contains the seeds of its own regeneration. It has social workers, preachers, artists, and political radicals—all, says Burgess, "obsessed with the vision of a new and better world." To this, we can add that in recent years financiers have seen value in this area and, in a process called *urban renewal*, they have demolished the buildings that were there, replacing them with office buildings, financial centers, stadiums, and luxury hotels. This is another movement *toward* the city center.

Because many cities diverge from Burgess' concentric zone model, his theory has many critics (Alihan 1938; Hoyt 1939; Harris and Ullman 1945; Palen and Schnore 1965; Berry and Kasarda 1977; La Gory 1980). All cities, however, have zones of functional specialties—areas of warehouses or those that specialize in selling and servicing automobiles or clusters of restaurants and shops. Cities also have zones that "specialize" in urban problems—skid rows, red-light districts, and high-crime, delinquency, and graffiti-marked areas.

It is significant that the functionalist approach implies that a city's problems are temporary. Over time, a city will absorb its dispossessed and poor and equip them for a better life.

CONFLICT THEORY

How Class Conflicts Create Urban Problems

Conflict theorists reply that the functionalists overlook the basic class conflict that underlies urban problems. Manuel Castells (1977, 1983, 1989), for example, says that the problems that our cities face are the consequence of our capitalistic system. Businesses began with mom-and-pop operations, but they outstripped those humble origins—expanding, merging, and growing powerful. Today, business leaders dictate government policy and tap the public treasury. By insuring home mortgages, for example, the government increases the profits of developers who build and market homes. By building interstate highways, the government finances a transportation system to move the goods that the wealthy manufacture.

As Castells points out, building interstate highways solved a major problem that confronted the wealthy. In the early 1900s, capitalists built multistory buildings to house their factories. When newer assembly-line techniques were developed, these buildings became obsolete: It was inefficient to move raw materials and manufactured goods from one floor to another. Interstate highways (or expressways), built at taxpayer expense, enabled factory owners to relocate their production to the suburbs, where land prices and taxes were lower. These highways also allowed the corporate elite to maintain access to the city, where they could use its marketing and financial institutions, as well as continue to enjoy its cultural benefits, such as professional sports, theaters, and concerts.

Moving factories and offices out of the city led to its decline. This flight by corporate management and skilled workers ravished the city's tax base, crippling the city's ability to maintain services and help the many poor who were left behind. To add insult to injury, after the corporate leaders moved their power base from city to suburb, they supported a coalition of rural and suburban districts that voted against proposals designed to aid cities. In effect, corporate leaders abandoned areas they no longer needed to the poor, about whom they did not care.

The Urban Renaissance and the New Underclass

A downtown cloaked in smoldering ruins, however, did not fit into the plans of the corporate elite, and they spearheaded plans to redevelop the downtown area. The bottom line of such redevelopment is profits through selling properties and operating businesses. To tourists—and indeed to a city's nearby comfortable suburbanites—the downtown area makes the city seem a phoenix, reborn from the ashes of destruction. The city, however, remains the repository of the poor and powerless. To the sides of the resurrected downtown live the huddled masses—the destitute in an affluent society. The poor are bypassed, some say oppressed, by leaders who pursue their own political and economic interests. This underclass, however, is not irrelevant, for if this group riots, it threatens the stability of society. This, in turn, threatens the powerful and privileged. As a consequence, the police keep a sharp eye on this group. A legion of social workers is also dispatched into their midst, not from altruism but to keep the poor quiet and to preserve the status quo.

Research Findings

Is the city inherently alienating? Let's first consider this question, and then look in depth at the decline of the inner city, urban violence, and the changes that are affecting U.S. cities.

IS THE CITY INHERENTLY ALIENATING?

Gemeinschaft* versus *Gesellschaft

From early on, sociologists were fascinated by the sharp contrast between the intimacy and neighborliness of village life and the anonymity and self-centeredness of urban life. In the 1880s, Ferdinand Tönnies noted that agricultural people share a sense of community because they share the same activities and values. Tönnies (1957) used the term *Gemeinschaft* to refer to such bonds of intimacy and shared tradition. He used the term *Gesellschaft* to refer to the impersonality and self-interest that are associated with urban areas. (In German, *Gemeinschaft* means "community"; *Gesellschaft* means "society.")

Extremes of Impersonality and Self-Interest

Impersonality and self-interest are ordinary characteristics of the city, but sometimes they are carried to extremes. When it occurred, the following event made national headlines and upset the entire country:

The Kitty Genovese Case

> Twenty-eight-year-old Catherine Genovese, who was known as Kitty in her Queens neighborhood, was returning home from work. After parking her car, a man grabbed her. Kitty screamed, "Oh my God! He stabbed me! Please help me!"
>
> For more than half an hour, thirty-eight respectable, law-abiding citizens watched the killer stalk and stab Kitty in three separate attacks. Twice the sudden glow from their bedroom lights frightened him off. Each time he returned, sought her out, and stabbed her again. Not one person telephoned the police during the assault.
>
> When interviewed by the police, the witnesses said: "I didn't want to get involved," "We thought it was a lovers' quarrel," "I don't know," and "I was tired. I went back to bed." (*New York Times*, March 26, 1964).

Road Rage

Even traffic accidents hold the danger of angry people whose wrath explodes:

> In 1995, in crowded traffic on a bridge going into Detroit, Deletha Word bumped the car ahead of her. The damage was minor, but the driver, Martell Welch, jumped out. Cursing, he pulled Deletha from her car, pushed her onto the hood, and began beating her. Martell's friends got out to watch. One of them held Deletha down while Martell took a car jack and

smashed Deletha's car. Scared for her life, Deletha broke away, fleeing to the bridge's railing. Martell and his friends taunted her, shouting, "Jump, bitch, jump!" Deletha plunged to her death. Whether she jumped or fell is unknown. (*Newsweek,* September 4, 1995)

How Cities Undermine Community

Why should the city be alienating? In a classic essay, sociologist Louis Wirth (1938) said that urban dwellers live anonymous lives marked by segmented and superficial encounters. This undermines kinship and neighborhood, the traditional bases of social control and solidarity. Urbanites then grow aloof and indifferent to other people's problems—as happened with Kitty Genovese's neighbors. In short, the personal freedom that the city offers comes at the cost of alienation.

Alienation and Community

The city is not inevitably alienating, however. Most drivers who witnessed the tragedy that befell Deletha Word did nothing. But after Deletha went over the railing, two motorists jumped in after her, risking injury and their own lives in a futile attempt to save her. Some urbanites, then, are far from alienated.

The Urban Villagers

The city also has enclaves of community. Sociologist Herbert Gans, a symbolic interactionist, did participant observation in the West End of Boston. He was so impressed with the sense of community that he titled his book *The Urban Villagers* (1962). Gans said:

> After a few weeks of living in the West End, my observations—and my perceptions of the area—changed drastically. The search for an apartment quickly indicated that the individual units were usually in much better condition than the outside or the hallways of the buildings. Subsequently, in wandering through the West End, and in using it as a resident, I developed a kind of selective perception, in which my eye focused only on those parts of the area that were actually being used by people. Vacant buildings and boarded-up stores were no longer so visible, and the totally deserted alleys or streets were outside the set of paths normally traversed, either by myself or by the West Enders. The dirt and spilled-over garbage remained, but, since they were concentrated in street gutters and empty lots, they were not really harmful to anyone and thus were not as noticeable as during my initial observations.
>
> Since much of the area's life took place on the street, faces became familiar very quickly. I met my neighbors on the stairs and in front of my building. And, once a shopping pattern developed, I saw the same storekeepers frequently, as well as the area's "characters" who wandered through the streets everyday on a fairly regular route and schedule. In short, the exotic quality of the stores and the residents also wore off as I became used to seeing them.

Slum or Low-Rent District?

In short, Gans found a community, people who identified with the area and with one another. Its residents enjoyed networks of friends and acquaintances. Despite the area's substandard buildings, most West Enders had chosen to live here. *To them, this was a low-rent district, not a slum.*

Most West Enders had low-paying, insecure jobs. Other residents were elderly, living on small pensions. Unlike the middle class, these people didn't care about their "address." The area's inconveniences were something they put up with in exchange for cheap housing. In general, they were content with their neighborhood.

As did Gans, sociologists who do participant observation document community in the city. They stress that the city is divided into little worlds that are knowable down to their smallest details (Lenz-Romeiss 1973; Karp and Yoels 1990; Keans 1991). People who feel that they fit in these little worlds experience emotional security.

Types of Urban Dwellers

What, then, is the answer? Is Wirth right? Is urban life a struggle for safety and survival, providing more threat than security? Or are these other sociologists correct? Not everyone in the city faces the same situation, and the answer depends on whom one is discussing. Let's look at the five types of urban dwellers that Gans (1962, 1968, 1991) identified. The first three live in the city by choice and are not alienated; the latter two are outcasts of industrial society who live in the city despairingly, without choice or hope.

Urban life can be alienating. To feel anonymous in a crowd of strangers can make people grow aloof and indifferent to other people's problems.

In Sum

Suburbs Also Have Problems

1. *The cosmopolites.* These are the intellectuals, professionals, and artists who have been attracted to the city. They value its conveniences and cultural benefits.
2. *The singles.* Roughly between the ages of 20 and 30, the singles have not decided to settle in the city permanently. For them, urban life is a stage in their life course. Businesses and services, such as singles bars and apartment complexes, cater to their needs and desires. After they marry, many singles move to the suburbs.
3. *The ethnic villagers.* Feeling a sense of identity, working-class members of the same ethnic group band together. They form tightly-knit neighborhoods that resemble villages and small towns. Family and peer oriented, they try to isolate themselves from the dangers and problems of urban life.
4. *The deprived.* Destitute, emotionally disturbed, and having little income, education, or work skills, the deprived live in neighborhoods that are more like urban jungles than urban villages. Like Hagan, some of them stalk those jungles in search of prey. Neither predator nor prey has much hope for anything better in life—for themselves or for their children. See the Thinking Critically box on danger and alienation in the city on the next page for an example of the deprived.
5. *The trapped.* These people don't live in the area by choice, either. Some were trapped when an ethnic group "invaded" their neighborhood and they could not afford to move. Others are "downwardly mobile"; they started in a higher social class but because of mental or physical illness, alcohol or other drug addiction, or other problems, they drifted downward. Many are elderly and are not wanted elsewhere. Like the deprived, the trapped suffer from high rates of assault, mugging, and rape.

Gans's typology illustrates the complexity of urban life. The city is a mosaic of social diversity, and not all urban dwellers experience the city in the same way. Each group has its own lifestyle, and each has distinct experiences. Some welcome the city's cultural diversity and mix with a lot of groups. Others find community by retreating into the security of ethnic enclaves. Some, in contrast, feel trapped and deprived. To them, the city is an urban jungle. It poses threats to their health and safety, and they live a life of despair.

THE DECLINE OF THE CENTRAL CITY

As people fled the central city for the suburbs, the city declined. It lost population, jobs, and political power. People moved out of U.S. cities to such an extent that more than half of Americans now live in the suburbs and twice as many manufacturing jobs are located in the suburbs than in the city (Palen 2002). Far from being utopias, the suburbs have their own problems, especially the older ones. From traffic congestion to street crime and eroding tax bases, they have problems commonly associated with the city. Suburbs even have **suburban sprawl,** the disappearance of open areas as a suburb expands into the countryside.

Thinking Critically about Social Problems

DANGER AND ALIENATION IN THE CITY

It is a summer afternoon in the Robert Taylor Homes, no different from most other days in the nation's largest public housing complex except for the intense heat.

Shots crackle from pistols near a play area. Laughter turns to screams as children dart for cover behind buildings and in stairwells crowded with craps shooters and winos.

The gunfire is soon over. The angry men bent on shooting each other have run off. The dice games and wine drinking resume. The basketball hoops again rattle above the scorching asphalt, and the children return to the dilapidated play equipment.

Fifteen blocks long and one block wide, Robert Taylor Homes is the world's largest public housing project. Taylor Homes consists of 28 identical red and cream 16-story towers surrounded on all sides by other impoverished neighborhoods. Many residents view Taylor Homes as a separate city within Chicago, an island of poverty adrift in a city of plenty.

Mrs. Wallace has lived in Taylor Homes since it was built. "There are a lot of good people here," she says. "They go to work, come home, and close their doors. They take the attitude that if nobody bothers them, they won't bother anybody. They try to get their kids to do the right thing, which is hard when so many parents don't."

John Smith remembers better times at Robert Taylor Homes. He has reared his children here. "And I sent all 12 to college," he says proudly with a deep, resonant voice. "I worked two jobs to do it, but I did it. I was firm with them and demanded that they do the right thing. They never gave me any trouble."

"But things are different now," 68-year-old Mr. Smith says from the chair in which he sits each day. "Things are tense now. The young people have nothing to do. No jobs. No recreation programs. So they are rowdy. They don't go to school. They make trouble."

As he talks, a young man walks by several times wielding a metal pipe. Mr. Smith pauses and gives the youth a stern look. The youth leaves.

"You have to watch them or they will hurt you," he said. "If they think you have something, they will slash you or knock you over the head and take it."

Asked why he doesn't move, Mr. Smith says, "Son, things are bad all over. It's not just here."

One hundred fifty thousand people live in Chicago's public housing. Single mothers occupy 94 percent of the units. Many buildings are controlled by gangs. The police have given up enforcing laws against drugs and burglaries. The head of Chicago's public housing put it this way:

As long as they don't go after and injure innocent people, it's fine. I can't stop them from using drugs. Everybody belongs to a gang. They are going to burglarize apartments to support their habits. You send a message. You don't say you can do these things, but over time they know that the only thing that's going to set me off is when they start hurting innocent people.

What do you think can be done to change this situation?

Based on Sheppard 1980; J. Anderson 1995.

Redlining and Disinvestment as Causes of Urban Decay

As we saw, conflict theorists trace the decline of the city to capitalists, whose policies damaged cities and encouraged suburbanization. Banks and savings and loan associations tightened this noose by **redlining,** refusing to lend money for mortgages in areas they considered undesirable (Squires 2003). (Loan officers used to draw a "red line" around neighborhoods they considered bad risks.) Redlined areas are usually either in the inner city or in neighborhoods undergoing integration.

As sociologist John Palen (2002) noted, redlining creates a *self-fulfilling prophecy.* Because banks refuse to finance the sale of homes in the area, only people with cash or those who are eligible for government loans are able to buy homes. With few buyers, the inventory of homes for sale builds up, and prices drop. With home prices dropping and banks refusing to make loans for improvements, homeowners stop remodeling and making repairs to their homes. As the neighborhood declines, it justifies the decisions of the lending officials to avoid the area because it was a "bad risk." Bankers, of course, insist that **disinvestment,** their withdrawal of investments from an area, is the *result* of deteriorating housing, not its cause.

Redlining is now illegal, but it is still practiced covertly. A banker in southern Illinois told me that he would loan no money in a certain area. He then added, "If you tell anyone that I said this, I will deny that the conversation ever took place."

The Landlords'/-ladies' Dilemma

"It just doesn't pay," said Linda Kutz as she looked mournfully around her. "This used to be a good business. I could get good rents and keep my building up. I knew my tenants, and they respected me. But now—nothing but animals!" Linda muttered as she looked despairingly at the shambles of what was a nice apartment just a few days before.

Like many other urban landlords, Linda Kutz is abandoning her apartment building. She is caught between the cross-pressures of high taxes, the city insisting that she bring her buildings into conformity with the housing code, tenants who damage her property and refuse to pay their rents, and a costly and long eviction process.

When she went to the police, they asked, "Did you see them (the renters) do it?" She said, "No, I wasn't there." Pointing to holes in the wall and feces in the floor ducts, she said, "But you can see for yourself what they did." Their response: "If you didn't see them do it, we can't do anything about it." With three of her apartments vandalized during the past year, Kutz says she has no choice but to walk away and let the banks foreclose on her building.

Abandonment. Each year, landlords abandon thousands of **housing units**—places of residence such as houses or apartments. Some of these buildings need only minor repairs. Why, then, are abandoned buildings part of the urban scene? As Kutz indicates, vandalism, high taxes, a slow eviction process, and housing codes that sometimes border on the quixotic all play a role. As another landlord told me:

"Look at this building," he said, indicating the workers on the roof. "I don't know how long I can keep this up. I want to provide a nice place for my renters. Then comes the city inspector who says I have to add rain gutters. Every time someone moves in, an inspector examines my building. No one's ever said anything about gutters before. The building is over a hundred years old and has never had rain gutters. Why does it suddenly need them now?"

All these factors add up to higher risk and, sometimes, financial loss. Unable to find a buyer, some landlords stop paying their property taxes or making repairs. They collect as much rent as long as possible, and then walk away from their buildings. The abandoned buildings become a dangerous playground for children, a shelter for junkies, a target for looters, fun for vandals, and profit for arsonists.

Arson

Some owners of buildings and businesses who face huge losses see fire as the solution. Those afraid to set the fire themselves hire "torches" (professional arsonists), who are seldom apprehended because arson often destroys the evidence of the crime. Many insurance companies prefer to pay off a blaze of "suspicious origin" and recover the cost in their general rates than fight a case in court and risk getting a reputation of not paying claims. Some cynically call arson the "modern way of refinancing."

Even when a company does fight a claim that is

Urban problems, including slums, are a worldwide problem. The waterway behind this slum in India is a sewer. The little attachments above the water are toilets, from which human waste drops directly into the water.

obviously arson, it can easily lose. As an insurance claims agent told me during an investigation:

> We won't have to pay on this one. The fire began in the basement on a pile of clothes. There was no source of fire [heating element or electricity] there. The insured was paid off on another fire just three years ago. The police have the case.
>
> I talked to the detective in charge of the case. The insured had lost his job, and the mortgage holder had begun foreclosure (the legal process of getting possession of the property), but the man stuck to his story. ("I don't know anything. I wasn't there.") The company paid.

Except when people are killed, urban arson receives little publicity or concern. The public shows little interest, and often neither do the police. Functionalists can well see the core truth in the statement that "arson is the modern way of refinancing." Perhaps it is functional for society to let entrepreneurs refinance their losses by spreading the cost over tens of thousands of policyholders.

URBAN VIOLENCE

In addition to a physical decline, our urban centers also face violence. We have already discussed this topic in chapters 5 and 6. Here we will examine violence by youth gangs, violence in the schools, and riots.

Why Lower-Class Boys Are Attracted to Gangs

Let's begin by looking at gangs, a topic that intrigues both the public and sociologists. In the 1920s, sociologist Frederic Thrasher did research on 1,313 gangs in Chicago. His report became a classic in sociology. Thrasher (1927) found that gangs start as ordinary play groups that compete for space in crowded and deteriorating areas of the city. Boys band together because their participation in a group gives them a valued identity. The group then becomes the impetus for criminal activities.

The Thrasher Study

The Cohen Study

Over and over, sociologists have documented what the public has perceived, that it is primarily lower-class boys who are involved in gangs. Why do gangs hold such an attraction for them? In another classic study, sociologist Albert Cohen (1955) found a key that helps us to understand this attraction: Lower-class boys are measured by middle-class standards, but they lack the socially approved means to meet those standards. The schools are run by middle-class teachers and administrators who judge the boys' speech, behavior, and test performance. The boys feel that they don't fit in, that their teachers look down on them. In self-defense, they form a subculture of like-minded boys in which they use different standards to judge one another, standards by which they can succeed. Their rejection of middle-class standards is so thorough that doing well in school becomes equated with girls and sissies, the opposite of the vibrant manliness and bravado that they expect of one another. As the boys twist norms, they also reject the standards of other authority figures and give approval to violating the law.

The Miller Study

In another classic study, sociologist Walter Miller (1958) also analyzed why gangs draw primarily lower-class boys. Not only do the boys reject middle-class values but also they build identities and confer status on one another on the basis of six contrary values: trouble, toughness, smartness, excitement, fate, and autonomy. Trouble provides excitement and relieves the monotony of everyday life. Through trouble, the boys can show that they are tough, smart, and autonomous (free from authority). The boys use fate to explain their lot in life: If you get hurt or killed, this is simply because your number came up. In short, gangs offer an arena in which lower-class boys not only reject the middle-class values that impinge so sharply on them but also one in which they develop a world of their own values.

"Supergangs"

For the most part, the gangs in these classic studies were groups of adolescents who did nothing worse than get high, skip school, write graffiti, steal from parked cars, get into a fight now and then, and vandalize property. I say "nothing worse" because now we have "supergangs" such as the Crips and Bloods. These gangs, and the many oth-

Although urban violence is decreasing, it remains a matter of major concern. With guns the major weapon used in killings, gun ownership has become one of the most controversial topics in U.S. society.

ers like them, are no play groups that occasionaly wander outside the law: Their members not only steal, but, like Hagan, a Crip, they also kill. The Crips and Bloods have gone national, and they now have affiliated gangs in most major cities, and even in some smaller ones.

Girl Gangs

Lower-class girls, coming from backgrounds similar to the boys, also find school oppressive and the contrarian values attractive. Although female gang members are expected to act tough and to be aggressive, they are also expected to be submissive to the boys (Vigil 2002). Here is one indication of how dominant the males in these groups are: When girls are initiated into the gang, the boys can require them to have sex with one or several of the male gang members. For the most part, girls play supportive roles in the boys' gangs, such as hiding weapons and drugs and providing alibis and sex.

All-girl gangs do exist, but almost all of them are auxiliaries of boy gangs (Vigil 2002). (Sociologist Dana Nurge [2003] found an exception to this in her study of girl gangs in Boston.) The few independent girl gangs last only a short while. In some cases, such as *Las Locas* (the Crazies) in Los Angeles, the girls were unpredictably dangerous, and the boys had to watch their step when they were around them. Although such cases are rare, the girls can be every bit as violent as the boys. Some girls kill another girl just to get her pair of earrings (Faison 1991).

Cultural Diversity of Urban Gangs

Youth gangs are culturally diverse. They are not limited to any race-ethnic group. Los Angeles has white gangs, African American gangs, Chicano gangs, even Colombian, San Salvadoran, and Vietnamese gangs. The boys (or girls) band together to attain identity and protection, friendship, a "family," anonymity, and group support in criminal activities—and to protect themselves from rival gangs. In some areas, it is dangerous *not* to be a gang member.

Violence in Gang Life

For gang members, violence is a tool. It is a means both for getting their way and for expressing themselves. Because gang members live in neighborhoods where violence is a normal part of their social world, they believe that people will be violent toward them and that they ought to be violent toward others. Life is cheap, violence routine, and killing normal. For some, like Hagan in the opening vignette, a victim doesn't have to be a gang member. Life can be destroyed for little or no provocation. Initiation into a gang can even require that the initiate do an anonymous drive-by shooting

(Vigil 2002). No revenge is involved; the gang drives up, and the initiate blindly shoots into a crowd.

As long as gangs limit their violence to their own area of the city, the public is seldom concerned. The common attitude is "let them kill each other." If violence spills into the downtown or some other area of the city that is used by the middle class, then the public demands that "something be done." Similar demands are made when there is an outrageous killing (a killing that the public does not define as "normal"). Such killings generate publicity, and youth gangs "become" a "problem." The killing of Ben Wilson is an example.

School Violence

> Ben Wilson, the 17-year-old star forward of the Illinois state champion basketball team, was walking with his girlfriend during a school lunch break. Three teenage gang members confronted them. As the 6-foot 8-inch Wilson tried to move past them, one youth turned to his companion and said, "This guy pushed me. Pop him." The teenager pulled out a .22-caliber pistol and fired two shots into Wilson's stomach. Wilson died a day later—on Thanksgiving eve. (Starr and Maier 1985)

We need to note that there is no such thing as *the* urban gang. There are many types of gangs, and not all of them are violent. In fact, not all of them are criminal. The purpose of some gangs is to protect their neighborhood, even to bring about social change that gives the poor a shot at the American dream—or at least makes life better for people who are clinging precariously to the edge of society (DiChiara and Chabot 2003; Martinez 2003).

That U.S. schools would need guards and metal detectors to protect their students used to be unimaginable. Yet what once was nonexistent has become common. The worst kids in school used to carry a switchblade, but today those kids take guns to class. Some bring guns to defend themselves from classmates who carry guns! As a 15-year-old in a Baltimore junior high school said, "You gotta be prepared—people shoot you for your coat, your rings, chains, anything." He then proudly displayed his "defensive" .25-caliber Beretta (Hackett 1988).

And then, of course, there is Columbine—and the other schools where students have gone on killing sprees. In their wake, they have left dead students and teachers—and fear on the part of students, parents, and entire communities.

In some grade schools, teachers practice "duck-and-cover" drills to protect children from neighborhood shootings (Mydens 1991). In some high schools and even junior highs, rapes and assaults go unreported. Guilt stops some teachers from reporting that they were attacked; they feel that the assault would not have occurred if they had somehow done a better job in the classroom. Some teachers find it easier to ignore an attack, because assault cases usually require at least three appearances in court. Others don't report attacks because they fear for their lives. Often there are no witnesses, and it is the teacher's word against the student's.

Except for incidents that cannot be hidden, such as shootings, school violence seldom comes to the attention of the police or public primarily because, like prison wardens—and I use this analogy purposefully—school administrators want to "run a nice, quiet school." The last thing they want is to arouse the community with stories about teachers versus students or to publicize unsafe conditions at school. Administrators hush up and downplay incidents. This relieves pressure on them and protects their jobs, for one sign of their success—or failure—is the amount of violence in their schools.

Riots in U.S. History

> The year was 1747. The place was the bustling port of Boston. The Royal Navy had been impressing (kidnapping legally) local men for forced service. Fed up, seamen and others armed themselves and rioted. For three days, they dominated the city, forcing the governor to flee. The mobs freed the impressed men, gaining another victory for the urban rioters of the time.

Urban riots, seemingly so modern, go far back in history. The book of Genesis in the Old Testament recounts a riot in the city of Gomorroh. Two thousand years ago, riots

Although riots are often thought of as a recent development in the United States, they are rooted in our history. Shown here is an engraving based on a newspaper account of the New York City Draft Riots of 1863. Until then, the Civil War's Union Army was made up of volunteers. Rioters protested the initiation of a draft. They also looted stores—another behavior that is not new.

occurred in the city of Rome. In the United States, riots have been with us since the 1700s. According to historian Richard Brown (1969), rioting by the lower-class urban population even helped start the American Revolution.

In their early history, Baltimore, Philadelphia, New York, and Boston were the sites of numerous riots. During the 1830s through the 1850s, at least 35 major riots and numerous minor ones took place in these cities. There were labor riots, anti-Catholic riots, and riots by volunteer firemen. Some riots were directed against the Irish, who were a despised immigrant group at this time. In protest against the flood of Irish immigrants, in 1835 mobs from Boston burned the Ursuline convent and school at Charlestown (Wyatt-Brown 2003).

Communal Riots

Then, too, there were what are called race riots. Competition for jobs underlie some of these, especially the riots of whites against blacks (Brown 1969). Until the 1960s, the most common type of race riot was the **communal riot.** In this type, also called a *contested area riot,* one group would contest another's control of an area of the city. According to sociologist Morris Janowitz (1970b), the cities in which communal riots occurred contained large numbers of migrants—both African American and white—who were living in segregated areas. The police had little capacity to deal with outbreaks of mass violence, and often conspired with white rioters against African Americans.

Background Factors and Precipitating Incidents

Sociologists have found that riots are preceded by rising tensions and minor outbursts of violence. Then comes a **precipitating incident,** something that triggers the riot. For example, between 1917 and 1919 whites bombed more than twenty-seven homes of Chicago blacks. None of these incidents led to riots. What did, however, was the death of a 17-year-old black youth who swam into an area of Lake Michigan used exclusively by whites. When other blacks challenged the whites' use of this part of the beach, crowds of blacks and whites began throwing stones at one another. The black youth, still in the water, drowned. Rumors abounded that he had been stoned to death, and blacks rioted. Thirty-eight people were killed, 537 injured, and about 1,000 left homeless.

Chief Background Factors in Commodity Riots

In the 1960s, something changed. Riots had been sporadic through the years, but at this time they erupted across the nation. Harlem, Brooklyn, Watts, Newark, and Detroit were hit. These riots were different. Instead of challenging the control of some area of the city, as in communal riots, the rioters looted stores. Because of this, they are referred to as **commodity riots** (Janowitz 1970a). Commodity riots peaked in 1967, with 41 major riots and 123 lesser ones.

The 1960s riots so upset the nation that President Johnson appointed a National Advisory Commission on Civil Disorders to study them. The commission identified five main background factors (Kerner 1968):

1. *Discrimination and segregation* in employment, education, and housing that excluded many blacks from economic benefits.
2. *Isolation*—due to black in-migration and white flight, poor blacks were concentrated in the city, with deteriorating facilities and services and unmet human needs.
3. *Destroyed opportunity* from segregation and poverty, which enforced failure on the young. Life in the ghetto often culminated in crime, drug addiction, welfare, and bitterness and resentment against society in general and white society in particular.
4. *Frustrated hopes*—stimulated by the judicial and legislative victories of the civil rights movement, unfulfilled hopes created frustration.
5. *Powerlessness,* combined with alienation and hostility to society, led to the conviction that only violence could change the "system."

These are *background* factors. By themselves, they do not cause riots. The poor and minorities are not strangers to discrimination, segregation, isolation, destroyed opportunity, frustrated hopes, and powerlessness. They encounter them as part of their everyday lives. Rioting, in contrast, is rare. Despite their disadvantage and oppression, poor people usually live lives of quiet desperation. To riot, their anger must rise to fever pitch (Piven and Cloward 1977). There has to be something that ignites their underlying anger and frustration. This spark is called a *precipitating incident.*

Precipitating Incidents That Raise the Level of Anger

But there always are incidents. Why does one incident set off a riot, whereas others do not? Social psychologists Kurt and Gladys Lang (1968) identified two necessary conditions for an incident to precipitate a riot: It must be perceived as a threat to the group's well-being and evoke moral outrage. The precipitating incident is often a confrontation between an African American and a white police officer. Rumors sweep the area, and the incident escalates in people's minds as they talk excitedly about it. As they conclude that "this time it has gone too far, and we won't take it any more," violence erupts.

The Los Angeles riot of 1992 followed this scenario perfectly. Background conditions were the long-term poverty of African Americans and Latinos and their oppression by the police. The precipitating incident that inflamed passions was the acquittal of the policemen who had been accused of assaulting Rodney King, an African American who was being arrested on traffic violations. A passerby had videotaped the police as they beat King. The videotape showed the officers as they savagely pounded King with their nightsticks. Television stations repeatedly broadcast the videotape to stunned audiences. *Everyone* knew that the police officers were guilty.

Within minutes of the verdict of acquittal, angry crowds gathered. That night, mobs set fire to businesses in south-central Los Angeles, and looting and arson began. The rioting spread to other cities—Atlanta, Tampa, and even Madison, Wisconsin, and Las Vegas, Nevada. Whites and Koreans were favorite targets. The LA riot was spectacular—4,000 fires; dramatic footage of looting and beatings; the president appearing on television federalizing the California National Guard and ordering the Seventh Infantry, SWAT teams, and the FBI into Los Angeles; and sixty dead, the most victims of a U.S. riot since the Civil War. The LA riot seemed different, but sociologically it was a "routine" riot. That is, it followed the patterns that sociologists have identified.

What Are Results of Riots?

Beyond the obvious—the burning, looting, and killing—what are the results of riots? First, rioting can have positive consequences: It may stimulate the flow of federal funds to the inner city. Most positive consequences, however, are short lived. Second, as sociologists George Simpson and Milton Yinger noted (1972), riots increase segregation, for whites flee the area. Although rioters may gain a sense of having struck a blow for freedom, they have only indicated their need for freedom: They have not shaken the basic institutions that support their oppression and enforce their poverty (Piven and Cloward 1977). Not one riot in the history of the United States has eliminated the underlying discrimination and poverty that are the background factors of riots. The sad truth is that because these background conditions remain and precipitating events are bound to occur, we are destined to have more riots.

THE CITY IN CHANGE

In addition to violence and general decline, U.S. cities face extensive change. In this section we will examine the transition in power, changes in urban government, the emerging megalopolis, and the brightening of the sun belt.

Are U.S. Cities Obsolete?

"Are U.S. cities becoming obsolete?" John Teaford (1986), an urban historian, posed this question. He was referring to the problems we have reviewed here and in earlier chapters—gangs, rape, murder, drug addiction—that often make U.S. cities threatening, alienating places to live. Our inner cities have become so fearful that they are avoided by all except those who live there and those who must transact business there. Locked in these pockets of poverty, many inner-city residents live short, brutal lives.

Challenges from the Suburbs

The suburbs may once have been bedrooms for the city, but no longer. Cities used to hold the jobs, but now the suburbs do. Nearly three-quarters of suburbanites work in the suburbs, not in the nearby city. Just as suburbanites used to commute to the city for work (and many still do), now many urbanites commute to the suburbs for work (Rybczynski 1999).

A Renewal?

Although the cities face severe challenges, no one need erect a grave marker over them. They are located on valuable land, which draws resources of renewal when the price is right. Just as the World Trade Center is replaced after its destruction, so U.S. cities are renewed after they reach a certain point of decay. Consider the reversal of fortunes in Harlem, the topic of the Thinking Critically box on the next page.

Urban Government

Regardless of its problems, the city must be governed. To help accomplish this task, the **political machine** emerged—an organization that operated behind the scenes to circumvent the city's official procedures. In return for loyalty, the machine distributed government jobs and favors. In a practice called patronage, the machine put its members on the city payroll. Their official job was a subterfuge; their real job was to promote the political machine.

Merton's Functional Analysis of the Political Machine

In a classic functional analysis, sociologist Robert Merton (1968) examined big-city "machine politics." He wanted to know why, despite attempts at reform, the machine continued year after year. Merton applied two basic assumptions of functionalism: (1) something does not exist in a society unless it contributes to that society, and (2) no part of society exists in isolation; each part is related to the other parts of the social system.

Merton found that the political machine helped the disadvantaged, businesspeople, and individuals who wanted to get ahead. The machine helped the disadvantaged obtain food, welfare, jobs, scholarships, and legal assistance when children ran afoul of the law or when bill collectors became too threatening. Those who received such favors knew without question whom to vote for in the next election.

Businesspeople also needed favors. They wanted to bypass building codes and the many bureaucratic regulations that impeded their efforts to expand. In return for under-the-table payoffs, the boss would pull strings at the appropriate government

Thinking Critically about Social Problems

RECLAIMING THE CITY: THE NEW HARLEM

The story is well known. The inner city is filled with crack, crime, and corruption. It stinks from foul, festering garbage strewn on the streets and piled up around burned-out buildings. Only those who have no choice live in this desolate, despairing environment where danger lurks around every corner.

What is not so well known is that affluent African Americans are reclaiming some of these areas.

Howard Sanders was living the American Dream. After earning a degree from Harvard Business School, he took a position with a Manhattan investment firm. He lived in an exclusive apartment on Central Park West, but he missed Harlem, where he had grown up. He moved back, along with his wife and daughter.

African American lawyers, doctors, professors, and bankers are doing the same.

What's the attraction? The first is nostalgia, a cultural identification with the Harlem of legend and folklore. It was here that black writers and artists lived in the 1920s, here that the blues and jazz attracted young and accomplished musicians.

The second reason is a more practical one. Harlem offers housing value. Five-bedroom homes with 6,000 square feet are available. Some feature Honduran mahogany. Some brownstones are only shells and have to be renovated; others are in perfect condition.

What is happening is the rebuilding of a community. Some people who "made" it want to be role models. They want children in the community to see them going to and returning from work.

When the middle class moved out of Harlem, so did its amenities. Now that young professionals are moving back in, the amenities are returning, too. There were no coffee shops, restaurants, jazz clubs, florists, copy centers, dentist and optometrist offices, or art galleries—the types of things urbanites take for granted. Now there are.

The same thing is happening on Chicago's West Side and in other U.S. cities.

The drive to find community—to connect with others and with one's roots—is strong. As an investment banker who migrated to Harlem said, "It feeds my soul."

Sources: Based on Cose 1999; McCormick 1999; Scott 2001; Taylor 2002; Leland 2003

---

agency. The boss served as a mediator between the demands of bureaucrats and the needs of modern business.

The machine also helped people move up the social class ladder. Ambitious people always confront obstacles in their pursuit of success, and the ambitious poor are no exception. They don't have the money to start their own businesses, and many don't have the grades to attend professional schools. In return for their loyalty, the machine helped some get jobs at local businesses. Others went to work for the machine.

In short, Merton found that the political machine existed because the official channels of society failed to provide needed services; the machine stepped in to fill the void left by the more culturally approved structures of society.

Functions to Some Are Dysfunctions to Others

As functionalists also stress, something that is functional for some may be a source of problems for others. The political machine passed over minorities when it handed out political favors. It also "contained" minorities to specified areas of the city, ordering real estate agents to keep designated areas "pure" (Royko 1971). Fire marshals and city inspectors enforced city and state codes strictly when property was scheduled to pass into the "wrong hands," but overlooked violations for buyers whose ethnicity was approved. The machine may also be dysfunctional to the general public if it sacks the city treasury or diverts tax monies while streets, sewers, bridges, lighting, libraries, and other public services deteriorate.

**The Decline
of the Political Machine**

The machine, which had dominated politics during the first half of the twentieth century, gradually declined. With the death of Chicago's Mayor Richard Daley in 1976, the last of the old-fashioned political machines began to pass into history. Here is why the political machine declined:

1. Immigration slowed to a trickle. This removed a major function of the machine (serving unmet needs in return for loyalty) and undermined one of its major bases of power.
2. Education increased. As many people moved into the mainstream of society, they became less dependent on favors from the machine.
3. Suburbanization occurred. As whites and jobs left the city, the machine lost the broad revenue base on which its power depended.
4. Civil service laws were passed. As city workers came under the protection of these laws, it became difficult for the machine to demand their loyalty.
5. Blacks migrated north. As African Americans moved from the South, the white power establishment held onto control until it was too late to pass to its political successors an intact, powerful machine.
6. New standards of city management came into vogue. The public wanted city agencies to be headed by professionals rather than given as rewards for political service.

The political machine may be down, but it isn't dead. After Richard Daley died, Richard Daley became mayor of Chicago. That is, the mayor's son, who was barely able to pass the Illinois bar exam, was elected mayor. He has been reelected several times. The machine that his father passed to him, though weakened, still functions. And rumors abound about political connections in Boston so corrupt that during the construction of a subway millions of dollars were siphoned off for payoffs. Today's high immigration, especially the millions of undocumented workers from Mexico and central and South America who have flooded our cities, may be planting the seeds for the renewal of the political machine.

**The New City
Management**

The professionalization of city management, which weakened the political machine, has also contributed to urban problems. Mayors or city managers head a network of departments. Each department is assigned a particular task and works fairly independently of the others. Communication breaks down, and with department chiefs and their workers being more loyal to their own department than they are to the city or the mayor, they perform their work without concern for how it fits into the larger picture (Lowi 1977). Here's an example from Granada, Spain. The rundown buildings on one of its main streets were an eyesore. To present a better image to tourists, the city spent huge amounts painting and repairing the concrete, iron, and stonework on these buildings. The results were impressive. The only problem was that another unit of the government had slated these same buildings for demolition (Arías 1993).

**The Transition
to Minority Leadership**

Another major change in city governance is the transition of power from whites to African Americans and Latinos. Statistics tell the story: In 1964, there were only 70 elected African American officials at all levels of government in the United States. Today there are 9,000. From 70 to 9,000 in 40 years! Latinos have also increased their total, to more than 4,000 (Eisinger 1980; *Statistical Abstract* 2003:Tables 417, 418). It should be obvious from these totals that Latinos have a lot farther to go in gaining similar power in U.S. cities.

Sociologist Peter Eisinger studied this transition of power. If a city is to be governed, its major groups must cooperate. If whites were to withdraw their cooperation from an elected minority mayor, winning control of the formal apparatus of government would be a hollow victory. To see what happened after African Americans were elected as mayors of Detroit and Atlanta, Eisinger interviewed the business, political, and social leaders of these cities. Instead of engaging in confrontational politics, the white elite had chosen to cooperate and build coalitions.

This transition of power, Eisinger says, can be compared with what happened in Boston a century ago. At that time the Yankees, the white settlers from England, controlled the city. When thousands of poor Irish immigrants flooded Boston in the 1800s, the Yankees felt threatened, and they held onto their power. By 1900, however, the Irish held the political reins of Boston. Eisinger concludes that we are in the midst of a similar process. Although the players have changed, the game is the same—and the results are proving to be similar.

THE MEGALOPOLIS

Separate Cities Are Merging into a Single Unit

Another major change is the development of the **megalopolis.** This term refers to urban areas spilling into one another. What once were small towns and cities become an interconnected mass. The first U.S. megalopolis was the area between New York, Boston, and Washington, D.C. It covers ten states, the District of Columbia, and hundreds of local governments. The areas between Chicago and Cleveland and between San Francisco and San Diego are becoming megalopolises.

These metropolitan areas are merging into a single unit. They are so intertwined that some people use air shuttles to taxi back and forth between the part of the megalopolis they work in and the part they live in. Air shuttles tie Washington, D.C., New York City, and Boston together. From dawn to dusk, commuters can catch a flight every few minutes between these cities. As sociologist John Palen (2002) says, some city-to-city air shuttles offer more frequent and faster transportation than the transportation available between parts of a single large city.

Regional Planning

As the fate of one city merges with that of others, regional governing structures are developing that supersede the boundaries of the individual cities and suburbs. The many urban units that make up a megalopolis find it difficult to give up their autonomy, but in an endeavor called *regional planning* they work together through county boards. The boards pass laws to regulate the larger region's transportation, environment, housing, policing, and growth. Cooperation does not come about without struggle. Often, each smaller urban unit clings to its historical rights, granted by state charter, and thinks of itself as independent. With profits at stake, there is little doubt about the outcome of these struggles: The larger governing unit will win out.

Edge Cities

Edge cities are another way that cities are expanding beyond their traditional political boundaries. This term refers to a clustering of buildings and services near the intersection of major highways (Garreau 1991; Leinberger 2001; Lang 2003). The shopping malls, hotels, office parks, and residential areas overlap political boundaries and include parts of several cities or towns. Edge cities are not cities in the traditional sense; that is, they are not political units with their own mayor or city manager. Yet, edge cities provide a sense of place to those who live or work there, and many of the nation's new jobs are developing in them. Two of the most well-known edge cities are those in Tysons Corner in Washington and those clustering along the LBJ Freeway in Dallas, Texas.

Restratification: Regional Shifts in Wealth and Power

Another major change in U.S. cities is **restratification,** a shift in their population, wealth, and power. Tables 12-2 and 12-3 depict this shift in population. As you can see from Table 12-2, all ten of our fastest-growing cities are in the West and South. Of the ten cities that lost the most population, all are in the Northeast (and Ohio, which borders this section of the United States). Table 12-3 on page 414 illustrates this restratification on a *regional* basis. You can see how greatly the South and the West have grown and how little increase there has been in the Northeast and the Midwest. About half of the country's total population growth occurred in just the western states.

The political implications of this regional shift are enormous. Only during one other period of U.S. history—the Civil War—has the balance of power among the states undergone such rapid and deep transformation. With more population comes more wealth and power. Regarding wealth: The tax base is growing dramatically faster in the West and the South than in other regions. Regarding power: The West and South are gaining representatives in Congress whereas the Northeast and Midwest are losing representatives.

Emerging Problems in the Sun Belt

The rapid growth of cities in the West and South, "the sun belt," has created the same problems that the older urban centers face: traffic congestion, air pollution, urban sprawl, and pressures on educational systems. The capital and human resources flowing from the old industrial centers to the sun-belt states, however, have given them greater resources to solve their urban problems. As in the older cities, many problems in these newly expanding urban areas of the West and South mostly affect the poor. Leaders in these expanding areas are not unlike their counterparts in the older industrial centers: Few are willing to devote many resources to help the poor.

Let's look at the potential for improving life in U.S. cities.

Social Policy

The Essential Condition for Success: Establishing Community

Many despair that the crises facing our cities can be solved. Some feel that the government has simply shuffled money from one fashionable urban program to another, with little, if anything, to show for it. Some even insist that government programs have made the problems worse. A few have given up on cities, saying their problems are too great, and we should disperse the urban population throughout the countryside, to new, planned-from-scratch small cities with designated maximum populations (Webber 1973).

TABLE 12-2 The Fastest-Growing and Shrinking U.S. Cities

THE FASTEST-GROWING CITIES

1. 83.3% Las Vegas, NV
2. 65.3% Naples, FL
3. 49.7% West Palm Beach–Boca Raton, FL
4. 48.5% McAllen–Edinburg–Mission, TX
5. 47.7% Austin–San Marcos, TX
6. 47.5% Fayetteville–Springdale–Rogers, AR
7. 46.1% Boise City, ID
8. 45.3% Phoenix–Mesa, AZ
9. 39.8% Provo–Orem, UT

THE SHRINKING CITIES

1. −5.3% Utica–Rome, NY
2. −4.6% Binghamton, NY
3. −2.2% Scranton–Wilkes Barre–Hasleton, PA
4. −1.6% Buffalo–Niagara Falls, NY
5. −1.5% Pittsburgh, PA
6. −1.4% Syracuse, NY
7. −1.0% Youngstown–Warren, OH
8. −0.3% New Bedford, MA
9. −0.1% Dayton–Springfield, OH

Note: The plus totals of the growing cities and the minus totals of the shrinking cities indicate the percentage of population change from 1990 to 2000.
Source: By the author, based on *Statistical Abstract of the United States* 2002:Table 30.

TABLE 12-3 Population Change of U.S. Regions

	MILLIONS OF PEOPLE				INCREASE IN MILLIONS	INCREASE IN PERCENTAGE
	1970	1980	1990	2000	1970–2000	1970–2000
Northeast	49	49	51	54	5	10%
Midwest	57	59	60	64	7	12%
South	63	75	85	100	37	59%
West	35	43	53	63	28	80%

Source: By the author, based on *Statistical Abstract of the United States,* various years and 2003:Table 23.

Short of such an extreme approach, whose outcome would be uncertain, what steps are reasonable? Sociologists stress that urban policy must create a sense of community (Karp et al. 1991). If social policy does not do this, it is doomed. To create community, we must preserve and develop neighborhoods. We must avoid "urban renewal" programs that destroy neighborhoods and social relationships, no matter what appealing names they may be given.

SPECIFIC PROGRAMS

Six Programs with Promise:

Programs to halt decline and revitalize urban areas are urban homesteading, reducing taxes for improving property, enterprise zones, job deconcentration, condominium in-filling, and regional planning. Let's begin with urban homesteading.

> Paul Gasparotti bought two abandoned adjacent houses from the city for a dollar each. After tearing everything out but the exterior bricks, roof rafters, and floor joists, he connected the two houses and dug out the basement (Kirkpatrick 1981).

1. Urban Homesteading

Urban homesteading is sometimes called "sweat equity," because people invest hard work rather than money in a building. In this program, a city sells (usually for $1) derelict housing that it has acquired by tax foreclosure. The buyer agrees to stay for some specified time, ordinarily at least three years, and to bring the house up to code within eighteen months. As the mayor of Wilmington, Delaware, said, "We are not trying to provide housing for people. We are trying to find people for [abandoned] housing."

This program aims to stabilize neighborhoods by inspiring confidence. The idea is that salvaging buildings will encourage neighbors to stay and to improve their own properties. Deterioration will stop, neighborhoods will be rebuilt, and people will be lured back from the suburbs. Despite its promise, however, a study of homesteading in forty-two locations showed that it did *not* stabilize neighborhoods (Varady 1986).

Urban homesteading is a mixed blessing, because it does not include the very poor. Only people with good incomes and credit can undertake the rehabilitation of buildings. How can the poor repay the loans, unless they have jobs? Even if times are prosperous and the unskilled poor get jobs, what happens when they lose them when the economy slows? Urban homesteading also threatens to displace the poor, for as a neighborhood is upgraded, rent and property values increase.

2. Reducing Taxes

Reducing taxes hold promise. No one wants to abandon buildings. Walking away from a property means losing huge amounts of money. To encourage homeowners and landlords to improve their properties, city and county officials can reduce taxes for a specified time, say three or five years. Because taxes are based on a percentage of a property's assessed value, when someone improves a property, the assessed value goes up and so do the taxes. Some may object that this policy helps landlords, but it also makes landlords a vehicle for improving and maintaining neighborhoods. Everyone wins. Social policies that penalize homeowners and landlords sow seeds of neighborhood destruction.

3. Enterprise Zones

The third program, **enterprise zones** (also known as empowerment zones), has been tried by most states. The general principles of enterprise zones are

1. Businesses that locate in a designated zone—a rundown area with high unemployment—receive tax credits for each full-time, qualified employee they hire.
2. Businesses in the enterprise zone that improve their facilities receive credits on their property tax.
3. Low-interest loans are available.

Enterprise zones are designed to stimulate economic growth and generate employment. A danger is that enticing businesses to move into the zone may create blight in the areas they leave behind. Another problem is that subsidizing some businesses in this fashion may create unfair competition for businesses not in the zone.

Evaluating the results of enterprise zones has been difficult. The basic problem facing researchers is this: If you measure employment, earnings, or poverty in an enterprise zone, how do you know what they would have been if the enterprise zone had not been there? In general, the results have been disappointing: Researcher have concluded that enterprise zones have had little impact on residents in the zone (Ferguson 2001).

4. Job Deconcentration

Job deconcentration is another promising policy. It presupposes a regional master plan and a regional authority to enforce it. Toronto has such a plan. Factories, offices, shopping centers, and housing subdivisions can be built only in specified areas adjacent to the city. This allows rational planning and helps control urban and suburban sprawl. Job deconcentration also lets planning bodies develop public transportation that serves workers outside the central city. If there is no regional authority, however, this policy is impossible. As policy analyst Jan Newitt said to me, "Can't you just see New York City adopting a policy of putting jobs in the suburbs!"

5. Condominium In-filling

The exodus of the young middle class is the snow-belt cities' major loss. To reverse this migration, Newitt proposes **condominium in-filling,** building small energy-efficient condominiums for older urban homeowners. Because many older people stay in the homes in which they reared their children, they often have more room than they need and more maintenance than they can handle. Building condominiums in the neighborhoods in which people reared their children—where many older people wish to remain—would give these older people a place to move to, while allowing them to remain in the area and help stabilize the neighborhood. The larger, older housing they vacate would be available to younger families with children, who have energy and enthusiasm to maintain and improve such homes. More younger adults would then remain in the city, often in the same neighborhoods where they spent their childhood. Of all programs, this has the most exciting potential, because it meets the sociological requirement to foster a sense of community.

6. Regional Authority

An overarching need to develop solid programs is *regional planning.* Metropolitan areas are fragmented into numerous small, competing political divisions. Each jealously guards its own turf against other jurisdictions. Governments responsible for regional development can be created without abolishing the individual, smaller governments. States, from which cities receive their charter to operate, can force cities to give some of their authority to regional bodies (such as water and sewer systems, police and fire protection, and building codes). These agencies would then implement policies for the region as a whole.

EDUCATING THE POOR

To be successful, however, any urban program must confront one of our major failures, the education of the poor. As sociologist Herbert Gans (1968:292) said:

The public-school system has never learned how to teach poor children, mainly because it has not needed to do so. In the past, those who could not or would not learn what the schools taught dropped out quietly and went to work. Today, such children drop out less quietly, and they cannot find work. Consequently, the schools have to learn how to hold them, not only when they drop out physically, but long before, in the early elementary grades, when they begin to drop out in spirit.

Principles for Success

Good schools for the poor require more than new buildings. Teachers must nourish the motivation to learn. Poor children don't lack the desire to learn when they begin school. As they stay in school, however, they often see school as irrelevant to their lives and future. To do a better job of educating the poor, Gans (1968) pointed out that we need

1. Motivated teachers
2. New teaching methods
3. Smaller classes
4. Innovative curriculums that build on the aspirations of inner-city youth
5. A more decentralized and less bureaucratized school system
6. Work-study programs
7. Scholarships to encourage adult dropouts to return to school

To produce an effective learning environment, violence and gang activity must also be reduced—or, better, eliminated.

ABC

ABC (A Better Chance) is a successful program. Financed by corporations, foundations, and individuals, ABC specializes in identifying and recruiting gifted inner-city students, starting in junior high school, and matching them with top prep schools. Given scholarships, these high-performing youngsters attend schools such as Phillips Academy in Andover, Massachusetts, and Cate Preparatory School in Carpinteria, California. The program is so successful that 99 percent of all graduates go to college or study abroad (Holden 1994; Kinnon 1997).

The Potential vs. Short-Term Solutions

ABC enrolls one or two thousand students, but we need to touch the lives of most poor children. As the Thinking Critically box on next page shows, we *can* design and implement successful programs. Although these programs appear expensive, they would pay back their cost many times over: Getting young people in school and out of criminal pursuits reduces the cost of crime and punishment. As working adults, former students would also pay taxes, The initial cost, however, would be high, and the basic question is where this money would come from. Both our leaders and the public have a short-term view of educating the poor and show little interest in solving fundamental problems.

The Basic Solution

In conclusion, if we have learned anything from the recent past, it is that *replacing buildings does not cure urban ills.* Dilapidated buildings are only surface appearances, not the basic social problems of the city. The real problems are street crime, poverty, unemployment, broken families, gang violence, riots, arson, drug addiction, mental illness, and juvenile delinquency—conditions whose origins are not local and that fixing or replacing old buildings does not solve. As sociologist William Julius Wilson (1987)

The United States is experiencing one of its largest waves of immigration (approximately a million immigrants a year). Earlier immigrants formed ethnic enclaves in which they maintained customs from their homeland while they adjusted to the norms of their new land. Today's immigrants are following this same pattern.

Thinking Critically about Social Problems

EDUCATING FOR SUCCESS: REESTABLISHING COMMUNITY IN THE LEARNING PROCESS

Education is in crisis. Children are being promoted from one grade to another whether they learn or not. Some students graduate from high school illiterate. Budgets are cut, programs trimmed, teachers burned out, and students unmotivated.

"Sow the wind and reap the whirlwind," said Hosea, an Old Testament prophet. And sowing a future of children having babies, unemployment, welfare dependency, crime, and despair will bring a whirlwind of shattered community—which can destroy a society.

Can education make a difference? How about for the most impoverished of society, the children of the inner city? To find out, a team from Yale worked with the staff and parents in two grade schools in New Haven, Connecticut. The schools were in low-income neighborhoods that were 99 percent black and marked by the usual inner-city problems. Student achievement, which had been the lowest in the city, soared to the third and fourth highest. As measured on standardized tests, the students' achievement levels jumped to nine months above their grade level in one school, and twelve months ahead in the other. Attendance and behavior also improved dramatically.

How was this accomplished? First, the team made a radical assumption—that the problem was not "poor students," but, rather, the educational system. This put the responsibility on the shoulders of the staff—they had to meet the needs that the children's background created. Second, the staff fostered a feeling of common cause. They transferred leadership from a central office to the grass roots, to participants who worked on problems and made decisions together. Third, parents, staff, and students interacted frequently. This allowed students to identify with adults who valued and encouraged learning, reflecting a solid educational principle that learning is based on modeling and imitation. Fourth, a sense of community was engendered as trust, mutual respect, and a sense of common cause developed among teachers, administrators, parents, and students.

Using this same assumption—that inadequate teaching, not inadequate students, is the reason the poor children do not do well in school—Jaime Escalante motivated his students in an East Los Angeles inner-city school to perform so well on national calculus tests that officials thought that they had cheated.

How would you apply these principles to change a troubled school in your area? What other principles from this text would you use?

Based on Comer 1986, Escalante and Dirmann 1990; Hilliard 1991.

says, the key to solving urban problems is a revitalized economic system that offers work. We need to note how these conditions are in balance: On the one hand, greater access to jobs, housing, education, and justice will reduce urban problems; on the other hand, urban problems will persist to the same degree that these inequalities persist.

The Future of the Problem

Twelve Trends Likely to Continue

Based on current trends, I foresee the following.

1. The continued segregation of poor and minorities in the inner city
2. Further rebuilding of downtown areas
3. The slum areas adjacent to downtown areas remaining slums with the same problems they have now
4. Poor young males still being attracted to gangs
5. More young females joining gangs and committing street crimes
6. Street crimes that continue to make parts of the city unsafe for visitors and residents
7. Continued fear and avoidance of the inner city by the middle class
8. More middle-class flight to the suburbs, by both whites and minorities
9. Maintenance of racial-ethnic neighborhoods

10. More migration from the snow belt to the sun belt
11. Financial crises for city governments and deteriorating services
12. More gentrification as the middle class is drawn to cheaper housing

A Lower Tax Base and Deferred Maintenance

The reduced tax base in the face of rising costs and demands for services is an urgent problem. Our cities depend on federal money to finance many programs, from urban transit to rehabilitating buildings and even supervising playgrounds. Some of that federal money has dried up. Caught in a financial squeeze, some cities have cut back on education, street cleaning, recreation programs, and activities for children and the elderly. Because reducing services upsets voters, urban governments have postponed maintenance—a cutback that is less visible and less subject to voter outcry. Deferred maintenance, however, borrows from the future, for the deterioration of bridges, sewers, and city buildings continues. Deferred maintenance is one of the most severe crises that U.S. cities face.

Race–Ethnic Neighborhoods

The maintenance of racial-ethnic neighborhoods flies in the face of predictions that sociologists used to make. As sociologist John Palen (2002) points out, for decades sociologists predicted the imminent disappearance of ethnic neighborhoods—but apparently no one told the people who live there. Neighborhoods based on race-ethnicity and social class will continue to provide a sense of community for their residents.

Skid Rows

Skid rows used to mark all our cities. Now many have faded away because the skid row population is recruited primarily from unskilled migratory workers, a dwindling group. In addition, speculators saw the value of this urban real estate and converted many skid rows into high-rise office buildings, upscale shops, and hotels. The reclaiming of New York City's Times Square from winos, pimps, pornographers, and the down-and-out by developers is such an example. The demise of skid row may be more appearance than substance, however, for its residents don't disappear, but instead, resurface in adjacent areas, less visible because they are dispersed.

The Homeless

The homeless will continue their sorry presence on our city streets, but they will be persecuted by city officials. To foster tourism and profits, politicians will disperse the homeless. This will create an outcry—not at the existence of such miserable poverty but at the presence of pitiful people in areas that the better-off would like to enjoy without having their consciences pricked. There will be calls to remove the homeless from sight, to put them in "asylums" somewhere, as though hiding them might solve the problem.

Pressures on Housing

Two major forces will increase the demand for and cost of housing. First, each year about 4 million Americans turn age 30, the typical first-time home-buying age (*Statistical Abstract* 2003:Table 13). Second, the American dream of owning a home is deep, and it is nourished by developers and financial institutions. Middle-class Americans, although they have few children, want larger homes with more amenities (large master baths with his and her sinks, jacuzzis, hot tubs, and so on). As long as times are prosperous, these two factors will feed urban sprawl and inflate the cost of housing.

Potential In-Migration

Higher home and commuting costs could lead to a turnaround for our cities. As couples face the high cost of commuting to the city for work, the lower-priced, solid houses in deteriorated areas of the city become attractive. Gentrification holds the potential of reversing the exodus from the city. It may also signal another major racial-ethnic change, for it may increase the proportion of whites in our central cities. Gentrification, of course, will fuel another controversy, for it will mean accommodating the middle class at the expense of the poor, who are displaced.

Restratification

The future of the city depends on what city we are talking about. Because our cities are undergoing restratification, their future will be region oriented. Sun-belt cities hold the brightest future. With their influx of capital, jobs, and workers, along with an expanding tax base, they appear best equipped to weather problems.

Principles for Successful Social Policy to Mold the Future

I need to stress that no particular future is inevitable. The future of our cities depends on trends yet unknown and on the social policies we adopt. The following three principles provide a solid foundation for shaping that future:

1. As a cultural center of work and play, the city offers vast potential for human happiness.
2. The city is a social creation, and so are its negative features. As such, they can be overcome.
3. To design a future that overcomes urban problems, our policies must incorporate basic human needs—social, psychological, physical, and spiritual.

The Potential for Our Urban Future

These three principles can help us forge a future that enhances the quality of life, maximizes human potential, and creates urban areas that satisfy the human need for community. Or we can ignore sound principles and long-term planning, deal with problems on a piecemeal, haphazard basis, and leave a failed legacy to future Americans. The choice is ours.

As a final note, I want to stress that if we do not solve the problem of the poor who are isolated in the inner city—desperate people with little hope, who descend into drugs and crime, turning savagely on one another and on anyone within their reach—at some point. U.S. cities will again go up in flames.

SUMMARY

1. The world is seeing an urban explosion. In 1900, about 13 percent of the world's population lived in *cities*. Today about 50 percent do. The U.S. figure is almost 80 percent.
2. Symbolic interactionists emphasize that areas of the city that appear undesirable, disorganized, and threatening to outsiders may be a viable community to its inhabitants. Slums are worlds in miniature, with their own hierarchies of status, standards, and controls over behavior. The insider's frame of reference provided by symbolic interactionism helps us to understand such worlds.
3. According to functionalists, specialized zones naturally develop as a city grows. Each zone meets certain needs of a city's residents, and people with distinctive characteristics live there. Antagonisms result from the *invasion-succession cycle*, as one group displaces another. Urban problems are generally concentrated in the area adjacent to the central business district.
4. According to the conflict perspective, business leaders caused the decline of the inner city. They influenced politicians to subsidize the relocation of their businesses to the suburbs and to build a transportation system to move their products. Suburban development came at the city's expense; it reduced the city's tax base and spurred the flight of the middle class.
5. Many people find cities alienating and experience intense problems in them. Some people, however, find in cities islands of intimacy that yield high personal satisfaction.
6. The quality of life in our cities deteriorated because of *redlining*, the abandonment of buildings, the poor being locked out of opportunities, and the flight of the middle class. Older suburbs have similar problems.
7. Violence is such a problem that youth gangs even control some areas of our cities. Violence is also common in our urban schools. Poverty and discrimination remain background factors, but riots require a *precipitating incident*.
8. Ethnic minorities have gained political clout in our urban areas, and the transition of power has gone quite smoothly. *Megalopolises,* interconnected metropolitan centers that once were a series of smaller towns and cities, have emerged. The move to the sun belt is forcing *restratification* of U.S. cities in terms of capital, human resources, and political power.
9. To meet human needs better, urban policy can preserve neighborhoods and encourage new ones. Social policies include *urban homesteading, enterprise zones, job deconcentration, condominium in-filling,* and regional authority. To succeed, an urban policy must develop a sense of community and meet the needs of the poor.
10. Our cities have a troubled future. We are now at the crossroads in making decisions that will affect future generations.

KEY TERMS

Chicago school of sociology   An approach to research that originated with the Department of Sociology at the University of Chicago in the 1920s. It emphases were participant observation, symbolic interactionism, and seeing things from an insider's point of view.
City   A large number of people who are permanently based and do not produce their own food.
Commodity riot   Collective violence that involves extensive looting.

Communal riot Collective violence between the residents of two areas for control of a contested area.

Community People identifying with an area and with one another, sensing that they belong and that others care about what happens to them.

Concentric zone theory A theory developed by Ernest Burgess suggesting that cities develop outward from their center, resulting in areas, or zones, that have specialized functions. The area closest to the central business district—the zone in transition—has the most severe urban problems.

Condominium in-filling An urban policy in which condominiums for older people are built in vacant areas of a neighborhood, whereas the larger homes they vacate are taken over by younger families.

Disinvestment Withholding investments from an area.

Enterprise zones An urban policy that attempts to encourage private enterprise (investment) in a designated area by reducing taxes and government regulations.

Gemeinschaft A group of people characterized by bonds of intimacy combined with a sense of tradition and belonging. See also *Gesellschaft*.

Gentrification The relatively affluent displacing the poor and renovating their homes.

Gesellschaft A group of people characterized by impersonality and the pursuit of self-interest. See also *Gemeinschaft*.

Housing unit A place of residence normally occupied by a family, individual, or group of people. Examples are a detached house, a mobile home, an apartment, and a condominium.

Invasion–succession cycle One group moving into an area that is inhabited by a group that has different characteristics. Moving in represents the invasion; dominating the area, the succession.

Job deconcentration An urban policy that moves jobs to specified areas adjacent to a city.

Machine See *Political machine*.

Megalopolis Urban areas spilling onto one another, making them an interconnected region.

Political machine A political organization that distributes government jobs or favors among its members. Essential to its operation is an informal, behind-the-scenes working arrangement that circumvents the official ways of handling a city's business.

Precipitating incident An incident that triggers a riot.

Redlining The refusal to service a designated area, such as a bank not offering mortgages or an insurance company not writing insurance.

Restratification A shift in the relative wealth and power of the parts of a society. The gains recently made by the sun belt are an example.

Skid row An area of the city that is inhabited by the poor, the homeless, and the social institutions catering to their needs, such as rescue missions and shelters.

Suburban sprawl The disappearance of open areas as a suburb expands into the countryside.

Urban crisis The interrelated problems of governing and financing our cities, including their poverty, violence, crime, and deterioration of services.

Urban homesteading An urban policy whereby a city gives tax-foreclosed property to an individual who agrees to bring it into compliance with city codes and to live in it for a designated period of time.

Urban sprawl The expansion of a city onto adjacent farmland.

THINKING CRITICALLY ABOUT CHAPTER 12

1. Do you think that symbolic interactionism, functionalism, or conflict theory does the best job of explaining urban problems? Why?

2. If a bank decides that a certain area of a city is "risky" to invest in and makes a business decision to "redline" the area (refusing to give loans to people who live or work in the area), do you think it is proper for government to ban such a practice? Explain.

3. Which of these programs do you think are the most appropriate and helpful in combatting urban decay?
   • Urban homesteading
   • Enterprise zones
   • Job deconcentration
   • Condominium in-filling
   Why?

CHAPTER 13

Population and Food

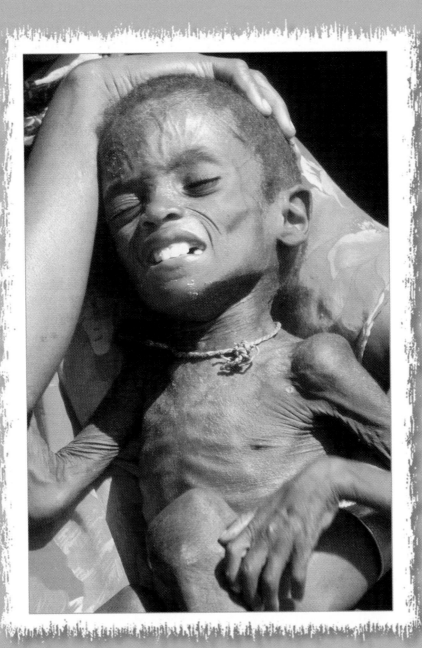

WITH HER VARICOSE VEINS AND HER blackened and missing teeth, Celia, only 30 years old, looked like an old woman. She beamed as she pointed to her distended stomach, indicating that her thirteenth child was on its way. Her oldest was only 14 years old! Looking at her smiling face, it was hard to imagine how she could be more delighted—even if she were expecting her first.

"The rich get richer—and the poor get children," I thought, as I looked around the tiny palapa, the single-room hut that housed this large family. I saw straw mats on the dirt floor where the older children slept, a double bed for the parents and younger children, and, for the oldest, a hammock strung between the poles that supported the thatched roof. The only furnishings were a stove, a cabinet where Celia stored her dishes and cooking utensils, and a table in the cooking area.

There were no chairs. This really startled me: The family was so poor that they could not afford even a single chair.

I found it difficult to swallow, as I ate the posole, swollen corn tasting something like hominy, that Celia and her husband, Angel, generously offered. "Surely the children are not receiving enough food on Angel's daily wage of $5," I thought. And the family obviously could not afford adequate medical care. They had lost one child to polio, while their oldest daughter had been left disfigured by an injury to her right eye. Vainly trying to conceal her disfigurement, this 13-year-old would constantly sweep stringy locks of hair over the ghastly eye.

I was living in Armería, Mexico, and I had gotten used to many things. But I found Celia's situation depressing. I looked at the haggard face of her oldest son. Only 14 years old, he worked in the fields with the men. Each day I watched these men, machetes in hand, dragging themselves home at twilight. This was his fate, to work exhaustingly in fields for pennies a day. But Celia could not have been more proud of him. He was doing his part to help pay for the family's needs. She was as thrilled about her son's working as a U.S. mother is when her child graduates from college.

And then there was the coming child. Celia and her husband were genuinely delighted about this latest pregnancy. I congratulated them on the coming blessed event and decided that I still had much to learn about this culture. "Why is their thinking so different from ours?" I wondered.

How could Celia have wanted so many children, especially when she lived in such poverty? That question bothered me. I couldn't let it go until I knew why.

This chapter helps to provide an answer.

The Problem in Sociological Perspective

What Is Demography?

The definition of **demography**—the study of the size, composition, growth, and distribution of human populations—makes it sound like a pretty dry subject. Yet this area of sociology is anything but dry, for demographers study some of the most far-reaching changes that are taking place in today's world. Some are even warning us that these changes might engulf us and our children and destroy our way of life.

Changes in population are especially important. For example, for most of history, the world's population increased at a snail's pace. When Jesus Christ was born 2,000 years ago, the population of the entire world was the same as that of the United States today. By 1750, all of Europe had only about 140 million inhabitants. Then there was an abrupt change: During just the next fifty years, Europe's population jumped by 48

Why Did Europe's Population Surge from 1750 to 1850?

million. Fifty years later, by 1850, it had shot up by another 68 million, reaching a total of 256 million. What caused this unprecedented change?

In 1926, G. T. Griffith argued that this increase was due to improved public health. Better medical knowledge, hospitals, housing, water, and sanitation, he said, lowered the *death rate,* the number of deaths per 1,000 people. More people lived longer, and the population jumped.

Griffith's explanation is widely accepted, but some demographers disagree. Thomas McKeown (1977), for example, claimed that the population of Europe remained low until 1750 because Europeans practiced **infanticide,** killing infants shortly after birth. This practice declined after 1750, he said.

If McKeown is right, why did infanticide decline? His answer is surprising—because of the potato! McKeown's explanation goes like this: Europeans practiced infanticide because their food supply could not support more people. Infanticide kept their population in balance with their food supply, preventing widespread starvation. When the Europeans' food supply suddenly changed, they stopped practicing infanticide, and their population shot upward.

Let's see why. When the Spaniards conquered South America in the 1500s, they discovered the potato, which was cultivated in the Andean highlands. When they brought the potato back home with them, Europeans first viewed this strange food with suspicion. Some grew it as a curiosity, and Europeans gradually began to see the potato as a good food. They then started to grow it in quantity. So sweeping was their change in attitude that by 1800 the potato had become the main food of the poor in northern and central Europe. This "miracle" vegetable enlarged Europe's food supply, allowing the population almost to double in a century.

Demography, then, emphasizes the relationship between population and environment. If a population increases dramatically, demographers look for changes in people's customs. These can range from the adoption of new medical and sanitation practices to simply a change in their diet.

The Gloomy Prophet: Thomas Malthus

Thomas Malthus, an English economist, took Europe's surge in population as a sign of doom. In 1798, he wrote an influential book, *An Essay on the Principle of Population.* Malthus argued that although population grows geometrically, that is, from 2 to 4 to 8 to 16 and so forth, the food supply increases only arithmetically, that is, from 1 to 2 to 3 to 4 and so on. This means, he said, that if births go unchecked, the population of a country, or even of the world, will outstrip its food supply.

The Pessimists: The New Malthusians

Malthus' conclusions were controversial at the time he made them, and they are still debated today. One group, whom we can call the *New Malthusians,* says that Malthus was right. We are still in the early stages of the process that Malthus identified, they say, and today's situation is as grim, if not grimmer, than he ever imagined. The world's population is out of control. It is following an **exponential growth curve.** This means that if growth doubles during approximately equal intervals of time, it suddenly accelerates.

To illustrate the implications of exponential growth, sociologist William Faunce (1981:84) told a parable about a man who saved a rich man's life. The rich man, of course, was very grateful, and he offered a reward:

> The man replied that he would like his reward to be spread out over a four-week period, with each day's amount being twice what he received on the preceding day. He also said he would be happy to receive only one penny on the first day. The rich man immediately handed over the penny and congratulated himself on how cheaply he had gotten by. At the end of the first week, the rich man checked to see how much he owed and was pleased to find that the total was only $1.27. By the end of the second week, he owed only $163.83. On the twenty-first day, however, the rich man was surprised to find that the total had grown to $20,971.51. When the twenty-eighth day arrived, the rich man was shocked to

discover that he owed $1,342,177.28 for that day alone and that the total reward had jumped to $2,684,354.56!

This is precisely what alarms the New Malthusians. They claim that we have just entered the "fourth week" of an exponential growth curve. Figure 13-1 shows why they think that the day of reckoning is just around the corner. It took from the beginning of time to 1800 for the world's population to reach its first billion. It then took only 130 years (1930) to add the second billion. Just thirty years later (1960), the world population hit 3 billion. The time it took to reach the fourth billion was cut in half, to only fifteen years (1975). Then just twelve years later (in 1987), the total reached 5 billion, and in another twelve years it hit 6 billion (in 1999).

On average, every minute of every day, 253 babies are born. As Figure 13-2 shows, at sunset the world has 217,000 more people than it did the day before. In one year, this amounts to an increase of 79 million people. In less than four years, the world adds the equivalent of the entire U.S. population (*Statistical Abstract* 2003:Table 1322; Haub 2004). You might think of it this way: *In just the next twelve years the world's population will increase as much as it did during the first 1,800 years after the birth of Christ.*

These figures terrify the New Malthusians. They are convinced that we are headed toward a showdown between population and food. In the year 2025, the population of just India, Pakistan, and Bangladesh is expected to be more than the entire world's population was 100 years ago (Haub 2004). It is obvious that we will run out of food if we don't curtail population growth. Soon we are going to see more pitiful, starving, Pakistani and Bangladeshi children on television.

The Optimists: The Anti-Malthusians

"You're wrong!" replies a much more optimistic group, which I call the Anti-Malthusians. "This is just scare talk," claims this group. "Ever since Malthus reached his faulty conclusions, like Chicken Little people have been running around claiming that the sky is falling—it is only a matter of time until the world is overpopulated and everybody starves. Year after year, the New Malthusians do the same song and dance, and, frankly, we're tired of it. Let's be realistic for a change."

FIGURE 13-1 *World Population: The Exponential Growth Curve*

Sources: Piotrow 1973:4; Haub 1995, 2004.

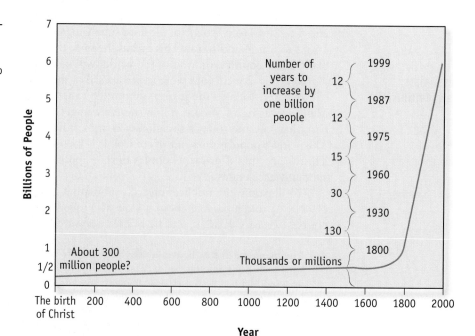

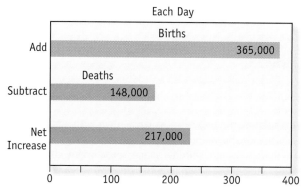

FIGURE 13-2 *How Fast Is the World's Population Growing?*

Source: Haub 2004.

And what is the counterargument of the Anti-Malthusians? They first point out that the way the New Malthusians perceive people is wrong, for the New Malthusians think of people as being comparable to germs that breed in a bucket:

> Assume there are two germs in the bottom of a bucket, and they double in number every hour. . . . If it takes one hundred hours for the bucket to be full of germs, at what point is the bucket one-half full of germs? A moment's thought will show that after ninety-nine hours the bucket is only half full. The title of this volume [*The 99th Hour*] is not intended to imply that the United States is half full of people but to emphasize that it is possible to have "plenty of space left" and still be precariously near the upper limit. (Price 1967:4)

Anti-Malthusians scoff at this image. They say that fitting the world's current population growth onto an exponential growth curve and then projecting it into the future indefinitely is totally incorrect. This ignores people's intelligence and their rational planning when it comes to having children. To understand what people really do, we need to study the historical record. Here we see an encouraging principle: People generally limit reproduction to match their available food. And this principle applies today, as shown in the Global Glimpse box on the next page. The current "explosion" in world population, then, is a hopeful sign. It means that the world is producing *more food* than ever before. As the Europeans did when they added the potato to their diet, people today are simply reacting to a growing food supply.

To understand the future, continue the Anti-Malthusians, consider Europe's **demographic transition.** As diagrammed in Figure 13-3 on the next page, Stage I consists of a fairly stable population—high death rates offset the high birthrates. Most of Europe's history was characterized by Stage I. Then came the "population explosion" of about 1750, which so frightened Malthus, and Europe entered Stage II. The population surged because death rates declined rapidly but birthrates remained high. Europe then moved to Stage III. Its population stabilized as people brought their birthrates in line with their lower death rates.

The demographic transition was so successful that European countries now worry about *not having enough babies.* Having moved into Stage IV of the demographic transition, Western European leaders fear **population shrinkage,** not producing enough children to replace people who die. Italy was the first country in the world to have more people over age 65 than children under age 15. The transition has been like a small stream that turns into a raging river. Of the 42 countries of Europe, 40 no longer produce enough children to maintain their populations (McDonald 2001). They all fill more coffins than cradles.

The Anti-Malthusians predict that this demographic transition will also occur in the poorer nations of the world. The rapid growth of these nations today is not a cause for concern, for it merely indicates that they have reached the second stage of the demographic transition. Already their growth rate has slowed. Look again at Figure 13-1 on page 424. It took the world's population 12 years to go from four to five billion, and then another 12 years to go from five to six billion. If population growth had kept accelerating as it had been doing, this last billion of people would have taken less than 12 years. Instead, population growth tapered off, the precise slowing that we would expect. These nations are just now penetrating the third stage of the demographic transition. Soon we will be wondering what all the fuss was about.

A Global Glimpse

"I'D LIKE TO HAVE TWENTY CHILDREN"

In 1976, an anthropologist who was making a documentary of an African village in Kenya, asked a 26-year-old mother of two how many children she wanted. The woman looked at her bulging stomach, giggled, and said, "I'd like to have twenty children."

The documentary then went into a freeze frame, with a subtitle stating that the woman had given birth to twins.

This image haunted John Tierney, a *New York Times* reporter. "What is wrong with her?" he wondered. "What would become of her family?" Ten years later he went to Kenya to follow up the story. He found the woman, Fanisi Kalusa, living in the same hut, the twins healthy, She was now 36, with seven children, aged 4 to 16.

When Tierney asked about her wanting twenty children, Fanisi laughed, and said, "I've rejected that idea because there is not enough food to meet the demand."

Most African men dislike birth control, but her husband had agreed to limit their family. He had his mother put a curse on his wife to make her barren—a standard practice in the area.

Fanisi went along with the curse—but without telling her husband, she visited a clinic for a free IUD.

Having twenty children made sense when children meant more hands to help farm the land and to support the parents in their old age. But now, children have become expensive in Kenya. For each child, parents must pay $10 a year in tuition, a burden in this poor land. In addition, many children are moving to the city, breaking the close family bonds and threatening the custom of adult children providing support for their aged parents.

Fanisi told her 16-year-old daughter to have only six children. Fanisi's daughter told Tierney that she thought four would be about right.

What do you think? Will Africa successfully make the demographic transition? The Anti-Malthusians point to Fanisi Kalusa as evidence that they will. But the New Malthusians retort that Kenya is growing at 2.3 percent each year—*four* times as fast as the United States.

Based on Tierney 1986; Haub 2004.

FIGURE 13-3 *The Demographic Transition*
Source: By the author.

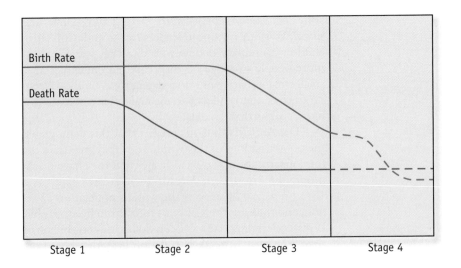

Note: The standard demographic transition is depicted in Stages 1–3. Stage 4 has recently been suggested by some Anti-Malthusians.

Experiencing the Demographic Transition

arl Haub, Senior Demographer at the Population Reference Bureau, became interested in population growth in the 1970s when he learned that the populations of some of the world's poorest nations would double in 23 years. He has conducted demographic research in Belarus, Honduras, India, Jamaica, Trinidad and Tobago, and Viet Nam.

The populations of the world's poorest nations began to grow rapidly when their death rates declined owing to such factors as immunization campaigns, but their birth rates remained high. As a result, their growth rates shot up. This was unlike Europe, where birth and death rates tended to decline together.

Most Least Industrialized Nations have adopted policies to slow their rates of growth. Without this, it would be impossible for them to improve health conditions and have any hope of feeding their people. A key point for demographers is the length of time it takes for a country's birth rate to decline to what we call the *replacement level*. This is achieved when couples average about two children each. When this happens, a country's population reaches zero growth, neither growing nor declining, since the average couple simply "replaces" itself.

Since most Least Industrialized Nations do not have thorough registration systems of their births and deaths, how do we know what a country's growth rate is? We glean trends in their population growth from their national census data. In addition, we take demographic surveys to fill the gaps in our knowledge.

Birth rates have declined remarkably in some countries, such as Brazil, South Korea, Thailand, and Tunisia. In others, especially the countries of sub-Saharan Africa, progress has been slow. In some sub-Saharan countries,

progress has even stopped. In Asia and Latin America, the story is mixed. India, with one billion people, has seen some success, especially in its more educated areas. But in Uttar Pradesh, India's largest state with 170 million people, women still give birth to nearly five children each. In Costa Rica, the birth rate has declined to the replacement level, but in Guatemala it remains high.

The Green Revolution was truly a revolution; it improved food supplies in the Least Industrialized Nations. But the story does not end there. Poverty remains widespread in these nations, and malnutrition is still common. Without declines in population growth, alleviating poverty will be difficult. Consider these two countries: In Yemen, a country of high poverty, women still average about seven children. In Thailand, where much of the population is still rural, women average less than two.

Two recent demographic developments are of major concern to demographers: HIV/AIDS and population shrinkage. HIV/AIDS has taken a toll, particularly in Africa, where, in some countries, over 30 percent of the population are infected. This has drastically changed the population outlook for these countries. The population of Africa, however, is still growing rapidly. In contrast, population shrinkage, not growth, is the situation in many of the Most Industrialized Nations. In all of Europe and in Japan, low birth rates are causing concern. In Germany and Italy, for example, women now average only 1.3 children. These low birth rates will lead to social problems.

Today's demographic trends will have significant impacts on society. The future will bring new developments, which will add to the developing demographic story.

One of the researchers whom I have referenced is Carl Haub, a demographer. As he discusses his work in the Spotlight on Research box above, he touches on many of the issues that we have reviewed.

The Scope of the Problem

How the New Malthusians See the Scope of the Problem

Let's suppose that the world's population doubles during the next 54 years, which it will if present growth rates continue. Can the world support twice its present population? The New Malthusians say that we can get the answer by looking at how the world is doing with its current population. They stress that famine and malnutrition stalk the earth. About one of every five people on earth lives in absolute poverty (Livernash and Rodenburg 1998). Eight hundred million people are malnourished and go to bed hungry each night (Pollack 2004). In some of the world's poorest nations, such as Bangladesh, *half* the population does not eat enough protein. Every year thousands of people in Africa, Asia, and Latin America are born deaf-mutes because of iodine deficiency. Several hundred million people survive on *less* than $1,000 a year. In Ethiopia, which is growing so fast that by the year 2050 it will be the tenth largest country in the world, the *average* income is just $100 for the entire year (*Statistical Abstract* 2003:Table 1333).

As bad as it is now, add the New Malthusians, the future looks even bleaker. Urban sprawl is devouring productive farmlands. In the United States alone, each year developers turn about 3 million acres of farmland into subdivisions and businesses. This is enough land to form a corridor a mile and a half wide stretching from San Francisco to New York. The land chewed up by urban sprawl is lost to food production, further sealing the fate of the world's malnourished.

How the Anti-Malthusians See the Scope of the Problem

"It isn't like that at all," reply the Anti-Malthusians. The idea that the United States is being "paved over" is absurd, argued economist Julian Simon (1981). The United States has about 2 billion acres. All the land taken up by cities, highways, roads, railroads, and airports amounts to only 75 million acres—less than 4 percent of our total land. We are in no danger of running out of farmland.

Urban sprawl has not even slowed food production, add the Anti-Malthusians, nor is it taking food out of the mouths of starving children, as the New Malthusians would have us believe. The problem of starvation has nothing to do with the earth having too many people, nor with the earth failing to produce enough food. The amount of food available for every person on earth has actually been *increasing*, not decreasing. Every country records how much food it produces. As Figure 13-4 shows, *despite the billions of people who have been added to the earth's population, more food is available*

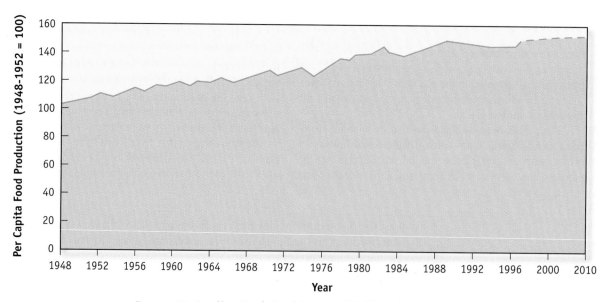

FIGURE 13-4   *How Much Food Does the World Produce Per Person?*

Source: U.S. Department of Agriculture. Simon 1981:58; *Statistical Abstract* 1988:Table 1411; 1998:Tables 1380, 1381, 1382, 1383; recomputed to 1948–52 base.

Note: Projections from 1997 are the author's.

per person now than in the past. The United States produces so much food that our problem is what to do with it all. The U.S. government even pays its farmers *not* to farm some land. Americans eat so much that obesity has become a major health problem. The bottom line is that efforts to reduce the world's population are misdirected.

If it isn't too many people or not enough food, then what causes starvation? The earth's abundance, continue the Anti-Malthusians, is not distributed adequately. If we were to redistribute a mere 3 to 5 percent of the grain grown in the Most Industrialized Nations, we could prevent *all* the malnutrition and starvation in the entire world (Conti 1980).

The African starvation that upsets the world does *not* occur because there are too many people, but because of drought and civil war. Africa is rich in resources, and it has *fewer people per square mile than either Europe or the United States* (Haub 2004). Those alarming images of starving children—scrawny bony arms, protruding stomachs, and flies crawling over their faces—are due to civil wars that disrupt food production and block humanitarian aid from reaching the dying (Gibbons 1991; MacKenzie 1998; Nelan 1998). The suffering shown in this chapter's opening photo is totally unnecessary. There is plenty of food to feed this child—and all others like her.

To look at the problem of starvation as too many people or the earth not producing enough food misses the mark entirely. The problem is a combination of agricultural inefficiency, inadequate incentives, political corruption, maldistribution of the earth's abundance, poor governments, and war—not too little food in the world.

Simon (1981) stressed that today's famines are even a sign that food production and distribution have improved. *Fewer* people starve today, he pointed out, than at any other point in history for which we have reasonable estimates. This means that the food supply for the poor is more stable than at any time in the past two or three centuries.

As far as those statistics about deaf-mutes go, the Anti-Malthusians agree that those are horrible figures. They point out, however, that these people are born deaf-mutes because they lack iodized food, not because they are "excess" people. Their situation has nothing to do with the earth being overpopulated. The problem is how to get iodized food to people, not how to reduce population.

In Sum   The New Malthusians and the Anti-Malthusians draw different conclusions from the same evidence. Much like the pessimists who look at the water in a glass and conclude that the glass is half empty, the New Malthusians conclude that we are about to run out of land and food. Like the optimists who consider the same glass of water half full, the Anti-Malthusians conclude that our era enjoys the greatest abundance and hope that the world has ever known. The scope of the population problem depends on one's perception—whether one sees the glass as half empty or half full.

No one can settle this for you. You will have to read the evidence and make up your own mind. As you do so, remember the symbolic interactionist principle that *facts never interpret themselves:* To interpret something, we place it within a framework that gives it meaning. As we consider issues of population and food in the coming pages, we will return to this basic principle from time to time. For now, let's apply the frameworks of understanding called sociological theories.

Looking at the Problem Theoretically

As usual, our three theoretical lenses provide contrasting perspectives. We will use symbolic interactionism to better understand why the population of the Least Industrialized Nations is growing so fast. Functionalism illuminates the relationship between modern medicine and the twin problems of population and food. Finally, conflict theory yields a controversial analysis of food, profits, and international relations. Together, these perspectives help us understand the whole.

With political conflicts common, the world is awash in refugees, who need to be fed, clothed, and sheltered. Their care is usually a temporary matter, as in this scene from Afghanistan, but in some instances the turmoil continues or the refugees' government refuses to allow them back into the country. In that case the "temporary" arrangement can continue for decades.

SYMBOLIC INTERACTIONISM

Why Do the Poor Have So Many Children?

Let's start with something that doesn't seem to make sense. Look at Figure 13-5. The population of the Least Industrialized Nations is increasing fast; that of the Most Industrialized Nations is standing still. You can see that *almost all* the increase in the world's population is coming from the Least Industrialized Nations.

This seems obvious: If you are poor, you should have few children. Yet you can see that the world's population growth is driven by the poor nations of the world. Why don't hunger and disease, starvation and death convince poor people to have fewer children? Do people in the Least Industrialized Nations *want* to have fewer children, but don't know how to prevent them? This is not the case. Cheap and effective birth control techniques are available, but many of the poor won't use them. They continue to have many children because they *want* large families (Burns 1994).

The focus of symbolic interactionism—trying to grasp people's perspective, to see the world as they see it—helps explain this. What to us seems to be irrational behavior takes different shape when we examine what children *mean* for people in the Least Industrialized Nations.

Taking the Role of the Other

Recall Celia and Angel in the chapter's opening vignette. As you could tell, it was difficult for me to understand Celia's joy at being pregnant with her thirteenth child when her oldest child was only 14 years old and she was just 30. I was viewing her situation from my framework, not as she and her husband saw it. Only by **taking the role of the other**—that is, seeing things from another person's perspective—can we make sense of people's experiences.

To understand Celia and Angel's desire for more children, then—and the desires of billions of poor people like them—we must move beyond our own culture. We first need to see that in the Least Industrialized Nations people's identities center around their children. Motherhood is the most exalted status that a woman can achieve. It is what she was born for. Through childbearing, she fulfills this destiny and finds personal fulfillment. The more children she bears, the more she fulfills the purpose for which she was born. Similarly, the more children that a man fathers, the

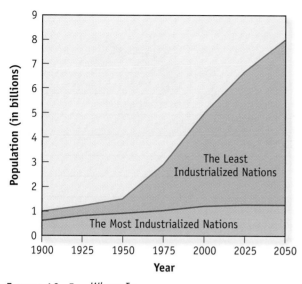

FIGURE 13-5 *Where Is the World's Population Growth Taking Place?*

Sources: World Population Profile 1985; Haub 2004.

more he proves his manhood. It is especially sons that he desires, for through them, his name lives on.

There is more to the explanation, though: Most of these people live in small communities where they share values and identify with one another. It is in this *Gemeinschaft* community of like-minded people that they are given or denied the status that matters—their rank in the family and among friends and neighbors. Having many children is taken as a sign of God's blessing on their lives. As people produce more children, then, the community grants them higher status. The barren woman, not the woman with a dozen children, is to be pitied.

These are strong motivations for bearing many children. But there is yet another: For the poor in the Least Industrialized Nations, children are *economic assets*. This, too, is difficult for us to grasp. We live in an urbanized, postindustrialized society where children are economic liabilities. Long ago, we left the agrarian world where children helped on the family farm. In our world, children have become luxuries. They are expensive to bear and to rear—and with our requirement of college, and even graduate school, for economic success, they remain so for many years. In the Most Industrialized Nations, young adults consider whether to have children in much the same way that they consider buying a new car: "Can we afford one?" or "Should we put it off until later?"

How, then, can poor people afford to have many children, and why do they view children as economic assets? These people live in a different world. They have no social security, no medical insurance, and no unemployment benefits. This motivates them to have *more* children, not fewer, for when parents become too old to work, they rely on their adult children to take care of them. Their children are their social security, and the more children they have, the firmer that security. In addition, children

As stressed in the text, events in life do not come with built-in meanings. All of us use frameworks of thought to interpret life's events. How do New Malthusians and Anti-Malthusians interpret this scene in India? Why do they see things so differently?

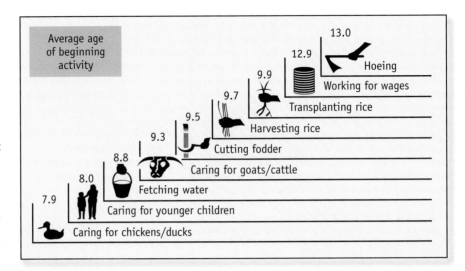

FIGURE 13-6 *Why the Poor in the Least Industrialized Nations Want Many Children*
Based on a survey in Indonesia, this figure shows how children are economic assets in the Least Industrialized Nations. Boys and girls can be net income earners for their families by the age of 9 or 10.
Source: U.N. Fund for Population Activities.

start to contribute financially to their family long before the parents are old. As you will recall, at age 14, the oldest son of Celia and Angel was contributing to his family. Figure 13-6 should help you take the role of the other, which is essential if we are to understand why the surge in the world's population is coming from the Least Industrialized Nations.

Our own situation in life, of course, is remarkably different, and for us it would be irrational to have many children. From the framework of the people involved, however—the essence of the symbolic interactionist position—having many children is rational. Consider this incident reported by a worker for the government of India:

> A water carrier . . . Thaman Singh. . . . welcomed me inside his home, gave me a cup of tea (with milk and "market" sugar, as he proudly pointed out later), and said: "You were trying to convince me . . . that I shouldn't have any more sons. Now, you see, I have six sons and two daughters and I sit at home in leisure. They are grown up, and they bring me money. One even works outside the village as a laborer. *You told me I was a poor man and couldn't support a large family. Now, you see, because of my large family I am a rich man.*" (Italics added) (Mamdani 1973:109)

In Sum

Our ideas of the right number of children make sense for us, for our perspectives match our life situation. To superimpose our ideas onto people in a different culture, however, is to overlook their situation and their perspectives. To understand the behavior of any group, we must see things as they see them, including—and perhaps especially—behavior that appears irrational to us.

FUNCTIONALISM

As we apply the functionalist perspective, keep in mind that functionalists want to determine *objectively* what the functions or consequences of events are, without the goal of judging those consequences as good or bad. As we saw in the instances of poverty, rape, murder, drug addiction, and racial-ethnic discrimination, functionalists find that even deviant, illegal, or abhorrent events have functions. With regard to the social problem of population and food, functionalists stress that war, natural disasters, disease, and famine are functional. Historically, these mass killers held the world's population

Catastrophes Are Functional

in check, keeping it to manageable levels and ensuring that humans did not outstrip their food supply.

Modern medicine, however, upset this precarious balance between population and food. The high death rates of the Least Industrialized Nations plunged as better nutrition, sanitation, and Western drugs brought the major killers—smallpox, diphtheria, typhoid, measles, and other communicable diseases—under control. The birthrates in the Least Industrialized Nations, however, remained high. Millions of people who otherwise would have died not only survived, but they also reproduced. This has forced the Least Industrialized Nations into the difficult second stage of the demographic transition (see Figure 13-3 on page 426).

If a country is in the second stage of the demographic transition, it has a lot of young people; if it is in the third or fourth stage, it has a lot of older people. Obviously, countries that have a lot of younger people are going to have higher birthrates. These different age structures, as demographers call them, produce different "shapes" of populations. To illustrate those shapes, demographers produce **population pyramids,** such as Figure 13-7, which contrasts Mexico, in Stage II of the demographic transition, with that of the United States, which is in advanced Stage III.

Let's consider one of the implications of Figure 13-7. If Mexico and the United States had the same number of people, Mexico would still grow faster than the United States. The reason? A lot more of its population are young, in the childbearing years. This is the case with all the Least Industrialized Nations, giving them what demographers call *population momentum.* What accounts for the growth that you saw in Figure 13-5 on page 431, then, isn't only that the families are larger in the Least Industrialized Nations. This is important, as we considered with Celia and Angel, but

The Latent Dysfunctions of Modern Medicine and Public Health Practices

Population Pyramids

Population Momentum

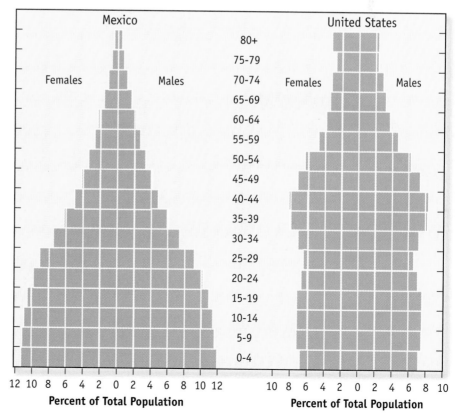

FIGURE 13-7 *Population Pyramids of Mexico and the United States*

Source: By the author. Computed from the U.S. Bureau of the Census, International Data Base, Table 94.

underlying this surge in growth is also the population momentum of the Least Industrialized Nations.

Doubling Times

Look at the consequence: The population growth of the Most Industrialized Nations averages 0.1 percent per year. At this rate; it will take 583 years for their population to double. The Least Industrialized Nations, in contrast, are growing *fifteen times faster,* and they will double in just 40 years (Haub and Cornelius 1999). The doubling time of the world's nations is shown on the Social Map below. Look at the extremes in Table 13-1: Chad will double its population in just 21 years, but it will take Austria 2,310 years to do so.

Implications of a Doubled Population

The implications of a doubled population are mind-boggling. *Just to stay even* a country must double its food production and factories; its medical and educational capacity; its transportation, communication, water, gas, sewer, and electrical systems; its housing, churches, civic buildings, stadiums, theaters, stores, and parks; its automobiles, electronics, and household appliances; as well as jobs and all else that constitutes "decent living standards." If not, a society's standard of living will fall.

The Contrast

The Least Industrialized Nations, then, appear destined to fall still farther behind the industrialized nations, for they start with less, and their swelling numbers drain their limited financial resources. In contrast, the Most Industrialized Nations, such as the United States, *can spend much more on fewer people.* With an annual growth rate of 0.9 percent, the United States is at the low end of the world's growth rate but at the high end of the rate for the Most Industrialized Nations. Half of the U.S. increase is due to immigration. The U.S. rate of natural increase (growth without immigration) is 0.6 percent (*Statistical Abstract* 2003:Table 4; Haub 2004).

Latent Dysfunctions of Medicine and Hygiene

Functionalists analyze how exporting modern medicine and public sanitation into the Least Industrialized Nations tipped a delicate balance. The unanticipated conse-

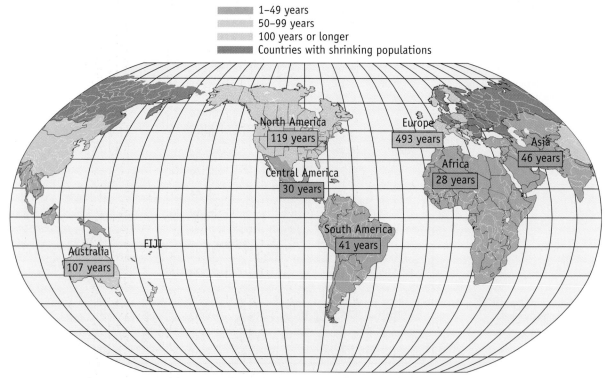

FIGURE 13-8 *Social Map: How Long Will It Take for Population to double?*
Source: Haub and Cornelius 1999.

TABLE 13-1 How Long Will It Take a Country to Double Its Population?

SOME MOST INDUSTRIALIZED NATIONS

COUNTRY	POPULATION (IN MILLIONS)	BIRTHS (PER 1,000 WOMEN)	DEATHS (PER 1,000 POPULATION)	ANNUAL NATURAL INCREASE	YEARS IT TAKES TO DOUBLE
United States	290	15	9	0.6	116
Canada	31	11	7	0.4	162
Japan	127	10	7	0.2	318
Great Britain	59	12	10	0.2	423
Denmark	5	12	11	0.1	472
Belgium	10	11	10	0.1	693
Austria	8	10	10	Slightly over 0	2,310

SOME LEAST INDUSTRIALIZED NATIONS

COUNTRY	POPULATION (IN MILLIONS)	BIRTHS (PER 1,000 WOMEN)	DEATHS (PER 1,000 POPULATION)	ANNUAL NATURAL INCREASE	YEARS IT TAKES TO DOUBLE
Chad	8	50	17	3.3	21
Nicaragua	5	38	6	3.2	22
Ethiopia	60	46	21	2.5	28
Algeria	31	30	6	2.4	29
Mexico	100	27	5	2.2	32
India	987	28	9	1.9	37
China	1,254	16	7	1.0	73

Source: By the author, based on Haub 2004.

quences of exporting these features from the West was a surge in their population as their natural killers were curtailed. As their rapid population growth outstripped their food supply, the resulting dysfunctions were malnutrition, mass starvation, and political unrest. Because these negative consequences were not anticipated or intended, sociologists call them **latent dysfunctions.**

But Could These Difficulties Actually Be Functional?

Where others see dysfunctions, the Anti-Malthusians see functions. They believe that in the long run the increase in the world's population is functional. The Least Industrialized Nations are fighting through the difficult second stage in their demographic transition, but they will enter the third stage and limit their populations. Some already have begun to do so. Their growing populations will stimulate them to industrialize and to apply technology to farming. Consequently, they will increase their food supply to match their growing populations. Warnings to reduce world population are unwarranted, and the population surge that some now find so upsetting will turn out to be functional for humanity.

CONFLICT THEORY

The Problem Is Not Nature, But Power: Arrangements that Favor the Most Industrialized Nations

Conflict theorists focus on the global distribution of power and resources. They stress that social and economic arrangements, not nature, produce poverty, hunger, and starvation. The Least Industrialized Nations have problems feeding their populations not because of Malthusian inevitabilities but because they have too little income. As sociologist Michael Harrington (1977) stressed, their income is restricted because global political and economic arrangements favor the rich nations.

Conflict theorists point out that the Most Industrialized Nations exploit the Least Industrialized Nations today just as the European powers used to exploit their colonies. They control the international markets so they can extract the mineral and agricultural wealth of the Least Industrialized Nations at low cost. Manipulating commodity markets, they determine what they will pay for tin from Bolivia, copper from Peru, sugar from Cuba, coffee from Brazil, and so forth.

The poor nations even contribute to the diet of the rich nations. For example, each year the United States imports about $42 billion of food, much of it from the Least Industrialized Nations (*Statistical Abstract* 2003:Table 825). Although the ultimate consumers of these foods pay dearly for them, the poor countries themselves receive little for the foods they sell. As Harrington (1977) pointed out, global arrangements put the real profits in the pockets of the middlemen in the Most Industrialized Nations.

Food Politics

The United States also exports about $53 billion of food (*Statistical Abstract* 2003:Table 824). Like other grain-exporting nations, it treats food as a money-making enterprise, not as a means of dealing with world hunger. The United States and Canada, which control about 60 percent of the world's wheat market, sell their wheat surpluses first to those that can pay the highest prices, not to the most needy (Conti 1980; *Statistical Abstract* 2003:Table 1353).

Why does the U.S. government pay farmers billions of dollars *not* to grow crops, even though people in some nations are starving? Conflict theorists say that the answer is *food politics,* controlling food production to control food prices. Paying farmers to leave their land fallow creates an artificial shortage and drives up grain prices. This also reduces the charges for storing grain—as there is less grain to store—and caters to the farm vote by keeping grain prices high. Food politics, stress conflict theorists, is pursued for political ends, with no concern for its moral implications. An indication that conflict theorists are correct is the U.S. government's own term for this practice: price supports.

In Sum

Conflict theorists conclude that food is a tool in the U.S. diplomatic kit. The food crisis that affects the undernourished masses of the world—and that so gnaws at our consciences as we see those shriveled bodies on television and in magazines—is the result of food politics, not Malthusian inevitabilities. Conflict theorists think in terms of a grain cartel headed by the United States and Canada, which is as damaging to the Least Industrialized Nations as the OPEC oil cartel was to the industrialized world before the United States bombed it into submission. The United States, say conflict theorists, is engaged in a struggle of "agripower" against "petropower."

Research Findings

Let's first examine the position of the New Malthusians: the harm to fisheries, forests, and grasslands; the threat of plant disease and the intensification of natural disasters; and the built-in momentum in world population growth. Then, after considering the views of the Anti-Malthusians, we'll conclude by examining why it is difficult to predict population growth accurately. We'll also consider whether the United States has a population problem.

THE NEW MALTHUSIANS

Three Natural Systems:

As you have seen, the New Malthusians are convinced that the world is outstripping its food supply. The world's huge population has put unsustainable pressure on the earth's three natural systems—its fishing grounds, forests, and grasslands—on which we all depend for food. Each has a *carrying capacity*, limits fixed by nature, and we are straining those limits.

1. The Fishing Grounds

It is folly to view the ocean, as some do, as an infinite source of food that only needs better harvesting techniques (Hayden 2003). Biologists Paul and Anne Ehrlich (1972) note that 90 percent of the ocean is a biological desert. The upper layer of open sea, which gets enough sunlight for photosynthesis, lacks nutrients for high productivity. Close to shore are the areas that supply us with virtually all our fish, but these are also the most polluted waters. Fishing fleets equipped with sonar and mile-long drift nets are devastating these fragile fish populations.

2. The Forests

The second natural system, the forests, seems eternally renewable. On one level, this is true. For every tree cut down, a tree can be planted. Each year, however, the world's forests shrink by an area the size of Cuba. In some places, the cutting is not accompanied by replanting. In Peru and Chile, for example, vast areas have been cut for firewood and farming. With the soil unprotected against wind and rain, some hills are as barren as the moon. Pressure on the world's forests continues to increase, as the demand for newsprint and packaging soars worldwide. Incredibly, it takes about 850 acres of timber to produce just the Sunday edition of the *New York Times* (Waddington 1978).

3. The Grasslands

The third global life-support system, the grasslands, is also under mounting pressure. Many U.S. farmers in the Midwest, for example, have bulldozed their windrows, the row of trees to break the wind that they had planted between their fields. By reducing the force of the wind, windrows keep topsoil from blowing away. Now that many are removed, some fear a repeat of the dust bowl of the 1930s. Back then, Oklahoma was the main victim; this time, much of the Midwest could be hit.

Much of the agricultural production of the Midwest and the West depends on the Ogallala aquifer, an extensive underground water system. Irrigation is depleting this reservoir. Wells are running dry, as we shall see in the next chapter. Soon we will have to curtail this extensive irrigation, which underlies much of the high productivity of the western United States.

Around the world, the pressing need for food is pushing into production land that is basically unsuitable for cultivation (Little and Horowitz 1987). The steep hillsides of Indonesia are being eroded; slash-and-burn agriculture is destroying tropical forests in many countries, including Brazil and the Philippines. Attempts to apply farming techniques that work in the temperate zone to the tropical soils of Brazil and Sudan have caused **laterization,** the transformation of soils into laterite, a rocklike material. This occurs when cultivation exposes certain soils to the air.

Two Major Dangers:

1. Disease of Specialized Strains

In addition to pressure on the world's three natural systems, the expanding population of the world faces two other dangers. First, the world's agricultural system now depends on only a few specialized strains of crops. In the quest for higher yields, a few specifically bred, high-yield strains have replaced the world's wide range of traditional varieties of wheat and rice. Although these high-yield varieties allow farmers to produce more food, they also increase the potential of widespread crop failure from insects and disease.

Biologists John Holdren and Paul Ehrlich (1974) warned that what happened in Ireland during the nineteenth century could happen to our generation, but on a much larger scale:

> The Irish potato famine of the last century is perhaps the best-known example of the collapse of a single agricultural ecosystem. The heavy reliance of the Irish population on a single, high productive crop led to 1.5 million deaths when the potato monoculture fell victim to a fungus.

In other words, if the right pest or plant disease comes along, we can have a worldwide calamity. Our extensive cultivation of single high-yield grains is "an accident waiting to happen." The benefits it now yields may come at the future cost of epidemic starvation, malnutrition, and disease. This could occur in surprising ways. For example, the 2004 hurricane season was one of the worst that the United States ever experienced. These hurricanes unexpectedly spread to the United States from South America a fungus that attacks soybeans.

2. Intensification of Natural Disasters

The second danger arises from the intensification of natural disasters. As human populations grow, they expand into areas less likely to protect them from the elements. The Ehrlichs (1972:243) provided this account of how overpopulation intensifies natural disasters:

> In November of 1970, a huge tidal wave driven by a cyclone swept over the Ganges Delta of East Pakistan. There a large, mostly destitute population lived exposed on flat lowland, in spite of the ever-present danger of climatic disaster for which the region is famous. They live in constant jeopardy because in grossly overpopulated East Pakistan the choice of places for them is greatly restricted. In November, 1970, 300,000 people died who need not have died if their nation had not been over-populated. This cataclysm has been described as the greatest documented national disaster in history.

In this poor, overcrowded nation, now called Bangladesh, evacuation was impossible. Because it was already nutritionally marginal, after the disaster people began to starve.

An Amazing Statistic

Now consider this statistic, which underscores the New Malthusians' point. Despite this huge death toll, in only five or six weeks new births made Bangladesh's population as large as it was before the catastrophe (Waddington 1978). In May 1991, a cyclone and its aftermath claimed about 200,000 Bangladeshi (Crossette 1991). It would take just a month to replace this number.

Thus the New Malthusians conclude that humanity must stop its population growth. Outstripping our food supply, they warn, will bring the worst catastrophe that the world has ever known. Some are so pessimistic that they say even an increased food supply will not buy much time. It would allow us to postpone, but not avoid, the inevitable disaster. The only solution is to stabilize world population (Miles 1970).

Zero Population Growth

Suppose that we achieve **zero population growth**—that is, adults reproducing only enough children to replace themselves. It seems obvious that the world's population problem would disappear, right? The obvious, however, is not true. *The population momentum that we discussed earlier would keep the world's population growing for 50 to 70 years before it leveled off.* By definition, zero population growth combined with the population continuing to grow are contradictory. Yet this strange combination is true. The reason for it is found in the population pyramids on page 433. In the Least Industrialized Nations, there are more people in the younger age groups than in the older age groups. For example, 42 percent of Africa's people are not yet age 15 (Haub 2004). Thus, more people will enter the reproductive ages each year than will leave them. Although the growth *rate* would fall during this 50- to 70-year period, population would increase before it eventually levelled off.

Even World Peace Is Threatened

The future looks desperate. Famine, malnutrition, and starvation are ready to strike the earth. We are also suffering from pollution and environmental destruction as too many people try to scratch a living from the earth's precarious surface. (We discuss this in the next chapter.) The world's swelling population also threatens world peace. When the governments of the Least Industrialized Nations cannot feed their people, riots will break out. Governments will topple, threatening the precarious balance of international power.

THE ANTI-MALTHUSIANS

Larger Populations Are Good

The Anti-Malthusians, of course, draw different conclusions. They insist that, in the long run, more people are *good* for a country; larger populations lead to *higher* standards of living (Simon 1977, 1982, 1991). This seems to fly in the face of reality. How can they possibly take this position? All we have to do is look at India, Bangladesh, and

China. To support their position, the anti-Malthusians make four points. First, population growth forces countries to use their land more efficiently, thereby increasing productivity. Second, a growing population means that more geniuses will be born, who will contribute to everyone's welfare. Third, larger populations create larger markets. This promotes more efficient manufacturing, lowering the production cost per unit. More goods become available more cheaply. Fourth, a larger population makes many social investments profitable, especially railroads, highways, irrigation systems, and ports. They don't pay off for sparse populations. These factors spur productivity and increase a country's capacity to deliver that productivity to its people.

Food Production Is Outpacing Population Growth

The Anti-Malthusians stress that we should not lose sight of how the world's food production. has *outpaced* the world's population growth. (Recall Figure 13-4 on page 428.) Today there is more food for each person in the entire world than there was 25, 50, or even 100 or 200 years ago. Moreover, this increase in per capita food occurred while the world's population "exploded." During this same time, the United States, the "breadbasket of the world," decreased the number of acres that it farmed. As Figure 13-9 shows, the United States now has *less* land under the plow than in 1920.

If the population increase is dramatic, then this food increase is more dramatic still. Even in the Least Industrialized Nations, agricultural production has outpaced population growth. Despite its surge in population, India, for example, produces more food per capita than it did years ago (Stevens 1994). As productivity in the Least Industrialized Nations increases, they, too, will need even less land to feed even more people (Simon 1981).

When it comes to fishing grounds, the Anti-Malthusians say that the numbers tell the story there, too. The world's fish harvest has not fallen, as one would expect from the New Malthusians' alarms. According to U.S. government records, the world's fish harvest is now 33 percent *higher* than it was in 1990 (*Statistical Abstract* 1998:Table 1341; 2003:Table 1354). This increase does not make good headlines, of course, as it does not spread fear and sell newspapers. Therefore, the mass media ignore the good news and try to find something to catch the public's attention by screaming the end of the world.

Not Even a Land Shortage

And running out of land? Not in any realistic future, say the Anti-Malthusians. According to the U.N. Food and Agricultural Organization, more than two billion

FIGURE 13-9 *Cropland Harvested in the United States*

Sources: By the author, based on *Statistical Abstract* 1991:Table 1154; 1998:Table 1126; 2003:Table 808. Broken line is the author's estimate.

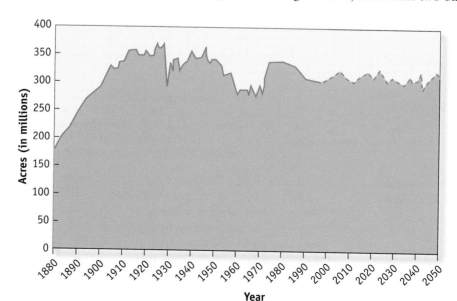

Food production has increased faster than population growth, and today the average person has more food than when the world had billions fewer people. New and Anti-Malthusians disagree sharply on what this means.

acres of rain-fed land go unfarmed (Livernash and Rodenburg 1998). Contrary to common belief, then, the world contains enough land to feed even more people. If we should ever farm all this unused land, and need more, then we could reclaim wasteland and make it productive. The best example is Holland, whose success shows the potential of human endeavor. Originally Holland belonged more to the sea than the land; one would expect it to be filled with lagoons and dominated by sea fowl and migratory birds. Instead, it is a prosperous country with one of the highest population densities in Europe.

HAS THE POPULATION EXPLOSION PEAKED?

The Anti-Malthusians

The Anti-Malthusians point out that the world's rate of population growth is slowing. The world's population grew 2 percent a year between 1965 and 1975. Then it dropped to 1.7 percent a year during the 1980s. Now it has dropped to 1.3 percent (*Statistical Abstract* 1991:Table 1434; Haub 2004). This means that the world's population is growing only two-thirds the rate that it was just 30 years ago. Population growth has slowed not only in the industrialized nations of Europe and North America but also in the poorer nations on all continents. Population growth is still speeding along, but it is slowing—just as we would expect according to the demographic transition. Perhaps the most startling statistic is this: Today's birth rate in the Least Industrialized Nations is only *half* what it was in the 1950s. Back then, the average woman in the Least Industrialized Nations gave birth to 6.2 children; today, she has just 3.1 children (Livernash and Rodenburg 1998; Haub 2004).

The New Malthusians

The advocates of zero population growth agree that these figures indicate that the *rate* of population growth has slowed, but they are quick to add that the world's population is still exploding. They stress that we have to look at absolute numbers: The world's population is soaring beyond anything history has ever seen; we are still adding about 79 million people a year to our planet.

PROBLEMS IN FORECASTING POPULATION GROWTH

The Pessimistic Prophets

To forecast population growth is to invite yourself to be wrong (Conner 1990). Consider this:

> During the depression of the late 1920s and early 1930s, birthrates plunged as unemployment reached unprecedented heights. Demographers issued warnings about the dangers of depopulation almost as alarmist as some of today's forecasts of overpopulation (Waddington 1978). Because each year fewer and fewer females would enter the childbearing years, they felt that the population of countries such as Great Britain would shrink.

Why Demographers Hedge Their Bets

Instead, with the end of the depression and the outbreak of World War II, the birthrate rose. After the war, both the United States and Britain had a "baby boom." The inaccuracy of the pessimistic prophecies of the 1930s has made some skeptical of demographic forecasts. Population growth depends on people's attitudes and behavior, and how can anyone know what those will be? To get around this, today's demographers hedge their bets. They make several predictions, each based on different assumptions. Figure 13-10 shows three of their projections about the U.S. population.

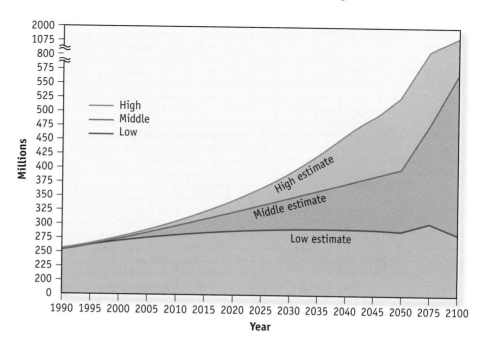

FIGURE 13-10 *Three Projections of the U.S. Population*

Source: *Statistical Abstract* 2003:Table 3.

Which projection will prove most accurate? As we saw, unforeseen trends upset population projections. Because some children die, for our population to stay even, the average woman must give birth to 2.1 children. (The usual way this is cited is 2,100 children per 1,000 women.). For probably 100 years, the U.S. birthrate has dropped (recall Figure 11-1 on page 354), and it has now reached its lowest point in our history: The average U.S. woman now gives birth to only 1.4 children (*Statistical Abstract* 2003:Table 85). If it weren't for immigration, our population would be shrinking.

Unlike the population of such countries as Italy and Spain, however, ours will not shrink. Our low rate of childbearing is more than offset by immigration. About 1 million immigrants a year enter the United States legally (*Statistical Abstract* 2003:Table 6), and even more than this enter illegally. This vast immigration is having dramatic effects on the United States. Figure 13-11 on the next page shows one of them, how immigration (combined with the natural increase from births minus deaths) is expected to affect the U.S. racial-ethnic makeup.

Do Immigrants Pay Their Way?

People worry that immigrants depress wages and take jobs away from citizens. Due to concerns that immigrants are a drain on taxpayers, in 1997 a federal law made immigrants ineligible for welfare benefits (Martin and Midgley 1999). Some economists claim that after subtracting what immigrants collect in welfare and adding what they produce in jobs and taxes, they make a positive contribution to the economy (Simon 1986). Others find an "immigrant deficit," concluding that immigrants are a drain on taxpayers (Huddle 1993).

The situation is complicated, but the key seems to be education (Smith and Edmonston 1997). The fairest summary seems to be this: Immigrants with low education collect more in benefits than they pay in taxes, whereas those with high education pay more in taxes than they collect in benefits. On average, each adult immigrant who has less than a high school education costs taxpayers $89,000 over his or her lifetime. Immigrants who have more than 12 years of schooling provide a $105,000 lifetime gain (Martin and Midgley 1999).

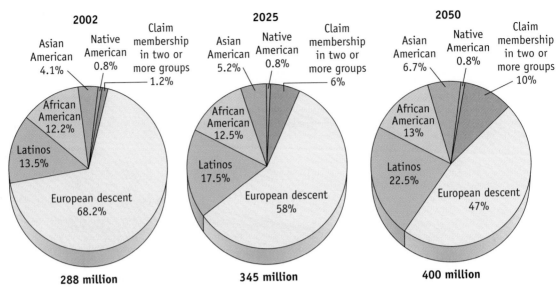

2002

Asian American 4.1%
Native American 0.8%
Claim membership in two or more groups 1.2%
African American 12.2%
Latinos 13.5%
European descent 68.2%

288 million

2025

Asian American 5.2%
Native American 0.8%
Claim membership in two or more groups 6%
African American 12.5%
Latinos 17.5%
European descent 58%

345 million

2050

Asian American 6.7%
Native American 0.8%
Claim membership in two or more groups 10%
African American 13%
Latinos 22.5%
European descent 47%

400 million

FIGURE 13-11   *U.S. Population by Race-Ethnicity*
Source: Henslin 2005.

DOES THE UNITED STATES HAVE A POPULATION PROBLEM?

The Anti-Malthusians

Let's conclude this section by considering whether the United States has a population problem. As Table 13-2 shows, in terms of available space and absolute numbers of people, it is difficult for anyone to make the case that we do. The Anti-Malthusians stress that even if immigration continues at a high pace, the country would have enough space, industry, and food to meet their needs. In fact, a larger population would prove an economic boom to the United States, because industries would have to supply what they needed. In short, say the Anti-Malthusians, the United States does *not* have *enough* people, and we ought to encourage immigration, especially of skilled people (Simon 1991).

The New Malthusians

The New Malthusians look at the same set of statistics differently, of course. They claim that we do have a population problem. It is not inadequate space, food, or industry, or even too many people, but, instead, the rate at which Americans deplete the world's resources and pollute the environment. The average American uses 5 times more energy than the average person in the world, 26 times more energy than a citizen of India (*Statistical Abstract* 2003:Table 1365). If each American costs the earth as much as 26 Indians, then in terms of energy our approximately 300 million inhabitants use the same amount as 8 billion Indians. Put somewhat differently, if the population of India multiplied until it was as large as the earth's total population is expected to be in the year 2050, only then would India put as much pressure on the earth's resources as we Americans do.

The Anti-Malthusians

This analogy, reply the Anti-Malthusians, is irrelevant. We need to focus on what Americans contribute to the earth. Our science, technology, financing, and industry give the world the capacity to increase production and enhance the standard of living of even the poorest nations. If we had more people, we would have more geniuses, spurring even more creativity. We would then develop more of our potential, increase our capacity for production, including food, and help the poorer nations even more (Simon 1981).

TABLE 13-2 Density of Selected Countries

COUNTRY	NUMBER OF PEOPLE PER SQUARE MILE
Macau	70,868
Monaco	41,423
Hong Kong	19,126
Singapore	18,482
Gibraltar	11,963
Malta	3,207
Bahrain	2,746
Bangladesh	2,624
South Korea	1,265
Holland	1,230
Puerto Rico	1,116
India	901
Japan	834
Israel	768
Philippines	721
Haiti	696
Great Britain	642
Germany	609
Italy	510
Pakistan	491
North Korea	478
Nigeria	371
China	355
Indonesia	331
Denmark	329
Poland	329
Guatemala	323
Portugal	285
France	284
Hungary	283
Cuba	262
Austria	255
Turkey	226
Greece	210
Spain	208
Egypt	191
Morocco	181
Ethiopia	151
Ireland	146
Iraq	143
Mexico	138
Afghanistan	111
Nicaragua	108
Iran	107
South Africa	91
United States	81
Venezuela	71
Peru	57
Sweden	56
Brazil	55
Chile	54
New Zealand	38
Norway	38
Argentina	36
Saudi Arabia	28
Congo	22
Russia	22
Canada	9
Libya	8
Australia	7
Mongolia	4

Source: By the author, based on *Statistical Abstract* 2003:Table 1322.

Not Objective Facts, but Definitions and Viewpoints

How should we look at the matter? As with the optimist and the pessimist, the question again depends on definitions and viewpoints. These clashing views highlight the relevance of symbolic interactionism, for conclusions on both sides depend on how people interpret objective conditions. Although those conditions may be objective, how we choose to interpret them is not. Accordingly, the conclusions of both the New Malthusians and the Anti-Malthusians are biased.

Social Policy

When it comes to social policy, the New and Anti-Malthusians again have differing viewpoints.

EXPORTING WESTERN AGRICULTURE

Why Don't We Export Western Agricultural Techniques to Solve the Problem?

Our farming techniques are so efficient that, as discussed, our problem is what to do with excess production. Because we have such advanced technology, why can't we solve the world's food problem once and for all by exporting our agricultural techniques to the Least Industrialized Nations? Everyone knows the proverb, "Give people a fish and you feed them for a day. Teach them to fish, and you feed them for a lifetime." If these nations adopt our techniques, which are tried and proven, couldn't they produce food in abundance?

This solution has initial appeal, but it is unworkable. The **green revolution**—the rapidly expanded food production that occurred in the 1950s and 1960s—originated during a period of cheap energy and seemingly unlimited amounts of fresh water. The development of high-yield wheat and rice, coupled with effective fertilizers, raised hopes that impoverished nations could abolish famine. The U.S. Midwest could be reproduced in India, China, and Africa.

It didn't happen. Water and fertilizer, essential to these high-yield plants, are in short supply in the poor nations. To maximize yields, fields must be dosed with up to 150 pounds of nitrogen fertilizer per acre, and they also require massive amounts of water to keep the fertilizer from burning the crops.

Nitrogen fertilizer is expensive. Even some U.S. farmers find its cost prohibitive, and few farmers in the poor nations can afford it at all. What rural poverty is like in the Least Industrialized Nations is difficult for Americans to imagine. Many farmers cannot afford even gasoline or electricity to irrigate their fields:

> "Oh, yes, we know about the green revolution," said Patal Mukherjee, a primary-school teacher in India who farms a few acres of rice and wheat. "But it does not change anything here. We are too poor."

Mukherjee's traditional farming methods are typical of India's 700 million village dwellers. He knows that different fertilizers will increase crops. And he knows how to apply them. But he rarely has the money to buy them. He is locked into an endless cycle of defeat. When he most needs fertilizers—to make up for a bad harvest—he cannot afford to buy them. Thus, skimpy harvests often follow bad harvests (Wallace 1980).

Another factor also prevents the exportation of Western farming methods. As functionalists emphasize, food production is only one item in an interconnected system. Abundance is not enough; agricultural products must be distributed quickly to consumers or they rot. Our vast network of railway and trucking, with many units refrigerated, allows us to do this. Our superhighways are subsidized by the federal government, which, in turn, depends on a vast system of tax collection. We also have regional and national systems of supermarkets to deliver products to consumers. It will not work to export one or two pieces of this interconnected, elaborate, and expensive support system of production, processing, and distribution to a poor nation (Harrington 1977).

Exporting our agricultural techniques is not the answer. Let's look at the policies that follow from the Anti-Malthusian and New Malthusian positions.

POLICY IMPLICATIONS OF THE ANTI-MALTHUSIANS

Although both the New and the Anti-Malthusians want to increase food production, they differ in most other respects.

Few Anti-Malthusians will like the policy implications of their position, but let's extrapolate the policies that follow from taking their position seriously. If larger populations are good for the world, then it follows that social policy ought to encourage larger families and to avoid polices that would discourage women from having children. To implement their position, we could take the following steps:

1. Reduce the age of consent to have sex to match the age at which girls are biologically able to reproduce. This would get more young women pregnant.
2. Encourage teenagers to experiment sexually.
3. Offer incentives for women to become mothers. These might include reduced taxes, paid maternity leave, subsidized housing, free nannies and child care, and free education and medical care. Cash bonuses could be paid, with larger bonuses for each successive child.
4. Make abortion and birth control illegal.
5. Offer incentives to encourage medicine, science, technology, industry, and agriculture. Developments here can help improve the standard of living of huge populations.
6. Export to the Least Industrialized Nations Western medicine, public health techniques, and technical assistance for building schools, hospitals, roads, railroads, heavy industry, and information technology.

Encouraging Population Growth and More Technology and Development

POLICY IMPLICATIONS OF THE NEW MALTHUSIANS

Similarly, few New Malthusians are likely to be pleased with the implications of their position, but let's also extrapolate the policies that follow from taking their position seriously. Because their views are more widely held, let's examine their policy implications in more detail.

Malthus's Machiavellian Proposal

Although Malthus's main suggestion for limiting population was sexual abstinence, in *An Essay on the Principle of Population* (1798) he proposed a solution that most would find outrageous:

> We should . . . encourage . . . destruction. . . . Instead of recommending cleanliness to the poor, we should encourage contrary habits. In our towns we should make the streets narrower, crowd more people into the houses, and court the return of the plague. In the country, we should build villages near stagnant pools, and particularly encourage settlements in all marshy and unwholesome situations. . . . But above all, we should reprobate (abandon, reject) specific remedies for ravaging diseases.

Today's Workable but Generally Unacceptable Solutions

If we were to take Malthus's recommendations seriously, we would withdraw modern medicine from the Least Industrialized Nations, especially vaccines and antibiotics. We would also refuse to train students from the Least Industrialized Nations and not send food to areas of famine and starvation. Other policy implications include

1. Encourage infanticide.
2. Raise the age of sexual consent and the age at which people are allowed to marry

3. Require a license to have children.
4. Require abortions for women who become pregnant without a license.
5. Encourage homosexual unions, since they don't produce children.
6. Sterilize enough baby girls to assure zero population growth.
7. Sterilize each woman who gives birth to a second child.
8. Establish a national system that provides free abortions on demand to any woman of any age for any reason.

Today's Gloomy Prophet

Actually, some New Malthusians take even more extreme positions than these. Pentti Linkola, a Finnish botanist, suggests that we annihilate most of the human race (Milbank 1994). He compares humanity to a sinking ship with 100 passengers and a lifeboat that can hold only 10. He says, "We need to end aid to the Third World, stop giving asylum to refugees—and a war would be good, too." To prove that he is serious, he adds, "If there were a button I could press that meant millions of people would die, I would gladly sacrifice myself."

For Dictators, Machiavelli Still Lives: The Example of China

Although most of these solutions seem too far-fetched to be implemented, we can note that legal abortion in the United States, once unthinkable, is now common. Similarly, homosexual relations were once punished by law, but now they are supported by law. It was once unthinkable for people of the same sex to marry, but such marriages are now legal in several countries. As society changes, what is perceived as outrageous to one generation can become acceptable to another generation. The other policy implications of the New Malthusians, then, can similarly become accepted over time. Consider China, where the government launched a national campaign to reduce its population. The policy is simple: "One couple, one child." Steven Mosher (1983), an anthropologist who did fieldwork in China, observed how this policy was implemented:

> "Each population unit, such as a rural collective, is limited to a certain number of births per year, which it allots to couples who have yet to have children." Women who have had their allotted quota of 1 who get pregnant "are forced to attend round-the-clock 'study courses' until they submit to an abortion." In some cases abortions are physically forced on resisting women, some of whom are nine months pregnant. (Erik 1982)

Mosher also reports that

families who actually have a second child must pay heavy fines, up to $2,000—several year's wages in mainland China—and run the risk of demotion or assignment to less desirable work as well.

One consequence is female infanticide:

Among the peasants, especially, sons are more valued, as they still provide for their aged parents in a society that has no old-age security insurance. A daughter, in contrast, takes up residence with her husband's family upon marriage, severing all economic ties with her natal family. The birth of a son signals a relaxed and secure old age, while the arrival of a daughter portends poverty in one's declining years. Consequently, many peasants decide in favor of their own security, and trade the infant's life for their own.

The authorities not only overlook female infanticide but also practice it. Mosher provides this example:

A young woman pregnant for the first time gave birth to twin boys. What should have been an occasion for rejoicing quickly turned tragic as the cadres (government representatives on the local level) present asked her which one she wanted. Both of them, she replied, but to no avail. One of the babies—she could not and would not choose which—was taken from her and put to death.

Chinese officials are serious about their "one couple—one child" policy. The Chinese landscape is dotted with billboards like this one—which translates to: "You will be happy and prosperous if you follow what the state says."

To solve social problems, leaders of an autocratic state can take steps that are out of bounds in a democracy. Remember that Hitler's murder of millions of Jews, Slavs, Gypsies, homosexuals, and people with disabilities was his "final solution" to what he saw as a social problem. Citizens of any nation that is ruled by a dictator, or any group that is not subject to the will of the people, can become captive to the *leaders' views of reality*. Although our system is far from perfect, it prevents leaders from enacting many policies that the people strongly oppose.

Zero Population Growth

The New Malthusians usually support zero population growth. To get people to go along with such a policy can be far from simple, however, for as we saw with Celia and Angel, peasant society produces strong motives for wanting many children. There, children are interwoven so intricately with identity and security that few of us who don't live in such a society can comprehend their attitudes toward children. They consider our ideas selfish and shortsighted: From their perspective, for the sake of a higher standard of living, we are refusing what God wants to give us. Nor can they connect their desire to reproduce with some apocalyptic vision of a desperately overpopulated, starving world. Most people decide to have fewer children not because of a world population problem—but because of the attitudes, beliefs, and values produced by their location in an industrial or postindustrial society.

A Change in Perception

For zero population growth to occur in the Least Industrialized Nations, small families must be workable; that is, they must meet people's needs. Adults must be confident that they do not need their grown children to take care of them when they are sick or old. Our perspective, though, is supported by a vast system of unemployment benefits, private and government retirement programs, and medical and disability insurance. With the exception of a few oil-rich nations such as Qatar, to have such a support system requires the development of industry.

Specific Proposals

Ways to achieve zero population growth include (Miles 1970; Bird 1977; Specter 1998a):

1. Encourage women to go to college and graduate school. The more education that women attain, the fewer children they bear.
2. Encourage women to want careers. Careers reduce commitment to motherhood: Women find satisfactions in their careers, and their families become dependent on their income for a higher standard of living.
3. Distribute free or low-cost birth control devices.
4. Teach zero population growth to schoolchildren.
5. Pay women to be sterilized. The payment can be small, as $20 or $30 in the Least Industrialized Nations goes a long way for people whose annual incomes are $200.
6. Tie medical intervention to measures to lower birthrates.
7. Tie food aid to agricultural reform.

This last principle was tried successfully in the 1960s. India faced mass starvation, and the United States used food to force agricultural reform: Each month's shipment depended on progress in meeting monthly goals. Today India can feed itself (Brown 1985).

The other Least Industrialized Nations also have the potential to produce enough food to feed themselves. Asia used to have famines that killed millions. Now Asia *exports* excess food. China broke up its communal farms and, using capitalist (profit-oriented) incentives, produces more food than it needs for its billion two or three hundred million people (Critchfield 1986).

Not a Panacea

Population control is not a panacea (Ehrlich and Ehrlich 1972). If the world's population were to stabilize exactly where it is, all the other social problems that we discuss in this text would remain—poverty, sexism, racism, ageism, urban blight, drug addiction, violence, discrimination, and environmental decay. The New Malthusians, however, believe that to try to solve these problems is a lost cause without population control.

RESTRUCTURING GLOBAL MARKETS

Some New and Anti-Malthusians agree that the root of the problem is poverty, and that to eradicate poverty we need to restructure global markets. To do this, however, would mean that the rich nations would have to redistribute their wealth (Burch 1971; Frank 1979; Wallerstein 1974, 1979, 1984). Why would they do this? Their people do not want to lower their standard of living.

Changing the Opportunity Structure

Michael Harrington (1977) suggested a more moderate program to redress the imbalance in global trade that loads crushing debt onto the Least Industrialized Nations. Harrington called for canceling their debt, increasing trade with them, and giving technical assistance to increase their food production. He also pointed out that nations with specialized economies (such as coffee or oil) suffer from fluctuations in the price they receive for their commodities. To stabilize prices, he said that we should create a world organization to buy commodities when the price dips below a specified level and to sell them when they rise to a certain point. He also suggested indexing, keying what the poor nations pay for industrial products to what they are paid for their own primary products. Indexing could lower the price that the poor nations pay for manufactured goods.

The Problem of Self-Interest and of Knowing What It Is

Such proposals require altruism on the part of the Most Industrialized Nations, which are more likely to act from self-interest. Long-term self-interest, however, is not always obvious. For example, it may well be in the interest of the wealthy nations to restructure global markets to give greater benefits to the Least Industrialized Nations. If they don't, they may face a more hostile world. The Iraqi invasion of Kuwait may have been an attempt by a Least Industrialized Nation to restructure global markets. The counterattack by the Western nations under the leadership of the United States (Desert Storm) may also have been an attempt by the Most Industrialized Nations to maintain the structure of global markets. Some conflict theorists say that the second invasion of Iraq had the same purpose. Regardless of those purposes, which have many different interpretations, as more Least Industrialized Nations gain access to nuclear, biological, and chemical weapons, it is going to be more difficult for the Most Industrialized Nations to maintain their control of global markets.

The Future of the Problem

The future of food and population problems is murky. Demographers cannot even agree what the future population of a given country will be, much less the future population of the world. With this caveat, let's plunge into the unknown.

THE NEW MALTHUSIAN VIEWPOINT

The Pessimistic View:

If the New Malthusians are right, our future will bring wall-to-wall people. Perhaps the life portrayed in the Global Glimpse box on the next page on population density in Hong Kong is to be the fate of the world.

Wall-to-Wall People

High Food Prices

If population outstrips food production, as the New Malthusians say it will, supply and demand will push the price of food upward. Some Americans already find food expensive, but the burden on the Least Industrialized Nations will be greater. Already poor, and burdened by debt to the Most Industrialized Nations, they cannot afford to import food.

Famines

If the New Malthusians are right, the famines of Africa are an omen of what is coming to other parts of the world. Millions of people will starve each year, and the

A Global Glimpse
WHERE WALL-TO-WALL MEANS PEOPLE

The Mong Kok section of Hong Kong may be the densest area on the face of the earth. Here, 200,000 people live in a bit more than half a square mile—a density rate of 300,000 people per square mile.

Officials have left a little strip of grass and a few wispy trees. People stand and stare at them. The trees are fenced off from the public.

How do the people feel about the crowding?

Winnie Choi, a hairdresser, says, "It's very crowded, but people like to live here because it's very convenient. It's a popular neighborhood." She adds that her family of five lived with two other families because her parents rented out two of the three rooms in their tiny apartment. Thirteen people shared one bathroom and a closet-sized kitchen. "But we didn't think we were crowded. The other families each stayed in their rooms, and we had ours."

Lee Chi-Kwong, a merchant, could move out of Mong Kok if he wants to. But he stays. He says, "I don't mind crowds. Crowds mean prosperity."

When asked about crowding, some residents just gave a quizzical look. They had difficulty understanding what the interviewer was trying to get at.

Based on Basler 1988.

Refugees

world will face a flood of economic refugees. Neither the Least Industrialized Nations nor the Most Industrialized Nations will be willing to accept the social stream of hundreds of thousands of poor, uneducated, culturally foreign people. To do so, if they can afford it, would deepen social tensions. Consequently, huge numbers of dislocated people will live in "temporary" camps.

Revolution and Repression

If efforts to stave off famine fail, or if there is insufficient food to feed the rural masses that are flocking to the cities in search of work, the Least Industrialized Nations will face riots and revolution. In response, these governments, controlled by their wealthy elites, will become more repressive. Because political and civil disorder could upset the global balance of power that the Most Industrialized Nations try desperately to control, these more powerful nations may well encourage such repression.

THE ANTI-MALTHUSIAN VIEWPOINT

The Optimistic View: The Future Is What We Make It

The Anti-Malthusians, of course, see a different future. The idea that famines are inevitable if the world's population grows is a bogeyman designed to scare people into having fewer children and to raise money for political purposes (Simon 1981). The earth can support several times more people than it does now. Whether famines will be avoided, however, depends on political and economic arrangements. The future is what we make it.

The Potential of Abundance

Biotechnology

Poorly managed, the earth's natural systems (fishing grounds, forests, and grasslands) can collapse, losing much of their productivity and bringing terrible suffering to humanity. Carefully managed, however, these renewable resources can produce all that the world, even a growing one, will ever need. In the coming *bioeconomy*, which some are calling the type of society that is presently emerging, bioengineering will produce pest-resistant plants that produce their own fertilizers. From gene splicing will come cereals that replace nitrogen in the soil, allowing farmers to bypass expensive petroleum-based fertilizers. We will produce low-fat cows and chickens that lay several eggs a day. Not only can the so-called inevitable cataclysm so widely touted by the New Malthusians be prevented, but also a future of abundance for all is within our capacity.

If any of this sounds far-fetched, we only have to note that the biotechnological future is already arriving. Not only can we clone animals, but also we have produced "designer animals," gene-spliced farm animals that produce more meat and milk. Consider what is on the drawing board (Elias 2001): Tobacco that fights cancer, corn that fights herpes and is a contraceptive, and goats whose milk contains spider silk. Science fiction? Not at all. We *already* have the goats that produce spider silk, as well as part-human animals that produce medicine (Kristoff 2002; Osborne 2002).

THE LONG-TERM ANTI-MALTHUSIAN VIEWPOINT

The Fourth Stage of the Demographic Transition Creates Controversy

To see the long term, we need to consider the nations that are in the latter stages of the demographic transition. As we saw earlier in this chapter, some nations have entered the fourth stage of the demographic transition and face population shrinkage. They confront a dilemma. Because of their low birthrates, they don't produce enough workers for their factories, and masses of unemployed young people in the Least Industrialized Nations want those jobs. The immigrants from the Least Industrialized Nations, however, bring with them different customs. This can upset a society. Germany and France, which have a lot of workers from Turkey, are experiencing this now. There, immigration has become a political hot potato. Because Germany is mindful of the Holocaust, it remains quiet about the controversy. Without such historical baggage, the French are more open in their opposition. One political party, whose slogan is "France for the French," has even made anti-immigration its cornerstone.

Fearful of a shrinking population and the arrival of more immigrants that don't share French culture, the French government has initiated **pronatalist policies,** policies that encourage women to bear children. It is trying to build attitudes and a political consensus to increase fertility: If French women bear more children, there will be more French to operate the offices and factories. It is too late. Several million immigrants from Northern Africa have become French citizens. If French officials offer women benefits for giving birth, these benefits must also go to the "new" French. This will increase births among a group that already has a high birth rate and one that is feared by the traditional French. The factors that create a low birthrate are firmly in place, and it is unlikely that government policy will deflect them. (See the Global Glimpse box on Sweden, on the next page.)

You can see why it is perilous to predict the future of populations. A nation may turn inward and exile immigrants, or it may welcome them. A nation may establish effective pronatalist policies. Any of these actions will affect its future. If the United States did not welcome immigrants, its population would be stagnant or shrinking. Only its million immigrants (or two million, counting those who immigrate illegally) a year keep it growing. The United States, however, is one of the largest countries in the world, and as we have seen, it is relatively unpopulated. Few countries face similar conditions.

A potential future is this: Today's Least Industrialized Nations follow the Western world and reach the fourth stage of the demographic transition. Their populations level off and then begin to decline as women do not bear enough children to replace those who die or emigrate. One day, governments that now despair over too many children will be offering incentives for women to give birth.

WHICH WILL IT BE?

Contradictory Potential Outcomes

Will the earth be filled with famine and suffering? Will such conditions spur vast political unrest that topples governments? Is African-style famine the world's fate? Without curtailing population growth, can the nations manage their resources, feed and

A Global Glimpse

THE LOPSIDED SOCIETY: PRONATALISM IN SWEDEN

"What is happening now has simply never happened before in the history of the world," said Nicholas Eberstadt, a demographer (Specter 1998). Never before has a country's birthrate plunged so low that its population shrank. But now the populations of several European countries are shrinking.

Are birthrates so low that they don't replenish a population really new in history? We have had instances in the past when a country's leaders thought that their nation had too few children. Usually this was because many young men had been killed in war, and they wanted new soldiers to replace them. Officials would then initiate *pronatalism,* policies that favor or promote births. They were successful. Men and women responded to the rewards and had more children.

Today's situation is different. Populations are shrinking not because of war but because women are bearing so few children that they aren't replacing the people who die. Sweden, one of these countries, helps us understand what is happening—and why pronatalism is failing.

If any country is pronatalistic, it is Sweden. Health care for mothers and children is free. Maternity centers offer free health checks and free courses in preparation for childbirth. When a child is born, the parents are eligible for fifteen months' leave of absence with pay. They can divide the leave between them any way they want, as long as the father gets at least one of the months. When a child is sick, either parent can stay home to care for it and receive full pay for missed work—up to sixty days a year per child (The Swedish Institute 1992; Froman 1994; Bernhardt and Goldscheider 2001).

Births should be booming, families growing larger, the baby carriage industry prosperous. Instead, Sweden is becoming a lopsided society, one in which there are more old people than young, one in which there will not be enough workers to pay for the health care and pensions of the elderly.

The culprit is prosperity and freedom. Women are staying in school longer, putting more emphasis on careers, marrying later—and having fewer children. Sweden's birthrate is the same as Japan's—and dropping.

Swedes, like the Germans, Italians, Spanish, and others in western Europe, are developing different ideas about children and about what they want out of life. Here are some of the Swedes' comments:

"People want their freedom. They see children as a burden, as an inconvenience."

"It's a sacrifice to have a child."

"Children cost more than they used to. Today you have to bring them to the pool, and you need to get a nanny, and they have to learn a foreign language. Children have more needs. Parents just didn't think of all these things before."

Ninni Lundblad, a biologist who works in Stockholm, said, "Did your parents sit down with a spreadsheet and figure out whether they could afford to have two or three children?"

No, they didn't. They just had them. But Ninni Lundblad, who said this so derisively, has no children (Specter 1998a).

So why don't Sweden's generous pronatalist policies work? Perhaps this statement by Jan Delanor of Stockholm best sums it up:

"I am supposed to have an extra child to help the system? Nonsense. I'll have a child if and when it makes sense to me, not because the government thinks it's a good idea."

Swedes are finding so much more that makes sense to them—education, travel, career, money, spending time with friends. All these things come before having children.

I wonder who is going to live in Sweden after the Swedes are gone? The government is wondering, too—as they anxiously look over their shoulder at the vast Muslim immigration into Europe.

clothe themselves, and provide a high standard of living for everyone? Or, could the problem of the future be not enough people?

I have no crystal ball. Like others, I must await the outcome. It certainly appears that the world has the potential to meet its nutritional needs, but this would require that the Most Industrialized Nations cooperate to meet the challenge. Perhaps they will rise to the occasion.

SUMMARY

1. *Demographers* study the size, composition, growth, and distribution of human populations. They disagree as to why Europe's population surged after 1750. They cite improved public health or a change in diet.
2. In 1798, Thomas Malthus predicted that the world's population would outstrip its food supply. His prediction is still controversial. The New Malthusians fear that the population of the world is entering the latter stages of an *exponential growth curve*, and most of this growth is in the nations least able to afford it. They favor an immediate cutback in population. The Anti-Malthusians claim that the world is producing more than enough food; the problem is the maldistribution of food due to political arrangements.
3. By applying symbolic interactionism, we can see why the birthrate is higher in the Least Industrialized Nations. There, children are viewed as a blessing from God, they give the parents status in the present, and they provide security for the future.
4. By applying functionalism, we can see that exporting medicine and public health techniques from the Most Industrialized Nations was a *latent dysfunction* for the Least Industrialized Nations. It created problems by upsetting the balance between their birth and death rates.
5. Conflict theorists stress that food problems are due to political and economic arrangements that favor the Most Industrialized Nations. Food politics creates and intensifies problems in the Least Industrialized Nations.
6. Demographers who take a New Malthusian position stress pressures on the earth's three natural systems: fishing grounds, forests, and grasslands. Two dangers are the

threat of famine as the result of our dependence on specialized strains of grains and the intensification of natural disasters. Even if we attain zero population growth, it would still take 50 to 75 years for the world's population to stabilize.
7. Demographers who take an Anti-Malthusian position argue that the earth can support many more people. Food production is outpacing population growth, fewer people are dying from famines, and much land remains uncultivated. A growing population can spur us to greater productivity.
8. Because of many cross trends, demographers cannot forecast population growth accurately.
9. The United States is not overpopulated, but Americans place relatively great pressures on the earth's resources.
10. The New Malthusians recommend social policies to curb population growth. The Anti-Malthusians advocate policies that encourage (or do not discourage) population growth. Both sides agree that we should stimulate agricultural development. Exporting Western agricultural techniques to the Least Industrialized Nations is not viable, because it requires a vast support system that these nations cannot afford.
11. The New and Anti-Malthusians envision different futures. The New Malthusians anticipate widespread famine in the Least Industrialized Nations, which may lead to more repression. The Anti-Malthusians stress that the world's nations hold the potential for meeting human needs, that one day the world will face the problem of population shrinkage.

KEY TERMS

Demographic transition A three-stage historical process of population growth. The first is high birthrates and high death rates; the second is high birthrates and low death rates; the third is low birthrates and low death rates. A fourth stage has emerged: Population shrinkage due to even lower birthrates.

Demography The study of the size, composition, growth, and distribution of human populations.

Exponential growth curve As growth doubles during approximately equal intervals, it accelerates in the latter stages.

Green revolution The world's rapidly expanded food production during the 1950s and 1960s as the result of new fertilizers and high-yield strains of wheat and rice.

Infanticide Killing infants shortly after birth, usually as a form of population control.

Latent dysfunctions Unplanned results that have negative or harmful effects.

Laterization The tendency of certain tropical soils to become laterite, a rocklike material, when they are exposed to the air.

Population pyramid A graphic representation of a population, divided, by sex, into age levels (see Figure 13-7 on page 433).

Population shrinkage A country's population shrinking because its birth rate and immigration are too low to replace the people who die or emigrate.

Pronatalist policies Social policies that encourage women to bear children.

Taking the role of the other Putting yourself in someone else's shoes to try to see things as that person sees them.

Zero population growth Women bearing only enough children to replace those who die.

THINKING CRITICALLY ABOUT CHAPTER 13

1. Which side do you agree with—the New Malthusians or the Anti-Malthusians? Explain.
2. Should the United States use its foreign policy to change the social and economic policies of other countries?
   - If yes, under what conditions and for what purposes? Under what conditions would you change your mind?
   - If no, why not? Under what conditions would you change your mind?
3. Should Russia, Germany, France, or any other nation use its foreign policy to change the social and economic policies of the United States?
   - If yes, under what conditions and for what purposes? Under what conditions would you change your mind?
   - If no, why not? Under what conditions would you change your mind?
   - If your answer to this question is different from your answer to question #2, why the differences?
4. Which perspective (symbolic interactionism, functionalism, or conflict theory) do you think best explains the world's problems of population and food? Explain.
5. What is your reaction to Pentti Linkola's suggestion that we annihilate most of the human race to save the rest of the world? If such a policy were enacted, who would choose who lives and who dies?

CHAPTER 14

The Environmental Crisis

HADN'T BEEN TEACHING VERY LONG AT Southern Illinois University, Edwardsville, when I decided that I wanted to move to a farm. I had purchased a small trailer and had been living in a low-rent, working-class mobile home park. By living there and driving a junker, for the first time in my adult life I had a money surplus.

I advertised for a farm in the county papers. When I visited the third one, I knew I had found what I was looking for. It was remote ("in the boonies," as the phrase goes here), filled with trees and pastures, with its own pond for swimming and fishing. (The pond was also my water source.) At $150 an acre, I knew I couldn't go wrong. My fellow professors were paying as much for a house as I would for the entire 165 acres.

Being a town boy, I had a lot to learn about farm life. Eventually, I owned a dog, a horse, a sheep, and twenty-five head of cattle. My inexperience led to several humorous events (at least I can laugh at them now): the sharpie farmer sticking me with the runt of his herd, the horse I bought refusing to let me ride her, the cattle breaking through the fence and running away.

One of my most insightful lessons in farm life came one Saturday morning, when I went to a cattle auction. This is where area farmers bring their excess cattle, and fellow farmers—and meat companies, as it turned out—bid on them.

Standing amidst men wearing hats emblazoned with "Allis-Chalmers," "John Deere," and "Nutra-Feeds," I felt myself entering a new culture. I was enjoying the moment, lost in reverie as I observed the auctioneer and the bidding. When one group of animals was brought into the ring, the auctioneer said, "Them's red-tagged, boys. Them's red-tagged."

I asked a man standing next to me what that meant. He said, "You can't buy 'em. They've got some disease. You can't take 'em back to your farm."

I nodded, then asked, "What happens to 'em, then?"

He replied, "Only guys from the meat packing plant can bid on 'em."

I let this sink in, relieved that I didn't eat much sandwich meat.

Then I recalled something my grandfather had told me when I was a child. He farmed on Minnesota's brutally cold Canadian border, and to earn money to buy his farm he had worked at a meat packing plant in St. Paul, Minnesota. I noticed that he always refused sandwich meat and had asked him about it. He said that it was because of what he had seen at the meat packing plant.

I suppose I was too young for my grandfather to explain his revulsion, but I think I felt something similar on that Saturday morning. Animals too diseased to live on farms were, under our government's supervision, judged perfectly acceptable to be turned into lunch meat.

The Problem in Sociological Perspective

Romantic Imagery: The Myth of the Noble Savage

In early history, humans lived in harmony with their environment. They considered themselves one with the water, earth, sky, animals, and plants. Unlike people today, who greedily destroy their environment, people used to use earth's resources wisely. Their presence did not disrupt the earth's natural systems. An old woman of the Wintu tribe explained:

> The White people never cared for land or deer or bear. When we Indians kill meat, we eat it all up. When we dig roots, we make little holes. . . . We shake down acorns and pine nuts. We don't chop down trees. We only use dead wood. But the White people plow up the

Many of our ideas of the past are shrouded in myth and painted in idyllic terms. An example is the common view that early Native Americans lived in harmonic balance with nature. The text explains why this view is a myth. Native Americans today treat the environment in the same thoughtless ways that most other Americans do. When I visited an Indian settlement on an Arizona mesa, I peered behind the houses. There, at the bottom of the ravine, lay heaps of garbage—easier to dump down the hillside than to discard properly.

ground, pull up the trees, kill everything. . . . How can the spirit of the earth like the White man?. . . Everywhere the White man has touched it, it is sore. (Lee 1959:163)

This view evokes a comforting warmth about some primitive past that is a part of us all: The good old days. The problem is that it just isn't true. Sociologist William Burch (1971) calls the image of "noble savages" a myth. He says that the social sciences should stop perpetuating romanticized views of the past and set the matter straight.

Okay. Let's try to do that.

The destruction of the environment has been going on as long as humans have lived on earth. Carnivorous kangaroos, giant lizards, and horned turtles the size of automobiles disappeared from Australia about the time that humans arrived there. Environmental historians believe that the humans destroyed these animals by setting fire to trees and shrubs to keep warm or to clear the land (Hotz 1999). The same thing happened in North America. Its early inhabitants burned forests to manage game, control mosquitos, or even for pleasure. The result: they wiped out three-fourths of the animals that weighed more than 100 pounds (Lutz 1959; Martin 1967; Hotz 1999). Prehistoric hunters may have exterminated more species of large animals than people have since then.

Human destruction of the environment in the past may have been so extensive that it brought down entire civilizations. Mesopotamia was located in the lush river basin of the Tigris and Euphrates, in what is now Iraq. Its fall has usually been attributed to invaders. But its destruction could have come from these people's abuse of the environment (Jacobsen and Adams 1958). The Mesopotamians developed an extensive irrigation system, which provided abundant food, and their civilization flourished. Their irrigation system, however, did not allow for drainage. As water evaporated, it left the remaining water salty. Over the centuries, as the water seeped into the earth, the underground water table rose, making the land too salty for crops. Eventually, the agriculture collapsed and, with it, the Mesopotamian civilization.

The great Mayan civilization of what is today Guatemala and Yucatan may have met a similar fate. This civilization developed for seventeen centuries, reaching its peak in agriculture, architecture, and science in 900 A.D. Then, within decades, 90 percent of its population disappeared, dropping from about five million to fewer than half a million. The cause may have been environmental destruction. Samples from lake beds indicate heavy soil erosion. As their population increased, the Mayans cleared the land of trees. The topsoil washed from the denuded land, and with it went the agricultural productivity on which their civilization depended (Deevey et al. 1979).

The story is the same for the Anasazi Indians in what is now Arizona and New Mexico (Budiansky 1987). The Anasazi built roads, an irrigation system, and pueblos of stone and masonry. Some pueblos were four or five stories high and had 800 rooms. The Anasazi cut down so many trees in the canyons that they had to travel fifty miles or more to gather wood for fuel. Having outstripped the forest's ability to replenish itself, their civilization collapsed.

Far from thoughtful, gentle conservationists, then, earlier humans were like us. They, too, destroyed thoughtlessly. Because our civilizations are larger, however, our capacity for destruction is greater. Many hope that there is another difference, too—that, having advance information about the destruction of the environment on which our civilizations depend, we will act before it is too late.

The reason for the collapse of the Mayan civilization is uncertain, but one theory is that it was due to the destruction of their environment. Shown here are Mayan ruins in Chichen Itza, Mexico.

"Everything Is Connected to Everything Else"

The Need to See the Environmental Crisis in Global Terms

Pollution

Unfortunately, self-interest (or selfishness, if you prefer) works against the logic of environmental preservation. Biologist Garrett Hardin (1968) used to tell a parable known as *the tragedy of the commons.*

> Let us picture a pasture open to everyone. The number of cattle exactly matches the amount of available grass. Each herdsman, however, will seek to maximize his own gain. He thinks to himself: "If I add a cow to my herd, I will receive *all* the proceeds from the sale of this additional animal. The little overgrazing that this extra animal causes will be shared by all the other herdsmen."

This herdsman adds another animal to his herd. He eventually adds another and another. And, for the same reason, the other herdsmen who share the commons do the same. Each is part of a system that rewards individuals for increasing the size of their herds. And therein lies the tragedy of the commons. The pasture is limited, and additional stress eventually causes it—and the civilization that depends on it—to fail. As each pursues his or her own interest, all rush to their collective ruin.

In sum, an irony of human existence is that our efforts to improve life can destroy the very environment on which life depends. Our environmental destruction joins a line that stretches into prehistory, for even the ancients confronted this dilemma. Today, however—with our new technology, incessant demands for an ever-rising standard of living, and more people on earth than ever before—we have magnified our destructive capacity.

The Scope of the Problem

None of us is isolated. Although the connections between ourselves and others may not be apparent, we all are part of a system that interrelates humanity, technology, and the environment. To think in terms of individual small units ignores reality. For example, although my grandfather, whom I mentioned in the opening vignette, lived on a remote farm in northern Minnesota, his actions had international consequences. He sprayed his fields with DDT, the practice at the time. The excess would run from his fields into a creek. The creek ran into a local river. That river led to a river that led to a river that ran into the Mississippi. From there, the chemicals flowed into New Orleans, helping to give its residents higher than average rates of cancer. From there, the chemicals flowed into the Atlantic, where they affected other nations.

Because all of us are part of a worldwide, interdependent system, we need to see the environment in global terms. The population explosion, industrialization, and the drive for higher living standards are upsetting our planet's precarious balance. If we deplete our natural resources, as some civilizations of the past did, our civilization, too, will collapse. This is the fear of some ecologists, scientists who study **ecology**—the relationship between living things and their environment.

For many, the primary concern is pollution. Although pollution by humans is not new—it occurred when the first fires were lit for warmth, cooking, or visual delight—it has intensified beyond anything the world has ever seen. Although the industrializing nations place increasing strain on the environment, its main polluters continue to be the world's industrial giants.

Defining Pollution

We all know what pollution is, but it is hard to define. A common definition of pollution is the accumulation in the air, water, and land of substances harmful to living things. This is a good definition, but for our purposes we want to look at pollution in *social* terms. Like all *social* problems, it is people who say that something is polluted, that they do not like what they see, and that they want to change it. Consequently, we can define **pollution** as the presence of substances that interfere with socially desired uses of the air, water, land, or food (Davies and Davies 1975).

Pollution Does Not Depend on Ideology

As the tragedy of the commons reveals, the depletion of resources is due to short-sighted self-interest. So, too, is pollution. Ideology makes no difference. In the former Soviet Union, pollution was treated as a state secret (Feshbach 1992). Scientists and journalists could not even mention pollution in public. To demonstrate against pollution, even peacefully, could bring two years in prison. With protest stifled, no environmental protection laws, and rigid production quotas, pollution was rampant. Citizens of Russia and those of the former Soviet states have been left a legacy of death—from abandoned factories that used to manufacture chemical and germ weapons to billions of pounds of nuclear waste that was simply dumped into rivers or holes in the ground (Garelik 1996; Miller 1999; Gessen 2001). Is the term "legacy of death" too strong? Consider this: Birth defects in Russia have jumped, and life expectancy has dropped. The life expectancy of Russian men is now 60 years, compared to 75 in the United States.

Looking at the Problem Theoretically

Each of our three theoretical perspectives helps us understand the environmental crisis. Using symbolic interactionism, we will examine how concerns about the environment arose and how the environment became a social problem. Through functionalism, we will focus on the interdependence of people and their environment. Through conflict theory, we will examine the conflicting interests of environmentalists and those who pollute.

Environmental decay in Russia is extensive. Shown here is one of the many leaks in the decrepit trans-Siberian oil pipe. The environmental costs of this pipeline, which is inadequate for withstanding the extreme freezing and thawing conditions of this region, may not be known for generations.

SYMBOLIC INTERACTIONISM

**The Natural History
of Environmental
Problems: The Creation
of a Social Problem**

How did the environment become a social problem? As we saw in Chapter 1, even if objective conditions are widespread and injurious, they are not automatically considered social problems. Objective conditions must be translated into subjective concerns.

This translation did not come easily. In the 1800s, when hundreds of steel plants in the United States polluted the air, no one considered this a social problem. Since the automobile was invented, people have discarded worn-out tires in gullies and creeks, but only recently have these actions been regarded as part of a social problem. This was also true with the disappearance of animal species, which began millennia ago: Many Anglos welcomed the near extinction of the bison, seeing it as a way to defeat the Indians. The passenger pigeon, during its mass annual migration, used to darken the skies for days. Its extinction in 1914 was seen as unfortunate—an interesting bit of history, perhaps, but not tragic.

Today, in contrast, people who have never seen a tropical rain forest are upset that they are disappearing. Around the world, people are bothered by the harm that is done to whales, seals, dolphins, and owls and by the loss of plants and animals whose names they can't even pronounce. A worldwide protest movement has evolved.

**How Did Attitudes
Change?**

**The Conservation
Movement**

How did we decide that environmental decay and destruction are a pressing, worldwide social problem? Sociologists Clay Schoenfeld, Robert Meier, and Robert Griffin (1979) investigated this question. They found that the 1960s were not the first time that Americans became concerned about the environment. Around 1900, Theodore Roosevelt (U.S. president from 1901 to 1909) spearheaded a conservation movement. He was concerned about vanishing wildlife in our wilderness areas (Morrison et al. 1972; Gale 1972). Roosevelt, who, ironically, roamed the United States and Africa killing big game, supported bills that established our national park system, setting aside millions of acres for public use. There is a vast difference, however, between conserving

*Humans have destroyed
many animal species, ex-
tinguishing some without
remorse. Few elephants
are left in the wild.
Poachers hunt them for
their tusks, selling the
ivory on the black market.
Soon, the only elephants
left will be those in zoos,
circuses, and on state
preserves.*

From Conservation to Environmental Concern

wilderness areas to make certain that hunters do not run out of moving targets and being concerned about the quality of our food, air, and water.

How did "conservation" change to "environmental concern"? Schoenfeld, Meier, and Griffin found that the change began with professionals and ended with an aroused public. Here are the five steps involved.

Five Steps in This Change

First, *professionals* became troubled by the environment. Knowing that we depend on natural resources, some professionals concluded that the situation was crucial. Geographers were the first. In 1959, they began to write journal articles about environmental problems and to present papers at their conventions. Then *interest groups* began to form around specific issues. Third, *government agencies,* aroused by the activities of the interest groups, began to issue environmental reports. Fourth, the *news media* discovered the issue. At first, reporters had difficulty understanding and communicating the idea that people, resources, and technology are all part of a larger system. They tended to see things in terms of single, unrelated news items, such as an oil spill. Gradually, they understood that "everything is connected to everything else," and they began to connect events.

Fifth, *the public* became concerned by the stories in the mass media. Three stories were significant. The first was Rachel Carson's *The Silent Spring,* published in 1962. Focusing on the dangers of pesticides, this blockbuster alerted Americans to environmental hazards. It was, however, a single-issue approach. People, including the media, still did not yet perceive interconnections among events. Then, in 1969 an oil well erupted off the coast of Santa Barbara, California. For weeks, environmental destruction riveted America's attention. Each day, 20,000 gallons of oil poured into the water. National headlines reported its drift to the coast, and people were outraged as twenty miles of beautiful beaches were blackened (Davies and Davies 1975). Later that same year came the single most effective environmental message of the century—the view from the moon of earth as a fragile, finite "spaceship." That first glimpse of us from the "outside" made it clear that we all are partners on a small planet.

Concerned about a decline in wildlife, Theodore Roosevelt, twenty-fifth president of the United States (1901–1909), launched a conservation movement. Though it seems ironic today, Roosevelt, who was instrumental in establishing our national park system, setting aside millions of acres for public use, was an avid hunter who roamed the United States and Africa in search of animals to kill. The text explains the process by which environmental concerns changed from "conserving" wilderness areas to prevent hunters from running out of moving targets to what they are today.

In Sum

Thus a social problem was "created," for over the course of these five steps people's perceptions changed. The general public began to see individual events as interconnected parts of the same problem. The more technical term for the interconnected system is **ecosystem**—all life on the planet is interconnected in the finely balanced cycles of the dynamic layer of the earth's surface. This concept has transformed our opinions of ourselves, our relationship with other living things, and even our place in the universe. This change in how we symbolize our world is still in process: We are still having a difficult time connecting what we do now with a distant future.

FUNCTIONALISM

Seeing Interconnections

The idea that everything is connected to everything else is becoming part of our intuitive understanding. We all know that though we are individuals, we are part of a larger group. We also know that the small groups to which we each belong are parts of a larger society, and that our nation is part of a global network. Slowly, we are coming to grasp that we all are part of a global social system, that what each of us does—whether individual, group, or nation—affects the others.

This picture of humanity forming a global network is a functional analysis. Each unit is part of a larger structure, with the activities of one part having functional or dysfunctional consequences for the other parts.

An Ecosystem

Both biologists and sociologists who work on environmental problems emphasize the interconnections between people and the earth's resources. No matter where we live on this globe, we need air, water, and soil to survive. We all are enmeshed in an intricate ecosystem. We have multiplied and expanded into every habitable region of the globe. Our cultures have permitted us to adapt to mountains and plains, to deserts and oceans, even to ice-bound regions. Our intelligence has allowed us to dominate the earth. We have domesticated plants and animals. To improve our lives, we have harnessed the energy of animals and rivers, the sun and the wind.

The steam engine increased productivity on a scale unknown in history. As we saw in Chapter 11, the Industrial Revolution that followed created countless new jobs and great wealth. Because of it, the average person today enjoys a standard of living that was previously attained only by the wealthy.

Dysfunctions of Industrialization

Industrialization, however, also brought dysfunctional consequences for the earth's ecosystem. Production of our material wealth damaged the air, water, and soil on which we depend. Our industrial wastes are toxic. In our drive to expand our industrial systems and create a better life, we are damaging the environment that allows us life in the first place.

Although we still have problems conceptualizing it, we have begun to think in terms of our being part of a complex, living machine called the environment. Our survival depends on the ecosystem. Green plants produce oxygen for human and animal life. Plants, animals, and microorganisms purify the water in lakes and streams. Biological processes in the soil provide food and fuel. Anything that disrupts the earth's ecosystem threatens these finely balanced cycles.

As with earlier civilizations such as the Mesopotamians, the Mayans, and the Anasazi, our economic and political systems depend on a fragile ecosystem that is mostly invisible to us. If it fails, our society will collapse.

CONFLICT THEORY

The Basic Conflict

Opposing sides are lining up on environmental issues. Some see us on the verge of catastrophe, and they act politically to protect the environment. Others resist what they consider arbitrary and irrational controls over their right to pollute. No one ever defends dirty water or filthy air, of course, for clean air and water have become like motherhood and apple pie. Nevertheless, some groups fight efforts to reduce pollution. Let's look at this conflict.

On One Side: Environmental Groups

On one side are the environmental action groups—organizations such as Greenpeace, the National Wildlife Federation, the Izaak Walton League, the Sierra Club, Americans for Safe Food, and Earth First!—that fight environmental threats. This statement from the Izaak Walton League expresses this position:

> There is no justification for water pollution. The people of the United States are entitled to wholesome surface and groundwater, usable for all human needs. At a minimum, surface water should be of suitable quality for both recreational contact and for the protection and propagation of fish and wildlife. . . . The public goal should be maximal removal of pollutants from all waters (Izaak Walton . . . 2000:11).

These groups have become a powerful force. With chapters across the nation, they maintain Washington lobbyists, aggressively promote legislation, and hire lawyers to fight environmental cases in the courts. Many politicians support their efforts.

On the Other Side: Polluters

Other groups oppose pollution control. At their core are the industrial polluters. Their dilemma is obvious. Pollution control is expensive and adds nothing to the value of their products. Manufacturers must compete with businesses in the Least Industrialized Nations. On top of their advantage of low-cost labor, they gain an additional edge from not having to pay for pollution controls in the manufacturing process.

Making It Profitable to Pollute

Manufacturers can't take a public stand in favor of pollution, of course. But they know how to work behind the scenes, and they have deep pockets. They lobby in Washington, influencing legislation. As the Technology and Social Problems box on the next page illustrates, in some instances they even have enough clout to get laws passed that allow them to profit from their own pollution. They also hire lawyers who specialize in finding loopholes in pollution controls. Consider the automobile industry:

The Power of U.S. Industry

> In 1951, when it was discovered that automobiles were the major cause of smog in Los Angeles, the suggestion was made to develop electric cars. The auto industry formed a committee to study this proposal. The White House stacked the committee with representatives from the auto and oil industries. Their "surprising" conclusion: a recommendation against research on electric vehicles (Davies and Davies 1975).
>
> While the car manufacturers were opposing the control of automobile emissions, another group of manufacturers tried to pass laws that would require pollution control devices. This group was made up of the businesses that manufacture the pollution control equipment. For them, the more regulation the better—more stringent laws mean more profit.

The automobile industry's fight against pollution controls and alternative transportation illustrates a basic principle of conflict theory—that society is composed of competing groups whose interests often collide. It isn't just the interests of business and the public that collide, but the interests of one business group can also conflict with those of another.

The efforts of environmentalists to eliminate what they see as dangers to the public welfare conflict with what other groups see as their inherent right—to make profits regardless of pollution. Those who campaign to develop what they consider to be a more livable, healthy,

The most extensive polluters are the wealthy, those who own the factories, but the poor are most frequently the victims. One consequence is environmental injustice, *discussed in the text. Shown here is a child in Matamoros, Mexico, playing in a drainage ditch. Most of this pollution comes from U.S. companies.*

Technology and Social Problems

HOW TO GET PAID TO POLLUTE: CORPORATE WELFARE AND BIG WELFARE BUCKS

Welfare is one of the most controversial topics in the United States. It arouses the ire of both wealthy and middle-class Americans, who view the poor who collect welfare as parasites. But have you heard about *corporate welfare?*

Corporate welfare refers to handouts given to corporations. A state may reduce a company's taxes if it will locate within the state or remain if it has threatened to leave. A state may even provide land and factories at bargain prices. The reason: jobs.

Corporate welfare even goes to companies that foul the land, water, and air. Borden Chemicals in Louisiana has buried hazardous wastes without a permit and released clouds of hazardous chemicals so thick that to protect drivers, the police have sometimes had to shut down the highway that runs near the plant. Borden even contaminated the groundwater beneath its plant, threatening the aquifer that provides drinking water for residents of Louisiana and Texas.

Borden's pollution has cost the company dearly: $3.6 million in fines, $3 million to clean up the groundwater, and $400,000 for local emergency response units. That's a hefty $7 million. But if we consider corporate welfare, the company didn't make out so badly. Its $15 million in reduced and canceled property taxes have brought Borden a net gain of $8 million (Bartlett and Steele 1998). And that's not counting the savings the company racked up by not having to properly dispose of its toxic wastes in the first place.

Louisiana has added a novel twist to corporate welfare. It offers an incentive to help start-up companies. This itself isn't novel; the owners of that little "mom-and-pop" grocery store on your corner may have gotten some benefits when they first opened. Louisiana's twist is what it counts as a start-up operation. One of these little start-up companies is called Exxon Corp. Although Exxon opened for business about 125 years ago, it had $213 million in property taxes canceled under this start-up program. Another little company that the state figured could use a nudge to help it get started was Shell Oil Co., which had $140 million slashed from its taxes (Bartlett and Steele 1998). Then there were International Paper, Dow Chemical, Union Carbide, Boise Cascade, Georgia Pacific, and another tiny one called Procter & Gamble.

Of course, you can always improve welfare programs. Can you imagine what a welfare program would be like if the recipients of welfare got to design them? You can be certain that they would come up with some interesting ideas. Consider this one:

> Let's suppose that poor people were burning their old tires, fouling the air all around them, and the state said: "We know that we can't stop you from burning tires, so we'll give you a certificate for each tire that you don't burn. Other people want to burn tires, so you can make money by selling these certificates to them, giving them the right to burn a tire for each one that you don't burn."

This would be nonsense.

Yet this is just what U.S. businesses arranged. When a treaty was negotiated in Kyoto, Japan, to reduce emissions of greenhouse gases, U.S. industries hit on a novel way to turn pollution on its head and reap billions of dollars. They proposed a new corporate welfare law. In this one, the government would issue credits to companies that reduce their emissions early—and even give them credits for reductions that took place years before the treaty. The companies could then sell the credits for billions of dollars to companies that didn't reduce their emissions, allowing them to continue to pollute (Cushman 1999). Now that's a great way to clean up—without cleaning up.

---

sane society run head on into the interests of powerful groups who see the cure as worse than the illness. This basic conflict runs throughout the environmental crisis.

Conflict and unequal power have led to what sociologists call **environmental injustice**—that pollution is more likely to hurt minorities and the poor (Hines 2001; Ramo 2003). This is because polluting industries locate where land is cheaper, and this takes them to places where the wealthy do not live. As a result, low-income communities, often inhabited by minorities, are more likely to be exposed to pollution. Sociologists have studied, formed, and joined environmental justice groups that fight to stop polluting plants and to block construction of polluting industries.

Research Findings

How badly has our environment deteriorated? To answer this question, we will first examine the pollution of our air, land, water, and food. Then we will look at energy and resources. Finally, let's consider whether the whole matter is exaggerated.

AIR POLLUTION

The Fearful Discovery

A mixture of fog and smoke settled over Donora, Pennsylvania, during the last five days of October 1948. By Sunday, October 31, wind and rain finally cleared the smog.

Of the 12,300 people who lived in this steel mill town, about half (5,910) soon became sick. Another 1,440 were "severely affected." Seventeen died.

Front-page news stories compared Donora to the Meuse Valley in Belgium, where 60 people died in 1930. Both were heavily industrialized, and both had a **thermal inversion,** a layer of cold air sealing in a lower layer of warm air. Thermal inversions trap smoke, exhaust, and particles.

By Tuesday, November 2, most of Donora's dead were buried. The residents' reactions sound hauntingly familiar. The local doctor described the deaths as murder. An air pollution expert from a nearby university said the lungs of the people in the valley had suffered chronic damage. The superintendent of the steel factory, however, said, "I can't conceive how our plant has anything to do with the condition. There has been no change in the process we use since 1915." The workers, who saw the dense smoke and fog as part of their way of life, said, "That smoke coming out of those stacks is putting bread and butter on our tables." And most of the public shrugged their shoulders and went about their business. (Bowen 1972)

A few years later, in 1952, a "killer smog" settled on London. In just 5 days, 4,000 people were dead (Thorsheim 2004). People became fearful. Slowly, facts about air pollution emerged. Air pollution is essentially a poison that accumulates in the human body. Besides causing eye, nose, and throat irritations, it causes bronchitis, emphysema, and lung cancer, which lead to a slow, agonizing death.

Three Main Sources of Air Pollution:

1. Burning of Fossil Fuels

What causes air pollution? The main cause is the burning of fossil fuels, that is, substances derived from living things—wood, coal, petroleum, and natural gas. To produce our electricity and the goods we consume, power plants and factories pour pollutants into the air. The worst polluter, however, is the internal combustion engine. The exhausts of cars, trucks, and buses emit poisons—sulphur dioxide, nitrogen oxide, hydrocarbons, and carbon monoxide. The vehicles also leave behind a **carcinogenic** (cancer-causing) trail from the asbestos particles in their brake linings.

On occasion, pollution is the result of deliberate, spiteful acts. The most dramatic example occurred in 1991, when Iraqi troops ignited 600 oil wells, storage tanks, and refineries in Kuwait. The soot from the fires circled the globe (Naj 1992).

2. Waste Incineration

Waste incineration is a second major source of air pollution. Burning plastics is especially damaging to our health because it creates PCBs (polychlorinated biphenyls), a potent toxin. Plastics are not **biodegradable;** that is, they do not disintegrate after being exposed to normal bacteria. Even steel rusts, but plastics endure almost indefinitely. Consequently, we burn them.

3. Fluorocarbon Gases

A third source of air pollution is fluorocarbon gases. These gases are suspected of damaging the **ozone shield,** the layer in the earth's upper stratosphere that screens out much of the sun's ultraviolet rays. High-intensity ultraviolet radiation harms most life forms. In humans, it causes skin cancer and cataracts; in plants, it reduces growth and causes genetic mutations. When the danger of fluorocarbon gases was realized, their use in aerosol cans, refrigerators, and air conditioners was reduced or eliminated. The damage to the ozone is expected to be repaired (U.S. Department of State 1997).

The Greenhouse Effect

Air pollution may lead to what is known as the **greenhouse effect.** Carbon dioxide and water vapor form an invisible blanket around the globe that allows the sun's light to enter, but traps the heat. Without this blanket, temperatures would plummet, and the earth would be unable to support life. If the blanket is too thick, however, it traps too much heat and has devastating consequences for our environment.

Global Warming

The blanket seems to be growing thicker. Because of the industrial revolution, we burn more fossil fuels than humans did in the past, releasing more carbon dioxide into the air. In effect, the carbon dioxide blocks the atmospheric window through which our earth's daily heat escapes to outer space. The increased temperature of the earth is known as **global warming.**

> Peru's 7.5-mile-long mountain glacier, the Quelcayya, is the world's largest tropical glacier. Sitting at 18,600 feet above sea level, it often gets snow but never rain. The Quelcayya is shrinking by about 100 feet a year. As the ice receded, researchers discovered a moss-like plant that had been frozen in the glacier. Carbon dating showed the plant to be over 5,000 years old.
>
> To get an idea of how extensive today's global warming is, consider this: The last time this plant wasn't covered with snow and ice, the Egyptians were busy inventing hieroglyphics (Regaldo 2004).

If global warming continues, some scientists say that it will disrupt the earth's climate and biological system (Smith and Tirpak 1988; Brown 2001; Parmesan and Yohe 2003). If so, they say that we can expect these consequences:

Potential Effects of Global Warming

1. Climate boundaries will move about 400 miles north, resulting in a longer growing season in the United States, Canada, and Russia.
2. The oceans will rise about two feet as the polar ice caps melt.
3. The world's shorelines will erode. (Most of the beaches on the U.S. east coast will be gone in a generation.)
4. Some small island nations will be destroyed, and the United States will lose an area of land the size of Massachusetts.
5. Coastal fisheries will be damaged.
6. Summers will be hotter, increasing the demand for electricity.
7. There will be more forest fires, droughts, floods, and outbreaks of pests.
8. There will be outbreaks of diseases—malaria, dengue fever, cholera.
9. Many species of plants and animals will become extinct.
10. Problems in the Least Industrialized Nations will be worse, as they have fewer resources to meet the crisis.

The Maldives are a little island nation of just 270,000 people. Their maximum altitude is about five feet above sea level. With the threat of the polar ice caps melting and the oceans rising, the ministry of tourism considered making their national slogan, "Come see us while we're still here" (Dickey and Rogers 2002).

Differences of Opinion

Because the earth goes through periods of warming and cooling (it was an ice age that formed the glaciers that once covered huge parts of North America), scientists disagree on whether global warming is due to natural or human causes (McFarling 2000). They point out that during the past 3,000 years the earth has had five extended periods that were warmer than today (Robinson and Robinson 1997; Stevens 1998b). Atmospheric temperatures are rising, but they have been rising for 300 years (from a cold period called "the Little Ice Age"), and current temperatures remain below the 3,000-year average. Some even conclude that if carbon dioxide increases, it may *lower* sea levels (Singer 1997): A warmer earth would increase evaporation from the warmer oceans, and more rain would fall over Greenland and the Antarctic. This would thicken the polar ice caps, removing vast amounts of water from the oceans.

In 1998, 15,000 scientists signed a petition asking that the United States revoke the Kyoto agreements to cut emissions of carbon dioxide. The petition was accompanied by a letter from a former president of the National Academy of Sciences. He said that higher carbon dioxide did not pose a threat to the climate, and that it might actually benefit the world. More carbon dioxide would increase plant growth and be "a wonderful and unexpected gift from the industrial revolution" (Stevens 1998b). Confused, members of Congress called the National Academy of Sciences; its current president assured them that the greenhouse effect poses a threat to the world.

This argument has heated up science: One side claims that the case for global warming is overblown, whereas those convinced about global warming call the other side silly (Vergano 2003). Because scientists who examine the same data disagree, we will have to await more data.

Changes in U.S. Air Pollution

With today's pollution control devices and the agitation of environmentalists, is our air getting cleaner? Figure 14-1 shows some striking improvements. The change in the amount of lead in our air is stunning; it is now only 2 percent of what it was in 1970. The primary reason for this welcome change is lead-free gasoline. But results are mixed: We now have slightly more nitrogen dioxide in our air than in 1970 (*Statistical Abstract* 2001:Table 356). Certainly the picture is far from rosy: Our air still contains 188 chemicals that have been linked to cancer, birth defects, and other serious health problems (Getter 1999).

LAND POLLUTION

It was such a beautiful day that Tamara and Bill decided to skip their social problems class and have a picnic on the beach. As they walked hand in hand, they found that they had to step around sewage that had washed ashore the night before. Their stomachs turned when they saw blood samples and contaminated needles that must have come from a hospital. All they could think of was AIDS.

They left hastily—without eating their lunch.

Cities and towns across the nation have to dispose of their waste. From Figure 14-2, which shows how much solid waste each American generates each *day*, you can see how our garbage has increased. At 4.4 pounds of solid waste per American per day, we produce *230 billion pounds* of garbage each year (*Statistical Abstract* 2003:Table

FIGURE 14-1 *U.S. Air Quality: The Emission of Pollutants*

Source: By the author, based on *Statistical Abstract* various years and 2003:Table 372. The last year that the source listed a measurement for lead is 1996.

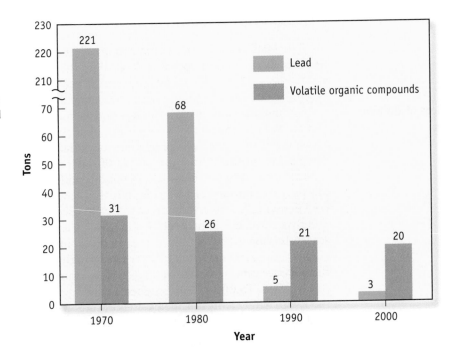

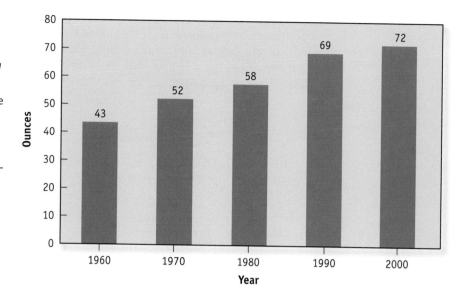

FIGURE 14-2 *Ounces of Solid Waste Each American Generates Each Day*

These totals are based on the solid wastes from residential and commercial trash collections. The totals do not include mining, agricultural, and industrial processing, demolition and construction wastes, sewage sludge, nor junked autos and obsolete equipment wastes.

Source: By the author, based on *Statistical Abstract* 1994:Table 370; 1998: Table 402; 2003:Table 375.

The Problem of Garbage

375). Some of this waste is recovered (paper, glass, metals, plastics, rubber, wood), but each day each American still sends 2½ pounds of solid waste to landfills.

Humans have always dumped their wastes around them. For example, we can identify many Stone Age villages by the mounds of oyster and mussel shells their inhabitants left behind. But modern industrial civilization produces so much trash that we no longer know what to do with it. Some trash can be burned in incinerators, but this creates air pollution. Gullies and swampy areas are sometimes used as dumping grounds, but areas convenient to urban centers are filling up—and groundwater contamination has become a problem. The land seems incapable of absorbing the huge amounts of garbage that we produce, and few want to turn the Grand Canyon into a giant landfill.

Many cities burn their waste, but no longer can they simply throw it in a pit and light it, as they once did. Now they must use garbage incinerators approved by the Environmental Protection Agency (EPA), which have been fancifully renamed resource recovery plants. These facilities solve the problem of what to do with waste, and they partly pay for themselves. Federal regulations require utilities to buy power from these garbage-burning plants. However,

> even with state-of-the-art pollution-control devices, garbage-burning plants still emit dangerous amounts of toxic gases such as dioxin. . . . As these toxic materials disperse on land and in air and water, they can become concentrated in the flesh of fish, wildlife and humans. . . . Ultimately, a plethora of ailments can result, including cancer, birth defects. (Paul 1986)

As a consequence, the EPA tightened its rules, threatened legal action against those who operated the incinerators it once approved, and began to require multimillion-dollar pollution controls. Unable to afford this bill, many communities abandoned their incinerators (Schneider 1994).

Some states tried to solve the problem by shipping their garbage to other states. When these states refused to accept the shipments, the case went to the Supreme Court. The Court ruled that the states to which the garbage was sent could not refuse the shipments. When landfills across the Midwest were opened to the hard-pressed, more populated eastern states (Bailey 1992), some midwestern states became the "garbage cans" of other states.

Strip Mining

Strip mining, which occurs where coal lies so close to the surface that it can be retrieved by stripping away the soil, has scarred more than 5 million acres of U.S. land.

West Virginia was a special target. Vast tracts of this state can no longer be farmed because, stripped bare of forest and plant life, salt from the coal poisoned the land. Although current federal regulations require mining companies to return land to its original condition, many believe that this is impossible. Today the western areas of the United States are vulnerable, for vast amounts of shale and coal lie just beneath the surface.

WATER POLLUTION

Acid Rain

> A silent spring has fallen over parts of the western Adirondacks. Brook trout have vanished from Big Moose Lake—along with crayfish and frogs, loons, kingfishers, and most of the swallows.
>
> Pollutants from Midwest factories, borne by rain, wind, and snow, have left more than 300 lakes devoid of fish. The acid rain is also killing the trees. (Blumenthal 1981; Ehrlich and Ehrlich 1981; Stevens 1996)

How do factory emissions in the Midwest destroy lakes in Canada and our northeastern states? Death at long distance begins when power plants in the Midwest burn coal and oil to generate electricity. Burning fossil fuels releases sulfur dioxide and nitrogen oxide into the atmosphere. Moisture in the air turns these emissions into sulfuric and nitric acid. After traveling hundreds of miles, they fall to the earth's surface as **acid rain.**

Acid rain is not new. Ice samples from glaciers show heavy concentrations of acids 350 years ago, probably from volcanic activity and organic decomposition (LaBastille 1979; Lynch 1980). Our intensified use of fossil fuels, however, has transformed acid rain into a global problem. To burn coal, utility companies in the Midwest built more than 175 smokestacks 500 feet tall or higher. These "megastacks" do a good job of reducing local pollution, but it is not as though the pollutants disappear as if by magic. Disgorged high into the air, these pollutants remain aloft for days, even weeks, before becoming part of a "chemical soup" that falls as rain on areas hundreds of miles away.

Canadians are upset by the U.S. "airborne sewer" that spills across their border. Acid rain has destroyed the fish and normal plant life of about 200 lakes in Ontario. Authorities there say that acid rain threatens 48,000 of their more than 180,000 lakes. Acid rain also damages crops and forests around the world, as well as such landmarks as the Colosseum in Rome, the Taj Mahal in India, the Parthenon in Athens, and the Lincoln Memorial in Washington. Acid rain also threatens human health. Apparently, acid rain produces chemical reactions that release toxic metals into the water table. From there, these metals go to the public water supply.

Although Congress required power companies to reduce their emissions of sulfur dioxide, which greatly reduced acid rain, the problem continues. Some lakes are regaining the chemical balance that will support plant and animals, but for reasons that scientists are trying to figure out, most of the affected lakes remain as acidic as ever (Roberts 1999).

Mercury Rain

Then there is mercury rain. Half of the nation's electricity comes from burning coal. As coal burns, it releases traces of mercury, which becomes part of the smoke that the coal-fired plants release. Some of the mercury stays airborne for two years, spreading around the globe. Some reacts with chlorine in the coal and falls with rain. This rain water washes into lakes, rivers, and oceans, where it is ingested by microorganisms. From there, it goes up the food chain into fish. As a result, some species of fish, especially swordfish and shark, are off limits to young children and to pregnant and nursing women (Levine 2004).

Drinking Water

As you can see, pollution also contaminates groundwater, the source of drinking water for millions (Lewis 1990; Raloff 1990; Bartlett and Steele 1998). Some of our drinking water contains arsenic, asbestos, benzene, carbon tetrachloride, chloroform, mercury, PCBs, and other chemical wastes. Some wells on which large populations depend have had to be closed. For example, a well in the San Gabriel Valley of California that supplied drinking water to 400,000 people was closed because it had become contaminated with the solvent TCE. Large portions of the water supplies of southern Michigan are so polluted that state officials have suggested that it might be "cheaper to simply write off the groundwater supplies" than to try to clean up the problem.

The Mississippi River is a special case in point. Although thousands of industries discharge their wastes into this river, hundreds of cities pump their drinking water out of this putrid cesspool. To "purify" the water they send to their customers, the water companies add more chemicals, a senseless process that one day must end. Thirty million Americans do not have access to drinking water that meets minimal health standards (Duskin 2003).

Lakes

The pollution of the Great Lakes is of special concern, for this giant network of waterways—Erie, Superior, Michigan, Huron, and Ontario—contains *one of every five gallons of the entire world's surface freshwater.* More than 900 toxic chemicals have been found in the Great Lakes (Ashworth 1987; Pearse 1987; Gorrie 1990). The pollution of these formerly pristine waters by industry is so bad that people are warned not to eat bottom-feeding fish (which are exposed to heavier concentrations of poisons in the lakes' sediment). Congress has mandated that the EPA clean up these lakes, and improvements are being made (EPA 1994, 1998).

Although lakes and streams can be cleaned up, when groundwater gets contaminated, it is permanent. Technically, it isn't actually permanent, but for all practical purposes it is. Groundwater recycles so slowly that it remains in aquifers for an average of 1,400 years (Bogo 2001).

Oil Spills

Like a junkie, our industrial machine demands a continuous supply of oil. Transporting those vast quantities of oil is risky. Although industry and government assured environmentalists that they could handle oil spills, those promises proved hollow in 1989 when the *Exxon Valdez,* a 1,000-foot-long supertanker, ran aground and ruptured. It spewed 11 million gallons of crude oil into the pristine waters of Alaska's Prince William Sound, soiling 1,300 miles of coastline (Wells and McCoy 1989; Rosen 1999). Left dead were 250,000 sea birds, 2,800 sea otters, 300 harbor seals, 250 bald eagles, 22 killer whales, and vast numbers of fish (Rosen 1999). Exxon spent over $2 billion to clean up the mess (Wells 1990). A surprise to many, Prince William Sound has largely recovered ("Parallelism . . ." 2001).

Unfortunately, oil spills in Russia dwarf the Exxon spill (Rosett 1994; Garelik 1996). In 1994, a cross-country oil pipeline burst in Siberia, dumping 300 million gallons onto the tundra and into rivers—27 times more oil than in the Exxon spill. Russia's rusting oil pipes continue to spew oil.

Toxic Chemicals

The pollutions we have discussed so far all involve chemicals. Chemicals are so poisonous to land, air, and water that it is difficult to overstate the extent to which they threaten our well-being.

Love Canal

Perhaps the most infamous case of chemical pollution in the United States is Love Canal, New York, where

> hundreds of families unwittingly purchased homes adjacent to a waste dump that had been covered over with clay. Over the years, deadly poisons seeped into their homes. Neurological damage was common. So were urinary tract infections, kidney damage, swollen joints, sleepiness, clumsiness, headaches, fragile bones, irritability, and loss of appetite. One third of Love Canal residents suffered chromosome damage (Brown n.d.). One child was born with

The Taj Mahal in Uttar Pradesh, India, is considered by many to be the most beautiful building in the world. This mausoleum built by Shah Jehan in 1630–1648 for himself and his favorite wife, Mumtaz Mahal, is made of white marble inlaid with semiprecious stones. Along with other architectural masterpieces the world over, the Taj Mahal is threatened by acid rain.

One Solution: Keep Doing What You've Been Doing, But Give It a New Name

The Profit Potential Has Attracted Organized Crime

two rows of teeth, another with one kidney, and a third with three ears (Shribman 1989).

Eventually, the federal government ordered all pregnant women and children under age 2 to move out of Love Canal (Brody 1976; Brown n.d.). In 1978, 239 families abandoned their homes, and in 1980 the federal government and the state of New York relocated another 710 families. The government bulldozed one hundred twenty-eight homes (Shribman 1989).

How did Love Canal get so polluted?

Beginning in the early 1940s, Hooker Chemical Company buried and covered with clay 44 million pounds of chemical wastes in a canal it owned (Mokhiber and Shen 1981). When Niagara Falls officials unwittingly chose the covered-over canal as the site for an elementary school, Hooker said that they had chosen a "desirable site" for the school and deeded the land to the city for a token $1. The company warned no one about the chemicals, but the deed stated that Hooker was not liable for any injuries or deaths that might occur at this site (Brown 1979).

"That account," replied Hooker, "is only part fact, combined with a lot of lies." The truth, claimed Hooker, is that "we warned the board about the risk. We even told them on what part of the property to locate the school so they would not disturb the buried chemicals." Moreover, when the board considered selling part of the property, Hooker sent an attorney to the board meeting to warn them that the buried chemicals could have a "serious deleterious effect on foundations, water lines, and sewer lines" and that it was "quite possible that personal injuries could result from contact therewith." The attorney also stated that "only the surface of the land" should be used because "the subsoil conditions make it very undesirable and possibly hazardous if excavations are to be made therein" (Wilcox 1957).

Despite these warnings, Niagara Falls' Board of Education approved that dirt be removed from the canal for top grading, the city constructed a storm sewer through the landfill, and the Department of Transportation built an expressway across part of the site. These construction projects disturbed industrial wastes that had been buried properly, causing the resulting damage, said Hooker.

Whoever is to blame—and there seems to be plenty of negligence and culpability to go around—Love Canal illustrates the danger of burying chemical wastes, the lack of adequate controls over disposing of chemicals, and the necessity of safeguarding people from harm.

How to dispose of chemical wastes properly is an enormous problem. U.S. industries produce about 200 billion pounds of hazardous chemical wastes each year (Brown n.d.). Just as companies used to simply discharge wastes into the air or dump them into rivers and the oceans, they now find it convenient to bury them. To help us feel better about this, the word *dump* has been changed to landfill. The containers buried in landfills disintegrate slowly, allowing lethal chemical wastes to rise to the surface or to leach into rivers and groundwater.

As officials have cracked down to make companies dispose of toxic wastes properly. This has opened opportunities for greedy money-grubbers—including members of organized crime (Brown n.d.). Legal disposal of a tankful of chemical wastes might cost $40,000, but underworld firms will do it for half that amount. Their disposal methods are a little different: They drive an 8,000-gallon tank truck full of waste to a wooded area and dump it in eight minutes flat. The industrial company that produced the waste (a legitimate business) feigns ignorance. On 21 acres of marshlands on Staten Island, men "well known to law enforcement agents" deposited 700,000 gallons of waste oil in barrels. There are even easier ways. In North Carolina, one "midnight dumper" simply opened the spigots on a tankload of PCBs and then drove until the tank was empty.

Time Bombs

With inadequate disposal and thousands of toxic dump sites, chemical wastes are a ticking time bomb. The Social Map shows the *worst* of the hazardous wastes sites in the United States, those designated as needing *immediate* attention.

NUCLEAR POLLUTION

The Kyshtym Disaster

In 1980, Zhores Medvedev, a Russian biologist and dissident who had fled his country, published a book in which he claimed that a devastating nuclear accident had occurred in 1957 in Kyshtym, in Russia's Ural River Valley. The Soviet government denied that an accident had taken place and would not allow Medvedev's book to be published in the Soviet Union. Some Western nuclear scientists joined in, calling Medvedev's account "science fiction." Medvedev was right, however, and the Russian government eventually acknowledged the accident (Clines 1998).

Because this area of the Urals is so remote, Soviet officials chose it to develop their first atomic bomb. They built a nuclear reactor to obtain plutonium, which produced millions of gallons of liquid waste. Accounts vary as to how the Soviets disposed of this nuclear waste. Some say they bored holes into the ground and poured down the liquid wastes (Solomon and Rather 1980). Others report that they piled the waste onto a dry lake bed (Clines 1998). In either case, a chemical reaction occurred, and in the winter of 1957 the waste exploded. Radioactive dust and materials shot high into the sky.

The fallout was devastating. Maps of the area before 1958 show 30 villages and towns around Kyshtym. On maps printed after 1958, those communities have disappeared. Thousands of people had to be evacuated permanently from a 1,000-square-kilometer area.

FIGURE 14-3 *Hazardous Waste Sites on the National Priority List*

Source: By the author, based on *Statistical Abstract* 2003:Table 381.

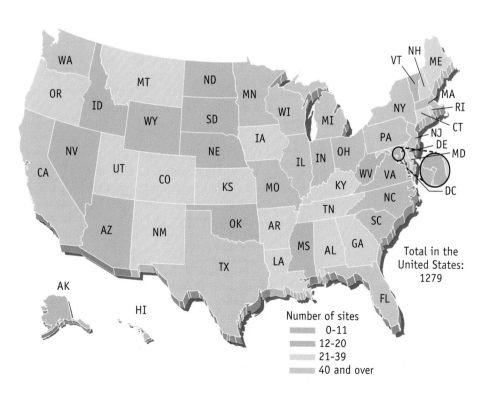

Three Mile Island

By comparison, the worst nuclear accident in the United States was puny. It occurred at Three Mile Island, Pennsylvania, in 1979. When a reactor leaked, 100,000 residents fled in panic (Rabinovitz 1998). The contamination was minimal, and today people live near the defunct reactor. Although some say that this accident may cause up to 50 people to die from cancer (Milvy 1979), Edward Teller (1980), the "father of the hydrogen bomb," claimed that "one person at some later time—one single person—may develop cancer." He added that this "single case has only 10 percent probability of occurring." Others even claim that the accident was simply a minor loss of coolant that exposed people to less radiation than they get at the dentist (Williams 1980).

The Chernobyl Disaster

Then there was Chernobyl, a nightmare that shocked the former Soviet Union in 1986:

> *Meltdown.* The word froze in the mouth of the operating engineer. No one wanted to even think it could happen. Yet the evidence was undeniable. An explosion had blown a 1,000-ton steel cover off a nuclear reactor. The containment structure was obliterated.
>
> It was too late to flee; the deadly radiation could not be outrun. For ten days, the world watched the drama and destruction play out, the fire raging and radioactive materials spewing into the air.
>
> Chernobyl's cloud of radioactive gases traveled slowly around the world. In two weeks, airborne radioactivity was detected in the United States and Tokyo (Flavin 1987). Canadians were advised not to drink rain water, and farmers in Great Britain were ordered not to grow certain crops because of the radioactive fallout. (Dufay n.d.)

About 336,000 people were evacuated (Jaworowski 2001). Despite emergency transplants of bone marrow and fetal liver cells by an international medical team, 31 people died during the first months. The real death count, however, comes in only as the years pass. The United Nations estimates that the radiation killed 15,000 to 30,000 people who were living in the contaminated zones, giving them various forms of cancer (Weir 2003). Others, in contrast, say that the radiation produced no general health problem, that the cancer rates of these people are within the usual range (Jaworowski 2001).

About 12,000 square miles of farm- and forestlands were made worthless for human use for at least two generations. Fearful that other reactors might explode, the Most Industrialized Nations provided money and engineers to improve the safety of Soviet nuclear plants (U.S. Department of State 1997). Unfortunately, about 600 elderly have moved back into the contaminated area around Chernobyl. They know the risk, but they still call it home (Dufay n.d.).

FOOD POLLUTION

Two Types of Food Pollution

A form of pollution that you and I face daily is **food pollution.** There are two types: disease-causing germs in our food, and chemicals added to food to process it, lengthen its shelf life, enhance its appearance, or alter its taste. Let's look at both types.

1. Disease

We can illustrate the first by noting how processing contaminates chicken (Ingersoll 1990). Slaughter lines run so fast that inspectors have two seconds to scrutinize each carcass, inside and out, for signs of disease and feces. "After a while, it gets to be a blur," says one inspector.

The way that chickens are processed *increases* contamination. In one plant, 57 percent of chickens arrived at the plant contaminated with disease-causing bacteria such as salmonella. This is horrible to contemplate, but listen to this: Seventy-six percent left the plant infected. The two primary sources of bird-to-bird contamination are automatic disemboweling knives, which spread feces, and vats of chilled water in which the chickens are dipped before going into the freezer. Says a microbiologist, "Even if you chlorinate the chill water, it's still like soaking birds in a toilet." To this, industry officials reassuringly reply, "It may spread bacteria from bird to bird, but it also dilutes the overall dose level."

Why Not Use Alternative Techniques?

Why doesn't the U.S. poultry industry switch to blasts of cold air, like in Europe? The reason is profits. Federal regulations allow each carcass to soak up to 8 percent of its weight in water, allowing the sale of hundreds of thousands of gallons of disease-ridden water at poultry prices.

How to Contaminate Chicken

Over one million Americans get sick each year from contaminated chicken. To find out why, scientists at *Consumer Reports* bought chickens at supermarkets in 25 cities nationwide ("Of Birds and Bacteria" 2003). These included the major brands, supermarket specialty brands, and chicken sold at health food stores. When they tested these chickens, they found that *half* were contaminated with salmonella or Campylobacter, bacteria that can make people sick. To not get sick from the filthy chickens that are sold in our stores, the researchers suggest that people buy chickens that are low in the freezer (where it is colder), separate raw chicken from other foods, don't let any foods touch the area where you prepare the chicken, and cook the chicken thoroughly. They also say to wash your hands thoroughly to remove chicken juices—the blood and the filthy water that the U.S. Department of Agriculture allows the chickens to absorb.

These sorts of standards make it easier to understand why some European nations refuse to import some food from the United States. For other reasons, see the Technology and Social Problems box on the next page.

The Danger Is Real

It isn't just chickens, of course, that present such a threat to our health. When hot dogs produced by a subsidiary of Sara Lee were contaminated with listeria monocytogenes, 20 people died. Jalisco brand soft cheese, also contaminated with listeria, killed 40 people (Burros 1999). A plant in Arkansas, which was producing 400,000 pounds of hot dogs a day, was shut down due to listeria contamination—but the contaminated meat had already been shipped nationwide and to South Korea and Russia (Associated Press, January 23, 1999). After eating Schwan's ice cream, 224,000 Americans became sick. The ice cream was tainted with salmonella, which was traced to trucks that carried ice cream mix in the same tanks that had been used to transport raw eggs (Neergaard 1998). Apple juice produced by Odwalla was infected with *E. coli* bacteria—14 children developed a life-threatening disease that ravages kidneys, and a 16-month-old girl died (Belluck 1998a). Each year, *30 million Americans get sick and nine thousand die from food-borne diseases* (Burros 1998).

2. Chemical Additives

Let's turn to the second type of food pollution. Food companies sprinkle our food with a lot of artificial additives. Just to flavor our foods, they use 2,000 different chemical compounds. The "cherry" flavor in soft drinks, pies, and shakes, for example, requires 13 different chemicals.

The relationship of food additives to safety is not reassuring. The U.S. agency that is responsible for overseeing the safety of food additives, the Food and Drug Administration (FDA), has a sad history in this regard. For example, Red Dye No. 2 used to

Food Coloring

be the most common food coloring in the United States. Because it enhances colors, the food industry added more than a million pounds to our food each year. In 1970, researchers discovered that rats and mice fed Red Dye No. 2 developed cancer. It took five years for the FDA to ban this dye—and only after the agency was flooded with petitions from public interest groups.

Many find little comfort in knowing that Red Dye Nos. 3, 8, 9, 19, 37, and 40 replaced No. 2 to color food. Some of these dyes also damage DNA and cause cancer in animals—yet the FDA allows them to be used (Brooks 1985, 1987; Tsuda 2001). Red dye No. 40, for example, has been banned in Austria, Belgium, France, Germany, Norway, Sweden, and Switzerland—yet it continues to be added to our foods (Hanssen 1997).

Then there are the hundreds of dyes to make the colors blue, green, and yellow.

Technology and Social Problems

"DO YOU EAT PLASTIC FOOD?" WHY EUROPEANS DON'T LIKE U.S. FOOD

I didn't know what to say when a friend in Spain asked me if Americans eat plastic food. I was amused by the phrase and perplexed by what the question could mean.

The reason for the question became apparent as I became more familiar with Spanish food. I noticed that the egg yolks were brighter, almost orange. Fruits and vegetables are picked ripe and sold and eaten fresh. The meat is more tender and tasty. It doesn't come prepackaged or frozen. Each grocery store has it own butcher; in small stores, the butcher is also the owner. Bread is freshly baked and purchased daily. The Spanish use a lot of fresh herbs—especially garlic and parsley. They also cook with olive oil—always.

All these things account for the better taste of Spanish food. And, as scientists have discovered, Spanish food is healthier. But plastic? A rumor had spread throughout Europe that U.S. food companies do a lot of strange things to our food, that it had become synthetic. The term *plastic* may have been my friend's, but unfortunately, it is not too far off the mark.

It isn't only the common folk who wonder about our food. (My friend, who asked this question, runs one of the thousands of mom-and-pop bar–restaurants on Spain's many beaches.) Officials of the European Union (EU) are also suspicious about U.S. food. EU scientists claim that a hormone fed to U.S. cattle to make them grow faster is carcinogenic. The EU has banned any beef with 17-beta-oestradiol. 17-beta oestradiol? I don't like the sound of that one. EU scientists haven't cleared the other five growth-promoting hormones that U.S. farmers use, either, but they don't have enough data yet to call them carcinogens (Wolf 1999).

Why don't our lawmakers insist that meat laced with carcinogens be labeled as such? (Can't you just see this label: "WARNING: This meat may give you cancer.") The U.S. food industry has a lot of political clout, and their lobbyists have told our lawmakers that the European test results are "bad science" (Bahree 1999). I don't have the expertise to judge those results, but I do know this: As conflict theorists remind us, many politicians are less concerned about our health than about how much money the food industry pumps into their political campaigns.

Some European countries refuse to import our genetically engineered grains as well. Their scientists say that these biofoods aren't safe. We don't get a label on those either.

The U.S. food industry isn't taking European resistance to its beef and biofoods lying down, of course. Its political arm, the U.S. government, slapped millions of dollars of punitive import taxes on goods imported from Europe (Bahree 1999). Guess that'll show 'em that our food is healthy.

Sulfites

The sulfites illustrate another example:

> The food industry has found sulfites to be a handy chemical, for they are antioxidants. Because they keep foods from discoloring, the sulfites are spread over raw fruits and vegetables, especially at salad bars, to keep them "looking fresh." Sulfites are also added to beer, wine, and bakery goods, sprinkled over shrimp and fish, mixed with dairy and grain products, and added to fruit juices and frozen potatoes.
>
> The problem is that the sulfites also make some people sick. A few even die from allergic reactions. Sulfites have been linked to deaths involving pizza, wine, and beer, and they pose a special danger to asthmatics. After years of complaints—and no regulation—the FDA decided to limit the amount of sulfites in our food and to require a warning label. (Dingell 1985; Ingersoll 1988; FDA 1994)

The Strange Case of Saccharin

To be fair to the FDA, its hands are tied when Congress speaks. And sometimes Congress utters some strange sounds. Saccharin, an artificial sweetener, is known to cause cancer, and the FDA banned it (FDA 1988; Smolinske 1992; Hanssen 1997). But Congress granted saccharine a "special exemption," and this chemical is still sold in food stores. Little cancer packets are also found in restaurants, conveniently placed next to the sugar. A label warns consumers that they may be killing themselves. It wouldn't be too harsh to assume that Congress's "special exemption" had something to do with campaign contributions from the food industry, would it?

The Problem of Synergism

Because they are **synergistic,** that is, they interact with one another, chemical food additives are a complicated hazard. For example, the nitrites that give hot dogs, ham, and bacon their inviting red color appear to be safe in and of themselves. In the presence of amines, however, nitrites become nitrosamines—potent carcinogens. Every organ in every species of experimental animal ever exposed to the nitrosamines has shown cancer. Amines are commonly added to beer, wine, cereals, tea, fish, cigarettes, streptomycin, Librium, and Contac. Thus, hot dogs and beer are an unhealthy combination, as are a ham sandwich and a cup of tea. See Figure 14-4 for another illustration of polluted food.

The Problem of Cumulative Effects

Many chemical additives are harmless until they build up in our bodies. When they reach a certain level, then they begin to destroy tissues and organs. That level varies from person to person.

Why Not Use Alternative Techniques?

The food industry adulterates our food with harmful chemicals not because it is necessary but because it is profitable. The chemicals retard spoilage and increase sales by making food appealing to the public's conditioned taste and sight. Because the food industry can use alternative ways to preserve food, from a conflict perspective we can say that those who control the food industry put profits ahead of health. Certainly the *food chain* is long—that is, getting food from grower to consumer is a lengthy process—and we must have effective ways to preserve food. Ways to do so without harming people's health include older techniques such as pickling, smoking, salting, canning, freezing, and drying, as well as newer ways such as freeze-drying and vacuum packing.

The Extent of Food Pollution

Some of our food is polluted before it is processed and marketed. To keep cows, chickens, and other animals from getting sick and to get them to the market faster, they are fed antibiotics, hormones, and growth-promoting drugs. These substances end up in our own bodies when we eat these animals or their products, such as milk and cheese. Similarly, farmers spray pesticides on fruits and vegetables to prevent insect damage. Because the fruits and vegetables absorb some of these chemicals, they enter our bodies when we eat them.

High Stakes

The stakes are high. Food is the largest industry in the United States. Sales in our 220,000 grocery stores amount to about $450 billion a year (*Statistical Abstract*

FIGURE 14-4 *Bon Appétit?*

APPLES		MILK
captan*		aflatoxin*
parathion*		clorsulon*
daminozide*		fenbendazole*
paraquat		thiabendazole*
		bacteria
POTATOES		GRAPES
chlorothalonil*		captan*
chlorpropham		parathion*
aldicarb		methyl bromide*
CARROTS		CHICKEN
trifluralin*		antibiotics
chlorothalonil*		gentian violet*
parathion*		nitrofurans*
linuron*		bacteria

These contaminants are often but not always in the items pictured above.
*Known or suspected carcinogen.

A Global Glimpse
WHERE NEW LIFE BRINGS DEATH

"The factories, they give us life, but they kill us at the same time," sighs Maria Alves, who awakens at night to the sounds of her six children gagging in the polluted air. "It isn't fair, but what can we do? We need to work."

This is Cubatao, Brazil, a village nestled in the Serr do Mar mountains. It was pretty 20 years ago. Today the people call it "the valley of death."

As nations rush to industrialize, they often skip health and safety standards. Their problems with hazardous chemicals don't grab the world's attention, but they still kill.

Cubatao is one of the most polluted cities on earth. With its factory pollutants and the worst acid rain ever recorded, half its 100,000 people have respiratory ailments.

A benzene gas leak caused hundreds of workers to develop leukopenia, an abnormality of the blood cells. Three developed leukemia and died. The company was fined $4,000.

The phosphates spewing from the fertilizer factories make it look like winter here—little white chemical flakes fluttering down, burning the skin.

Adimar dos Santos Lima, who works in a steel plant for $70 a month and is happy to have a job, says, "I make a living. But I live in a sewer."

A slum neighborhood blew up after gasoline leaked from an underground pipe owned by Petrobras, the national oil company. They found 90 bodies. Another 500 had been incinerated.

Based on Schuster 1985.

2003:Table 1038). Adulterating our food is so profitable that our food industry adds more than 1 billion pounds of chemicals to our food each year—about five pounds of chemicals for every man, woman, and child in the United States. Researchers associate these chemicals with our high rates of cancer.

POLLUTION IN THE INDUSTRIALIZING NATIONS

Although most pollution occurs in the industrialized nations, the nations that are industrializing also contribute to this problem. The air in Mexico City, for example, was so bad that 25 percent of the city's children had symptoms of asthma (U.S. Department of State 1997). After the United Nations declared that Mexico City had the worst air in the world, authorities banned leaded gasoline, shut down some factories, and embarked on a tree-planting program (Mandel-Campbell 2001). Mexico City's air improved, and there now are fewer hacking patients admitted to hospitals. For a snapshot of how harmful conditions can get in these nations, see the Global Glimpse box above.

Four Factors that Increase Pollution in the Industrializing Nations

1. Use of Dangerous Chemicals

Four factors underlie pollution in the industrializing nations: First, chemicals that are outlawed in the industrialized nations remain legal in many of the industrializing countries. Our chemical companies still manufacture these chemicals, although they cannot be used here. They ship them to the industrializing nations, where they are used by workers who cannot read the warnings on the label. The chemicals poison the workers, the land, and the water. In a strange twist, they also often poison the food that you and I eat, for they return to us in our coffee, fruit, nuts, and so on.

The EPA banned domestic use of the pesticide ethylene dioromide (EDB) because it causes cancer. The State Department, whose concern is foreign relations, fearing bad relations with Mexico and Haiti, and, not incidentally, damages to U.S.-financed mango growers in Belize and Guatemala, pressured the EPA to allow foreign mango growers to continue using the pesticide. (Meier 1987a)

2. The Manufacture of Dangerous Chemicals

Second, the industrializing nations manufacture chemicals that the United States bans or that can be made cheaper in those nations—often in factories that U.S. corporations own. Those factories mean jobs, and if an industrializing nation were to insist on stringent safeguards in manufacturing or in pollution controls, it would cut its own economic throat. Other nations would welcome the company—without the safeguards.

The cost of such practices, however, can be high. Consider Bhopal:

It was an unseasonably cold night in Central India. In the shantytowns of Bhopal, thousands of poor families were asleep. At a nearby railway station, a scattering of people waited for early-morning trains. At the local Union Carbide plant, a maintenance worker noticed that a storage tank holding methyl isocyanate (MIC), a chemical used in making pesticides, was showing a high pressure reading. The worker heard rumbling in the tank, then the sound of cracking concrete. The plant superintendent was notified, and he sounded an alarm. But it was too late. A noxious white gas had started seeping from the tank and had begun to spread through the region on the northwesterly winds.

At the Vijoy Hotel near the railroad, sociologist Swapan Saha, 33, woke up with a terrible pain in his chest. "It was both a burning and a suffocating sensation," he said. "It was like breathing fire." Wrapping a damp towel around his nose and mouth, Saha went outside to investigate. Scores of victims lay dead on the platform at the train station. "I thought at first there must have been a gigantic railway accident," he recalled. Then he noticed a pall of white smoke on the ground, and an acrid smell in the air. People were running helter-skelter, retching, vomiting, and defecating uncontrollably. Many collapsed and died. Dogs, cows, and water buffaloes also lay on the ground, twitching in death agonies. Saha made his way to the railway office, only to find the stationmaster slumped over his desk. For a moment, he thought that an atom bomb had hit Bhopal. Staggering back to the hotel, half blind himself by now, he sat down to write a farewell letter to his wife.

Saha survived. More than 2,500 others did not. (Whitaker 1984; Spaeth 1989)

This accident took place in India, but it could happen here. "The only reason we haven't had a release with the same disastrous effect is that we've been lucky," said one EPA official (Beck 1984). An expert on workplace safety put it this way, "It's like a giant roulette wheel. This time the marble came to a stop in a little place in India. But the next time it could be the United States" (Whitaker 1984).

3. The Rush to Industrialize

The third factor is the pollution that these nations produce. As they industrialize, which they are desperate to do, they will produce ever-increasing amounts of pollution. Their pressing concern at the moment is to increase their standard of living and their position in the global power structure, not to manage pollution. China and India, the two most populous nations in the world, are industrializing at such a furious pace that they may well become the world's two largest polluters.

4. Some of These Nations Are Turned Into Toxic Waste Dumps

Fourth, the industrialized nations have found that the Least Industrialized Nations are a convenient dump for their toxic wastes. Our corporate leaders make deals with dictators and weak governments and ship them chemical wastes that under our regulations make them expensive to dispose of (Bartlett and Steele 1998). We even send them the ships that we discard. In Alang, India, 35,000 men work for $1.50 a day breaking up ships whose parts are laden with asbestos, PCBs, lead, and toxic sludge (Englund and Cohn 1997b). The men work unprotected, and many workers die from accidents. Without seeing such conditions firsthand, it is difficult to grasp the desperate misery that these people face on a daily basis. One man who works in this setting, earning $1.50 for a full day's toil with the smell of death hovering over his work, said: "It is better to work and die than starve and die."

GETTING THE OTHER SIDE

A More Optimistic View

Some experts, whom I shall call the optimistic environmentalists, say that alarmist doomsayers have captured the attention of the media and exaggerated the negative aspects of the environment. Isolated incidents such as Bhopal, although tragic, have been blown out of proportion. If we take a more realistic, dispassionate view, they say, we will see that things are not so bad.

This group believes that improved technology will solve whatever threat pollution may pose to the environment. We have had predictions of disaster in the past, they argue, and our technology has always seen us through. The present is no exception. Some of them point to the pollution that people faced in 1900. At that time, horses were common, and so was their manure. Huge amounts were piling up on city streets. That problem disappeared when horses were replaced by automobiles, trucks, and streetcars. The present is no different, and we will develop technology to counter threats to our environment.

Do Environmentalists Cause Disease?

The optimistic environmentalists also claim that many so-called solutions can do more harm than good. Edward Teller (1980), the man most responsible for the hydrogen bomb, said that strict environmental regulations are not only expensive but also they create poverty and disease in the poor nations. He made this point: When environmentalists raised their objections and DDT was removed from Sri Lanka, 2 million people came down with malaria. To combat this disease, DDT had to be brought back. Teller said, "I challenge anybody to show me a case where lack of environmental protection has made 2 million people as seriously sick as the disease caused by the environmentalists."

Life Expectancy as an Indicator That the Environment Is Improving

The optimistic environmentalists also make this point: The best single indicator of the condition of the environment is life expectancy. When the environment deteriorates, life expectancy drops, such as it did in Russia. If an environment improves, life expectancy increases. Figure 14-5 shows the upward march in U.S. life expectancy. Americans are living longer because our environment has improved, not deteriorated (Simon

FIGURE 14-5 *Life Expectancy in the United States, by Year of Birth*

Sources: By the author, based on *Statistical History* 1976:Table B 116, 117; *Statistical Abstract* 1989:Table 106; 2003:Table 105.

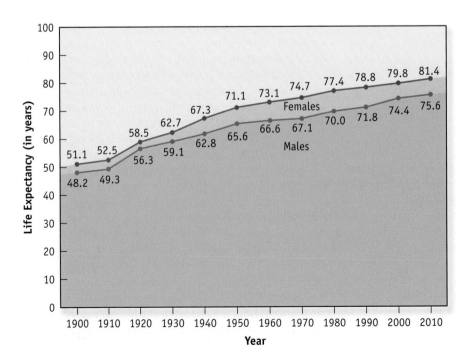

1981). We should stop worrying about what *might* go wrong, much less twist reality in order to match a woeful view of life. Life is getting better, so let's enjoy it.

IN SUM

Three Essential Aspects of Pollution

Whether we take the optimistic or pessimistic view, we confront three aspects of environmental pollution (Faunce 1981):

1. Pollutants are being introduced at an exponential rate.
2. The earth has a finite capacity to absorb pollutants.
3. A long delay often occurs between the introduction of a pollutant and indications that it is doing harm.

Reasonable Concerns: The Extinction of Species

We need not be alarmists to see that, at a minimum, we must deal with toxic wastes, provide wholesome food, and learn how to preserve, create, or—at least—not destroy a healthy environment. We also need not be alarmists to be concerned about the extinction of plant and animal species. The destruction of the tropical rain forests is especially ominous for humanity's future.

The Tropical Rain Forests and the Future of Humanity

The rain forests have been called the lungs of the world. Like our lungs, they help to regulate the earth's exchange of oxygen and carbon dioxide; they absorb carbon gases that create global warming and release oxygen into the air. They also help keep the earth's climate in balance by giving off water vapor that keeps the ground from drying out. Those lungs are gasping, and as the environmental pessimists would say, if action is not taken soon, they will collapse.

The Pessimistic Environmentalists

Although the rain forests cover just 7 percent of the earth's land area, they are home to *one-third to one-half* of all plant and animal species. Many species of plants, still unstudied, could possess medicinal or nutritional value (Linden 1991; Cheng 1995; Simons 2005). Some of the discoveries from the rain forests have been astounding: A flower from Madagascar is used in the treatment of leukemia, and a frog in Peru produces a painkiller more powerful, but less addictive, than morphine (Wolfensohn and Fuller 1998).

Ecotourism has developed to educate people about the environment and to generate profits to help sustain the environment. Shown here is a guide in the Sabah Rainforest of the Danum Valley, Malaysia.

Despite our knowledge that the rain forests are essential for humanity's welfare, we seem bent on destroying them. For the sake of timber and farms, we keep clearing them. In the process, we extinguish thousands of plant and animal species (Durning 1990; Wolfensohn and Fuller 1998; "The Price of Success" 2004). As biologists remind us, a species lost is gone forever.

Like Esau who exchanged his birthright for a bowl of porridge, we exchange our future for some lumber, farms, and pastures.

Let's turn to resource depletion. Here we find more disagreement among the experts.

ENERGY AND RESOURCES

Americans used to think that gasoline was limitless. We even had "gas wars," in which gas stations kept undercutting one another's price. To attract people to buy their gas, stations used to give away glasses and dishes with a gasoline purchase. This ended abruptly. In the late 1970s, OPEC (Organization of Petroleum Exporting Countries) surprised the West with an oil embargo. Overnight, long lines appeared at U.S. gas stations, and for a moment, Americans became acutely aware of how fragile their energy supply was. But only for a moment.

Although a few changes were permanent, such as more fuel-efficient cars and better-insulated homes, when the embargoes were removed, we mostly went back to our old habits.

Two Views

How concerned should we be about energy and resources? It depends on whom you listen to. Let's examine the views.

The Pessimistic Environmentalists

One group of experts feels that we are facing energy shortages so vast that we will shatter the foundations of the industrialized world. Our civilization depends on materials whose supply is limited. There is only so much petroleum and natural gas, and one day we shall run out of these substances. This group is also disturbed by how quickly we are depleting water and minerals. Although freshwater appears to be endless, 97 percent of all the water on earth is saltwater. A little over 2 percent is frozen in glacial ice. This leaves about 1 percent for all agricultural, industrial, and personal uses. Industrial societies are making huge demands on this limited supply of freshwater.

To illustrate the coming crisis, consider the Ogallala aquifer. This aquifer, shown in Figure 14-6, runs from South Dakota to Texas. It waters nearly 12 percent of the nation's corn, cotton, grain sorghum, and wheat (Frazier and Schlender 1980; Brown 1987). In this area, ranchers raise nearly half the nation's cattle. Yet we are depleting this underground formation ("Ogallala Water..." 2003). Some say that the natural condition of much of this area, now in pasture and farmlands, is Sahara-like desert, that eventually its outstanding characteristic will be its giant sand dunes (Stevens 1996). Frank Popper, the head of the Department of Urban Studies at Rutgers University, says that one day hardly anyone will live in this region. He suggests that the federal government buy huge chunks of the land, replant the native prairie grasses, reintroduce the buffalo, and turn off the lights (Farney 1989).

FIGURE 14-6 *The Ogallala Aquifer*

The Ogallala Aquifer

The pessimistic environmentalists conclude that our needs may soon outpace our water supply. They also foresee a bleak outlook for essential minerals. Although the quantities of minerals are finite, their demand is growing. We have moved from an era of abundance to an era of scarcity. Soon we will run out of the metals that we need to maintain our societies.

We are facing the end of the industrialized world. Although substitute materials may buy us some time, we are reaching limits that will stop the expansion of business. As Barry Commoner (1972) warned, we are playing out a fundamental paradox of human life: Our economy has a built-in need to grow, but its growth depends on irreplaceable, essential resources—and these are not growing. We're cruising along at 90 mph, with the top down and the radio tuned to our favorite station—and we don't see the brick wall ahead.

The Optimistic Environmentalists

Such a view misreads and distorts the evidence, reply the optimistic environmentalists. Economist Julian Simon, for example, insisted that raw materials are *not* getting scarcer. This led to one of history's famous bets, which is recounted in the Thinking Critically box on the next page. Simon said that when something in demand grows scarce, its price increases. To see if raw materials are becoming scarcer, look at their price. The long-term trend is lower prices, which means *less scarcity*. Here is how Simon put it (1980:11):

The cost trends of almost every natural resource—whether measured in labor time required to produce the resource, or even in the price relative to other consumer goods—have been downward over the course of recorded history.

Thinking Critically about Social Problems

PUT YOUR MONEY WHERE YOUR MOUTH IS: THE SIMON–EHRLICH BET

To say that Professors Julian Simon and Paul Ehrlich didn't like each other would be an understatement. *Detest* would be a more appropriate description. Simon was an economist who taught at the University of Maryland. Ehrlich, a demographer and ornithologist, taught at Stanford.

Ordinarily, their paths would not have crossed. They worked in different fields, and they lived a continent apart.

But then life changed for both of them.

Ehrlich came out swinging. In 1968, he wrote a book that scared millions of people and fueled the environmental movement. He said that populations were growing so fast that scarcity of food was on the horizon. Prices were going to soar, and life expectancy would drop. *The Population Bomb* sold three million copies, scared the American public, and made Ehrlich rich. He was sought after as a guest on talk shows.

Fame and fortune. A prestigious job at Stanford. Unless he started to sexually harass his students or come to class drunk, how could that be spoiled?

Then came Simon. Simon started grumbling in public, muttering that Ehrlich's book was a piece of, well, you know what—rotten codfish. Simon claimed that the truth was the opposite of what Ehrlich had said. Larger populations, asserted Simon, would mean more abundance, not less. Prices would drop, not increase. Life expectancy wouldn't drop, but, instead, increase.

Simon and Ehrlich began to call each other names. They wrote nasty comments about one another in academic journals.

Ehrlich still had the public on his side. He kept repeating his predictions of doomsday. He was a founder of Earth Day, where he spoke to a crowd of 200,000.

Simon was there, too, telling his side of the story. He had an audience of 16.

Simon didn't like this, but there wasn't much he could do about the public latching on to Ehrlich's ideas, not his.

Then Simon made an intriguing proposal. He challenged any pessimistic environmentalist (or New Malthusian) to a bet (Toth 1990). They could select *any* commodity, and Simon would bet that its price would drop. "After all," he said, "contrary to common sense, resources are growing more plentiful, and they will drop in price."

"Put your money where your mouth is," Simon boasted, none too gently.

This was too much for Ehrlich—who knew that he was the target of the challenge. In October 1980, he accepted the bet, then he did a little boasting of his own. He said, "I'll accept Simon's astonishing offer before other greedy people jump in" (Tierney 1998).

The bet—on chrome, copper, nickel, tin, and tungsten—was publicized widely. If the prices were higher in 10 years, Ehrlich would win; if they were lower, Simon would win. To be sure there were no misunderstandings, the two signed a contract.

During the ensuing years, the two kept attacking each other, and the world's population kept growing—soaring by more than 800 million people, the greatest increase in history.

Ten years later to the day, the two checked prices.

Ehrlich was chagrined. The price of all five metals had dropped. He quietly sent Simon a check; he enclosed no letter.

Simon gloated publicly. "Now you know who's right," he said. "And if you think this was just a fluke, let's do it again. And this time, let's put up some real money. How about $20,000?"

Ehrlich refused, saying that the matter was of minor importance.

Simon laughed and continued to poke fun at Ehrlich. Then students started to do the same, calling Ehrlich Stanford's nuttiest professor.

Julian Simon died at age 65 in 1990. Paul Ehrlich stayed on at Stanford, where he still teaches. The two never reconciled.

An hour's work in the United States has brought increasingly more of copper, wheat, and oil (representative and important raw materials) from 1800 to the present. . . . These trends imply that the raw materials have been getting increasingly available and less scarce relative to the most important and most fundamental element of life, human work time.

To illustrate how the prices of raw materials have been falling relative to wages, Simon used the example of copper. As Figure 14-7 illustrates, it takes less and less time to earn enough to buy a pound of copper.

The optimistic environmentalists also count on technology. If we should ever exhaust a particular resource, our technology will produce a substitute. New technology will exploit materials that were useless to older technology. In fact, technology is rushing so headlong into the future that it even produces new materials before the old ones are threatened. A recent example is how fiber optic cable is replacing copper wire for the transmission of sound and images. Just a few years ago, they point out, the pessimists were saying that we would run out of copper. Take another look at Figure 14-7.

And energy? Here too, Simon stressed, the answer lies in long-term price trends. Short-term trends can yield a distorted picture. The escalation of oil prices in the 1970s, for example, did not indicate scarcity, but the futile attempt of a cartel to control prices. OPEC saw its chance at monopoly and took it. As Figure 14-8 makes clear, OPEC's effort was but a blip on a long-term trend of declining oil prices. The higher oil prices of the early 2000s will prove to be the same—increases because of war, political instability, and the manipulation of output. The prices of electricity and coal are also downward, indicating an increasing and stable supply of energy.

THE COMING RESOLUTION

Frameworks of Interpretation

As with population and food, the experts fall into opposing camps. As symbolic interactionists stress, the framework into which we fit data colors our conclusions—and that applies to "experts" and "nonexperts" alike. If we assume that the environment is deteriorating and our vital resources are disappearing, we interpret data one way. If we assume that resources are infinitely abundant and will not shrink, other interpretations follow.

What usually happens in science is that, barring political interference, opposing sides present their evidence, air their views, try to disprove the other, and the best data win out. This isn't always the case, mind you, but usually it is. In this instance, as scientists produce more data, the exaggerations of each side should become apparent, and which position has the better data should become evident.

FIGURE 14-7   *The Price of Copper Relative to Wages*

Sources: *Historical Statistics of the U.S.: Colonial Times to 1970,* 1976; *Statistical Abstract* 2003:Tables 641, 871.

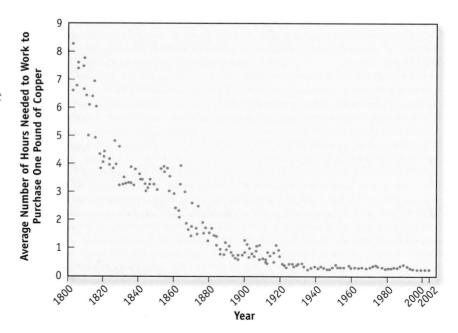

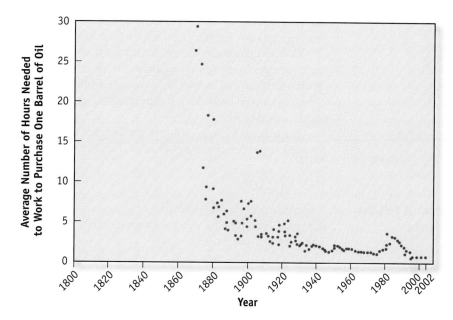

FIGURE 14-8 *The Price of Oil Relative to Wages*

Sources: *Historical Statistics of the U.S.: Colonial Times to 1970,* 1976; *Statistical Abstract,* various years, including 2003:Tables 641, 873.

The Need for Continued Debate

Meanwhile, we must draw our own conclusions—which affect how we perceive the problem and evaluate solutions. On an individual level, our conclusions color our choices about energy use and lifestyles. On the level of governments, the conclusions have greater implications: The well-being of billions of people depend on them—including future generations. It is to everyone's benefit that this debate and its related research continue, unencumbered by politics, so that governmental policies can be based on sound argument and data. We now turn to social policies.

Social Policy

THE STEADY STATE SOCIETY

Comparing the Pessimists and the Optimists: Steady State or Scaled-Back Society?

Before we examine specific social policies, let's look at an overarching solution that the pessimistic environmentalists propose. It is folly, they say, to expect the world's economies and our standards of living to increase endlessly. We must develop a **steady state society;** that is, we must stabilize industrial output approximately where it is now. If we do this, we will decrease the rate at which we pollute the environment and use up resources. This means, though, that we must curb our growing appetite for the material goods that support our current lifestyles.

Some pessimists go further. They say that we must develop a scaled-back society. We can't stabilize our industrial output until we first reduce it. Only after we cut back to an optimal level can we move to a steady state society. This will require sacrifice: All of us, except the poorest, must learn to get by with less. To lower our material

To save the environment, some insist that we must drastically reduce the world's population and our standard of living. Few of us, however, want to live like this hermit in Desolation Canyon of southern Utah. There must be a balance that we can strike between population, standard of living, and the environment.

standards so we can reduce our dependence on depleting fossil fuels, we must scale back our expectations. Simpler, less-materialistic lifestyles, they add, will be more satisfying.

The optimistic environmentalists scoff at such arguments. They say that we can solve the environmental crisis and at the same time enjoy a high standard of living, increase our industrial output, and create a world of even greater material abundance. It is foolish to even consider a steady state society. Such a society would deny billions of people a better life.

Regardless of the position that one takes on a steady state or scaled-back society, we need social policies for pollution and energy. Let's consider them.

POLLUTION

Four Potential Policies for Pollution:

A pressing problem is the misuse of toxic chemicals. As the Global Glimpse box on the next page highlights, it is not enough to ban the use of a chemical in the United States. The chemical will return to us by way of a food chain that stretches to us from the Least Industrialized Nations. U.S. companies and their subsidiaries should not be allowed to manufacture chemicals whose use is banned in the United States. Because other countries also produce toxic chemicals, the United States can call a summit to enact international controls.

1. Preventing the Misuse of Toxic Chemicals

To prevent misuse, industry must be held accountable. To protect the people of the industrializing nations, where harmful chemicals are used in food production, all chemicals need to be labeled in the language of the country to which they are shipped, their dangers clearly stated in plain words. To make industry accountable, Congress passed the *Community Right to Know Act* in 1986. It requires companies to annually submit to a state agency and to local fire departments a list of the hazardous chemicals they use or manufacture. Some states have passed their own right-to-know laws, requiring businesses to inform their employees of the hazardous chemicals they will be exposed to at work.

Some environmentalists say that this is not enough, They want a comprehensive policy for toxic chemicals. In this "cradle-to-grave" approach, all toxic chemicals would be approved for sale and use, registered as they enter the marketplace, and monitored throughout their lifetime. Lists of chemical releases would be available to the public, and the names of the worst polluters would be publicized (Friends of the Earth, 2004).

2. Preventing Food Pollution

A second pressing problem is food pollution. Recall the chapter's opening vignette. No compelling reason exists to allow diseases to be transmitted in foods. With our alternative forms of food processing and preservation, there also is no compelling reason to adulterate food chemically to make it look or taste better, to make its transportation easier, or to lengthen its shelf life. At a minimum, no chemical should be added to our food until it is proven safe for human consumption. State-of-the-art testing procedures can be used to detect banned chemicals in our food, whether imported or domestic. We can shut down U.S. companies that violate chemical restrictions and ban food imports from countries that do so. To be effective, the legal penalties need to be directed against the *managers and directors* of companies that violate such laws.

In their pursuit of profit, many industries lack a sense of social responsibility. Instead of grappling with the severe consequences of their pollution, they prefer to ignore, dissimulate, and use public relations to misdirect the public.

A Global Glimpse
THE CIRCLE OF POISON

In U.S. ports from Gulfport, Mississippi, to Oakland, California, you can watch forklifts loading 55-gallon drums onto the decks of vessels bound for Central and South America.

What's in the drums? Heptachlor, chlordane, BHC, and other chemicals on their way to the plantations of Latin America.

These pesticides, linked to cancer and sterility, are banned or restricted severely in the United States. U.S. companies, however, manufacture them here and in other nations and market them in the industrializing countries. There, most workers who handle these chemicals cannot read. They have no idea what the warnings on the labels say. Yet these chemicals will contaminate them, their family, and their food.

Pesticides that are banned here don't disappear—they come back to haunt us. The fruit grown in these countries appears on our kitchen tables—along with the poisons used to protect them from insects. BHC comes back in your coffee. DDT, applied to cotton in El Salvador, shows up in beef carcasses imported through Miami. Nearly half of the green coffee beans we import are contaminated with pesticides, potential carcinogens. And the situation worsens, for the free trade zones that stimulate the globalization of capitalism increase the importation of these products.

Based on a newsletter from Frances Moore Lappe, founder of Food First; Ingersoll 1990; Allen 1991; "U.S. Pesticide Exports" 1994.

3. Disposing of Industrial Wastes

A third pressing problem is how to safely dispose of the unwanted by-products of industrialization. We already know how to detoxify most industrial wastes. We probably could learn to detoxify the rest. Recycling waste products is especially promising because it turns noxious waste into safe and usable products. To develop better technology to recycle and detoxify wastes, we could establish a superfund to finance cooperative research by scientists. Through a crash program—a "Manhattan Project" of industrial wastes—we might be able to decontaminate the world's chemical time bombs before they go off.

Scattered across the nation are thousands of hazardous waste sites where we have discarded oil, battery acid, PCBs, pesticides, paint, and radioactive wastes. The EPA has drawn up a National Priority List of the most dangerous waste sites. Earlier, you saw where these sites are located (Figure 14-3 on page 471). Table 14-1 on page 487 ranks the states on the basis of the number of priority waste sites they contain. Congress established a superfund to clean up these sites and has spent $20 billion to begin the cleanup. Some estimate that the bill for cleaning up these sites will run $50 billion; others say that it will total $500 billion. No one knows, of course, but if the lower total is correct, that's $160 for every person in the United States. If the higher figure is right, the cleanup will cost each of us $1,600.

The Special Problem of Nuclear Wastes

Because they stay lethal for thousands of years, leftover plutonium and other nuclear wastes have perplexed the experts. For decades, while scientists debated how to store something that was beyond human experience, *millions* of pounds of radioactive waste have been stored in temporary containers (Campbell 1987; Schneider 1992). The waste's new home is supposed to be in Yucca Mountain near Las Vegas, Nevada. Storage chambers have been carved from an ancient salt bed, nearly half a mile below ground. Geologists assure us that this salt deposit has been stable for 250 million years (Brooke 1999). Critics point out that this may be so, but the waste will be stored in stainless steel containers lined with lead. No one knows if those containers will last a thousand years, much less ten thousand years. Others say that we have so much waste waiting to be buried that even this depository won't hold it all (Ashley 2002). The issue is so controversial that Las Vegas officials have weighed in on the issue. They swear that they won't allow the waste to pass through their city on the way to the mountain, that, if necessary, they'll use armed force to stop the trucks and railroad cars carrying the waste.

4. Solving the Greenhouse Effect

The greenhouse effect is a fourth pressing problem. An immediate step would be to plant vast numbers of trees around the world, for they thrive on carbon dioxide. To the extent that carbon dioxide is a danger to the world, nations must reduce the amounts that they produce. The 1997 environmental treaty approved by 160 nations in Kyoto, Japan, was a giant step in this direction. As mentioned, the treaty proved controversial. Fearful that compliance with the treaty could cost millions of jobs, the United States withdrew from it (Associated Press 2004). We will have to see what the future holds in this regard.

Protecting the Rain Forests

We must also develop social policies to help stop the destruction of the world's rain forests. I propose two policies. The first is to make it illegal to import timber that comes from these forests. This will require an international agreement, for it is not sufficient for only a nation here and there to pass such laws. The second is for the industrialized nations to *purchase the rights to not develop the rain forests*. Because most of the rain forests are in nations that have not industrialized, those funds could pay off their huge debts, thus helping to solve another problem. This policy would preserve millions of acres and thousands of plant and animal species for future generations. The rights would extend indefinitely and be overseen by an international watchdog agency.

Is the United States Preparing to Invade Other Nations to Enforce Environmental Policies?

No social policy is simple, of course, and policies concerning the rain forests bring their own complications. Brazil, for example, which has extensive rain forests, knows that the United States prospered by cutting down most of its forests for farmland. Brazilian officials find it ironic that the United States wants them to preserve Brazil's forests for the benefit of Americans. Some Brazilian officials even fear that the concern the United States has expressed is a prelude to an invasion, and they have trained jungle forces to repel it (Goering 1998). Paranoia? We only have to look at the long history of U.S. intervention in Latin America to see why they have such fears.

The Overarching Solution

An overarching solution to pollution is to produce less of what harms the environment (Ball 1999; Dye 1999). We can do this by changing our production techniques and equipment, redesigning our products, and doing more in-process recycling. We have the capacity to take these steps, but to take them we must be convinced that our fragile environment is being harmed and that it is worth the effort and cost to change our ways.

ENERGY

Two Types of Solutions:

Aside from discovering new deposits of gas and petroleum, only two types of solutions for energy exist: alternative forms of energy and energy conservation.

1. Finding Alternatives

Let's first consider alternative forms of energy. One alternative to oil and petroleum has already been mentioned—coal. We have enough coal in the United States to satisfy our energy needs for centuries. We can transform coal into liquids and gases. South Africa operates a coal liquefaction plant that produces a fuel competitive with petroleum. We would have to assure that such plants did not contribute to pollution.

Synfnels

"Synfuels" can be developed from garbage, sawdust, and other waste. The decay of organic substances, such as sewage and straw, produces methane and methanol, gases that motors can burn efficiently. One day we may solve two problems at once: the disposal of our organic garbage and the production of alternative fuels. We may see fields of common milkweed turn into flourishing "petroleum farms" as factories extract hydrocarbons—the backbone of motor fuels, lubricants, turpentine, and rubber—from those plants.

TABLE 14-1 How the States Rank in Number of Hazardous Waste Sites
on the National Priority List

STATE	NUMBER OF SITES	STATE	NUMBER OF SITES
1. New Jersey	115	26. Alabama	15
2. California	98	27. Georgia	15
3. Pennsylvania	96	28. Montana	15
4. New York	91	29. Iowa	14
5. Michigan	69	30. Kentucky	14
6. Florida	52	31. Tennessee	13
7. Washington	47	32. Arkansas	12
8. Illinois	45	33. Kansas	12
9. Wisconsin	40	34. Maine	12
10. Texas	43	35. New Mexico	12
11. Ohio	33	36. Oregon	12
12. Massachusetts	32	37. Rhode Island	12
13. Virginia	30	38. Oklahoma	11
14. Indiana	29	39. Nebraska	11
15. North Carolina	28	40. Idaho	10
16. Minnesota	24	41. Arizona	9
17. Missouri	23	42. West Virginia	9
18. South Carolina	21	43. Vermont	9
19. Utah	20	44. Alaska	6
20. New Hampshire	19	45. Hawaii	3
21. Maryland	19	46. Mississippi	4
22. Colorado	17	47. South Dakota	2
23. Connecticut	16	48. Wyoming	2
24. Delaware	15	49. Nevada	1
25. Louisiana	15	50. North Dakota	0
			Total 1,278

Source: By the author, based on *Statistical Abstract* 2003:Table 381.

Hydrogen and Solar Power

Hydrogen, too, holds great potential. As a basic component of air and water, hydrogen is available in limitless amounts. Other alternative sources of energy include the sun, wind, ocean tides, geothermal energy (heat from beneath the earth's crust), and nuclear fusion (combining atoms, as opposed to nuclear fission, which splits atoms). The most promising alternative is harnessing the sun. Solar power is infinite, and technologies, such as the photovoltaic cell, which changes sunlight into electricity, can trap it. Developing alternative sources of energy is promising, but the political climate is not. If gasoline hits $4 or $5 a gallon, it is likely that Americans will get serious about alternative forms of energy.

Legal Scams

Whenever scammers smell profits, they jump in with both feet. So it has been with synfuels. To encourage the development and production of synfuels, Congress offered huge tax breaks. This drew the scammers out of the woodwork. To spray pine tar or latex on coal meets the IRS requirement that the new product be chemically different from the original. Although there is no new product, no real synfuel, the spraying meets the letter of the law and qualifies for the tax break. The companies that do this spraying have to sell their coated coal at a loss—otherwise, the utility companies they sell to could simply burn coal that doesn't have this coating. Although these supposed synfuel companies lose money on their fake product, they reap real profits from the tax credits that they sell to wealthy investors (Biddle 2001; Hogan 2001). The losers in this sweet setup are the taxpayers who eventually have to ante up the taxes that the IRS doesn't collect from those who profit from this legal scam.

2. Conservation

Another step is to conserve energy. This involves everything from insulating homes, businesses, and factories to working four ten-hour shifts instead of five eight-hour shifts a week. Such a change in working patterns would cut commuting expenses by 20 percent and allow factories to fire up their boilers less often. The potential of conservation is dramatic, but it does involve changing patterns of behavior that are rooted firmly in culture, hardly an easy matter.

Our homes and cars have become more energy efficient, but we still have a long way to go. The "Lo-Cal" house, developed at the University of Illinois, can cut fuel bills by about two-thirds. These savings are made simply through the design of the house, without help from solar equipment. About 85 percent of the total window area in the house faces south, the house is heavily insulated, and its roof overhangs by 30 inches, letting sunshine in during the winter but excluding it during the summer. Another home design is the "solar envelope." This house is built within a second set of walls that provide a "skin" to trap and distribute the sun's heat. Even in northern climates, a furnace is needed on only the cloudiest days of winter. Its ingenious design also cools the house in the summer by drawing in cool air from a chamber under the house.

Another form of conservation is **cogeneration,** producing electricity as part of normal operations, such as generating electricity from the heat and steam that industrial boilers produce. This is not a new idea. In 1900, cogenerators produced more than half of the nation's electricity. Now they produce only about 3 percent. To encourage cogeneration, federal law requires that utility companies purchase a firm's excess production at the utility's standard costs (Paul 1987). The advantage for utility companies is that they can add to their capacity to provide electricity without having to invest in building new power plants (Devine 2004).

An Underlying Conflict

Alternative forms of energy and conservation should guarantee that we never run out of energy. Solar energy, for example, is endless. We need only harvest it. We must keep in mind, however, what conflict theorists stress: Both conservation and alternative forms of energy threaten politically powerful oil companies—and they do not take threats to their profits lightly.

Again, the Optimists

Finally, we should note that if the optimists are right, we will develop alternative forms of energy as we need them. Market forces will take over: If we run out of one form of energy, in their pursuit of profits, people will develop the technologies to tap alternative sources. Those who are convinced of this view say: Just don't interfere with those market forces, and the balance will occur naturally (Simon 1986).

DETERMINING NATIONAL PRIORITIES

No Perfect Solutions

As with all social policy, every choice exacts its costs. So it is with resources and energy. Each choice forgoes some alternative. No choice is *the* perfect solution. All choices are limited by technology, politics, and imperfect knowledge. No society is a heaven on earth, where all pollution and poverty, brutality and evil, have been eliminated. And I do not foresee such a society as ever existing on earth.

The Need for Global Cooperation

Because the environmental problem is global, its solution requires global cooperation. If the industrialized nations dedicate their resources, we can solve our environmental problems. Consider the potential of technology.

The Technological Fix

Some technology that can solve environmental problems sounds as though it comes straight out of science fiction: Already we can grow a fungus that eats the heavy metals (mercury, uranium, lead, nickel, silver, and zinc) that pollute our waterways (Roberts 1987; Naj 1988, 1989a, 1989b; Siwolop 1988). By genetically altering strains of bacteria, we can develop "superbugs" to neutralize hazardous wastes, even radioactive wastes (Daly and Minton 1998). We can convert cellulose, a common waste product of many manufacturing processes, into an acid that can be used to produce fuels and fertilizer (Dye 1999).

Fuel-Cell Powered Cars

It even seems within our grasp to dethrone the king of power, the internal combustion engine. Although the automobile industry dragged its feet, after California mandated that 10 percent of the vehicles sold in that state be essentially pollution free, car companies began researching alternatives in earnest. Their main innovation is the hybrid car, even hybrid SUVs. Using both electricity and gasoline to propel them, hybrid cars burn about 25 percent less gasoline than regular cars. They even convert the car's motion to electricity when the brakes are applied ("Hybrid Car..." 2004). Other hybrids burn hydrogen. Toyota has developed a car that can travel 300 miles on a single tank of compressed hydrogen (Murphy 2003). As hybrid cars and trucks become economically competitive and standards of pollution control become stricter, the internal combustion engine might become obsolete. Propelling cars by burning hydrogen can even reduce global warming, because water flows out of the exhaust, instead of carbon dioxide.

Taking the Lead and Determining Policies

The Dilemma

The United States could take the lead in solving environmental problems by proposing international laws to benefit all nations. It is likely to continue down an ethnocentric path, however, and propose laws biased in its own interests. Another problem is that such laws could conflict with the individual sovereignty of nations, making some likely to reject such legislation as violating their national interest. This would bring us face-to-face with a basic, philosophical, moral problem. Is there a fundamental right of some nations to enforce their will on others? If so, what is the basis of that right? Some "greater good" for the world's benefit? If so, who decides what that "greater good" is and how it should be enforced? Assumptions of a "greater good," as conflict theorists remind us, can be excuses for the Most Industrialized Nations to bully the world.

Establishing National Priorities

Perhaps the best social policy is to set an example. For this, we need to establish national priorities. Without them, we follow current dictates of the market, which are circular; that is, public demand is based on advertising, which, in turn, is based on the need to sell what we produce. To establish national priorities requires a vision of the future, and we seem to have little agreement on either our destination or our route for getting there.

The Future of the Problem

As we discussed social policy, we touched on the future. At this point, let's first examine energy conservation and pollution. Then we'll again look through the eyes of the pessimists and optimists.

The Outlook for Energy

We continuously increase our demands for energy. Since 1970, the average size of a new home has risen from 1,600 square feet to over 2,100—even as the average household has shrunk to 3 people from 3.6. We also furnish our homes with more energy-eating appliances. In the 1970s, 40 percent of new homes had central air conditioning; now 87 percent do (Myerson 1998; *Statistical Abstract* 2003:Table 944). Dishwashers have gone from being luxuries to being "necessities." Although our cars get better mileage, we burn gasoline as though there were no tomorrow—with more fuel being used per person than was used in the 1970s (Myerson 1998). The conservation movement has stagnated, and without higher prices at the gas pump and higher bills from the power company, we and the rest of the industrialized world will continue our energy-wasteful ways. And why not continue on our merry way? In the United States, gasoline is cheaper than bottled water.

For energy, the future is rosy. We possess vast reserves of coal and oil. We can also use technology to harness alternative forms of energy, making these sources of energy

The Marriage of Community and Environment

Robert Gottlieb, Professor of Urban Environmental Policy at Occidental College, has found that something new is happening in the environmental movement. He calls it a marriage of community and environment. Living in Los Angeles and writing and teaching about the urban environment make this "marriage" particularly compelling for him.

When I first arrived in Los Angeles in 1969, the city, with its sprawling landscapes of subdivisions and freeways, had a reputation as the "antienvironment." I never focused on the fact that Los Angeles had a river until the 1980s, when one of my students brought to my attention the growing advocacy around the revitalization of the asphalt-and-concrete-encased Los Angeles River. Since then, I've been able to document the creation in Los Angeles of a new kind of community-based environmentalism: where urban rivers and streams and other green spaces and community places in the City are re-envisioned.

This marriage of community and environment has made an impact on environmental groups. Open space has long referred to places outside urban areas or at the urban edge where there is little or no development. Earlier battles for open space sought to *preserve* environmental assets, such as habitat, wildlife, and other forms of biodiversity. Their focus was not on built environments where there is little or no existing green space, where den-

sity is high, where the land is contaminated, and where the acquisition of land for parks or recreation seems only a distant possibility.

That's changing. Environmental advocates have begun to redefine the issue of open space as the need to re-envision *community spaces* and to reclaim rather than simply preserve such places. Now embraced by many environmentalists are community gardens, farmers markets in low-income communities, relandscaping projects, and recreational opportunities in densely populated areas. I had the opportunity to direct an educational program on the Los Angeles River—the very symbol of both the antienvironment and efforts to re-envision the river as a community and environmental asset.

If you define the marriage of community and environment as an effort to re-envision—or reconstruct or reclaim—these kinds of community and environmental assets, then a different kind of environmental agenda begins to emerge. This would be an agenda that focuses on a neighborhood's transportation needs, on access to and quality of food, on health concerns like asthma, and on schools as relandscaped, livable places rather than fortresslike, asphalt jungles. In this marriage, the greening agenda becomes a justice agenda. It leads us to understand that nature belongs in the city as well as outside it.

widely available at low prices. Doubtless, the international oil companies will turn the alternative forms into profitable enterprises.

The Outlook for Pollution   The picture for pollution is less positive. We continue to approach pollution on an emergency basis: When the leaching of a chemical dump or some other matter of pollution becomes too public to ignore, we apply an environmental Band-Aid. We have no overarching plan for chemical and nuclear pollution that ensures the long-range health of our population.

If bringing pollution under control required only law and technology, we could assume a future that becomes ever more pollution free. But more is required—particularly a national determination to make our environment as free of pollution as possible. Although this depends on public awareness, which ebbs and flows, it also depends on politics; any administration can strengthen or weaken standards.

The Greens   Environmentalists in Germany have formed their own political party. The Green Party, as it is called, holds seats in the German parliament, and in several of Germany's states it has become a key player in coalition governments. The United States, too, has a Green Party, but it has a difficult time mustering enough support to get on the ballot, much less to win a major election. Support for Ralph Nader, the closest we have had to a national Green candidate, always weak, dried up in the 2004 elections. That the U.S. Greens have not been able to muster strong political support does not mean that this will continue indefinitely. Some unexpected event could etch the environment into the national consciousness, making it a top political issue. In the meantime, as Robert Gottlieb discusses in the Spotlight on Research box on the previous page, the environmentalists are applying their perspective to urban areas.

An Unfolding Coalition of Interests

As conflict theorists would predict, the future of pollution depends on the balance of power among groups whose interests collide. The environmental movement may be picking up key strength at this point in our history, however, for people around the globe have become increasingly concerned about the world they will leave for their children. A coalition of religious groups has even made the environment a top priority (Watanabe 1998). With missionary zeal, Christians and Jews are joining forces under the banner "Creation Care." They stress that "we are called to be stewards, not exploiters, of the earth."

The Picture Painted by the Pessimists

Finally, let's look at the future through the eyes of the two groups who see practically nothing alike. The pessimists paint a gloomy future, of course. Pollution will continue with only superficial improvements here and there, and the depletion of resources will accelerate. The countdown has already begun, and "RDP Day" (Resource-Depletion and Pollution Day) is on its way—the day when we have depleted our vital resources and pollution has gone so far that we can't fix it. With its industrial base undermined, modern society will disintegrate. Desperate, people will flee. But to where? Even the countryside will be too polluted to support anything but a minimum of life.

Can this gloomy future be averted? Yes, reply the pessimists, but only if we develop a steady state society. To reduce our energy consumption and eliminate much of our material gadgetry, however, will be like taking the bottle away from an alcoholic. We will go through a painful adjustment, because we have built a society on the assumption of inexhaustible resources. But once we recover from the initial shock of having our lifestyle drastically changed, we may find that a simpler way of life is rewarding: we will be less rushed, enjoy social relationships more, and feel less compulsion to own things.

The Picture Painted by the Optimists

And what does the future look like to the optimists? Instead of using the gray and black colors of the pessimists, the optimists paint with rosy colors. Our present path is fine. We already have more resources than we need for the foreseeable future, but scientists will continue to make breakthroughs that will put even more energy at our disposal. Their developments in hydrogen storage and fusion, for example, hold the potential of giving us energy in unlimited quantities. From this source alone, we can meet all the world's needs now and in the future (Bishop and Wells 1989; Stevens 1989).

For the optimists, neither is pollution a fearsome problem, not even nuclear waste. Scientists have discovered a bacteria that has adapted to 15 times the dose of radiation that it takes to kill humans. This bacteria, an

Out of environmental degradation, and the potential that conditions will worsen, has arisen an international environmental movement. Some feel that people who use extreme measures to get their message across are crazy, whereas many environmentalists feel that people who put profits ahead of the world's health are crazy. Greenpeace uses attention-getting tactics to get its message to the world.

extremophile, will be able to eat nuclear wastes, breaking them down into relatively harmless components (Fialka 2004).

The principle is this: Pollution will be solved to the extent that people demand a cleaner environment and are willing to pay for prevention and cleanup. Because people are demanding it, the environment is already getting cleaner—and it will continue to improve. Consequently, the future promises a healthier environment, an even higher standard of living, and a continued lengthening of our life expectancy.

Who Is Right?

Who is right? What *is* the future of the environmental crisis? Is humanity at a crossroads, as the pessimists insist, with our current course destining us to destruction? Or are the optimists right, and our current course is taking us to a delightful future? Could the future turn out to be even gloomier than imagined, with nuclear war, the worst pollution of all, destroying our ecosystem—and humanity? We consider that possibility in the following chapter.

We who are audience—and either beneficiaries or victims—of this unfolding drama will have to await its outcome.

SUMMARY

1. The destruction of the environment began millennia ago and may even have destroyed ancient civilizations. Industrialization has intensified this process.

2. The nations of the world share a common *ecosystem.* The environmental crisis is a global matter: Individual acts of *pollution* can have international consequences. Pollution comes primarily from industrialization and is not dependent on ideology. Pollution is common in both capitalist and socialist nations.

3. Symbolic interactionists have studied how the environment became a social problem, how objective conditions were translated into subjective concerns. Concerns about the environment began with professionals, were picked up by interest groups and government agencies, and then by the press, which aroused the public.

4. Functionalists stress that all life on earth is interdependent. ("Everything is connected to everything else.") We all are part of a huge, complex living machine called the environment. Industrialization has dysfunctional consequences for the ecosystem.

5. Conflict theorists stress the conflict between environmentalists, who battle to reduce environmental threat, and industrial leaders, who fight for the right to pollute while earning a profit.

6. Some measures of air and water pollution show improvement, but the results are mixed, and pollution continues. The *greenhouse effect* could cause climatic change that would have far-ranging consequences for humanity.

7. Strip mining and the disposal of solid wastes despoil the land. Industrial wastes threaten our drinking water and many of our lakes and rivers. *Acid* and *mercury rain* imperil animal and plant life.

8. Chemical pollutants pervade our environment. Leaching from landfills is extensive. Nuclear pollution is ominous, as illustrated by the Kyshtym and Chernobyl disasters. Food additives are another form of pollution.

9. Alarmed at the environmental crisis, pessimists advocate a *steady state society*—one based on no economic growth or even controlled shrinkage of the economy. Optimists are convinced that we can continue industrial growth and use technology to solve environmental problems. Regardless of who is right, pollution is a global problem that requires international social policies.

10. With our coal and oil reserves, technology, and alternative forms of energy, our energy future looks positive. The outlook for pollution, however, is less positive. Chemical pollution especially will plague us.

KEY TERMS

Acid rain   Rain with heavy concentrations of sulfuric and nitric acids.

Biodegradable   Capable of disintegrating in outdoor weather.

Carcinogen   A cancer-causing substance.

Cogeneration   Producing electricity as a by-product of one's ordinary operations.

Corporate welfare   Handouts given to corporations, usually in the form of tax breaks; may also be reductions in rent or bargain-priced real estate.

Ecology   The study of the relationship between living things and their environment.

Ecosystem The interconnection of life on the planet's outer surface.

Environmental injustice Polluting industries located in places inhabited primarily by the poor and minorities.

Food pollution (also called food contamination) The transmission of disease during food processing and the addition of chemicals to food to help process it, lengthen its shelf life, or enhance its appearance or taste.

Global warming An increase in the earth's temperature because of the greenhouse effect.

Greenhouse effect The concentration of gases in the atmosphere that allows sunlight to enter but inhibits the release of heat. It is thought to hold the potential of warming the earth's climate.

Ozone shield A layer of the earth's upper stratosphere that screens out a high proportion of the sun's ultraviolet rays.

Pollution The presence of substances that interfere with socially desired uses of the air, water, land, or food.

Steady state society A society in which the economy does not grow or shrink.

Synergistic (literally, "working together") Applied to chemicals, it refers to their interactions.

Thermal inversion A layer of cold air sealing in a lower layer of warm air.

THINKING CRITICALLY ABOUT CHAPTER 14

1. Which of the perspectives (symbolic interactionism, functionalism, or conflict theory) do you think does the best job of explaining environmental pollution? Explain.
2. How far do you think the government should go to reduce pollution? Should individuals who run polluting corporations be jailed? Should the government shut down polluters? What else could or should the government do?
3. The scientists represented by, among others, the conservative think tank, the Heritage Foundation, argue that environmental and scarcity problems are best solved by free enterprise. They believe that the market is much more likely and better equipped than governments to solve these problems. What do you think of their position? Explain.
4. Do you think that U.S. corporations should be allowed to manufacture and export chemicals that are banned in the United States to other countries? Explain.
5. Do you think that the U.S. government has the power or authority to demand a steady state society? Do you think it is advisable? Why or why not?

CHAPTER 15

War, Terrorism, and the Balance of Power

MOST OF US CAN REMEMBER VIVIDLY where we were on September 11, 2001, a day that has become emblazoned on our own memories—and seared into the national consciousness. This day, which began like so many before it—a bright dawn, shining sun, and people going about their everyday lives—was destined to change the United States. No longer would our assumptions about life be the same.

When the commercial jets that had been transformed into lethal missiles struck the Twin Towers and the Pentagon, the United States was shaken to its roots. At dawn, these two global symbols, one of capitalism and the other of military power, had stood tall and proud. Just a few hours later, the one had been destroyed, the other crippled.

Americans shook their heads in dismay and confusion. Why had they been attacked? And by what enemy? As confusion turned into anger, and the face of the enemy was beamed to Americans and the world, the response of the United States was swift and violent. Amidst missiles directed from remote lo-cations, along with the direct intervention of U.S. Special Forces, Al-Qaeda was quickly routed from Afghanistan.

The United States declared war on terrorism—as it steeled itself against further attacks by an enemy that hit suddenly and without warning. Where would this unseen enemy strike next? The White House? A nuclear plant? Some NFL football game? Even the local mall?

Just as in 1941, this surprise attack led to war. This time, though, it was a different kind of war. Instead of a country to counterattack, the enemy consists of small groups in many countries. One fear is sleeper cells in the United States, with attacks launched at any time, from almost anywhere.

And how will we know when this war has ended? After all, will there ever be an end to people who hold grudges against the United States? Will the United States try to track down groups around the world, without end?

It's a strange war—and strange times we live in.

The Problem in Sociological Perspective

The Magnitude of Today's Threat

From the end of World War II in 1945 until the end of the 1980s, the Soviet Union and the West were caught up in an **arms race.** Each furiously developed and produced new weapons, trying to outmatch the other's war capabilities. During these decades, called the **Cold War,** the West and the Soviet Union built arsenals of nuclear weapons that have the capacity to destroy the world many times over. The Cold War is over, but the nuclear weapons that these nations developed still threaten human existence. In an instant, these weapons could reduce major cities to rubble and transform world powers into barren deserts. If we piled together all of the catastrophes that the world has experienced throughout history, they would pale in comparison with nuclear war.

Why Is War Common?

Although the magnitude of the threat is new, war itself is not. Human groups have always fought each other. Because war has been common in human history, some anthropologists suggest that humans possess an instinct for aggression. Konrad Lorenz (1966) said that aggressive energy accumulates inside us. Like steam in a closed container, this energy builds up pressure and demands release. Long ago, Lorenz says, this instinct helped ensure that only the fittest survived. It also forced humans to colonize the whole world as they fled from one another's innate aggression. Today, however, as Lorenz put it, this instinct is a "hereditary evil of modern society."

The Sociological Perspective: Societies Channel Aggression

To find the answer to warfare, sociologists and most anthropologists do not look *within* people. Whether humans have an instinct for aggression is not the point. Conflicts always arise among people who live together. *What is significant are the norms that groups establish to deal with those conflicts.* Let's look at two extremes. One is the nourishment of aggression. The Yanomamö, discussed in the Global Glimpse box on the next page, represent this extreme. The other is represented by the Eskimos of East Greenland. Instead of fighting, their norms require that hostile individuals sing to one another! Actually, they sing about their grievances in a contest that goes like this:

> The singing style is highly conventionalized. The successful singer uses the traditional patterns of composition which he attempts to deliver with such finesse as to delight the audience to enthusiastic applause. He who is most heartily applauded is "winner.". . . One of the advantages of the song duel carried on at length is that it gives the public time to come to a consensus about who is correct or who should admit guilt in the dispute. . . . Gradually more people are laughing a little harder at one of the duelist's verses than at the other's, until it becomes apparent where the sympathy of the community lies, and then opinion quickly becomes unanimous and the loser retires. (Fromm 1973)

Other groups channel aggression into ritualistic violence. Here is an example of a spear-throwing duel among the Tiwi of north Australia:

> When a dispute is between an accuser and a defendant, which is commonly the case, the accuser ritually hurls the spears from a prescribed distance, while the defendant dodges them. The public can applaud the speed, force, and accuracy of the accuser as he hurls his spears, or they can applaud the adroitness with which the defendant dodges them. After a time unanimity is achieved as the approval for one or the other's skill gradually becomes overwhelming. When the defendant realizes that the community is finally considering him guilty, he is supposed to fail to dodge a spear and allow himself to be wounded in some fleshy part of his body. Conversely, the accuser simply stops throwing the spears when he becomes aware that public opinion is going against him. (Fromm 1973)

War Is Not Universal

Although hostilities, aggression, and even murder characterize all human groups, war does not. War is just one option that groups have for settling disagreements, and not all societies choose this option. The Mission Indians of North America, the Arunta

The origins of warfare go back to the origins of history. Because war is so common, some theorists suggest that aggression is a part of human nature. If so, it is socially channeled into cultural forms. Shown here are men of a Yanomamö tribe competing with spears while wearing traditional body paint.

A Global Glimpse
WHY MEN FIGHT: THE YANOMAMÖ

Yanomamö men often attack neighboring villages, killing the men and kidnapping the women. They also fight with one another. Fights often begin about sex: infidelity, seductions, or failure to give a promised girl in marriage. Sometimes the men challenge one another to a duel. One man stands there while the other hits him once in the chest or pounds him once over the head with a long wooden club. Then the other man gets his turn. This continues until one man can no longer return the blow. At other times, the men use axes and machetes and neglect to await their turn. When relatives are drawn in, fights turn into brawls. These games can trigger feuds between villages. When someone is killed, relatives seek revenge. A feud is self-feeding, for each killing requires retaliation.

Why do the men fight like this? Anthropologist Napoleon Chagnon, who lived with the Yanomamö, believes that the basic reason is access to women. He found that the men in this northern Venezuelan jungle who have killed

at least one other person have more wives and children than those who have never killed. An especially successful warrior may have six wives.

It works this way: Because violence is considered to be the mark of a true man, a reputation for violence gives a Yanomamö man high status. This makes him an attractive candidate for marriages—which are arranged by the men.

"How primitive they are!" we might say. The Yanomamö are not that different from us, however, as Chagnon points out. Although we don't reward our war heroes with additional wives, we do give them medals, seats in the U.S. Senate, and even the presidency. As Chagnon points out and is well known, the military record of candidates is important in U.S. political races.

Are we any different, then, from the Yanomamö—aside from being more indirect in rewarding "war behaviors"?

Based on Allman 1988; Chagnon 1988.

of Australia, the Andaman Islanders of the South Pacific, and the Eskimos of the Arctic, for example, have established ways to handle quarrels, but they do not have organized battles that pit one tribe against another. These groups don't even have a word for war (Lesser 1968).

Why Do Some Groups Choose War?

War—an organized form of aggression that involves armed conflict between politically distinct groups—is often part of national policy. Why do some groups choose war to handle disputes when less drastic measures are available?

Three Essential Conditions of War

Sociologist Nicholas Timasheff became interested in this question. After studying armed conflicts, he (1965) identified three essential conditions of war. The *first* is a cultural tradition of war. Because war is a part of a people's thinking, they see war as a way to resolve conflict with another nation. The *second* is an antagonistic situation in which states confront incompatible objectives. Each, for example, might want the same land or resources. A cultural tradition for war and an antagonistic situation are essential, but they are not enough. They provide the fuel, but there also has to be a spark to ignite it. This *third* condition moves the nations from thinking about war to actually engaging in it.

Seven "Sparks" of War

To find these sparks that ignite the fuel, Timasheff studied wars throughout history. He found seven "sparks" that ignite the antagonistic situation, causing it to flame into war. They are the opportunity to

1. Get revenge (to settle "old scores" from previous conflicts)
2. Dictate one's will to a weaker nation
3. Protect or enhance prestige (to preserve the nation's "honor")

4. Unite rival groups within one's country
5. Protect or exalt the nation's leaders
6. Satisfy the national aspirations of ethnic groups (to bring "our people" who are living in another country into our borders)
7. Convert others to religious and ideological beliefs

In Sum: The Sociological Perspective

In sum, to understand war, sociologists do not look for factors within humans. Instead, they look for social causes—conditions in society that encourage or discourage aggression and that shape aggression into organized combat between nations.

The Scope of the Problem

War in the History of the West

The evening news always seems to include a war somewhere. And the United States always seems to be sending troops somewhere, sometimes to countries we can't even pronounce or spell, and, frankly, that most of us don't care about. Did countries fight this much in the past?

To find out how common war has been, sociologist Pitirim Sorokin (1937) listed the wars in Europe from 500 B.C. to A.D. 1925. He identified 967 wars, an average of one war every two to three years. Counting years or parts of a year in which a country was at war, Germany had the least warfare, at 28 percent; Spain had the highest, at 67 percent.

Sorokin found that Russia, the land of his birth, had experienced only one peaceful quarter century during the previous 1,000 years. Since William the Conqueror took power in 1066, England had been at war for 56 of each 100 years. Spain had fought even more often.

The United States: One of the Most Warlike Nations in the World

And the United States? From 1850 to about 1980, we intervened militarily around the world more than 150 times (Kohn 1988). That's more than once a year. At our current rate, it won't be long until the total reaches 200. Although we have been "at war" with no nation, in recent years we have "intervened" (as U.S. politicians like to call it) in El Salvador, Honduras, Libya, Grenada, Panama, Afghanistan, Iraq, Somalia, Haiti, Bosnia, Sudan, Kosovo—and then back again to Afghanistan and Iraq. Military operations from our declared war on terrorism, then, are not new, but, rather, they continue a long-standing pattern.

Measuring Wars in Terms of Deaths

War may be hell, as William T. Sherman said, but some wars are more hellish than others. Consider the killing. Since 1829, there have been approximately

80 wars in which 3,000 to 30,000 people died
42 wars in which 30,000 to 300,000 people died
11 wars in which 300,000 to 3,000,000 people died
2 wars (World Wars I and II) in which 3,000,000 to 31,000,000 people died (Richardson 1960; updated)

If your father or mother dies in a war, of course, it matters little that there were 30,000 or 3 million other victims of that war. On a personal level, we measure things by how they affect us.

The Growing Capacity to Kill

Nevertheless, it is important to know how industrialization has increased our capacity to kill. Consider bombs. During World War I, of every 100,000 people in England and Germany, fewer than 3 died from bombs. During the next twenty years, scientists "advanced" this technique of human destruction, and during World War II bombs killed about 300 of every 100,000 English and Germans (Hart 1957). Scientists have continued to "advance" our technology in killing, and if nations were to unleash nuclear weapons against one another today, the deaths of past wars would seem as nothing. Some of our more "advanced" weapons supposedly have the capacity to destroy every living thing on earth.

The Continuing Slaughter

What about education? Education has expanded across the globe, so one might suppose that war would have become a relic of a primitive past. We should have reached a more advanced state, able now to look back uncomprehendingly, and with a bit of smug superiority, at how humans used to slaughter one another. As we all know, however, this doesn't even come close to describing life today. A generation or so ago, the United States fought in Vietnam for about seven years—at a cost of 58,000 American lives and a couple of hundred thousand Vietnamese. The death toll of the Soviet Union's nine-year war in Afghanistan ran about 1 million Afghanistani and perhaps 20,000 Soviet soldiers (Armitage 1989). Iran and Iraq fought an eight-year war at a cost of 400,000 lives. We don't know the death tolls of our "interventions" in Afghanistan and Iraq.

In Sum   War, then, as Sorokin sadly concluded in the 1930s, is normal. That is, war is a regular part of the world's history. Sorokin added that his era was one of the bloodiest, most turbulent periods in the history of Western civilization—and perhaps in the history of humanity. Our era certainly provides no reason to correct Sorokin's judgment. We have seen Serbs kill Bosnians, and Bosnians kill Serbs—each claiming rightful revenge for atrocities of years past. After generations and even hundreds of years, these groups claim the right to hate eternally—and to pass their nasty heritage to their children. Israelis and Palestinians do the same. They, too, continue to kill one another—each absolutely convinced that its views are just and that God is on its side. Among other nations, India and Pakistan also claim their right to perpetuate ancient hatreds—and to threaten to nuke one another to hell. The soldiers of the United States, NATO, Russia, and the European Union are armed and ready to battle their own "righteous" causes. On top of all this, as 9/11 shows, individuals who head private organizations have gotten into the act: Sending suicide bombers to blow up civilians, they initiate the launching of armies across the globe.

Looking at the Problem Theoretically

Let's use our three theoretical perspectives to focus on the social problem of war. Using symbolic interactionism, we will examine the symbolic basis of the nuclear arms race. Using functionalism, we will consider why nations go to war. Through conflict theory, we will explore how conflicting interests and the desire for more territory lead to war.

SYMBOLIC INTERACTIONISM

The Role of Perceptions   Symbolic interactionists emphasize the signficance of *perceptions* in war. They stress how courses of action depend on how leaders see the odds for winning or losing, and how this depends on how they evaluate their own nation's strengths relative to that of their enemy.

During the Cold War, the United States and the Soviet Union had to decide which weapons to build and how much to spend on them. To underestimate the enemy could prove fatal, so each magnified the evil intentions and destructive capability of the other. Without hard information, each had to guess what the other intended, and they then used their guesses to choose what seemed to be the most practical response.

In Medieval times in Europe, war was considered a gentlemen's exercise, a grand game fought according to established rituals. This painting from 1470 shows a joust (or contest) among knights. During jousts, a form of preparing for war, knights exhibited their fighting skills. The royalty is watching and evaluating the contestants. This painting is in the British Library in London.

This led to an arms race. When one superpower thought that the other might build a certain weapon, it began to build that weapon itself. Sometimes, however, the other nation had no intention of building the weapon, and the so-called countermeasure turned out to be an aggressive step that forced the other nation to build the weapon. Robert McNamara explained how such a mistaken perception led to the United States increasing its supply of nuclear warheads (Kurth 1974).

> In 1961 when I became Secretary of Defense, the Soviet Union possessed a very small operational arsenal of intercontinental missiles. However, they did possess the technological and industrial capacity to enlarge that arsenal very substantially over the succeeding several years. We had no evidence that the Soviets did plan, in fact, fully to use that capability. But, as I have pointed out, a strategic planner must be conservative in his calculations; that is, he must prepare for the worst plausible case and not be content to hope and prepare merely for the most probable.
>
> Since we could not be certain of Soviet intentions, since we could not be sure that they would not undertake a massive buildup, we had to insure against such an eventuality by undertaking ourselves a major buildup of the Minuteman and Polaris forces. But the blunt fact remains that if we had more accurate information about planned Soviet strategic forces, we simply would not have needed to build as large a nuclear arsenal as we have today.

Symbols Are Central to Human Behavior— Including War

This event illustrates a primary principle of symbolic interactionism—symbols are central to human behavior. Based on how we perceived Soviet plans, we decided to build intercontinental ballistic missiles (ICBMs). Our decision, in turn, signaled to the Soviets that they needed to build ICBMs right away. The nuclear arms race was based on symbolic interpretations of what the enemy might do.

Symbols Determine Reality

This example also shows us that *symbols can take on a life of their own;* once put into play, symbols wield power over human affairs. Although McNamara's initial perception of Soviet intentions might have been wrong, our buildup of missiles became proof to the Soviets that they needed to build more missiles. This, in turn, became proof to us that our interpretation was right—and that we needed to build even more powerful weapons. *Perception, not facts, usually guides human behavior.*

Perception Determines Peace or War

Symbolic interaction underlies war in another way. As long as two rival nations perceive war as a no-win situation, they are likely to avoid it. If there is hatred and fear between them, however, and one nation thinks that striking first can destroy the other's capacity to strike back, that nation is encouraged to strike first. During the Cold War, U.S. Air Force generals advocated a "first-strike" if it meant that they could win the war (Kurth 1974). Apparently Soviet generals did the same. You can see how tense and dangerous the situation was. Each nation felt that it had to let the other know that it could not win, that a first strike would be foolish. As a result, both the Soviet Union and the United States would let information slip about their new weapons, or defense systems like "Star Wars." It is scary to think that our lives—and those of the world—depended on mutual fear and the correct interpretation of one another's signals!

FUNCTIONALISM

Ten Functions of War:

1. Extension of Territory

In 1939, the world was in turmoil. Hitler's tanks and *Luftwaffe* were rampaging through Europe. Japan had invaded China and was threatening the South Pacific. His sociological imagination piqued, Robert Park (1941) decided to analyze war's social functions. He surveyed the literature on war and found that the world's countries (or states) had been born in war. Our countries came about as one group extended its political boundaries by subjugating other groups. What is today's United States, for example, would not exist if it weren't for the Indian wars, and wars against France, Great Britain, Spain, and Mexico. A major function of war, said Park, is the *extension of territory,* an enlargement of a group's political power.

2. Social Integration

Another function of war is *social integration*. If groups within a country are in conflict, war can give them a mutual enemy. The groups put aside their differences, close ranks, and cooperate to repel their common threat (Coser 1956; Timasheff 1965; Shibutani 1970; Blainey 1973). After the war, the factions turn back to unfinished business and try to settle old scores. Afghanistan had groups bitterly divided according to religious, class, tribal, and clan loyalties. When the Soviets invaded, these groups cooperated to repel their common enemy, but as soon as they defeated the Soviets, they turned on one another. Today, the United States looks on in dismay as it tries to produce from the territory of Afghanistan a country in its own image. It is similarly the case with Iraq.

3. Social Change

Sociologist Georg Simmel (1904) identified *social change* as a third function of war. Warfare can stimulate the development of science and technology. Five centuries ago, for example, Leonardo da Vinci designed war machines for his patron. Today, we owe our interstate highways to war. In case the Soviets attacked, President Eisenhower wanted to be able to rapidly move soldiers, weapons, and supplies. War has also prompted aerodynamic designs, the harnessing of nuclear energy, surgical techniques, satellites, and the Internet.

Even losers can benefit from the changes stimulated by war. The Japanese, for example, after their defeat in World War II, embraced Western technology. This not only increased their standard of living and life expectancy, but also it gained them the world leadership that they had failed to win by war. No social change is without its dysfunctions, however, and Japan's, too, has come at a price: the disruption of its traditional ways of life.

4. Economic Gain

A fourth function of war is *economic gain:* access to treasure, trade routes, markets, raw materials such as oil, and outlets for investment (Pruitt and Snyder 1969). Industrialization has put a new twist on this function—increasing production, profits, and employment. The best example is how World War II put millions of unemployed people to work and helped lift the United States out of the Great Depression. Even the threat of war can bring economic gain. As sociologist C. Wright Mills (1958) noted back in the 1950s, "war readiness" requires high spending that benefits big corporations. This is still true today.

5. Ideology

A fifth function of war is *ideological*—advancing a political or religious system or suppressing an opposing one. An example is the Crusades by European Christians between the eleventh and fourteenth centuries to recover the Holy Land from Islam. Al-Qaeda and supporters have a similar agenda. A sixth function is *vengeance* or *punishment*—teaching another nation "a lesson" or avenging an injury or insult (Pruitt and Snyder 1969). Much of the warfare in Bosnia and Kosovo, including the rapes and other atrocities, served this function. A seventh function is to increase *military security*. That is, a nation does not desire an asset in and of itself, but attacks to prevent an enemy from using that asset against it. This is why Israel bombed Iraq's nuclear plants in 1981, and why trigger fingers have become itchy concerning Iran's nuclear capability. An eighth function of war is to *increase the credibility* of a nation's threats or guarantees. By going to war, other nations will see that a nation means what it says.

6. Vengeance

7. Military Security

8. Establish Credibility

Functions for Individuals

War also has functions for soldiers and leaders. Soldiers often report that battle presents them with a challenge to "see what I'm made of." Some even report an excitement that verges on sexual arousal. More significant, however, are the satisfactions that war brings its leaders. Although most leaders bemoan war, much of this is posturing, done for the sake of a public image. Officers who plan battles derive intense satisfaction from outmaneuvering the enemy, gaining advantage through unexpected strategies, and being acclaimed as the victor. War can also be an avenue of social mobility. Generals George Washington, Ulysses S. Grant, and Dwight D. Eisenhower, for example, moved from being generals in the Army to being presidents of the United States. Colin Powell went from general to National Security Advisor and then to Secretary of State, one of the most powerful positions in the world.

No War Serves a Single Function

No war serves a single function. The same war can involve territory, revenge, ideology, and military security. If war is drawn out, functions can even change. The Crusades began in 1095 when Pope Urban II exhorted Christians to go to war, promising that their journey to the Holy Land would ensure forgiveness of sins. Ideological purposes may have dominated at first, but the Crusades also functioned to provide treasure and territory. Nine Crusades and 200 years later, all the functions of war had become part of this prolonged war.

War Is Usually Functional for the Victors

War is usually highly functional for the victors. Rome, for example, conquered most of the known world, subjugating one people after another and exploiting their resources. To the acclaim of citizens and Caesar alike, generals would return in triumph to Rome, laden with treasure and slaves. The treasure enriched the government and its elite, and the captives did their grunt work. Educated Greeks were enslaved, too. They served as tutors for the elite's children. In the latter part of the empire, the slaves provided drama, their deaths in the Coliseum yielding pleasure for Rome's jaded and bloodthirsty citizens.

Dysfunctions of War

Standing in stark contrast are the dysfunctions of war. Defeat is its most well-known dysfunction: among so many other things, the destruction of cities, the deaths and maiming, the interruption of education, and the bitterness. Even military victory, however, can be dysfunctional. The victor can grow dependent on the exploitation of subjugated peoples; when that control ends, as it inevitably does, the economic pain is severe. Spain experienced this dysfunction when it lost its colonies in the 1820s. It has never fully recovered from that experience. For decades, Great Britain suffered withdrawal pains after the loss of its many colonies. Russia is undergoing this same dysfunction today. No longer can bureaucrats dispatch an order from Moscow, and minions in satellite nations unquestioningly send the specified materials. The spigot has been turned off.

CONFLICT THEORY

Four Causes of War

1. Conflict over Resources

Conflict theorists provide four major explanations of the cause of war. Ibn Khaldun of Tunis, whom some count as one of the earliest sociologists, proposed the first explanation in the 1300s. He stressed that all human groups struggle to survive. As they compete for scarce resources and strive to expand their power, they inevitably come into conflict with one another. War is simply one form that human conflict takes.

2. Conflicting Interests of the Bourgeoisie

The second explanation is based on what conflict theorists see as the central force in human history. In each society, some group takes control. This group, which they call the *bourgeoisie,* uses the resources of society to keep itself in power and to exploit the less powerful. As the bourgeoisie expand their power beyond their country, they come into conflict with one another. As a result, they sometimes decide to go to war. The bourgeoisie don't fight, of course. They send the groups that they control (the poor, the workers, the *proletariat*) to battle for them. The German's term for the young men of the poor who died in such outrageous numbers in their wars was "cannon fodder."

3. Imperialism

The third explanation focuses on the expansion of markets. In 1902, John Hobson, an economist, said that capitalist nations develop surplus capital, and business leaders want to expand their markets so they can invest this capital. They then persuade the government to go to war and take over other lands. The result is **imperialism,** the pursuit of expansion by war and threat of war.

4. A Military Machine

Another economist, Joseph Schumpeter, proposed a fourth explanation in 1919. He said (1955) that the military and political elite build a strong military machine because it brings them power and prestige. This encourages war, because the military is there to be used, and its use brings more prestige to the elite.

Conflict Theorists Build on These Ideas: The War Machine

Today's conflict theorists have built on these explanations. They, too, stress how a war machine has increased the threat of war. They note that after World War I the

United States dismantled its military, and U.S. war industries returned to their peace-time pursuits (Barber 1972). World War II, however, was a turning point. When this war was over, the United States did not dismantle its war machine (Eisenhower 1972). Instead, the United States has maintained a couple of million soldiers and has pumped vast amounts of money into upgrading its weapons and equipment. The Soviet Union, Great Britain, France, and others did the same. The telling moment came after the fall of the Soviet Union. With its enemy supposedly transformed into a capitalist ally, the West has continued to pay and arm millions. In an ironic twist, it has now even incorporated Russia into NATO, the organization it founded to fight the Soviets.

Using the War Machine to Promote Global Capitalism

To understand why such huge armies have become a fact of contemporary life, conflict theorists say that we need to look at the top levels of power. There we see the *power elite*—the military, business leaders, and politicians. And if we look closely, we can see how their interests have merged. The generals always want a more powerful military, of course: This is their reason for being, and greater power bolsters their position. Generals also perceive enemies on every side, so they give endless reasons for expansion. This isn't new. But to this old picture has been added global capitalism. To protect their worldwide investments, today's business leaders, too, want a powerful military. To protect their investments, they might need armed intervention at home—or on the other side of the globe. Politicians are sensitive to what the business elite wants, because, as conflict theorists stress, they owe their positions to the business elite. If business withdraws its support, they have little chance of being reelected. Consequently, politicians find it in their interest to support a strong military: In the name of national security (an effective phrase at budget time, deflecting opposition by both politicians and ordinary citizens), politicians levy taxes to finance the military machine desired by the generals and business leaders.

Today, stress conflict theorists, the U.S. military machine is used to advance capitalism around the globe. When you see U.S. armed forces in action, alone or, when not quarreling, accompanied by the United States' international capitalist partners—Great Britain, France, Canada, and Australia—you can be sure that the world is being made safe for capitalism. The result, says Mills (1958:2), is that "war is no longer an interruption of peace; in our time, peace itself has become an uneasy interlude between wars. . . ."

Research Findings

With war so common—and with today's weapons jeopardizing even the existence of humanity—what factors reduce the likelihood that nations will go to war? After looking at this question, we will then examine the costs of war, both economic and human, and the U.S. military machine. Finally, we'll consider the possibility of accidental war, biological and chemical warfare, and terrorism.

Religion, land, riches, revenge, and glory became intermixed in one of the world's strangest wars, the Crusades, which were fought between the 11th and 13th centuries. The Christians' stated purpose was to recover the Holy Land, particularly Jerusalem, from the Muslims, but these other motives became intertwined. In 1212, the Children's Crusade took place. In this, the most pathetic of the Crusades, thousands of children set out from France for the Holy Land. The ships' captains sold them to the Muslims as slaves. German children met a different fate. Going overland, they died of hunger and disease.

WHAT REDUCES WAR?

Seven Major Findings about War and Peace

To see what reduces war, Quincy Wright (1942), a professor of international law, looked at war throughout history and tallied the important battles. His findings, combined with those of physicist–mathematician Lewis Richardson (1960), are not encouraging. They can be summarized this way (Nettler 1976):

1. Type of religion does not reduce warfare. A nation in which Christianity is dominant does not go to war less than a nation in which Islam is dominant.
2. Type of government does not reduce warfare. Democracies and republics are neither more nor less peaceful than dictatorships and monarchies.
3. Prosperity does not reduce warfare. Prosperous nations are neither more nor less peaceful than poor nations. Nor do periods of prosperity reduce fighting.
4. A shared religion does not reduce warfare between nations.
5. A common language does not reduce warfare.
6. Being "neighbors" does not reduce warfare. The opposite is true: Shared boundaries stimulate fights over territory, and war increases in proportion to the number of boundaries that countries share.
7. Education does not reduce warfare. Education does not create an "enlightened" preference for peace; countries with high education are as likely to go to war as those with low education.

No Trend Toward Peace

When we attempt to discover what reduces war, then, we are forced to conclude that we don't know. Contrary to common sense, democracy, prosperity, increased education, and a shared religion don't reduce war. Experts can make up fancy sounding terms such as "conflict resolution," but the world's nations aren't becoming more peaceful. Instead, wars have become more intense, killing more people than ever. As sociologist Gwynn Nettler (1976) ruefully observed, the Nobel Peace Prize usually goes to a citizen of a nation with a long history of recent war. He said that perhaps we should consider this prize as awarded on the basis of need, rather than as a recognition of achievement.

THE COSTS OF WAR

What the United States Spends on War

It is an understatement to say that war is costly. Table 15-1 summarizes what the United States has spent on its nine major wars. This huge amount does not include the billions of dollars spent on Iraq War I and Iraq War II. Nor does it count what it cost

TABLE 15-1 What Has the United States Spent on Its Wars?

War of 1812	$600,000,000
Mexican War	$1,100,000,000
American Revolution	$2,000,000,000
Spanish–American War	$6,000,000,000
Civil War	$46,000,000,000
Korean War	$260,000,000,000
World War I	$370,000,000,000
Vietnam War	$553,000,000,000
World War II	$3,000,000,000,000
Total	$4,200,000,000,000

Note: In the source, the costs are listed in 1967 dollars. To account for inflation, I increased these amounts by 350 percent, and added the costs of service-connected benefits. Where a range was listed, the mean was used.
The costs of the many "military interventions" such as in Grenada, Panama, Somalia, and Haiti are not listed in the source, nor are the more expensive Gulf Wars I and II. The costs do *not* include interest payments on war loans, nor are they reduced by the financial benefits to the United States, such as the acquisition of California and Texas in the Mexican War.
Source: By the author, based on *Statistical Abstract* 1993:Table 553; this table was dropped after 1993.

to "intervene" in places such as Bosnia, Kosovo, and Afghanistan. If you look at Figure 15-1, you will see how much the United States spends each year to operate its military. The totals are in constant dollars, so you can easily compare one year to another. The higher spending during 1970 and 1990 represents expenditures for the war in Vietnam and the ICBM defense called Star Wars. Today's high spending represents the war on terrorism.

The expenditures shown in Figure 15-1 include the costs of veterans' benefits, but a more realistic total of what we spend on war and preparing for war would also include the costs of running the Central Intelligence Agency, the National Aeronautics and Space Administration, the Agency for International Development, and the Department of Homeland Security. A case could also be made to include what we spend on the Overseas Private Investment Corporation, the International Monetary Fund, and the World Bank (Greenberger 1994).

On average, since 1960 we have spent $270 billion a year on what is euphemistically called national defense. Such numbers roll easily off the tongue—with little realization of what they mean. This is because the concept of 1 billion of anything is beyond our experience. To gain an idea of how much we are spending, consider this (Shaffer 1986):

> If we were to lay a million dollar bills end to end, we could just about cover the distance from New York to Philadelphia. If we laid a billion dollar bills end to end, we would circle the earth four times around the equator.

Now if we laid the dollar bills of our average annual defense budget end to end, they would circle the earth 1,100 times! Today's expenditures, in current dollars, would make it around the earth 1,500 times.

The Cost of War Preparations in Terms of Alternative Purchases

Another way to measure our military expenditures is to compare them with what else we could buy with the same money. I could not find a comparison with today's dollars and have to rely on costs from the 1980s, but the same principle applies:

1. For the price of one aircraft carrier, we could build 12,000 high schools.
2. For the price of one naval weapons plant, we could build twenty-six 160-bed hospitals.
3. For the price of one jet bomber, we could provide school lunches for 1 million children for a year.
4. For the price of one new prototype bomber, we could pay the annual salaries of 250,000 teachers (de Silva 1980).

FIGURE 15-1 *How Much Does the United States Spend on Its Military?*

Source: By the author, based on *Statistical Abstract* 2003:Table 509.

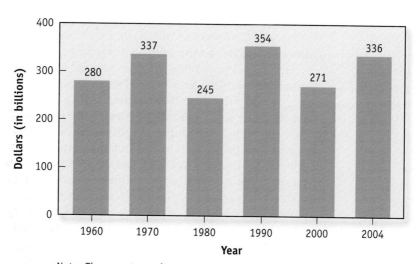

Note: These costs are in constant, 1996, dollars.

Money goes a lot further in the Least Industrialized Nations. There, the price of one tank would buy 1,000 classrooms. Many people dream of a world in which military dollars go to education, medicine, and the enlightenment of nations, but we certainly do not live in such a world—and from all indications, we never will.

Money spent on payrolls also represents alternative purchases that we did not make. Our armed forces employ about 1.4 million military personnel and about 600,000 civilians. Add the 1.1 million men and women in the reserves and national guard, and the total comes to almost 3 million people (*Statistical Abstract* 2003:Tables 516, 517). For what it costs to pay these people for war, we could pay 3 million people to work for the public good. We are already sending tens of thousands of soldiers abroad each year, so for the same cost we could send tens of thousands of people to other countries to build schools and hospitals and to reduce the suffering of refugees.

Like other nations, the United States finds itself boxed in. Although the military is costly in money spent and benefits foregone, not spending this money would leave us vulnerable to attack. In light of the world's bellicose history, an assumption of danger appears well founded. Only if all nations miraculously become pacifists and all dangers of attack cease would military preparedness become unnecessary. No such miracle seems in the offing.

The Incredible Amounts that Nations Spend on War

The nations of the world spend about $800 billion a year to arm themselves (*Statistical Abstract* 2003:Table 1383). This is about $135 a year for every man, woman, and child on the entire planet. Laid end to end, these dollars would stretch around the earth 3,200 times. Or you could lay them end to end and reach the moon—and then you could make that trip a hundred times!

Any way you look at it, that's a lot of money.

Table 15-2 shows which countries spend the most and least on their military. The table holds some surprises. On a per capita basis, six of these countries outspend the United States. Sweden, hardly a bellicose nation, is in the top ten of spenders. As you can see, the nations that spend the least have little industrialization. Although what they spend for their military on a per capita basis is tiny, these are poor nations. Most of their citizens live in poverty, and they need every dollar they can get for basic necessities.

The Costs of War in Terms of Deaths

War's greatest cost, of course, is not dollars, but lives lost. During the 1700s, wars were fought according to aristocratic ideals. Small professional armies waged short, limited campaigns. In battle, the soldiers marched in formation, accompanied by flags, drums, and other musical instruments. War was like a chess game, with generals matching wits with opponents who came from similar social class backgrounds. Some opposing generals had even been trained in the same military schools. Officers considered warfare a test of bravery and referred to battle as the "field of honor." If townspeople knew when a battle would be fought, they rode in carriages to the site, eating picnic lunches and drinking wine while they watched the entertainment.

Napoleon changed this when he initiated **total war,** "no-holds-barred" warfare (Finsterbusch and Greisman 1975). This came home to us with the American Civil War. During four brutal years, 620,000 Americans died, more than in all our other wars combined, from the Revolution to the present. No longer is there a field of honor, if ever there was one. U.S. civilians were shocked by the actions of the U.S. military in Vietnam, and their protests led to a shortening of that brutal war. In Kosovo, U.S. planes bombed civilian targets to undermine support for the country's regime. The war was too short to initiate anything but feeble protest. With today's mass armies, and the capacity to deliver wholesale death, with industries spewing out weapons, and with civilians not spared, an image of pageantry and games is far from reality.

Most fearful of all, today's weapons are so destructive that they threaten human existence itself. Although killing in the past was inefficient, since 1700 over 100 million people have died in war (Gartner 1988). Today, that many could die from just one

TABLE 15-2 What Countries Spend on Their Military

WHAT COUNTRIES SPEND THE MOST ON THEIR MILITARY?

RANK	COUNTRY	PER CAPITA	AS A PERCENTAGE OF GROSS NATIONAL PRODUCT
1.	Israel	$1,510	8.8
2.	Kuwait	$1,410	7.7
3	Singapore	$1,100	4.8
4.	United States	$1,030	3.0
5.	Saudi Arabia	$996	14.9
6.	Taiwan	$690	5.2
7.	France	$658	2.7
8	Great Britain	$615	2.5
9.	Sweden	$601	2.3
10.	Greece	$573	4.7

WHAT COUNTRIES SPEND THE LEAST ON THEIR MILITARY?

RANK	COUNTRY	PER CAPITA	AS A PERCENTAGE OF GROSS NATIONAL PRODUCT
1.	Tanzania	$4	1.4
2.	Bangladesh	$5	1.3
3.	Indonesia	$7	1.1
4.	Kenya	$7	1.9
5.	India	$11	2.5
6.	Nigeria	$13	1.6
7.	Philippines	$14	1.4
8.	Pakistan	$25	5.9
9.	Mexico	$27	0.6
10.	Egypt	$36	2.7

Source: By the author, based on *Statistical Abstract of the United States* 2003:Table 1383.

nuclear blast. If ever there were another world war, deaths could number in the hundreds of millions—if, indeed, anyone were left to count them.

The Costs of War in Quality of Life

The costs of war in terms of quality of life.   Although we can measure war in terms of money and deaths, war involves more than such gross measures. Among war's other costs is a loss in people's "quality of life." This is impossible to measure accurately, but at the very minimum war increases insecurity, paranoia, fear, and worry. Even everyday life becomes uncertain, as war breaks down the norms that regulate human behavior. It becomes difficult to plan for the future, and the ordinary expectations of what life is like begin to unravel.

Dehumanization

Morality is also part of our "quality of life," and war erodes this, too. Soldiers who are exposed to brutality and killing tend to **dehumanize** their opponents. They come to see them as objects, not as people. This removes the obligation to treat them as human beings. Consciences become so numbed that ordinary people can dissociate even acts of torture from their "normal self." Torture and killing, though remaining perhaps disagreeable, become "dirty work" that has to be done. Those who do this "dirty work" think of themselves as having the duty to obey orders, not to question them. "Those who make the decisions are responsible, not I, a simple soldier is just following orders."

Four Characteristics of Dehumanization

Dehumanization was studied by physicians Viola Bernard, Perry Ottenberg, and Fritz Redl (1971). They identified these four characteristics:

1. *Increased emotional distance from others.* The individual stops identifying with others, seeing them as lacking basic human qualities. They become not people, but an object called "the enemy."
2. *An emphasis on following procedures.* Regulations become all-important. Those who do the "dirty work" do not question their orders, even if they involve atrocities. A person will say, "I don't like it, but it's necessary," or "We all have to die some day."
3. *Inability to resist pressures.* Fears of losing their job or the respect of their group, or of having their integrity and loyalty questioned become more important than morality.
4. *Diminished personal responsibility.* They see themselves as a small cog in a large machine. They are not responsible, because they have no choice. They are simply obeying orders. The superiors know best, for they have the information to judge what is right and wrong. The individuals reason, "Who am I to question this?"

The Symbolic Transformation of Prolonged Struggles

Sociologist Tamotsu Shibutani (1970) pointed out that dehumanization is helped along by the tendency for prolonged conflicts to be transformed into a struggle between good and evil. We don't want to do these things, but because the survival of good (democracy, freedom, the nation) hangs in the balance, we must suspend moral standards. War, then, exalts treachery, brutality, and killing—and we give medals to glorify behavior that we would otherwise condemn.

World War II: The Nazis and the Japanese

To participate in such acts, soldiers distance themselves from their earlier socialization. They try to neutralize the morality that they learned as children. This often is effective. For instance, it enabled ordinary Germans to staff the concentration camps. Surgeons who had been educated at top universities, whose profession called for them to be highly sensitive to people's needs, denied that the inmates they experimented on were fully human. Methodically and dispassionately, they mutilated patients just to study the results. Some doctors immersed Jews in vats of ice water in freezing weather, considering their deaths insignificant because the results of the studies would be used to save the lives of German pilots shot down over the North Atlantic (Gellhorn 1959).

Despite the horrors of the Nazis, the Japanese matched their atrocities with prisoners of war. They beheaded U.S. prisoners of war, and buried others alive (Watanabe 1999). They also tortured prisoners and performed medical experiments on them (Davis 1994). In one experiment, Japanese doctors pumped U.S. prisoners full of horse blood. In another, they injected them with typhus, typhoid, smallpox, and other diseases. In one test, they lined up ten prisoners "behind a protective screen with their naked buttocks exposed while a fragmentation bomb was detonated" (Leighty 1981). In China, the Japanese conducted germ warfare experiments, killing perhaps hundreds of thousands of Chinese with anthrax, typhoid, and plague (Harris 1994).

The War in Vietnam: The Americans

The Germans and Japanese carried dehumanization to horrifying limits, but they were not unique. U.S. soldiers in Vietnam also dehumanized their victims. The Vietnamese became less than people; they became "gooks," "dinks," and "slants." Shooting into villages and shooting at mothers trying to flee with their babies were dissociated from the self. It was better not to question the morality of the act, better to think of the act as part of the larger scheme of things, saving a people from communism—or as rightful retaliation for buddies who had been killed: "I don't like this, but, after all, this is war."

When Dehumanization Fails

Although such techniques can protect the self, they are not foolproof, and their failure can lead to crippling guilt. Tim, for example, whose statement follows, was a Marine interrogator in Vietnam. Beating prisoners to elicit information became a way of

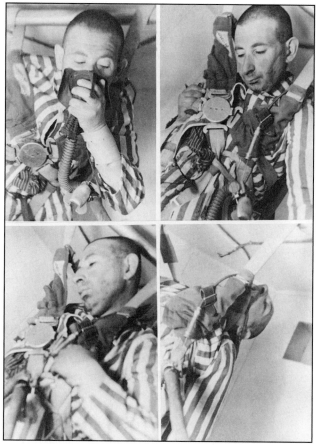

The extent that dehumanization can take is incredible. To measure the effects of compression and decompression, German doctors placed this inmate of a concentration camp in a pressure chamber. As the doctors manipulated the air pressure, they observed and photographed the man's death.

life for him. When beating did not work, he would use electric shocks, attaching "two wires of a field telephone usually to the earlobe or the cheek or the temple, sometimes the balls or the crotch" (Smith 1980:27). Tim did not enjoy his work, and one day as he was beating a 16- or 17-year-old girl, he began to think:

> Why are we killing all these people? These aren't soldiers. I'm beating on this girl—and it all hit me. I'm beating up this girl, what for? Who am I? . . . It was as if for the first time I was looking at myself. Here's this guy, slapping, beating on this girl—for what?

No longer seeing this prisoner as an object, Tim insightfully added: "For the first time I was looking at this person, a detainee, as a real human being, not as a source of information." This change of perspective directly affected Tim's job performance. As he said: "I wasn't a very good interrogator from that time on. I lost all motivation."

Being surrounded by army buddies who agree that the enemy is less than human helps maintain definitions that justify cruelty. After returning home, however, the former soldiers go back to more routine norms, and these definitions tend to break down. As a result, many former soldiers are disturbed by what they did in the war. Before putting a bullet in his head, a soldier from California wrote:

> I can't sleep anymore. When I was in Vietnam, we came across a North Vietnamese soldier with a man, a woman, and a 3- or 4-year-old girl. We had to shoot them all. I can't get the little girl's face out of my mind. I hope that God will forgive me. I hope the people in this country who made millions of dollars off the men, women, and children that died in that war can sleep at night (I can't, and I didn't make a cent). (Smith 1980:15)

It made international news when some Japanese soldiers, who had kept quiet for fifty years, publicly confessed their mass rapes and killings. Their neutralization techniques, too, failed.

Let's turn from what has been a symbolic interaction analysis to a conflict perspective and examine how organizations and profit underlie modern warfare.

THE MILITARY-INDUSTRIAL COMPLEX

The Cold War

As we discussed, the United States did not disarm after World War II. During the period of hostilities known as the Cold War, the West and the Soviet Union tried to "contain" one another's influence on the world. Our leaders were convinced, as were theirs, that to prevent an attack we had to develop the most advanced weapons and show a willingness to use them.

The Military as a Powerful Economic Force

The military requires a vast industrial backup. Those industries that specialize in armaments—the guidance systems, bombs, missiles, tanks, planes, guns, ships, submarines, and other weapons—have become a powerful force in the U.S. economy. Military weapons are like personal computers; they quickly become obsolete, forcing their continuous replacement with a new generation of even more powerful and sophisticated ones. As you can imagine, this is expensive: About one of every six dollars spent by the federal government goes to the Department of Defense and the Department of Veterans' Affairs (*Statistical Abstract* 2003:Table 509).

Like other businesses, the corporations that manufacture our armaments want to increase their profits. Unlike other businesses, however, their main customer is the Department of Defense. This leads to a cozy relationship. The defense industry hires top-ranking military officers when they retire, people who know the military system inside and out. Some of them are even on a first-name basis with the officers who are in charge of military purchases, who may themselves be eyeing well-paying jobs in the defense industry after their own retirement.

"Pentagon Capitalism"

With their interests merged, the military and defense industries have become a power to be reckoned with by Congress. The **military-industrial complex,** as it is known, pressures key members of Congress to increase military spending. Congress listens, because the Defense Department can channel profitable contracts into their districts. Seymour Melman (1970) called this interlocking relationship between Pentagon armaments and U.S. business **pentagon capitalism.**

Table 15-3 shows how important the military has become to the U.S. economy. Ten states receive at least $5 billion each in military contracts. The several hundred thousand employees of the military also spend huge sums for local purchases. Consider how Virginia, an average-size state (7 million people), brings in $18 billion in military contracts. The 168,000 military and civilian workers located in Virginia bring in another $13 billion a year. With such sums at statke, the threat to close a military base unites local governments, Chambers of Commerce, and unions, who send lobbyists to Washington to fight to keep the base. NIMBY (Not In My Back Yard) has changed to KIMBY (Keepit In My Back Yard).

Growing Capacity to Inflict Death

During the arms race, the West and the Soviet Union feverishly stockpiled nuclear weapons, continuously increasing their explosive power and the efficiency of their delivery systems. Our capacity for inflicting death grew so sharply that *if a bomb the size of the one dropped on Hiroshima had exploded every single day from the birth of Christ*

This is Hamburg, Germany, in July of 1943, following allied bombing. The real destruction of war, however, is the loss of human lives: The toll from World War II was about 31 million men, women, and children. When I visited Hamburg for an international sociology conference, my hosts escorted me through the city. It has been meticulously restored.

TABLE 15-3 Where Defense Contracts Go: The Top 20 Winners

RANK	STATE	AMOUNT OF CONTRACTS	MILITARY PERSONNEL	CIVILIAN EMPLOYEES*
1.	California	$23,800,000,000	124,000	58,000
2.	Virginia	$18,100,000,000	91,000	77,000
3.	Texas	$13,700,000,000	115,000	37,000
4.	Florida	$7,100,000,000	56,000	27,000
5.	Arizona	$6,700,000,000	22,000	8,000
6.	Maryland	$6,500,000,000	31,000	32,000
7.	Missouri	$5,800,000,000	16,000	9,000
8.	Georgia	$5,800,000,000	64,000	31,000
9.	Connecticut	$5,600,000,000	4,000	3,000
10.	Massachusetts	$4,900,000,000	2,000	7,000
11.	Alabama	$4,700,000,000	11,000	21,000
12.	Pennsylvania	$4,600,000,000	3,000	25,000
13.	New York	$4,400,000,000	21,000	11,000
14.	New Jersey	$3,500,000,000	6,000	14,000
15.	Ohio	$3,400,000,000	7,000	22,000
16.	Washington	$2,800,000,000	39,000	23,000
17.	Colorado	$2,600,000,000	30,000	10,000
18.	District of Columbia	$2,400,000,000	13,000	16,000
19.	Kentucky	$2,300,000,000	34,000	8,000
20.	Mississippi	$2,300,000,000	14,000	9,000

*These are civilians directly employed by the military. The totals do not include workers in the defense industries who fulfill the military contracts listed in column 3.

Source: By the author, based on *Statistical Abstract of the United States* 2003:Table 513.

until now, the total force of those bombs would be less than the destructive capacity of the United States (Melman 1970).

That's just the United States. To this, we can add the nuclear weapons of Russia, France, Great Britain, and others. It is almost impossible to grasp the destructive capacity of the nuclear powers, but imagery sometimes helps. Consider this. The explosive energy of nuclear weapons is measured in megatons. If you had 1 million tons of TNT, you would have one **megaton.** The United States has over 3,000 megatons of explosive power. Think of a freight train filled with gunpowder that stretches from earth to the moon. Now *triple* that—make the train 925,000 miles long—and you have an image of the destructive power of the United States (see *Nucleus* 1981).

The length of the U.S. train is a matter of alarm for many. But then there is also this statistic: Russia has a train of about the same size. France and Great Britain also have trains, although theirs are shorter. Israel, India, Pakistan, China, and a few other nations have them as well. Still other nations, envious that they aren't in the nuclear club, are frantically trying to build their own trains.

The Cold War has bequeathed us trains that are running along the edge of a cliff. There has been a downpour, and a washout could be ahead. Yet the trains steam forward full speed into the darkness. At any time, one of them might hit a washout, plunge off the cliff, and obliterate humanity.

A Glimmer of Hope?

In the midst of this dark futility lies a glimmer of hope. Like a train's engineer who has seen a washout ahead and is furiously waving a warning lantern, Russia and the United States have been heeding the danger. They have negotiated agreements to eliminate ICBMs with multiple warheads and to reduce their nuclear stockpiles. No longer do Russia and the United States target each other's major cities. (Since ICBMs

Political Instability in Russia

have to be aimed somewhere, just where are those nuclear missiles targeted?) Although Russia and the United Sates have destroyed a few weapons, this is not disarmament. This is really only *a reduction of excess capacity:* Each nation can still destroy the other many times over.

Not only do we still face the possibility of nuclear warfare, but also the likelihood that nuclear weapons will be used may have *increased.* When Russia lost its colonies, ethnic conflicts resurfaced. The former Soviet Union suppressed ethnic conflicts with an iron hand. As its empire broke up, throughout its former borders those simmering ethnic rivalries and hatreds erupted. At the same time, religious fundamentalism and terrorism have grown. All this is accompanied by nuclear proliferation and the capacity to smuggle nuclear weapons across borders.

Is it any wonder that some see our civilization ending in one gigantic mushroom cloud? Before we examine that possibility, look at the Social Map on pages 514–515. There you can see the major sources of this danger.

THE POSSIBILITY OF ACCIDENTAL WAR

The Possibility of Accidental War

Only with disarmament, which we discuss later, will the world be safe from nuclear destruction. As things now stand, we face not only the potential of some leader launching a nuclear attack and of terrorists detonating nuclear weapons, but also the possibility of missiles being unleashed accidentally. Consider how close we have come in the past:

Computer Failure

> Back in 1980, a military computer reported that Russia had fired missiles at the United States. The United States immediately went to red alert. U.S. bombers plotted courses toward preselected targets in the Soviet Union, and we prepared our missiles for launching. The countdown toward nuclear devastation had begun. (*U.S. News & World Report*, June 24, 1980)

Russia had *not* launched any missiles. A computer had malfunctioned. It's a chilling thought—the end of the world due to a computer malfunction.

Operator Failure

The obliteration of humanity could also come from a simple human error. Here's another real-life event:

> On October 28, 1962, the North American Defense Command was informed that Cuba had launched a nuclear missile. It was about to hit Tampa, Florida. The U.S. began a countdown for its retaliatory strike. Then someone noticed that there had been no explosion in Tampa (Sagan 1994).

It turned out that a radar operator had accidentally inserted into the system a test tape that simulated an attack from Cuba. If the United States had launched immediately, instead of waiting a few minutes, Cuba would have been destroyed. The Soviet Union, Cuba's ally at the time, might have responded with salvos of its own—and you probably would not be here to read this book.

Nuclear Accidents

Or the end might come because a nuclear weapon detonates accidentally. Consider these accidents that Rear Admiral Gene LaRocque, U.S. Navy (retired) summarized:

> The *George Washington,* a missile submarine, ran into a Japanese ship and sank it. The *Scorpion* and the *Thresher,* two other nuclear attack submarines, sank in the ocean. When a mechanic dropped a wrench in a missile silo in Arkansas, a missile was launched. Several nuclear weapons have fallen out of planes, through open bomb bays.
> A nuclear weapon fell from a plane into a swamp in the Carolinas. The Air Force was unable to find it. The Defense Department bought the land, put a fence around it and, in Orwellian fashion, called it a "nuclear safety area." (Keyes n.d.)

In none of these incidents did a nuclear weapon detonate. We have no assurance that similar accidents will not happen again, and, if they occur, that the weapons will not explode.

Nuclear Sabotage

The U.S. government has repeatedly assured us—and the world—that a missile cannot be launched without proper authorization. Any talk to the contrary, they say, is alarmist. Such assurances are lies:

> The year was 1962. Kennedy had backed down in the Bay of Pigs invasion of Cuba, and the Soviet military thought that Kennedy would be a pushover. Khrushchev, the premier of the Soviet Union, decided to ship missiles to Cuba. The CIA reported that the missiles would be capable of destroying the Pentagon, New York City, and other U.S. cities. Kennedy warned Khrushchev to order the ships back and set up a blockade to intercept them. The world waited tensely, television reporting the location of the ships as they neared the blockade.

All the preceding is well known. What is not well known is this:

> At the height of the Cuban crisis, officers at Malmstrom Air Force Base in Montana, who also doubted the resolve of President Kennedy to give the order to bomb the Soviets, did what was supposedly impossible: They jerry-rigged their Minutemen missiles so they could launch them on their own.
>
> After the crisis, the air force investigated the jerry-rigging. It then altered the evidence to prevent higher authorities from learning that officers at Malmstrom had given themselves the ability to launch missiles. (Sagan 1994)

The Significance of Symbolic Interaction

This hair-raising event demonstrates the significance of symbolic interaction. To have meaning, all events in life must be interpreted. If a missile were launched, or a city destroyed, as could happen with a computer malfunction or an unauthorized launch, this question would have to be answered: Is this an accident, an unauthorized attack by a madman, or the opening of an orchestrated attack? On that interpretation hangs the fate of the world.

Fortunately, the United States and Russia have agreed to notify the other if either spots a missile—and to help each other track and destroy it (Greenberger 1992). Their intention is to protect one another against missile attacks by third nations, but such cooperation also helps prevent accidental nuclear war.

The proliferation of nuclear weapons, however, has expanded the possibility of accidental war. India and Pakistan, two neighbors with a history of warfare and unresolved territorial disputes, joined the nuclear club some years ago. Each hates and fears the other, and each sees the other's possession of nuclear weapons as a direct threat to its own existence. Although they know that their weapons can destroy each other, India and Pakistan continue to hurl threats across the thin line that separates them.

BIOLOGICAL AND CHEMICAL WARFARE

The Origin of This Type of Warfare

It sometimes is difficult to fathom the human mind. One of the strangest quirks in human thinking is this: To kill by bullets and bombs is considered normal, but to kill by gas is deemed abnormal. During World War I, the French and Germans shocked the world by using poison gas. After that war, in 1925, the major powers met in Geneva where they signed an agreement banning the use of poison gases in warfare. In 1972, they agreed not to use biological weapons (Seib 1981). In 1989, 145 nations met to try to ban chemical weapons (Revzin 1989). They failed.

The Use of These Weapons

A few nations have used biological and chemical agents during war. In World War I, the opposing forces unleashed mustard gas. In the 1980s, Iran and Iraq used this gas on each other. In the 1960s and 1970s, the United States rained chemical defoliants on the jungles of Vietnam. These chemicals were not intended as a weapon but as a tool to destroy crops and clear terrain. Spraying stopped when Vietnamese women began giving birth to deformed babies, such as the children shown in the photo on page 516.

Agent Orange

After the war, thousands of U.S. Vietnam veterans claimed that Agent Orange had damaged their health. The Veterans Administration (VA) insisted that the defoliant was not the cause of the "cancer, birth defects in their children, miscarriages by their

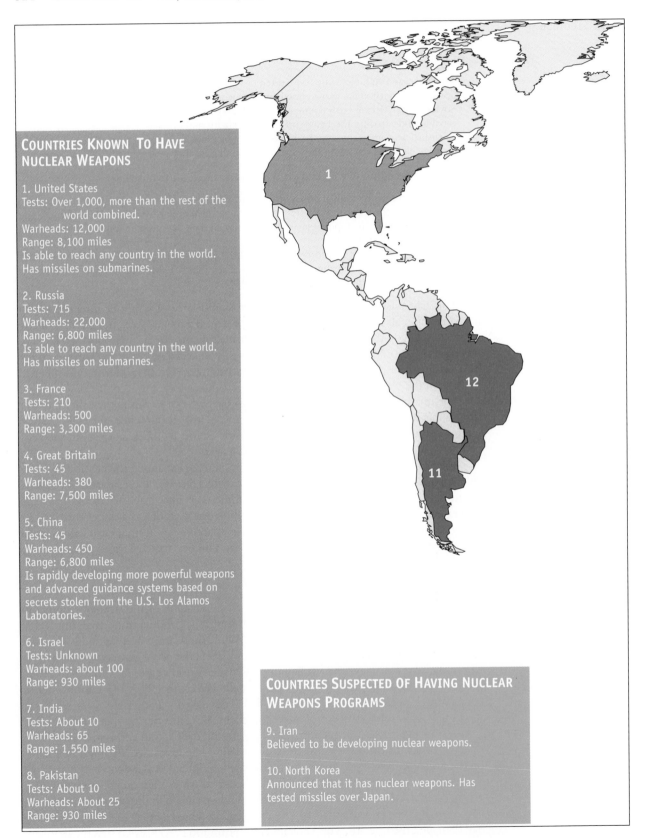

COUNTRIES KNOWN TO HAVE NUCLEAR WEAPONS

1. United States
Tests: Over 1,000, more than the rest of the world combined.
Warheads: 12,000
Range: 8,100 miles
Is able to reach any country in the world.
Has missiles on submarines.

2. Russia
Tests: 715
Warheads: 22,000
Range: 6,800 miles
Is able to reach any country in the world.
Has missiles on submarines.

3. France
Tests: 210
Warheads: 500
Range: 3,300 miles

4. Great Britain
Tests: 45
Warheads: 380
Range: 7,500 miles

5. China
Tests: 45
Warheads: 450
Range: 6,800 miles
Is rapidly developing more powerful weapons and advanced guidance systems based on secrets stolen from the U.S. Los Alamos Laboratories.

6. Israel
Tests: Unknown
Warheads: about 100
Range: 930 miles

7. India
Tests: About 10
Warheads: 65
Range: 1,550 miles

8. Pakistan
Tests: About 10
Warheads: About 25
Range: 930 miles

COUNTRIES SUSPECTED OF HAVING NUCLEAR WEAPONS PROGRAMS

9. Iran
Believed to be developing nuclear weapons.

10. North Korea
Announced that it has nuclear weapons. Has tested missiles over Japan.

FIGURE 15-2 *The Nuclear Club*

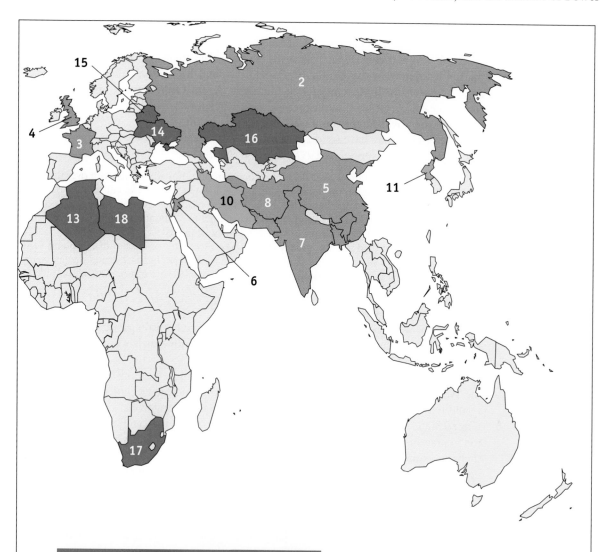

COUNTRIES THAT GAVE UP NUCLEAR WEAPONS

11. Argentina
Stopped nuclear weapons development in 1990 and signed a nuclear weapons-free zone in Latin America.

12. Brazil
Stopped nuclear weapons development in 1990 and signed a nuclear weapons-free zone in Latin America.

13. Algeria
Stopped its program in 1991 and signed the Nuclear Proliferation Treaty.

14. Ukraine
Gave up the weapons the Soviet Union left when it broke up.

15. Belarus
Gave up the weapons the Soviet Union left when it broke up.

16. Kazakhstan
Gave up the weapons the Soviet Union left when it broke up.

17. South Africa
Dismantled its nuclear arsenal in 1991 and signed the Nuclear Proliferation Treaty.

18. Libya
Gave up its nuclear program in the face of economic sanctions.

wives, impotency, respiratory problems, and liver, skin, nerve, and emotional disorders" (Feinsilber 1981). The VA claimed that Agent Orange caused only a "severe skin rash." When the Department of Health and Human Services investigated the matter, it found that the United States had dropped 12 million gallons of Agent Orange on Vietnam. In 41 emergency situations, Agent Orange was dumped "directly over or near U.S. air bases and other military installations." In 1989, each soldier who had sued the government was awarded about $12,000.

Afghanistan and Laos

The Soviets may have used chemicals in Afghanistan and Laos, not against plants but against people (Douglass 1998). Here is one account:

> The biplane came out of a clear sky at 9:30 one morning. It made a single run over the Laotian village of Va Houng, unleashing a stream of yellow gas that fell like rain along a one-kilometer strip and formed droplets on the ground. To the villagers, it smelled like burning peppers.
>
> According to Gnia Pao Vang, a subdistrict chief in Vientiane Province, the gas killed 83 of his village's 473 residents, as well as all village animals.
>
> The people died in pain, usually after two or three days of intense diarrhea and vomiting. Like other survivors, Mr. Gnia suffered for weeks from headaches and dizziness, impaired vision, a runny nose, painful breathing and a swollen throat. For days he spit phlegm and blood. (Wain 1981)

The former Soviet Union denies the allegations.

Iraq

It seems well documented that Saddam Hussein used poison gas against the Kurds. Hussein denied the charge, but the images of dead Iraqi Kurds went a long way toward gaining U.S. support for Gulf War II.

The Chemical Arms Race

The justification for producing biological and chemical weapons was the same that the West and the Soviet Union gave for producing nuclear weapons. The Pentagon would tell Congress: "The Soviet Union has achieved a dangerous advantage over the United States." Congress would then fund a new program to "catch up." At one point, the Pentagon reported that we were behind in **binary chemical weapons.** These are shells or bombs in which two benign chemicals are kept in separate chambers. When the weapon is detonated, the chemicals mix, releasing a lethal agent. We caught up, of course—and pushed ahead a bit. And, of course, the Soviet Union then had to rush to catch up, producing even more destructive agents. This, in turn, forced us to move into even higher gear—and so the weapons race was given push after push.

Because the Pentagon does not have money of its own, it has to go to Congress to finance its weapons. In true Orwellian fashion, the Pentagon once told Congress that chemical weapons could help bring about peace. If we develop more powerful chemical

The human costs of war far outnumber the soldiers who are killed and maimed. Shown here are two victims of Agent Orange, a defoliant used by U.S. troops in Vietnam to clear the forests and disrupt the movement of troops and supplies from the north. Birth defects, especially the absence of vital organs (brains, eyes, kidneys, and so on) were a major factor in terminating the massive use of chemical defoliants during this war.

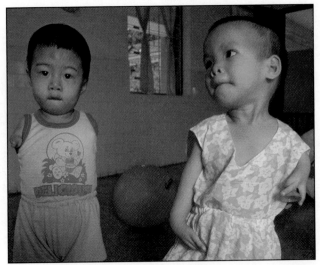

weapons, they said, this might force the Soviets to agree to "a complete and verifiable ban on the development, production, and stockpiling of chemical weapons by dangling the threat of retaliation over the heads of the Soviets" (*Wall Street Journal,* February 9, 1982). Apparently, the irony of producing chemical weapons in order to stop the production of chemical weapons was lost on Congress, the Pentagon, and the Politburo.

In 1993, the United States, Russia, and other nations signed a Chemical Weapons Convention. In this treaty, they agreed not to produce, stockpile, or use chemical weaons. By 2012, the nations are to have destroyed their total supply of chemical weapons. Biological weapons are not covered by the treaty.

The Biological Arms Race

Although the Cold War ended, the United States and Russia have continued their research to develop even more lethal biological weapons. Russia announced that it has genetically engineered an anthrax microbe that attacks blood cells, making vaccines useless against it (Broad and Miller 1998). A defector reported that Russia has ICBMs with warheads loaded with plague, anthrax, and smallpox intended for delivery against U.S. cities (Douglass 1998). If so, we can assume that the United States has done the same—its missiles pointed the other way, of course. With Russia now a part of NATO, it is likely that this race toward mutual biological destruction will stop. It is also likely that the ICBM warheads will be directed toward other targets. After all, why waste a perfectly good ICBM?

A major danger is that terrorists will get their hands on some of these weapons. Let's consider this possibility.

POLITICAL TERRORISM

Terrorism Today

Terrorism is today's nightmare. Hostages and kidnappings used to be the main worries, but with 9/11 the world changed. Officials are concerned that terrorists lurk around the corner. Nuclear plants appear vulnerable, and stadiums filled with spectators could be blown up. Boarding a plane used to be a simple matter, but no longer. Armed security agents scrutinize our baggage and person, while screening devices do the same. Billions of dollars have been spent to fortify our embassies around the world, and yet they remain subject to attack.

Three Types of Political Terrorism:

Political terrorism is similar to warfare. Although it is not war between nations, **political terrorism** is the use of the means of war—intimidation, coercion, threats, and violence—to achieve political objectives (Boston et al. 1977). Political terrorists use violence to sow fear. They do not recognize civilians as "noncombatants." On the contrary, they often target civilians because they are easier to reach, and the apparent randomness of the attack creates fear. The three types of political terrorism are revolutionary, repressive, and state-sponsored. Let's look at each.

1. Revolutionary Terrorism

In the *first* type, **revolutionary terrorism,** enemies of the state use terrorism to try to overthrow the political system. Walter Laqueur (1977), a political scientist, found these background factors in revolutionary terrorism:

1. Existence of a segregated ethnic, cultural, or religious minority
2. Perceptions of being deprived or oppressed
3. Unemployment or inflation
4. External encouragement (often from an ethnic, cultural, or religious counterpart living elsewhere)
5. An historical "them" (a group they blame for their oppressed condition)
6. Frustrated elites who provide leadership and justify ideological violence

The Goals of Revolutionary Terrorism

The first act of terrorism doesn't appear spontaneously in a social vacuum. The group (whichever it is) has usually tried legal channels to change its situation. Finding the government unresponsive, the group turns to revolutionary terrorism. The group chooses targets designed to

1. Publicize the group and its grievances
2. Demonstrate the government's vulnerability
3. Force political and social change

Because publicity is often a key objective of a terrorist act, terrorism is sometimes called "political theater." As political scientist Brian Jenkins (1987) put it: "Terrorists want a lot of people watching, not a lot of people dead." Consequently, terrorists choose targets that will attract the media. In light of 9/11, I would modify Jenkins's observation. Some political terrorists do want a lot of people dead. It depends on their message. Suleiman Abu Ghaith, a spokesman for Al-Qaeda, has said that Al-Qaeda's goal is to kill 4 million Americans. After that, the rest can convert to Al-Qaeda's brand of Islam (Simon 2004).

A Fourth Goal: Conversion and Recruitment

Some terrorists have a fourth purpose. Communist terrorists believed that the masses were deluded by "false consciousness," blinding them to their oppression. What Trotsky called the "theater of terrorism" was designed to provoke the capitalist rulers to overreact. The harshness and brutality of their reaction would then expose the repressive system and arouse the masses (Rubenstein 1987). Al-Qaeda, too, tries to entice a brutal reaction from the West to expose what they see as the true nature of Western civilization. If, in response to Al-Qaeda's attacks, the West oppresses Arabs in its midst or invades Arab countries, the Arab masses will recognize the true hostility that the West harbors against Islam and will join in the *jihad* that will bring about Islamic world dominance.

Examples in the United States

Americans lost their innocence concerning terrorism when a truck bomb exploded in Oklahoma City in 1995. The destruction of a federal building and the deaths of almost 200 people, including 19 children in a day-care center, opened their eyes to a new form of warfare. Up to that time, they assumed that terrorism only happened "over there."

Then, as recounted in this chapter's opening vignette, an even more shocking act of terrorism on U.S. soil was the destruction of the World Trade Center in New York City on September 11, 2001. This attack, accompanied by the simultaneous attack on the Pentagon in Washington, caused several thousand deaths. These two targets were not random choices. The leaders of Al-Qaeda chose the World Trade Center because it symbolized the U.S. dominance of global capitalism. The Pentagon was targeted because it symbolized the U.S. military. To strike at the heart of two major symbols exposed the vulnerability of the United States. The attack struck fear in Americans, for they knew that nothing was safe.

The attack of 9/11 also served as theater, in precisely the way that analysts had indicated. The timing—a Tuesday morning—meant that a huge audience would gather immediately. The act went beyond the terrorists' dream, of course, for none could have anticipated the dramatic collapse of the Twin Towers. Yet they did collapse and, in even more dramatic fashion, took with them several hundred firefighters. The message could not have been clearer, nor an audience so large as quickly summoned.

Convictions of Moral Superiority

The terrorists' acts of bloodshed are immoral to outsiders and victims, but to their perpetrators they are righteous acts. Using a neutralization technique we reviewed in Chapter 6, terrorists appeal to a higher morality to justify their killings. Despite almost everyone else in the world viewing their actions as evil, the terrorists are convinced of their moral superiority. As they see it, their "cause" justifies mass, indiscriminate killing of civilians, for these can help usher in their apocalyptic vision of Islamic society.

Combined with Self-Sacrificing Dedication

It is this conviction (the cause, seeming so righteous, justifies any act, no matter how heinous) that makes revolutionary terrorists such formidable opponents of the established order. Some revolutionaries become as dedicated to "the cause" as any monk to his god. Listen to Karari Mjama, a Mau Mau insurgent:

> No one can serve two masters. In order to become a strong faithful warrior who would persevere to the last minute, one had to renounce all worldly wealth, including his family. . . . In fact, I had said to my wife . . . not to expect any sort of help from me for at least ten years' time. I had instructed her to take care of herself and our beloved daughter. I had trained myself to think of the fight, and the African Government; and nothing of the country's progress before independence. I had learned to forget all pleasures and imagination of the past. I confined my thoughts (to) the fight only—the end of which would open my thoughts to the normal world. (Schreiber 1978:32)

Targets and Weapons Everywhere

As with 9/11, terrorists often strike without warning. Japan had prided itself on being a "community nation" that was insulated from the "profane" social problems of the West. Its soothing, self-serving myth was shattered by a renegade religious leader who launched a poison gas attack on Tokyo subways. Twelve people died, and 5,000 were injured (Miller and Broad 1999). The gas, sarin, can be manufactured from chemicals used in pesticides that you can buy at your local hardware store. Other frightening recipes for poisons have turned up on the Internet—a sort of Betty Crocker cookbook on how to poison the world (Greenberger and Bishop 1995).

2. Repressive Terrorism

Repressive terrorism, a *second* type, is terrorism waged by a government against its own citizens. For example:

> Diana, a dedicated Christian, worked among the poor in Buenos Aires. One midnight, soldiers broke down her door, rushed in, and knocked her to the floor. They blindfolded her and beat her across the head. They then threw her into a car and drove to a building with an underground chamber. Here she was threatened, tortured, and interrogated for six straight hours about church leaders, the Vatican Council, and the Jews.
>
> Beaten beyond all tears, she suddenly blurted, "Good God, aren't you Christians?"
>
> Abrupt silence followed. One of the soldiers grabbed her hand and pressed her fingers to a metal cross on his chest. Afterward, they seemed to give up on her. "I'm convinced that small incident saved my life," she says. "The man apparently wanted to be recognized as a person rather than a torturer. He couldn't have that recognition without making me a person, too, rather than an object to be disposed of."
>
> Diana was later taken back to her apartment and held there for two more days by four officers who took turns raping her. The police then released her. (Cornell 1981)

The Case of Argentina

The reason for the massive brutality and killing in Argentina was typical of repressive terrorism: The government felt weak and vulnerable, unable to respond to social change. Fearful of its own collapse, it became afraid of ideas. Like Diana, between 1976 and 1983 tens of thousands of Argentines were arrested. Thousands were tortured and executed. Some bodies were dumped in public places, a mute warning to others. Some captives were dropped alive from airplanes into the ocean. Thousands of parents never knew what happened to their children.

The Case of Cambodia

Pol Pot, the dictator of Cambodia, directed perhaps the most ruinous terrorism that any government has ever inflicted on its people. The extent of his regime's devastation is mind-boggling. For almost four years, from April 1975 to January 1979, Cambodia was Pol Pot's slaughterhouse. On an average day, 1,500 Cambodians died. In just forty-five months, the government killed about 2 million Cambodians (Wain 1981). Death often came by rubber hoses and bamboo sticks. Some victims were tortured for weeks before their death. Others were killed on the spot. *All* intellectuals were marked for death, for they represented an elite, and the Pol Pot government was supposedly ushering in a classless society (Miles 1980). Being able to speak a foreign language was enough to merit execution. In one area of Cambodia, members of the ruling group, the Khmer Rouge, could count only to 10. Anyone who could count higher was an "intellectual." To ferret them out, the Khmer Rouge would have someone count other people—they executed those who counted to 20, instead of counting two groups of 10. Only 50 of Cambodia's 800 doctors survived.

On a visit to the killing fields of Cambodia, I saw one of Pol Pot's slaughterhouses. Today, on the outskirts of Phnom Penh, the capital of Cambodia, the buildings are maintained as a sort of museum, so the people won't forget. I could see the metal cots on which the prisoners had been chained, the torture devices used to break the men, women, and children before they were executed. Emblazoned on my mind is the cabinet of skulls—the larger ones of adults and the smaller ones of children—each cracked where someone had struck a blow into that living person. So, too, is the huge vat that once had a wooden bar above it. The vat was filled with water, and the victims, hung upside down, were lowered slowly head first into the water. They could be immersed as many times as the torturers wanted, until they finally were forced to drink their death.

The Case of the Soviet Union

To dictators, who hold power uneasily and have few checks on what they can do, repressive terrorism allows them to silence criticism and suppress ideas they don't like. Soviet officials were sensitive to criticism of any sort, and they even persecuted poets who expressed "incorrect" political thought. They also felt threatened by religion, with party leaders referring to the Church as "the enemy within" (Ra'anan et al. 1986). Andrei Sakharov (1977), a dissenter who drew attention to "the persecution of Baptists, of the True Orthodox church, of Pentecostals, and uniates, and others" said,

> It is a common practice of the Russian government to take children away from parents who are evangelical; that is, they believe that Jesus of Nazareth is God incarnate or the Savior who should be placed ahead of the State. Pastors of underground churches are regularly arrested, beaten, tortured, and killed.

3. State-Sponsored Terrorism

In the *third* type, **state-sponsored terrorism,** a government finances, trains, and arms terrorists. Colonel Moammar Gadhafi of Libya saw terrorism as a legitimate extension of the state. He bankrolled terrorist groups and provided training camps for them. After the U.S. Air Force tried to kill him by bombing his palace, Gadhafi became more clandestine in his support of terrorism. Then after years of economic sanctions that worsened conditions in his country, Gadhafi renounced his support of terrorism and invited international inspectors to verify that he had dismantled his efforts to produce nuclear weapons. The Taliban government of Afghanistan supported Osama bin Laden, the terrorist most wanted by the U.S. government. This protection allowed bin Laden, who has sworn to kill U.S. civilians no matter where they are, to operate openly. Bin Laden's safe haven was removed when the United States attacked Afghanistan in retaliation for 9/11 and destroyed the Taliban government.

Criminal Terrorism

In addition to political terrorism, there is **criminal terrorism.** The most widely known example today of criminals using terrorism to attain their objectives is the Russian Mafia. To maintain their control, these gangsters intimidate and kill anyone who opposes them. They terrorize both the public and government into submission. The Russian Mafia guns down bankers who won't launder money for them, and, as the executions of reporters, prosecutors, and judges attest, violent death awaits anyone who dares to investigate or prosecute them.

Narco-Terrorism

Narco-terrorism is criminal terrorism that centers on drugs. Some narco-terrorists have political goals, and they use drug dealing to finance their ambitions. Mehemet Ali Agca, for example, sold drugs to finance his attempted assassination of Pope John Paul II (Oakley 1985; Ehrenfeld 1990). For other narco-terrorists, money is the primary objective; terrorism is simply a way to protect their drug operations. In Colombia, international drug dealers hired thugs to assassinate the justices of the Colombian supreme court. They also terrorized the Colombian government to cancel its extradition treaty with the United States.

A development in narco-terrorism that worries officials is the uniting of the sophisticated Russian Mafia with the Colombian drug cartel (Farah 1997). The Russian Mafia, with former KGB (Russian secret police) agents and members with Ph.D.s, has opened banks in the Caribbean to launder Colombian drug money. The Russian Mafia has also sold the Colombian drug cartel sophisticated weapons—AK-47 assault rifles, rocket-propelled grenades, helicopters, and surface-to-air missiles. The Colombian drug dealers have become so powerful that, with the aid of guerrillas, they control large areas of Colombia.

Nuclear and Biological Terrorism

Nuclear and *biological terrorism* are in a class by themselves. Let's look at each.

Because plutonium can be used to manufacture nuclear weapons, you would think it would be guarded carefully. This will sound as though I am making it up, but about 5,000 pounds—two and a half tons—of plutonium are missing from U.S. nuclear facilities. A former security agent reported that protective measures at the Rocky Flats weapons factory near Denver were so lax that it was "like having a window in a bank vault" (Hosenball 1999). When the missing plutonium was made public, officials took a cavalier attitude. "What's to worry?" they asked. After all, the plutonium "probably got stuck in pipes and manufacturing tools." The solution? Simple. They suspended the individual who revealed that the plutonium was missing.

In light of 9/11, such a cavalier attitude is a sign of gross incompetence, one that can lead to tens of thousands of deaths.

The danger of nuclear terrorism has grown worse since the breakup of the Soviet empire. Seeing its opportunity, the "Russian Mafia" stepped into the void of legitimate power. With apparently no morality to hold their desires in check, these gangsters stole plutonium and uranium and offered them for sale to Iraq and other dictatorships ("The Wild Wild East" 1995). The United States is helping to make Russia's nuclear material more secure, but problems abound in keeping it out of the hands of terrorists. The Soviet Union produced 1,300 tons of enriched uranium and 220 tons of plutonium, which are scattered throughout the former Soviet Union at 40 to 50 locations (Gordon 1996). Some enriched uranium has been smuggled out of nuclear plants and naval facilities. One worker simply hid nuclear material in his protective gloves and walked out the gate (Zaitseva and Hand 2003).

This terrorist threat is amplified by Russia's dire economic situation. Conditions have deteriorated to the point that for a few dollars guards at some nuclear facilities can be bribed to turn off security systems (Zaitseva and Hand 2003). Many of Russia's nuclear scientists are unemployed, whereas others work for wages paid to common laborers—and even these go unpaid for months at a time. Both U.S. and Russian leaders fear that offers from states that want to become nuclear powers will tempt some nuclear scientists to defect. To prevent this, the United States has given Russia money to pay these scientists, to retrain them in business ventures, and to turn nuclear production facilities into factories to manufacture automobiles and other consumer items.

This photo, taken at the former Tuol Sleng Prison (now a tourist attraction) outside Phnom Penh, illustrates just a few of the many thousands of people tortured and killed at this prison.

One nightmare facing the West is that a dictatorship will develop nuclear-tipped missiles and, unrestrained by the checks and balances built into democracies, terrorize an entire region—and, with advanced delivery systems, perhaps the world. One scenario is that North Korea, an iron-fisted dictatorship whose rulers have proved willing to sacrifice millions of their people to starvation, will blackmail the West by threatening to destroy Seoul and Tokyo (Ricks 1999). Another scenario is that Iran will develop nuclear weapons and, regardless of the consequences, will bomb Israel. By stealing nuclear secrets from an incredibly insecure Los Alamos, China was able to miniaturize its nuclear warheads and develop precise guidance systems. It now has the capacity to threaten the world's nations, including the United States and the countries of Europe (Risen and Gerth 1999). At the moment, the nuclear weapons picture is as grim, if not grimmer, as it was during the Cold War.

The nightmare grows. The "father of the Pakistani bomb," Abdul Qadeer Khan, who headed Pakistan's nuclear program, sold blueprints and parts for making nuclear bombs (Rubin 2004). Among his customers were Iran and North Korea. Evidently, there

Before he masterminded 9/11, Osama bin Laden had financed other attacks against the United States, such as the bombing of the U.S. embassies in Nairobi and Dar Al Salam. Bin Laden wants to reclaim Arab grandeur and power and drive the United States and other Western nations from the Middle East. As this book goes to press, bin Laden is directing operations from caves on the Afghani-Pakistani border.

The Need to Avoid Encouraging Terrorists

Eight Promising Policies

is a global network of suppliers and middlemen—with agents in Germany and brokers in Dubai—for procuring nuclear weapons (Omestad and Latif 2004).

Because the potential destruction is enormous, at some point nuclear terrorists could hold major governments, including that of the United States, captive. Without even possessing advanced delivery systems, terrorists could smuggle nuclear weapons into the country. Few of the thousands of containers arriving at U.S. ports are searched. What would U.S. officials do if terrorists threatened to detonate a nuclear weapon in the heart of New York City or Atlanta or Los Angeles? The thought of nuclear weapons in the hands of a ruthless, hell-bent-for-destruction dictator sends chills down the back of the industrialized nations.

Biological terrorism presents perhaps an even greater threat. Biological weapons such as anthrax, smallpox, and the plague are cheaper to produce, their components are easier to obtain, and they can be transported in tiny containers. Terrorists could infiltrate the United States or any other country and simultaneously release anthrax or other killer germs in several cities. If this occurs in the United States, a large proportion of Americans could die. As I write this, the perpetrator of the anthrax scare through the U.S. mail remains unknown. The fingerprint of the anthrax should reveal the laboratory in which it was produced, and, from there, telltale clues should point to the killer. But after years of frustrating search, the FBI has come up short.

The continuing threat of biological terrorism is the topic of the Technology and Social Problems box on the next page.

Social Policy

Let's look at social policies on the two major problems we have reviewed in this chapter, nuclear war and political terrorism.

POLITICAL TERRORISM

The first principle for dealing with terrorists is to not give in to their demands, for this only encourages terrorists. As one analyst said, "You cannot permit terrorism to become a profitable tactic unless you want more of it" (Bremer 1988).

Legal and government experts suggest the following as effective social policies (Oakley 1985; Bush 1986; Bremer 1988; Clawson 1988; Ehrenfeld 1990; FBI 1998):

1. Promise anything during negotiations. Promises made under threat are not valid.
2. Make no distinction between terrorists and their state sponsors. States that sponsor terrorists are not neutral and should not be treated as neutrals. This principle allows both retaliatory and preemptive acts.
3. Use economic and political sanctions to break the connection between terrorists and the states that provide them weapons, financing, safe houses, training areas, and identity documents in return for terrorism done on their behalf.
4. Treat terrorists as war criminals. Track them, arrest them, and punish them. Bomb them, if that is what it takes.
5. Discourage media coverage because publicity is a prime terrorist goal. It should be illegal for the media to pay terrorists for interviews.
6. Establish an international extradition or prosecution agreement: If terrorists are caught anywhere, they would be extradited or tried.

Technology and Social Problems

OUR FUTURE: BIOLOGICAL TERRORISM IN THE TWENTY-FIRST CENTURY

Consider this scenario:

> Over a period of years, agents of a nation whose leader hates the United States and has a score to settle quietly infiltrate the United States. Most gain admission as students at universities around the country. All have been trained by their country's secret police. On a predetermined day, at a specified hour, they release anthrax and smallpox into the air of twenty major cities. Within days, a third of Americans are dead.

Scenarios like this haunt U.S. officials. Few safeguards exist to protect against such an attack. Some think that one has already been planned, the agents awaiting their instructions. There will be no warning, no attempt to hold the United States hostage in order to extort billions of dollars. Money will not be the goal. The motive will be revenge for humiliations suffered at U.S. hands. The goal will be no less than to wipe out the United States itself.

The secret agents know that they will sacrifice their lives, for they, too, will be infected by the diseases they release. But they have been assured that they will obtain immediate entry into heaven, for they will become martyrs for a holy cause. Just in case that promise is insufficient motivation, they've been told that their families will be tortured and killed if they change their minds.

U.S. officials are scared. They fear that such a scenario is not theoretical. The White House conducted a secret exercise to play out what would happen if terrorists struck with genetically modified germs. The president and other officials were alarmed at the results (Broad and Miller 1998). How seriously officials are taking this threat is indicated by the federal budget: Several billion dollars are earmarked for civil defense in the event of such an attack (Department of Homeland Security 2004). Officials have stockpiled vaccines around the country, and emergency medical teams have been trained in major cities. All military personnel, active and reserve, are being vaccinated against anthrax, as well as all civilian employees of the Department of Defense who are designated essential workers ("Anthrax Vaccination . . ." 2004).

The president has issued secret directives. Top officials have developed plans, not to evacuate populations, but to block roads and stop people at gunpoint from fleeing cities and spreading the disease. The president wants Congress to approve a military takeover of state and local governments to fight the chaos that would result from such an attack (Miller and Broad 1999). Reading between the lines, it is certain that the secret directives include Pentagon control of the United States.

An ancient Chinese proverb says: "May you live in exciting times." This simple saying is actually a curse, for it expresses the hope that an enemy's life will be chaotic. We live in exciting times. Let's hope that the curse with which we live—weapons of mass destruction, hatreds engendered by foreign domination, and retaliatory action by terrorists—does not mean our destruction.

7. Develop an international organization to combat terrorism. This organization would coordinate worldwide intelligence and advise nations. It would also direct international teams to respond to specific events—such as freeing hostages or locating evidence to identify sponsors of terrorists.
8. Offer large rewards for information leading to the disabling of known terrorists. Just as in the old West, rewards can be paid on a "dead-or-alive" basis. With rewards of $50,000, or $1 million, or $5 million, terrorists will never know if associates can be trusted. Informants should also be offered new identities.

Some of these policies are controversial—and disturbing. With Iraq War II, for example, the policy of preemptive strikes has been put into practice. An additional application of this policy is targeted killings. The CIA determines that X individual is responsible for a terrorist attack, or is planning one, and he is put on a "hit list," marked for assassination (Risen and Johnston 2002). Lest you think that I am exaggerating—

9/11 has had far-reaching effects on the United States. Whether the country ever returns to its more easy going ways based on feelings of internal security remains to be seen. The anti-terrorism laws passed after 9/11 give the police more authority than they have had since the Civil War.

since trials, evidence, judges, and juries are an essential part of our heritage—the CIA has already done this. In Djibouti, the CIA launched a Predator, an unmanned plane, and in Yemen fired a Hellfire missile into an automobile carrying six suspected terrorists. All six were killed (Hersh 2002).

NUCLEAR WARFARE AND THE ELUSIVE PATH TO PEACE

The Strange Path to Peace

The primary policy that the United States and the former Soviet Union pursued after World War II was **mutual deterrence**—using threats and the fear of mutual destruction to prevent the other from striking first. Each was afraid to use its nuclear arsenal, because each had developed doomsday safeguards—that is, if a country were attacked and destroyed, even out of the ashes missiles would be launched that would destroy the other. Because neither country would survive, there was no benefit to attacking the other. The resulting balance of power was called Mutual Assured Destruction (MAD).

MAD

The path to peace, then, has been a strange one. Each superpower armed itself to the teeth, stockpiled nuclear, chemical, and biological weapons, and signaled to its counterpart that it would unleash those weapons if necessary. Thus the superpowers struck a balance of power—or terror—that kept them from attacking each other. Sociologist Nicholas Timasheff (1965:291) explained how it worked:

> Each party may consider that it has a fair chance to win, but each party also knows that the cost of victory would be prohibitive; physical destruction of 90–95 percent of the total population, almost complete destruction of industrial equipment, transformation of almost the total territory into an uninhabitable area because of radiation, contamination of air, water, plants and animals and other natural resources. Under these circumstances victory can be worse than the most crucial defeat before this atomic age. Each of the parties to the possible conflict has full reason to refrain from attack.

G8 and the Precarious Balance of World Domination

G8, the world's eight most powerful industrialized nations, is working out a new balance of power—sometimes called the New World Order. The balance, however, is precarious. Of its many sources of disequilibrium, perhaps the most disturbing is the

1. Spreading Nuclear Capacity

proliferation of nuclear weapons. Poor nations may not be able to make it to G8's bargaining table, but if they join the nuclear club, G8 will listen to them. With some poor nations now possessing or building nuclear weapons, the nuclear balance of power is precarious. India has developed a missile system that can be fired from mobile launchers. Not only can India's missiles hit any target in Pakistan, its neighboring enemy, but also they can reach Beijing and Shanghai (Bearak 1999a). Look at the Social Map on pages 514–515.

2. Spreading Conflicts

Even local conflicts can upset G8's balance of power. If a local conflict heats up, other nations may become involved. This is one reason that NATO (North Atlantic Treaty Organization) was so quick to take action against Serbia. Bombs speak louder than words, as Milosevic discovered. If a minor, hostile power even comes close to possessing nuclear weapons, as was thought to be the case of Hussein's Iraq, G8 will bomb now and ask questions later. If G8 won't act, the United States will.

3. Gross Incompetence

Our current balance of power is more fragile than most of us realize. It could even be upset by incompetence at a low level. Consider this event from the 1970s:

> For nearly four years the public library of the Los Alamos Scientific Laboratory in New Mexico had on its shelves a report that provided precise details of the devices that trigger hydrogen bombs (Mintz 1979). Only a few pages of the report were supposed to have been declassified, but through a "clerical error" the entire report was made available to the public, both Americans and foreigners, for inspection and copying. A nuclear expert, Dimitri Rotow, who copied this report, was quoted as saying: "It was easier than getting something out of the Library of Congress. At the Library of Congress, they at least check your briefcase" (AP May 25, 1979).

Three Potential Policies:

Policies that could help ensure peace include disarmament, interlocking networks of mutual interests, and international law. Let's look at each.

1. Disarmament

Proponents of disarmament are of two major types. Some propose **bilateral disarmament;** that is, both sides agree to disarm simultaneously. Others favor **unilateral disarmament:** One nation would announce its intention to disarm, and begin to dismantle some weapons system. When its antagonist sees that it has made itself more vulnerable, it supposedly would begin to disarm, too. Just as each step of armament led to the escalation and proliferation of weapons systems, so each step of disarmament would reduce and ultimately eliminate that stockpile.

Another group argues that only a strong military and the will to use it can make a nation secure. Those who favor this position oppose disarmament. Although full military preparedness may indeed prevent war, extremists carry this argument to logical absurdities. They argue that the nuclear powers should help other nations build nuclear weapons (Sagan 1994). Because nuclear weapons kept the superpowers from attacking one another, they will also restrain smaller nations. The more the merrier!

Russia and the United States have signed treaties to reduce their stockpiles of nuclear weapons. This is not disarmament, however, as neither intends to rid itself of nuclear weapons, just to reduce the number it possesses. The huge cost of maintaining these weapons, however, has led some of the top military to favor unilateral reduction. Maintaining them is taking money from other projects that the military favors (Myers 1998).

2. Interlocking Networks of Mutual Interests

Some feel that the key to peace is to develop interlocking networks of mutual interest. It is thought that the more a nation depends on another for its own well-being, the less likely it will be to destroy that nation. The principle is sound, but the route to such dependence may come as a surprise, for it involves global capitalism. The expansion of capitalism has produced a **global economy,** one that links the world's nations to one another. As a nation's trading partners increase, its affairs become more linked to those nations. To develop further interlocking interests, then, we should encourage

3. International Law

trade among the world's nations. To stimulate peace, we also would encourage communication, including travel and scientific and cultural exchanges.

International law is essential for world peace. If each nation is a law unto itself and feels free to wage war when its goals are frustrated, we can never have peace. The major obstacle to implementing international law is the unwillingness of nations to yield sovereignty to an international organization. The rule of law, as represented by the United Nations, was dealt a severe blow when NATO bombed Kosovo. Despite the official reason given for the bombing, with which most of us can agree—to prevent further ethnic slaughter—NATO placed itself above international law by attacking without the approval of the United Nations. It was dealt a further blow by the refusal of the United States to submit to the World Court of the United Nations. Officials of the United States fear that they could be charged with war crimes. This is not so far-fetched, for "one person's freedom fighter is another person's terrorist."

The Mutual Benefit of Survival

In the end, perhaps the desire for self-preservation is what will prevent the nuclear annihilation of humanity. Leaders don't want themselves, their families, or their own country destroyed. Unfortunately, there are exceptions—madmen who want to dominate the world and, failing to do so, want to destroy it. As Albert Speer (1970), one of Hitler's close associates, noted, Hitler held onto the illusion of victory until the end. When he saw that the war was lost, he blamed failure on a lack of will on the part of the Germans, and he wanted to destroy his country. If Hitler had had nuclear bombs, the history of the world may have been written with a different hand.

The Need to Focus on This Problem

Most of us ignore the proliferation of nuclear weapons and the threat of nuclear war. We have enough concerns in our daily lives without trying to shoulder problems of world peace. Besides, this problem is scary, and we would rather think about pleasant things. Yet, I suggest that because the survival of humanity hangs in the balance, we need to think about it—and to do what we can to halt nuclear and biological destruction and proliferation. If we don't, who will?

THE FUTURE OF THE PROBLEM

More Wars

There is no indication that war will disappear. On the contrary, it appears that wars will continue indefinitely. Look at Table 15-4, which lists the top merchants of death. The United States takes an easy lead, selling five times as many weapons as its nearest competitor. With borders in jeopardy and dictators needing to prop up their sagging regimes, there is no end to eager buyers. Where profit comes in, for some, morality goes out. With greed being what it is, it is unlikely that this profitable merchandising in death will diminish—regardless of the destruction of human life that ensues.

The International Arms Trade

As Table 15-4 also shows, poor nations pay huge amounts for arms. Some customers, such as Egypt and Malaysia, are dirt poor. They are using money that they need to feed, house, and educate their people.

More Political Terrorism

What about political terrorism? Indications are that it will increase. The unshackling of the central dictatorship in the former Soviet Union unleashed ethnic antagonisms that are rooted in centuries of animosity and that had been bottled up for decades. Groups that we had never heard of are at each other's throats. In the former Yugoslavia, for example, Serbs, Croats, Muslims, and Albanians tried to eliminate each other. Groups in India and Pakistan fight one another—both killing and dying over the same sliver of disputed land.

Ethnic Antagonisms Unleashed

More Revolutionary Terrorism

Revolutionary terrorists, such as those who bombed the World Trade Center in New York in 2001, will acquire more sophisticated weapons. Available on the black market are shoulder-fired, precision-guided surface-to-air missiles that can bring down jumbo jets. If terrorists acquire systems that can target cars in a motorcade several miles away, few political leaders will be safe. That we will face weapons of mass de-

TABLE 15-4 The Global Arms Trade: Buying and Selling the Weapons of Death

THE TOP EXPORTERS	AMOUNT SOLD
1. United States	$31,800,000,000
2. United Kingdom	$6,600,000,000
3. France	$5,900,000,000
4. Russia	$2,300,000,000
5. China: Mainland	$1,100,000,000
6. Sweden	$900,000,000

THE TOP IMPORTERS: THE MOST INDUSTRIALIZED NATIONS	AMOUNT PURCHASED
1. China, Taiwan	$9,200,000,000
2. Japan	$2,600,000,000
3. United Kingdom	$2,100,000,000
4. United States	$1,600,000,000
5. Israel	$1,100,000,000
6. Australia	$925,000,000
7. Germany	$750,000,000
8. Netherlands	$460,000,000
9. Spain	$430,000,000
10. Italy	$430,000,000

THE TOP IMPORTERS: THE INDUSTRIALIZING AND LEAST INDUSTRIALIZED NATIONS	AMOUNT PURCHASED
1. Saudi Arabia	$11,600,000,000
2. Kuwait	$2,000,000,000
3. Turkey	$1,600,000,000
4. Egypt	$1,600,000,000
5. United Arab Emirates	$1,400,000,000
6. Korea, South	$1,100,000,000
7. Thailand	$950,000,000
8. Greece	$850,000,000
9. Iran	$850,000,000
10. Malaysia	$725,000,000

Source: By the author, based on *Statistical Abstract of the United States* 2001:Table 496. This table was dropped in later editions.

struction—nuclear, chemical, and biological weapons—is also likely. With advances in genetic engineering, the potential of biological weapons that could launch global plagues haunts humanity.

More Repressive Terrorism

Despite democratic crosscurrents, repressive terrorism will continue, particularly in China, Central and South America, Africa, and the Middle East. Government repression, in turn, will stimulate resistance groups—and the bloody struggles will continue.

The Wild Card: Russia

Russia holds fascinating prospects. After seven decades of persecution, its people gained freedom of speech, press, politics, education, religion, and the arts. Increased trade and cultural exchanges with the West reduced suspicions and hostilities on both sides. The acceptance of Russia into NATO, albeit as a junior partner at first, also allows us to visualize a better future. Nothing about Russia is certain, however. Its leaders may slap their repressive hats firmly on their heads. Their arduous experiment with democracy may prove too threatening—inflation, poverty, the Russian Mafia, and open criticism and even defiance of leaders. On one side are the hard-liners, straining to seize power and make repression state policy. They are restrained only with difficulty.

After the September 11, 2001 attacks on New York City and Washington, D.C., anthrax was spread via powder in packages sent through the U.S. mail. These hazardous materials workers are preparing to enter a mail facility in Washington, D.C.

On the other side is the potential for anarchy. If the government fails to regain control and to legitimate its authority, the state may dissolve. With an arsenal of nuclear weapons hanging in the balance, either hard-liners or anarchy threatens world peace.

SUMMARY

1. The three essential conditions of *war* are a cultural tradition for war, an antagonistic situation, and a "spark" that sets off the war. War is common in history, but today's wars are much more destructive.

2. Symbolic interactionists analyze how symbols (perceptions) underlie war. The West and the Soviets saw each other as mortal enemies arming for deadly combat. Each felt obliged to arm itself, setting off a nuclear arms race. Nuclear weapons are not intended to be used, but to symbolize a country's capacity to destroy an enemy.

3. Functionalists identify these functions of war: the extension of political boundaries, social integration, economic gain, social change, ideology, vengeance, military security, and credibility. The dysfunctions of war are defeat, dependence, and destruction.

4. Conflict theorists identify four causes of war: competition for resources, a conflict of interests, a surplus of capital, and the dominance of a military machine.

5. Humans are no more peaceful today than in earlier times. The following do *not* diminish the chances of warfare: the type of government, the group's religion, prosperity, a common language, shared political boundaries, or level of education.

6. Modern weapons are expensive and come at the cost of alternative benefits. A major cost of war is *dehumanization*.

7. Both the military and business gain from producing, selling, and using weapons. The *military-industrial complex* is a powerful force in promoting war.

8. One of the more serious threats facing humanity is biological and chemical warfare. Unless effective international controls are put into place, these weapons will proliferate, one day leading to vast destruction. Today's nations are vulnerable to these forms of *terrorism*.

9. *Political terrorism*, that is, the use of war to achieve political objectives, is of three types: *revolutionary terrorism*, waged by individual groups against the state; *repressive terrorism*, waged by the state against its own people; and *state-sponsored terrorism*, waged by one state against another. *Criminal terrorism* cuts across these types.

10. Disarmament, international law, and growing interlocking interests among the nations of the world could increase the chances for peace.

11. The future holds more terrorism and war. All-out nuclear war is unlikely because of mutual destruction. Revolutionary terrorism will continue. This, in turn, will stimu-

late repressive terrorism. The ethnic antagonisms unleashed in the former Soviet Union will lead to more terrorism. Al-Qaeda—or at least its supporters and successors—are likely to continue their terrorism. The Russian Mafia is likely to be brought under control, but political instabilities may bring hard-liners back into power. Control of Russia's nuclear weapons hangs in the balance.

KEY TERMS

Arms race   The attempt by the West and the Soviets to match one another's war capabilities.

Bilateral disarmament   Two or more nations disarming simultaneously.

Binary chemical weapons   Shells or bombs in which two benign chemicals are kept in separate chambers in the weapon. Upon detonation, they mix, forming a lethal agent.

Cold War   A period of hostilities between the former Soviet Union and nations of the West.

Criminal terrorism   Organized crime using terrorism to achieve its objectives.

Dehumanization   Viewing and treating a person as an object that does not deserve the treatment ordinarily accorded humans.

Global economy   The economic interdependence of the nations of the world such that economic events are no longer isolated but have far-reaching ramifications on many nations.

Imperialism   The pursuit of unlimited geographic expansion.

Megaton   The explosive power of 1 million tons of TNT.

Military-industrial complex   The combined interests of the military and business to produce armaments. The military-industrial complex has become a potent political force in the contemporary world.

Mutual deterrence   Preventing a first strike by making the enemy fear that a massive retaliation would also destroy them.

Narco-terrorism   The combining of drug dealing and terrorism.

Pentagon capitalism   A term coined by Seymour Melman to refer to the influence of the Pentagon's armaments programs on the economy of the United States. Roughly equivalent to the military-industrial complex.

Political terrorism   Using the means of war to try to achieve political objectives. It is of four types: repressive terrorism, revolutionary terrorism, state-sponsored terrorism, and criminal terrorism.

Repressive terrorism   Terrorism directed by a government against its own citizens.

Revolutionary terrorism   Terrorism used in the attempt to bring about change in the political structure.

State-sponsored terrorism   A country supporting terrorism against another nation.

Total war   No-holds-barred warfare.

Unilateral disarmament   One nation disarming itself. When used to refer to a social policy, it generally means one nation taking some dramatic step in disarmament in order to encourage a similar step by the enemy.

War   Violent armed conflict between countries.

THINKING CRITICALLY ABOUT CHAPTER 15

1. Sociologist Nicholas Timasheff identified three essential conditions of war and seven "sparks" that can explode these conditions into war. Analyze two wars that the United States has participated in. In these two examples, what were the essential conditions and the sparks?

2. Which of the three perspectives (symbolic interactionism, functionalism, or conflict theory) do you think best explains why countries go to war? Explain.

3. The functions of war are summarized on pages 500–502. Apply these functions to the U.S. war on terrorism. How about the dysfunctions?

4. Do you think that the United States would ever be able to trust the other nuclear countries of the world if a worldwide treaty to destroy all nuclear weapons were signed? How would we be able to protect ourselves if just one country decided to secretly retain their weapons?

5. Do you think that it is justified for the United States to intervene in another country to protect our economic or political interests? Under what conditions is intervention justified? Explain.

6. Do you think that it is justified for another country to intervene in the United States to protect its economic or political interest? Under what conditions is intervention justified? Explain.

7. Do you think that nuclear war is more or less likely now than it was during the Cold War? Explain.

BIBLIOGRAPHY

"AA Fact File." Alcoholics Anonymous. Online, 2004.

Achenbaum, W. Andrew. *Old Age in the New Land: The American Experience Since 1970.* Baltimore: Johns Hopkins University Press, 1978

Alder, Christine. "Violence, Gender, and Social Change." *International Social Science Journal, 44,* 132, May, 1992:267–276.

Adler, Stephen J. "Lawyers Advise Concerns to Provide Precise Written Policy to Employees." *Wall Street Journal,* October 9, 1991:B1, B4.

Alihan, Milla A. *Social Ecology.* New York: Columbia University Press, 1938.

Allen, Charlotte Low. "Anti-Abortion Movement's Anti-Establishment Face." *Wall Street Journal,* December 8, 1988:A14.

Allen, Frank Edward. "Environment." *Wall Street Journal,* May 28, 1991.

Allman, William F., " A Laboratory of Human Conflict." *U.S. News & World Report,* April 11, 1988:57-58.

Allport, Gordon. *The Nature of Prejudice.* Reading, Mass.: Addison-Wesley, 1954.

Altman, Lawrence K. "Deadly Strain of Tuberculosis Is Spreading Fast, U.S. Finds." *New York Times,* January 24, 1991:A1, A10.

Amábile-Cuevas, Carlos. "New Antibiotics and New Resistance." *American Scientist Online,* March–April 2003.

American Civil Liberties Union. "ACLU Says Court Case Exposes America's Dirty Little Secret: The Criminal Justice System is Racially Biased." "Freedom Network." Online. February 26, 1996.

American Fact Finder. Washington, D.C.: U.S. Bureau of the Census, 2003.

American Lung Association. "Search Lung USA." November 2003.

American Savings Education Council. "Personal Savings Rate, 1929–1998." Online, 1999.

Amott, Teresa, and Julie Matthaei. *Race, Gender, and Work: A Multicultural Economic History of Women in the United States.* Boston: South End, 1991.

Andersen, Margaret L. *Thinking About Women: Sociological Perspectives on Sex and Gender.* New York: Macmillan, 1988.

Anderson, Elijah. *A Place on the Corner.* Chicago: University of Chicago Press, 1978.

Anderson, Elijah. *Streetwise: Race, Class, and Change in an Urban Community.* Chicago: University of Chicago Press, 1990.

Anderson, Elijah. "Streetwise." In *Down-to-Earth Sociology: Introductory Readings,* 10th ed., James M. Henslin, ed. New York: Free Press, 1999:193–202.

Anderson, Jack. "Chicago's Public Housing Official Tries to Thwart Gangs." *Alton Telegraph,* March 24, 1995:A6.

Anderson, Jack, and Jan Moller. "Gorton Under Republican Fire for Indian Wars." January 1998.

Anderson, Robert T. "From Mafia to Cosa Nostra." *American Journal of Sociology, 71,* November 1965:302–310.

Anslinger, Harry J., and Courtney Ryley Cooper. "Marijuana: Assassin of Youth." *American Magazine,* July 1937.

Anthrax Vaccination Immunization Program. Online, November 14, 2004.

Arías, Jesús. "La Junta rehabilita en Grenada casas que deberá tirar por ruina." *El Pais,* January 2, 1993:1.

Aries, Philippe. *Centuries of Childhood: A Social History of Family Life.* Robert Baldick (trans.). New York: Vintage, 1962.

Arlacchi, P. *Mafia, Peasants and Great Estates: Society in Traditional Calabria.* Cambridge: Cambridge University Press, 1980.

Armitage, Richard L. "Red Army Retreat Doesn't Signal End of U.S. Obligation." *Wall Street Journal,* February 7, 1989:A20.

Ashley, Richard. *Cocaine: Its History, Uses, and Effects.* New York: St. Martin's, 1975.

Ashley, Steven. "Divide and Vitrify." *Scientific American, 286,* 6, June 2002.

Ashworth, William. "The Great and Fragile Lakes." *Sierra,* November–December 1987:42–50.

Associated Press. "Father's Persistence Pays Off." February 12, 1995.

Associated Press. "Possible Listeria Contamination Prompts Meat and Poultry Recall." January 23, 1999.

Associated Press. "Bush Stands by Rejection of Kyoto Treaty." *New York Times,* November 6, 2004.

Aston, G., and V. Foubister. "MD and Physician Extender Turf War." *The American Medical News, 41,* 1998:27, 9–10.

Atchley, Robert C. "Dimensions of Widowhood in Later Life." *The Gerontologist, 15,* April 1975: 176–178.

Athens, Lonnie H. *Violent Criminal Acts and Actors: A Symbolic Interactionist Study.* Boston: Routledge, 1980.

Auerbach, Judith D. "Employer-Supported Child Care as a Women-Responsive Policy." *Journal of Family Issues, 11,* 4, December 1990:384–400.

Bagne, Paul. "High-Tech Breeding." In *Marriage and Family in a Changing Society,* 4th ed., James M. Henslin, ed. New York: Free Press, 1992:226–234.

Bahree, Bhushan. "U.S., Canada Can Penalize EU Over Its Ban on Beef." *Wall Street Journal,* July 13, 1999.

Bai, Matt. "Anatomy of a Massacre." *Newsweek,* May 3, 1999:25–31.

Bailey, Jeff. "Economics of Trash Shift as Cities Learn Dumps Aren't So Full." *Wall Street Journal,* June 2, 1992:A1, A7.

Ball, Jeffrey. "Auto Makers Race to Sell Cars Powered by Fuel Cells." *Wall Street Journal,* March 15, 1999.

Bandura, Albert, and Richard H. Walters. *Social Learning and Personality Development.* New York: Holt, 1963.

Barber, James Allen, Jr. "The Military-Industrial Complex." In *The Military and American Society: Essays and Readings,* Stephen E. Ambrose and James A. Barber, Jr., eds. New York: Free Press, 1972.

Bardwick, Judith M. *Psychology of Women: A Study of Bio-cultural Conflicts.* New York: Harper & Row, 1971.

Barnes, Edward, and William Shebar. "Quitting the Mafia." *Life,* December 1987:108–112.

Baron, Larry. "Immoral, Inviolate or Inconclusive?" *Society,* July/August 1987:6–12.

Bart, Pauline B., and Patricia H. O'Brien. "How the Women Stopped Their Rapes." *Signs, 10,* 1984.

Bart, Pauline B., and Patricia H. O'Brien. *Stopping Rape: Successful Survival Strategies.* New York: Pergamon, 1985.

Bartlett, Donald L., and James B. Steele. "Paying a Price for Polluters." *Time,* November 23, 1998:72–80.

Bartoi, Marla Green, and Bill N. Kinder. "Effects of Child and Adult Sexual Abuse on Adult Sexuality." *Journal of Sex & Marital Therapy, 24,* 1998:75–90.

Basler, Barbara. "Where Wall-to-Wall Means People." *New York Times,* October 3, 1988:A4.

Bayles, Fred. "Mass. to Allow Gay Marriage Monday." *USA Today,* May 17, 2004.

Beals, Ralph L., and Harry Hoijer. *An Introduction to Anthropology,* 3rd ed. New York: Macmillan, 1965.

Bearak, Barry. "India Tests Missile Able to Hit Deep Into Neighbor Lands." *New York Times,* April 12, 1999.

Beasley, Berrin, and Tracy Collins Standley. "Shirts vs. Skins: Clothing as an Indicator of Gender Role Stereotyping in Video Games." *Mass Communication and Society, 5,* 3, 2002:279–293.

Beck, Melinda. "Could It Happen in America?" *Newsweek,* December 17, 1984:38, 40, 44.

Becker, Howard S. "Editor's Introduction." In *Social Problems: A Modern Approach.* Howard S. Becker, ed. New York: Wiley, 1966:1–31.

Becker, Howard S. "History, Culture, and Subjective Experience: An Exploration of the Social Bases of Drug Induced Experiences." *Journal of Health and Social Behavior, 7,* June 1967:163–176.

Beddoe, Christine, C., Michael Hall, and Chris Ryan. *The Incidence of Sexual Exploitation of Children in Tourism.* Madrid: World Tourism Organization, 2001.

Beech, Hannah. "Unhappy Returns." *Time,* July 26–August 2, 2004.

Beeghley, Leonard. *The Structure of Social Stratification in the United States,* 4th ed. Boston: Allyn and Bacon, 2005.

Beirne, Piers, and Richard Quinney, eds. *Marxism and Law.* New York: Wiley, 1982.

Bell, Alan P., Martin S. Weinberg, and Sue Kiefer Hammersmith. *Sexual Preference: Its Development in Men and Women.* Bloomington: Indiana University Press, 1981.

Bell, Daniel. *The End of Ideology.* New York: Free Press, 1960.

Bell, David A. 1991. "An American Success Story: The Triumph of Asian-Americans." In *Sociological Footprints: Introductory Readings in Sociology,* 5th ed., Leonard Cargan and Jeanne H. Ballantine, eds. Belmont, Calif.: Wadsworth, 1991:308–316.

Belluck, Pam. "First-Ever Criminal Conviction Levied in Food Poisoning Case." *New York Times,* July 24, 1998a.

Belluck, Pam. "Forget Prisons: Americans Cry Out for the Pillory." *New York Times,* October 4, 1998b.

Bengtson, Vern L., Carolyn Rosenthal, and Linda Burton. "Families and Aging: Diversity and Heterogeneity." In *Handbook of Aging and the Social Sciences,* 3rd ed., Robert H. Binstock and Linda K.

George, eds. San Diego: Academic Press, 1990: 263–287.

Bengtson, Vern L., Gerardo Marti, and Robert E. L. Roberts. "Age-Group Relationships: Generational Equity and Inequity." In *Parent-Child Relations Throughout Life*, Karl Pillemer and Kathleen Mc-Cartney, eds. Hillsdale, N.J.: Lawrence Erlbaum Associates, 1991:253–278.

Benson, Michael L. "Denying the Guilty Mind: Accounting for Involvement in White-Collar Crime." *Criminology, 23,* November 1985:585–607.

Bergström, Hans. "Pressures Behind the Swedish Health Reforms." *Viewpoint Sweden, 12,* July 1992: 1–5.

Bernard, Jessie. *Women and the Public Interest: An Essay on Policy and Protest.* Chicago: Aldine-Atherton, 1971.

Bernard, Viola W., Perry Ottenberg, and Fritz Redl. "Dehumanization: A Composite Psychological Defense in Relation to Modern War." In *The Triple Revolution Emerging: Social Problems in Depth,* Robert Perucci and Marc Pilisuk, eds. Boston: Little, Brown, 1961:17–34.

Bernhardt, Eva M., and Frances K. Goldscheider. "Men, Resources, and Family Living: The Determination of Union and Parental Status in the United States and Sweden." *Journal of Marriage and the Family, 63,* 3, August 2001:793-803.

Bernstein, Deborah S. "Expanding the Split Labor Market Theory: Between and Within Sectors of the Split Labor Market of Mandatory Palestine." *Comparative Studies in Society and History, 38,* 2, April 1996:243–266.

Bernstein, Robert, and Mike Bergman. "Hispanic Population Reaches All-Time High of 38.8 Million, New Census Bureau Estimates Show." *U.S. Department of Commerce News,* June 18, 2003.

Berry, Brian J. L., and John D. Kasarda. *Contemporary Urban Ecology.* New York: Macmillan, 1977.

Bianchi, Suzanne M., Melissa A. Milkie, Liana C. Sayer, and John P. Robinson. "Is Anyone Doing the Housework? Trends in the Gender Division of Household Labor." *Social Forces, 79,* 1, September 2000:191–228.

Biddle, RiShawn. "The Ghost of Energy Crisis Past." *Reason,* April 1, 2001.

Bird, David. "Population: Winning the War." *New York Times,* January 30, 1977:Section 12, 22.

"Births, Marriages, and Divorce." National Center for Health Statistics. *National Vital Statistics, 52,* 3, February 13, 2004: Table A.

Bishop, Jerry E., and Ken Wells. "Two Scientists Claim Breakthrough in Quest for Fusion Energy." *Wall Street Journal,* March 24, 1989:A1, A5.

Blackstone, Sir William. *Commentaries on the Laws of England,* 4th ed., Thomas M. Cooley, ed. Chicago: Callaghan and Co., 1899.

Blainey, Geoffrey. *The Causes of War.* New York: Free Press, 1973.

Blakely, Mary Kay. "Is One Woman's Sexuality Another Woman's Pornography?" *Ms.,* April 1985:37–47.

Blau, Francine D. "Women in the Labor Force: An Overview." In *Women: A Feminist Perspective,* Jo Freeman, ed. Palo Alto, Calif.: Mayfield, 1975: 211–226.

Block, Richard, and Wesley G. Skogan. "Resistance and Outcome in Robbery and Rape: Nonfatal, Stranger to Stranger Violence." Mimeo, 1982.

Blok, Anton. *The Mafia of a Sicilian Village: A Study of Violent Peasant Entrepreneurs.* New York: Harper Torchbooks, 1974.

Blum, Richard H., and Associates. *Drugs I, Society and Drugs: Social and Cultural Observations.* San Francisco: Jossey-Bass, 1969.

Blum, Richard H., Eva Blum, and E. Garfield. *Drug Education: Results and Recommendations.* Lexington, Mass.: Heath, 1976.

Blumberg, Abraham S. "The Practice of Law as Confidence Game: Organizational Cooptation of a Profession." *Law and Social Review, 1,* 1967:15–39.

Blumemthal, Ralph. "Polluted Midwest Rain Is Killing New York Lakes." *Alton Telegraph,* June 8, 1981.

Blumstein, Alfred, and Jacqueline Cohen. "Characterizing Criminal Careers." *Science, 237,* August 1987: 985–991.

Bogo, Jennifer. "Consider the Source: How Clean Is Your Bottled Water?" *E/The Environmental Magazine,* March 1, 2001.

Bonow, Robert O., and Robert H. Eckel. "Diet, Obesity, and Cardiovascular Risk." *New England Journal of Medicine, 348,* 17, May 22, 2003:2057–2058.

Boot, Max. "Your Money or Your Life? That Depends." *Wall Street Journal,* March 4, 1998:A18.

Booth, Alan, and James M. Dabbs, Jr. "Testosterone and Men's Marriages." *Social Forces, 72,* 2, December 1993: 463–477.

Boston, Guy D., Kevin O'Brien, and Joanne Palumbo, *Terrorism: A Selected Bibliography,* 2nd ed. Washington, D. C.: National Institute of Law Enforcement and Criminal Justice, March 1977.

Bowen, Crosswell. "Donora, Pennsylvania." In *Society and Environment: The Coming Collision,* Rex R.

Campbell and Jerry L. Wade, eds. Boston: Allyn & Bacon, 1972:163–168.

Boyle, Elizabeth Heger, Fortunata Songora, and Gail Foss. "International Discourse and Local Politics: Anti-Female-Genital-Cutting Laws in Egypt, Tanzania, and the United States." *Social Problems, 48,* 4, November 2001:524–544.

Brace, Charles Loring. *The Dangerous Classes of New York and Twenty Years' Work Among Them,* 3rd ed. New York: Wynkoop and Hallenbeck, 1880.

Bramlett, M. D., and W. D. Mosher. "Cohabitation, Marriage, Divorce, and Remarriage in the United States." Hyatsville, Md.: National Center for Health Statistics, Vital Health Statistics, Series 23, Number 22, July 2002.

Brannigan, Augustine. "Is Obscenity Criminogenic?" *Society,* July/August 1987:12–19.

Brecher, Edward M., and the Editors of *Consumer Reports. Licit and Illicit Drugs.* Boston: Little, Brown, 1972.

Bremer, L. Paul III. "Terrorism: Myths and Reality." *Department of State Bulletin,* May 1988:63.

Bridges, George S., and Sara Stein. "Racial Disparities in Official Assessments of Juvenile Offenders: Attributional Stereotypes as Mediating Mechanisms." *American Sociological Review, 63,* August 1998: 554–570.

Brinkhoff, Thomas. "City Population." http://www.citypopulation.de, 2004.

Broad, William J., and Judith Miller. "Rocky Start for U.S. Plan to Stockpile Vaccines to Fight Germ Warfare." *New York Times,* August 7, 1998.

Brockerhoff, Martin P. "An Urbanizing World." *Population Bulletin, 55,* 3, September 2000:1–44.

Broder, M. S., D. E. Kanouse, B. S. Mittman, and S. J. Bernstein. "The Appropriateness of Recommendations for Hysterectomy." *Obstetrics and Gynecology, 95,* February 2000:199–205.

Brody, Elaine M. "The Aging of the Family." *Annals of the American Academy of Political and Social Science, 438,* July 1978:13–27.

Brody, Jane E. "1,100 Tested in Michigan for Effects of Toxin That Poisoned Food in '73." *New York Times,* November 5, 1976.

Broff, Nancy. Statements supplied to the author from NARAL, January 1989.

Brooke, James. "Deep Desert Grave Awaits First Load of Nuclear Waste." *New York Times,* March 26, 1999.

Brooks, Jack. *HHS' Failure to Enforce the Food, Drug, and Cosmetic Act: The Case of Cancer-Causing Color Additives.* Eleventh Report of the Committee on Government Operations. Washington, D.C.: U.S. Government Printing Office, 1985.

Brooks, Jack. *FDA Continues to Permit the Illegal Marketing of Carcinogenic Additives.* Twenty-fifth Report of the Committee on Government Operations. Washington, D.C.: U.S. Government Printing Office, 1987.

Brooks, Virginia R. "Sex Differences in Student Dominance Behavior in Female and Male Professors' Classrooms." *Sex Roles, 8,* 7, 1982:683–690.

Brown, Donald A. "The Ethical Dimensions of Global Environmental Issues." *Daedalus, 130,* 4, Fall 2001: 59–69.

Brown, Janet Welsh. *Environmental Defense Fund Letter.* New York, n.d.

Brown, Lester R. "'Human Element,' Not Drought, Causes Famine." *U.S. News & World Report,* February 25, 1985:71–72.

Brown, Lester R. "Food Growth Slowdown: Danger Signal for the Future." In *Food Policy: Integrating Supply, Distribution, and Consumption,* J. Price Gittinger, Joanne Leslie, and Caroline Hoisington, eds. Baltimore: Johns Hopkins University Press, 1987:89–102.

Brown, Michael H. "Love Canal and the Poisoning of America." *The Atlantic, 235,* December 1979: 33–47.

Brown, Richard Maxwell. "Historical Patterns of Violence in America." In *Violence in America: Historical and Comparative Perspectives.* Hugh Davis Graham and Ted Robert Gurr, eds. New York: Bantam, 1969.

Brownfield, David, and Ann Marie Sorenson. "Self-Control and Juvenile Delinquency: Theoretical Issues and an Empirical Assessment of Selected Elements of a General Theory of Crime." *Deviant Behavior, 14,* July–September 1993:243–264.

Brownmiller, Susan. *Against Our Will: Men, Women, and Rape.* New York: Simon & Schuster, 1975.

Buck, K. J. "Recent Progress Toward the Identification of Genes Related to Risk for Alcoholism." *Mamm Genome, 12,* December 9, 1998:927–928.

Budiansky, Stephen A. "The Trees Fell—And So Did the People." *U.S. News & World Report,* February 9, 1987:75.

Buff, Stephen A. "Lois Lee Takes Back Children from the Night." *ASA Footnotes, 15,* 5, May, 1987:1, 2.

Bulkeley, William M. "Untested Treatments, Cures Find Stronghold on On-Line Services." *Wall Street Journal,* February 27, 1995:A1, A7.

Bullock, Henry A. "Significance of the Racial Factor in the Length of Prison Sentences." *Journal of Criminal Law, Criminology, and Police Science, 52,* September–October 1961:411–417.

Burch, William R., Jr. *Daydreams and Nightmares: A Sociological Essay on the American Environment.* New York: Harper & Row, 1971.

Burgess, Ann Wolbert, and Lynda Lytle Holmstrom. "Rape Trauma Syndrome." *American Journal of Psychiatry, 131,* 1974:981–986.

Burgess, Ernest W. "The Growth of the City: An Introduction to a Research Project." In *The City,* Robert E. Park, Ernest W. Burgess, and Roderick D. McKenzie, eds. Chicago: University of Chicago Press, 1925 (pages 47–62 in the 1967 edition).

Burns, John F. "Bangladesh, Still Poor, Cuts Birth Rate Sharply." *New York Times,* September 13, 1994:A10.

Burros, Marian. "Clinton Pressures Congress for Money to Ensure Safety of Food." *New York Times,* July 4, 1998.

Burros, Marian. "Experts Worry About the Return of a Deadly Germ in Cold Cuts." *New York Times,* March 14, 1999.

Burroughs, William. "Excerpts from 'Deposition: Testimony Concerning a Sickness.'" In *Drugs in American Life,* Morrow Wilson and Suzanne Wilson, eds. New York: Wilson, 1975:133–158.

Burton, Velmer S., Jr., Francis T. Cullen, T. David Evans, Leanne Fiftal Alarid, and R. Gregory Dunaway. "Gender, Self-Control, and Crime." *Journal of Research in Crime and Delinquency, 35,* 2, May 1998:123–147.

Bush, George. *Public Report of the Vice President's Task Force on Combatting Terrorism.* Washington, D.C.: U.S. Government Printing Office, February 1986.

Butterfield, Fox. "Prison Population Increases as Release of Inmates Slows." *New York Times,* January 11, 1999.

Cain, Glen G., and Douglas A. Wissoker. "A Re-analysis of Marital Stability in the Seattle–Denver Income-Maintenance Experiment." *American Journal of Sociology, 95,* 5, March 1990:1235–1269.

Calle, Eugenia E., Carmen Rodriguez, Kimberly Walker-Thurmond, and Michael J. Thun. "Overweight, Obesity, and Mortality from Cancer in a Prospectively Studied Cohort of U.S. Adults." *New England Journal of Medicine, 348,* 17, April 24, 2003.

Campbell, Duncan. "Electronic Tagging May be Used for Prisoners Released on Parole." *The Guardian,* August 12, 1995.

Campbell, John L. "The State and the Nuclear Waste Crisis: An Institutional Analysis of Policy Constraints." *Social Problems, 34,* 1, February 1987: 18–33.

Campo-Flores, Arian. "A Crackdown on Call Girls." *Newsweek,* September 2, 2002.

"Canada Tries to Bar Pro-Nazi View on the Internet." *New York Times,* August 2, 1998.

Cancian, Maria, Marieka M. Klawitter, Daniel R. Meyer, Ann Rangarajan, Geoffrey Wallace, and Robert G. Wood. "Income and Program Participation Among Early TANF Recipients: The Evidence from New Jersey, Washington, and Wisconsin." *Focus, 22,* 3, Summer 2003:2–10.

Caplow, Theodore. *Middletown Families: Fifty Years of Change and Continuity.* Minneapolis: University of Minnesota Press, 1982.

Carlson, Kenneth, and Jan Chaiken. "White Collar Crime." Special Report of the Bureau of Justice Statistics. Washington, D.C.: U.S. Department of Justice, September 1987.

Carlson, Lewis H., and George A. Colburn. *In their Place: White America Defines Her Minorities, 1850–1950.* New York: Wiley, 1972.

Carlson, Rick J. *The End of Medicine.* New York: Wiley, 1975.

Carnevale, Mary Lu. "New Jolt for Nynex: Bawdy 'Conventions' of Buyers, Suppliers." *Wall Street Journal,* July 12, 1990:A1, A6.

Carroll, Charles R. *Drugs in Modern Society,* 5th ed. Boston: McGraw-Hill, 2000.

Carroll, Peter N., and David W. Noble. *The Free and the Unfree: A New History of the United States.* New York: Penguin, 1977.

Carton, Barbara. "At Jenny Craig, Men Are Ones Who Claim Sex Discrimination." *Wall Street Journal,* November 29, 12994:A1, A7.

Cass, Vivienne C. "Homosexual Identity Formation: A Theoretical Model." *Journal of Homosexuality, 4,* Spring 1979:219–235.

Castaneda, Carlos. *The Teachings of Don Juan: A Yaqui Way of Knowledge.* New York: Ballantine, 1968.

Castaneda, Carlos. *A Separate Reality: Further Conversations with Don Juan.* New York: Simon & Schuster, 1971.

Castaneda, Carlos. *Tales of Power.* New York: Simon & Schuster, 1974.

Castells, Manuel. *The Urban Question: A Marxist Approach.* Alan Sheridan, trans. Cambridge, Mass.: MIT Press, 1977.

Castells, Manuel. *The City and the Grass Roots.* Berkeley: University of California Press, 1983.

Castells, Manuel. *The Informational City*. Oxford, England: Blackwell, 1989.

Catanzaro, Raimondo. *Men of Respect: A Social History of the Mafia*. New York: Free Press, 1992.

Cates, Jim A., and Jeffrey Markley. "Demographic, Clinical, and Personality Variables Associated with Male Prostitution By Choice." *Adolescence, 27,* 107, Fall 1992:695–706.

Centers for Disease Control. "HIV/AIDS Surveillance—General Epidemiology," 2004.

Chafetz, Janet Saltzman. *Gender Equity: An Integrated Theory of Stability and Change*. Newbury Park, Calif.: Sage, 1990.

Chagnon, Napoleon A. "Life Histories, Blood Revenge, and Warfare in a Tribal Population." *Science*, February 26, 1988:985–992.

Chalkey, Kate. "Female Genital Mutilation: New Laws, Programs Try to End Practice." *Population Today, 25,* 10, October 1997:4–5.

Chambliss, William J. "The Saints and the Roughnecks." In *Down-to-Earth Sociology: Introductory Readings,* 13th ed., James M. Henslin, ed. New York: Free Press, 2005:281–296.

Cheng, V. "328 Useful Drugs Are Said to Lie Hidden in Tropical Forests." *New York Times,* June 27, 1995:C4.

Cherlin, Andrew J. "A 'Quieting' of Change." *Contexts, 1,* 1, Spring 2002:67–68.

Chernoff, Nina W., and Rita J. Simon. "Women and Crime the World Over." *Gender Issues, 18,* 3, Summer 2000:5–20.

Chesler, Mark A., Barbara Chesney, and Benjamin Gidron. "Israel and U.S. Orientations Toward Self-Help Groups for Families in Crisis." *Non-profit and Voluntary Sector Quarterly, 19,* 3, Fall 1990: 251–262.

Chilman, Catherine S. "Public Policies and Families." In *Mental Illness, Delinquency, Addictions, and Neglect,* Elam W. Nunnally, Catherine S. Chilman, and Fred M. Cox, eds. Newbury Park, Calif.: Sage, 1988: 189–197.

Cho, Eunyoung, et al. "Dairy Foods, Calcium, and Colorectal Cancer: A Pooled Analysis of 10 Cohort Studies." *Journal of the National Cancer Institute, 96,* 13, July 7, 2004:1015–1022.

Churchill, Ward, and Jim Vander Wall. 1990. *Agents of Repression: The FBI's Secret Wars Against the Black Panther Party and the American Indian Movement*. Boston: South End Press.

"Citibank Thieves Transferred $12M." 1995. Online.

Clarke, Steve. "Earnings of Men and Women in the EU: The Gap Narrowing But Only Slowly." *Eurostat: Statistics in Focus: Population and Social Conditions,* 2001.

Clausing, Jeri. "Senate Adds Internet Proposals to Spending Bill." *New York Times Bulletin,* July 22, 1998.

Clawson, Patrick. "Terrorism in Decline?" *Orbis, 32,* Spring 1988:263–276.

Cleaver, Eldridge. *Soul on Ice*. New York: McGraw-Hill, 1968.

Clinard, Marshall B. *Corporate Corruption: The Abuse of Power*. New York: Praeger, 1990.

Clinard, Marshall B., Peter C. Yeager, Jeanne Brisette, David Petrashek, and Elizabeth harries. *Illegal Corporate Behavior*. Washington, D.C.: U.S. Department of Justice, 1979.

Clines, Francis X. "Soviets Now Admit '57 Nuclear Blast." *New York Times,* June 18, 1998.

Clinton, Hillary Rodham. *It Takes a Village: And Other Lessons Children Teach Us*. New York: Touchstone Books, 1997.

Cloward, Richard A., and Lloyd E. Ohlin. *Delinquency and Opportunity: A Theory of Delinquent Gangs*. New York: Free Press, 1960.

CNN. "Supreme Court Strikes Down Texas Sodomy Law." November 18, 2003.

CNN. "Massachusetts Court Rules Ban on Gay Marriage Unconstitutional." February 4, 2004.

Cockerham, William C. *This Aging Society*. Englewood Cliffs, N.J.: Prentice Hall, 1991.

Cockerham, William C. "The Social Determinants of the Decline of Life Expectancy in Russia and Eastern Europe: A Lifestyle Explanation." *Journal of Health and Social Behavior, 38,* June 1997:117–130.

Cohen, Albert K. *Delinquent Boys: The Culture of the Gang*. New York: Free Press, 1955.

Cohen, Elizabeth. "Shrinks Aplenty Online, But Are They Credible?" *New York Times,* January 17, 1997.

Cohen, Jacqueline. "The Incapacitative Effect of Imprisonment: A Critical Review of the Literature." In *Deterrence and Incapacitation: Estimating the Effects of Criminal Sanctions on Crime Rates,* Alfred Blumstein, Jacqueline Cohen, and Daniel Nagin, eds. Washington, D.C.: National Academy of Sciences, 1978.

Cohen, Morris R. "Moral Aspects of the Criminal Law." *Yale Law Journal, 49,* April 1940:1009–1026.

Cohen, Murray, Theoharis Seghorn, and Wilfred Calamas. "Sociometric Study of the Sex Offender." *Journal of Abnormal Psychology, 74,* April 1969: 249–255.

Colarossi, A. "Judge Orders Man With TB Into Hospital." *Orlando Sentinel,* February 22, 2001.

Coleman, James William. *The Criminal Elite: The Sociology of White Collar Crime*. New York: St. Martin's, 1989.

Coleman, James William. "Politics and the Abuse of Power." In *Down-to-Earth Sociology: Introductory Readings,* 8th ed., James M. Henslin, ed. New York: Free Press, 1995:442–450.

Coltrane, Scott, and Melinda Messineo. "The Perpetuation of Subtle Prejudice: Race and Gender Imagery in 1990s Television Advertising." *Sex Roles: A Journal of Research,* 2000.

Comer, James P. "Education for Community." In *Common Decency: Domestic Policies After Reagan,* Alvin L. Schorr, ed. New Haven, Conn.: Yale University Press, 1986:186-209.

Commoner, Barry. *The Closing Circle: Nature, Man, and Technology.* New York: Bantam, 1972.

Comons, Marlene. "Scientists Study Gender Gap in Drug Response." *Los Angeles Times,* June 6, 1999.

"Congress Looks to Fund Efforts to Beat Back Fetal Alcohol Syndrome." *The Nation's Health, 24,* 3, March 1994:5.

Conley, Dalton. "Capital for College: Parental Assets and Postsecondary Schooling." *Sociology of Education, 74,* 1, January 2001:59–68.

Conner, Roger L. "Demographic Doomsayers: Five Myths About Population." *Current,* February 1990: 21–25.

Conrad, Peter. "The Discovery of Hyperkinesis: Notes on the Medicalization of Deviant Behavior." *Social Problems, 23,* October 1975:12–21.

Conrad, Peter. "Learning to Doctor: Reflections on Medical School." In *Down-to-Earth Sociology: Introductory Readings,* 8th ed., James M. Henslin, ed. New York: Free Press, 1995:420–430.

Conti, Massimo. "The Famine Controversy." *World Press Review, 27,* January 1980:56.

Convensky, Milton. "Postindustrial Society and the Family." University of California, University Extension, Courses by Newspapers, San Diego, 1980.

Corcoran, Mary, Greg J. Duncan, Gerald Gurin, and Patricia Gurin. "Myth and Reality: The Causes and Persistence of Poverty." *Journal of Policy Analysis and Management, 4,* 4, 1985:516–536.

Cornell, George W. "Modern Persecutions Mirror Those of Jesus." AP, April 13, 1981.

Corzine, Jay, and Richard Kirby. "Cruising the Truckers: Sexual Encounters in a Highway Rest Area." *Urban Life, 6,* July 1977:171–192.

Cose, Ellis. "The Good News About Black America." *Newsweek,* June 7, 1999:29–40.

Coser, Lewis A. *The Functions of Social Conflict.* New York: Free Press, 1956.

Coser, Lewis A. *Masters of Sociological Thought: Ideas in Historical and Social Context.* New York: Harcourt, 1977.

Cowley, Joyce. *Pioneers of Women's Liberation.* New York: Merit, 1969.

Cressey, Donald R. *Other People's Money.* New York: Free Press, 1953.

Cressey, Donald R. "Methodological Problems in the Study of Organized Crime as a Social Problem." *Annals of the American Academy of Political and Social Science, 347,* November 1967:101–122.

Cressey, Donald R. *Theft of the Nation: The Structure and Operations of Organized Crime in America.* New York: Harper & Row, 1969.

Crider, Raquel. "Phencyclidine: Changing Abuse Patterns." In *Phencyclidine: An Update,* Doris H. Clouet, ed. Rockville, Md.: National Institute on Drug Abuse, 1986:163–173.

Crisp, Anthony D. "Making Substance Abuse Prevention Relevant for Low-Income Black Neighborhoods." *Journal of Psychedelic Drugs, 12,* January–March 1980:13–19.

Critchfield, Richard. "China's Agricultural Success Story." *Wall Street Journal,* January 13, 1986:25.

Crossette, Barbara. "Official Toll Reaches 92,000 in Bangladesh Cyclone." *New York Times,* May 4, 1991:A1.

Cuffel, B., W. Goldman, and H. Schlesinger. "Does Managing Behavioral Health Care Services Increase the Cost of Providing Medical Care? *Journal of Behavioral Health Services and Research* 26, 4, 1999:372–380.

Cumming, Elaine, and William E. Henry. *Growing Old: The Process of Disengagement.* New York: Basic Books, 1961.

Currie, Elliott. *Confronting Crime: An American Challenge.* New York: Pantheon, 1985.

Cushman, John H. "Industries Press Plan for Credits in Emissions Control." *New York Times,* January 3, 1999.

Dabbs, James M., Jr., and Robin Morris. "Testosterone, Social Class, and Antisocial Behavior in a Sample of 4,462 Men." *Psychological Science, 1,* 3, May 1990: 209–211.

Dahrendorf, Ralf. *Class and Class Conflict in Industrial Society.* Stanford, Calif.: Stanford University Press, 1959.

Dahrendorf, Ralf. "Toward a Theory of Social Conflict." In *Social Change: Sources, Patterns, and Consequences,* Amitai Etzioni and Eva Etzioni, eds. New York: Basic Books, 1973.

Daly, Martin, and Margo Wilson. *Homicide.* New York: Aldine de Gruyter, 1988.

Daly, Michael, and Kenneth Minton. "Conan the Bacterium." *The Sciences.* July—August, 1998.

Daniels, Roger. *The Decision to Relocate the Japanese Americans.* Philadelphia: Lippincott, 1975.

Dao, James. "U.S. Government Joins Oneida Indians' Suit Against New York State." *New York Times,* January 13, 1999.

Dash, Leon. "When Children Want Children." *Society,* 27, 5, July–August 1990:17–19.

Davey, Monica. "Missourians Back Ban on Same-Sex Marriage." *New York Times,* August 4, 2004.

Davies, J. Clarence, III, and Barbara S. Davies. *The Politics of Pollution,* 2nd ed. Indianapolis, Ind.: Bobbs-Merrill, 1975.

Davis, Angela. *Angela Davis: An Autobiography.* New York: Random House, 1974.

Davis, Kingsley. "The Sociology of Prostitution." *American Sociological Review, 2,* October 1937: 744–755.

Davis, Kingsley. "Sexual Behavior." In *Contemporary Social Problems,* 2nd ed., Robert Merton and Robert Nisbet, eds. New York: Harcourt, 1966.

Davis, Nancy J., and Robert V. Robinson. "Class Identification of Men and Women in the 1970s and 1980s." *American Sociological Review, 53,* February 1988:103–112.

Davis, Nanette J. "Prostitution: Identity, Career, and Legal-Economic Enterprise." In *The Sociology of Sex: An Introductory Reader,* James M. Henslin and Edward Sagarin (eds.). New York: Schocken, 1978: 297–322.

Davis, Natalie Zemon. "Families in the Past." University of California, San Diego, Courses by Newspaper, University Extension, 1980.

Daws, Gavin. *Prisoners of the Japanese: POWs of World War II in the Pacific.* New York: Morrow, 1994.

Day, Charles R., Jr. "Tear Up the Tracks." *Industry Week, 239,* 5, March 5, 1990:5.

De Beauvoir, Simone. *The Second Sex.* New York: Knopf, 1953.

Deevey, E. S., Don S. Rice, Prudence M. Rice, H. H. Vaughan, Mark Brennes, and M. S. Flannery. "Mayan Urbanism: Impact on a Tropical Karst Environment." *Science,* October 19, 1979:298–306.

Delph, Edward William. *The Silent Community: Public Homosexual Encounters.* Beverly Hills, Calif.: Sage, 1978.

De Mott, Benjamin. "The Pro-Incest Lobby." *Psychology Today, 13,* March 1980:11–12, 15–16.

Denes, Magda. *In Necessity and Sorrow: Life and Death in an Abortion Hospital.* New York: Basic Books, 1976.

DeOilos, Ione Y., and Carolyn A. Kapinus. "Aging Childless Individuals and Couples: Suggestions for New Directions in Research." *Sociological Inquiry, 72,* 1, Winter 2002:72–80.

Department of Homeland Security, online, home page, November 14, 2004.

DeRios, Marlene Dobkin, and David E. Smith. "Drug Use and Abuse in Cross-Cultural Perspective." *Human Organization, 36,* 1977:14–21.

de Silva, Rex. 1980. "Developing the Third World." *World Press Review,* May 1980:48.

DeSouza, Eros, and A. Gigi Fansler. "Contrapower Sexual Harassment: A Survey of Students and Faculty Members." *Sex Roles, 48,* 11/12, June 2003: 529–542.

Devine, Michael A. "A Fresh Look at Cogeneration." *Energy User News, 29,* 1, September 2004:13–15.

Diamond, Milton, and Ayako Uchiyama. "Pornography, Rape, and Sex Crimes in Japan." *International Journal of Law and Psychiatry, 22,* 1, 1999:1–22.

Diaz-Calderon, Joseph. "Letters to the author." September 1996 and March 1997.

DiChiara, Albert, and Russell Chabot. "Gangs and the Contemporary Urban Struggle: An Unappreciated Aspect of Change." In *Gangs and Society: Alternative Perspectives,* Louis Kontos, David Brotherton, and Luis Barrios, eds. New York: Columbia University Press, 2003:77–94.

Dickey, Christopher, and Adam Rogers. "Smoke and Mirrors." *Newsweek,* February 25, 2002.

Dickson, Donald T. "Bureaucracy and Morality: An Organizational Perspective on a Moral Crusade." *Social Problems, 16,* Fall 1968:143–156.

DiEugenio, James. "The Posthumous Assassination of JFK, Part II." *Probe, 5,* 1, November—December, 1997.

Digest of Education Statistics. Washington, D.C.: U.S. Department of Education, November 1991.

DiIulio, John J., Jr. "The Value of Prisons." *Wall Street Journal,* May 13, 1992:A16.

Dingell, John D. *Sulfites: Hearing Before the Subcommittee on Oversight and Investigations of the Committee on Energy and Commerce, House of Representatives.* Washington, D.C.: U.S. Government Printing Office, March 27, 1985.

Dobyns, Henry F. *Their Numbers Became Thinned: Native American Population Dynamics in Eastern*

North America. Knoxville: University of Tennessee Press, 1983.

Doerner, William G. "The Index of Southernness Revisited: The Influence of Wherefrom upon Whodunnit." *Criminology, 16,* May 1978:47–56.

Dollard, John, Neal E. Miller, Leonard W. Doob, O. H. Mowrer, and Robert R. Sears. *Frustration and Aggression*. New Haven, Conn.: Yale University Press, 1961 (originally published in 1939).

Domhoff, G. William. *The Bohemian Grove and Other Retreats: A Study in Ruling-Class Cohesiveness*. New York: Harper & Row, 1974.

Domhoff, G. William. *The Powers That Be*. New York: Random House, 1978a.

Domhoff, G. William. *Who Really Rules?* New Brunswick, N.J.: Transaction, 1978b.

Domhoff, G. William. *The Power Elite and the State: How Policy Is Made in America*. New York: Aldine de Gruyter, 1990.

Domhoff, G. William. *Who Rules America? Power and Politics in the Year 2000,* 3rd ed. Mountain View, Calif.: Mayfield Publishers, 1998.

Donaldson, Samuel. "World News Tonight." May 25, 1992.

Douglass, Joseph D. "A Biological Weapons Threat Worse Than Saddam." *Wall Street Journal,* March 10, 1998:A22.

Douvan, Elizabeth. "Is the American Family Obsolete?" University of California, University Extension, Courses by Newspaper, San Diego, 1980.

Dove, Adrian. "Soul folk 'Chitling' Test or the Dove Counterbalance Intelligence Test." Mimeo, n.d..

Dowie, Mark. "Pinto Madness." *Mother Jones, 2,* September–October 1977:18–32.

Dowie, Mark. 1979. "The Corporate Crime of the Century." *Mother Jones, 4,* November 1979:23–25, 37.

Draper, R. "The History of Advertising in America." *New York Review of Books 33,* June 26, 1986: 14–18.

Drug Dependence in Pregnancy: Clinical Management of Mother and Child. Rockville, Md.: U.S. Department of Health, Education, and Welfare, 1979.

Dubar, Helen. "American Discovers Child Pornography." In *Human Sexuality 80/81,* James R. Barbour (ed.). Guilford, Conn.: Dushkin, 1980.

Dufay, Joanne. "Ten Years After Chernobyl: A Witness to the Devastation." Greenpeace online, n.d..

Durkheim, Emile. *The Division of Labor in Society,* George Simpson, trans. New York: Free Press, 1964 (originally published in 1893).

Durkheim, Emile. *Suicide,* John A. Spaulding and George Simpson, trans. New York: Free Press, 1951 (originally published in 1897).

Durkheim, Emile. *The Rules of Sociological Method,* Sir George E. G. Catlin, ed. New York: Macmillan, 1938. Originally published in 1904. (8th ed. 1950)

Durkheim, Emile. *Elementary Forms of the Religious Life,* Joseph Weld Swain, trans. New York: Free Press, 1965 (originally published in 1912).

Durning, Alan. "Cradles of Life." In *Social Problems 90/91,* Leroy W. Barnes, ed. Guilford, Conn.: Dushkin, 1990:231–241.

Duskin, Edgar W. "Environment Continues to Get Better." *Southwest Farm Press,* August 7, 2003.

Duster, Troy. *The Legalization of Morality: Law, Drugs, and Moral Judgment*. New York: Free Press, 1970.

Duster, Troy. "From Structural Analysis to Public Policy." *Contemporary Sociology, 17,* 3, May 1988: 287–290.

Dye, Lee. "Tiny Firm Sees Process as Big Answer to Waste." *Los Angeles Times,* March 1, 1999.

Eastland, Terry. "Weed and Seed: Root Out Crime, Nurture Poor." *Wall Street Journal,* May 14, 1992:A14.

Eberstadt, Nick. *The Poverty of Communism*. New Brunswick, N.J.: Transaction, 1988.

Ebomoyi, Ehigie. "The Prevalence of Female Circumcision in Two Nigerian Communities." *Sex Roles, 17,* 3/4, 1987:139–151.

eDrugstore.MD. Online pharmacy. July 5, 2004.

Ehrenfeld, Rachel. *Narcoterrorism*. New York: Basic Books, 1990.

Ehrenreich, Barbara, and Deirdre English. *Witches, Midwives, and Nurses: A History of Women Healers*. Old Westbury, N.Y.: Feminist Press, 1973.

Ehrlich, Elizabeth. "The Mommy Track." *Business Week,* March 20, 1989:126–134.

Ehrlich, Paul R., and Anne H. Ehrlich. *Population, Resources, and Environment: Issues in Human Ecology,* 2nd ed. San Francisco: Freeman, 1972.

Ehrlich, Paul R., and Anne H. Ehrlich. *Extinction: The Causes and Consequences of the Disappearance of Species*. New York: Random House, 1981.

Eisenhart, R. Wayne. "You Can't Hack It, Little Girl: A Discussion of the Covert Psychological Agenda of Modern Combat Training." *Journal of Social Issues, 31,* Fall 1975:13–23.

Eisenhower, Dwight D. "From 'Farewell Address to the Nation,' January 17, 1961." In *The Military and American Society: Essays and Readings,* Stephen E. Ambrose and James A. Barber, Jr., eds. New York: Free Press, 1972:61–63.

Eisinger, Peter K. *The Politics of Displacement: Racial and Ethnic Transition in Three American Cities.* Campbell Calif.: Academic Press, 1980.

Elias, Paul. "Molecular Pharmers' Hope to Raise Human Proteins in Crop Plants." *St. Louis Post-Dispatch,* October 28, 2001:F7.

Ellis, Havelock. "Mescal: A New Artificial Paradise." *Annual Report of the Smithsonian Institution, 52,* 1897:547–548.

Ellis, Havelock. "Mescal: A Study of a Divine Plant." *Popular Science Monthly, 61,* 1902:52–71.

Engelmayer, Paul A. "Violence by Students, from Rape to Racism, Raises College Worries." *Wall Street Journal,* November 21, 1983:1, 18.

Englund, Will, and Gary Cohn. "A Third World Dump for America's Ships?" *Baltimore Sun,* December 9, 1997.

Environmental Protection Agency. "The Great Lakes: Report to Congress on the Great Lakes Ecosystem." February 1994.

Environmental Protection Agency. "Reduction of Toxic Loadings to the Niagara River From Hazardous Waste Sites in the United States." November 1998.

Epstein, Cynthia Fuchs. "Inevitabilities of Prejudice." *Society,* September–October 1986:7–13.

Epstein, Cynthia Fuchs. *Deceptive Distinctions: Sex, Gender, and the Social Order.* New Haven, Conn.: Yale University Press, 1988.

Epstein, Cynthia Fuchs. Letter to the author, January 26, 1989.

Epstein, Samuel S. "International Scientific Committee Warns of Serious Risk of Breast and Prostate Cancer from Monsanto's Hormonal Milk." Press Release, March 21, 1999.

Erik, John. "China's Policy on Births." *New York Times,* January 3, 1982:IV, 19.

Escalante, Jaime, and Jack Dirmann. "The Jaime Escalante Math Program." *Journal of Negro Education, 59,* 3, Summer 1990:407–423.

Espenshade, Thomas J. "A Short History of U.S. Policy toward Illegal Immigration." *Population Today,* February 1990:6–9.

Etzioni, Amitai. "Letter to the Editor: Porn Filters Are a Net Benefit." *Wall Street Journal,* November 3, 1998:A23.

Faison, Seth, Jr. "Friend Says Girl Killed on Train Resisted Robbery of Other Girls." *New York Times,* September 22, 1991:34.

Farah, Douglas. "Russian Gangs Amplify Drug Threat." *The Seattle Times,* September 29, 1999.

Farah, Judy. "Crime and Creative Punishment." *Wall Street Journal,* March 15, 1995:A15.

Faris, R. E. L., and W. W. Dunham. *Mental Disorders in Urban Areas.* Chicago: University of Chicago Press, 1939.

Farney, Dennis. "On the Great Plains, Life Becomes a Fight for Water and Survival." *Wall Street Journal,* August 16, 1989:A1, A12.

Farney, Dennis. "They Hold the Cards, But After All, They Do Own the Casino." *Wall Street Journal,* February 5, 1998:A1, A6.

Faunce, William A. *Problems of an Industrial Society,* 2nd ed. New York: McGraw-Hill, 1981.

Faupel, Charles E., and Carl B. Klockars. "Drugs-Crime Connections: Elaborations from the Life Histories of Hard-Core Addicts." *Social Problems, 34,* 1, February 1987:54–68.

FBI Uniform Crime Reports. Washington, D.C.: U.S. Government Printing Office, annual.

Federal Bureau of Investigation. *Terrorism in the United States, 1997.* Washington, D.C.: U.S. Department of Justice, 1998.

Feinsilber, Mike. "Agent Orange May Have Fallen Near U.S. Bases." AP, September 24, 1981.

Feldman, Harvey M. "Background and Purpose of the Ethnographers' Policymakers' Symposium." In *Ethnography: A Research Tool for Policymakers in the Drug and Alcohol Fields,* Karl Akins and George Beschner, eds. Rockville, Md.: Department of Health and Human Services, 1985.

Felsenthal, Edward. "Justices' Ruling Further Defines Sex Harassment." *Wall Street Journal,* March 5, 1998:B1, B2.

Ferguson, Ronald E. "Community Revitalization, Jobs, and the Well-Being of the Inner-City Poor." In *Understanding Poverty,* Sheldon H. Danziger and Robert H. Haveman, eds. New York: Russell Sage, 2001:417–443.

Feshbach, Murray. "Russia's Farms, Too Poisoned for the Plow." *Wall Street Journal,* May 14, 1992:A14.

Fialka, John J. "Pentagon Outlines Plans to Use Troops to Join Border 'War' Against Drugs." *Wall Street Journal,* February 23, 1988:A10.

Fialka, John J. "Global Warming Treaty Is Approved." *Wall Street Journal,* December 11, 1997:A2.

Fialka, John J. "Position Available: Indestructible Bugs To Eat Nuclear Waste." *Wall Street Journal,* November 16, 2004:A1.

Field, Mark G. "The Health Crisis in the Former Soviet Union: A Report from the 'Post-War' Zone. In *Readings in Medical Sociology,* William C. Cockerham, Michael Glasser, and Linda S. Heuser, eds. Upper Saddle River, New Jersey, N.J.: Prentice Hall, 1998:506–519.

Fields, George. "Racism Is Accepted Practice in Japan." *Wall Street Journal,* November 10, 1986:19.

Finckenauer, James O. *Scared Straight and the Panacea Phenomenon.* Englewood Cliffs, N.J.: Prentice Hall, 1982.

Finkelhor, David, and Kersti Yllo. *License to Rape: Sexual Abuse of Wives.* New York: Holt, 1985.

Finkelhor, David, and Kersti Yllo. "Marital Rape: The Myth versus the Reality." In *Marriage and Family in a Changing Society,* James M. Henslin, ed. New York: Free Press, 1989:382–391.

Finsterbusch, Kurt, and H. C. Greisman. "The Unprofitability of Warfare in the Twentieth Century." *Social Problems, 22,* February 1975:450–463.

Firestone, Shulamith. *The Dialectic of Sex: The Case for Feminist Revolution.* New York: Morrow, 1970.

Fischer, Claude S. *The Urban Experience.* New York: Harcourt, 1976.

Fish, Jefferson M. "Mixed Blood." *Psychology Today, 28,* 6, November-December 1995:55–58, 60, 61, 76, 80.

Fisher, Gordon M. "Setting American Standards of Poverty: A Look Back." *Focus, 19,* 2, Spring 1988:47–52.

Fisher, Sue. *In the Patient's Best Interest: Women and the Politics of Medical Decisions.* New Brunswick, N.J.: Rutgers University Press, 1986.

Fisse, Brent, and John Braithwaite. "The Impact of Publicity on Corporate Offenders: Ford Motor Company and the Pinto Papers." In *Corporate and Governmental Deviance: Problems of Organizational Behavior in Contemporary Society,* 3rd ed., M. David Ermann and Richard J. Lundman, eds. New York: Oxford University Press, 1987:244–262.

Flavin, Christopher. "Reassessing Nuclear Power." In *State of the World,* Lester R. Brown, ed. New York: Norton, 1987:57–80.

Food and Drug Administration. "A Primer on Food Additives," 1988

Food and Drug Administration. "Food Allergies—Rare But Risky." *FDA Consumer,* May 1994.

Foley, Douglas E. "The Great American Football Ritual." In *Society: Readings to Accompany Core Concepts,* James M. Henslin, ed. Boston: Allyn and Bacon, 2006:64–76.

Ford, Clellan S., and Frank A. Beach. *Patterns of Sexual Behavior.* New York: Harper Colophon, 1972.

Forney, Mary Ann, James A. Inciardi, and Dorothy Lockwood. "Exchanging Sex for Crack-Cocaine: A Comparison of Women from Rural and Urban Communities." *Journal of Community Health, 17,* 2, April 1992:73–85.

Forward, Susan, and Craig Buck. *Betrayal of Innocence: Incest and Its Devastation.* New York: Penguin, 1978.

Fouts, Gregory, and Kimberley Burggraf. "Television Situation Comedies: Female Body Images and Verbal Reinforcements." *Sex Roles: A Journal of Research,* March 1999.

Fox, John W. "Social Class, Mental Illness, and Social Mobility: The Social Selection-Drift Hypothesis for Serious Mental Illness." *Journal of Health and Social Behavior, 31,* 4, December 1990:344–353.

Frank, Andre Gunder. *Dependent Accumulation and Underdevelopment.* New York: Monthly Review, 1979.

Frankenberg, Erica, and Chungmei Lee. "Rapidly Resegregating School Districts." The Civil Rights Project. Cambridge, MA: Harvard University, August 2002.

Frazier, Steve, and Brenton R. Schlender. "Huge Area in Midwest Relying on Irrigation Is Depleting Its Water." *Wall Street Journal,* August 6, 1980:1.

Freed, Anne O. "How Japanese Families Cope with Fragile Elderly." In *Perspectives in Social Gerontology,* Robert B. Enright, Jr., ed. Boston: Allyn & Bacon, 1994:76–86.

Freedman, Alix M. "How a Tobacco Giant Doctors Snuff Brands to Boost Their 'Kick.'" *Wall Street Journal,* October 26, 1994:A1, A6.

Freidson, Eliot. *Patient's Views of Medical Practice.* New York: Russell Sage, 1961.

"Frequent Tobacco Use Among U.S. Youth Declines." *Smokers' Advocate,* February 1992.

Freund, Matthew, Nancy Lee, and Terri Leonard. *Journal of Sex Research, 28,* 4, November 1991: 579–591.

Friedan, Betty. *The Feminine Mystique.* New York: Norton, 1963.

Friedl, Ernestine. "Society and Sex Roles." In *Conformity and Conflict: Readings in Cultural Anthropology.* James P. Spradley and David W. McCurdy, eds. Glenview Ill.: Scott, Foresman, 1990: 229–238.

Friends of the Earth. Press release, online 2004.

Froman, Ingmarie. "Sweden for Women." *Current Sweden, 407,* November 1994:1–4.

Fromm, Erich. *The Anatomy of Human Destructiveness.* New York: Holt, 1973.

Fuller, Rex, and Richard Schoenberger. "The Gender Salary Gap: Do Academic Achievement, Internship Experience, and College Major Make a Difference?" *Social Science Quarterly, 72,* 4, December 1991: 715–726.

Galbraith, John Kenneth. *The Nature of Mass Poverty.* Cambridge, Mass.: Harvard University Press, 1979.

Gale, Richard P. "From Sit-In to Hike-In: A Comparison of the Civil Rights and Environmental Movements." In *Social Behavior, Natural Resources, and the Environment,* William R. Burch, Jr., Neil H. Cheek, Jr., and Lee Taylor, eds. New York: Harper & Row, 1972:280–305.

Galinsky, Ellen, and Peter J. Stein. "The Impact of Human Resource Policies on Employees: Balancing Work/Family Life." *Journal of Family Issues, 11,* 4, December 1990:368–383.

Galliher, John R., and Allyn Walker. "The Puzzle of the Social Origins of the Marihuana Tax Act of 1937." *Social Problems, 24,* February 1977: 367–376.

Ganahl, Dennis J., Thomas J. Prinsen, and Sara Baker Netzley. "A Content Analysis of Prime Time Commercials: A Contextual Framework of Gender Representation." *Sex Roles, 49,* 9/10, November 2003: 545–551.

Gans, Herbert J. *The Urban villagers.* New York: Free Press, 1962.

Gans, Herbert J. *People and Plans: Essays on Urban Problems and Solutions.* New York: Basic Books, 1968.

Gans, Herbert J. "The Uses of Poverty: The Poor Pay All." In *Down to Earth Sociology: Introductory Readings,* 13th ed., James M. Henslin, ed. New York: The Free Press, 2005. Originally appeared in *Social Policy,* July/August 1971:20–24.

Gans, Herbert J. "The Way We'll Live Soon." *Washington Post,* September 1, 1991:BW3.

"GAO Delineates State Use of Tobacco Funds." *Alcoholism and Drug Abuse Weekly, 15,* 10, March 10, 2003:3.

Garbarino, Merwin S. *American Indian Heritage.* Boston: Little, Brown, 1976.

Gardner, Sandra. "Coping with a Daughter's Murder." *New York Times.* January 5, 1992:NJ3.

Garelik, Glenn. "Russia's Legacy of Death." *National Wildlife,* June–July 1996.

Garreau, Joel. *Edge City: Life on the New Frontier.* New York: Doubleday, 1991.

Garrett, Laurie. "Global Warning." *Los Angeles Times,* March 1, 1999.

Gartner, Michael. "A Dream of Peace, the Reality of Never-ending Wars." *Wall Street Journal,* December 22, 1988:A13.

Gattari, P., L. Spizzichino, C. Valenzi, M. Zaccarelli, and G. Rezza. "Behavioural Patterns and HIV Infection Among Drug Using Transvestites Practising Prostitution in Rome." *AIDS Care, 4,* 1, 1992: 83–87.

Gaufberg, Slava V. "Russia." E-Medicine, March 11, 2004.

Gay, Jill. "The 'Patriotic' Prostitute." *The Progressive,* February 1985:34–36.

Gaylin, Willard. *Partial Justice: A Study of Bias in Sentencing.* New York: Knopf, 1974.

Gelles, Richard I. "The Myth of Battered Husbands and New Facts About Family Violence." In *Social Problems 80–81,* Robert L. David, ed. Guilford, Conn.: Dushkin, 1980.

Gellhorn, Martha. *The Face of War.* New York: Simon & Schuster, 1959.

Gemme, Robert. "Prostitution: A Legal, Criminological, and Sexological Perspective." *Canadian Journal of Human Sexuality, 2,* 4, Winter 1993: 227–237.

Gerbner, George. "The 1998 Screen Actors Guild Report: Casting the American Scene." Online. December 1998.

Gerlin, Andrea. "Quirky Sentences make Bad Guys Squirm." *Wall Street Journal,* August 4, 1994:B1, B2.

Gerth, Jeff. "Two Companies Pay Penalties for Improving China Rockets." *New York Times,* March 3, 2003.

Gessen, Masha. "The Nuclear Wasteland." *U.S. News and World Report,* February 26, 2001.

Gest, Ted. "Teaching Convicts Real Street Smarts." *U.S. News & World Report,* May 18, 1987:72.

Getter, Lisa. "Cancer Risk From Air Pollution Still High, Study Says." *Los Angeles Times,* March 1, 1999.

"Getting the Message." Children Now. Online, 1997.

Gibbons, Ann. "Famine: Blame Policy, Not Nature." *Science, 254,* 5033, November 8, 1991:790.

Gibbs, Nancy. "In Sorrow and Disbelief." May 3, 1999:25–36.

Giddens, Anthony. "Georg Simmel." In *The Founding Fathers of Social Science,* Timothy Raison, ed. Baltimore: Penguin, 1969:165–173.

Giele, Janet Zollinger. *Women and the Future: Changing Sex Roles in Modern America.* New York: Free Press, 1978.

Gilham, Steven A. "The Marines Build Men: Resocialization in Recruit Training." In *The Sociological Outlook: A Text with Readings,* 2nd ed., Reid Luhman, ed. San Diego, Calif.: Collegiate Press, 1989: 232–244.

Gillespie, Terry. "Virtual Violence? Pornography and Violence Against Women on the Internet." In *Women, Violence and Strategies for Action: Feminist Research, Policy and Practice*. Philadelphia: Open University Press, 2000:40–56. The quote is on page 53.

Gilmartin-Zena, Pat. "Rape Impact: Immediately and Two Months Later." *Deviant Behavior, 6,* 1985:347–361.

Gilmore, David G. *Manhood in the Making: Cultural Concepts of Masculinity*. New Haven, Conn.: Yale University Press, 1990.

Glascock, Jack. "Gender Roles on Prime-Time Network Television: Demographics and Behaviors." *Journal of Broadcasting and Electronics Media, 45,* Fall 2001:656–669.

Glaser, Daniel. *Crime in Our Changing Society*. New York: Holt, 1978.

Goering, Laurie. "Paranoia Pervasive in Amazon." *Seattle Times,* August 28, 1998.

Goetting, Ann. *Getting Out: Life Stories of Women Who Left Abusive Men*. New York: Columbia University Press, 2001.

Goldberg, Carey, and Sophia Kishkovsky. "Russia's Doctors Are Beggars at Work, Paupers at Home." *New York Times,* December 16, 2000.

Goldberg, Steven. *The Inevitability of Patriarchy*, rev. ed. New York: Morrow, 1974.

Goldberg, Steven. "Reaffirming the Obvious." *Society,* September–October 1986:4–7.

Goldberg, Steven. Letter to the Author. January 18, 1989.

Goldberg, Susan, and Michael, Lewis. "Play Behavior in the Year-Old Infant: Early Sex Differences." *Child Development, 40,* March 1969:21–31.

Goleman, Daniel. "Girls and Math: Is Biology Really Destiny?" *New York Times,* August 2, 1987:42–44, 46.

Goode, Erich. *Drugs in American Society*, 3rd ed. New York: Knopf, 1989.

Gooden, Angela M., and Mark A. Gooden. "Gender Representation in Notable Children's Picture Books: 1995–1999." *Sex Roles, 45,* 1/2, July 2001: 89–101.

Gordon, Michael R. "Russia Struggles in Long Race to Prevent an Atomic Theft." *New York Times,* April 20, 1996.

Gordon, Milton. *Assimilation in American Life*. New York: Oxford University Press, 1964.

Gosch, Martin A., and Richard Hammer. *The Last Testament of Lucky Luciano*. New York: Dell, 1975.

Gottfredson, Michael, and Travis Hirschi. *A General Theory of Crime*. Stanford, CA.: Stanford University Press, 1990.

"GPS Creates Global Jail." Online, April 8, 1998.

Grady, Denise. "Bacteria Resistant to Powerful Antibiotics Are Discovered in Chicken Feed." *New York Times,* February 26, 1999.

Graven, Kathryn. "Sex Harassment at the Office Stirs Up Japan." *Wall Street Journal,* March 21, 1990:B1, B7.

Green, Gary S. "White-Collar Crime and the Study of Embezzlement." *Annals of the American Academy of Political and Social Sciences, 525,* January 1993:95–106.

Greenberg, David F. "The Incapacitative Effect of Imprisonment: Some Estimates." *Law and Society Review, 9,* Summer 1975:541–579.

Greenberger, Robert S. "U.S., Russia Will Explore Joint System for Early Warning of Missile Attacks." *Wall Street Journal,* February 19,1992:A7.

Greenberger, Robert S. "U.S., Russia Agree to Faster Timetable for Destruction of Nuclear Arsenals." *Wall Street Journal,* September 29, 1994:A22.

Greenberger, Robert S., and Jerry E. Bishop. "Suspected Toxic Agent in Attack Is Made of Chemicals Easily Available in U.S." *Wall Street Journal,* March 21,1995:A12.

Greenfield, Lawrence A. "Capital Punishment 1990." *Bureau of Justice Statistics Bulletin,* September 1991.

Greenhouse, Steven. "Doctors, Under Pressure from H.M.O.'s, Are Ready Union Recruits." *New York Times,* February 4, 1999.

Greer, Germaine. *The Female Eunuch*. New York: Bantam, 1972.

Grella, Christine E. "Irreconcilable Differences: Women Defining Class after Divorce and Downward Mobility." *Gender and Society, 4,* 1, March 1990:41–55.

"Guardian of Brazil Indians Faces Many Foes." Reuters online, June 10, 1997.

Gudkov, Yuri. "The 'Respectable' Mafia." *World Press Review, 27,* January 1980:51.

Gurvich, Tatyana, and Janet A. Cunningham. "Appropriate Use of Psychotropic Drugs in Nursing Homes." *American Family Physician, 6,* 2000: 1437–1446.

Gusfield, Joseph R. *Symbolic Crusade: Status Politics and the American Temperance Movement*. Urbana: University of Illinois Press, 1963.

Haas, Jack, and William Shaffir. "The Cloak of Competence." In *Down-to-Earth Sociology: Introductory*

Readings, 7th ed., James M. Henslin, ed. New York: Free Press, 1993.

Hacker, Helen Mayer. "Women as a Minority Group." *Social Forces, 30,* October 1951:60–69.

Hackett, George. "Kids: Deadly Force." *Newsweek,* January 11, 1988:18–19.

Hadden, Jeffrey K., and Josef J. Barton. "An Image That Will Not Die: Thoughts on the History of Anti-Urban Ideology." In *The Urbanization of the Suburbs,* Louis H. Masoti and Jeffrey K. Hadden, eds. Beverly Hills, Calif.: Sage, 1973:79–116.

Hale, Marion. "In Courts, Defendant's Color Counts." *Fort Lauderdale News,* October 3, 1980.

Hall, Susan. *Gentleman of Leisure: A Year in the Life of a Pimp.* New York: New American Library, 1972.

Hamer, Dean H., Stella Hu, Victoria L. Magnuson, Nan Hu, and Angela M. L. Pattatucci. "A Linkage Between DNA Markers on the X Chromosome and Male Sexual Orientation." *Science, 261,* July 16, 1993:321–327.

Hanson, David J. *Preventing Alcohol Abuse: Alcohol, Culture, and Control.* Westport, Conn.: Praeger, 1995.

Hanson, Kitty. "Victims of Violence." *Daily News,* October 3, 4, and 5, 1977.

Hanssen, M. *The New Additive Code Breaker.* Port Melbourne, Australia: Lothian Books, 1997.

Hardin, Garrett. "The Tragedy of the Commons." *Science, 162,* December 1968:1243–1248.

Hardy, Quentin. "Hitting Slavery Where It Hurts." *Forbes, 172,* 14, Jan. 12, 2004:76.

Harlan, Christi. "Come Out with Your Hands Up and No Funny Stuff with the Peas." *Wall Street Journal,* November 4, 1988:B1.

Harrington, Michael. *The Vast Majority: A Journey to the World's Poor.* New York: Simon & Schuster, 1977.

Harris, Chauncy, and Edward Ullman. "The Nature of Cities." *Annals of the American Academy of Political and Social Science, 242,* November 1945: 7–17.

Harris, Marvin. "Why Men Dominate Women." *New York Times Magazine,* November 13, 1977:46, 115, 117, 123.

Harris, Sheldon H. *Factories of Death.* New York: Routledge, 1994.

Harrison, Bruce. "Pressing or Passe?" *Public Relations Journal, 43,* March 1987:4–6.

Hart, C. W. M., and Arnold R. Pilling. *The Tiwi of North Australia,* Fieldwork Edition. New York: Holt, Rinehart and Winston, 1979.

Hart, Hornell. "Acceleration in Social Change." In *Technology and Social Change,* Francis R. Allen, Hornell Hart, Delbert C. Miller, William F. Ogburn, and Meyer F. Nimkoff, eds. New York: Appleton, 1957.

Haub, Carl. "Demographic Upheavals in the Former USSR." *Population Today, 23,* 1, January 1995: 1–2.

Haub, Carl, and Diana Cornelius. "World Population Data Sheet." Population Reference Bureau, 2004.

Hauser, Philip, and Leo Schnore, eds. *The Study of Urbanization.* New York: Wiley, 1965.

Haveman, Robert H., and John Karl Scholz. "The Clinton Welfare Reform Plan: Will It End Poverty as We Know It?" *Focus, 16,* 2, Winter 1994–95:1–11.

Hayden, F. Gregory, Kellee R. Wood, and Asuman Kaya. "The Use of Power Blocs of Integrated Corporate Directorships to Articulate a Power Structure: Case Study and Research Recommendations." *Journal of Economic Issues, 36,* 3, September 2002: 671–706.

Hayden, Thomas. "Fished Out." *U.S. News and World Report.* June 9, 2003.

Hayes, Arthur S. "How the Courts Define Harassment." *Wall Street Journal,* October 11, 1991:B1, B3.

Healy, Patrick. "Hoisting Rainbow Flags, Wearing Campaign Buttons." *New York Times,* June 28, 2004.

Heckathorn, Douglas D. "Collective Sanctions and Compliance Norms: A Formal Theory of Group-Medicated Social Control." *American Sociological Review, 55,* June 1990:366–384.

Heins, Marjorie. "The War on Nudity, Continued." *Playboy,* November 1991:53.

Hellinger, Daniel, and Dennis R. Judd. *The Democratic Facade.* Pacific Grove, Calif.: Brooks/Cole, 1991.

Helmer, J. *Drugs and Minority Oppression.* New York: Seabury, 1975.

Hendin, Herbert. "Euthanasia and Physician-Assisted Suicide in the Netherlands." *New England Journal of Medicine, 336,* 19, May 8, 1997:1385–1387.

Hendin, Herbert. "Suicide, Assisted Suicide, and Mental Illness." *Harvard Mental Health Letter, 16,* 7, January 2000:4–7.

Henriques, Fernando. *Prostitution and Society.* New York: Grove, 1966.

Henslin, James M. "Guilt and Guilt Neutralization: Response and Adjustment to Suicide." In *Deviance and Respectability: The Social Construction of Moral Mean-*

ings, Jack D. Douglas, ed. New York: Basic Books, 1970.

Henslin, James M. "Cohabitation: Its Context and Meaning." In *Marriage and Family in a Changing Society,* James M. Henslin, ed. New York: The Free Press, 1980:101–115.

Henslin, James M. "Centuries of Childhood." In *Marriage and Family in a Changing Society,* 4th ed., James M. Henslin, ed. New York: Basic Books, 1992:214–225.

Henslin, James M. *Essentials of Sociology: A Down-to-Earth Approach,* 6th ed. Boston: Allyn and Bacon, 2005.

Henslin, James M., and Mae A. Biggs, "Behavior in Pubic Places: The Sociology of the Vaginal Examination." In *Down to Earth Sociology: Introductory Readings,* 13th ed., James M. Henslin, ed. New York: The Free Press, 2005:211–223.

Herbert, Bob. "The Hate Virus." *New York Times,* August 10, 1988.

Herbert, Bob. "Don't Flunk the Future." *New York Times,* August 13, 1998.

Hersh, Seymour. "Manhunt." *The New Yorker,* December 23, 2002.

Heyl, Barbara Sherman. *The Madam as Entrepreneur: Career Management in House Prostitution.* New Brunswick, N.J.: Transaction, 1979.

Hibbert, Christopher. *The Roots of Evil: A Social History of Crime and Punishment.* New York: Minerva, 1963.

Hilliard, Asa, III. "Do We Have the *Will* to Educate All Children?" *Educational Leadership, 49,* September 1991:31–36.

Hills, Stuart L. *Demystifying Social Deviance.* New York: McGraw-Hill, 1980.

Hills, Stuart L., ed. *Corporate Violence: Injury and Death for Profit.* Totowa, N.J.: Rowman & Littlefield, 1987.

Hiltz, Starr Roxanne. "Widowhood." In *Marriage and Family in a Changing Society,* James M. Henslin, ed. New York: Free Press, 1989:521–531.

Himmelhoch, Jerome, and Sylvia Fleis Fava (eds.). *Sexual Behavior in American Society: An Appraisal of the First Two Kinsey Reports.* New York: Norton, 1955.

Hindelang, Michael J. "Race and Involvement in Common Personal Crimes." *American Sociological Review, 43,* February 1978:93–109.

Hines, Revathi I. "African Americans' Struggle for Environmental Justice and the Case of the Shintech Plant: Lessons Learned from a War Waged."

Journal of Black Studies, 31, 6, July 2001: 777–789.

Hirschi, Travis. *Causes of Delinquency.* Berkeley: University of California Press, 1969.

Hochschild, Arlie, and Anne Machung. "Men Who Share 'The Second Shift.'" In *Down-to-Earth Sociology: Introductory Readings,* 8th ed., James M. Henslin, ed. New York: Free Press, 1995: 383–397.

Hodgson, James F. *Games Pimps Play: Pimps, Players and Wives-In-Law.* Toronto: Canadian Scholars' Press, 1997.

Hoffman, Albert. "Psychotomimetic Agents." In *Drugs Affecting the Central Nervous System* (vol. 2). New York: Marcel Dekker, 1968.

Hogan, Bill. "The Wages of Synfuels." *Mother Jones,* September 1, 2001.

Holden, Benjamin A. "In Elite Schools, Students See Hope of a Ticket Out." *Wall Street Journal,* August 15, 1994:B1, B4.

Holdren, John P., and Paul R. Ehrlich. "Human Population and the Global Environment." *American Scientist, 62,* May–June 1974:282–292.

Holman, Richard L. "World Wire." *Wall Street Journal,* July 28, 1994:A10.

Holmstrom, Lynda Lytle, and Ann Wolbert Burgess. "Rape and Everyday Life." In *Deviance in American Life,* James M. Henslin, ed. New Brunswick, N.J.: Transaction, 1989:349–371.

Holtzman, Abraham. *The Townsend Movement: A Political Study.* New York: Bookman, 1963.

Homblin, Dora Jane. *The First Cities.* Boston: Little, Brown, Time-Life Books, 1973.

Hooker, Evelyn. "The Adjustment of the Male Overt Homosexual." *Journal of Projective Techniques, 21,* March 1957:18–31.

Hooton, Earnest A. *Crime and the Man.* Cambridge, Mass.: Harvard University Press, 1939.

Hope, Christine A., and Ronald G. Stover. "Gender Status, Monotheism, and Social Complexity." *Social Forces, 65,* 1987:1132–1138.

Hornblower, Margot. "The Skin Trade." *Time,* June 21, 1993:45–51.

Horowitz, Ruth. *Honor and the American Dream: Culture and Identity in a Chicano Community.* New Brunswick, N.J.: Rutgers University Press, 1983.

Hosenball, Mark. "A Plutonium Mystery." *Newsweek,* May 3, 1999:62–64.

Hotchkiss, Sandy. "The Realities of Rape." *Human Behavior, 12,* December 1978:18–23.

Hotz, Robert Lee. "Early Humans' Fire Use Linked to Extinctions." *Los Angeles Times,* January 8, 1999.

Howard, Jan, and Anselm Strauss (eds.). *Humanizing Health Care.* New York: Wiley, 1975.

Hoyt, Homer. *The Structure and Growth of Residential Neighborhoods in American Cities.* Washington, D.C.: U.S. Federal Housing Administration, 1939.

Hsu, Francis L. K. *The Challenge of the American Dream: The Chinese in the United States.* Belmont, Calif.: Wadsworth, 1971.

Huber, Joan. "Micro-Macro Links in Gender Stratification." *American Sociological Review, 55,* February 1990:1–10.

Huddle, Donald. "The Net National Cost of Immigration." Washington, D.C.: Carrying Capacity Network, 1993.

Hudson, Robert B. "The 'Graying' of the Federal Budget and Its Consequences for Old-Age Policy." *The Gerontologist, 18,* October 1978428–440.

Huff-Corzine, Lin, Jay Corzine, and David C. Moore. "Southern Exposure: Deciphering the South's Influence on Homicide Rates." *Social Forces, 64,* 1986:906–924.

Huff-Corzine, Lin, Jay Corzine, and David C. Moore. "Deadly Connections: Culture, Poverty, and the Direction of Lethal Violence." *Social Forces, 69, 3,* March 1991:715–732.

Huggins, Martha K. "Lost Childhood: Assassinations of Youth in Democratizing Brazil." Paper presented at the annual meetings of the American Sociological Association, 1993.

Hull, Jon D. "Life and Death with the Gangs." *Time,* August 24, 1987:21–22.

Humphreys, Laud. *Tearoom Trade.* Chicago: Aldine, 1970. (Expanded version, Chicago: Aldine-Atherton, 1975.)

Humphries, Drew, John Dawson, Valerie Cronin, Phyllis Keating, Christ Wisniewski, and Jennine Eichfeld. "Mothers and Children, Drugs and Crack: Reactions to Maternal Drug Dependency." *Women and Criminal Justice, 3, 2,* 1992:81–99.

Huxley, Aldous. *The Doors of Perception.* New York: Harper & Row, 1954.

"Hybrid Car Market Revs Up." *USA Today,* May 3, 2004.

Ianni, Francis A. J., and Elizabeth Reuss-Ianni, eds. *The Crime Society: Organized Crime and Corruption in America.* New York: New American Library, 1976.

Inciardi, James A. *The War on Drugs: Heroin, Cocaine, Crime, and Public Policy.* Mountain View, Calif.: Mayfield, 1986.

Inciardi, James A., and Anne E. Pottieger. "Crack-Cocaine Use and Street Crime." *Journal of Drug Issues, 24, 2,* Winter 1994:273–292.

Ingersoll, Bruce. "FDA Is Proposing Limits on Sulfites in Range of Foods." *Wall Street Journal,* December 20, 1988:C21.

Ingersoll, Bruce. "Faster Slaughter Lines Are Contaminating Much U.S. Poultry." *Wall Street Journal,* November 16, 1990:A1, A6.

Isbell, Harris. "Historical Development of Attitudes Toward Opiate Addiction in the United States." In *Man and Civilization: Conflict, and Creativity,* Seymour M. Farber and Roger H. L. Wilson, eds. New York: McGraw-Hill, 1969:154–170.

Izaak Walton League of America. "Conservation Policies," 2000.

Izumi, Lance T. "Cutting Through the Smoke: Facts on Cigarette Tax." November 18, 1997.

Jacobs, David. "Inequality and the Legal Order: An Ecological Test of the Conflict Model." *Social problems, 25,* June 1978:515–525.

Jacobsen, Thorkild, and Robert M. Adams. "Salt and Silt in Ancient Mesopotamian Agriculture." *Science,* November 21, 1958:1251–1258.

Jaffe, Jerome H. "Drug Addiction and Drug Abuse." In *The Pharmacological Basis of Therapeutics,* Louis S. Goodman and Alfred Gilmann, eds. New York: Macmillan, 1965:285–311.

James, Jennifer, and J. Meyerding. "Early Sexual Experiences in Prostitution." *Archives of Sexual Behavior, 7,* 1977:31–42.

James, Jennifer, and Nanette J. Davis. "Contingencies in Female Sexual Role Deviance: The Case of Prostitution." *Human Organization, 41, 4,* Winter 1982:345–350.

Janowitz, Morris. "The Twentieth-Century Race Riot, Commodity Type: The Summer of 1967." In *American Violence,* Richard Maxwell, ed. Englewood Cliffs, N.J.: Prentice Hall, 1970a: 147–155.

Janowitz, Morris. "The Twentieth-Century Race Riot, Communal Type: Chicago, 1919." In *American Violence,* Richard Maxwell, ed. Englewood Cliffs, N.J.: Prentice Hall, 1970b:126–136.

Jaworowski, Zbigniew. "UNSCEAR on the Health Effects from Chornobyl." *Science, 293,* 5530, July 27, 2001.

Jefferson, Thomas. *Notes on the State of Virginia*, Bernard Wishy and William C. Leuchtenburg, eds. New York: Harper & Row, 1977.

Jekielek, Susan M. "Parental Conflict, Marital Disruption and Children's Emotional Well-Being." *Social Forces, 76*, 3, March 1998:905–935.

Jenkins, Brian Michael. "Future Trends in International Terrorism." *Symposium on International Terrorism.* Washington, D.C.: Defense Intelligence Agency, December 2–3, 1985.

Joffe, Carole. "What Haven? For Whom?" *Social Policy, 9*, May–June 1978:58–60.

Johnson, Bruce D., Kevin Anderson, and Eric D. Wish. "A Day in the Life of 105 Drug Addicts and Abusers: Crimes Committed and How the Money Was Spent." *Sociology and Social Research, 72*, 3, April 1988:185–191.

Johnson, Bruce D., Paul J. Goldstein, Edward Preble, James Schmeidler, Douglas S. Lipton, Barry Spunt, and Thomas Miller. *Taking Care of Business: The Economics of Crime by Heroin Abusers.* Lexington, Mass.: Lexington Books, 1985.

Johnson, Danny R. "Tobacco Stains: Cigarette Firms Buy into African-American Groups." *The Progressive, 56*, 12, December 1992:26–28.

Johnson, Dirk. "Murder Charges Are Met by Cries of Compassion." *New York Times*, August 8, 1988:A14.

Johnson, Terry R., Randall J. Pozdena, and Gary Steiger. *The Impact of Alternative Negative Income Tax Programs on Non-durable Consumption.* Menlo Park, Calif.: SRI International, October 1979.

Johnston, Lloyd D., Patrick M. O'Malley, Jerald G. Bachman, and John E. Schulenberg. *Monitoring the Future: National Results on Adolescent Drug Use.* Washington, D.C.: U.S. Department of Health and Human Services, 2003a.

Johnston, Lloyd D., Patrick M. O'Malley, and Jerald G. Bachman. *Monitoring the Future: National Survey Results on Drug Use, 1975–2000, Volume 1: Secondary Students.* Washington, D.C.: U.S. Department of Health and Human Services, 2003b.

Jordan, Jan. "Worlds Apart? Women, Rape and the Police Reporting Process." *British Journal of Criminology, 41*, 2001:679–706.

Josephy, Alvin M., Jr. "Indians in History." *Atlantic Monthly,* June 1970:67–72.

Julien, Robert M. *A Primer of Drug Action.* New York: Worth Publishers, 2001.

Juvenile Justice Bulletin. Washington, D.C.: U.S. Government Printing Office.

Kalb, Claudia. "Drugged-Out Toddlers." *Newsweek,* March 6, 2000.

Kamin, Leon. "Schizophrenia." Unpublished. Princeton University, Department of Psychology, 1981.

Kanin, Eugene J. "Date Rapists: Differential Sexual Socialization and Relative Deprivation." In *Violence and Society: A Reader,* Matthew Silberman, ed. Upper Saddle River, N.J.: Prentice Hall, 2003: 207–225.

Kantor, Glenda Kaufman, and Murray A. Straus. "The 'Drunken Bum' Theory of Wife Beating." *Social Problems, 34*, 3, June 1987:213–230.

Kaplan, Carl. S. "Anti-Porn Law Enters Court; Delay Soon Follows." *New York Times,* November 20, 1998.

Kaplan, Sidney. "Historical Efforts to Encourage White-Indian Intermarriage in the United States and Canada." *International Social Science Review, 65*, 3, Summe,1990: 126–132.

Karlen, Arno. "Homosexuality: The Scene and Its Students." In *The Sociology of Sex: An Introductory Reader,* rev. ed., James M. Henslin and Edward Sagarin, eds. New York: Schocken, 1978: 223–248.

Karlen, Neal, and Barbara Burgower. "Dumping the Mentally Ill." *Newsweek, 105*, January 7, 1985:17.

Karmen, Andrew. "The Narcotics Problem: Views from the Left." In *Is America Possible? Social Problems from Conservative, Liberal, and Socialist Perspectives,* 2nd ed., Henry Etzkowitz, ed. St. Paul, Minn.: West, 1980:171–180.

Karp, David A., Gregory P. Stone, and William C. Yoels. *Being Urban: A Sociology of City Life,* 2nd ed. New York: Praeger, 1991.

Karp, David A., and William C. Yoels. "Sport and Urban Life." *Journal of Sport and Social Issues, 14*, 2, 1990:77–102.

Katz, Michael B. *The Undeserving Poor: From the War on Poverty to the War on Welfare.* New York: Pantheon, 1989.

Keans, Carl. "Socioenvironmental Determinants of Community Formation." *Environment and Behavior, 23*, 1, January 1991:27–46.

Keil, Thomas J., and Gennaro F. Vito. "Race, Homicide Severity, and Application of the Death Penalty: A Consideration of the Barnett Scale." *Criminology, 27*, 3, 1989:511–535.

Kelley, Kitty. "The Dark Side of Camelot." *People Magazine,* February 28, 1988:107–114.

Kemp, Jack. "Tackling Poverty: Market-Based Policies to Empower the Poor." *Policy Review, 51*, Winter 1990:2–5.

Kenchaiah, Satish, et. al. "Obesity and the Risk of Heart Failure." *New England Journal of Medicine, 347,* August 1, 2002:305–313.

Kerner, Otto. *Report of the National Advisory Commission on Civil Disorders.* Washington, D.C.: U.S. Government Printing Office, 1968.

Kettl, Donald F. "The Savings-and-Loan Bailout: The Mismatch Between the Headlines and the Issues." *PS, 24,* 3, September 1991:441–447.

Keyes, Ken, Jr. *The Hundredth Monkey.* St. Mary, Ky.: Vision Books, n.d.

"Kids Count Data Sheet." Baltimore, Md.: Annie E. Casey Foundation, 2004.

Kilborn, Peter T. "Reality of H.M.O. System Does Not Live Up to Hopes for Health Care." *New York Times,* October 5, 1998.

King, Martin Luther, Jr. *Stride Toward Freedom: The Montgomery Story.* New York: Harper, 1958.

King, Storm A., and Stephan T. Poulos. "Ethical Guidelines for On-line Therapy." In *How to Use Computers and Cyberspace in the Clinical Practice of Psychotherapy,* Jeri Fink, ed. Lanham, Md.: Jason Aronson, 1999:121–132.

Kinkade, Ward. "Population Trends: Russia." Washington, D.C.: U.S. Department of Commerce, February 1997.

Kinnon, Joy Bennett. "A Better Chance." *Ebony, 52, 7,* May 1997:44–48.

Kinsey, Alfred C., Wardell B. Pomeroy, and Clyde E. Martin. *Sexual Behavior in the Human Male.* Philadelphia: Saunders, 1948.

Kinsey, Alfred C., Wardell B. Pomeroy, Clyde E. Mantin, and Paul H. Gebhard. *Sexual Behavior in the Human Female.* New York: Saunders, 1953.

Kirkham, George L. "Homosexuality in Prison." In *Studies in the Sociology of Sex,* James M. Henslin, ed. New York: Appleton, 1971:325–349.

Kirkpatrick, Melanie. "On the Abortion Barricades." *Wall Street Journal,* April 23, 1992:A14.

Kirkpatrick, Terry. "A New Breed of Pioneers Are Homesteading America's cities." *Alton Telegraph.* June 26, 1981.

Kitano, Harry H. L. *Race Relations.* Englewood Cliffs N.J.: Prentice Hall, 1974.

Kleck, Gary, and Susan Sayles. "Rape and Resistance." *Social Problems, 37,* 2, May 1990:149–162.

Klein, Stephen, Joan Petersilia, and Susan Turner. "Race and Imprisonment Decisions in California." *Science, 247,* 4944, February 16, 1990:812–816.

Kleinman, Paul H., Eric D. Wish, Shreey Deren, Gregory Rainone, and Ellen Morehouse. "Daily Marijuana Use and Problem Behaviors Among Adolescents." *International Journal of the Addictions, 22,* 12, 1987.

Knights, Roger. "Electronic Tagging in Practice." *Teleconnect,* January 22, 1999.

Knowles, Louis L., and Kenneth Prewitt. *Institutionalized Racism in America.* Englewood Cliffs, N.J.: Prentice Hall, 1969.

Kohn, Alfie. "Make Love, Not War." *Psychology Today,* June 1988:35–38.

Komisar, Lucy. "The Image of Woman in Advertising." In *Woman in Sexist Society: Studies in Power and Powerlessness.* Vivian Gornick and Barbara K. Moran, eds. New York: Basic Books, 1971:207–217.

Korda, Michael. *Male Chauvinism: How It Works.* New York: Random House, 1973.

Kornhauser, William. "'Power Elite' or 'Veto Groups'?" In *Culture and Social Character,* Seymour Martin Lipset and Leo Lowenthal, eds. Glencoe, Ill.: Free Press, 1961:252–267.

Kotlowitz, Alex. "Chicago Street Gangs Treat Public Housing as Private Fortresses." *Wall Street Journal,* September 30, 1988:1, 2.

Kozel, Nicholas J. *Epidemiologic Trends in Drug Abuse. Community Epidemiology Work Group.* Bethesda, Maryland: National Institutes of Health, June, 1996.

Kozol, Jonathan. "Savage Inequalities." In *Down-to-Earth Sociology: Introductory Readings,* 10th ed., James M. Henslin, ed. New York: Free Press, 1999: 343–351.

Krieger, Lisa. "Abortion Foes, Proponents Intensify Battle." *American Medical News, 28,* June 7, 1985:2–3.

Kristoff, Nicholas D. "Interview with a Humanoid." *New York Times,* July 23, 2002.

Kuczynski, Jurgen. *A Short History of Labour Conditions Under Industrial Capitalism in the United States of America, 1789–1946,* 2nd ed. New York: Barnes & Noble, 1946.

Kurth, James R. "American Military Policy and Advanced Weapons." In *Social Problems and Public Policy: Inequality and Justice,* Lee Rainwater, ed. Chicago: Aldine, 1974:336–352.

Kusum. "The Use of Pre-natal Diagnostic Techniques for Sex Selection: The Indian Scene." *Bioethics, 7,* 2–3, April 1993:149–165.

Kutchinsky, Berl. "The Effects of Easy Availability of Pornography on the Incidence of Sex Crimes in Copenhagen: The Danish Experience." *Journal of Social Issues, 29,* 1973:163–181.

La Barre, Weston. *The Human Animal.* Chicago: University of Chicago Press, 1954.

LaBastille, Anne. "The Deadly Toll of Acid Rain: All of Nature Is Suffering." *Science Digest, 86,* October 1979:61–66.

Lacayo, Richard. "Crusading Against the Pro-Choice Movement." *Time,* October 21, 1991.

Lacey, Marc. "African Activists Urge End to Female Mutilation." *International Herald Tribune,* February 7, 2003:10.

LaFree, Gary D. "The Effect of Sexual Stratification by Race on Official Reactions to Rape." *American Sociological Review, 45,* October 1980:842–854.

La Gory, Mark, Russell Ward, and Thomas Juravich. "The Age Segregation Process." *Urban Affairs Quarterly, 16,* 1980:59–80.

Lamar, Jacob V., Jr. "An Inmate and a Gentleman." *Time,* August 11, 1986:17.

Landes, David S. *The Wealth and Poverty of Nations: Why Some Are Rich and Some So Poor.* New York: W.W. Norton, 1998.

Lang, Kurt, and Gladys Lang. "Racial Disturbances as Collective Protest." In *Riots and Rebellion: Civil Violence in the Urban community,* Louis H. Masotti, and Don R. Bowen, eds. Beverly Hills, Calif.: Sage, 1968:121–130.

Lang, Robert E. *Edgeless Cities: Exploring the Elusive Metropolis.* Washington, D.C.: Brookings Institution Press, 2003.

Langan, Patrick A., and Mark A. Cunniff. "Recidivism of Felons on Probation, 1986–1989." Bureau of Justice Statistics Special Report, Washington, D.C., February, 1992.

Laqueur, Walter. *Terrorism.* Boston: Little, Brown, 1977.

Larned, Deborah. "The Epidemic in Unnecessary Hysterectomies." In *Seizing Our Bodies: The Politics of Women's Health,* Claudia Dreyfus, ed. New York: Random House, 1977.

Larson, Mary Strom. "Interactions, Activities and Gender in Children's Television Commercials: A Content Analysis." *Journal of Broadcasting and Electronic Media, 45,* Winter 2001:41–51.

Lasch, Christopher. *Haven in a Heartless World: The Family Besieged.* New York: Basic Books, 1977.

Laslett, Barbara. "Family, Social Change Can Often Spell Trouble." University of California, University Extension, Course by Newspaper, San Diego, 1980.

Laumann, Edward O., John H. Gagnon, Robert T. Michael, and Stuart Michaels. *The Social Organization of Sexuality: Sexual Practices in the United States.* Chicago: University of Chicago Press, 1994.

"Law Enacted to Protect Ainu Culture, Tradition." Foreign Press Center of Japan, June 19, 1997.

Leaf, Clifton. "Enough Is Enough." In *Sociology,* 33rd ed., Kurt Finsterbusch, ed. Dubuque, Ia: McGraw-Hill/Dushkin, 2004:52–59.

Lee, Dorothy. *Freedom and Culture.* Englewood Cliffs, N.J.: Prentice Hall, 1959.

Lee, Rex E. *A Lawyer Looks at the Equal Rights Amendment.* Provo, Utah: Brigham Young University Press, 1980.

Lee, Sharon M. "Asian Americans: Diverse and Growing." *Population Bulletin, 53,* 2, June 1998:1–39.

Leighty, Keith E. "Germ Testing by Japanese Killed POWs." AP, October 31, 1981.

Leinberger, Christopher R. *Financing Progressive Development.* Washington, D.C.: Brookings Institution Press, 2001.

Leinwand, Donna. "Judges Write Creative Sentences." *USA Today,* February 24, 2004.

Leland, John. "A New Harlem Gentry in Search of Its Latte." *New York Times,* August 7, 2003.

Lender, Mark Edward, and James Kirby Martin. *Drinking in America: A History.* New York: Free Press, 1982.

Lenz-Romeiss, Felizitas. *The City: New Town or Home Town?* Edith Kustner and J. A. Underwood, trans. New York: Praeger, 1973.

Leonard, Rebecca, and Don C. Locke. "Communication Stereotypes: Is Interracial Communication Possible?" *Journal of Black Studies, 23,* 3, March 19933:32–343.

Lerner, Gerda. *The Creation of Patriarchy.* New York: Oxford University Press, 1986.

Lerner, Robert, Althea K. Nagai, and Stanley Rothman. "Abortion and Social Change in America." *Society, 2, 27,* January–February 1990:8–15.

Lesser, Alexander. "War and the State." In *War: The Anthropology of Armed Conflict and Aggression,* Morton Fried, Marvin Harris, and Robert Murphy, eds. Garden City, N.Y.: Natural History, 1968.

Lester, David. "Incest." *Journal of Sex Research, 8,* November 1972:268–285.

Leuchtag, Alice. "Human Rights, Sex Trafficking, and Prostitution." In *Social Problems,* 32nd ed., Kurt Pinsterbusch, ed. Boston: McGraw-Hill/Dushkin, 2004:88–93.

LeVay, Simon. *The Sexual Brain.* Cambridge, Mass.: MIT Press, 1993.

Levin, Jack, and James Alan Fox. *Mass Murder: America's Growing Menace.* New York: Plenum, 1985.

Levine, Art. "Drug Education Gets an F." *U.S. News & World Report,* October 13, 1986:63–64.

Levine, Samantha. "Who'll Stop the Mercury Rain?" *U.S. News and World Report,* April 5, 2004.

Lewin, Tamar. "1 in 8 Boys of High-School Age Has Been Abused, Survey Says." *New York Times,* June 26, 1998.

Lewis, David L. "Bias in Drug Sentences." *National Law Journal,* February 5, 1996.

Lewis, Jack. "The Ogallala Aquifer: An Underground Sea." *EPA Journal, 16,* 6, November 1990:42–44.

Lewis, Karen J. "Abortion: Judicial Control." Washington, D.C.: Congressional Research Service, American Law Division. Mimeo. September 13, 1988.

Lewis, Oscar. *Five Families.* New York: Basic Books, 1959.

Lewis, Oscar. "The Culture of Poverty." *Scientific American, 115,* October 1966:19–25.

Lewis, Peter W., and Kenneth D. Peoples. *The Supreme Court and the Criminal Process: Cases and Comments.* Philadelphia: Saunders, 1978.

Liazos, Alex. "Corporate Crime and Capitalism." Paper presented at the annual meeting of the Society for the Study of Social Problems, 1981.

Library of Congress, Federal Research Division, *Russia: A Country Study, 1999.* online.

Light, Donald W., Jr. "Treating Suicide: The Illusions of a Professional Movement." *International Social Science Journal, 25,* 1973:473–488.

Light, Donald W., Jr. "Perestroika for Russian Health Care." *Footnotes, 20,* 3, March 1992:7, 9.

Lightfoot-Klein, H. "Rites of Purification and Their Effects: Some Psychological Aspects of Female Genital Circumcision and Infibulation (Pharaonic Circumcision) in an Afro-Arab Society (Sudan)." *Journal of Psychological Human Sexuality, 2,* 1989:61–78.

Linden, Eugene. "Lost Tribes, Lost Knowledge." *Time,* September 23, 1991:46, 48, 50, 52, 54, 56.

Linton, Ralph. *The Study of Man.* New York: Appleton, 1936.

Linz, Daniel, Edward Donnerstein, and Steven Penrod. "The Findings and Recommendations of the Attorney General's Commission on Pornography: Do the Psychological 'Facts' Fit the Political Fury?" *American Psychologist,* October 1987:946–953.

Little, Peter D., and Michael M. Horowitz (eds.). *Lands at Risk in the Third World: Local-Level Perspectives.* Boulder, Colo.: Westview, 1987.

Livernash, Robert, and Eric Rodenburg. "Population Change, Resources, and the Environment." *Population Bulletin, 53,* 1, March, 1998:1–40.

Locy, Toni, and Joan Biskupic. "Anti-Porn Filters in Libraries Upheld." *USA Today.* June 23, 2003.

Lohn, Martiga. "Minnesota May Expand Meth Boot Camp Program." Associated Press, February 17, 2005.

Lombroso, Cesare. *Crime: Its Causes and Remedies,* H. P. Horton, trans. Boston: Little, Brown. "The Long Losing Battle Against Drugs." *The Economist.* March 5, 1988:23–24.

Lopez, Adalberto (ed.). *The Puerto Ricans: Their History, Culture, and Society.* Cambridge, Mass.: Schenkman, 1980.

Lorber, Judith. "Beyond Equality of the Sexes: The Question of Children." In *Marriage and Family in a Changing Society,* James M. Henslin, ed. New York: Free Press, 1980:522–533.

Lorenz, Konrad. *On Aggression.* New York: Harcourt, 1966.

Lowenstein, Sophie Freud. "Understanding Lesbian Women." *Social Casework, 61,* January 1980:29–38.

Lowi, Theodore J. "Machine Politics—Old and New." In *City Scenes: Problems and Prospects,* J. John Palen, ed. Boston: Little, Brown, 1977.

Luckenbill, David F. "Deviant Career Mobility: The Case of Male Prostitutes." *Social Problems 33,* 4, April 1986: 283–296.

Luker, Kristen. *Taking Chances: Abortion and the Decision Not to Contracept.* Berkeley: University of California Press, 1975.

Lundberg, Ollie. "Causal Explanations for Class Inequality in Health: An Empirical Analysis." *Social Science and Medicine, 32,* 4, 1991:385–393.

Lutz, Harold J. *Aboriginal Man and White Man as Historical Causes of Fires in the Boreal Forest, with Particular Reference to Alaska.* New Haven, Conn.: Yale University School of Forestry. No. 65, 1959 [as referenced in Burch 1971].

Luy, Mary Lynn M. "Rape: Not a Sex Act—A Violent Crime, An Interview with Dr. Dorothy J. Hicks." *Modern Medicine.* February 15, 1977:36–41.

Lynch, Mitchell C. "Old Ice Indicates Acid Was Present in Rain Long Ago." *Wall Street Journal,* September 18, 1980:13.

Lynd, Robert S., and Helen M. Lynd. *Middletown.* New York: Harcourt, 1929.

Lynd, Robert S., and Helen M Lynd. *Middletown in Transition.* New York: Harcourt, 1937.

Mackellar, Landis, and David Horlacher. "Population Ageing in Japan: A Brief Survey." *The European Journal of Social Sciences, 13,* 4, December 2000.

MacKenzie, Doris Layton, and Claire Souryal. "Inmate Attitude Change During Incarceration: A Comparison of Boot Camp With Traditional Prison." *Justice Quarterly, 12,* 2 1995.

MacKenzie, Hilary. "Enmeshed in Conflict and Drought, Southern Sudan Starves." *New York Times,* July 22, 1998.

MacKinnon, Catharine A. *Sexual Harassment of Working Women: A Case of Sex Discrimination.* New Haven, Conn.: Yale University Press, 1979.

MacNamara, Donal E. J., and Edward Sagarin. *Sex, Crime, and the Law.* New York: Free Press. 1977.

Madigan, Lee, and Nancy Gamble. *The Second Rape: Society's Continued Betrayal of the Victim.* New York: Free Press, 1991.

Mahran, M. *Proceedings of the Third International Congress of Medical Sexology.* Littleton, Mass.: PSG, 1978.

Mahran, M. "Medical Dangers of Female Circumcision." *International Planned Parenthood Federation Medical Bulletin, 2,* 1981:1–2.

Malamuth, Neil M., Tamara Addison, and Mary Koss. "Pornography and Sexual Aggression: Are There Reliable Effects and Can We Understand Them? *Annual Review of Sex Research, 11,* 2000:26–91.

Malthus, Thomas Robert. *First Essay on Population.* London: Macmillan, 1926. Originally published in 1798.

Mamdani, Mahmood. *The Myth of Population Control: Family, Caste, and Class in an Indian Village.* New York: Monthly Review, 1973 [as contained in Simon 1981].

Mandel-Campbell, Andrea. "A Breath of Fresh(er) Air." *U.S. News and World Report,* June 25, 2001.

Manpower Report to the President. Washington, D.C.: U.S. Department of Labor, Manpower Administration, April 1971.

Manski, Charles F. "Income and Higher Education." *Focus, 14,* 3, Winter 1992–93:14–19.

Marger, Martin N. *Elites and Masses: An Introduction to Political Sociology,* 2nd ed. Belmont, Calif.: Wadsworth, 1987.

Martin, Paul Schultz. "Prehistoric Overkill." In *Pleistocene Extinctions: The Search for a Cause,* Paul Schultz Martin and H. E. Wright, Jr., eds. New Haven, Conn.: Yale University Press, 1967.

Martin, Philip, and Elizabeth Midgley. "Immigration to the United States." *Population Bulletin, 54,* 2, June 1999:1–43.

Martinez, Juan Francisco Esteva. "Urban Street Activists: Gang and Community Efforts to Bring Peace and Justice to Los Angeles Neighborhoods." In *Gangs and Society: Alternative Perspectives,* Louis Kontos, David Brotherton, and Luis Barrios, eds. New York: Columbia University Press, 2003: 95–115.

Marx, Karl. *Das Kapital.* New York: International, 1967 (originally published in 1867–1895).

Marx, Karl, and Friedrich Engels. *Capital: A Critique of Political Economy,* E. Aveling, trans. Chicago: Charles Kerr, 1906.

Marx, Karl, and Friedrich Engels. *The Communist Manifesto,* S. Moore, trans. New York: Washington Square, 1964 (originally published in 1848).

Massey, Douglas S. As quoted in *Footnotes,* September/October 2001:6.

Masters, William, and Virginia Johnson. *Homosexuality in Perspective.* Boston: Little, Brown, 1979.

Maynard, Douglas W. *Inside Plea Bargaining: The Language of Negotiation.* New York: Plenum, 1984.

Mayne, Susan Taylor, Dwight T. Janerich, Peter Greenwald, Sherry Chorost, Cathy Tucci, Muhammad B. Zaman, Myron R. Melamed, Maureen Kiely, and Martin F. McKneally. "Dietary Beta Carotene and Lung Cancer Risk in U.S. Nonsmokers." *Journal of the National Cancer Institute, 86,* 1, January 5, 1995:33–38.

McCain, Chiree. "The Pros of Preventing Cons." *Business First of Columbus,* June 25, 2004.

McCarthy, Bill, and John Hagan. "Mean Streets: The Theoretical Significance of Situational Delinquency Among Homeless Youths." *American Journal of Sociology, 98,* 3, November 1992:597–627.

McCarthy, Michael. "Report Finds Abuse in U.S. Nursing Homes Goes Unreported and Unpunished." *The Lancet, 359,* 9309, March 9, 2002.

McCormick, John. "Change Has Taken Place." *Newsweek,* June 7, 1999:34.

McDonald, Peter. "Low Fertility Not Politically Sustainable." *Population Today,* August–September 2001:3, 8.

McDowell, Bart. "Mexico City: An Alarming Giant." *National Geographic, 166,* 1984:139–174.

McFarling, Usha Lee. "Climate is Warming at Steep Rate, Study Says." *Los Angeles Times,* February 23, 2000.

McGarigle, Bill. "Satellite Tracking for House Arrest." *Geo Info,* May 1997.

McGinley, Laurie. "Health-Care Debate Heats Up Over Control of Medical Decisions." *Wall Street Journal,* February 18, 1999.

McIntyre, Jennie, Thelma Myint, and Lynn Curtis. "Sexual Assault Outcomes: Completed and Attempted Rapes." Paper presented at the annual meeting of the American Sociological Association. Boston, 1979.

McKeown, Thomas. *The Modern Rise of Population.* New York: Academic Press, 1977.

McKeown, Thomas. *The Role of Medicine: Dream, Mirage, or Nemesis?* Princeton, N.J.: Princeton University Press, 1980.

McManus, Michael J. "Introduction." In *Final Report of the Attorney General's Commission on Pornography.* Nashville, Tenn.: Rutledge Hill, 1986: ix–l.

McNeely, R. L., and Carl E. Pope. "Socioeconomic and Racial Issues in the Measurement of Criminal Involvement." In *Race, Crime, and Criminal Justice,* R. L. McNeely and Carl E. Pope, eds. Beverly Hills, Calif.: Sage, 1981:31–47.

Meese Commission. Final Report of the Attorney General's Commission on Pornography. Washington, D.C.: U.S. Department of Justice, 1986.

Meier, Barry. "Tobacco Windfall Begins Tug-of-War Among Lawmakers." *New York Times,* January 10, 1999.

Melloan, George. "Europe Struggles with the Burdens of Old Age." *Wall Street Journal,* December 12, 1994:A15.

Melman, Seymour. *Pentagon Capitalism.* New York: McGraw-Hill, 1970.

Melody, G. F. "Chronic Pelvic Congestion in Prostitutes." *Medical Aspects of Human Sexuality, 3,* November 1969:103–104.

Mendels, Pamela. "Judge Rules Against Filters at Library." *New York Times,* November 23, 1998a.

Merton, Robert K. *Social Theory and Social Structure,* enlarged ed. New York: Free Press, 1968.

Merton, Robert K., and Robert Nisbet (eds.). *Contemporary Social Problems,* 4th ed. New York: Harcourt, 1976.

Merwine, Maynard H. "How Africa Understands Female Circumcision." *New York Times,* November 24, 1993.

Messner, Michael A., Margaret Carlisle Duncan, and Cheryl Cooky. "Silence, Sports Bras, and Wrestling Porn." *Journal of Sport and Social Issues, 27,* 1, February 2003:38–51.

Messner, Steven F. "Regional and Racial Effects on the Urban Homicide Rate: The Subculture of Violence Revisited." *American Journal of Sociology, 88,* 1983:997–1007.

Meyer, H. *Old English Coffee Houses.* Emmaus, Pa.: Rodale, 1954.

Miall, Charlene E. "The Stigma of Involuntary Childlessness." *Social Problems, 33,* 4, April 1986: 268–282.

Michelman, Kate. As quoted in "NARAL," pamphlet published by the National Abortion Rights Action League, 1988:1.

Milbank, Dana. "In His Solitude, A Finnish Thinker Posits Cataclysms." *Wall Street Journal,* May 20, 1994:A1, A8.

Miles, Rufus E., Jr. "The Population Challenge of the 70's: Achieving a Stationary Population." In *The Crisis of Survival,* editors of *The Progressive,* eds. Glenview, Ill.: Scott Foresman, 1970:122–140.

Miles, Steven. "Intellectualism Meant Death in Cambodia." *St. Louis Post-Dispatch,* April 8, 1980:D3.

Millar, Heather. "For 'Neurosis,' Press 'Enter.'" *Business Week,* October 27, 1997.

Miller, Judith. "U.S. and Uzbeks Agree on Chemical Arms Plant Cleanup." *New York Times,* May 25, 1999.

Miller, Judith, and William J. Broad. "Clinton Describes Terrorism Threat for 21st Century." *New York Times,* January 22, 1999.

Miller, Laura L. "Women in the Military." In *Down to Earth Sociology: Introductory Readings,* 13th ed., James M. Henslin, ed. New York: The Free Press, 2005:520–536.

Miller, Michael W. "Quality Stuff: Firm Is Peddling Cocaine, and Deals Are Legit." *Wall Street Journal,* October 27, 1994:A1, A8.

Miller, Walter B. "Lower-Class Culture as a Generating Milieu of Gang Delinquency." *Journal of Social Issues, 14,* 1958:5–19.

Millett, Kate. *Sexual Politics.* Garden City, N.Y.: Doubleday, 1970.

Millett, Kate. *The Prostitution Papers: A Candid Dialogue.* New York: Avon, 1973.

Mills, C. Wright. *The Causes of World War Three.* New York: Simon & Schuster, 1958.

Mills, C. Wright. *The Power Elite.* New York: Oxford University Press, 1959a.

Mills, C. Wright. *The Sociological Imagination.* New York: Oxford University Press, 1959b.

Mills, Karen M., and Thomas J. Palumbo. *A Statistical Portrait of Women in the United States: 1978.* Washington, D.C.: U.S. Government Printing Office, 1980.

Milner, Christina, and Richard Milner. *Black Players*. Boston: Little Brown, 1972.

Milvy, Paul. "Cancer from the Radiation." *New York Times,* April 12, 1979:19.

"Minneapolis Judge Lets Victim Set Punishment." *Jet, 17,* January 30, 1989:24.

Mintz, Morton. "Error Placed H-Bomb Secrets on Library Shelf." *St. Louis Globe-Democrat,* May 18, 1979:5a.

Mokdad A. H., J. S. Marks, D. F. Stroup, and J. L. Gerberding. "Actual Causes of Death in the United States." *Journal of the American Medical Association, 291,* 2004:1238–1245.

Mokhiber, Russell, and Leonard Shen. "Love Canal." In *Who's Poisoning America: Corporate Polluters and Their Victims in the Chemical Age,* Ralph Nader, Ronald Brownstein, and John Richard, eds. San Francisco: Sierra Club Books, 1981:268–310.

Montagu, M. F. Ashley. *The Concept of Race.* New York: Free Press, 1964.

Moore, Gwen. "The Structure of a National Elite Network." *American Sociological Review, 44,* October 1979:673–691.

Moore, Joan W. *Homeboys: Gangs, Drugs, and Prison in the Barrios of Los Angeles.* Philadelphia: Temple University Press, 1978.

Moore, Stephen D., and Ron Winslow. "Health-Care Systems in 12 Countries Near Crisis, Drug Maker Study Says." *Wall Street Journal,* September 15, 1993:B6.

Morash, Merry A., and Etta A. Anderson. "Liberal Thinking on Rehabilitation: A Work-Able Solution to Crime." *Social Problems, 25,* June 1978: 556–563.

Morash, Merry, and Lila Rucker. "A Critical Look at the Idea of Boot Camp as a Correctional Reform." *Crime and Delinquency, 36,* 2, April 1990:204–222.

Morgan, Patricia A. "The Legislation of Drug Law: Economic Crisis and Social Control." *Journal of Drug Issues, 8,* Winter 1978:54–62.

Morrison, Denton E., Kenneth E. Hornback, and W. Keith Warner. "The Environmental Movement: Some Preliminary Observations and Predictions." In *Social Behavior, Natural Resources, and the Environment,* William R. Burch, Jr., Neil H. Cheek, Jr., and Lee Taylor. eds. New York: Harper & Row, 1972:259–279.

Mosher, Steven W. "Why Are Baby Girls Being Killed in China?" *Wall Street Journal,* July 25, 1983:9.

"Movie Spurs Jamaica Tourism." Associated Press, December 13, 1998.

Muecke, Marjorie A. "Mother Sold Food, Daughter Sells Her Body: The Cultural Continuity of Prostitution." *Social Science and Medicine, 35,* 7, October 1992:891–901.

Muehlenhard, Charlene L., and Melaney A. Linton. "Date Rape: Familiar Strangers." *Journal of Counseling Psychology, 34,* 1987:186–196.

Mulvihill, Donald J., Melvin M. Tumin, and Lynn A. Curtis. *Crimes of Violence: A Staff Report to the National Commission on the Causes and Prevention of Violence.* Washington, D.C.: U.S. Government Printing Office, 1969.

Muminovic, Mirza. "Psychiatric Association to Investigate Abuse in China." *BMJ,* September 7, 2002: 513.

Murnen, Sarah K., Carrie Wright, and Gretchen Kaluzny. "If 'Boys Will Be Boys,' Then Girls Will Be Victims? A Meta-Analytic Review of the Research That Relates Masculine Ideology to Sexual Aggression." *Sex Roles, 46,* 11/12, June 2002: 359–375.

Murphy, Kim. "Last Stand of an Aging Aryan." *Los Angeles Times,* January 10, 1999.

Murphy, Tom. "Hybrids, FCVs, Oddities Abound." *Ward's Auto World,* December 1, 2003.

Murray, Rosie. "First Death, Then Shag." Business Telegraph. February 1, 2004.

Mydens, Seth. "Bullets and Crayons: Children Learn Lessons of the 90s." *New York Times,* June 16, 1991:14.

Myers, Martha A., and Susette M. Talarico. "The Social Contexts of Racial Discrimination in Sentencing." *Social Problems, 33,* 3, February 1986:236–251.

Myers, Steven Lee. "Pentagon Ready to Shrink Arsenal of Nuclear Bombs." *New York Times,* November 23, 1998.

Myerson, Allen R. "U.S. Splurging on Energy After Falling Off Its Diet." *New York Times,* October 22, 1998.

Myrdal, Gunnar. *An American Dilemma.* New York: Harper, 1944.

Naj, Amal Kumar. "Battle Against Toxic PCBs Gains Ground as Bacteria Are Found That Eat Them." *Wall Street Journal,* November 9, 1988:B5.

Naj, Amal Kumar. "Lab Notes." *Wall Street Journal,* February 1, 1989a:B1.

Naj, Amal Kumar. "'Super' Microbes Offer Way to Treat Hazardous Waste." *Wall Street Journal,* January 25, 1989B:B1.

Naj, Amal Kumar. "Kuwait Oil-Well Fires Did Little Damage to the Global Environment, Study Says." *Wall Street Journal*, May 15, 1992:B5.

Nash, Gary B. *The Urban Crucible*. Cambridge, Mass.: Harvard University Press, 1979.

National Women's Political Caucus. "News & Opinions: 1998 Election Results." November 5, 1998.

Neergaard, Lauran. "Strong Tainted Food Warnings Urged." Associated Press, December 31, 1998.

Nelan, Bruce W. "Sudan: Why Is This Happening Again?" *Time*, July 27, 1998:29–32.

Nettler, Gwynn. "Embezzlement Without Problems." *British Journal of Criminology*, 14, January 1974:70–77.

Nettler, Gwynn. *Social Concerns*. New York: McGraw-Hill, 1976.

New York Times. "First Death Sentence Under New Drug Law." May 15, 1991:A24.

Newdorf, David. "Bailout Agencies Like to Do it in Secret." *Washington Journalism Review*, 13, 4, May 1991:15–16.

Newman, Donald J. *Conviction: The Determination of Guilt or Innocence Without Trial*. Boston: Little, Brown, 1966.

Newman, Dorothy K., Nancy J. Amidei, Barbara L. Cater, Dawn Day, William J. Kruvant, and Jack S. Russell. *Protest, Politics, and Prosperity: Black Americans and White Institutions, 1940–1975*. New York: Pantheon, 1978.

1969 Handbook on Women Workers. Washington, D.C.: U.S. Department of Labor, Woman's Bureau, 1969.

Nishio, Harry Kaneharu. "Japan's Welfare Vision: Dealing with a Rapidly Increasing Elderly Population." In *The Graying of the World: Who Will Care for the Frail Elderly?* New York: Haworth, 1994:233–260.

Nucleus: A Report to Union of Concerned Scientists Sponsors. 3, Spring–Summer 1981.

Nuland, Sherwin. "The Debate over Dying." *USA Weekend*, February 3–5, 1995:4–6.

Nurge, Dana. "Liberating Yet Limiting: The Paradox of Female Gang Membership." In *Gangs and Society: Alternative Perspectives*, Louis Kontos, David Brotherton, and Luis Barrios, eds. New York: Columbia University Press, 2003:161–182.

Oakley, Robert B. "Combating International Terrorism." *Department of State Bulletin*, June 1985:73–78.

O'Connell, Pamela Licalzi. "Web Erotica Aims for New Female Customers." *New York Times*, August 13, 1998.

"Of Birds and Bacteria." *Consumer Reports*, January 2003.

"Ogallala Water Level Drop Talked." *Southwest Farm Press*, September 4, 2003.

O'Hare, William P. "America's Minorities: The Demographics of Diversity." *Population Bulletin*, 47, 4, December 1992:1–47.

Oliver, Melvin L., and Thomas M. Shapiro. *Black Wealth/White Wealth: A New Perspective on Racial Inequality*. New York: Routledge, 1995.

Olivo, Antonio. "Doctor Shortage Severe in Poor Areas." *Los Angeles Times*, April 19, 1999.

Olson, James S., Mark Baxter, Jason M. Tetzloff, and Darren Pierson. *Encyclopedia of American Indian Civil Rights*. Westport, Conn.: Greenwood Press, 1997.

Olson, Walter K. "Give It Back to the Indians?" *City Journal*, Autumn 2002.

Omestad, Thomas, and Aamir Latif. "Selling the Bomb." *U.S. News and World Report*, February 16, 2004.

Onion, Amanda. "Getting Better . . . Virtually." ABC News online, July 7, 2004.

Organized Crime: Report of the Task Force on Organized Crime, Washington, D.C.: National Advisory Committee on Criminal Justice Standards and Goals, 1976.

Osborne, Lawrence. "Got Silk?" *New York Times Magazine*, June 15, 2002.

Otten, Alan L. "People Patterns." *Wall Street Journal*, January 27, 1995:B1.

Oyserman, Daphna, and Hazel Markus. "Possible Selves in Balance: Implications for Delinquency." *Journal of Social Issues*, 46, 2, 1990:141–157.

Paddock, Richard C. "Patient Deaths Point to Depth of Russian Crisis." *Los Angeles Times*, March 13, 1999.

Pagelow, Mildred Daley. "Protecting the Fetus From Its Mom: A New Form of Social Control." Paper presented at the annual meeting of the society for the Study of Social Problems, 1992.

Palen, J. John., and Leo F. Schnore. "Color Composition and City-Suburban Status Difference." *Land Economics, 41*, February 1965:87–91.

Palen, J. John. *The Urban World*, 6th ed., Boston: McGraw-Hill, 2002.

Pamuck, Elsie. A study for the National Centre for Health Statistics, as reported in America Online, "Rich Get Richer, Poor Get Sicker in U.S." July 30, 1998.

"Parallelism in Infaunal Abundance." Office of Response and Restoration, National Ocean Service, National Oceanic and Atmospheric Administration, 2001.

Park, Robert E. "The Social Function of War." *American Journal of Sociology, 46,* January 1941: 551–570.

Parmesan, Camille, and Gary Yohe. "A Globally Coherent Fingerprint of Climate Change Impacts Across Natural Systems." *Nature,* January 2003: 37–42.

Partington, Donald H. "The Incidence of the Death Penalty for Rape in Virginia." *Washington and Lee Law Review, 22,* 1965:43–75.

Passell, Peter. "Race, Mortgages and Statistics." *New York Times,* May 10, 1996:D1, D4.

Paul, Bill. "Burning Trash is Becoming Big Business." *Wall Street Journal,* October 13, 1986:6.

Paul, Bill. "Cogeneration Is Rapidly Coming of Age." *Wall Street Journal,* March 2, 1987:6.

Paul, William, James D. Weinrich, John C. Gonsiorek, and Mary E. Hotvedt. *Homosexuality: Social, Psychological, and Biological Issues.* Beverly Hills, Calif.: Sage, 1982.

Pearse, Peter H. "The Environment Revisited." *Au Courant, 7,* Winter 1987:7.

Peele, Stanton. "The Addiction Experience." In *Social Problems: A Critical Thinking Approach,* Paul J. Baker and Louis E. Anderson, eds. Belmont, Calif.: Wadsworth, 1987:210–218.

Penn, Stanley. "Organized Crime Finds Rich Pickings in Rise of Union Health Plans." *Wall Street Journal,* October 5, 1982:1, 26.

Penn, Stanley. "How Public Defenders Deal with the Pressure of the Crowded Courts." *Wall Street Journal,* July 5, 1985:1, 22.

Peplau, Letitia Anne, and Hortensia Amaro. "Understanding Lesbian Relationships." In *Homosexuality: Social, Psychological and Biological Issues.* William Paul, James D. Weinrich, John C. Gonsiorek, and Mary E. Hotvedt, eds. Beverly Hills, Calif.: Sage, 1982:233–247.

Pereira, Joseph. "Toys 'R' Us Decides to Pull Night Trap from Store Shelves." *Wall Street Journal,* December 17, 1993:A9A.

Persell, Caroline Hodges, Sophia Catsambis, and Peter W. Cookson, Jr. "Family Background, School Type, and College Attendance: A Conjoint System of Cultural Capital Transmission." *Journal of Research on Adolescence, 2,* 1, 1992:1–23.

Persell, Caroline Hodges, and Peter W. Cookson, Jr. "Where the Power Starts." *Signature,* August 1985:51–57.

Petersilia, Joan. *Racial Disparities in the Criminal Justice System.* Santa Monica, Calif.: Rand, June 1983.

Pettigrew, Thomas. "How the People Really Feel." *The Center Magazine, 9,* January–February 1976:35.

Phelps, Orme Wheelock. *The Legislative Background of the Fair Labor Standards Act: A Study of the Growth of National Sentiment in Favor of Government Regulation of Wages, Hours, and Child Labor.* Chicago: University of Chicago Press, 1939.

Piliavin, Irving, and Scott Briar. "Police Encounters with Juveniles." *American Journal of Sociology, 70,* September 1964:206–214.

Pillemer, Karl, and David W. Moore. "Abuse of Patients in Nursing Homes: Findings from a Survey of Staff." *The Gerontologist, 29,* 3, 1989:314–320.

Piotrow, Phylis Tilson. *World Population Crisis: The United States' Response.* New York: Praeger, 1973.

Pittman, David J. "The Male House of Prostitution." *Transaction, 8,* March–April 1971:21–27.

Piven, Frances Fox, and Richard A. Cloward. *Regulating the Poor.* New York: Vintage, 1971.

Piven, Frances Fox, and Richard A. Cloward. *Poor People's Movements: Why They Succeed, How They Fail.* New York: Pantheon, 1977.

Piven, Frances Fox, and Richard A. Cloward. *The New Class War: Reagan's Attack on the Welfare State and Its Consequences.* New York: Pantheon, 1982.

Piven, Frances Fox, and Richard A. Cloward. *Why Americans Don't Vote.* New York: Random House, 1989.

Piven, Frances Fox, and Richard A. Cloward. *The Breaking of the American Social Compact.* New York: New Press, 1997.

Platt, Anthony M. *The Child Savers.* Chicago: University of Chicago Press, 1979.

Polenberg, Richard. *One Nation Divisible: Class, Race, and Ethnicity in the United States Since 1938.* New York: Penguin, 1980.

Pollack, Andrew. "U.N. Unit Sees Great Promise in Biotech Research on Crops." *New York Times,* May 18, 2004.

Pollay, Richard W. "Hacks, Flacks, and Counter-Attacks: Cigarette Advertising, Sponsored Research, and Controversy." *Journal of Social Issues, 53,* 1, 1997:43–74.

Pope, Carl E. "The Family, Delinquency, and Crime." In *Mental Illness, Delinquency, Addictions, and Ne-*

glect, Elam W. Nunnally, Catherine S. Chilmam, and Fred M. Cox, eds. Newbury Park, Calif.: Sage, 1988:108–127.

Potterat, John J., Donald E. Woodhouse, John B. Muth, and Stephen Q. Muth. "Estimating the Prevalence and Career Longevity of Prostitute Women." *Journal of Sex Research, 27,* 2, May 1990:233–243.

Pozdena, Randall J., and Terry R. Johnson. *Income Maintenance and Asset Demand.* Menlo Park, Calif.: SRI International, March, 1979.

Preidt, Robert. "Smoking Claimed 5 Million Lives in 2000." *HealthDay,* September 11, 2003a.

Preidt, Robert. "Tobacco Companies Target Women in Developing Countries." *HealthDay,* August 7, 2003b.

Prescott, Carol A. *Alcoholism: Clinical and Experimental Research,* January 2004.

Price, Daniel O., ed. *The 99th Hour.* Chapel Hill: University of North Carolina Press, 1967 (as contained in Simon 1981).

"The Price of Success." *Economist, 371,* 8371, April 17, 2004.

Pruitt, Dean G., and Richard C. Snyder. "Motives and Perceptions Underlying Entry into War." In *Theory and Research on the Causes of War,* Dean G. Pruitt and Richard C. Synder, eds. Englewood Cliffs, N.J.: Prentice Hall, 1969.

Prus, Robert, and Styllianoss Irini. *Hookers, Rounders, and Desk Clerks: The Social Organization of the Hotel Community.* Salem, Wis.: Sheffield, 1988.

Public Health, Seattle and King County. "Gay, Lesbian, Bisexual and Transgender Health." February 1, 2002.

Ra'anan, Uri, Robert L. Pfaltzgraff, Jr., Richard H. Shultz, Ernst Halperin, and Igor Lukes, eds. *Hydra of Carnage: The International Linkages of Terrorism and Other Low-Intensity Operations, The Witnesses Speak.* Lexington, Ky.: Lexington Books, 1986.

Rabinovitz, Jonathan. "For Sale: Used Nuclear Reactor." *New York Times,* July 7, 1998.

Rabinowitz, Dorothy. *No Crueler Tyrannies: Accusation, False Witness, and Other Terrors of Our Times.* New York: Simon and Schuster, 2004.

Raghunathan, V. K. "Millions of Baby Girls Killed in India." *The Straits Times,* February 8, 2003.

Rakow, Lana F. "'Don't Hate Me Because I'm Beautiful': Feminist Resistance to Advertising's Irresistible Meanings." *Southern Communication Journal, 57,* 2, Winter 1992:132–142.

Raloff, Janet. "The Colloid Threat." *Science News, 137,* 11, March 17, 1990:169–170.

Ramo, Alan. "The Environmental Justice Clinic at the Golden Gate University School of Law." *Human Rights, 30,* 4, Fall 2003:6.

Ray, Oakley S. *Drugs, Society, and Human Behavior,* 8th ed. Boston: McGraw-Hill, 1998.

Ray, Oakley S., and Charles J. Ksir. *Drugs, Society, and Human Behavior,* 10th ed. Boston: McGraw-Hill, 2003.

Reasons, Charles E. (ed.). *The Criminologist: Crime and the Criminal.* Pacific Palisades, Calif.: Goodyear, 1974.

Reay, Diane, Jacqueline Davies, Miriam David, and Stephen J. Ball. "Choice of Degrees or Degrees of Choice? Class, 'Race,' and the Higher Education Choice Process." *Sociology, 35,* 4, November 2001: 855–876.

Reckless, Walter C. *The Crime Problem,* 5th ed. New York: Appleton, 1973.

Redlich, Fritz, and Stephen R. Kellert. "Trends in American Mental Health." *American Journal of Psychiatry, 135,* January 1978:22–28.

Reeves, Terrance, and Claudette Bennett. "The Asian and Pacific Islander Population in the United States: March 2002." *Current Population Reports,* 2003.

Regaldo, Antonio. "When a Plant Emerges From Melting Glacier, Is It Global Warming?" *Wall Street Journal,* October 22, 2004:B1.

Rehm, Jurgen, Gerhard Gmel, Christopher T. Sempos, and Maurizio Trevisan. "Alcohol-Related Morbidity and Mortality." *Alcohol Research and Health, 27,* 1, 2003:39–51.

Reich, Michael. "The Economics of Racism." In *The Capitalist System,* Richard C. Edwards, Michael Reich, and Thomas E. Weiskopf, eds. Englewood Cliffs, N.J.: Prentice Hall, 1972:313–326.

Reich, Michael. "The Economic Impact in the Postwar Period." In *Impacts of Racism on White Americans,* Benjamin P. Bowser and Raymond G. Hunt, eds. Beverly Hills, Calif.: Sage, 1981:165–176.

Reichert, Loren D., and James H. Frey. "The Organization of Bell Desk Prostitution." *Sociology and Social Research, 69,* 4, July 1985:516–526.

Reiss, Albert J. "The Sociological Integration of Queers and Peers." *Social Problems, 9,* Fall 1961:102–120.

Ressler, Robert K., and Tom Shachtman. *Whoever Fights Monsters.* New York: St. Martin's, 1992.

Revzin, Philip. "U.S. Claims Progress at Global Meeting Discussing Ban on Chemical Weapons." *Wall Street Journal,* January 9, 1989:A3.

Reynolds, Janice. "The Medical Institution: The Death and Disease-producing Appendage." In *American Society: A Critical Analysis,* Larry T. Reynolds and James M. Henslin, eds. New York: McKay, 1973:198–224.

Reynolds, Janice. "Rape as Social Control." In *Social Problems in American Society,* 2nd ed., James M. Henslin and Larry T. Reynolds, eds. Boston: Holbrook, 1976:79–86.

Richardson, Lewis F. *Statistics of Deadly Quarrels.* Chicago: Quadrangle, 1960.

Ricks, Thomas E. "Prospect of Nuclear Rogue State Makes North Korea Worrisome." *Wall Street Journal,* February 3, 1999.

Riesel, Victor. "Crackdown on Mobsters." Syndicated column, January 16, 1982a.

Riesel, Victor. "Racketeers Infest New Jersey Construction Trade." Syndicated column, January 25, 1982b.

Riesman, David, Nathan Glazer, and Reuel Denney. *The Lonely Crowd: A Study of the Changing American Character.* New Haven, Conn.: Yale University Press, 1951.

Riley, K. Jack. "Crack, Powder Cocaine, and Heroin. Drug Purchase and Use Patterns in Six U.S. Cities." National Institute of Justice, online, December 12, 1998.

Risen, James, and David Johnston. "Bush Has Widened Authority of C.I.A. to Kill Terrorists." *New York Times,* December 15, 2002.

Risen, James, and Jeff Gerth. "China Stole Nuclear Secrets From Los Alamos, U.S. Officials Say." *New York Times,* March 6, 1999.

Roberts, Leslie. "Discovering Microbes with a Taste for PCBs." *Science, 237,* August 28, 1987:975–977.

Robinson, Arthur B., and Zachary W. Robinson. "Science Has Spoken: Global Warming Is a Myth." *Wall Street Journal,* December 4, 1997:A22.

Rockett, Ian R. H. "Population and Health: An Introduction to Epidemiology." *Population Bulletin, 49,* 3, November 1994:1–47.

Rockwell, Don. "Social Problems: Alcohol and Marijuana." *Journal of Psychedelic Drugs, 5,* Fall 1972:49–55.

Roe, Kathleen M. "Private Troubles and Public Issues: Providing Abortion Amid Competing Definitions." *Social Science and Medicine, 29,* 10, 1989:1191–1198.

Rogers, Joseph W. *Why Are You Not a Criminal?* Englewood Cliffs, N.J.: Prentice Hall, 1977.

Rolo, Mark Anthony. "Marked Media." *The Circle.* Online, n.d.

Rosaldo, Michelle Zimbalist. "Women, Culture, and Society: A Theoretical Overview." In *Women, Culture, and Society,* Michelle Zimbalist Rosaldo and Louise Lamphere, eds. Stanford, Calif.: Stanford University Press, 1974.

Rosen, Lawrence, Leonard Savitz, Michael Lalli, and Stanley Turner. "Early Delinquency, High School Graduation, and Adult Criminality." *Sociological Viewpoints, 7,* Fall 1991:37–60.

Rosen, Yereth. "Exxon Valdez Oil Spill of 1989 Crippled Sound, Alaskans Say." Reuters, March 14, 1999.

Rosenberg, Charles E. *The Care of Strangers: The Rise of America's Hospital System.* New York: Basic Books, 1987.

Rosenfeld, Rachel A., and Arne L. Kalleberg. "A Cross-National Comparison of the Gender Gap in Income." *American Journal of Sociology, 96,* 1, July 1990:69–106.

Rosett, Claudia. "Big Oil-Pipeline Spill in Russia May Be a Sign of Things to Come." *Wall Street Journal,* October 27, 1994:A14.

Rothman, David J. *The Discovery of the Asylum.* Boston: Little, Brown, 1971.

Rothman, David J., and Sheila M. Rothman. *On Their Own.* Reading, Mass.: Addison-Wesley, 1972.

Royko, Mike. *Boss: Richard J. Daly of Chicago.* New York: Dutton, 1971.

Rubenstein, Richard E. *Alchemists of Revolution: Terrorism in the Modern World.* London: I. B. Tauris, 1987.

Rubin, Trudy. "Nuclear 'Supermarket' Another Concern for U.S." *The Philadelphia Inquirer,* February 8, 2004.

Ruggles, Patricia. "Short and Long Term Poverty in the United States: Measuring the American 'Underclass.'" Washington, D.C.: Urban Institute, June 1989.

Ruggles, Patricia. *Drawing the Line: Alternative Poverty Measures and Their Implication for Public Policy.* Washington, D.C.: Urban Institute, 1990.

Ruggles, Patricia. "Measuring Poverty." *Focus, 14,* 1, Spring 1992:1–5.

Rumbaut, Ruben G., and John R. Weeks. "Unraveling a Public Health Enigma: Why Do Immigrants Experience Superior Perinatal Health Outcomes?" Paper presented at the annual meeting of the American Public Health Association, 1994.

Russell, Diana E. H. "On Pornography." *Chrysalis, 4,* 1977:11–15.

Russell, Diana E. H. *The Politics of Rape: The Victim's Perspective.* New York: Scarborough, 1979.

Russell, Diana E. H. "Rape in Marriage: A Case Against Legalized Crime." Paper presented at the annual meeting of the American Society of Criminology, 1980.

Russell, Diana E. H. *The Secret Trauma: Incest in the Lives of Girls and Women.* New York: Basic Books, 1986.

Rybczynski, Witold. "The Virtues of Suburban Sprawl." *Wall Street Journal,* May 25, 1999.

Sagan, Scott D. "The Perils of Proliferation: Organization Theory, Deterrence Theory, and the Spread of Nuclear Weapons." *International Security, 18,* 4, Spring 1994: 66–107.

Sager, Ira, Ben Elgin, Peter Elstrom, Faith Keenan, and Pallavi Gogoi. "The Under Ground Web." *Business Week,* September 2, 2002.

Sakharov, Andrei. "Text of Sakharov Letter to Carter on Human Rights." *New York Times,* January 29, 1977.

Salas, Rosalinda. "Letter to the author." May 1996.

Sampson, Catherine. "Corrupt Care." *World Press Review, 39,* 5, May 1992:46.

Santora, Marc, and Lawrence K. Altman. "Rare and Aggressive H.I.V. Reported in New York." *New York Times,* February 12, 2005.

Sawhill, Isabel V. "Poverty in the U.S.: Why Is It So Persistent?" *Journal of Economic Literature, 26,* 3, September 1988:1073–1119.

Schaefer, Richard T. *Racial and Ethnic Groups,* 9th ed. Upper Saddle River, N.J.: Prentice Hall, 2004.

Schlafly, Phyllis. "The Phyllis Schlafly Report." 13, November 1979.

Schmidt, Gunter, and Volkmar Sigusch. "Sex Differences in Response to Psychosexual Stimulation by Films and Slides." *Journal of Sex Research, 6,* November, 268–283.

Schmitt, Richard B. "Some Towns Jail Indigents Illegally and Get Free Labor." *Wall Street Journal,* February 2 1982:1, 16.

Schneider, Keith. "Nuclear Disarmament Raises Fear on Storage of 'Triggers.'" *New York Times,* February 26, 1992:A1.

Schneider, Keith. "Burning Trash for Energy: Is It an Endangered Industry?" *New York Times,* October 11, 1994:A18.

Schoenfeld, A. Clay, Robert F. Meier, and Robert J. Griffin. "Constructing a Social Problem: The Press and the Environment." *Social Problems, 27,* October 1979:38–61.

Schottland, Charles I. *The Social Security Plan in the U.S.* New York: Appleton, 1963.

Schreiber, Jan. *The Ultimate Weapon: Terrorists and the World Order.* New York: Morrow, 1978.

Schrieke, Bertram J. *Alien Americans.* New York: Viking, 1936.

Schumpeter, Joseph A. *The Sociology of Imperialism.* New York: Meridian, 1955 (first published in 1919).

Schuster, Lynda. "Industrialization of Brazilian Village Brings Jobs at Cost of Heavy Pollution and Even Death." *Wall Street Journal,* April 15, 1985:28.

Schwartz, Felice N. "Management Women and the New Facts of Life." *Harvard Business Review, 89,* 1, January–February 1989:65–76.

Schwendinger, Julia R., and Herman Schwendinger. *Rape and Inequality.* Beverly Hills, Calif.: Sage, 1983.

Schwidrowski, Klaus. "Italy's Mafia Blight." *World Press Review, 17,* March 1980:56.

Scott, Janny. "White Flight: This Time Toward Harlem." *New York Times,* February 25, 2001.

Scully, Diana, and Joseph Marolla. "'Riding the Bull at Gilley's': Convicted Rapists Describe the Rewards of Rape." In *Down to Earth Sociology: Introductory Readings,* 13th ed., James M. Henslin, ed. New York: The Free Press, 2005:48–62. Originally appeared in *Social Problems, 32,* 3, February 1985:251–263.

Scully, Diana. *Understanding Sexual Violence: A Study of Convicted Rapists.* Boston: Unwin Hyman, 1990.

Scully, Diana. "Negotiating to Do Surgery." In *Dominant Issues in Medical Sociology,* 3rd ed. Howard D. Schwartz, ed. New York: McGraw-Hill, 1994:146–152.

Seib, Gerald F. "U.S. Aides Say Toxins on a Cambodian Leaf Hint at Chemical War." *Wall Street Journal,* September 15, 1981:22.

Seligmann, Jean. "The Date Who Rapes." *Newsweek,* April 9, 1984:91–92.

Sellin, Thorsten. "The Negro Criminal: A Statistical Note." *Annals of the American Academy of Political and Social Sciences, 140,* Part II, November 1928:52–64.

Seventh Special Report to the U.S. Congress on Alcohol and Health. Rockville, Md.: U.S. Department of Health and Human Services, 1990.

Shaffer, Harry G. "$1,000,000,000,000." *Republic,* May 1986:24.

Shafir, Gershon. "Split Labor Market and the Sources of National Separatism in the Israeli-Palestinian Conflict." In *Racism and the Labour Market: Historical Studies,* Marcel Van Der Linden and Jan Lucassen, eds. Bern: Peter Lang, 1995:437–456.

Shafir, Gershon, and Yoav Peled. "Citizenship and Stratification in an Ethnic Democracy." *Ethnic and Racial Studies, 21,* 3, May 1998:408–427.

Shapiro, Joseph P. "Euthanasia's Home: What the Dutch Experience Can Teach Americans about Assisted Suicide." *U.S. News Online,* January 17, 1997.

Shaw, Sue. "Wretched of the Earth." *New Statesman, 20,* March 1987:19–20.

Sheehy, Gail. *Hustling: Prostitution in Our Wide-Open Society.* New York: Dell, 1973.

Shellenbarger, Sue. "Companies Help Solve Day-Care Problems." *Wall Street Journal,* July 22, 1994:B1.

Shellenbarger, Sue. "Sales Offers Women Fairer Pay, but Bias Lingers." *Wall Street Journal,* January 24, 1995:B1, B14.

Sheppard, Nathaniel, Jr. "Chicago Project Dwellers Live Under Siege." *New York Times,* August 6, 1980:A14.

Shibutani, Tamotsu. "On the Personification of Adversaries." In *Human Nature and Collective Behavior,* Tamotsu Shibutani, ed. Englewood Cliffs, N.J.: Prentice Hall, 1970:223–233.

Shilts, Randy. *And the Band Played On: People, Politics and the AIDS Epidemic.* New York: St. Martin's, 1987.

Shim, Kelly H., and Marshall DeBerry. *Criminal Victimization in the United States, 1986.* Washington, D.C.: U.S. Department of Justice, Bureau of Justice Statistics, August 1988.

Shinnar, Revel, and Shlomo Shinnar. "The Effects of the Criminal Justice System on the Control of Crime: A Quantitative Approach." *Law and Society Review, 9,* Summer 1975:581–611.

Shively, JoEllen. "Cowboys and Indians." In *Down-to-Earth Sociology: Introductory Readings,* 10th ed., James M. Henslin, ed. New York: Free Press, 1999:104–116.

Shribman, David. "Even After 10 Years, Victims of Love Canal Can't Quite Escape It." *Wall Street Journal,* March 9, 1989:A1, A8.

Silver, Jonathan M. "Medical Terms—A Two-Way Block?" *Colloquy: The Journal of Physician-Patient Communications,* November 1979:4–10.

Silverman, Deidre. "Sexual Harassment: The Working Women's Dilemma." *Building Feminist Theory: Essays from Quest.* New York: Longman, 1981: 84–93.

Simmel, Georg. "The Sociology of Conflict." *American Journal of Sociology, 9,* January 1904:490–525; March 1904:672–689; and May 1904:798–811.

Simon, David R. "The Political Economy of Crime." In *Political Economy: A Critique of American Society,* Scott G. McNall, ed. Glenview, Ill.: Scott Foresman, 1981: 347–366.

Simon, Julian L. *The Economics of Population Growth.* Princeton, N.J.: Princeton University Press, 1977.

Simon, Julian L. "Global Confusion, 1980: A Hard Look at the Global 2000 Report." *Public Interest, 62,* Winter 1980:3–20.

Simon, Julian L. *The Ultimate Resource.* Princeton, N.J.: Princeton University Press, 1981.

Simon, Julian L. Conversation with the author. March 23, 1982.

Simon, Julian L. *Theory of Population and Economic Growth.* New York: Blackwell, 1986.

Simon, Julian L. "The Case for Greatly Increased Immigration." *The Public Interest, 102,* Winter 1991:89–103.

Simon, Steven. "The New Terrorism: Securing the Nation Against a Messianic Foe." In *Sociology,* 33rd ed., Kurt Finsterbusch, ed., Dubuque, Iowa: McGraw-Hill/Dushkin, 2004:215–220.

Simons, Marlise. "Social Change and Amazon Indians." In *Life in Society: Readings to Accompany Sociology: A Down-to-Earth Approach, 7th ed.* James M. Henslin, ed. Boston: Allyn and Bacon, 2005: 158–165.

Simpson, George Eaton, and J. Milton Yinger. *Racial and Cultural Minorities: An Analysis of Prejudice and Discrimination,* 4th ed. New York: Harper & Row, 1972.

Sindler, Allan P. *Bakke, De Funis, and Minority Admissions: The Quest for Equal Opportunity.* New York: Longman, 1978.

Singer, S. Fred. "The Sky Isn't Falling, and the Ocean Isn't Rising." *Wall Street Journal,* November 10, 1997:A22.

Sitomer, Curtis J. "Fencing Out Pornography Without Fencing in Free Speech." *Christian Science Monitor,* March 13, 1986:23.

Siwolop, Sana. "Developments to Watch." *Business Week,* April 11, 1988:123.

Skinner, B. F. *Walden Two.* New York: Macmillan, 1948.

Skinner, B. F. *Science and Human Behavior.* New York: Macmillan, 1953.

Skinner, B. F. *Beyond Freedom and Dignity.* New York: Knopf, 1971.

Skinner, Jonathan, James N. Weinstein, Scott M. Sporer, and John E. Wennberg. "Racial, Ethnic, and Geographic Disparities in Rates of Knee Arthroplasty Among Medicare Patients." *New England Journal of Medicine, 349,* 14, October 2, 2003: 1350–1359.

Slikker, William, Jr. "Behavioral, Neurochemical, and Neurohistological Effects of Chronic Marijuana Smoke Exposure in the Nonhuman Primate." In *Marijuana Cannabinoids Neurobiology and Neurophysiology,* Laura Murphy and Andrzej Bartke, eds. Boca Raton, Florida: CRC Press, 1992.

Smedley, Brian D., Adrienne Y. Stith, and Alan R. Nelson, eds. *Unequal Treatment: Confronting Racial and Ethnic Disparities in Health Care.* Washington, D.C.: The National Academies Press, 2003.

Smith, Barbara Ellen. *Digging Our Own Graves: Coal Miners and the Struggle over Black Lung Disease.* Philadelphia: Temple University Press, 1987.

Smith, Clark. "Oral History as 'Therapy': Combatants' Accounts of Vietnam War." In *Strangers at Home: Vietnam Veterans Since the War,* Charles R. Figley and Seymore Leventman (eds.). New York: Praeger, 1980:9–34.

Smith, Douglas A., and Christy A. Visher. "Street-Level Justice: Situational Determinants of Police Arrest Decisions." *Social Problems, 29,* December 1981: 167–177.

Smith, Harold, "A Colossal Cover-Up." *Christianity Today,* December 1986:16–17.

Smith, James P., and Barry Edmonston, eds. *The New American: Economic, Demographic, and Fiscal Effects of Immigration.* Washington, D.C.: National Academy Press, 1997.

Smith, Joel B., and Dennis A. Tirpak. *The Potential Effects of Global Climate Change on the United States.* Washington, D.C.: U.S. Environmental Protection Agency, October 1988.

Smith, Kristen F., and Vern L. Bengtson. "Positive Consequences of Institutionalization: Solidarity Between Elderly Parents and Their Middle-Aged Children." *The Gerontologist, 19,* October 1979:438–447.

Smith, Wesley J. "Dependence or Death? Oregonians Make a Chilling Choice." *Wall Street Journal,* February 25, 1999.

Smith-Lovin Lynn, and Charles Brody. "Interruptions in Group Discussions: The Effects of Gender and Group Composition." *American Sociological Review, 54,* 1989:424–435.

Smolinske, S. *Handbook of Food, Drug, and Cosmetic Excipients.* Boca Raton, Florida: CRC Press, 1992.

Snipp, C. Matthew, and Alan L. Sorkin, "American Indian Housing: An Overview of Conditions and Public Policy." In *Race, Ethnicity, and Minority Housing in the United States,* Jamshid A. Momeni, ed. New York: Greenwood, 1986:147–175.

Snow, Ronald W., and Orville R. Cunningham. "Age, Machismo, and the Drinking Locations of Drunken Drivers: A Research Note." *Deviant Behavior, 6,* 1985:57–66.

Snyder, Howard. *Court Careers of Juvenile Offenders.* Washington, D.C.: Office of Juvenile Justice and Delinquency Prevention, 1988.

"Social Darwinism in Sweden." *Report* (Alberta Edition), *28,* 14, July 9, 2001:4.

Solomon, Jeanne, and Dan Rather. "The Kyshtym Disaster." A segment of *60 Minutes,* November 9, 1980 (Jean Solomon, producer, and Dan Rather, interviewer).

Solomon, Jolie. "Companies Try Measuring Cost Savings from New Types of Corporate Benefits." *Wall Street Journal,* December 29, 1988:B1.

Sorensen, Jesper B. "Perceptions of Women's Opportunity in Five Industrialized Nations." *European Sociological Review, 6,* 2, September 1990: 151–164.

Sorokin, Pitrim A. *Social and Cultural Dynamics,* 4 vols. New York: American Book, 1937, 1941.

Sourcebook of Criminal Justice Statistics. Washington, D.C.: U.S. Government Printing Office, annual.

Spaeth, Anthony. "Court Settlement Stuns Bhopal Survivors." *Wall Street Journal,* February 22, 1989:A10.

Specter, Michael. "TB Carriers See Clash of Liberty and Health." *New York Times,* October 14, 1992:A1, A20.

Specter, Michael. "Plunging Life Expectancy Puzzles Russians." *New York Times,* August 1, 1995:A1, A6.

Specter, Michael. "Population Implosion Worries a Graying Europe." *New York Times,* July 10, 1998.

Speer, Albert. *Inside the Third Reich,* Richard and Clara Winston (trans.). New York: Avon, 1970.

Spitzer, Steven. "Toward a Marxian Theory of Deviance." *Social Problems, 22,* June 1975:608–619.

Spivak, Jonathan. "Israel's Discrimination Problem." *Wall Street Journal,* December 3, 1980:28.

Spunt, Barry. "The Current New York City Heroin Scene." *Substance Use and Misuse, 38,* 10, 2003: 1539–1549.

Squires, Gregory D. "Racial Profiling, Insurance Style: Insurance Redlining and the Uneven Development of Metropolitan Areas." *Journal of Urban Affairs, 25,* 4, 2003:391–410.

Srisang, Koson. "The Ecumenical Coalition on Third World Tourism." *Annals of Tourism Research, 16,* 1, 1989:119–121.

Srole, Leo, et al. *Mental Health in the Metropolis: The Midtown Manhattan Study.* New York: New York University Press, 1978.

Stafford, Linda, Sonya R. Kennedy, JoAnne E. Lehman, and Gail Arnold. "Wealth in America." *ISR Newsletter,* Winter 1986–87.

Stanford, Sally. "Madambood as a Vocation." In *In Their Own Behalf: Voices from the Margin,* Charles H. McCaghy, James K. Skipper, Jr., and Mark Lefton, eds. New York: Appleton, 1968:204–207.

Starfield, Barbara, Judy Robertson, and Anne W. Riley. "Social Class Gradients and Health in Childhood." *Ambulatory Pediatrics,* July–August 2002.

Starr, Mark, and Frank Maier. "Chicago's Gang Warfare." *Newsweek,* January 28, 1985:32.

Statistical Abstract of the United States. Washington, D.C.: U.S. Bureau of the Census, annual.

The Statistical History of the United States: From Colonial Times to the Present. New York: Basic Books, 1976.

Stein, Peter J. "The Diverse World of Single Adults." In *Marriage and Family in a Changing Society,* 4th ed., James M. Henslin, ed. New York: Free Press, 1992: 93–103.

Steinhauer, Jennifer. "Angry at Managed Care, Doctors Start Fighting Back." *New York Times,* January 10, 1999a.

Steinhauer, Jennifer. "For Women in Medicine, a Road to Compromise, Not Perks." *New York Times,* March 1, 1999b.

Steinhauer, Jennifer. "So, the Tumor Is on the Left, Right?" *New York Times,* April 1, 2001.

Steinhauer, Jennifer, and Ford Fessenden. "Medical Retreads: Doctors Punished by State But Prized at the Hospitals." *New York Times,* March 27, 2001.

Steinhoff, Patricia G., and Milton Diamond. *Abortion Politics: The Hawaii Experience.* Honolulu: University press of Hawaii, 1977.

Steinmetz, Greg, and Cacilie Rohwedder. "Green Party Grows Strong on Soil Peculiar to Germany." *Wall Street Journal,* April 20, 1998:A15.

Steinmetz, Suzanne K. *Duty Bound: Elder Abuse and Family Care.* Newbury Park, Calif.: Sage, 1988.

Steinmetz, Suzanne K., and Murray A. Straus (eds.). *Violence in the Family.* New York: Dodd Mead, 1974.

Stevens, Amy. "Sensible Victims Will Be Hoping Their Burglar Drives Up in a Rolls." *Wall Street Journal,* April 8, 1992:B1.

Stevens, Charles W. "Integration Is Elusive Despite Recent Gains; Social Barriers Remain." *Wall Street Journal,* September 29, 1980:1.

Stevens, Charles W. "Advance in Hydrogen Storage May Make Use of Abundant Element More Practical." *Wall Street Journal,* March 8, 1989:B4.

Stevens, Rosemary. *American Medicine and the Public Interest.* New Haven, Conn.: Yale University Press, 1971.

Stevens, William K. "Green Revolution Is Not Enough, Study Finds." *New York Times,* September 6, 1994.

Stevens, William K. "Great Plains or Great Desert?" *New York Times,* May 28, 1996.

Stevens, William K. "As Alaska Melts, Scientists Consider the Reasons Why." *New York Times,* August 18, 1998a.

Stevens, William K. "Linking Health Effects to Changes in Climate." *New York Times,* August 10, 1998b.

Stevens, William K. "Science Academy Disputes Attack on Global Warming." *New York Times, April 22, 1998c.*

Stockard, Jean, and Miriam M. Johnson. *Sex Roles: Sex Inequality and Sex Role Development.* Englewood Cliffs, N.J.: Prentice Hall, 1980.

Stolberg, Sheryl Gay. "AIDS Is Becoming an Epidemic of Silence Among Blacks." *New York Times,* June 29, 1998a.

Stolberg, Sheryl Gay. "Superbugs." *New York Times,* August 2, 1998b.

Stolberg, Sheryl Gay. "Blacks Found on Short End of Heart Attack Procedure." *New York Times,* May 10, 2001.

Stone, Alan A., and Harvey M. Stein. "Psychotherapy of the Hospitalized Suicide Patient." *American Journal of Psychotherapy, 22,* January 1968:15–25.

Stouffer, Samuel A., Arthur A. Lumsdaine, Marion Harper Lumsdaine, Robin M. Williams, Jr., M. Brewster Smith, Irving L. Janis, Shirley A. Star, and Leonard S. Cottrell, Jr. *The American Soldier: Combat and Its Aftermath,* vol. 2. New York: Wiley, 1949.

Straus, Murray A. "Victims and Aggressors in Marital Violence." *American Behavioral Scientist, 23,* May–June 1980:681–704.

Straus, Murray A. "Explaining Family Violence." *Marriage and Family in a Changing Society,* 4th ed., James M. Henslin, ed. New York: Free Press, 1992:344–356.

Straus, Murray A., and Richard J. Gelles. "Violence in American Families: How Much Is There and Why Does It Occur?" In *Troubled Relationships,* Elam W. Nunnally, Catherine S. Chilman, and Fred M. Cox, eds. Newbury Park, Calif.: Sage, 1988:141–162.

Straus, Murray A., Richard J. Gelles, and Suzanne K. Steinmetz. *Behind Closed Doors: Violence in the American Family.* New York: Anchor/Doubleday, 1980.

Strobel, Lee. *Reckless Homicide: Ford's Pinto Trial.* South Bend, Ind.: And Books, 1980.

Sugimura, T. "Food and Cancer." *Toxicology.* December 27, 2002:17–21.

"Suicide Rates." United Nations: World Health Organization, 2004.

"Suit Settled by Neil Bush." *New York Times,* March 29, 1992:A43.

Surgeon General of the United States. "Surgeon General's Report: A Call for Action." Washington, D.C.: Centers for Disease Control, April 3, 2003.

Sutherland, Edwin H. *The Professional Thief.* Chicago: University of Chicago Press, 1937.

Sutherland, Edwin H. *Principles of Criminology,* 4th ed. Philadelphia: Lippincott, 1947.

Sutherland, Edwin H. *White Collar Crime.* New York: Dryden, 1949.

Suttles, Gerald D. *The Social Order of the Slum: Ethnicity and Territory in the Inner City.* Chicago: University of Chicago Press, 1968.

Suzuki, Bob H. "Asian-American Families." In *Marriage and Family in a Changing Society,* 2nd ed., James M. Henslin, ed. New York: Free Press, 1985:104–119.

"Swedish Health Care in the 1990s." Stockholm: Federation of Swedish County Councils, July 2002.

Swedish Institute, The. "Fact Sheets on Sweden." February 1992.

Sykes, Gresham M. *Criminology.* New York: Harcourt, 1978.

Sykes, Gresham M., and David Matza. "Techniques of Neutralization: A Theory of Delinquency." *American Sociological Review, 22,* December 1957:664–670.

Szasz, Thomas. *The Myth of Mental Illness.* Harper & Row, 1961.

Szasz, Thomas. *Ceremonial Chemistry: The Ritual Persecution of Drugs, Addicts, and Pushers.* Garden City, N.Y.: Anchor, 1975.

Tannen, Deborah. "But What Do You Mean? Women and Men in Conversation." In *Down to Earth Sociology: Introductory Readings,* 13th ed., James M. Henslin, ed. New York: The Free Press, 2005: 174–180.

Tannen, Deborah. *You Don't Understand: Women and Men in Conversation.* New York: Morrow, 1990.

Tanouye, Elyse. "Price Markups on Generic Can Top Brand-Name Drugs." *Wall Street Journal,* December 31, 1998.

Tarmann, Allison. "Obesity in the United States: Reaching a Critical Mass." *Population Bulletin, 57,* Population Reference Bureau, December 2002:17.

Tax Foundation. "Tax Freedom Day Arrives April 11 in 2004, Earliest Since 1967," 2004.

Taylor, Monique M. *Harlem: Between Heaven and Hell.* Minneapolis: University of Minnesota, Press, 2002.

Teaford, John. *The Twentieth Century American City.* Baltimore: Johns Hopkins University Press, 1986.

Teller, Edward. "The Energy Crisis: No Contingency Plan." San Diego, Calif.: World Research, 1980.

Teresa, Vincent, with Thomas C. Renner. *My Life in the Mafia.* Greenwich, Conn.: Fawcett, 1973.

Thayer, Frederick C. "The Holy War on Surplus Americans: Soviet Dogma, Old-time Religion and Classical Economics." *Social Policy, 28,* 1, Fall 1997:8–18.

Thio, Alex. *Deviant Behavior.* Boston: Houghton Mifflin, 1978.

Thomas, Paulette. "Boston Fed Finds Racial Discrimination in Mortgage Lending Is Still Widespread." *Wall Street Journal,* October 9, 1992:A3.

Thompson, Hunter. *Hell's Angels.* New York: Random House, 1967.

Thornton, Russell. *American Indian Holocaust and Survival: A Population History Since 1492.* Norman: University of Oklahoma Press, 1987.

Thorsheim, Peter. "Interpreting the London Fog Disaster of 1952." In *Smoke and Mirrors: The Politics and Culture of Air Pollution,* E. Malanie DuPuis, ed. New York: New York University Press, 2004:154–169.

Thrasher, Frederic M. *The Gang*. Chicago: University of Chicago Press, 1927.

Tierney, John. "The Population Crisis Revisited." *Wall Street Journal*, January 20, 1986:16.

Tierney, John. "Betting on the Planet." *New York Times*. December 2, 1990.

Tiger, Lionel, and Robin Fox. *The Imperial Animal*. New York: Holt, 1971.

Timasheff, Nicholas S. *War and Revolution*. Joseph F. Scheuer, ed. New York: Sheed & Ward, 1965.

Tinker, John N. "Ethnic Bias in California Courts: A Case Study of Chicano and Anglo Felony Defendants." Paper presented at the annual meeting of the Society for the Study of Social Problems." 1981.

Toffler, Alvin. *Future Shock*. New York: Bantam, 1971.

Tolchin, Martin. "Mildest Possible Penalty Is Imposed on Neil Bush." *New York Times*, April 19, 1991a:D2.

Tolchin, Martin. "Fund Established to Help Pay Legal Fees for President's Son." *New York Times*, June 9, 1991b:1–31.

Tönnies, Ferdinand. *Community and Society*. East Lansing: Michigan State University, 1957 (originally published in 1887).

Toth, Mike. "According to Professor Ehrlich, Shouldn't the World Be Over By Now?" *Stanford Review*, March 10, 1998.

Trebach, Arnold S. *The Great Drug War: And Radical Proposals That Could Make America Safe Again*. New York: Macmillan, 1987.

Troiano, R. P. "Physical Activity Among Young People." *New England Journal of Medicine, 347,* September 5, 2002:706–707.

Trust, Cathy. "Presidential Panel Says 4 Major Unions Have Connections to Organized Crime." *Wall Street Journal*, January 15, 1986:48.

Tsuda, S., M. Murakami, N. Matsusaka, K. Kano, K. Taniguchi, Y. F. Sasaki. *Toxicol Sci. 61,* 1, May 2001:92-9:

Turner, Jonathan H. *The Structure of Sociological Theory*. Homewood, Ill.: Dorsey, 1978.

Ullman, Sarah E. "Does Offender Violence Escalate When Rape Victims Fight Back?" *Journal of Interpersonal Violence, 13,* 2, April 1998:179–192.

United Nations. "Fact Sheet: Sub-Saharan Africa." 2002.

United States Department of State. "Environmental Diplomacy: The Environment and U.S. Foreign Policy," April 22, 1997.

"U.S. Pesticide Exports and the Circle of Poison." Committee on Foreign Affairs, Subcommittee on Economic Policy, Trade and Environment, House of Representatives, January 26, 1994.

Use and Misuse of Benzodiazepines: Hearing Before the Subcommittee on Health and Scientific Research of the Committee on Labor and Human Resources, September 10, 1979. Washington, D.C.: U.S. Government Printing Office, 1980.

Useem, Michael. "The Social Organization of the American Business Elite." *American Sociological Review, 44,* August 1979:553–572.

Useem, Michael. *The Inner Circle: Large Corporations and the Rise of Business Political Activity in the U.S. and U.K.* New York: Oxford University Press, 1984.

Valocchi, Steve. "The Racial Basis of Capitalism and the State, and the Impact of the New Deal on African Americans." *Social Problems, 41,* 3, August 1994:347–362.

van den Haag, Ernest. *Punishing Criminals: Concerning a Very Old and Painful Question*. New York: Basic Books, 1975.

van den Haag, Ernest, and John P. Conrad. *The Death Penalty: A Debate*. New York: Plenum, 1983.

Varady, David. *Neighborhood Upgrading: A Realistic Assessment*. Albany: SUNY Press, 1986.

Vatz, Richard E. "Attention Deficit Delirium." *Wall Street Journal*, July 27, 1994:A14.

Veevers, Jean E. "Voluntarily Childless Wives." *Sociology and Social Research, 57,* April 1973:356–366.

Veevers, Jean E. *Childless by Choice*. Toronto: Butterworths, 1980.

Verespei, Michael A. "Drug Users, Not Testing, Anger Workers." *Industry Week, 241,* 4, February 17, 1992:33–34.

Vergano, Dan. "Global-Warming Debate Heats Up All the Way to Capitol Hill." *USA Today,* November 19, 2003.

Vidal, David. "Bilingual Education Is Thriving but Criticized." *New York Times,* January 30, 1977.

Vigil, James Diego. *A Rainbow of Gangs: Street Cultures in the Mega-City*. Austin: University of Texas Press, 2002.

Waddington, Conrad H. *The Man-Made Future*. New York: St. Martin's, 1978.

Wagley, Charles, and Marvin Harris. *Minorities in the New World*. New York: Columbia University Press, 1958.

Wagman, Robert. "Is Japanese Mafia Threat to U.S.?" Syndicated column, November 27, 1981.

Wain, Barry. "Cambodia: What Remains of the Killing Ground." *Wall Street Journal,* January 29, 1981: 24.

Waitzkin, Howard, and Barbara Waterman. *The Exploitation of Illness in Capitalist Society.* New York: Bobbs-Merrill, 1974.

Wald, Patricia M. "Making Sense Out of 12 Rights of Youth." *Human Rights, 4,* Fall 1974:13–29.

Walker, Alice, and Pratibha Parmar. *Warrior Marks: Female Genital Mutilation and the Sexual Binding of Women.* New York: Harcourt Brace, 1993.

Wallace, James N. "Green Revolution Hits Double Trouble." *U.S. News & World Report,* July 28, 1980:37, 40.

Wallerstein, Immanuel. *The Modern World System: Capitalist Agriculture and the Origins of the European World-Economy in the Sixteenth Century.* New York: Academic Press, 1974.

Wallerstein, Immanuel. *The Capitalist World-Economy.* New York: Cambridge University Press, 1979.

Wallerstein, Immanuel. *The Politics of the World-Economy: The States, the Movements, and the Civilizations.* Cambridge: Cambridge University Press, 1984.

Walsh, Mark. "Supreme Court Refuses to Weigh Race-Based College Admissions." *Education Week on the WEB,* July 1, 1996.

Ward, Russell A. "Patient-Provider Ties and Satisfaction with Health Care." *Research in the Sociology of Health Care, 9,* 1991:169–190.

Watanabe, Teresa. "The Green Movement Is Getting Religion." *Los Angeles Times,* December 25, 1998.

Wax, Murray L. *Indian Americans: Unity and Diversity.* Englewood Cliffs, N.J.: Prentice Hall, 1971.

Wax, Murray L., and Rosalie H. Wax. "Cultural Deprivation as an Educational Ideology." *Journal of American Indian Education, 3,* January 15–18, 1964.

Wax, Murray L., and Rosalie H. Wax. "Indian Education for What?" *Midcontinent American Studies Journal, 6,* Fall 1965:164–170.

Wax, Rosalie H. "The Warrior Dropouts." *Trans-Action, 4,* May 1967:40–46.

Wayne, Julie Holiday, Christine M. Riordan, and Kecia M. Thomas. "Is All Sexual Harassment Viewed the Same? Mock Juror Decisions in Same- and Cross-Gender Cases." *Journal of Applied Psychology, 86,* 2, April 2001:179–187.

Webber, Melvin M. "Urbanization and Communications." In *Communications Technology and Social Policy; Understanding the New Cultural Revolution.*

George Gerbner, Larry P. Gross, and William H. Melody, eds. New York: John Wiley, 1973.

Weinberg, S. Kirson, and Henry Arond. "The Occupational Culture of the Boxer." *American Journal of Sociology, 57,* March 1953:460–469.

Weir, Fred. "Russia and Ukraine Bicker Over Chernobyl." *Christian Science Monitor, 95,* 105, April 25, 2003.

Weissbourd, R. *The Vulnerable Child: What Really Hurts America's Children and What We Can Do About It.* Reading, Mass.: Addison-Wesley, 1996.

Weitz, Rose. *Life with AIDS.* New Brunswick, N.J.: Rutgers University Press, 1991.

Weitz, Rose, and Deborah A. Sullivan. "The Politics of Childbirth: The Re-Emergence of Mid-Wifery in Arizona." *Social Problems, 33,* 3, February 1986: 163–175.

Weitzer, Ronald, ed. *Sex for Sale: Prostitution, Pornography, and the Sex Industry.* New York: Routledge, 2000.

Weitzman, Lenore J., Deborah Eifler, Elizabeth Hokada, and Catherine Ross. "Sex Role Socialization in Picture Books for Pre-School Children." *American Journal of Sociology, 77,* May 1972: 1125–1150.

Weitzstein, Cheryl. "Gays Poised to Wed Legally." *Washington Times.* May 16, 2004.

Wells, John Warren. *Tricks of the Trade.* New York: New American Library, 1970.

Wells, Ken. "Hazelwood is Acquitted of Most Charges." *Wall Street Journal.* March 23, 1990:A3, A4.

Wells, Ken, and Charles McCoy. "Exxon Says Fast Containment of Oil Spill in Alaska Could Have Caused Explosion." *Wall Street Journal,* April 5, 1989:A3.

Wenneker, Mark B., and Arnold M. Epstein. "Racial Inequalities in the Use of Procedures for Patients with Ischemic Heart Disease in Massachusetts." *Journal of American Medical Association, 261,* 2, January 13, 1989:253–257.

Wertheimer, David M. "Victims of Violence: A Rising Tide of Anti-Gay Sentiment." *USA Today,* January 1988:52–54.

West, Candace, and Angela Garcia. "Conversational Shift Work: A Study of Topical Transitions Between Women and Men." *Social Problems, 35,* 1988:551–575.

West, Richard W., and Gary Steiger. *The Effects of the Seattle and Denver Income Management Experiments on Alternative Measures of Labor Supply.* Menlo Park,

Calif.: SRI International Research Memorandum, 72, May 1980.

Westley, William A. "Violence and the Police." *American Journal of Sociology, 59,* July 1953:34–41.

Whitaker, Jennifer Seymour. *How Can Africa Survive?* New York: Harper & Row, 1988.

Whitaker, Mark. "'It Was Like Breathing Fire . . .'" *Newsweek,* December 17, 1984:26–32.

White, Helene Raskin. "Marijuana Use and Delinquency: A Test of the 'Independent Cause' Hypothesis." *Journal of Drug Issues, 21,* 2, Spring 1991:231–256.

Whitehurst, Carol A. *Women in America: The Oppressed Majority.* Santa Monica, Calif.: Goodyear, 1977.

Whyte, William Foote. *Street Corner Society.* Chicago: University of Chicago Press, 1943.

Whyte, William Foote. "Street Corner Society." In *Down to Earth Sociology: Introductory Readings,* 8th ed., James M. Henslin, ed. New York: Free Press, 1995:59-67.

Wilcox, Ansley II. 1957. Letter from Hooker Electrochemical Company to the President of the Niagara Falls Board of Education, November 21, 1957.

"The Wild Wild East." CNN, March 12, 1995.

Willhelm, Sidney M. "Can Marxism Explain America's Racism?" *Social Problems, 28,* December 1980:98–112.

Williams, Robert C. "Three Mile Island as History." *Washington University Magazine, 50,* October 1980:56, 58–59, 61–63.

Williams, Terry M., and William Kornblum. *Growing Up Poor.* Lexington, Mass.: Lexington Books, 1985.

Williamson, John B., Judith A. Shindul, and Linda Evans. *Aging and Social Policy: Social Control or Social Justice?* Springfield, Ill.: Charles C. Thomas, 1985.

Willing, Richard. "U.S. Prisons to End Boot Camp Program." *USA Today,* February 4, 2005.

Wilson, James Q. "Lock 'Em Up and Other Thoughts on Crime." *New York Times Magazine,* March 9, 1975:11, 44–48.

Wilson, William Julius. *The Declining Significance of Race: Blacks and Changing American Institutions.* Chicago: University of Chicago Press, 1978.

Wilson, William Julius. *The Truly Disadvantaged: The Inner City, the Underclass, and Public Policy.* Chicago: University of Chicago Press, 1987.

Wilson, William Julius. Scholar in Residence Lecture at Southern Illinois University, Edwardsville, June 14, 1992.

Winick, Charles. "Physician Narcotic Addicts." *Social Problems, 9,* Fall 1961:174–186.

Winick, Charles, and Paul M. Kinsie. *The Lively Commerce: Prostitution in the United States.* Chicago: Quadrangle, 1971.

Winslow, Ron. "Heroin Remedy to Be Marketed for Alcoholism." *Wall Street Journal,* January 17, 1995:B1, B5.

Wirth, Louis. "Urbanism as a Way of Life." *American Journal of Sociology, 44,* July 1938:1–24.

Wirth, Louis. "The Problem of Minority Groups." In *The Science of Man in the World Crisis,* Ralph Linton, ed. New York: Columbia University Press, 1945.

Wolf, Deborah Goleman. *The Lesbian Community.* Berkeley: University of California Press, 1979.

Wolf, Julie. "EU Scientists Contend Hormone Fed to U.S. Cattle Is Carcinogenic." *Wall Street Journal,* May 4, 1999.

Wolfensohn, James D., and Kathryn S. Fuller. "Making Common Cause: Seeing the Forest for the Trees." *International Herald Tribune,* May 27, 1998:11.

Wolfgang, Marvin E. *Patterns in Criminal Homicide.* Philadelphia: University of Pennsylvania Press, 1958.

Wolfgang, Marvin, E., and Marc Reidel. "Rape, Race, and the Death Penalty." *American Journal of Orthopsychiatry, 45,* July 1975:658–668.

"Women in the Riksdag." Online, December 7.

World Population Profile. Washington, D.C.: Bureau of the Census, U.S. Department of Commerce, various years.

Wren, Christopher S. "Methadone Use Emerged in City Where It Is Now Challenged." *New York Times,* October 3, 1998.

Wright, Erik Olin. *Class Structure and Income Determination.* New York: Academic Press, 1979.

Wright, Eric. *Class.* London: Verso, 1985.

Wright, Quincy. *A Study of War,* 2 vols. Chicago: University of Chicago Press, 1942.

Wyatt-Brown, Bertram. "Anatomy of a Wife-Killing." In *Violence and Society: A Reader,* Matthew Silberman, ed. Upper Saddle River, N.J.: Prentice Hall, 2003:182–189.

Yablonsky, Judy. "Survey Finds World Trend Toward More Liberal Abortion Laws." AP, May 20, 1981.

Young, T. R. "Social Problems: A Radical Agenda for the 80's and 90's." *SSSP Newsletter, 16,* Summer 1985:7–11.

Yuan, D. Y. "Voluntary Segregation: A Study of New York Chinatown." *Phylon, 24,* Fall 1963:255–265.

Zaitseva, Lyudmila, and Kevin Hand. "Nuclear Smuggling Chains: Suppliers, Intermediaries, and End-Users." *American Behavioral Scientist, 46, 6,* February 2003:822–844.

Zawitz, Marianne W., ed. *Report to the Nation on Crime and Justice,* 2nd ed. Washington, D.C.: U.S. Department of Justice, Bureau of Justice Statistics, July 1988.

Zimbardo, Philip G. "The Pathology of Imprisonment." *Society, 9,* 6, April 1972:4–8.

Zimbardo, Philip G. "The Pathology of Imprisonment." In *Down-to-Earth Sociology: Introductory Readings,* 8th ed., James M. Henslin, ed. New York: Free Press, 1995:278–283.

Zinn, Maxine Baca, and D. Stanley Eitzen. *Diversity in Families,* 2nd ed. New York: HarperCollins, 1990.

Zoucha-Jensen, Janice M., and Ann Coyne. "The Effects of Resistance Strategies on Rape." *American Journal of Public Health, 83,* 11, November 1993: 1633–1634.

PHOTO CREDITS

Hope, Stover, 285
Horlacher, D., 36
Hornback, K. E., 459
Hornblower, M., 67
Horowitz, M. M., 437
Horowitz, R., 134
Horowitz, Ruth, 135
Hosenball, M., 521
Hotchkiss, S., 142
Hotz, R. L., 456
Hoyt, H., 398
Hsu, F. L. K., 270
Hu, N., 59
Hu, S., 59
Huber, J., 285
Huberty, James, 154
Huddle, D., 441
Hudo, Cindy, 374–375
Hudson, Buddy, 165–166
Hudson, R. B., 40
Huff-Corzine, L., 154
Huggins, M., 231
Hull, J. D., 389
Humphreys, L., 55–56
Humphreys, Laud, 55–56
Humphries, D., 111
Huxley, A., 112

I
Ianni, F. A. J., 187
Inciardi, J. A., 63, 88, 110, 116
Ingersoll, B., 472, 474, 485
Irini, S., 65, 66
Isbell, H., 88
Izumi, L. T., 118

J
Jacobs, D., 173
Jacobsen, T., 456
Jaffe, J., 117
James, J., 68, 69
James, William, 29
Janowitz, M., 407, 408
Jawarowski, Z., 472
Jefferson, T., 392
Jekielek, S. M., 357
Jenkins, B., 517
Joffe, C., 383, 384
John, Elton, 82
Johnson, B., 115, 116, 295
Johnson, Clyde, 165–166
Johnson, D., 118

Johnson, D. R., 109
Johnson, Lyndon, 215
Johnson, M., 291
Johnson, T. R., 237
Johnson, V., 59
Johnston, D., 523
Johnston, L. D., 100
Jordan, J., 144
Josephy, A. M., Jr., 261
Judd, D. R., 175
Julien, R. M., 111, 114

K
Kalb, C., 98
Kalleberg, A. L., 299
Kaluzny, G., 140
Kamin, L., 335
Kanin, E. J., 143
Kanouse, D. E., 327
Kantor, G., 374
Kapinus, C. A., 371
Kaplan, C. S., 83
Kaplan, S., 261
Kapur, Promilla, 279
Karlen, A., 50
Karlen, N., 321
Karmen, A., 95, 97
Karp, D. A., 400, 414
Kasarda, J. D., 398
Katz, M., 211
Kaya, A., 229
Keans, C., 400
Keating, P., 111
Keenan, F., 76
Keil, T. J., 191
Kellert, S., 337
Kelley, K., 187
Kemp, J., 299
Kenchaiah, S., 343
Kennedy, John F., 187, 215, 513
Kennedy, S. R., 214
Kerner, O., 408
Kettl, D. F., 183
Kevorkian, Jack, 348
Keyes, K., Jr., 512
Khan, Abdul Qadeer, 521–522
Kibria, Nazli, 249
King, Martin Luther, Jr., 266, 267–268
King, Rodney, 408
Kilborn, P. T., 316, 339
Kinder, B. N., 377

King, 242
King, M. L., Jr., 267
King, S. A., 337
Kinkade, W., 14
Kinnon, J. B., 416
Kinsey, A., 55, 76
Kinsie, P. M., 62
Kirby, R., 56
Kirkham, G., 56
Kirkpatrick, M., 10
Kirkpatrick, T., 414
Kishkovsky, S., 344, 345
Kitano, H. H. L., 261
Klawitter, M. M., 235
Kleck, G., 141
Klein, S., 191
Kleinman, P. H., 107
Klockars, C., 122
Knights, R., 201
Knowles, L. L., 253
Kohn, A., 498
Kolata, Gini, 57
Komisar, L., 295
Korda, M., 290
Kornblum, W., 68
Kornhauser, W., 228
Koss, M., 77
Kotlowitz, A., 179
Kozel, N. J., 111
Kozol, J., 171, 216
Krieger, L., 11
Kristoff, N. D., 450
Ksir, C. J., 87, 88, 99, 110, 113, 114
Kuczynski, J., 174
Kurth, J. R., 500
Kusum, 5
Kutchinsy, B., 77
Kutz, Linda, 403

L
La Barre, W., 376
LaBastille, A., 468
Lacayo, R., 10
Lacey, M., 286
LaFree, G., 191
Lamar, J. V., Jr., 199
Landes, D. S., 232
Lang, G., 408, 412
Lang, K., 408
Langan, P. A., 198
Lappe, F. M., 485